THE
CAMBRIDGE EDIT[...]
THE LETTERS AND W[...]S OF
D. H. LAWRENCE

THE LETTERS OF D. H. LAWRENCE

Vol. I: September 1901 – May 1913
James T. Boulton

Vol. II: June 1913 – October 1916
George J. Zytaruk and James T. Boulton

Vol. III: October 1916 – June 1921
James T. Boulton and Andrew Robertson

Vol. IV: June 1921 – March 1924
Warren Roberts, James T. Boulton and Elizabeth Mansfield

Vol. V: March 1924 – March 1927
James T. Boulton and Lindeth Vasey

Vol. VI: March 1927 – November 1928
James T. Boulton and Margaret H. Boulton, with Gerald M. Lacy

Vol. VII: November 1928 – February 1930
Keith Sagar and James T. Boulton

Vol. VIII: Previously Uncollected Letters and General Index
James T. Boulton

All published

THE LETTERS OF D. H. LAWRENCE

GENERAL EDITOR
James T. Boulton

THE LETTERS OF
D. H. LAWRENCE

VOLUME VII
November 1928–February 1930

EDITED BY
KEITH SAGAR
AND
JAMES T. BOULTON

CAMBRIDGE
UNIVERSITY PRESS

PUBLISHED BY THE PRESS SYNDICATE OF THE UNIVERSITY OF CAMBRIDGE
The Pitt Building, Trumpington Street, Cambridge, United Kingdom

CAMBRIDGE UNIVERSITY PRESS
The Edinburgh Building, Cambridge CB2 2RU, UK
40 West 20th Street, New York NY 10011–4211, USA
10 Stamford Road, Oakleigh, VIC 3166, Australia
Ruiz de Alarcón 13, 28014 Madrid, Spain
Dock House, The Waterfront, Cape Town 8001, South Africa

http://www.cambridge.org

First published 1993
First published in paperback 2002

*Cataloguing in publication records for this book are
available from the British Library and the Library of Congress*

ISBN 0 521 23116 7 hardback
ISBN 0 521 00699 6 paperback

CE

CONTENTS

ILLUSTRATIONS

ACKNOWLEDGEMENTS

The volume editors once again acknowledge with gratitude the generosity of manuscript holders: their names will be found in the list of cue-titles.

Willing assistance has been readily forthcoming from members of the Editorial Board. The scholarship and meticulous attention to detail of Lindeth Vasey have been especially appreciated. The University of Birmingham, through its Librarian and his staff, have continued liberally to support the edition. Andrew Brown and his staff at Cambridge University Press have been unstinting in their advice and practical help.

The editors are indebted to Cornelia Rumpf-Worthen and John Worthen for translations of Lawrence's letters in German; to Simonetta de Filippis for translations of those in Italian; to Jim Davies for photographic work; to Elma Forbes for the published index; and to Margaret Boulton for checking the text of Lawrence's letters throughout the volume and for reading proof.

The following individuals also deserve the editors' thanks for a multitude of kindnesses: Anna Lou Ashby; Melanie Aspey; Winston Atkins; Ben Benedikz; Robert J. Bertholf; Wendy Bowersock; David Bradshaw; Ellen A. Buie; Rebecca Campbell Cape; W. H. Clarke; Desmond Costa; Lori N. Curtis; Keith Cushman; Harry Davis; Emile Delavenay; Paul Eggert; W. Forster; R. A. Gekoski; Norman Gentieu; Howard B. Gotleib; Bonnie Hardwick; John Harris; Lilace Hatayama; Cathy Henderson; Kurt W. Hettler; the late Enid Hilton; David J. Holmes; Patricia Howell; Dennis Jackson; Dorothy B. Johnston; Mara Kalnins; Saki Karavas; Joan King; Mark Kinkead-Weekes; Gerald Lacy; Oonagh Lahr; Peter and Iris Law; George Lazarus; Sheila Leslie; Myriam Librach; Elizabeth A. Linn; Derek Lomax; Linda J. Long; Dieter Mehl; Franck M. Mercurio; the late Lilian Miller; C. H. Milsom; Leslie Morris; Craig Munro; Margaret Needham; Luis Orioli; Ruth Ostroff; Sigfrid P. Perry; the late Harwood Brewster Picard; Arthur Pollard; Gerald Pollinger; Christopher Pollnitz; Elizabeth Powis; Jean F. Preston; Clive Probyn; Martin Rogers; Natania Rosenfeld; Sheila Ryan; Wilbur Scott; G. F. Sims; Michael Squires; Beth Tate; J. R. Watson; Marjorie Watts; Rosalind Wells; Wilfred van der Will; David Wishart; Nigel Wood.

For the use of copyright material in annotation the editors wish to acknowledge the kindness of the Harry Ransom Humanities Research Center, University of Texas at Austin; Doris B. Mason; the Pierpont Morgan Library; the Rosenbach Museum & Library; University of Southern Illinois.

The editors are indebted to the following for the illustrations in this volume: Yvette Bailey; John Carswell; Express Newspapers Ltd; Brewster

Ghiselin; Harry Ransom Humanities Research Center, University of Texas; Morris Library, University of Southern Illinois; Ruth Ostroff; Julian Potter; the Rosenbach Museum & Library; Mala Rubinstein; the P. R. Stephensen Collection, Fryer Library, University of Queensland, and Craig Munro; University of Illinois Library at Urbana-Champaign.

NOTE ON THE TEXT

A full statement of the 'Rules of Transcription' and an explanation of the 'Editorial Apparatus' are provided in Volume I, pp. xviii–xx. The reader may, however, like to be reminded that the following symbols are used:

[   ]   indicates a defect in the MS making it impossible even to conjecture what Lawrence had written. Where a reconstruction can be hazarded or a fault corrected, the conjecture or correction is shown within the square brackets.

[. . .]   indicates a deletion which cannot be deciphered or a postmark which is wholly or partly illegible

MSC   = autograph manuscript copy

TMS   = typed manuscript

TMSC = typed manuscript copy

TSCC = typescript carbon copy

Maps are provided to show the principal places which Lawrence visited during the period covered by this volume. No attempt has been made fully to repeat information given on the maps in earlier volumes.

CUE-TITLES

Cue-titles are employed both for manuscript locations and for printed works. The following appear in this volume.

A. Manuscript locations

Anon	Anonymous
Besterman	the late Theodore Besterman
BL	British Library
Brill	the late Dr Edmund R. Brill
BucU	Bucknell University
Clarke	Mr W. H. Clarke
ColU	Columbia University
Faber	Faber & Faber
Forster	Mr W. Forster
Ghiselin	Mr Brewster Ghiselin
Halévy	M. Jean-Pierre Halévy
HMohr	Mrs Eva Humbert-Mohr
Holt	Mrs Frances Holt

HU	Harvard University
Huelin	Miss Lucy Huelin
Hughes-Stanton	Mrs Ida Hughes-Stanton
Hutchinson	Lord Hutchinson of Lullington
Huxley	Juliette, Lady Huxley
IEduc	Iowa State Education Association
Jeffrey	Mr Frederick Jeffrey
Jenner	Ms Heather Jenner
Lazarus	Mr George Lazarus
Mason	Mrs Doris Mason
Moore	Mrs Beatrice Moore
NCL	Nottinghamshire County Libraries
NWU	Northwestern University
NYPL	New York Public Library
PM	Pierpont Morgan Library
PU	Princeton University
Rosenbach	Rosenbach Museum & Library
Sagar	Dr Keith Sagar
Schlaefle	Mrs Susan Schlaefle-Nicholas
SIU	Southern Illinois University
StaU	Stanford University
SVerlag	Suhrkamp Verlag
UCB	University of California at Berkeley
UCin	University of Cincinnati
UCLA	University of California at Los Angeles
UD	University of Delaware
UIll	University of Illinois
UInd	University of Indiana
ULon	University of London
UN	University of Nottingham
UNYB	University of New York at Buffalo
UR	University of Reading
UT	University of Texas at Austin
UTul	University of Tulsa
VL	State Library of Victoria (Melbourne, Australia)
WAPL	Western Australia Public Library
YU	Yale University

B. Printed Works
(The place of publication, here and throughout, is London unless otherwise stated.)

Apocalypse	D. H. Lawrence. *Apocalypse and the Writings on Revelation.* Ed. Mara Kalnins. Cambridge: Cambridge University Press, 1980
Brewster	Earl Brewster and Achsah Brewster. *D. H. Lawrence: Reminiscences and Correspondence.* Secker, 1934
Chambers	Maria Cristina Chambers, 'Afternoons in Italy with D. H. Lawrence', *Texas Quarterly*, vii (Winter 1964), 114–20
Complete Poems	D. H. Lawrence. *The Complete Poems of D. H. Lawrence.* Ed. Vivian de Sola Pinto and Warren Roberts. 2 volumes. 3rd edn. Heinemann, 1972
DHL Review	*The D. H. Lawrence Review.* Fayetteville: University of Arkansas, 1968–83; Newark: University of Delaware, 1984–
Frieda Lawrence	Frieda Lawrence. *"Not I, But the Wind...".* Santa Fe: Rydal Press, 1934
Huxley	Aldous Huxley, ed. *The Letters of D. H. Lawrence.* Heinemann, 1932
Lacy, *Escaped Cock*	D. H. Lawrence. *The Escaped Cock.* Ed. Gerald M. Lacy. Los Angeles: Black Sparrow Press, 1973
Lawrence–Gelder	Ada Lawrence and G. Stuart Gelder. *Young Lorenzo: Early Life of D. H. Lawrence.* Florence: G. Orioli, [1931]
Letters, i.	James T. Boulton, ed. *The Letters of D. H. Lawrence.* Volume I, September 1901–May 1913. Cambridge: Cambridge University Press, 1979
Letters, ii.	George J. Zytaruk and James T. Boulton, eds. *The Letters of D. H. Lawrence.* Volume II, June 1913–October 1916. Cambridge: Cambridge University Press, 1981
Letters, iii.	James T. Boulton and Andrew Robertson, eds. *The Letters of D. H. Lawrence.* Volume III, October 1916–June 1921. Cambridge: Cambridge University Press, 1984

Letters, iv.	Warren Roberts, James T. Boulton and Elizabeth Mansfield, eds. *The Letters of D. H. Lawrence.* Volume IV, June 1921–March 1924. Cambridge: Cambridge University Press, 1987
Letters, v.	James T. Boulton and Lindeth Vasey, eds. *The Letters of D. H. Lawrence.* Volume V, March 1924–March 1927. Cambridge: Cambridge University Press, 1989
Letters, vi.	James T. Boulton and Margaret H. Boulton, with Gerald M. Lacy, eds. *The Letters of D. H. Lawrence.* Volume VI, March 1927–November 1928. Cambridge: Cambridge University Press, 1991
Luhan	Mabel Dodge Luhan. *Lorenzo in Taos.* New York: Knopf, 1932
Mohr, Briefe	'Briefe an Max Mohr von D. H. Lawrence', *Die Neue Rundschau*, xliv (April 1933), 527–40
Mohr	Max Mohr, 'The Unpublished Letters of D. H. Lawrence to Max Mohr', *T'ien Hsia Monthly*, i (August 1935), 21–36; i (September 1935), 166–79
Moore, *Intelligent Heart*	Harry T. Moore. *The Intelligent Heart: The Story of D. H. Lawrence.* New York: Farrar, Straus, and Young, 1954
Moore, *Poste Restante*	Harry T. Moore. *Poste Restante: A Lawrence Travel Calendar.* Berkeley and Los Angeles: University of California Press, 1956
Moore	Harry T. Moore, ed. *The Collected Letters of D. H. Lawrence.* 2 volumes. Heinemann, 1962
Munro	Craig Munro, 'The D. H. Lawrence–P. R. Stephensen Letters', *Australian Literary Studies*, xi (May 1984), 291–315
Nehls	Edward Nehls, ed. *D. H. Lawrence: A Composite Biography.* 3 volumes. Madison: University of Wisconsin Press, 1957–9
Paintings	*The Paintings of D. H. Lawrence.* Mandrake Press, 1929
Phoenix	Edward McDonald, ed. *Phoenix: The Posthumous Papers of D. H. Lawrence.* Heinemann, 1936

Roberts	Warren Roberts. *A Bibliography of D. H. Lawrence.* 2nd edn. Cambridge: Cambridge University Press, 1982
Schorer	Mark Schorer, 'I Will Send Address: Unpublished Letters of D. H. Lawrence', *London Magazine*, iii (February 1956), 44–67
Secker	Martin Secker, ed. *Letters from D. H. Lawrence to Martin Secker 1911–1930.* [Bridgefoot, Iver] 1970
Smith	Grover Smith, ed. *Letters of Aldous Huxley.* Chatto & Windus, 1969
Zytaruk	George J. Zytaruk, ed. *The Quest for Rananim: D. H. Lawrence's Letters to S. S. Koteliansky 1914 to 1930.* Montreal: McGill–Queen's University Press, 1970

MONETARY TERMS

tanner = sixpence (6d) = 2½p.
bob = one shilling (1/-) = 5p.
half-a-crown = 2/6 = 12½p.
quid = £1.
guinea = £1/1/- = £1.05.

LAWRENCE: A CHRONOLOGY, 1928–1930

November 1928	'Insouciance' in *Atlantic Monthly*
17 November 1928– 11 March 1929	At Hotel Beau Rivage, Bandol
22 November 1928	Has lengthened *Rawdon's Roof* as requested; 'The Blue Moccasins' in *Eve: The Lady's Pictorial*
24 November 1928	'Enslaved by Civilisation' sent to Nancy Pearn for *Sunday Dispatch*
25 November 1928	'Sex Locked Out' in *Sunday Dispatch*
29 November 1928	'Is England Still A Man's Country?' in *Daily Express*
29 November– 2 December 1928	Visit by Rhys Davies
3 December 1928	Returns to Mollie Skinner MS of her (unpublished) novel, 'Eve in the Land of Nod'
9 December 1928	Sends to Nancy Pearn 'Oh These Women!' ('Give Her a Pattern'); tells her that he has been writing 'Poems – Pensées' (*Pansies*)
14 December 1928	Reports gross profits of £1024 on *Lady Chatterley's Lover*
18–22 (or ?24) December 1928	Visit by Rhys Davies; P. R. Stephensen also stays 18–19 December
19 December 1928	Receives MS of Edward Dahlberg's novel, *Bottom Dogs*; sends comments on 22 December
24 December 1928	First draft of introduction to *Pansies* written
25 December 1928	'New Mexico' sent to Nancy Pearn for *Survey Graphic*, New York (published 1 May 1931)
January 1929	'Cocksure Women and Hensure Men' in *Forum*
1–2 January 1929	Julian and Juliette Huxley visit on their way to see H. G. Wells at Grasse
2–12 January 1929	Barbara Weekley stays with the Lawrences
4–15 January 1929	Visit from Brewster Ghiselin to whom Lawrence shows *Leda* and *Renascence of Men* (completed by 2 January)
5 January 1929	Reads to Barbara Weekley and Ghiselin the revised and longer introduction for *Pansies*

7 January 1929	Sends two copies of *Pansies* to Laurence Pollinger in Curtis Brown's London office; Stephensen visits (from Nice)
10 January 1929	In Toulon
11 January 1929	Has completed black-and-white frontispiece (revised version in water-colour c. 13 January) for Norman Douglas's *Venus in the Kitchen*, 'Introduction to These Paintings' and the drawing, *Electric Nudes*, which becomes the end-piece in *The Paintings of D. H. Lawrence*
12 January 1929	Sends poem, 'Henriette', to Juliette Huxley
14 January 1929	Sends MS of 'Introduction to These Paintings' to Pollinger
18 January 1929	Sends 'Ships in Bottles' to Pollinger; police inform Pollinger that six copies of *Lady Chatterley's Lover* have been seized
21 January–1 February 1929	Aldous and Maria Huxley, en route for Florence, stay with the Lawrences
23 January 1929	Police tell Pollinger that typescript of *Pansies* seized as 'obscene and indecent'
24 January 1929	The painting, *Spring* (begun c. 15 January), finished; Lawrence working on *Summer Dawn* (finished c. 7 February)
February 1929	'The Blue Moccasins' in *Plain Talk*
1 February 1929	Has completed 'about a third' of *Pansies* typescript; 'nearly done' on 7 February
5 February 1929	Returns typescript of 'Introduction to These Paintings' to Pollinger
7 February 1929	Attends 'Bandol philharmonic concert'
11 February 1929	Sends copy of *Pansies* TS to Marianne Moore of the *Dial*, with a new introduction
12 February 1929	His sister, Ada Clarke, arrives for holiday with Lawrences; autographed sheets for *Rawdon's Roof* returned to Elkin Mathews
17 February 1929	'Myself Revealed', accompanied by sketch of Lawrence, in *Sunday Dispatch*
19 February 1929	Proofs of 'Mother and Daughter' arrive from and are returned on 20th to Nancy Pearn
22 February 1929	Ada Clarke returns to England, taking with her paintings, *Spring* and *Summer Dawn*, and typescript of revised *Pansies*

8 May 1929	Goes by car to Valldemosa and Soller
10–13? May 1929	Spends weekend at Cala Ratjada
14 May 1929	Further proofs of *Paintings* received
18 May 1929	Returns signed sheets for *Paintings*, to Stephensen
20 May 1929	Presents Harry Crosby with MS of first part of *Escaped Cock*
25 May 1929	Sends two pages of 'one or two of the *Pansies* poems' in rough draft, as gift to David Lederhandler
26 May 1929	Has outing by car along island coast
31 May 1929	Receives agreement with Knopf for US edn of *Pansies*, but refuses to sign it
June 1929	Stephensen publishes *The Paintings of D. H. Lawrence*; pocket edn of *The Rainbow* (Secker)
6 June 1929	Outing by car along east coast of Mallorca
7 June 1929	MS of *The Escaped Cock*, Part II, sent to Crosby by Enid Hilton
8 June 1929	Tauchnitz edn of *Sons and Lovers*
12 June 1929	*Paintings* 'ready today'; copy received 17 June
14 June 1929	Exhibition of Lawrence's paintings at the Warren Gallery opens with private view; it closed in September
15 June 1929	Signed sheets for *Pansies* sent to Secker
18 June 1929	Leaves Mallorca by boat for Marseille
22 June 1929	Arrives at Pensione Giuliani, Forte dei Marmi (Huxleys nearby at 'Il Canneto'); Frieda in London
23 June 1929	Instructs Brett to place all his MSS at Kiowa Ranch in the Taos bank
25 June 1929	Dines with Baroness Franchetti
26 June 1929	Agrees to Harold Monro's request for poems to include in anthology, *Twentieth Century Poetry*
29?-30? June 1929	Visit by Giuseppe Orioli arranged for weekend
30? June 1929	Maria Cristina Chambers arrives at Pensione Giuliani
July 1929	First US impression of *Collected Poems*; Secker publishes expurgated *Pansies*; 'Making Pictures' in *Creative Art* and *Studio*; 'To Let Go Or Hold On – ?' (ten poems) in *Dial*

5 July 1929	Police raid Warren Gallery and seize thirteen of Lawrence's pictures
6 July 1929	Goes by road (Maria Huxley driving) to Pisa; by train to Florence
6–16 July 1929	Stays in Orioli's flat, 6 Lungarno Corsini
8–9 July 1929	Ill, in bed
11 July 1929	Frieda returns to Florence from London
15 July 1929	*My Skirmish with Jolly Roger* (New York, Random House)
16 July 1929	Orioli sends 'None of That' to Lederhandler
16–18 July 1929	Travels with Frieda by train, via Milan and Basel, to Baden-Baden
18–23 July 1929	At Hotel Löwen, Lichtenthal, Baden-Baden, with Frieda and her mother
23 July–3 August 1929	At Hotel Plättig, Bühl, with Frieda and her mother
28 July 1929	Has begun translation of Grazzini's *Second Supper*; 'More Paintings by D. H. Lawrence' announced in the Warren Gallery
29 July 1929	Returns proofs of *The Story of Doctor Manente* to Orioli
August 1929	Lahr's (nominally Stephensen's) unexpurgated edn of *Pansies*
1 August 1929	Receives MS of first version of *Lady Chatterley's Lover* from Orioli
2 August 1929	Sends essay 'The Risen Lord' to Nancy Pearn
3–25 August 1929	At Hotel Löwen, Lichtenthal
5 August 1929	Sends article 'Men and Women' ('Men Must Work and Women as Well') to Nancy Pearn; receives copy of Lahr's *Pansies* (ordinary edn)
7 August 1929	Returns more *Manente* proofs to Orioli, more on 10 August and still more on 19th
8 August 1929	Proofs of *The Escaped Cock* arrive; receives copy of Lahr's special edn of *Pansies*; magistrate's judgement delivered on police seizure of Lawrence's pictures and copies of *Paintings*
10 August 1929	Sends poems in MS and TSCC to Hilda Aldington; the six poems in MS appeared in the *Imagist Anthology* (1930)
11 August 1929	Celebration for Frieda's fiftieth birthday

15 August 1929	Returns proofs of *The Escaped Cock* to Caresse Crosby, together with his water-colour decorations
16 August 1929	Receives 3810 francs ($150) from Titus as half of fee from Random House for publishing *My Skirmish with Jolly Roger*
23 August 1929	Sends Lahr several *Nettles* poems
25 August 1929	Leaves Lichtenthal for Munich
26 August– 18 September 1929	At Kaffee Angermeier, Rottach-am-Tegernsee (to visit Max Mohr)
30 August 1929	Receives contract for Gallimard's French translation of *Lady Chatterley's Lover*
September 1929	*The Escaped Cock* published by Crosby in Paris; 'Pornography and Obscenity' in *This Quarter*, July–September; 'The Manufacture of Good Little Boys' ('Enslaved by Civilisation') in *Vanity Fair*
2 September 1929	Visit from Else Jaffe
8 September 1929	Sends additional material to Pollinger for Faber edn of *Pornography and Obscenity*
13 September 1929	Returns to Orioli proofs of notes to *Manente*
16 September 1929	Receives cheque from Dorothy Warren for pictures sold in Warren Gallery exhibition
17 September 1929	Sends signed sheets for *The Escaped Cock* to Caresse Crosby
18 September 1929	Leaves Rottach for Bandol (23 September) via Munich and Marseille
23 September– 1 October 1929	At Hotel Beau Rivage, Bandol
27 September 1929	Receives, signs and returns to Orioli sheets for *Manente*; Knopf publishes American edn of *Pansies*
October 1929	*The Life of J. Middleton Murry* privately printed by Lahr
1 October 1929– 6 February 1930	At Villa Beau Soleil, Bandol
3 October 1929	'The Risen Lord' in *Everyman*
4 October 1929	Returns proofs of 'Men and Women' to Nancy Pearn

5 October 1929	Writes 'newspaper article' (probably 'We Need One Another')
11 October 1929	Returns to Pollinger the signed contract for Faber's edn of *Pornography and Obscenity*
15 October 1929	'feeling rotten. I'll have to go into a sanatorium if [my health] doesn't pick up'; receives copy of *The Escaped Cock*
18? October 1929	Brewsters arrive from Naples
21 October 1929	Mohr departs for home (having been in Hotel Goëlands since c. 29 September)
November 1929	Five poems in Harold Monro's *Twentieth Century Poetry*; 'Introduction' in Edward Dahlberg's *Bottom Dogs*; 'Men and Women' in *Star Review*
1 November 1929	Returns to Pollinger agreement for Cresset Press edn of *Birds, Beasts and Flowers*, along with proofs of *Pornography and Obscenity* and MS of *A Propos of "Lady Chatterley's Lover"*
4 November 1929	Sends three articles to Nancy Pearn for *Vanity Fair*
7 November 1929	Review of Rozanov's *Fallen Leaves* sent to Nancy Pearn
9 November 1929	Receives copies of *Doctor Manente*
12 November 1929	Sends 'Notes for *Birds, Beasts and Flowers*' to Blair Hughes-Stanton for Cresset Press edn
14 November 1929	*Pornography and Obscenity* published by Faber: sold 'over 6,000' by 10 December
ante 20–30 November 1929	Frederick Carter stays at Hotel Beau Rivage in order to visit Lawrence
December 1929	'Chaos in Poetry' in *Echanges*; 'Dead Pictures on the Wall' ('Pictures on the Wall') in *Vanity Fair*
3 December 1929	Sends four poems to Nancy Pearn for possible inclusion in Faber's *Ariel Poems* series
ante 9 December 1929	Anna and Ferdinando di Chiara and Ida Rauh arrive and stay at Hotel Beau Rivage
10 December 1929	Harry Crosby commits suicide in New York
13 December 1929	Sends MS of *Nettles* to Pollinger
15 December 1929	Has finished draft introduction for Carter's 'Revelation of St. John the Divine'
17 December 1929	Has lunch in Hotel Beau Rivage

18 December 1929	Signs and returns to Curtis Brown's office agreement for German translation (by Herlitschka) of *Lady Chatterley's Lover*
c. 28 December 1929	Sends text for *Assorted Articles* to Pollinger
6 January 1930	Sends rewritten 'Introduction' for Carter's *Dragon of the Apocalypse* to Curtis Brown's office for typing
15–20 January 1930	Pollinger at Hotel Beau Rivage; on his return takes Lawrence's 'Introduction' to *The Grand Inquisitor*
17–26 January 1930	Else Jaffe stays with Lawrences
20–1 January 1930	Dr Andrew Morland and his wife at Hotel Beau Rivage; he orders Lawrence to rest 'for some months'
23 January 1930	Review of Rozanov's *Fallen Leaves* in *Everyman*
c. 30 January 1930	Barbara Weekley arrives to stay with Lawrences
3 February 1930	Returns contract for *Nettles* to Pollinger
6 February 1930	Hughes-Stanton drives Lawrences from Nice to Vence
6 February–1 March 1930	In sanatorium 'Ad Astra', Vence; Frieda at Hotel Nouvel, 6–15 February, then – with Barbara Weekley and Ida Rauh – at Casa dei Sogni, Cagnes till 1 March
13 February 1930	Visit from Earl Brewster
24 February 1930	Visited by H. G. Wells
25 and 28 February 1930	Visits from Aldous and Maria Huxley
26 February 1930	Jo Davidson makes bust of Lawrence
27 February 1930	Visit from Aga Khan and his wife
1 March 1930	Moves from Ad Astra to Villa Robermond, Vence
2 March 1930	Lawrence dies
13 March 1930	*Nettles*
April 1930	*Assorted Articles*
17 May 1930	*The Virgin and the Gipsy* (Florence)
25 November 1930	*Love Among the Haystacks & Other Pieces*
March 1931	*The Man Who Died* (*The Escaped Cock*)
3 June 1931	*Apocalypse* (Florence)
September 1932	*Etruscan Places*
1 October 1932	*Last Poems* (Florence)

MAPS

N

Soller

Valldemosa

San
Agustin Palma

*Mallorca
(Majorca)*

Cala
Ratjada

0   10 Miles
0   16 Kilometres

Biarritz

Burgos

PORTUGAL

SPAIN

Madrid

Toledo

Valencia

Cordoba

Alicante

Sevilla

Granada

O Orléans

N

FRANCE

O Lyons

ITALY

Genoa O

O Toulouse

Carcassonne O

Marseille
St Cyr-s
-mer
Les Lecques O

Perpignan O

Barcelona O

MEDITERRANEAN SEA

SEE INSET

Menorca
(Minorca)

Palma O

Mallorca
(Majorca)

Ibiza

Balearic Islands

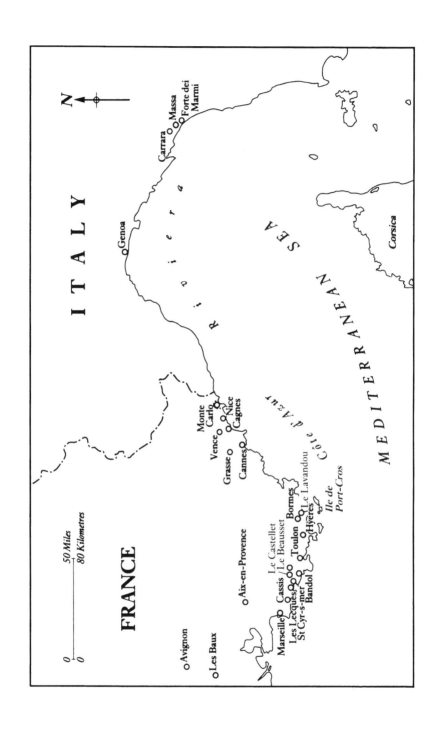

FRANCE

ITALY

MEDITERRANEAN SEA

Riviera

Côte d'Azur

Corsica

50 Miles
80 Kilometres

N

Avignon

Les Baux

Aix-en-Provence

Le Castellet
Le Beausset
Marseille
Cassis
Les Lecques
St Cyr-s-mer
Bandol
Toulon
Bormes
Hyères
Le Lavandou
Ile de
Port-Cros

Grasse
Vence
Cannes
Cagnes
Nice
Monte
Carlo

Genoa

Carrara
Massa
Forte dei
Marmi

INTRODUCTION

This volume differs from its predecessors in several ways. It covers a shorter period of Lawrence's life, a mere fifteen months, and records a greater than usual density of correspondence. The explanation is probably not that Lawrence wrote more letters in this period than in any other; rather that a higher proportion has survived. Whole archives of business letters were kept intact: not only those involving the staff of Curtis Brown Ltd, Lawrence's literary agents, especially Laurence Pollinger and Nancy Pearn; but also those of Giuseppe Orioli, publisher of *Lady Chatterley's Lover* and *The Story of Doctor Manente*; Charles Lahr, publisher of *Pansies*; P. R. Stephensen, publisher of *The Paintings of D. H. Lawrence* and *A Propos of "Lady Chatterley's Lover"*; and Edward Titus, publisher of the Paris popular edition of *Lady Chatterley's Lover*. Lawrence's private correspondents, aware of his distinction, also felt under some obligation – perhaps prompted by affection, respect, knowledge of his terminal illness or, occasionally, self-interest – to preserve everything he wrote, even the most casual notes. For some of the same reasons the volume contains a higher proportion, a large majority, of unpublished letters. Indeed, perhaps remarkably few of the letters Lawrence wrote in this period are not printed here.

However it must be acknowledged that in terms of expressive and imaginative vigour there is some falling off. Partly because such a large quantity of the letters are of the 'business' kind, though when it is recognised that those people to whom Lawrence wrote most frequently – Orioli, Pollinger and Lahr – became friends as well as publishers or agent, the normal connotations of 'business' are too restrictive; partly because there is no fictional work-in-progress to be discussed; and partly because of Lawrence's loss of energy as he enters the last phase of his illness: for such reasons the letters of these last months are relatively lacking in the vitality which characterises the best of those written earlier, though it sparkles here and there. Lawrence himself was sadly aware of this. In November 1929 he remarked to his sister Emily: 'so many letters to write, I get tired to death of them'; and in the following month to Koteliansky: 'Excuse this poor letter ...'[1] Yet even the relatively poor, drained letters have their place in tracing the shape of a life. As Aldous Huxley wrote in the Introduction to his volume of Lawrence's *Letters*: 'How tragically the splendid curve of the letters droops, at the end, towards the darkness!'[2]

---

[1] Letters 5409, 5461.   [2] Huxley xxxi–xxxii.

Yet in spite of this, there continue to be numerous examples of Lawrence's characteristic virtues as a letter-writer: spontaneity, freshness, evocative and flexible prose, playful humour, stinging wit ('How are the puny risen!') and, perhaps most important, sensitivity, the delicate adjustment to the occasion and the recipient. This was stressed by Rebecca West in a tribute to Lawrence after his death. She mentioned the splendid letter he wrote to her in April 1929, encouraging her to renew her 'energy like the eagle':

... a few months ago I received a letter from him thanking me for some little tribute I had paid him during the trouble about his pictures in London. This letter showed the utmost humility in him to take notice of such a small courtesy; and it showed more than that. With marvellous sensitiveness he had deduced from a phrase or two in my article that I was troubled by a certain problem, and he said words that in their affectionate encouragement and exquisite appositeness could not have been bettered if we had spent the ten years that had intervened since our meeting in the closest friendship.[1]

That is a perceptive summing-up: 'words that in their affectionate encouragement and exquisite appositeness could not have been bettered'. Nowhere do these qualities shine out more than in his letters to people who were, in some sense, vulnerable, such as the young, or the socially or economically deprived or the bereaved. There is the tender regard in letters to the Pini family, the peasants who had been turned off from the Mirenda estate; or the concern he reveals for the expatriate American teenager, Harwood Brewster, in an English boarding-school, growing in independence from her parents; or the compassionate advice in his letter to Caresse Crosby (written only a week before Lawrence entered the Ad Astra sanatorium), whose husband had committed suicide after killing his mistress:

Oh yes, don't you try to recover yourself too soon – it is much better to be a little blind and stunned for a time longer, and not make efforts to see or to feel. Work is the best, and a certain numbness, a merciful numbness. It was too dreadful a blow – and it was wrong.[2]

Lawrence himself was vulnerable in many respects, not least in his sensitivity to public hostility in the shape of prosecution, vilification and censorship of various kinds. One consequence was his increasing reliance on private publication and limited editions though he strongly objected to this type of publishing. But one principle had to give way to another: 'when a thing *can't* appear publicly, it shall appear privately, and that's all'.[3] This defiance was directly responsible for the relationships he developed with several private publishers.

[1] Letters 5477, 5046; Nehls, ii. 65–6.   [2] Letter 5501.   [3] Letter 5354.

The most significant among these new correspondents was the left-wing, eccentric London bookseller, Charles Lahr. The two men never met. Had Lawrence visited the 'Progressive Bookshop' in Red Lion Street (hence Lahr's nickname, 'the Lion'), he might have encountered such figures as the Scottish poet Hugh MacDiarmid; the young Welsh novelist and short-story writer Rhys Davies (who was later introduced to Lawrence through Lahr); the antipodeans Eric Partridge and Jack Lindsay; or the poet Anna Wickham (whom he had previously known through the Garnetts). Kenneth Hopkins recalled that 'more or less ankle deep all over the floor, were the letters Charles had received from D. H. Lawrence, and T. F. Powys, and Liam O'Flaherty and Norman Douglas, and practically every other prominent writer of the 'twenties'.[1] Lahr had already unhesitatingly distributed copies of *Lady Chatterley's Lover* and was prepared to handle the 200 copies of the cheap paper issue; Lawrence thought him 'very good, and ... absolutely honest', a man who would sympathise with his idea 'to publish two or three poems on a sheet of paper and sell them for 2d or 3d'. Lahr was, then, just the right publisher for the unexpurgated *Pansies*, in a limited edition, though, when it came in August 1929, Lawrence was bitterly disappointed by the book's appearance: 'it looks as if the one idea had been to economise paper ... all so crowded, some pages look like a Hansard's report'. Yet, in spite of that, and though Lahr was 'a wee bit of a muddler, and careless in details ... he is a man in ten thousand'. Lawrence was 'very grateful to him for his pluck and energy'.[2]

These were the qualities Lawrence looked for in his publishers and because they were so often lacking – Martin Secker, his main English publisher, for example, would publish only an expurgated *Pansies* – he had increasingly to act as his own agent and salesman. (Much of the voluminous correspondence with his agents, Curtis Brown, is concerned with urging Pollinger to stir Secker and Lawrence's main American publisher, Alfred Knopf, into energetic action.) Most of his principal works from the last years were handled by Lawrence himself; no general publisher would dare to be associated with them. The private edition of *Lady Chatterley's Lover* is the chief example; it earned Lawrence more than any other of his books. To

---

[1] Kenneth Hopkins, *The Corruption of a Poet* (1954), p. 128.

[2] Letters 4788, 4869, 5246, 5315. In his unpublished history of the *Pansies* typescript (Roberts E302g), John Taylor Caldwell claims that – before Lahr agreed to publish the volume – DHL had viewed Guy Alfred Aldred (1886–1963), the voluminous, Communist author, as a possibility. The champion of a free press, Aldred had been prosecuted for publishing seditious works, but private publishing for gain would not have appealed to him. (No mention is made of any correspondence with DHL in Aldred's autobiography, *No Traitor's Gait*, Glasgow, 1955–63.)

circumvent the efforts of 'censor-morons' he took great pains (including a health-sapping visit to Paris) to find a publisher for a cheap 'popular' edition of the same work. The Crosbys published *The Escaped Cock* on their Black Sun Press in Paris, with the author's water-colour decorations (perhaps the most beautiful edition of any Lawrence book). Stephensen took on Lawrence's paintings as the first publication by his Mandrake Press, and another handsome volume resulted.

In his personal dealings with these private publishers Lawrence demanded fair terms and scrupulous accounting, reflected, for example in his letter to Caresse Crosby, 12 August 1929, or the opening paragraph of his last letter to Titus:[1] he had been taken in too often in the past. The deceit and dilatoriness of commercial publishers, especially in the USA, incensed him. It was doubt-less his bitterness as well as Frieda's which burst out in her letter to Titus, 5 February 1930: 'It does'nt seem to matter, *who* has the books, but that this priceless & unique property should bring us not *200* dollars a year in America & Lawr having sweatted his guts out for this filthy humanity, that does'nt even pay him back in money *not* to *speak* of *life*, there he gets *nothing* – It makes me quite furious'.[2]

As Lawrence grew physically ever weaker and devoted so much of his limited energy to 'business', he had little left for creative work. He had hoped to finish *Sketches of Etruscan Places* but never did; he declined Mollie Skinner's request for a new collaboration on another novel; his imagination was fired by his own proposal to start (with Lahr) a magazine, 'The Squib', intended to satirise pretentiousness and hypocrisy, but it came to nothing; he tried to interest other writers in Orioli's Lungarno Renaissance series, but his own *Story of Doctor Manente* remained its sole publication. Lawrence wrote no fiction in his last fifteen months. Apart from *Apocalypse* and four impor-tant essays – *A Propos of "Lady Chatterley's Lover"*, *Pornography and Obscenity*, 'New Mexico' and 'Nottingham and the Mining Countryside' – he wrote only poems and short articles. Some of the latter were intended for *Vanity Fair* whose managing editor, Donald Freeman, was hoping – as late as January 1930 – to persuade Lawrence to accept a year's contract as a regular contributor to his magazine. The *Architectural Review*, the Freedom Associ-ation and the *Star Review* were other competitors for his attention. He was unenthusiastic about what became the posthumous volume, *Assorted Articles* – 'if it was left to me, I should say don't do it' – but he acquiesced, submitted the material in late December 1929 and corrected proof. 'As for work, I haven't felt like doing anything at all, and I am still that way. I neither write

---

[1] Letters 5257, 5524.   [2] MS SIU ('Wednesday').

nor paint':[1] the dejection and weariness in that remark, made in November 1929, find recurring echoes in this volume.

* * *

When, in mid-November 1928, the Lawrences left 'that poky island', the Ile de Port-Cros, they had little idea where they wanted to go. As Lawrence had told the Brewsters, 'I think we shall only just go over to Bandol, on the coast between Toulon and Marseilles, for a little while, just to gather our wits and decide where to go.'[2] Frieda wanted a house – she became bored in the hotel – but could not decide whether it should be on Lake Garda, at Taormina or the ranch which she owned near Taos, New Mexico; Lawrence preferred to return to Italy to do more work on the Etruscans, or to visit Spain – he even fantasised about Zululand as he had done some years earlier.[3] In the event, life was so easy and comfortable, though a little dull, at the Hotel Beau Rivage that they stayed there all winter, until March 1929. Frieda recalled:

A sunny hotel by the sea, friendly and easy as only Provence can be ... Lawrence wrote 'Pansies' in his room in the morning, then we went to have our aperitif before lunch in a cafe on the sea-front ... We knew all the dogs of the small place, we saw the boats come in, their silvery loads of sardines glittering on the sand of the shores. Lawrence ... watched the men playing 'boccia' on the shore, after lunch. We seemed to share the life of the little town, running along so easily ... Yes, easy and sunny was this winter in Bandol.[4]

Lawrence's health improved. He spent not a single day in bed that winter. He wrote some newspaper articles and an introduction to Edward Dahlberg's novel, *Bottom Dogs*; he completed several paintings. And there was a stream of visitors: his sister Ada, Frieda's daughter Barbara, Rhys Davies, Aldous and Maria, Julian and Juliette Huxley, P. R. Stephensen and the young American critic and painter Brewster Ghiselin.

The calm was shattered on 21 January: news arrived from Pollinger that, three days earlier, the police had seized six copies of *Lady Chatterley's Lover* addressed to him. More important, the typescript of *Pansies* was also intercepted in the post and once again, after fourteen years, Lawrence's affairs became matters of political debate. In the Commons on 28 February 1929 Mr Pethick-Lawrence, on behalf of the Labour M.P., Miss Ellen Wilkinson, asked the Home Secretary 'whether he gave instructions for a manuscript of poems sent by Mr. D. H. Lawrence to his literary agent to be seized before any question of publication arose'. Sir W. Joynson Hicks (popularly known as 'Jix') replied that he gave no such instructions. He went on to explain:

[1] Letters 5285, 5362, 5471 and n. 1; 5244 and nn. 1 and 2; 5399; 5468; 5403.
[2] Letter 4752; *Letters*, vi. 608.
[3] Letter 4762; cf. *Letters*, iii. 416–17, 449.   [4] Frieda Lawrence 211.

Under the Post Office Act of 1908 the duty is laid upon the Postmaster-General to refuse to take part in the conveyance of any indecent matter, and the Postal Union Convention of Stockholm, 1924, also prohibits the transmission through the post of indecent matter. In this case the typescripts were sent through the open book post from abroad and were detected in the course of the examination to which a proportion of such packets are subjected for the purpose of detecting whether letters or other matter not conveyed at that rate are contained in the packet. The typescripts were sent to the Home Office and by my directions were then forwarded to the Director of Public Prosecutions. I am advised that there is no possible doubt whatever that these contain indecent matter and, as such, are liable to seizure. I have, however, given instructions that they shall be detained for two months to enable the author to establish the contrary if he desires to do so.[1]

Joynson Hicks then had the effrontery to assert that 'there is nothing which can properly be described as a literary censorship in this country'. In answer to a further question he admitted that 'nobody, no official of the State, can open a sealed packet without the direct warrant of the Secretary of State': Lawrence's typescript had been mailed by sealed and registered letter post. As Lawrence had told Orioli the week before: 'the blow has fallen!'[2]

He had been afraid of police intervention for some months and was not therefore taken by surprise. Though he dismissed the notion that the police were reading his mail, in December 1928 he suggested to Lahr that he could 'address the letters to my wife ... there must be thousands of Mrs Lawrences'.[3] He was apprehensive that he would face arrest if he returned to England and this made him sensitive to the situation elsewhere: he hesitated about going to Spain, for example, because the country was politically disturbed, the police were on the alert 'everywhere wanting to look at people's papers'. The fear of arrest in England persisted; as a result he took the decision in May 1929 not to attend the Warren Gallery exhibition of his paintings. (In July Nancy Pearn advised Frieda to consult their friend, the barrister St John Hutchinson, 'as to the advisability or otherwise' of Lawrence's coming to England.) Later, in August, when Lahr's unexpurgated *Pansies* was published, Lawrence told Titus: 'I have to keep quiet about it as the police are getting fierce because I defy them.'[4] Not surprisingly paranoia appears to have exacerbated his physical decline.

Piracies of his work were another source of anxiety. Victor Gollancz, the radical publisher who had recently founded his own firm, agreed to consider issuing a cheap edition of *Lady Chatterley's Lover* to undercut the pirates, but nothing came of it. Eventually Lawrence decided to seek publication of such

[1] Nehls, iii. 311–12.   [2] Letter 4898.   [3] Cf. *Letters*, vi. 12–13; Letter 4783.
[4] Letters 5000, 4926, 5094; letter from Nancy Pearn to Frieda Lawrence, 2 July 1929, TMSC UT; Letter 5268.

an edition in Paris where he arrived, with Rhys Davies, on 11 March. He was obliged to stay a month to complete his business; he quickly succumbed to what he called 'Paris grippe'[1] and his health never recovered. After unsuccessful negotiations with Sylvia Beach, who had published *Ulysses*, he came to terms with another American-expatriate bookseller, Edward Titus, who published and quickly disposed of 3,000 copies of 'Our Lady' as they subsequently called the novel. While in Paris, staying with Aldous and Maria Huxley, his hosts introduced him to a number of the leading literary figures, especially those associated with the *Nouvelle Revue Française*. Lawrence was unimpressed. The Lawrences also paid several visits to the rich American playboy and publisher, Harry Crosby and his wife Caresse at their Moulin du Soleil, to discuss the publication of *The Escaped Cock*.

It was on one of these visits that Lawrence came close to meeting James Joyce. On 3 April the Crosbys left Lawrence with Aldous Huxley at their home to rush off to a business meeting with Joyce. They invited him to return with them but 'he didn't want to meet Lawrence – said his eye hurt him – he is very timid'.[2] He may have had other reasons for not wishing to meet Lawrence of whom he remarked to the Italian writer, Nino Frank: 'Cet homme écrit vraiment très mal.' When Stuart Gilbert later read him some pages from *Lady Chatterley's Lover*, Joyce responded with the single word 'Lush!'; he wrote to Harriet Weaver in December 1931: 'I read the first 2 pages of the usual sloppy English, and S.G. read me a lyrical bit about nudism in a wood and the end which is a piece of propaganda in favour of something which, outside of D.H.L.'s country at any rate, makes all the propaganda for itself.'[3] Lawrence had an even lower opinion of *Ulysses*: 'The last part of it is the dirtiest, most indecent, obscene thing ever written.' And of *Finnegans Wake* Brewster learned: 'What a stupid *olla podrida* of the Bible and so forth ... just stewed-up fragments of quotation in the sauce of a would-be-dirty mind. Such effort! Such exertion! sforzato davvero!'[4]

At last, on 7 April, the Lawrences were able to escape from Paris – 'that city of dreadful night' – to Mallorca – 'a wonderful place for doing nothing'.[5] They remained there till mid-June when Lawrence joined the Huxleys at Forte dei Marmi, while Frieda was in London to see the exhibition in the Warren Gallery. That opened on 14 June; on 5 July the police removed, of the twenty-five paintings, thirteen which were judged by the police officer,

[1] Letter 5035.
[2] Harry Crosby, *Shadows of the Sun*, ed. E. Germain (Santa Barbara, 1977), p. 245.
[3] Richard Ellmann, *James Joyce* (1982 edn), p. 615 and n. (Joyce to Frank: 'This man really writes very badly.')
[4] Dorothy Brett, *Lawrence and Brett* (Philadelphia, 1933), p. 81; *Letters*, vi. 507.
[5] Letters 5041, 5113.

Inspector Hester, to be obscene because they depicted pubic hair. The police also seized copies of the Mandrake edition of the *Paintings* (which included Lawrence's lengthy introduction), together with a copy of George Grosz's *Ecce Homo* portfolio. Blake's *Pencil Drawings* was also impounded but was returned by Hester in response to jibes from the public.[1] On the same day as the raid in London, Lawrence in Forte was taken violently ill with stomach pains. He struggled to Florence the next day and Orioli was so concerned that he took Lawrence to his own flat and telegraphed to Frieda to come at once. After a few days he was well enough to travel with her to Baden-Baden.

The prosecution at Marlborough Street Magistrates' Court, arising from the seizure of the paintings, was directed against the Gallery owners, but a solicitor, Percy Robinson, was engaged to safeguard Lawrence's interests. He proposed that, so long as the paintings were returned by the police unharmed, Dorothy Warren and Philip Trotter should undertake not to exhibit them again; they, however, wanted to fight for the complete vindication of the paintings and their right to display them, even at the risk that the pictures might be destroyed. They enlisted the support of many prominent artists and writers for their cause, including Lytton Strachey, Roger Fry, Leonard and Virginia Woolf, Clive and Vanessa Bell, Duncan Grant, Maynard Keynes, Augustus and Gwen John, Jacob Epstein and Vita Sackville-West. Lawrence's position was clear: 'I do not want my pictures to be burned, under any circumstance or for any cause. The law, of course, must be altered – it is blatantly obvious. Why burn my pictures to prove it? There is something sacred to me about my pictures, and I will not have them burnt, for all the liberty of England.' They were returned and have never since been exhibited in England (though they would no longer be in danger of seizure). A few were sold, some given to friends, others disappeared. Newspaper reports on the exhibition left Lawrence disgusted and insulted: 'I shall not forgive it easily, to my white-livered nation ... Thank God I needn't live amongst them, even to hear their beastly mingy British voices.'[2]

Lawrence's physical condition had for some time alarmed his friends; his own reluctance to admit it coupled with his seeming ignorance about it both astonished and distressed them. Aldous Huxley provides the clearest evidence of this in a letter to his brother, Julian, on 13 July 1929, shortly after Lawrence's visit to Forte dei Marmi. It is worth quoting at length.

Lawrence was here a few days and is gone again. If you knew the struggles we had had with him about his health – but quite in vain. When he was in Paris, before he went to

---

[1] See the account by Philip Trotter in Nehls, iii. 342–52.

[2] Letter 5200; those pictures which remained in Frieda's possession are now housed in La Fonda in Taos, New Mexico, while others are in the Harry Ransom Humanities Research Center, University of Texas at Austin; Letter 5261.

Majorca, we actually got him to agree to undertake a treatment, alone, *minus* Frieda, and we also actually got him to go to a doctor in Paris. He was to go back to the Dr. to be X-rayed. (Meanwhile, however, the Dr. told M that, from just sounding him he could hear that one lung was practically gone and the other affected. He doubted whether very much cd be done.) Then Frieda, who had been in London, returned. L felt himself reinforced. He refused to go back to the Dr., refused to think of the treatment and set off with Frieda (of whom he had bitterly complained when he was alone with us) to Majorca. So that's that. It's no good. He doesn't *want* to know how ill he is: that, I believe, is the fundamental reason why he won't go to Doctors and homes. He only went in Paris because he was feeling iller than usual and was even more frightened of dying at once than of hearing how ill he was. He rationalizes the fear in all kinds of ways which are, of course, quite irrelevant. And meantime he just wanders about, very tired and at bottom wretched, from one place to another, imagining that the next place will make him feel better and, when he gets [to] the next place, regretting the one before and looking back on it as a paradise. But of course no place will make him feel any better than any other now that he's as ill as he is. He's a great deal worse than he was when you saw him at Diablerets – coughs more, breathes very quickly and shallowly, has no energy. (It's pathetic to see the way he just sits and does nothing. He hasn't written a line or painted a stroke for the last 3 months. Just lack of vital strength.) He still talks a good deal and can get amused and excited into the semblance of health for an hour or two at a time. But it is only a semblance, I'm afraid. I think he's even worse than he was in Paris in March (when he had a touch of flu to complicate matters). The Doctor told M that he might drag on for quite a little time like this, unless he got a cold which turned into bronchitis or pneumonia, when he'd simply be asphyxiated. He has gone to Germany now – or is just going: for he has been in Florence these last days – of all places in this weather! We have given up trying to persuade him to be reasonable. He doesn't want to be and no one can persuade him to be – except possibly Frieda. But Frieda is worse than he is. We've told her that she's a fool and a criminal; but it has no more effect than telling an elephant. So it's hopeless. Short of handcuffing him and taking him to a sanatorium by force, there's nothing to be done.[1]

Three days after Huxley wrote his letter Lawrence and Frieda set off by train for Germany. Baden's moist heat, however, made him 'limp and raggy' so they, with Frieda's mother, moved up to the Kurhaus Plättig at about 2,600 feet; there it was so cold that Lawrence had to stay in bed under a great feather bolster in order to keep warm. He was irritable, almost truculent with Titus and on the edge of being tetchy with the Crosbys,[2] but the clearest sign of near-despair over his health was the change in his attitude to Frieda's mother. No longer was she 'Meine liebe Schwiegermutter' who had formerly been addressed with such affection. In November 1928, for example, Lawrence had been sympathetic and tender when he remonstrated with her for being over-active: '... you're not a light young thing any more. Just don't

---

[1] Smith 313–14.   [2] Letters 5223, 5227, 5236.

walk so far ... No no, just be wise and gentle. Exertion is not for you.' Now, ten months later, he found her 'rather awful ... thinking her time to die may be coming on. So she fights in the ugliest fashion, greedy and horrible, to get everything that will keep her alive'. Orioli was told that 'she would see me or anyone else die ten times over, to give her a bit more strength to drag on a few more meaningless years'.[1] This was the reaction of a man who had secretly acknowledged the terminal nature of his condition and was seeing his own face in the mirror held up to another supposed victim. Confirmation is found in the defiant, superficially jocular remarks to Orioli in August 1929: 'How they do all like to dwell on the thought of my being dead! but everybody alike. They have determined I shall die. So of course I shall live a hundred years, and put wreaths on all their graves.'[2] As if to prove it, he wrote articles – 'The Risen Lord' for *Everyman*, 'Men and Women' for *Star Review* – and read proof on *The Story of Doctor Manente* and *The Escaped Cock*.

It is noticeable, however, that for the first time Lawrence became seriously concerned for the whereabouts and safety of his manuscripts and sensitive to their monetary value. He had gently enquired of Dorothy Brett in March 1929 about the manuscripts which he believed to be in a cupboard at Frieda's ranch where Brett was living: 'They are getting valuable now, they may come in so handy some rainy day.' Pressure on her intensified in June when Lawrence heard that some manuscripts were being offered for sale by dealers: 'I want you to tell me exactly what manuscripts I gave to you: and which exactly you sold to Mrs Hare: and how much she paid ... I need to keep track of my manuscripts ... So please answer me quite plainly and definitely, or I shan't know what to think.' Frieda added her weight with letters of extreme bitterness reflecting years of resentment: 'Do stop your monkey tricks about the ranch, the manuscripts & all the rest – ... You can live at the ranch for nothing, unless you wont hand over the manuscripts and any other things we want – We can turn you out, you know lock stock & barrel quite ignom-iniously –'[3] It was not until 29 September that Lawrence fully admitted his error: 'Of course I knew quite well you would not sell my MSS, in spite of what anybody said.' He was himself offered $3,000 for the manuscript of *Lady Chatterley's Lover* and refused it; when his sister Ada discovered the *Rainbow* manuscript in her attic, he was clearly delighted and asked for details of its provenance: and it was to her that he declared the reasons, both immedi-ate and long-term, for his keenness to preserve and safeguard his property: 'I want to keep them for the present, because they increase in value and they

[1] *Letters*, vi. 615; Letters 5235, 5237.   [2] Letter 5256.
[3] Letters 4972, 5158; letter, Frieda Lawrence to Dorothy Brett, 20 August 1929, MS UCin: see also p. 385 n. 1.

represent my capital . . . if I died, the MSS and pictures would have to be sold to secure something of an income for Frieda.'[1]

Meanwhile, in Germany, Lawrence longed for 'the olive trees and the Mediterranean';[2] he planned to look for a house perhaps on Lake Como. But a few days later he received and promptly accepted an invitation to visit Max Mohr at Rottach in Bavaria. He liked Mohr but at this moment was additionally drawn to him by the fact that Mohr was a doctor as well as a writer. At Rottach Lawrence was so weak that he had to confront the probability that he was dying. Frieda remembered:

My sister Else came to see him, and Alfred Weber. When he was alone with Alfred Weber, he said to him: 'Do you see those leaves falling from the apple tree? When the leaves want to fall you must let them fall.' Max Mohr had brought some doctors from Munich, but medicine did not help Lawrence. His organism was too frail and sensitive. I remember some autumn nights when the end seemed to have come. I listened for his breath through the open door, all night long, an owl hooting ominously from the walnut tree outside. In the dim dawn an enormous bunch of gentians I had put on the floor by his bed seemed the only living thing in the room.[3]

It was at this time that Lawrence wrote the first drafts of 'Bavarian Gentians' and 'The Ship of Death'. The doctors put him on a diet, of which he approved, but also prescribed arsenic which made him much worse. He must have suspected that his forty-fourth birthday on 11 September (remembered only by the Brewsters, overlooked even by his sisters) would be his last. Temporarily, however, he did recover sufficiently to move on; he decided that he had been so well in Bandol that it would be wise to return there.

Lawrence was delighted to be back on the Mediterranean. On 1 October he and Frieda moved into the Villa Beau Soleil; externally it was rather like a little railway station, he thought, but ideally situated overlooking the sea, and with central-heating. He was much happier now but his health did not improve. On 15 October he felt so ill that, for the first time, he mentioned to two correspondents the possibility that he might enter a sanatorium. The Brewsters arrived in Bandol (Lawrence wanted them as neighbours) and subsequently saw him nearly every day. 'Earl massaged him with cocoanut oil until Lawrence's blue fingers began to take on a hue of life.'[4]

The letters now become fewer and more subdued, full of complaints about his enforced inactivity. He insisted on having the shutters and curtains open every night so that he could see the sky as he lay awake, coughing. Frieda recalled:

---

[1] Letters 5355; 5217, 5365; 5300.   [2] Letter 5226.   [3] Frieda Lawrence 213.
[4] Letters 5379, 5380; Brewster 304.

But then at dawn I believe he felt grateful that another day had been given him. 'Come when the sun rises,' he said, and when I came he was glad, so very glad, as if he would say: 'See, another day is given me.'

The sun rose magnificently opposite his bed in red and gold across the bay and the fishermen standing up in their boats looked like eternal mythological figures dark and alive against the lit-up splendour of the sea and sky ... And his courage and unflinching spirit doing their level best to live as long as he possibly could in this world he loved so much, gave me courage too.[1]

Lawrence's imagination was attracted now to the vast and eternal and mythological. He read avidly all the books he could obtain about Revelation, in preparation for writing an introduction to a book by Frederick Carter; the introduction outgrew its purpose and became his last work, *Apocalypse*.

There was some slight improvement in November. Lawrence began to take short walks. He was cheered by the sales of his pamphlet *Pornography and Obscenity* – 1,200 a week he reported in early December – and by R. A. Barclay's review of it in the *New Statesman*, 'standing up for me boldly'. He talked of a return to the ranch in the spring, but by Christmas he was in bed again. According to Achsah Brewster, New Year's Day was critical: 'Lawrence attended a New Year's luncheon given by the Di Chiaras which he enjoyed with his usual zest, but he lingered overlong, and walked to the village to sit down in a cutting wind. From that time he steadily lost flesh.'[2]

In November his old friend Koteliansky had told Lawrence that Dr Andrew Morland, resident physician at Mundesley sanatorium (where the painter Mark Gertler had been treated for tuberculosis with some success) would be in the south of France in January 1930 and would be willing to visit him. Lawrence replied guardedly, but Frieda wrote: 'Tell that doctor how glad I would be if he came to see Lawr.' Morland examined Lawrence on 20 January. He told Lawrence that the bronchitis was acute and aggravated by the lung, and that he 'must lie still and see no one and do no work'. He recommended the Ad Astra sanatorium in Vence. To Frieda, Morland was more outspoken, as she told Titus on 5 February: 'The doctor (Moreland) said: If he did'nt go into a sanatorium, he would be dead in 3 months. But 6 years ago they told me he would be dead in a year, or two –'[3] Lawrence tried to follow the medical advice; he wrote to Morland on 30 January that whether he entered the sanatorium would depend on his progress; but within three days he had decided to go. He moved in on 6 February. Five days later Morland wrote to Kot:

---

[1] Frieda Lawrence 302.   [2] Letters 5442, 5434; Brewster 308.
[3] Letter 5428; *Frieda Lawrence: The Memoirs and Correspondence*, ed. E. W. Tedlock (1961), p. 239; Letter 5492; MS SIU.

I am indeed relieved to hear Lawrence has gone to Vence. It is not that his treatment will be so very much different up there but one feels so much happier to think that he will have proper nursing & attention. I am particularly glad he has gone so soon; when I wrote last week I again advised him to go so I hope it is this rather than any relapse on his part that has made him decide. He had almost consented to go previously.

I will certainly give him any help I can in the way of advice – I am afraid a really long period of strict rest is the only possible treatment now & it will not be easy to get him to submit to it.

I have written to the doctor who will be looking after him & hope to get a report from him before long.

The sanatorium was not a success, as Morland later admitted: 'I wish now that I had never urged him to go to Vence as I am afraid my efforts only made his last weeks more unhappy.'[1] Lawrence became more and more dependent on Frieda. On 15 February she told Titus: 'Lawr is so sad, cant eat & does'nt gain weight, only 44½ kili he weighs – I try hard to think of things to comfort him, but when I said yesterday, you see we ll have some jolly times yet, he said: that will be in heaven my dear – I dont care about heaven, but perhaps it may be alright –'[2] After a fortnight at Ad Astra Lawrence wrote to Maria Huxley: 'I am rather worse here – such bad nights, and cough, and heart, and pain decidedly worse here – and miserable ... It's not a good place – shan't stay long – I'm better in a house – I'm miserable.' Aldous Huxley was working on Lawrence's behalf in Paris, exercising all the influence he could muster to head off the possibility of action against *Lady Chatterley's Lover* by the French police. In this he succeeded. When the Huxleys arrived in Vence on 25 February they were shocked by Lawrence's appearance: 'he was such a miserable wreck of himself and suffering so much pain ... the illness had reduced him to an appalling state of emaciation'.[3] Also on the 25th Morland passed on to Gertler the report he had received about Lawrence from Dr Medinier in Vence:

Both lungs appear to be affected with moderate severity but it is his general condition which is causing the greatest amount of anxiety; his appetite is poor & he does not seem to be responding to treatment. It is obvious that his case is not suitable for any special treatment & that reliance will have to be placed on prolonged rest & good food. I feel that for the present he is best in the sanatorium but doubt if he will stay there very long. I do not think much of French sanatoria & think that it would not be wise to urge him to stay on there very much longer. The difficulty will be to know what to do when he leaves. If he would consent to come to Mundesley I think that would be best provided he is not too ill to travel ... If Mundesley cannot be arranged I suppose he

[1] Letter 5495; Zytaruk 402, 404.   [2] MS SIU ('Saturday').
[3] Letter 5530; Sybille Bedford, *Aldous Huxley* (1973), i. 222–3; Smith 330–1.

would take a villa somewhere near Vence. Should he do this I think it important that he should have a good nurse & a good cook. I could probably find the former.

Lawrence had himself already decided to move into a nearby villa. With great difficulty Frieda and her daughter Barbara rented the Villa Robermond 'on the hill just above Vence. It was a comfortable house, with a little cottage where an Italian peasant lived with his wife, who acted as concierge.'[1] They also engaged an English nurse from Nice and a new, Corsican, doctor.

Lawrence had taken no books with him to the sanatorium. Earl Brewster scoured the unpromising Ad Astra library for him and found a 'life of Columbus' (possibly Washington Irving's *Life and Voyages of Columbus*) remembered by Frieda and by Barbara.[2] Lawrence was still reading this on the day he died. He attempted only one piece of writing there, his unfinished review of Eric Gill's *Art Nonsense*, written a few days before his death.

In his last week at Ad Astra he had several visitors. H. G. Wells came from Grasse on 24 February but Lawrence's dislike of him ('a common temporary soul') was not diminished when Wells said that he thought his illness was mainly hysteria. Another visitor was the American sculptor, Jo Davidson who was then, with his wife Yvonne, in Grasse; Wells had urged Lawrence to sit for him. Thus, on the 26th the Davidsons travelled to Vence; they found Lawrence lunching on a terrace and expecting them. Davidson recalled:

After lunch I started to work, while we talked of mutual friends. I knew Lawrence had painted, and I asked him if he had ever done any modeling. He had – once, in plasteline. But he hated the material, its feel and odor, and never touched it again. I gave him a piece of my clay. He liked the feel of it – because it was clean and cool. I promised to send him the very clay I was using as soon as the bust was completed. He thought he would like to do some little animals in clay.

After I worked for about an hour or so, Lawrence suggested that I had better go down and have some lunch, while he had a nap.

A little later a servant came down and said that Mr. Lawrence was awake and had asked for me. When I went up, I found him in bed. He asked me if I could work if he sat up in bed. I told him it did not matter. If he would rather, I would come back tomorrow or any other time. He stayed in bed and I worked for another hour.

When I told Lawrence I had been experimenting in polychrome sculpture, he asked me to do him in color, and not to forget the blue of his dressing gown, of which he was very fond.

Davidson later told Julian and Juliette Huxley: 'it was not a bad head; but who could ever fix that face ... Lawrence was waiting for Aldous and Maria – talked only of that, waiting to die when they had come.'[3] In addition to the

[1] Zytaruk 403; Nehls, iii. 434–5. [2] Brewster 229; Nehls, iii. 435, 442.
[3] Letter 5534; Nehls, iii. 433–4; Juliette Huxley, *Leaves of the Tulip Tree* (1986), p. 210.

Huxleys, Frieda's daughter Barbara and a few other close friends, Lawrence had another visitor: the Aga Khan, who came with his wife on the 27th. He wanted to discuss a plan for mounting an exhibition of Lawrence's paintings in Paris; he also showed himself interested in the possibility of buying some of the paintings – but neither project was realised.

On 1 March Lawrence was taken to the Villa Robermond. The new doctor examined him and commented to Frieda and Barby: 'It is very grave. There is not much hope. Do not let him see that you know.' On the 2nd, Aldous and Maria Huxley came again; they returned in the evening. Lawrence was now crying out for morphia and claimed to see his own body on a table across the room. The superintendent of the sanatorium administered morphia at nine.[1] Lawrence slept. At ten o'clock he died.

Frieda, writing on 6 March to Nancy Pearn, described the scene and her own feelings:

His death was so splendid, so bravely he fought right to the last, he knew quite well about himself, & then he asked for morphine I think he knew it was the end, then he lay down & said: 'I am better now' & soon breathed his last, slow breaths – Dead he looked fulfilled and splendid, all the suffering gone – I am so full of admiration for his unconquerable spirit that my grief has no bitterness or misery in it – He has left me all his love & all his love for the world – I see him only now as a whole in his simple greatness.[2]

[1] Nehls, iii. 435–6.   [2] MS Lazarus.

THE LETTERS

4750. To Emily King, [17 November 1928]
Text: MS Sagar; PC v. Côte d'Azur – BANDOL – Quai du Port; Postmark, Bandol 19[. . .];
Unpublished.

Hotel Beau-Rivage, *Bandol.* Var.

Sat.

– We got here today – think we shall stay fifteen or twenty days – had such a
rough crossing from Port-Cros, hated it – we weren't ill, but *felt* it.

How are you all?[1]

DHL

4751. To Ada Clarke, [17 November 1928]
Text: MS Clarke; PC v. Côte d'Azur – BANDOL – Quai du Port; Postmark, Bandol 19[. . .];
Unpublished.

Hotel Beau-Rivage, *Bandol.* Var.

Sat.

[2]We had such a rough crossing from that island[3] – but all right. Think we
shall stay here at least two weeks – the others all gone to Paris. Still sunny and
warm here.

DHL

---

[1] DHL's elder sister Emily Una ('Pamela') King (1882–1962), her husband Samuel Taylor King
(1880–1965) and their daughters Margaret ('Peg' or 'Peggy') Emily (b. 1909) and Joan Frieda
(b. 1920).

[2] DHL's correspondent was his younger sister Lettice Ada Clarke (1887–1948). m. 1913,
William Edwin ('Eddie') Clarke (1889–1964).

[3] The Lawrences spent the previous month with the novelist Richard Aldington (1892–1962),
his mistress Dorothy ('Arabella') Yorke (1892–), and Brigit Patmore (1882–1965) – the
estranged wife of John Deighton Patmore – who became Aldington's mistress (see *Letters,* vi.
42 n. 3, 590 n.). They had all lived at La Vigie, Ile de Port-Cros, which Aldington had rented
from Jean Paulhan, editor of *Nouvelle Revue Française* (Nehls, iii. 254).

18   *[17 November 1928]*

4752. To S. S. Koteliansky, [17 November 1928]
Text: MS BL; PC v. Côte d'Azur – BANDOL – Quai du Port; Postmark, [...] 19[...];
Zytaruk 365.

Hotel Beau-Rivage, *Bandol.* Var.
Saturday
– ¹Got here today – think we shall stay the month out. Glad to be off that
poky island – but we had such a bad crossing, still feel shaky inside. Will write
– I had your letters – no news here.

DHL

4753. To Laurence Pollinger, 17 November 1928
Text: MS UT; Unpublished.

Hotel Beau-Rivage, *Bandol.* Var.
17² Novem 1928
Dear Pollinger³
We got here today – a nasty little crossing from that island, feel I'm still
standing on my head – but sunny and warm here.
This is to send you the address – will you please give it to all the other depts
too –
What about Elkin Mathews' people and the *Rawdon's Roof* story?⁴ –
Imagine Secker adding up to £165.⁵ – Hope you get this soon.

ever! D. H. Lawrence

¹ DHL's correspondent was Samuel Solomonovich Koteliansky ('Kot') (1880–1955), Russian-
born but naturalised British. He produced over thirty translations of Russian works, some of
them in collaboration with DHL. Kot was a close friend and correspondent of DHL's,
1914–30. See *Letters,* ii. 205 n. 4.
² 17] 27
³ Laurence Edward Pollinger (1898–1976) was on the staff of DHL's agent, Curtis Brown Ltd.
He was responsible for the publication of DHL's books in English. See *Letters,* vi. 29 n. 1.
⁴ *Rawdon's Roof* was published by Elkin Mathews & Marrot, but the date of publication is
uncertain. The title-page includes the statement: 'This is number seven of the Woburn Books
... published at London in 1928 ... '; yet DHL did not return the signed sheets to Mathews,
for the limited edn of 530 copies, until 12 February 1929 (Letter 4932); and he instructed
Pollinger about distributing his complimentary copies on 28 March (Letter 5018).
⁵ Pollinger had just informed DHL that his royalties for the previous year from his English
publisher Martin Secker amounted to this meagre sum.

4754. To Giuseppe Orioli, 17 November 1928
Text: MS UCLA; Unpublished.

Hotel Beau-Rivage. *Bandol.* Var.

17 Novem 1928

Dear Pino[1]

I haven't heard from you for three weeks – whatever is it? Do write at once, and tell me what news of *Lady C.* Apparently the fuss in *John Bull* didn't cut much ice[2] – but do hope you're all right. – I sent you the Lasca story – do as you like about it.[3] I think I *wouldn't* print Italian text, anyhow. – Did you get my poems, ordered for you?[4] – I saw Adrian Kent in Toulon; apparently his aunt Miss Kent, who once attacked you in fierce Italian,[5] wants to sell the Villa Bronciliano at Vingone – a nice villa – and go to live in the Mirenda![6] So we'd have a successor. – Do write!

DHL

4755. To Achsah Brewster, [18 November 1928]
Text: MS UT; Brewster 185–6.

Hotel Beau-Rivage. *Bandol,* Var.

Sunday

Dear Achsah[7]

Just a line to send you the address – we got here yesterday, quite nice: beastly crossing from that island. I think we shall stay here about two weeks – then perhaps come to Italy to finish my *Etruscans*[8] – or perhaps go to Spain. Quite *hot* and sunny here – only 2 days rain since we left you – yet endless torrents in Florence, so I hear. Hope you had the *poems* – I sent them. And I

---

[1] Giuseppe ('Pino') Orioli (1884–1942), Florentine bookseller who acted as publisher for *Lady Chatterley's Lover* in July 1928. See *Letters*, v. 450 n. 3.

[2] *John Bull* condemned *Lady Chatterley's Lover* as 'the most evil outpouring that has ever besmirched the literature of our country' (see *Letters*, vi. 598 n. 2).

[3] DHL had translated the *Terza Cena* by A. F. Grazzini ('Il Lasca') (see *Letters*, vi. 595 n. 1). Orioli published it as *The Story of Doctor Manente* in November 1929 (Roberts A45).

[4] DHL's *Collected Poems* had been published by Secker in September 1928 (Roberts A43).

[5] Little is known of the Kents beyond the incident to which DHL refers (see *Letters*, vi. 420 and n. 1).

[6] The Lawrences lived at the Villa Mirenda, Scandicci, near Florence, May 1926–June 1928.

[7] DHL had met the American painters Earl Henry Brewster (1878–1957), his wife Achsah (1878–1945) and their daughter Harwood (1912–90) on Capri in April 1921. See *Letters*, iii. 711 n. 1.

[8] In the spring of 1927 DHL and Earl Brewster had visited the Etruscan tombs at Cerveteri, Tarquinia, Vulci and Volterra, and DHL had already written the essays which were to be published posthumously as *Etruscan Places* (Roberts A60). But at this time it was still his intention (frustrated by his declining health) to extend the collection of essays after making a tour of other Etruscan sites. See *Letters*, vi. 566, 575.

hope you didn't think I was like Rampion – such a gas-bag.[1] If I'm like that
I'll shut up.

tante cose!   DHL
BANDOL is the place   Côte d'Azur.

4756. To Giuseppe Orioli, [21 November 1928]
Text: MS UCLA; Unpublished.

Hotel Beau Rivage, *Bandol.* Var.
22 November 1928[2]

Dear Pino

Your letter this morning – am so sorry you are not well. I suppose it is the
bad weather.

Bad luck about those 19 copies to the Centaur.[3] I can hardly believe it. –
Lawrence Gomme wrote to Mabel that there was a pirated edition out in
Philadelphia, but I hardly believe it.[4]

You might send two copies to Pollinger at two guineas. I had promised him
them. – And will you answer this woman, in a *plain* envelope.[5] Use plain
envelopes and plain parcel-labels now.

Write and ask Aldous if he would translate a few stories by Sacchetti or

[1] Mark Rampion, a character in the recently published novel *Point Counter Point* by DHL's close
friend, Aldous Huxley (1894–1963). See *Letters,* vi. 77 n. 2, 600–1.
[2] DHL's date is unlikely to have been correct. The letter following (from a MS now lost) also
refers to his having heard from Orioli; it is dated 'Wed.', the day when Orioli's letter arrived;
Letters 4756 and 4757 were therefore both written on the same day, Wednesday 21 November
1928.
[3] Harold Trump Mason's Centaur Book Shop in Philadelphia; Mason (1893–1983) had advised
DHL against directing copies of *Lady Chatterley's Lover* to the Book Shop; but apparently the
advice had been disregarded and nineteen copies had been lost (see *Letters,* vi. 363 n. 1); see also
Letter 4919. (Mason's Centaur Press had published Edward D. McDonald's *Bibliography of the
Writings of D. H. Lawrence* and DHL's *Reflections on the Death of a Porcupine and Other Essays,*
both in 1925.)
[4] Laurence James Gomme (1882–1974), 'Consulting Bookseller' in New York. On 16 October
1928 he had written to Mabel Dodge Luhan (1879–1962) in Taos, with whom he and DHL
were both acquainted, claiming to have seen 'an edition of Lady Chatterley printed and
published in Philadelphia' (*Letters,* vi. 608 n. 1). On Mabel Luhan see *Letters,* iv. 110 n. 4.
[5] DHL's letter is on the verso of the letter from 'this woman' (of whom nothing is known):

Belgrave House, Eccleston Sq. S.W.1
Nov. 15, 1928
D. H. Lawrence Esq.
Dear Sir,
    Will you tell me if & where it is possible to obtain a copy of your book, "Lady Chatterley's
Lover", which was published in Italy. And what is the price of same?
faithfully yours   (Mrs) Eve Midgley

Bandelli – about 15,000 words.[1] I think he would. But I hear his novel *Point Counter Point* has sold 80,000 copies in America.[2] If that is so, he will be very lordly and uppish, no answering for him.
I sent you the MS of the Lasca story from Port-Cros. That you have not got it proves that it is being detained in the post. I sent it registered. I hope it will turn up.
I think perhaps in ten days time, or a fortnight, Frieda and I will come to Florence, and I will go to the Etruscan towns to finish my Etruscan essays. Then we can talk about everything – the Lasca and all. – Probably in Florence we would stay in Hotel Porta Rossa. But I'll write again. And I do hope you'll be feeling better. Don't take too much wine. You must set about publishing another book. You are *much* better in health when you are busy. – Did you get my poems?

                                                                        DHL
I shall tell Pollinger you are sending him two copies.
L. E. Pollinger, Curtis Brown Ltd. 6 Henrietta St, Covent Garden, W.C. 2.
By the way, will you see that Haskards[3] put my sterling cheques to my sterling account. I see on the bordereau[4] they turned the last lot into Liras, and I don't want a lot of Liras.

4757. To Maria Huxley, [21 November 1928]
Text: Huxley 762.
                                                            Beau Rivage, Bandol, Var.
                                                                        Wed.
Dear Maria, –[5]
It is incredibly lovely weather, and the place very lovely, swimming with milky gold light at sunset, and white boats half melted on the white twilight sea, and palm trees frizzing their tops in the rosy west, and their thick dark columns down in the dark where we are, with shadowy boys running and calling, and tiny orange lamps under foliage, in the under dusk. Then we come in and have tea in my room looking south where the moon is, and get sticky with the jammy cake.

[1] Huxley did not accept the challenge to translate stories by Franco Sacchetti (1332?–1400) or Matteo Bandello (1485–1561) for the series of 'Italian Renaissance Novelists' which DHL had proposed to Orioli in October 1928 and for which he had translated *The Story of Doctor Manente*.
[2] By the end of 1928 10,000 copies of *Point Counter Point* had been sold (Sybille Bedford, *Aldous Huxley*, 1973, i. 198).
[3] Haskard & Casardi Ltd, DHL's bank in Florence.   [4] 'bank statement'.
[5] Maria Huxley, née Nys (1898–1955). m. 1919, Aldous Huxley. See *Letters*, v. 519 n. 1.

I think we shall go to Italy end of the[1] month, to finish my *Etruscans*, which they pester me about all the time. And if I get them done, perhaps Xmas on Capri. And then see what next. Orioli writes he is not well – liver. He wants to publish a series of Italian Renaissance stories, and wants to know if Aldous would do him 12,000 or 15,000 words of *Sachetti* or *Bandello* or anybody he likes. I am doing *Lasca* – quite amusing.

I do hope your house is getting shipshape, and a *cook*. You must have a cook. Food quite good and imaginative, here, especially nice fishes which I like so much. It's so hot, we can't believe it.

DHL

4758. To Emily King, 22 November 1928
Text: MS Lazarus; Postmark, Bandol 22[...]; Unpublished.

Hotel Beau-Rivage. *Bandol.* Var.
22 Nov. 1928

My dear Pamela

We came here on Saturday – it's a little port on the sea not far from Toulon – and very pretty. The hotel is really quite good, only 40 francs a day, and good food. It's been wonderful weather since we are here – hot sun all day long, and lovely evenings. But the sea has kept pretty rough, and I have been glad we were not crossing again from that island.

Tell Peg I have done no work to speak of lately. What bit I did in Port Cros Arabella typed for me. And now I'm doing a bit of verse.[2] The publishers are worrying me for a book, pestering me to finish the Etruscan book I have half done. I may go to Italy at the end of this month, to finish it. Then we'd stay over Christmas – perhaps Christmas in Capri with the Brewsters, who are having Anna di Chiara's villa.[3]

There's no news – all seems quiet – and it's getting late, so I'll add this to Friedas and go to bed.[4]

How are you all? How is Joan? And how is the immortal shop doing?[5] You must have taken stock by now. Let me know.

love   DHL

[1] Huxley reads 'other'.
[2] To be published in the volume entitled *Pansies* (July/August 1929); they were sometimes referred to by DHL as 'pensées' (perhaps in allusion to Pascal's *Pensées sur la Réligion*, 1669).
[3] Villa Giulia, Anacapri. Anna di Chiara and DHL met in Capri in 1920. An American from Hagerstown, Maryland, she was a particularly cultured woman with a reputation as a distinguished hostess; she was a close friend of the Brewsters. m. Ferdinando di Chiara, a Neapolitan.
[4] Frieda's contribution is missing.
[5] In July 1927 Sam King had bought a grocery and hardware shop in Bulwell, Nottingham (*Letters*, vi. 97 n. 1).

4759. To Charles Lahr, 22 November 1928
Text: MS UNYB; Postmark, Bandol 2[…]–11 28; Unpublished.

Hotel Beau-Rivage. *Bandol.* Var.
22 Nov. 1928

Dear Mr Lahr[1]

I have your letter this morning. If you would send me Rhys Davies' address, I might see him on my way to Italy, in about ten days time – if he wishes, that is.[2] You might perhaps send him this address.

About the German translations, the Insel Verlag hold the rights to all the *books*, but not to the periodical stuff. So the Galsworthy essay would be free.[3] – I don't know if the Insel Verlag want to do *Lady Chatterley*.[4]

Is there any further alarm about the book, by the way? I saw *John Bull's* rather affected squealy bellow – but I can't learn of any single copy which has been confiscated by customs – certainly none sent from Florence.

– My agent is Curtis Brown – and Miss Jean Watson manages the Foreign Dept. – 6 Henrietta St. Covent Garden.

sincerely   D. H. Lawrence

4760. To Laurence Pollinger, 22 November 1928
Text: MS UT; Unpublished.

Hotel Beau-Rivage. *Bandol.* Var
22 Nov 1928

Dear Pollinger

All right about the Elkin Mathews story – though I resent strongly signing. But I'll send the MS. – I lengthened it in a good hour. – Tell them though not to send any sheets to sign till I'm more settled.

I think by the end of the month I'll go back to Italy to finish those Etruscan essays. If I get that done, there's a nice book. – As for a novel, I'm not in a good humour for one.

All right about Miss Pearn's copy of the *Poems*.[5] You might have bagged one for yourself, had I thought of it: or you: –

More anon   D. H. Lawrence

[1] Charles Lahr (1895–1971), radical bookseller in Red Lion Square, Holborn (where he had sold many copies of *Lady Chatterley's Lover*). He later published the unexpurgated edn of *Pansies*. m. Esther Archer. See *Letters*, v. 572 n. 1.

[2] Rhys Davies (1903–78), Welsh novelist and short-story writer, and close friend of Lahr's, was living in Nice. In August 1928 Lahr had sent DHL a copy of Davies' first novel, *The Withered Root*; DHL wrote a generally favourable response (*Letters*, vi. 533–4 and n. 1). The story of Davies' relationship with DHL is told in his autobiography, *Print of a Hare's Foot* (1969).

[3] 'John Galsworthy' had been published in *Scrutinies by Various Writers* in March 1928 (Roberts B24).

[4] Insel Verlag of Leipzig never published the novel.

[5] Annie ('Nancy') Ross Pearn (1892–1950), manager of the periodicals department at Curtis Brown Ltd (London). See *Letters*, v. 57 n. 3.

I again asked Orioli to send you two copies of *Lady C.* at £2–2–0. This time I hope I'll be effective. His price is really £4.

4761. To Hon. Dorothy Brett, 23 November 1928
Text: MS UCin; Postmark, [. . .] 28; Moore 1101–2.
Hotel Beau-Rivage. *Bandol.* Var. France
23 Novem 1928
Dear Brett[1]
I meant to write before, but expected all the time to hear from you in New York. Yesterday I had your letter saying you were leaving Taos on the 4th. – so I suppose you must be there now all right. It will be a change for you to be in a city – I don't suppose you'll like it for very long. – I hope Stieglitz will do something with your pictures:[2] judging from his letters he is a pleasant-spoken but cautious and canny bird, anxious to whistle the dernier cri in art, but afraid of committing himself or giving himself away at all: at the same time, afraid of missing anything. So I hope your things will 'suit' his 'Room.' I wish you might make 20,000 dollars, but fear you won't. – Dorothy Warren keeps my pictures hanging in her gallery, and shows them to God knows who, but doesn't open her exhibition – is said now to have postponed it to the New Year.[3] I suppose she is nervous, because *John Bull* and the *Sunday Chronicle* came out with blasts against *Lady C.* If she doesn't soon make up her mind, I shall go to London and fetch the things away.

I had Mabel's cuttings about Andrew.[4] Ida is a fool anyhow, with her hysteria and her nagging about intimate companionship. What does she mean, anyhow, by intimate companionship, beyond a lot of nasty squashy *talk* about herself and personalities. As for Andrew, he has played the bully trick on her – serve her right, for being so self-important. But I should think by

---

[1] Hon. Dorothy Eugenie Brett (1883–1977), painter, daughter of Reginald Baliol Brett, 2nd Viscount Esher; first met DHL in 1915. She had lived with the Lawrences at the Kiowa Ranch, near Taos, New Mexico, in 1924 and remained there when they returned to Europe in 1925. (See *Letters*, ii. 427 n. 2.)

[2] Alfred Stieglitz (1864–1946), leading American photographer and art expert (see *Letters*, iv. 499 n. 2). He had offered to arrange an exhibition of DHL's paintings in New York; DHL urged him to consider exhibiting Brett's too (*Letters*, vi. 506); Stieglitz had opened 'The Room' 'to promote contemporary American art and in particular, that of Georgia O'Keefe, his young wife' (Sean Hignett, *Brett*, 1984, p. 200).

[3] Dorothy Cecil Wynter Warren (1896–1954), niece of Lady Ottoline Morrell and owner of the Warren Gallery in London which housed the exhibition of DHL's paintings, June–September 1929; she had already once postponed the opening of the exhibition. m. November 1928, Philip Coutts Trotter. See *Letters*, vi. 127 n. 3.

[4] Andrew Michael Dasburg (1887–1979), a Taos artist; 1922–8 he lived with the actress Ida Rauh (1877–1970); he married his second wife, Nancy Lane, in 1928. See *Letters*, v. 28 n. 2; 159 n. 1.

now he too is rather the worse for wear. I don't envy the Denver young woman.

I also had your letter enclosing that of Laurence Gomme. I don't trust that young man for a moment. I have heard no sound of any pirated edition either in Philadelphia or elsewhere. Mr Gomme wanted us to send him 50 copies, *at my risk*. I refused – and sent him six: which he has neither acknowledged nor paid for.[1] If you see him, kindly remind him of the fact. He must have received them, as he sent Spud a copy.[2] – As for his famous idea of sending by Express, the books go through Customs just the same, and are even more suspiciously examined. That young man must expect roast chickens to fly into his mouth. – You might ask Mabel to enquire round, if there *is* a pirated edition in existence. – And ask Mr Gomme if he intends to pay for his copies of *Lady C.*

About the gold, I am of course a sceptic – and now anyhow there is nothing to be done till spring.[3]

We are here on the Mediterranean near Toulon. The Villa Mirenda is given up, finished with. But I think I shall have to go back to Italy just now, to complete those Etruscan essays. The publishers nag at me for the book, so I may as well go and do it. In that case we should stay in Italy over Christmas, perhaps Christmas in Capri. The Brewsters are back there, moving in December into Anna di Chiara's house.

But I don't want to take a house, myself. I prefer, for the time being, to remain free. I wish so often we were at the ranch. But at present I feel America is rather hostile to me, and they might do something mean to one, if one came over. Then again there is the question of passports and visas. It isn't much good coming with the ordinary six-months visa. I would like to be able to stay, if we come, for at least a year. – You say you would have a lot of fuss with papers and permits, even if you came to Europe. I'm afraid I'd have a lot more fuss. Then if they *wanted* to be spiteful, they'd hold me up about my health. Altogether it seems too much of a coil and fuss. – But if it were simple and friendly-feeling, I guess we'd slip over soon:[4] I feel there's nowhere to go, in Europe. And I feel you are wise not to come over. What is it, but mere straying around.

I've not done any painting for a long time. One needs a proper place, to

[1] See *Letters*, vi. 444 and nn.; 456 and n. 1; 608.
[2] Willard ('Spud' or 'Spoodle') Johnson (1897–1968), friend of DHL from the New Mexico period (see *Letters*, iv. 316 n. 5).
[3] See *Letters*, vi. 550.
[4] Immediately on receipt of this letter, Brett wrote to Herbert J. Seligmann (see following letter and p. 27 n. 2) suggesting that they should meet 'and over a simple meal at a Caffetteria discuss how we best can help [DHL]' (MS PM).

paint in. I've done little articles for newspapers, and so on – make a little money to go on with. Anyhow I've got all I need – and am not bothering. I hope you are out of debt, too. You did get the fifty dollars I sent some little while ago, didn't you?[1] You didn't mention it.

On the whole, I think my health is a lot better. The cough is still a bore, but then it always was, more or less. I feel a good deal better in myself, though.

It is quite pleasant here, for a time – sunny, and – blue sea, and warm still days. It isn't the real Riviera – it's near Marseilles – very few tourists. But I suppose we shall go to Italy at the end of this month, to visit those Etruscan places.

I want to know how you both are, and how you like New York. Did you go in the car, I wonder? Tell me what it's like.

                                                                    DHL

4762. To Hon. Dorothy Brett, 24 November 1928
Text: MS UT; Huxley 763.

                                   Hotel Beau Rivage – *Bandol*, Var – France
                                                                    24 Nov 1928
Dear Brett

I wrote you a couple of days ago and posted it to Taos – all the news, which is none. Today comes your letter from New York. Glad you got there safely and easily. I can tell you are pining for Taos, but I suppose that will wear off. I wish I were there too – but feel the Americans hostile to me: and I don't feel I love *them*, at the moment.

We are here on the coast near Toulon – pleasant and warm and quiet. But I think I shall have to go back to Italy in December to finish those Etruscan essays – they nag at me for them – publishers always want 'a book.' They want a novel, but I'm not going to give them one. What's the good of writing books? – in England the government now takes 20% of all royalties of persons living abroad – and Curtis Brown 10%. So they take £30 on every £100. And their royalties damn little. What's the good? It pays me far, far better to write little newspaper articles, and the papers want them now. Imagine me appearing regularly – irregularly, as a matter of fact – in *The Evening News*, *Sunday Despatch, Daily Express*! But the *Sunday Despatch* gives me £25. for a 2000 word article, written in an hour and a half – and nobody would even publish a story like 'None of That'.[2] – I haven't painted anything real for a long while. That bitch Dorothy Warren has my pictures hung all ready, but

---

[1] DHL sent $50 on 20 July 1928 'for horses and taxes etc.' (*Letters*, vi. 469).

[2] It was not placed in any periodical; collected in *The Woman Who Rode Away and Other Stories* (1928) (see *Letters*, vi. 70 n. 3; 176).

seems scared to open. She's getting married. Says she'll open in New Year. Hell have her! The *Collected Poems* do fairly well – I'll order you a copy now I have your address. Knopf wouldn't trouble to do them in America – but we are arranging with somebody else.[1] I've got to get copyrights clear. I've asked Seligman about it.[2] I want him to get Seltzer to release me *Birds Beasts and Flowers*.[3] You talk to him too – Seligman. Because I'm bent on rescuing my poems in America, and doing a collected edition. – If Seligman knows Edwin Rich, Curtis Brown's manager, you meet him and tell me what he's like.[4] – About money I'm all right – we live very moderately over here – the hotel costs only 40 frs. pension, less than $2. a day – and *very* nice. If you get stumped I'll lend you some. – Have you seen Aldous' book *Point Counter Point*. Mark Rampion is supposed to be me! Poor me! And *poor you*!! Do you recognise yourself? Aldous knows about as much as a pump, about us or anybody. Truly wall-eyed. – They've got a little house at Suresnes outside Paris, and are bored – at least Maria is.

– If we come over after Christmas, what is the best way of doing it, as regards passports, permits etc. That business is a great bore. I don't want to take a house, because after Christmas I'd really like to sail away. America is so irritating. I feel I'd like to go to Zululand, and paint Zulus. Climate supposed to be perfect.

Give Mabel all the news – and I do hope you'll have a nice time. My cough is perennial – but I'm better, stronger. Hope Nina helps your ears! but I would be wary of[5] Nina's help.[6] I'm deaf too – must go and be syringed.

DHL

---

[1] Alfred Abraham Knopf (1892–1984), first acted as DHL's American publisher in 1925 with *St. Mawr* (see *Letters*, iii. 471 n. 1). The first American impression of *Collected Poems* was published by Jonathan Cape and Harrison Smith in July 1929 (Roberts A43).

[2] Herbert Jacob Seligmann (1891–1984), author of the first American book on DHL, in 1924; he reviewed *Lady Chatterley's Lover* very favourably in the *New York Sun* on 1 September 1928 and was never employed by the *Sun* as a reviewer thereafter (see *Letters*, vi. 607 n. 1).

[3] Thomas Seltzer (1875–1943), DHL's chief American publisher 1920–5; he published *Birds, Beasts and Flowers* in 1923. (See Gerald M. Lacy, ed., *D. H. Lawrence: Letters to Thomas and Adele Seltzer*, Santa Barbara, 1976, pp. 171ff.)

[4] In mid-1927 Edwin G. Rich became manager of Curtis Brown's New York office (*Letters*, vi. 222 n. 1); he replaced the Yorkshireman, Arthur Barmby with whom DHL had established a particularly friendly rapport.

[5] MS reads 'as'.

[6] Cornelia ('Nina') Rumsey Wilcox Witt (1880–1968), known to DHL since 1922 (see *Letters*, iv. 332 n. 4).

4763. To Achsah Brewster, [24 November 1928]
Text: MS UT; Brewster 186–7.

Hotel Beau Rivage, *Bandol*, Var
Sat.

Dear Achsah

What a shame we forgot your birthday[1] – what a mercy the poems arrived that day. I am buying you a little african basket – only like a big tumbler – from upper congo – I like it very much, so if it leaves you cold you give it me back and I give you something else.[2] – But I'll bring it to Italy.

I did write you from here. Did you get it? Our plans are to go early in December to Florence, *do those etruscan essays*, because the publishers bother me for them – and then perhaps sit in your Bella Vista in Anacapri for Christmas. Shall we do that? – I have an awful feeling I want to go to Africa, South Africa, which has a good climate, Natal, and paint Zulus. I have a strong feeling that way. After Christmas. But Achsah dear, you sit tight in Capri, whatever Earl or the others of us does or do. On revient toujours etc.[3] Don't you be lured off to *any* foreign parts. Sit calm in Capri and let the child study with Old Pa Reynolds, and let Time Itself dash along with a smoothing iron.[4] Why bother!

The *Evening News* printed 'Hymns in a Man's Life', but only gave me 15 quid. The *Atlantic Monthly* put our little old ladies of Chexbres in its contributors column this month – Nov. – But the *Sunday Despatch* is doing my 'Sex Appeal' article tomorrow and gives me 25 quid.[5]

I shall copy you out two of my poems in my best handwriting – that is to say, Frieda calls them poems but I call them *pensées*.

Well achsah dear it's late for your birthday, but Earl said you were dashing

---

[1] On 12 November.   [2] it me ... something else.] me something else.
[3] 'One always returns'.
[4] Richard William Reynolds (1867–1948) had taught Classics, English and History at King Edward's School, Birmingham, before he left England in 1922 for Egypt, then Capri, on account of the health of his wife Dorothea (née Deakin). After her death in 1925 he made himself largely responsible for teaching his three daughters together with Harwood Brewster, whenever she was in Capri (cf. *Letters*, v. 627 n. 3). DHL would meet Reynolds when staying with the Brewsters on Capri in March 1926. The final allusion is to the folk-song 'Dashing away with the smoothing-iron'.
[5] 'Hymns in a Man's Life' appeared in the *Evening News*, 13 October 1928; 'Insouciance' – written while DHL was staying with the Brewsters in an hotel at Chexbres-sur-Vevey, Switzerland – was published first as 'Over-Earnest Ladies' in the *Evening News*, 12 July 1928 (Roberts C171), and then anonymously in 'The Contributors' Club' section of *Atlantic Monthly*, cxlii (November 1928), 710–12; 'Sex Locked Out' was published in the *Sunday Despatch*, 25 November (Roberts C179). The editor of the *Sunday Despatch* was so enthusiastic about the article that he voluntarily increased the fee from 15 to 25 guineas (letter from Nancy Pearn to DHL, 15 November 1928; TMSC UT).

along with a smoothing-iron, so let's hope you smooth it all out.

A rivederci, cara[1]   DHL

4764. To Nancy Pearn, [24 November 1928]
Text: MS UT; Unpublished.

Hotel Beau Rivage, *BANDOL*. Var. France.

Sat.

Dear Nancy Pearn

Your letter came on very late: perhaps the address not quite right. Good-O! for the *Sunday Despatch* – Here's another article they can have if they like.[2] I'll do a next one on civilised savages I have seen in the wide wide world. – And I'll send you a few little 'poems' – which I call *pensées*. – I like doing 2,000 word articles much more than 1000 – gives me more swing. They can cut out what they like – but do save me a complete copy, for a book later. – I'll write in the copy of *Collected Poems* when I come.[3]

DHL

4765. To Carl Seelig, 24 November 1928
Text: MS SIU; Moore 1103.

Hotel Beau-Rivage. *Bandol*. Var. *France*.

24 Nov 1928

Dear Carl Seelig[4]

Your letter came this morning. So you are divorced, and want to set out into the world! But what a choice of places! Russia, Liberia, South Sea Islands.

I don't much want to go to Russia any more. My health has been very bad since I saw you, bad bronchial trouble, and cough. I daren't go to Russia, and I daren't go to Liberia, for that is tropical and dangerous even to healthy people. I thought in the spring we might go back to New Mexico, to the ranch: or if not there, to South Africa, to Natal. I don't know.

---

[1] 'Until we meet again, dear'.

[2] The editor of the *Sunday Dispatch* had suggested that DHL might like to submit a piece on 'why and how man is becoming enslaved by civilisation'; DHL's response, 'Enslaved by Civilisation', was enclosed with this letter. It did not appear in the *Sunday Dispatch* (though see p. 251 n. 2), but in *Vanity Fair*, September 1929, as 'The Manufacture of Good Little Boys'; it was collected in *Assorted Articles* under the original title. The piece on 'civilised savages' seems not to have been written.

[3] Cf. Letter 4760.

[4] Karl ('Carl') Wilhelm Seelig (1894–1962), Swiss journalist, editor and critic. The Lawrences had stayed with Seelig and his then wife, Maria Margareta (1898–), in mid-November 1925, at their home in Kastanienbaum near Lucerne; DHL had remarked on the incompatibility of the Seeligs in an earlier letter (see *Letters*, v. 314 n. 1, 371).

But early in December we must go back to Italy, to Florence. I want to finish a book of essays on the Etruscans. If you were in Florence we could anyhow talk things over. I think we shall stay here till about 3rd December, then to Nice and Florence.

So let me know. – I think it is just as well you are divorced – you didn't fit with your wife.

My wife sends many greetings, with mine.

D. H. Lawrence

4766. To Charles Lahr, 26 November 1928
Text: MS StaU; Unpublished.

Hotel Beau Rivage. *Bandol.* Var. France.
26 Nov 1928

Dear Mr Lahr

Many thanks for your letter and the stories. I think *Bed of Feathers* excellent, as far as I've got[1] – the books only came this morning. I think I shall ask Rhys Davies here, as I'm not sure about my movements.

I had heard rumours of a pirated edition in America, but yours is the first *definite* news.[2] Alas! But it was bound to happen. I wish I could forestall them. – There was only enough type in Florence to set up *half Lady C.* – so we had to print the first half, and break it all up for the second half. But I had the printer print 200 copies on plain paper – and they are bound up in paper covers. There they lie in Florence, and I would sell them at 21/- if I knew how. But it means a lot of fuss, and Orioli is ill, and I can't go to Florence and fag over it. – Of the 1000 copies of the proper edition, I kept 25 copies and Orioli kept 100 copies, and he has put up the price to £4. – and refused to supply Galignani[3] even at 2 gns. net. I don't know if it was wise. I don't like to go back on him. But I'd as leave have sold right out at the original price, rather than have the thing drag out. – We sold all the rest – except that in America a number were confiscated in customs. What would you do?

I would be quite glad to have a 7/6 expurgated edition – but who would do it? – and could the thing be successfully expurgated? What a tangle one gets into when one tries to do anything a bit off the lines! And of course agents,

---

[1] Rhys Davies' latest book, to be published by the Mandrake Press in June 1929. Lahr must have sent DHL a copy of the MS.
[2] On the *Lady Chatterley's Lover* piracies see DHL's *A Propos of "Lady Chatterley's Lover"*, and Jay A. Gertzman, 'The Piracies of *Lady Chatterley's Lover*: 1928–1950', *DHL Review*, xix (Fall 1987), 267–99.
[3] A large Paris book shop.

publishers, booksellers are all delighted to see one getting into a tangle. Damn 'em all!

I didn't know anything about the *London Aphrodite* or Fanfrolico Press – am glad to have this copy of No 2.[1]

Sincerely D. H. Lawrence

4767. To Rhys Davies, [26 November 1928]
Text: MS UT; Postmark, Bandol 26–11 28; Rhys Davies, 'D. H. Lawrence in Bandol', *Horizon*, ii (October 1940), 191.

Hotel Beau Rivage. *Bandol.* Var
Monday

Dear Rhys Davies

Mr. Lahr sent me your address. Would you care to come here and be my guest in this small and inexpensive hotel for a few days? Bandol is about 20 minutes on the Marseilles side of Toulon: 20 mins. from Toulon. – My wife and I would both be pleased if you came. I'm not quite sure how long we shall stay here – but anyhow ten days.

Sincerely D. H. Lawrence

4768. To Rhys Davies, [28 November 1928]
Text: MS UT; Postmark, Bandol 28–11 [...]; Unpublished.

Hotel Beau Rivage. *Bandol,* Var
Wed

Dear Rhys Davies

We shall be pleased to see you on Thursday, which is tomorrow. If you catch the 12.5 in Nice, you change at Toulon 15.43, and leave by the small train 16.10, which gets you to Bandol 16.37. It seems a long time, for not very far. But you can easily travel third – if you wish.

If we are not at the station to meet you, get in the Beau Rivage omnibus and come on.

D. H. Lawrence

---

[1] John ('Jack') Lindsay (1900–90), Australian, came to London in 1926 to start the Fanfrolico Press. The following year he appointed another Australian, Percy Reginald Stephensen (1901–65), manager of the Press. In August 1928 they launched the *London Aphrodite* in accordance with the aesthetics of Lindsay's father Norman Alfred William Lindsay (1879–), Australian artist, novelist and theorist, and in opposition to J. C. Squire's *London Mercury*; it ran for six issues, till July 1929. See Lindsay in Nehls, iii. 300–3; Craig Munro, *Wild Man of Letters: The Story of P. R. Stephensen* (Melbourne, 1984), pp. 46–67; Lindsay obituary, *Independent*, 13 March 1990.

4769. To Jean Watson, 28 November 1928
Text: MS Forster; Unpublished.

Hotel Beau Rivage. *Bandol.* BANDOL. Var. France

28 Nov 1928

Dear Miss Watson[1]

I enclose the Swedish agreement.[2] – Have you made up a new agreement
with Kippenberg, or aren't we signing one?[3]

Now Orioli is ill, and I hope it hasn't developed seriously – if it has I shall
have to go to Florence. But don't worry, I'll see you get your copy of *Lady C.*
– even if there is a bit of delay.

Sincerely   D. H. Lawrence

4770. To Giuseppe Orioli, [30 November 1928]
Text: MS UCLA; Unpublished.

Hotel Beau-Rivage. Bandol. Var.

Friday

Dear Pino

Do send these two copies to this man – they were promised long ago, so we
shall have to let him have them for the £2. each. I have his cheque for £4.

tante cose!   DHL

F. A. Voigt (c.o. H. Seaton),[4] (bei von Karger), Nürnbergerstrasse 7 II,
Berlin. W. S. O.

4771. To Giulia Pini, 30 November 1928
Text: MS UT; Unpublished.

Hotel Beau Rivage, *Bandol* (Var), Francia

30 novem. 1928

Cara Giulia

Come andate tutti ora? lavorate al podere nuovo, e c'è sempre una bella vita
lassù, e molto divertimento? Noi siamo sempre qui al mare, in un posto bello,
e stiamo tutte e due bene. Non ho cercato ancora un'altra casa – mi piace stare

---

[1] Jean Watson, manager of the Foreign Department of Curtis Brown Ltd (London). m 1929,
Spencer Curtis Brown.

[2] Possibly for the Swedish translation of *The Woman Who Rode Away and Other Stories*
published in 1930 (Roberts D248).

[3] Dr Anton Kippenberg (1874–1950), head of the Leipzig publishing house Insel Verlag which
had published translations of five of DHL's books since 1922 (Roberts D73, 75–8).

[4] DHL...H. Seaton] DHL   P.T.O.   the address is Herrn F. A. Voigt bei H. Seaton. (Voigt is
unidentified; his cheque was dated 28 November 1928 ('Memoranda', MS NWU); hence the
conjectural date of this letter.)

un poco in albergo, senza i fastidii. Ma credo che alla Signora le rincresce, lei vorrebbe essere a casa sua.

Quando vai a Firenze, domanda un po' del Signor Orioli, come sta. Mi scrisse che stava male, coll'influenza e col fegato, e dopo quindici giorni non ho ricevuto nessuna lettera, non so niente. – Anche quando il babbo va a Firenze, dagli questa assegna per dare al Maggiore. La Signora mi diceva l'altro giorno che aveva promesso di mandargli, al Maggiore, cento Lire, e non l'ha mai fatto. Dice che mi rincresce che non l'abbia fatto prima: io non sapeva niente.

Pensiamo molto a San Paolo – vorrei e non vorrei essere là. Veramente per la salute, sto meglio altrove che là. Ma siamo un poco soli qui, dove non conosciamo la gente.

Fra poco sarà Natale, e quest'anno non ci sarà l'albero. Ma voi avete il podere nuovo in mente, e la vita bella che avrete tutti là. Non ho un franco-bollo italiano – ma ti mando una busta indirizzata – scriveci dunque qualche parola per dirci tutto che c'è di nuovo. E per Natale ti scriverò per certo.

affettuosamente. D. H. Lawrence

[Dear Giulia[1]

How are you all now? Are you working on the new farm, and is there always a good life up there, and lots of fun? We are still here at the seaside, in a beautiful place, and we are both well. I haven't looked for a new house yet – I like being in an hotel for a while without problems. But I think that my wife is displeased, she would like to be in her own house.

When you go to Florence, make a discreet enquiry about Mr Orioli, how he is. He wrote to tell me that he was unwell, with flu and a liver complaint, and a fortnight later I have received no letter. I know nothing. Also, when your father goes to Florence, give him this cheque to give to the Major.[2] My wife told me the other day that she had promised to send one hundred lire to the Major, and she never did. She says she's sorry she didn't do it earlier: I knew nothing about it.

We think a lot about San Paolo – I would and I would not like to be there. Actually, as far as my health is concerned, I'm better anywhere else than there. But here we are a little isolated, and we know nobody.

Soon, it will be Christmas, and this year there will be no tree.[3] But you

[1] Giulia Pini, daughter of the family of contadini who farmed the Villa Mirenda estate; she had been employed by the Lawrences as a servant. See Frieda Lawrence 202; *Letters*, vi. 75 n.3.

[2] 'Major' Raul Mirenda, owner of the Mirenda (*Letters*, v. 459 n. 2).

[3] Giulia's half-brother, Pietro, presented the Lawrences with a stolen tree for Christmas in 1926 and 1927 (*Letters*, v. 616 and n. 1; vi. 235); see Letter 4829.

have your new farm on your mind and the good life that you all have there. I
have no Italian stamp but I enclose an addressed envelope – so write a few
words to us to tell us all the news. And we will certainly write to you by
Christmas.

affectionately.   D. H. Lawrence]

4772. To Nellie Morrison, 1 December 1928
Text: TMSC NWU; Unpublished.

Hotel Beau Rivage, Bandol, Var. France.
1st. Dec. 1928.

Dear Nelly Morrison,[1]

I had your letter and postcard, and glad to know all is well with you. By
now I expect it has stopped raining. On this coast we've only had about five
days rain in two months – sunny all the time. But just now it's turned cold. I
quite like it here, without loving it at all. But we are very puzzled to know
what to do next, whether really to look for a house, and where. Not on this
coast I think. Frieda thinks Lago di Garda, but I am vague as to what I want.

The Brewsters are back in Capri and want us to go there but I don't want
to. Where *does* one want to live? The Huxleys are just outside Paris and don't
like it very much. What a hard lot to please we are!

How is Florence socially? How is Miss Moller?[2] Did she ever cut her copy
of *Lady C.?* Or has she burnt it, or better still, sold it? I suppose you heard
John Bull let off a mighty squeak against it, but I think Jane Cow took very
little notice. Bah! It's a good and proper book in spite of em all.

Do you know how Orioli is? He wrote two weeks ago he wasn't well, since
then, not a sound. Do ask about him, and if it's anything at all serious, do let
me know.

Well, when shall we meet again? Before long I hope. Frieda and I may
come to Florence from here. Anyway, all good wishes to you, and remember
us to Gino[3] and Miss Moller,

D. H. Lawrence

---

[1] DHL had met Nellie Morrison on Capri in 1921; she had temporarily provided him and Frieda
with a home at her flat at 32 Via dei Bardi in Florence. More recently she had begun, but soon
abandoned in disgust, the typing of *Lady Chatterley's Lover.* (See *Letters*, iii. 720 n. 1; vi.
259–60.)

[2] Muriel Moller lived at 22 Lungarno Acciaioli, Florence; little is known about her (cf. *Letters*,
vi. 334 and n. 1).

[3] Gino Sansani, Nellie Morrison's constant companion (cf. *Letters*, v. 454; vi. 61).

4773. To Alfred Stieglitz, 3 December 1928
Text: MS YU; Postmark, [. . .]; Unpublished.

Hotel Beau-Rivage. *Bandol.* Var.
(c/o Curtis Brown, 6 Henrietta St. Covent Garden, London W.C.2.)
3 Decem. 1928

Dear Stieglitz

Your letter this morning about the pirated editions. All I know about the matter is that a man called Jacob something-or-other of the *Vanguard Press* wrote me in June he had two friends who would very much like to print privately, for subscribers only, a thousand copies of *Lady C.* at 10 dollars, giving me 10%.[1] I said – since I knew I couldn't get copies in to U.S.A. – it seemed to me a good idea. Then he wrote he wanted to get the promise of my future works, for the Vanguard Press. I said he must arrange this with my agents, Curtis Brown. Since then I heard no more: but Edwin Rich, of Curtis Brown, has written me that this Jacob X has behaved in a shifty bullying manner, and refused to come to any terms at all: in fact the fellow seems to have annoyed Rich considerably. The upshot is, nothing has been agreed, no consent given, and as far as I know, nothing done. But apparently the pirated editions are out – I heard of one copy sold in London for thirty shillings.

Now about Holliday – he ordered 35 copies through the London agent, and the London agent wouldn't supply him.[2] So he wrote me – not long ago in September – and I said all right, I would sell him the last copies I would send to America, if he paid in advance. His cheque for 297 dollars came, and Orioli is shipping, as Holliday requested, five copies at a time. The first five Holliday cabled he received – the second five were sent. But I don't know if they arrived; because apparently Orioli is ill, I can't get a word from him. I'm afraid I shall have to go to Florence. I don't know if he sent you that last copy, which I *expressly* asked him to send. But don't bother about it anyhow. – Only later I'll let you know, just for the satisfaction of knowing if it *was* confiscated.

The Centaur Bookshop wrote that *all* the nineteen copies I sent (unpaid) to the private addresses of their clients, were lost. There is something fishy there, because to the Drexel Institute in Philadelphia two copies arrived – and others in that town – only the nineteen whose addresses Harold Mason sent are *all* lost. – And I heard that a pirated edition was produced in Philadelphia.

You must be bored by all this. If you want any particulars of that Jacob man of the Vanguard Press, do ask Edwin Rich of Curtis Brown Ltd, 116 West 39 St. – and he'll tell you.

---

[1] Jacob Baker, managing editor of Vanguard Press (see *Letters*, vi. 525 n. 1, 568, 572).
[2] Terence B. Holliday, a New York bookseller; he ordered copies of *Lady Chatterley's Lover* through the London book exporter, William Jackson who refused to handle that 'obscene and disgusting' work (*Letters*, vi. 518 n. 3, 568).

It seems laws are specially and exceedingly necessary in U.S.A.

And I don't think I should be happy, coming over just now.

It's awfully good of you to give Brett's pictures a shove. It'll mean so much to her, a bit of success.

As for my show, the scatterbrained Dorothy Warren has postponed it till New Year, chiefly because she's a scatterbrain, and is getting married again – and perhaps she's a bit frightened.

Don't you go thundering if you aren't strong enough. My regards to O'Keefe – I wish I was seeing you both.[1]

D. H. Lawrence

4774. To Mollie Skinner, 3 December 1928
Text: MS WAPL; cited in Katharine Prichard, 'Lawrence in Australia', *Meanjin* ix (Summer 1950), 258.

Hotel Beau Rivage. *Bandol.* Var, France.
3 Decem. 1928

Dear Molly Skinner[2]

Your MS. came on here, and I have read it all, and am returning it to you.[3] I can't do with it as I did with *Boy in the Bush* – that was a *tour de force* which one can do once, but not twice. And you see I know nothing of gold-camps, never saw a black boy except in the streets of Sydney, and know nothing of medicine. How can I re-create an atmosphere of which I know nothing? I should only make silly howlers. I suspect you of making a few. A mine, for example, would, I feel sure, be much more difficult to fake. – And then I really don't like your Jim men – who appeal to women by their exquisite pathos. Exquisite pathos puts me dead off men. – Still, the book has good points, and in a way is the most developed of your efforts. If I were to suggest anything, I should suggest that its form might be the form of a sort of diary – use the *I* again – and write in little sections, no chapters, just those little flashes of scenes and incidents, made briefer and more poignant, following one another with the hap-hazard of event. If you set about it, you could do two or three little sections a week, and make each brief, poignant, telling. Cut

---

[1] Stieglitz had recently married the painter Georgia O'Keefe (1887–1986). Cf. p. 24 n. 2.

[2] Shortly after his arrival in Australia in the spring of 1922, DHL stayed at a guesthouse run by two nurses, Ellen ('Nellie') Beakbane and Mary Louisa ('Mollie') Skinner (1876–1955). Skinner showed him the MS of a novel which he later rewrote as *The Boy in the Bush* (1924). She published a second novel, *Black Swans* (1925) which DHL disliked (*Letters*, v. 113 and n., 359, 419).

[3] This third novel, 'Eve in the Land of Nod', has remained unpublished. For an account of the considerable effort DHL made to restructure the novel before he gave up the struggle, see 'Introduction' to *The Boy in the Bush*, ed. Paul Eggert (Cambridge, 1990), p. li and nn. 119, 120.

out what you don't want – the man dying in the buggy, at the very beginning, for example, it has no point. Make it all a little more inward and
personal. Don't make your Nurse Leigh quite so sprightly – make her
loneliness a bit more poignant. Put in more of the *ugliness* – and the pain of
the ugliness – more of the rather repulsive quality of people of that camp
sort. Don't be so swimmily sympathetic and rather school-teacherishly
good. And you might make a real book of it, much better than *Black Swans.*
Buy a nice exercise book, and do it fragment by fragment, as an intimate
experience.

There, you won't thank me for all this unasked-for advice which you get in
place of more strenuous help. But I'm sorry to see you disappointed, I'm
sorry I can't really do what you wish. – Remember us both to Miss
Beakbane, and all our good wishes to you.

D. H. Lawrence[1]

4775. To Blanche Knopf, 3 December 1928
Text: MS UT; Unpublished.

Hotel Beau Rivage. Bandol, Var.
3 Dec. 1928

Dear Mrs Knopf[2]

The letter you wrote from BadenBaden in July reached me yesterday – five
months, rather a record.

It was about my coming to you, to your English branch, with my books. I
would do it if I were leaving Secker, but he has been decent to me, in his own
small way, and I don't feel like turning him down.

We have left the Villa Mirenda for good – it didn't suit my health. I think
we shall try Spain now. So if ever there is occasion to write to me, address me
c/o Curtis Brown, London.

You will understand now why I didn't answer your letter. You addressed it
wrong, and heaven knows where it went.

Sincerely   D. H. Lawrence

---

[1] Mollie Skinner's reaction to this letter was to think: 'That's that. I'll give it up and concentrate
on nursing – it pays better, and gives me much greater satisfaction' (Mollie Skinner, *The Fifth
Sparrow*, Sydney, 1972, p. 168).
[2] Blanche Knopf, née Wolf (1894–1966), wife of Alfred Knopf; 1921–57 she was Vice-President,
and 1957–66, President, of her husband's company.

4776. To Thomas Seltzer, 3 December 1928
Text: MS UT; Lacy, *Letters to Thomas and Adele Seltzer*, pp. 153–5.

Hotel Beau Rivage, Bandol. Var.
3 Decem. 1928

Dear Seltzer

Seligman sent me your address – I want to ask you if you will release to me the copyright of *BirdsBeasts And Flowers* – which contains *Tortoises*.[1] You may have seen Secker's *Collected Poems* of me: I want very much to rescue in America my scattered and submerged poetry, and bring out *Collected Poems* there too. I can do it if I can get the copyrights back into my own hands. I am negotiating with the Viking Press. So please say[2] you will let me have *BirdsBeasts* – the right to include it in *Collected Poems* – you can still go on selling your copies, when you can – and we can knock something off that old debt to me.[3]

I think of you and Adele often, and always with affection.[4] People are so fond of blaming one another – and they blame you for this that and the other. But I know it was neither your fault nor mine. It is just that we are neither of us in line with modern business. I don't intend to be – and you can't be. I hate modern business, and always did. You wanted to make a success in it – and it's not really in your nature. You aren't tough enough. I can afford *not* to succeed – but you, being in business, needed to. Which makes me very sorry things went as they did. I myself know I shall never be a real business success. But I can always make as much money as I need: so why should I bother. I care about my books – I want them to stand four-square *there*, even if they don't sell many. That's why I want to rescue my poems.

How are you both? I hope, well. How is Adele? is she good and cheerful? – I was ill last year with bad bronchial hemorrhages, and am still slowly getting better. But I *am* getting better, nearly my old self. We have given up the Italian villa, which was not good for my health – and now I don't quite know what next.

You have heard of *Lady Chatterley* – wonder if you read it. I lost most of the copies sent to America – and now there are *two* pirated editions, I hear –

---

[1] DHL appears to have confused the two edns of *Birds, Beasts and Flowers*. The poems published separately by Seltzer as *Tortoises* (1921) were not included in his edn of *Birds, Beasts and Flowers*, whereas they were included in Secker's. Cf. p. 166 n. 5.
[2] please say] please let me say
[3] By 1925 Seltzer had lost so much money through litigation that he was no longer able to pay his authors their full royalties. DHL left him for Knopf at that time. The following year Seltzer's business collapsed and was taken over by his nephews, the Boni brothers. DHL reckoned that Seltzer owed him over $4,000 in accrued royalties.
[4] Seltzer's wife Adele, née Szold (1876–1940).

3 December 1928   39

so there we are, same old story. But I sold the bulk to England – and lost
nothing – and put the book into the world.
   Do you still have the 96 St. flat? and Carrie?[1] and those good baked hams so
shiny? – Why didn't things turn out nicer?
                        remembrances from us both to you both   D. H. Lawrence
      write me
      c/o Curtis Brown. 6 Henrietta St. Covent Garden. London W.C. 2

4777. To S. S. Koteliansky, 3 December 1928
Text: MS BL; Postmark, Ba[ndol] 5–12 28; Zytaruk 366.

                                          Hotel Beau Rivage. *Bandol.* Var. France
                                                                    3 Dec 1928
My dear Kot
   How are you now, and how are things? We have been sitting here quietly,
with good sunny weather, this last fortnight, and really I think I'm getting
stronger. Only my cough is a curse, but my real health seems genuinely
better. Which to me is the chief thing.
   Lady C. continues her sad course. I hear there are *two* pirated editions out
in America – Lahr – the Red Lion St bookseller – wrote me he bought a copy
for 30/- – and Stieglitz wrote they are selling it in New York, the pirated
edition, as the original, at $10: pretending it is the original. So you see my
plan to agree with the Vanguard people to take 10% would have been best,
since now I get *nothing*, and they do as they like. –
   Then I hear nothing lately from Orioli – he was not well when he last wrote
– and any copies I asked him to send out, lately, he has *not* sent. Something is
wrong. I expect I shall have to go to Florence.
   Did I tell you that when I printed *Lady C.* – as they had only enough type
to do *half* the book at a time, I had them print two hundred copies on ordinary
paper. These 200 copies are bound up in paper binding – brochure – and I
wish I could put them on the market at £1. – to undersell the private pirated
copies. I wrote to Charles Lahr about it, as he seemed friendly – you remember you once went there 'Miss Archer'[2] – but he hasn't answered.
   How has Aldous' book gone in England? I heard it sold 80,000 in America.
It's the modern sort of melodrama, what *East Lynne* was in its day.[3]
   I am hung up here waiting to see if I've got to go to Florence. I don't want

---

[1] Possibly the 'huge, jolly negro cook' whom Frieda and Brett encountered when they stayed in
the Seltzers' apartment in March 1924 (Dorothy Brett, *Lawrence and Brett*, Philadelphia, 1933,
p. 38; *Letters*, v. 17).
[2] Lahr conducted his business under his wife's maiden name, E. [Esther] Archer.
[3] *East Lynne* (1861) was a hugely successful novel by Mrs Henry Wood (1814–87).

to go. If I needn't, I think we shall go to Spain. Unless also I am forced to come to London to take my pictures away from Dorothy Warren – I can't have her keeping them there in this fashion. I may have to come just for Christmas – though I dread London, with its darkness and squalor.

How are you all? Sonia and Grisha and Ghita?[1] Things don't get much brighter in the world, do they? That's why one sticks to the Mediterranean, with its sun. But I hope you are well. The thought of St. John's Wood is gloomy to me.

DHL

4778. To Martin Secker, 3 December 1928
Text: MS UInd; Postmark, Bandol [...] 2 28; Secker 111–12.

Hotel Beau Rivage. Bandol. BANDOL, Var. France
3 Dec 1928

Dear Secker.[2]

Long since I've written – but nothing new in the world. We left that island – too uncomfortable. It's pretty and very pleasant here, nice little hotel for 40 frs. But of course, dull – a bit like Spotorno.[3] We've had sunshine all the time, and are sheltered when the cold wind blows. It seems to suit me pretty well – and the French here are very nice in their way, so self-sufficient and free. It's about 10 miles from Toulon.

I wanted to go to Tuscany and finish the Etruscan essays, but am a bit scared of tombs in winter. Orioli though worries me a bit – I don't hear from him, he doesn't send out *Lady C.* when she's ordered – I'm afraid he's really ill. Afraid I shall have to go to Florence and see to things. I don't really want to. We want to go to Spain – it's not very far. – Have you heard of the pirated editions of *Lady C.* – apparently two out in America – and a man bought a copy in London for 30/-. – I suppose it was bound to happen, especially over there.

I had a letter from Mrs Knopf asking if I thought of leaving you and going over to their English branch with my forthcoming books. I said No.

---

[1] Sonia Issayevna and Michael S. ('Grisha') Farbman and their daughter Ghita, with whom Kot lived at 5 Acacia Avenue, St John's Wood, London. Michael Farbman (1880?–1933) was a Russian journalist. See *Letters*, ii. 570 n. 3.

[2] Martin Secker (1882–1978) had been DHL's English publisher since 1918. See *Letters*, i. 275 n. 1.

[3] The Lawrences and the Seckers had spent a good deal of time together at Spotorno, on the Italian Riviera, where the Lawrences lived, November 1925–April 1926, and where the parents of Caterina Maria ('Rina') Secker, née Capellero (1896–1969), had a house.

Everybody likes the *Collected Poems* so much – and so do I. I hope they are doing well. I saw the reviews in the *Times Sup.* and the *Observer*.[1]

Lately they've taken to asking me for little articles for the newspapers. It amuses me, when I feel like it – which isn't always, I assure you. But it seems *far* the best way of making money.

Did you read Aldous' *Counter-Point?* My word, the modern melodrama – *East Lynne* up to date! I thought the Rampions an unreal and wordy couple, but I suppose he meant well.

Frieda gets rather bored without a house – but I don't know *where* I want to settle – and I do want to go to Spain before we decide on anywhere. – How is Bridgefoot?[2] – is it wintry? I can hardly believe it, it is so sunny here. How is the boy? – getting a real big lad now.[3] It is three years since Spotorno! Remember us to Rina.

D. H. Lawrence

4779. To Maria Huxley, 5 December 1928
Text: Huxley 764.

Beau Rivage, Bandol, Var.
5 Dec., 1928.

Dear Maria, –

Well, of all the duds, to go and poison yourselves with alum, if you don't take the biscuit! What your insides must have felt like! Do for goodness' sake sit quite calm and get your wits about you, and keep them there. Dear Maria, the only thing to do in life is to gather oneself together and keep oneself together in spite of everything and everybody. You do get far too much tangled up in other people's presences: though it's damned hard not to: but it is disastrous. It causes the modern hysteria, which affects men even worse than women, and which I find *nauseating*: worse than your alum.

I'm glad you'll get money out of your *Counterpane*[4] – sounds quite a lot – you'll be able to squirt around. Here there's no news. When it comes to the point of going to Florence, I find I don't want to go. I expect one of these days we shall move on to Spain. But it's sunny here all the time, and quiet and very pleasant: the people are all very nice: why should one hurry away to something worse! Only Frieda gets fidgety, wanting a house to keep. Why can't women be peaceful? Hanno il diavolo nel corpo.[5]

[1] Both are reprinted in R. P. Draper, ed., *D. H. Lawrence: The Critical Heritage* (1970), pp. 299–305.
[2] The Seckers lived at Bridgefoot, Iver, Bucks.   [3] Adrian Secker (b. 1924).
[4] I.e. Huxley's *Point Counter Point*.
[5] 'They have the devil within them.'

Paul Morand and the Greek wife sound quite attractive[1] – but I don't think I want their house, marble or otherwise: though it's nice of them to say we could have it.

I suppose Aldous is back with you? you don't say. – As for plans, they'll have to make themselves, when the time comes.

DHL

4780. To Giuseppe Orioli, [5 December 1928]
Text: MS (Photocopy) HU; Moore 1103–4.

Hotel Beau Rivage. Bandol. Var, France.
5 Sept. 1928[2]

Dear Pino

I am so relieved to hear from you this morning. I was so afraid you were seriously ill with that liver. Do please another time send me a post card.

I'm glad it's business, though, and not illness, and I hope you'll sell Mrs Lawson's[3] library at a good profit, without a lot of trouble.

Do please send that copy of *Lady C.* to Curtis Browns office at once. Isn't it Miss Jean Watson who ordered it? I certainly promised it her.

Good about the orders at £4. But we shall have to start selling the one-guinea lot – the 200. Lahr wrote me he bought a *pirated* (Amer.) copy at thirty shillings, and another pirated lot was arriving in London on Dec. 5th – today. We must sell the two hundred at a guinea, to undersell them. I am writing now to Lahr to ask him if he will take a number. If he will sell a number – say 100 – at the real price, a guinea, he can have his one-third discount. It will stop the sale of the pirated editions.

Because I hear from Stieglitz there are *two* pirated editions, photographed from my edition, and with forged signatures: but done rather messily. I have not given any authorisation – and shall not see a penny, of course. Those Vanguard Press people must have gone behind my back and cheated me. Those three copies *Joy Go With You!!*[4] – Stieglitz said Holliday is selling the pirated edition at $10. and pretending it is the original. So if he loses some of my copies, I am not sorry. What cheats they all are!

[1] Paul Morand (1888–1976), wealthy French novelist and travel writer; see Letter 4781.
[2] The contents of the letter undoubtedly point to December rather than 'Sept.'; see fourth paragraph.
[3] Unidentified, but see letter following.
[4] On 27 August 1928 DHL had suggested to Orioli that false jackets and title-pages should be printed for three inspection copies of *Lady Chatterley's Lover* to ensure their safe arrival at the Vanguard Press (*Letters,* vi. 525). They were to read: *Joy Go With You – by Norman Kranzler.* (*The Ponte Press*).

Did you send Stieglitz that last copy – his third – as I said? – or didn't you? He hasn't got it.

It is sunny all the time here, so if you are well I don't think we shall come to Florence just now.

When you send me the last accounts, I'll add up again and send you your per-centage. I must be owing you some now.

What are your ideas about the second edition – the 200? I would like best to sell them in London, and quick – if I had someone to handle them.

tante cose!¹ DHL

4781. To Rhys Davies, [5 December 1928]
Text: TMSC NWU; Unpublished.

Hotel Beau Rivage, Bandol, Var.
Wed.

Dear Rhys Davies,

At last I hear from Florence – Orioli has been away all this time buried in the country buying a private library – which he's done – and like an Italian, losing his head and forgetting everything else *entirely*. He seems to be *half* there again now – in Florence. And he says it's cold there and pouring with rain. I feel a bit annoyed altogether, and shan't go.

I haven't heard from Lahr, but I'm going to write to him now and ask him if he'll handle the 200 *Lady C*'s at a guinea – or some of them. Perhaps he won't want to – but then he can say so.

Still sunny here – why should one hurry away to something worse! If we stay till Christmas, perhaps you'll come again and see us – unless you hate the long journey. Did you get back all right on Sunday? I hear Paul Morand, who is rich, offers me his house about 100 miles from Paris. But I don't want it.

Hope the novel is getting on.²

Regards from us both. D. H. Lawrence

4782. To Charles Lahr, 5 December 1928
Text: MS UNYB; Unpublished.

Hotel Beau Rivage, *Bandol*. Var. France
5 Decem. 1928

Dear Mr Lahr

Rhys Davies was here a few days and we both liked him, and if we stay I hope he'll come again.

I wrote you about *Lady C*. – those pirated editions stick in my throat. I

¹ 'all the best' (literally 'many things'). ² Possibly *Rings on her Fingers* (1930).

hear from New York there are two. Alfred Stieglitz says they are messily produced – do you think so? – But what I wanted if possible was to put my second edition of 200 copies unsigned on the market, at a guinea. I wondered if you could handle them, or some of them for me, taking the usual bookseller's discount on them? I should like if possible to undersell those pirated editions in London: if it's any use.

And I don't think there's much risk with the book, is there? It has not been suppressed – and as far as *I* know, no single copy has been confiscated in customs: certainly none that were sent from Florence.

Anyhow I should be glad of a word of advice on the matter – I rather thought you'd have written me in answer to my other letter.

I hear from Orioli that Paris has begun buying the first edition at £4. – so we must stick to that price now.

I hope this isn't a bore to you.

Sincerely   D. H. Lawrence

4783. To Charles Lahr, 6 December 1928
Text: MS StaU; Unpublished.

Hotel Beau Rivage. *Bandol.* Var.
6 Dec. 1928

Dear Lahr

Good of you to take so much trouble over *Lady C.* I think Gollancz would be a good man to do an expurgated edition,[1] and if you sent me a marked copy with suggestions, I would look at it at once to get it ship-shape: rather a miserable job, but worth doing.

I am writing Orioli now to send you *at once* three copies of the 200 edition – and if you get them all right, would you send the addresses to him direct:

Signor G. Orioli, 6 Lungarno Corsini, *Florence.*

If you want any copies for your shop, I will tell Orioli to give you the regular trade discount, whatever it is. But I think Galignani and the rest will have to be content with 15% the same as before.

I don't really want to go to Florence – hear it's cold and wet there, and it never suits my health. If Orioli will only get these things off.

I don't believe my mail is touched – it comes too quickly. But you could address the letters to my wife – Mrs Frieda Lawrence – there must be thousands of Mrs Lawrences.

Again with thanks for all the trouble you take.

Sincerely   D. H. Lawrence

[1] Victor B. Gollancz (1893–1967), radical publisher who – after an association with Benn Bros – had recently founded his own firm. No correspondence between him and Lahr or DHL about an edn of *Lady Chatterley's Lover* has survived.

4784. To Giuseppe Orioli, 6 December 1928
Text: MS UCLA; Unpublished.

Hotel Beau Rivage. *Bandol.* Var, Francia
6 Decem. 1928

Dear Pino

Will you please send to Lahr *at once* three copies of the 200-edition, registered, in plain paper. I enclose his letter.[1] – I have told him I will give him the ordinary trade discount on any copies he orders for his shop. But private orders will be *nett*, and to other booksellers we will give only the 15% as before. – I want to be as quick as possible, and put a spoke in the pirates' wheel.

Did you send the copy to Miss Watson of Curtis Brown? – you said Mrs Curtis Brown.[2]

I am going to try to get an expurgated edition out – for the public – then we are safe. Hope you are well. This in a hurry.

DHL

The letters you said you were forwarding have not come.

4785. To Laurence Pollinger, 7 December 1928
Text: MS UT; Unpublished.

Hotel Beau Rivage. *Bandol.* Var. France
7 Decem. 1928

Dear Pollinger

I hope you got the enlarged MS. of *Rawdon's Roof*, which I sent a week ago.

I've written to Seltzer and the Viking Press about the poems: as yet I have no answer: but when I have I'll tell you, and then you can carry on if you'll be so good.

I got the enclosed from Mrs Knopf two days ago:[3] and *five months late.* She'd addressed it all wrong. But I wrote and told her I wasn't thinking of leaving Secker.

At last, after being ill and taking cures and so forth, Orioli is back in Florence and will *I hope* attend to things. I trust by now he has sent[4] Miss Watson her copy of *Lady C.* I am going to have a number of copies – my last 25 – sent to London, where they can be delivered by hand. But the price has to be £4. now unless, as with Miss Watson, it is someone I know – even if only by letter – and who isn't rich.

Have you heard there are *two* pirated editions out in America – and I heard of a man buying a copy of one at 30/-: and the other is three guineas. Makes

[1] The enclosure is missing.   [2] See p. 32 n. 1.   [3] The enclosure is missing.
[4] MS reads 'send'.

one groan. – When the book was set up, there was only enough type for half at a time – so Orioli urged me to have more copies printed on common paper. So I had two hundred done before the first half of the type was dispersed. And now I'm going to sell these at a guinea. They are unsigned, and only bound in paper, and on ordinary paper. They'll be sold in a jiffey once I offer them to the booksellers, so if you want any – that is if you know of anybody who wants a copy – you might send a list of addresses. – I can have copies of the *original* delivered by hand in London, but at £4. – Orioli is sending a few copies this week of the 200 edition to a certain London bookseller. If they go through all right, he'll continue. – You see no legal action has been taken against the book, so there's no danger there. And as far as *I* am concerned no copy has been stopped in customs – and I've heard of none. So – we can try again. And if Orioli doesn't post the copies, I shall go to Florence myself and see to it. I'm going to have *all* my 25 copies of the original edition in London, and sell them and have done with them. Then he can please himself.

DHL

4786. To Enid Hilton, 7 December 1928
Text: MS UCLA; Huxley 764–5.

Hotel Beau Rivage. *Bandol.* Var
7 Decem 1928

Dear Enid[1]

Your letter tonight. I ought to have written you before, but somehow I felt we might be moving on. It is really blank indecision keeps us here – though really Bandol is quite nice now there are no people. Anyhow the hotel is really pleasant and the food really good – 40 frs. – so it's not worth while changing. Frieda gets fidgetty wanting a place of her own to spread out in. But where? Where does one really want to live? Can you tell me? Even Frieda doesn't really know – she oscillates between Lago di Garda and Taormina, and isn't sure of either. I say the best thing would be to go to Spain and try it, anyhow before settling anything. But she has left the trunks in Florence – and Orioli seems to have gone very vague. I ought to go there. And one of us ought to come[2] to London to see Dorothy Warren. And in this state of complex indecision we just sit still here and do nothing. But anyhow it has been sunny all the time, till today, which is grey –really lovely weather. I feel I am pretty well off – as you say, the sun is worth a lot. So why fret.

---

[1] Enid Hilton (1896–1992), daughter of William ('Willie') Edward Hopkin (1862–1951) and his wife Sarah Annie ('Sallie') (1867–1922), DHL's old Eastwood friends. See *Letters*, i. 176 nn. 2, 5. m. 1921, Laurence Edward Hilton (1885–1966), civil servant and amateur painter.
[2] come] go

I'm sorry about your nose – what was it? – Damn London, it seems to depress everybody.

By the way, since the fuss over *Lady C.* has died down, do you feel you could keep twenty or twenty-five copies in your flat?[1] If you do, I'll ask Orioli to send them along, a few at a time. And you can keep them till we get orders again – you know the price[2] is now £4., as there aren't many copies left. – But I did a small edition of 200 on common paper, to be sold at a guinea. I am going to send a number to Lahr to sell, because the Americans have got out *two* pirated editions, robbing me completely, and I want to undersell them.

Well I do hope you'll keep pretty fit. One of us might possibly be in England soon.

Remember me to Lawrence.

DHL

4787. To Charles Lahr, 9 December 1928
Text: MS UNYB; Postmark, Bandol 10–12 28; Unpublished.

Hotel Beau Rivage. *Bandol.* Var. France
9 Dec 1928

Dear Lahr

Many thanks for the letter dated 7th. Very good of you to trouble about the 200. I expect Orioli has written you already about them – or at least posted you the three copies. He has written to Galignani and Allen & Co about them too, so he says (why, I don't know, for I told him I was asking you about it) – but if you think you can handle the 200, I shall tell him not to supply anybody else. Your terms are generous. –

About the £4. edition – I have some copies already in London, with a friend S. Koteliansky. He can supply you a few. He is a black Russian Jew and a bit Jehovahish sometimes, but I have known him for many years. I shall ask him to call on you and talk about the book – and he can then bring you what copies of the £4. edition you wish to take: and you can, if you like, pay the money into my account in the Westminster Bank, Aldwych Branch – as you wish – and just send me the bank's receipt.

I am interested to know what Gollancz will say – And I want to get after those pirates in America.

If you send addresses for the 200 edition, will you send them direct to Orioli? – or, if you would rather send to Davies, ask him if he'll forward them to Orioli, as it saves time. You have the address –

Sig. G. Orioli. 6 Lungarno Corsini. Florence.

[1] She had acted as a principal 'courier' in storing and delivering copies of *Lady Chatterley's Lover* when DHL feared repressive action by the police (cf. *Letters*, vi. 477–8, 489–90, etc.).

[2] the price] the London price

We are staying on at Bandol for the present – Florence is in for one of her spells of bad weather and sickness.

Sincerely   D. H. Lawrence

Orioli says the people of the Fanfrolico Press said they would like to do a portfolio of reproductions of my paintings, which are in Dorothy Warrens gallery awaiting exhibition. Do you know who the Fanfrolicos are? I don't.

4788. To Giuseppe Orioli, [9 December 1928]
Text: MS UCLA; Unpublished.

Hotel Beau Rivage. Bandol. Var
Sunday.

Dear Pino

I enclose Lahr's letter. He seems very good, and I believe he's absolutely honest. If he gives us 21/- for each of the 200 edition, we won't sell any to Galignani nor to Allen & Co, we'll deal only with Lahr. – I'll send the addresses when they come along.

Meanwhile I am going to ask *Kot* to go to him and supply him with the £4. copies he wants. And you can make up Kot's 25 later. Also I think we'd better send 25 copies to Enid Hilton. It will be well, when they start going again, to have copies in London. But I'll write *definitely* about that in a day or two. We need to hear if the copies arrived to Curtis Browns office.

Will you send a copy of the 200 edit. to.

Mr. E. H. Brewster, Villa Giulia, *Anacapri* (Napoli)

and a copy to

Herrn Max Mohr, Wolfsgrube, *Rottach am Tegernsee*, Baviera. Germania[1]

They are both gifts – I had promised them.

I think it might be fun to do a portfolio of my pictures with the Fanfrolico people. But I haven't heard from them. Have you their address? Who are they?

Yes, we must try and get after the American pirates. I've already written about it.

I'm *not* going to supply copies the Amer. Govt. have confiscated.

Awfully sorry about Perceval, poor devil.[2] He has no luck. And your poor wretched Gebhard.[3]

---

[1] Max Mohr (1891–1944), German doctor, dramatist and novelist whom DHL met at Irschenhausen in 1927 (see *Letters*, vi. 156). With his wife, Käthe, and daughter, Eve ('Eva'), Mohr lived at Wolfsgrube near Rottach. His novel, *Die Freundschaft von Ladiz* (Berlin, 1931), was dedicated to DHL.

[2] Deane Perceval, formerly Secretary of the British Institute of Florence (*Letters*, iii. 575 n. 2).

[3] Unidentified.

I think we'll come to Florence after Christmas. I want to do my Etruscans
– but daren't risk bad weather. Here it's been so good. Do keep well yourself.

                                                                        DHL

4789. To S. S. Koteliansky, [9 December 1928]
Text: MS BL; Postmark, B[andol] 10–12 28; Zytaruk 368.

                                                    Hotel Beau Rivage. *Bandol.* Var
                                                                        Sunday
My dear Kot.
   I heard today from Charles Lahr, 68 Red Lion St. W.C.1. He says he can
handle *all* the 200 edition: give me 21/-, and sell to the trade for 24/-, and to
private people for 30/-.
   Also he says he can dispose of several of the £4.- copies: give me £4. and
sell for £5.- – I believe he is absolutely honest, and I like the sound of him.
Rhys Davies, a young Welsh writer, was here a few days – nice fellow. He
knows Lahr very well and has a great respect for him.
   I told Lahr I would ask you to call and see him. Will you go? – and supply
him with a few of your copies if he wants them. But go and talk to him. – I
told him if you let him have copies he could put the money in the bank.
   Then Orioli could fill up your 25 again. And I am asking Enid if she'll take
25. Somehow I feel now as if I'd rather have the books in London. Orioli is
perhaps not so interested any more.
   I told Lahr I had only a few copies of the first edition – that Orioli was
responsible for the last hundred. So stick to that.
   No, I've heard of no copy confiscated.
   Orioli says the men of the Fanfrolico Press told him they would like to do a
portfolio of reproductions of my pictures. What do you think? I would have
to get them photographed.
   Today it's rainy here too – but not unpleasant. We may stay here over
Christmas. Not a bad place. Remember me to Sonia and Grisha.

                                                                        DHL

4790. To Rhys Davies, [9 December 1928]
Text: TMSC NWU; Moore, *Intelligent Heart* 394–5.

                                                    Hotel Beau Rivage, *Bandol*, Var.
                                                                        Sunday.
Dear Rhys Davies,
   So now it rains – so I stop all morning in bed and do my correspondence. I
suppose you do your novel. I think you are wise not to try to rush it out.
People always trip you up when you're in a hurry.

Lahr wrote very nicely and will look after my *Lady C.* business. The idea is to print an expurgated edition for the public – not to set up the unexpurgated again. But later on I shall try to set up the unexpurgated in Paris, if I know anyone who'll take charge.

Orioli wrote me that the Fanfrolico people would do a portfolio of reproductions of my paintings, which hang in Dorothy Warren's gallery waiting to be exhibited. That would be rather fun. But I've heard nothing direct. If you write to the *London Aphrodite* people, you might mention it – if they are Fanfrolico.[1] Because if the thing were going to come off, we'd have to hurry and get the pictures photographed before Dorothy W. shows them, in the New Year. But the idea of a portfolio amuses me very much.

My wife is rather sad, with inflammation in her eye. I expect its a chill, with the winds. But she never has anything wrong, so when she *does*, she minds.

I hear weather is very bad in Florence and many people are sick. Glad I didn't go.

I bought you the other African cap, but it's a bit bigger than mine, a bit too big for me. You'll have to have it when you come, or when *we* come to Nice. Hope it'll fit.

Au revoir then   DHL

4791. To Max Mohr, 9 December 1928
Text: MS HMohr; Mohr 32–3.

Hotel Beau Rivage – BANDOL. Var. France.
9 Dec 1928

Dear Max Mohr

It's a shame we've never written to you. But it becomes such an effort to write when one isn't absolutely obliged to. I get so tired of words.

We have been here on this coast since the beginning of October, and it's been wonderfully fine and sunny. Our Villa Mirenda is given up – fertig[2] – so we have no home, and must live in hotels. I don't mind, for a while, but my wife gets uneasy and wants a place of her own. I expect we shall stay here over Christmas, then perhaps go to Spain. If I knew *where* I wanted to live, I'd look for another house. But I don't know. Only I know I want to be in the sun. It has been wonderfully sunny all the time we have been here, till yesterday, now it has started to rain.

I have asked Orioli to send you from Florence a copy of *Lady Chatterley's Lover*, so I hope it will arrive safely. The first edition of 1000 is almost all sold

---

[1] See Letter 4766 and p. 31 n. 1.   [2] 'finished'.

out – the few remaining copies he sells at £4 – Mark 80. This little edition they will sell in London at Mark 30.

Did you read *Die Frau die davon ritt?*[1] I would have sent you a copy, but old Kippenberg was so angry with me for saying I would leave him, that I thought I'd keep quiet. Curtis Brown *almost* fixed it up for me to go to S. Fischer Verlag – then at the last moment it was broken off, so the Insel Verlag will go on publishing me. I am just as well pleased. I don't think Fischer would have been any better.

How is the Jungfrau Max? By now, no doubt, she is fat and full-sized, perhaps even printed.[2] How is it at Wolfsgrube? I must say I dread the northern winter, so dark and dismal.

Many regards from us both to you three. D. H. Lawrence

4792. To Nancy Pearn, 9 December 1928
Text: MS UT; Unpublished.

Hotel Beau Rivage. *Bandol.* Var. France
9 Dec 1928

Dear Nancy Pearn

Here is the article for the *Daily Express* or whoever it is.[3]

I am going to send you the MS. of the poems – if you call them Poems – Pensées – which I have been doing. This M. S. is strictly privately for you and your use. I don't want anyone else to see it. Send out any poems you think *really* suitable. If you like you can leave out a verse or a line or anything of a poem, for periodical use. I don't care what you do for the periodicals. But I keep a complete MS. for a book later.

Yes, do keep these little MSS for me. I'm a bad keeper.

Raining here – for the first time since we are here.

Perfect consideration,[4] as the French so sillily say.

DHL

---

[1] *The Woman Who Rode Away and Other Stories*, tr. by Frieda's sister, Else Jaffe (1874–1973), had just been published by Insel Verlag (Roberts D78).

[2] Mohr's novel was published in 1929 as *Die Heiden*.

[3] On 6 December 1928 (TMSC UT) Nancy Pearn forwarded to DHL a cutting received from the *Daily Express*, taken from an American magazine and entitled 'And We Marry These Women'. The *Express* asked whether he would be willing 'to write a special article conveying some of these comments in a manner to suit [him]self'. In response, with this letter, DHL enclosed his essay 'Oh These Women!'; it appeared in *Vanity Fair*, May 1929, as 'Woman in Man's Image', and in the *Express*, 19 June 1929, as 'The Real Trouble About Women'. It was collected in *Assorted Articles* as 'Give Her a Pattern' (Roberts C187). (The title 'Oh these Women' is written on DHL's letter probably by Nancy Pearn's assistant.)

[4] I.e. 'Ma parfaite considération' – 'yours very truly'.

4793. To Laurence Pollinger, 9 December 1928
Text: MS UT; Unpublished.

Hotel Beau Rivage. *Bandol,* Var.
9 Dec. 1928

Dear Pollinger

I enclose the letter from the Viking Press.[1] I told them that, personally, I should like them to do the book – the *Collected Poems.* – I wrote to Seltzer asking him to release *BirdsBeasts and Flowers.* There remains only *Love Poems and Others,* the very first vol. – and does anybody hold the copyright? I believe Mitchell Kennerley bought sheets from Duckworth, but I believe he doesn't have any rights now.[2] One would have to make sure – he's a slippery one.

Today I hear from Orioli that he has *sent* you your two copies of the novel, and Miss Watson hers. I do hope they arrive. At last my urgings have had effect. – But I'm going to get my remaining copies to London, if possible, to have them under my control.

I think the Vikings are all right, don't you?

Sincerely   D. H. Lawrence

4794. To Emily King, [10 December 1928]
Text: MS Lazarus; Postmark, B[andol] 10–[. . .]28; Unpublished.

Hotel Beau Rivage. Bandol. Var. France.
Monday

My dear Pamela

Well we are still here. I thought we should have moved before now – but I hear that in Florence the weather is very bad, many people ill, and as I always get flu there, I thought I'd better stay away. Here it has rained these last two days, but today is sunny again, so we can't grumble. Frieda gets tired of being in an hotel with nothing to do. One is really too comfortable. But of course I have my writing. Frieda hasn't any work, so she gets fidgetty. The worst of it is she doesn't know where she really *wants* a house. I say to her, if there's any place you definitely want to go and live in, I'll go and look for a place. Then she varies from Lago di Garda to Taormina, and doesn't know of anywhere. Myself I feel like going to Spain. It seems to suit me now to go on to new places, and I've no real desire to settle down. So we shall see. The Brewsters

---

[1] Cf. Letter 4785.
[2] Mitchell Kennerley (1878–1950), New York publisher of the first American edns of *The Trespasser* (1912), *Love Poems and Others* (1913) and *Sons and Lovers* (1913), and the first edition of *The Widowing of Mrs Holroyd* (1914). DHL had long regarded him as untrustworthy: see *Letters,* iii. 612 and n. 2.

are expecting us in Capri for Christmas – but it is an infernal long way. Barcelona is much nearer.

I'm not going to send any christmas parcels, the mail is such a curse. And please don't send me anything. Rhys Davies had a 2/6 cake sent from England – it arrived smashed to bits and he had to pay another 2/3 on it. What's the good! I'll send a little money. By the way, you never said how the shop is going. Rhys Davies, a young Welsh writer, was here for a few days – he says South Wales is horribly depressing. – So do tell me about the shop, what the result of the whole year is.

I'm sorry you all had colds. We had them mildly, with the winds, and Frieda has got an inflamed eye, but it's getting better. I don't like the turn of the year – shall be glad when it's New Year again.

The exhibition of pictures is still vague. I think Dorothy Warren is now actually married – but the bitch has never written to me. However it's just as well the show was delayed, as there was the fuss in *John Bull* over my novel – such rot! Anyhow another gallery now wants to show them. And a man said he'd like to publish a portfolio of the black-and white reproductions – done from photographs.[1] That might be rather fun – but I'm not at all sure about it.

Frieda's daughter Barby has had flu – and F. has asked her here for ten days.[2] I don't know if she'll come. If she does, I expect we shall stay over Christmas – and then set off for Spain. Frieda has always had such a desire to go to Majorca – which is another island, off Barcelona – but I'm by no means keen on islands.

Peg's German letter was very good – she's got on wonderfully. F. is going to answer it. – I find it bores me so to have to speak French. I don't know why, but the French don't really interest me, and I never want to speak to them. They are rather self-centred smallish people – though I must say, everyone is very nice.

I do hope you're all well – and send me the news.

love. DHL

4795. To Earl and Achsah Brewster, 10 December 1928
Text: MS UT; Brewster 187–8.

Hotel Beau-Rivage. *Bandol.* Var
Monday 10 Dec. 1928

Dear Earl and Achsah

We had your nice letters – am so glad you are pretty happy on Capri. And

---

[1] Jack Lindsay.
[2] Frieda's youngest child, Barbara Joy ('Barby') Weekley (b. 1904), the most frequent visitor of Frieda's family to the Lawrences.

by now you will be in the Villa Giulia. And I'm afraid we shan't come for Christmas, after all. Frieda's daughter Barbara had flu and wrote dismally, so Frieda has asked her here for Christmas. She might possibly not come – but I expect she will. – And I hear the weather in Florence is bad, and many people sick. Here we really have had wonderful weather – Saturday and yesterday it rained a lot – now today is sunny again, and fresh. This coast really seems to have a good winter climate.

I myself want to go to Spain. It's quite near, nearer to Barcelona than to Rome, a lot. And I think new things, new scenes are good for me – and Spain isn't too great an effort. It's nice here, the hotel is very pleasant, though it doesn't work out cheap. And the people are very nice. But somehow they aren't very interesting. They seem a bit small and pettifogging, too [domes]ticated,[1] too close on their own little centres. There's nothing thrilling about the French – their lives are too neat, though their sewage arrangements are pretty awful, and their taste is even worse than modern Italian taste. Still they are pleasant superficially, and they leave one very free. I like them for a time – but not for keeps. And now I feel I want to try Spain. There it lies, like destiny. And if we don't like Spain, then we'll come back to Italy. That settles it.

I asked Orioli to send you a copy of *Lady C.* – just one of the little 200 edition – because it isn't in your line, either of you – neither Buddha nor Mary – but you needn't read it if you don't want to.

Brett and Mabel are in New York for the winter – have you heard from them? I suppose they'll enjoy themselves seeing a lot of people, but Brett will get sick of it. She says she won't come over to Europe – in which she's wise – but I fear if she gets bored in New York, she will. It depends what sort of attitude her people take.

I wonder if Earl went to Florence. I'm sure he didn't want to. Frieda had a cold and an inflamed eye, but it's getting better. She says she wants a house – when I say right-o! she says: not here – perhaps Lago di Garda: perhaps Taormina: perhaps the ranch. So there you are – you can't take a house at that rate.

Well I'm sorry we shan't be seeing you soon – I was looking forward to Christmas and charades. But I feel it won't be very long.

love.   DHL

[1] The word is partly obscured by an ink blot.

4796. To Hon. Dorothy Brett, 10 December 1928
Text: MS UCin; Postmark, Bandol 13[. . .]28; Moore 1105.

Hotel Beau Rivage, *Bandol*, Var
10 Dec 1928

Dear Brett

I wish you would send a line to
Mrs Maria Cristina Chambers, 43 Hillside Rd. Elm Point,
Great Neck, Long Island. N. Y.[1]
I think she is a nice woman and you would like her. She is wife of the editor of the *Literary Digest*, and she is Mexican – she knows about the ranch and all – tell her I told you.

Nothing new here – I hear London and Paris are both selling the pirated editions of *Lady C* – at £3. and £2. – So I am done in the eye. Only I have a little edition of 200, printed from the original plates, which I am now selling at 21/- and 30/-. If only I had 2000 I could cut out the pirates, but I have only 200.

How are your pictures? – no further news of mine – except a man said he might do a portfolio of reproductions.

We linger on here – rather dull – but I don't want a house, and though Frieda wants one, she doesn't know where, so it amounts to the same thing. She talks again of the ranch, now. But I feel America very hostile to me.

I am doing some little *Pensées* – sort of poems, but really *thoughts* – all in snatches: rather amusing. Impossible to paint in poky hotel rooms. And France doesn't inspire me anyhow – the people are too tight.

Did you ask Lawr. Gomme why he never *paid* for his 6 copies of *Lady C*. I'm sick of being swindled.

I hear Katharine's letters sell largely, yet Murry whines about poverty.[2] And I hear he *inserts* the most poignant passages himself: Ottoline declares that in the letters to her,[3] large pieces are inserted, most movingly. Quelle blague![4] – Did you read Aldous' book? a bit cheap sensational I thought.

I wonder how you like New York. Anyhow it must be better than London. If we don't come to N. Mexico we shall go to Spain, it is so near, and I feel like something a bit new.

[1] Maria Cristina Chambers, née Mena (d. 1965), short-story writer. m. Henry Kellett Chambers who had published a version of one of DHL's Mexican essays in the *Literary Digest*. See *Letters*, vi. 210 and n. 3.
[2] DHL's erstwhile friend, John Middleton Murry (1889–1957), critic and journalist, had published *Letters of Katherine Mansfield*, 2 vols (October 1928).
[3] Lady Ottoline Violet Anne Morrell (1873–1938), well-known hostess and patroness of the arts; a close friend of DHL 1915–17 and they had re-established contact in May 1928. See *Letters*, ii. 253 n. 3; iv. 33 n. 2; vi. 394.
[4] 'What a humbug!'

How is Mabel? I do hope she's keeping pretty well. It's true, one suffers agonies from *noise*, in a town. I am just the same. But I am sorry to think of 'the hill' let out as a dude ranch.

Well, we'll see what next.

DHL

4797. To Earl and Achsah Brewster, [10 December 1928]
Text: MS UT; Brewster 188–9.

Hotel Beau Rivage, *Bandol*, Var. France
Monday

Dear Earl and Achsah

I felt so disappointed when I wrote you this morning that we wouldn't come to Capri, that now I've written to Frieda's daughters[1] to say, if they'd like it I'll try and get a ship *Marseilles to Naples* and we'll all come to Capri for Christmas – stay in the Bella Vista or Lauro or whatever you think best. Wouldn't it be fun! – if we can get a ship, that is – I can't bear the rail journey. And if the daughters want to do it. So wait a bit and I'll let you know. What fun, though! We could sail from Naples to Spain later.

DHL

4798. To Giuseppe Orioli, [10 December 1928]
Text: MS UCLA; Unpublished.

Hotel Beau Rivage. *Bandol*. Var, France.
Monday

Dear Pino

This in answer to yours of this morning.

Of course if Galignani is selling *Lady C.* for £3. he is selling the *pirated* edition. And if your other man doesn't send you the money for the eight copies, it's because he's got the pirated edition too. If only, if only we had 2000 of the cheap edition! – to sell at 21/- or at *any* price, to cut out the pirates! – Now what can we do? Paris is no doubt stocked with the pirated edition.

DHL

---

[1] Elsa Agnes Frieda Weekley (1902–85), and Barbara Weekley. DHL's letter(s) is/are missing.

4799. To Maria and Aldous Huxley, [10 December 1928]
Text: Huxley 767.

Beau Rivage, Bandol.
Monday.

My dear Maria and Aldous, –

Would you or Aldous do a little thing for me when you are in Paris? There have come out *two* pirated editions of *Lady C.* in America: they are being sold in London at £3 and one I heard at 30/- but usually £3. I believe they are being sold in Paris too, in Galignani's and other shops – is there one Castiglione? I do wish when you are in town you would ask at these shops if they have copies of the book, at how much, and ask to see one – then examine it and tell me if it's the pirated editions – and tell them, the brutes. The pirated editions were *photographed* from my edition, so they may look superficially the same. But paper and binding are different.

I've got a little paper-bound edition of 200 which I'm selling privately now – just going to – at 21/-, and the booksellers in London are going to ask 30/- for it. If only I had 2,000 I could kill the pirates – but I've only 200. Pino has them.

The first edition has about a hundred left, and they are now £4, London booksellers charge £5. But of course this pirated lot stops those too. I'm done in the eye! And such a lot of mine have been confiscated in America.

But if you are in town do find out for me. I must do something if I can.

Frieda had an inflamed eye, and was sad. She's asked her daughter Barby here. We might possibly go by ship to Capri (Naples) for Christmas.

DHL[1]

---

[1] Maria Huxley appears to have replied by return of post, on 11 December 1928. Her undated letter (first printed – by courtesy of Mrs Rosalind Wells – in Michael Squires, 'Two Newly Discovered Letters to D. H. Lawrence', *DHL Review*, xxiii, Spring 1991, 34–5) reads as follows:

Dearest Lawrence –

I am in a rage – the dogs are realy dirty – more than you thought – I asked this evening at the librairie Castiglione rue de Castiglione If they had your book – they said yes & went up to fetch it while the woman – respectable old lady & gent – told me "Ça vaut cher ça –" ['That's expensive'] & I knowing it was "Je sais bien" ['Yes I know'] – Arrived the book very like the real one – but paper thinner & cover in broad uneven shades – I suggested it was not the real one & they seemed genuinely hurt because they showed me the signature – also that it was *very* difficult to get & would not tell me where from – but unsuspecting, told me they had been forbidden to put it in window "because the Heroine – Madame Chatterley – was staying with a friend at the Ritz["] – & they said your book was unpublisheable because of libel! – they were friendly in spite of the assurances it was not the original – but the dirtiest to come – 5000 frs!!

I suppose they would take much less but still – Aldous will write himself about what he thinks – anyhow tomorrow I go back with my copy & compare it so as to make sure – it was No 130 – & had I not know or studied it, very convincing –

4800. To Charles Wilson, 11 December 1928
Text: MS YU; Unpublished.

Hotel Beau Rivage. BANDOL. Var. France
11 Dec 1928

Dear Charles Wilson[1]

Your very battered letter arrived here this morning. It looked as if it had had something enclosed in it, but the something had disappeared, whatever it was.

Yes, we have given up the Florence house, the climate wasn't good for me. Now we are wondering where to go next – and where to settle. But probably we shan't try to settle, at least this winter – perhaps go to Spain. I shan't come to England anyhow in winter.

I have asked Orioli to send you a copy of the novel, but of the second edition of 200, which costs a guinea. It is printed from the same plates as the first, but on cheaper paper. I hope you'll get it all right. Do let me know. – I don't think any serious people were affected by *John Bull*'s noise.

I expect the miners are doing just as badly as in the Midlands. It makes me so mad, for their sakes.

All good wishes   D. H. Lawrence

Next week we are going to Belgium so write there after 20th – 19 Grand Place – St Trond – but do tell me when & where you will be at Xmas as soon as you know – How I wish we were with you – If Frieda's eye remains troublesome I will send her an excellent "drops" who – I asked – can hurt in no case – & so far did me & everyone good –

This is a quick letter in a hurry – but it sends love & indignation. I will write to Frieda soon – next week. Terrificly busy with house & Xmas – house gets on & have Italian cook – also spare bedroom after Xmas – does it tempt you – love again

M–

Huxley replied on 12 December 1928 (Smith 304–5). His letter begins:

Dear Lawrence,

What an intolerable business about the pirating of *Lady C.*! M[aria] has seen a copy of the spurious edition, for which they ask 5000 francs. Wdn't it be worth while for Orioli to come to Paris, interview the booksellers and get rid of his remaining stock at some reasonable rate between the original 2 guineas and the 5000 francs asked by the pirates? He would undersell the devils at the same time turn an honest penny. Also he'd be able to get rid of the paper bound copies at the same time. I feel that Paris is a good centre owing to absence of censor-nonsense and presence of large numbers of English and Americans. If you want to multiply your own edition remember that the photographic process is simple and ... cheap.... If you can't get it done in Italy you cd certainly find some firm who'd do it in Paris. That's why I think Orioli wd be well advised to come here and explore the ground. I think there's much to be done – and it needs doing quickly if the pirates are not to get away with the loot. I don't know anybody in the bookselling trade here, or else I'd suggest. Is Sylvia Beach reliable? I have a prejudice against her, probably quite unfounded. But she might be useful.

[1] Charles Wilson (1891–1968), free-lance journalist, poet (known as 'The Pitman Poet') and adult-educationalist; he and DHL had never met but had exchanged letters for a year (see *Letters*, vi. 229 and n. 2).

4801. To Giuseppe Orioli, 11 December 1928
Text: MS UCLA; Unpublished.

Hotel Beau Rivage. *Bandol*, Var. France
Tuesday 11 Dec. 1928

Dear Pino

Here is the list from Lahr, for the copies of the 200-edition.[1] And there is one address I have added – Charles Wilson – I long ago asked you to send him a copy of the first edition, but I suppose you never sent it. However, let him have this one. The letter with the pipe?? was from him – it arrived this morning, but no pipe in it – nothing!

I hope these go through all right. Send them as soon as you can, will you – when you hear if Lahr has got the first three safely.

What are you doing for Christmas?

DHL

4802. To Laurence Pollinger, 14 December 1928
Text: MS UT; Unpublished.

Hotel Beau Rivage. *Bandol.* Var.
Friday 14 Dec. 1928

Dear Pollinger

Here is the registered receipt of the MS. of *Rawdons Roof,*[2] which I sent two weeks ago – perhaps 30 Nov. – from Bandol, here. Apparently the girl sent it as letter, though it was marked Manuscript. It's a very harum-scarum post-office, here.

I shall tell my friend S. Koteliansky to call on you – he's got a few copies of *Lady C.* – and bring you what you want.[3] Orioli *said* he'd *sent* you two copies, and Miss Watson hers. I hope none of these are lost. He's very un-satisfactory lately. – I'll get him to send a few prospectuses of the guinea edition. The booksellers are paying me a guinea, and charging private people 30/-.

Gollancz said if I'd submit to him an expurgated version of *Lady C* he'd give it sympathetic consideration. I wonder if it's worth while?

Awfully good of you to dispose of her Ladyship for me as you do.

DHL

---

[1] The list is missing.   [2] The receipt is attached to the letter (UT).
[3] you what you want.] them you.

4803. To Jack Lindsay, 14 December 1928
Text: MS VL; Unpublished.

Hotel Beau Rivage, BANDOL. Var. France
14 Dec 1928

Dear Mr Lindsay

Orioli wrote me from Florence that the Fanfrolico Press might do a port-folio of reproductions of my pictures, that hang now in Dorothy Warren's gallery. I think the idea is fun, if you'd really care to do it. I would write a little introductory essay on painting, modern painting, if you wished.

Would you let me know if you actually think of going on with the thing? I've heard of the Fanfrolico from Rhys Davies – hope you're having a good time with it.

Yours Sincerely   D. H. Lawrence

4804. To S. S. Koteliansky, 14 December 1928
Text: MS BL; Postmark, Bandol 14–12 28; Zytaruk 369.

Hotel Beau Rivage. Bandol. Var. France.
14 Dec 1928

My dear Kot

Yours today – hope you got on all right with Lahr.

Could you post me the enclosed letter to Jack Lindsay?[1] I leave it open for you to read.

Would you either go and see L. E. Pollinger of Curtis Browns, and take him three copies of *Lady C.* – or just leave the copies for him? He pays the £4. into my bank and is perfectly safe. I told him you'd call, but if you'd prefer merely to leave the books, do that. And I'll ask Orioli to send you ten more copies.

And you *must* let me pay you, some way.

DHL

4805. To Charles Lahr, 14 December 1928
Text: MS UNYB; Postmark, Bandol 14–12 28; Unpublished.

Hotel Beau Rivage. *Bandol.* Var.
14 Dec 1928

Dear Lahr

Do get Russell Green to go through *Lady C* and write his suggestions.[2] Naturally Gollancz can't make any promises till he sees at least a possible MS.

[1] The preceding letter.
[2] Russell Green (1893–) had edited *Coterie* in 1920, and *New Coterie* with Lahr, 1925–7; he acted as Lahr's copy-editor on other occasions. He was also the author of several semi-autobio-graphical romans à clef. Lahr acted on DHL's request: see p. 95 n. 2.

But *do you think* it can be made possible? Does Russell Green think so, seriously? Because I don't want to sweat at altering it, all to no purpose.

I've written Jack Lindsay – we'll see what he says.

Did you get the three copies of the 200 edit.? I haven't heard from Orioli whether he has sent out the orders on your list.

Wonder how you got on with Kot. – I think he's a bit of a terror, if you don't know him.

Sincerely   D. H. Lawrence

4806. To Giuseppe Orioli, 14 December 1928
Text: MS UCLA; Unpublished.

Hotel Beau Rivage, Bandol. Var. France
14 Dec. 1928

Dear Pino

Will you start sending *Kot.* ten more copies of the first edition.

Lahr writes it will be best to sell the 200 edition to other booksellers, but not to accept less than 21/- from booksellers: so perhaps we must make it 30/- to the private people. What do you think? Let me know.

Lahr does not say if he received his three copies – have you heard?

I have added up the accounts, and the profits are just about £1000, so I shall send you another £25. in my next, when I hear from you. I keep check of everything I know of: Pollinger and all.

DHL[1]

4807. To Giuseppe Orioli, 14 December 1928
Text: MS UCLA; Unpublished.

Hotel Beau Rivage. Bandol. Var, France
14 Dec 1928

Dear Pino

Your letter with borderaux this evening.

Yes, if Galignani want 50 copies at 21/-, let them have them.

---

[1] DHL's letter was written on a copy of a letter from Pollinger to Orioli, 10 December 1928:

Dear Sir,

   This will acknowledge with many thanks the receipt of yours of December 3rd, and copy of "Lady Chatterley". I should be glad to have the other copy, at your early convenience.

   By the bye, Miss Jean Watson, the Manager of our Foreign Department, tells me she sent you about a month ago her cheque for £2.2.0. but up to the time of writing, copy of the book has not reached her. Would you kindly send her copy, together with my other copy, as quickly as possible.

   Thanking you in anticipation,

Yours very truly,

Alongside the first sentence of paragraph 2, DHL wrote: 'Did you send it?'

Send Kot. *ten copies* of the first edition. I haven't heard from Enid yet. Send Holliday ten copies to London, then wait to see if he gets them. And then, if we wish, we can refuse to let him have any more, and re-fund for fifteen copies.

I enclose Maria's letter, and Aldous'.[1] So you see how Paris is. I wish she'd tried Galignani. I'll ask her, too.

I do wish I knew a Paris bookseller who would do as Aldous says, print from photograph and sell publicly. *Do you know anybody?* Of course you can't go to Paris. But I am making enquiries. I am asking Aldous to sound Sylvia Beach.[2] Of course I don't like her – but if she'd do a Paris edition and keep it going as she has done *Ulysses*, it would be very valuable.

Send her a note and ask her if she'd like any of the 200 edition at one guinea net, to stop the pirates: then we'll see what she says.

Send Pollinger *two* copies of the 200 edit.

We are still here – it's good sunny weather, and it suits me. I don't know if Frieda's daughters will come out for Christmas: if they don't, we may leave, perhaps for Spain.

I do hope it's not a great nuisance to you, bothering with *Lady C.* just when you want to be busy with the library you bought. But I think we'd better get all these copies sent out as soon as possible.

The MS. of *The Escaped Cock* is still in America. But I'll ask for it back, since the swine decide nothing. But do something else before you do any more me – either Faith McKenzie's cookery book[3] – or Douglas' story. *Is* Douglas story any good? I hear many complaints about his last two books.[4] – I am getting together a book of Poems – *Pensées* – which probably I'll publish next year – another possibility for you.

Amitiés.[5]   DHL

[1] See p. 57 n. 1. On 18 December Huxley wrote to Charles Prentice, his editor at Chatto & Windus, asking about the photographic process on DHL's behalf (Smith 305–6).
[2] Sylvia Woodbridge Beach (1887–1962), American publisher; operated Shakespeare & Co., 1919–41, the celebrated Paris bookshop and publishing house. Published Joyce's *Ulysses* (1922). See *Letters*, iv. 569 n.
[3] Faith Compton Mackenzie (1888–1960), biographer, wife of (Sir) Edward Montague Compton Mackenzie (1883–1972), novelist.
[4] George Norman Douglas (1868–1952), novelist and essayist; neighbour and close friend of Orioli. (See *Letters*, iii. 409 n. 3.) His previous two books (both published by Orioli) were the novel *In the Beginning* (1927), and a critical anthology, *Some Limericks* (1928). The 'story' was *Nerinda* which Orioli published in 1929.
[5] 'Kind regards.'

4808. To Giuseppe Orioli, 14 December 1928
Text: MS UCLA; Unpublished.

Gross profits on *Lady C.* to Dec. 14. 1928 = £*1024..0..0*
to Pino. £*27..10..0.* making in all £*102..10..0*
for Carletto £*1.*[1]
sent in Liras – 2,635.00 – Dec.14.1928

Hotel Beau Rivage, *Bandol.* Var. France.
14 Dec. 1928

Dear Pino

Above is my statement of profits as near as I can figure it. It includes Pollingers last £4..4..0, and your statements received this evening. In Haskards bank, on Monday, they inform me I have £603..13..11 sterling and Liras 5665/45. It doesn't quite fit, but I put some cheques in London, and I may have made a mistake there.

I enclose a cheque for Liras 2,635.00,[2] of which please give Liras 100 to Carletto from me.

What about postage? What do I owe you there? Please deduct it out of Liras that may be paid you in the shop.

this is just a money note.

DHL

I'm sending you Liras, as I shan't be using them – is it right, as equivalent for £28..10..0.? (counting the exchange as 92.40).

Say if it's all right.

4809. To Aldous and Maria Huxley, 15 December 1928
Text: Huxley 765–6.

Hôtel Beau Rivage, Bandol.
15 Dec., 1928.

Dear Aldous and Maria,–

It has been quite cold, but the sun rose brilliant, all bright and crystal, and is shining on me as I sit in bed writing. It makes me *not* want to come north – ever. My feeling now is, I would like to go real south, to get a house: either Sicily again or south Spain: and I'd like to look at the South of Spain first. But my instinct is to go south, not to come north. Of course it would mean going away in summer – but one does that even in Florence. I should think Suresnes would be a summer place rather than winter. It is quite nice here – but

---

[1] Carletto ('Carlo') Zanotti was Orioli's 'boy' or factotum. His mother was Orioli's cook.
[2] Liras 2,635.00] £28.10.0.

what a *mess* the French make of their places – perfect slums of villadom, appallingly without order, or form, or *place*. A ghastly slummy nowhereness – but France seems all like that. And the people, though nice and tidy in themselves, as a whole make a slummy impression, no bigger life at all – a bit thin and boring, too house-keeperishly individual. I don't think I'd want to live in France.

I have been doing a book of Pensées, which I call pansies, a sort of loose little poem form; Frieda says with joy: real doggerel. – But meant for Pensées, not poetry, especially not lyrical poetry. I think they'd amuse you, Maria. There's a little one to you, half catty –

> Thank you, dear Maria,
> for helping with *Lady C.*, etc.

but probably I shan't put it in.[1]

If you saw Sylvia Beach, and she seemed a bit warm, you might say I'd mentioned her – but I feel very doubtful of her.[2]

Glad the house is coming right.[3] Of course as soon as it's quite right you'll want to go away. But you can always go back to it. I suppose we'll see it one day – perhaps soon. But if we have to be in Paris, perhaps best stay in town. What little hotel would you suggest?

Love,   DHL

Of course I could put up the expenses of a Paris edition myself.

Pino would be no use in Paris – I have to hold his hand – or his head – all the time even in Florence. One wants somebody on the spot.

I am enclosing a letter to the Beach,[4] read it, leave it to your discretion; is her address right?

4810. To Nancy Pearn, 15 December 1928
Text: MS UT; Unpublished.

Hotel Beau Rivage. *Bandol*. BANDOL,[5] Var. France.
15 Dec 1928

Dear Nancy Pearn

I don't mind if they use about 1,500 words of that Autobiographical article,

---

[1] The poem was included in *Pansies* as 'To Clarinda' (*Letters*, vi. 273, 293).
[2] Huxley did see Sylvia Beach but was unable to persuade her to publish *Lady Chatterley's Lover*.
[3] In October the Huxleys had moved to 3 Rue du Bac, Suresnes (Seine). In his letter to DHL, 12 December 1928, Huxley had said: 'The house now begins to look like a house' (Smith 305).
[4] The letter is missing.
[5] On several occasions DHL attempted by this means to ensure the correct spelling by his correspondents.

but I do hope I've said nothing in it that I shall repent – have I? Don't let them print anything that I shall wish to God I'd never said.[1]

The *Pansies* – you're not to call them poems, really, I want them to be *Pensées*, only that's not an English word – are nearly done – and I'll send them, since you'll be discreet with them.[2] But a number of them I guess you'll hate. My wife joyfully says they are doggerel.

This unhappy word Bandol, everybody spells it wrong – but luckily the letters come. But a registered MS. I sent to Pollinger seems to be lost.

Ever   D. H. Lawrence

4811. To Edward Dahlberg, [15 December 1928]
Text: MS UTul; Postmark, [. . .]; Unpublished.

Hotel Beau Rivage, Bandol. Var, France
Sat.

Dear Mr Dahlberg[3]

Your letter has just come. I will of course read your MS. if you wish it, but please don't send it here, unless I write again, as we may be leaving next week, and I have already lost one registered MS. in French mail, and don't want to lose yours – or be in any way responsible for its loss.

Sincerely   D. H. Lawrence

4812. To Laurence Pollinger, [16 December 1928]
Text: MS UT; Unpublished.

Hotel Beau Rivage. Bandol. Var. France
Sunday

Dear Pollinger

You'll have to tell Cape that the Viking Press wouldn't release the *three* books they hold: *Amores*, *Look We Have Come Through*, and *New Poems*. They wouldn't, and of that I'm sure, once they had decided they might do the *Collected Poems* themselves. But let us wait first till the Viking have come to a

---

[1] DHL was responding to Nancy Pearn's letter, 12 December 1928 (TMSC UT) in which she said that the *Sunday Dispatch* wanted to extract about 1,500 words from the autobiographical sketch he 'wrote a few years ago for some German publication'. (She was referring to a piece requested by Insel Verlag in January 1927: see *Letters*, v. 620 and n. 4.) The *Sunday Dispatch* published 'Myself Revealed' on 17 February 1929 (collected in *Assorted Articles* as 'Autobiographical Sketch') (Roberts C182; see also C217).

[2] DHL enclosed one typed poem, 'No! Mr Lawrence!'

[3] Edward Dahlberg (1900–77), American novelist, poet and critic, had asked DHL if he might send the MS of his first, as yet untitled, novel, which was published by Putnam in November 1929 as *Bottom Dogs*, with an introduction by DHL (Roberts B26); reprinted in *Phoenix*. See Nehls, iii. 710 n. 85.

66 [*16 December 1928*]

definite agreement. – Besides, Cape's was only just a tentative suggestion, wasn't it? I wouldn't like to offend him, as he's been very friendly to me.[1] – Seltzer owes me about $4000.00 – rather more, alas. I haven't had time to hear from him. But I suppose we could knock off some of the non-existent dollars, for the rights to *BirdsBeasts and Flowers*. There remains Kennerley – but I've lost all track of him. Whether I *ever* had any money from him, I don't know. Whether he *ever* kept *Love Poems and Others* in print, I don't know. Even Duckworth had it out of print for a long time. – The first cheque I ever had from America was from Kennerley, in 1913, for £20: great rejoicing: but he'd altered the date, so the bank wouldn't cash it, and never did. What a blow in those days![2]

I hope you've got your second copy of *Lady C*. – as Orioli has certainly sent it.

And I do hope you've got the MS. of *Rawdon's Roof*. By great good luck it was a typed copy, as a friend at the Vigie[3] typed it for me. Usually I post my original copy. – So if this is lost – but *how*? – I can send you the duplicate.

There is talk too of the Fanfrolico press producing a portfolio of reproductions of my pictures, which hang in Dorothy Warren's gallery awaiting exhibition, when she's finished getting married and God knows what. I shall probably see the man Stephenson down here. I don't think much of the *London Aphrodite* – but I hear they are rich Australians, these Lindsays and Stephenson – and therefore a bit colonial and ramshackle. If they do the portfolio I expect it will be a limited edition at two guineas or something. But I hear they are doubtful payers – so I shall turn them over to you to look after them, if their plan materialises.

Koteliansky says that *England my England* is on Simpkin & Marshall's remainder list – when it has been selling at the dealers for a long time for 30/- and £1. – he is certain of his facts – and he wants to know who then has been supplying the dealers – and thinks you ought to know. – Did you see him, by the way? You might speak with him about it. He is in connection with booksellers and people who handle first editions and all that. – He dislikes Secker, though. And he's a Russian Jew, not tolerant at all.

Secker by the way has gone very quiet lately – not answered my letters.

I have asked Orioli to send you 2 copies of the 200. edition – to be sold in the shops at 30/-. But if your second copy of *Lady C* doesn't come, perhaps better stop him. If you'd like one of these copies for yourself, do please keep it

---

[1] Jonathan Cape had published the first English edition of *Mastro-don Gesualdo* (1925) and *Cavalleria Rusticana and Other Stories* (1928). He had now expressed an interest in publishing an American edition of the *Collected Poems* (Secker, 1928), and was to do so in July 1929.
[2] See *Letters*, iii. 74 and n. 4, iv. 131 and n. 2.   [3] Brigit Patmore.

as a token from me, and make me write in it when I'm in London. But if you'd rather have the *Collected Poems* from Secker I'll order you those from Secker and write in them when I come. Tell me then.

Maria Huxley went into the Castiglione librairie in Paris for a copy of *Lady C.* and they asked her 5,000 frs. Oh la-la-la! the swine! At the same time they are ordering four copies at £4. – But Galignani is selling the pirated edition at £3. – I must really try to get the book produced in Paris and sold like *Ulysses* at about 100[1] frs. – no use leaving *all* the field to the pirates – the pirated editions are selling in London.

4813. To Rhys Davies, [16 December 1928]
Text: TMSC NWU; Unpublished.

                                          Hotel Beau Rivage – Bandol – Var.
                                                                      Sunday.
Dear Rhys Davies,

Your letter this morning. Do come on Tuesday for a few days and be my guest as before – and bring Stephensen along if he cares to come – tell him I should like to talk over the pictures plan with him.

We've been waiting very undecidedly to hear if my wifes daughters are coming for Christmas – and if they would like to sail from Marseilles to Naples and Christmas on Capri where we have friends. But so far no sound from them. So I don't suppose *anyhow* we shall sail to Naples – won't be time to arrange it. Then I *may* have to go to Paris, to see if I can fix up the producing of a cheaper edition there – something like Joyce's *Ulysses* – sell at 100frs or so. I've got to find a bookseller or someone who'd do the work – and I don't know anybody but Sylvia Beach, who is absorbed in Joyce and considers me a sort of rival show. Altogether very vague. And I begin to feel I'd like to move on from Bandol – to Spain if not the other places.

But come on Tuesday by the same train – and I expect the bus will be at the station, if by chance we're not. It will be fun seeing you again. My wife's eye is better.

                                                      Au revoir,   DHL

---

[1] 100] 200

4814. To Achsah Brewster, [17 December 1928]
Text: MS UT; Brewster 189.

                                        Hotel Beau Rivage, *Bandol.* Var, France
                                                                    Monday
Dear Achsah
     Just heard from Frieda's daughters – Elsa can only come for just a week –
her job is at its busiest, and it finishes end of Feb. So Capri is too far – we
shall just have to stay here – which is sad, for I've about had enough of it, and
was thinking how jolly it would be in Anacapri.
     But we shall have to see what we can do after Christmas. Perhaps Barby
will stay some time with us. Anyhow you'll have a nice time.
     I shall write again properly. This is only a note of warning and sadness.
                                                                    DHL

4815. To Giuseppe Orioli, [18 December 1928]
Text: MS UCLA; Unpublished.

                                            Hotel Beau Rivage. Bandol. Var.
                                                                    Tuesday
Dear Pino
     Since my sisters know all about *Lady C.* from the fuss in *John Bull* etc, I
have to give them a copy, for they are mortally offended.
     So will you send them a copy of the first edition to
          1. Mrs. W. E. Clarke, Broadway, *Ripley near Derby*, England
          1. Mrs S. King, 16 Brooklands Rd, Sneinton Hill, *Nottingham.* England
     Don't send them, of course, if anything has gone wrong, with Customs or
anything – I'm a bit anxious about Pollinger's second copy.
     When you aren't so busy I want to make all those people in England *pay*
who haven't paid – there are about 25 copies, why shouldn't we get that
money? Kot. said he would help – but I thought first we would write to them,
especially *Miller & Gill* and those, saying we should publish their names in a
public list of requests for payment.[1] Could one do that? The *London Aphrodite*
would publish their names – and they'd pay rather than be exposed. After all,
why lose about £50.
     Then Mrs Chambers would chase the New York booksellers, if I had their
addresses. They must not get away with it.
     Hope you had my letter with cheque to you and all enclosures.
                                                                    DHL

---

[1] Orioli had been reminded on 17 August 1928 that Miller & Gill had '*4 copies not paid*' (*Letters*,
vi. 515).

4816. To Edward Dahlberg, [19 December 1928]
Text: MS UTul; Postmark, Bandol 19–12 28; Unpublished.

Hotel Beau Rivage, *Bandol*, Var
Wed.

Dear Mr Dahlberg

Your MS. arrived safely this morning, I will read it and let you know how it strikes me. – I think we are staying on here till New Year.

Yours Sincerely   D. H. Lawrence

4817. To Emily King, 19 December 1928
Text: MS Lazarus; Postmark, Bandol [...] 28; Unpublished.

Hotel Beau Rivage. *Bandol*. Var
19 Dec 1928

My dear Pamela

I had your letter, and glad everything goes pretty well – It will be an anxious moment when Sam takes stock.[1] But no good thinking of that just now.

I have ordered you for Christmas a copy of my novel *Lady Chatterley* – it is being sold in the shops now at £5..5..0. But if I were you I wouldn't read it, you'll find it mostly rather heavy. And don't let Peg read it either – just keep it uncut, its value is then higher. – And I enclose £2. – one for Joan and one for Peg. And I hope you'll have a nice time, though your programme doesn't sound exactly thrilling.

We shall stay here now. Elsa Weekley may come for Christmas week – don't know yet – with her Teddy[2] and perhaps Barby. She, Barby, has been ill, gone very weak, they say. Elsa wants to get married to her Teddy in March or April – but not wildly keen, I'm afraid – like the moderns.

It's very sunny and hot in the sun here, and sharp cold in the shade. I find that gets my bronchials – it always does – I'll have to be wary of the sudden change. – We've got a young Welsh writer staying till Saturday – Rhys Davies. He is quiet and not tiring. His grandfather was a Welsh miner, but his father has a shop in the village. He brought us a good plum cake from Nice, so we are already a bit Christmassy, at tea-time. There are a few English people here – but Nice is now getting full, thousands of them. It is amazing what a lot of money the English have, really.

I hope you are all well. The poor King, how depressing his illness is,

---

[1] See Letter 4758 and n. 4.
[2] Bernal Edward ('Teddy') de Martelly Seaman (1900–90), an officer in the Royal Navy to whom Elsa Weekley had been engaged since 1926; they married on 6 April 1929.

dragging on so long.[1] He'll be a wreck even if he recovers. But as many doctors as that would kill any man, seems to me – and as many remedies. Anyhow it's very depressing.

But I hope you'll have a jolly christmas, and much love to you all.

DHL

4818. To Dorothy Warren, 19 December 1928
Text: MS UN; Nehls, iii. 269–70.

Hotel Beau Rivage, *Bandol*, Var. France
19 Dec 1928

Dear Dorothy Warren

I think you've been a bit cool, keeping my pictures there all the time and merely doing nothing. However – now the men of the Fanfrolico Press – Jack Lindsay and P. R. Stephensen – say they want to do a book of reproductions of my paintings as early as possible in the New Year – So they want to have the pictures photographed *at once.* So will you please see that the photographer has access to them as soon as he is ready. – If you are hesitating at all about the exhibition, don't have it, as I have someone else who would like to exhibit them. But if you still want to show them, perhaps you could arrange with Mr. Lindsay to have the show at about the same time as their book is ready: perhaps in February. They are doing the book very *de luxe*, probably at ten guineas.

Let me know about this – and if I shall send to have the pictures removed from your gallery.

I hear you are married, and hope you are feeling jolly, and my best wishes. But I'm annoyed at not having heard a single word from you.

Sincerely   D.H. Lawrence

4819. To Giuseppe Orioli, [19 December 1928]
Text: MS (Photocopy) HU; Unpublished.

[Hotel Beau Rivage, Bandol, Var.]
Wed[2]

Dear Pino

Do you know what this man means, with his second five dollars?[3] Have you sent him a copy of the book?

---

[1] The illness of the king, George V (1865–1936), had been widely reported in the press since 22 November.

[2] Dated from Stephensen's arrival on Tuesday, 18 December.

[3] DHL's letter is written on one to him dated 3 December:
   Dear Sir:-
   A money order for the sum of $5.0 of the ten for *Lady Chatterley's Lover* is being dispatched to you by the Post Office.

I hope you have sent the 27 orders from Lahr – I only meant we would sell *also* to other booksellers – but Lahr says he will handle 150 copies. I *hope* the post is safe. *I haven't heard if Pollinger got his second copy*. Miss Watson had hers some time ago. It will be a great nuisance if the post begins bothering us – the customs. – I *don't* think it is worth while printing a prospectus for the 2nd edit. – you will have had Lahr's letter saying he got the three copies and liked the format very much. I hope you have my letter of Sat. with cheque to you, and enclosures. Stephensen of the Fanfrolico is here, and I think they will do my pictures in a *book* at ten guineas!

The Fanfrolico will change into the Mandrake Press, backed by Edward Goldston of Museum St, and be more *serious*.[1]

DHL

4820. To Mabel Dodge Luhan, 19 December 1928
Text: MS Brill; Luhan 338–9.

Hotel Beau Rivage, *Bandol*, Var
19 Dec. 1928

Dear Mabel

Yours about the article for the *Survey Graphic* came today. I'll have a shot at the article when I can get a bit of time[2] – people here now. –

My pictures are being kept back a bit – I think they are going to be reproduced in a book, rather expensively $50.00.

We are staying rather vaguely here – can't make up our minds what to do. We are expecting Frieda's daughters for Christmas – so shall stay here over the New Year anyhow, I suppose.

Tell Brett I wrote her three letters – hope she got some of them.

How do you like New York? Do you feel you've come a bit unstuck from the world altogether? – that's how I feel.

We'll have to see what breeze the gods will blow into our sails, to start us on a new move.

DHL

Thank you for accepting this unique method of payment. I would have been unable otherwise to possess the book.

Sincerely yours Jarell B. French
138 Home Ave. Rutherford, N.J., U.S.A.

[1] Edward Goldston, a London book dealer, who had made a great deal of money from the purchase of a Gutenberg Bible from a monastery in Europe and the sale of it in New York. In February 1929 he became Stephensen's partner in the Mandrake Press (Craig Munro, *Wild Man of Letters*, Melbourne, 1984, p. 77). See Letter 5047.

[2] 'New Mexico', completed by 25 December (Letter 4843), appeared in the *Survey Graphic*, 1 May 1931 (Roberts C206).

4821. To Martin Secker, 19 December 1928
Text: MS UInd; Postmark, Bandol 20–12 28; Secker 112.

Hotel Beau Rivage. *Bandol*, Var. France.
19 Dec. 1928

Dear Secker

A long time since I heard from you – you didn't answer my last letter.

We are still here by the sea – sunny bright weather, but a cold wind – and it gets my bronchials a bit. It's always risky. – Elsa and Barby may be coming out for Christmas – we shall hear tomorrow. Elsa would only stay a week, she has her job – but Barby may stay longer, she doesn't seem at all well, according to reports.

I think after Christmas we shall perhaps go to Spain for a bit. Italy has sounded so cold and wet, I didn't want to risk my chest in etruscan tombs. We keep saying we'll look for a house, but we don't do it. I suppose we can't really want to.

Would you please send a copy of the *Collected Poems*, and a 3/6 copy of *Sons and Lovers* to:

Herrn Max Hunger, 11. Niebuhrstr. *Berlin – Charlottenburg*[1]

I wonder how you all are – Rina and the boy – and Bridgefoot? I hear in Baden deep snow – Frieda's mother not so well, and feeling a bit afraid, suddenly, of her age.[2] – Have you read anything by Rhys Davies, a young welshman – he is staying here till Saturday – and very nice and simple. No news in our world. – I do hope you'll all have a gay Christmas – send a line, anyhow.

DHL

4822. To Baroness Anna von Richthofen, 19 December 1928
Text: MS UCB; Frieda Lawrence 284–5.

Hotel Beau Rivage. *Bandol*, Var.
19 Dec. 1928

Meine liebe Schwiegermutter

Heut' Abend sind Schlips und Kalendar gekommen. Der freundliche Kalendar, wir kennen ihn so gut, er macht heimweh. Wir müssen wirklich ein Haus suchen, nur um ihn auf den Wand zu hangen. Wir wissen aber immer nicht, wo wir wohnen wollen. Es ist ganz nett hier, so sonnig und freundlich. Jetzt warten wir bis Weihnacht vorbei ist.

Vielleicht kommen die Elsa und Barby – morgen werden wir wissen. Die Elsa aber arbeitet bis ende Februar, und so kann nur 8 Tagen bleiben, wenn

---

[1] The husband of DHL's cousin Ethel, née Staynes. See *Letters*, i. 184.
[2] Baroness Anna von Richthofen (1851–1930).

sie kommt. Sie sagt, sie will in März kommen, vor sie heiratet: weil endlich, sagt sie, sie will heiraten. Der Barby geht es nicht sehr gut – vielleicht wird sie für ein Paar wochen zu uns kommen.

Wir haben einen Freund hier, einen jungen Schriftsteller, ganz nett und treu. Erst hatte die Frieda ihn nicht gern, weil er nicht schön war: jetzt aber findet sie ihn schöner, und magt ihn. Wir hatten auch einen jungen Australier zwei Tagen hier – ist heut nachtmittag nach Nizza gefahren. Er macht, in London, diese schöne teuere Bücher die jetzt gesammelt werden – Und er sagt, in Neujahr will er meine Bilder als Buch machen – alle Bilder mit einem Vorwort von mir – und wird es verkaufen an 10 guineas die Exemplär – 210 Mark jedes Stück. Es kommt mir wahnsinnig vor – aber es ist sein Geld, und er wird mich auch gut zahlen. Wenn er es thut. Aber wie die Leute verrückt sind – es ist eine ganz grosse Commerce jetzt, Bucher *de luxe* die kosten 40 M. oder 100 M. oder auch 500 Mark. Ich hass' es.

Der Rhys Davies – der Freund der hier ist – ist Welscher,[1] von Wales – und sein grossvater war auch Kohlengrubarbeiter.

Der Max Mohr schrieb etwas traurig von seinem Wolfsgrube – sagt er muss immer mit seinen Verlegern kämpfen, und hat wenig Geld. Dort in Bayern liegt tiefe Schnee.

Ich bin froh dass es dir besser geht. Mir auch – aber heisse Sonne und kalter Wind finden meine Bronchien, die ein wenig roh fühlen. Es ist immer so, bei solchem Wetter –

Die Else wird da sein, bei dir. Sie wird dir 100 Mark. von mir geben, die sie hat vom *Jugend* – und sie behaltet noch die 20 Mark die übrig sind, für sich. Du wirst eine gute stille glückliche Weinacht haben – bleib' nur innerlich still.

Du sollst alle grüssen von mir. Und die Nusch? – sie wird nicht mehr da sein. Ich schreibe an ihr und an Emil. Und ich hoffe wir sehen sie diese Fruhling,[2] hier am Mittelmeer, wo die Sonne so hell ist und das Wasser so blau und die kleine Schiffe so weiss und tanzend. Sehr freundlich finde ich auch diese Franzoser – und sie lassen man in Ruhe, hangen nicht so schwer an. Doch sehnt sich die Frieda immer nach Italien, ich glaube.

So lebe wohl, Schwiegermutter – Merry Christmas! – Grüsse Frau Kugler und Frau Oberin – und ist die Gusterl wieder da? – Was hast du für Blumen? hier sind viele Narzissen in den Feldern.

Merry Christmas! Merry Christmas!   DHL

---

[1] DHL's word 'Welscher' means someone from France, Spain or Italy; he may only have been trying to insist that it applied to someone from Wales.
[2] Fruhling,] Weihacht.

[My dear Schwiegermutter

Tonight came the tie and the calendar. The friendly calendar, we know it so well, it makes us homesick. We really must look for a house, just so as to be able to hang it on the wall. But we still don't know where we want to live. It's really nice here, so sunny and friendly. Now we'll wait until Christmas is over. Perhaps Elsa and Barby are coming – tomorrow we'll know. But Elsa has a job till the end of February, and so can only stay for a week, if she comes. She says she wants to come in March, before she gets married: because, she says, at last she wants to get married. Barby isn't very well – perhaps she will come to us for a couple of weeks.

We have a friend here, a young writer, very nice and faithful. To begin with Frieda didn't like him, because he wasn't good-looking: but now she finds him better-looking, and likes him. We also had a young Australian here for two days – he left this afternoon for Nice. In London he produces those lovely expensive books which people collect these days – And he says, in the New Year he wants to bring out my pictures as a book – all the pictures with a foreword by me – and will sell it at 10 guineas a copy – 210 Marks each. It seems mad to me – but it's his money, and he'll also pay me well. If he does it. But how crazy people are – it's a really big trade these days, *de luxe* books costing 40 M. or 100 M. or even 500 Marks. I hate it.

Rhys Davies – the friend who's here – is a Welshman, from Wales – and his grandfather was a miner too.

Max Mohr wrote a little sadly from his Wolfsgrube – says he always has to fight with his publishers, and has little money. Over in Bavaria there's deep snow.

I am glad that you are better. I am too – but hot sun and cold wind get to my bronchials, which feel a bit raw. It's always like that, in such weather –

Else will be there, with you. She will give you 100 Marks from me, which she got from *Jugend*[1] – and she'll keep the 20 Marks left over, for herself. You'll be having a good, quiet happy Christmas – just stay quiet in yourself.

You must greet everyone from me. And Nusch?[2] – she will have left by now. I'm writing to her and to Emil. And I hope we'll see her this spring, here on the Mediterranean, where the sun is so bright and the water so blue and the little boats so white and dancing. I find these French people very friendly, too – and they leave one in peace, don't cling so tightly to one. But Frieda is still longing for Italy, I believe.

[1] Else Jaffe's translation of DHL's story 'Rex' had appeared in *Jugend*, October 1928 (Roberts C77).

[2] Frieda's sister, Helene Johanna Mathilde ('Nusch') von Krug (1882–1971); her husband, Emil von Krug (1870–1944) was a Berlin banker. See *Letters*, v. 266 n. 2.

So farewell then, Schwiegermutter – Merry Christmas! – Greetings to Frau Kugler and to the Mother Superior – and is Gusterl[1] back yet? – What kind of flowers do you have there? here we have lots of narcissus in the fields.

Merry Christmas! Merry Christmas! DHL]

4823. To Sylvia Beach, 19 December 1928
Text: MS PU; Postmark, Bandol 24-12 28; Unpublished.

Hotel Beau Rivage. *Bandol*, Var.
19 Dec 1928

Dear Miss Beach

Aldous Huxley wrote that you would put some of my second edition of *Lady Chatterley* in your shop. We have only about 160 now – and are selling at a guinea to the booksellers in London, who are supposed to be charging thirty shillings to their customers. Anyhow that is our arrangement – we charge 30/- to private purchasers, and sell to the bookseller at 21/-. Is that all right for you? Anyhow I am asking Orioli to send you ten copies at once, to stop the pirates as far as possible.

I suppose Aldous told you of the Castiglione people ridiculously asking 5000 frs. for the original edition – Orioli is selling the few remaining copies at £4. each – and one honest bookseller in London retails at five guineas. If you want a couple of those, would you tell Orioli. He only sells for cash now – but we know you would not let us down. And I would like to know the book was being offered at about 700 francs, anyhow. So you could settle accounts monthly, if that is as you prefer.

I shall have to try the Pegasus people, to put on the market a regular edition at about 100 or 120 frs.[2] I know nothing about them, though. Still, I'm sure it would be a paying thing: and I want the book to be sold, I want the public to get it, and not too dear either.

I hope you aren't bored by all this. I hope Orioli will send you the ten cheap copies *at once*.

All good wishes. D. H. Lawrence

---

[1] Frau Kugler and Gusterl are unidentified; presumably the Baroness's friends at the Stift. Possibly the person in charge of the Stift was known as 'the Mother Superior' (Frau Oberin).

[2] The Pegasus Press in Paris, founded (in 1927) and directed by John Holroyd-Reece (1897–1969), publisher and journalist. See Letter 4845.

4824. To Ada Clarke, 19 December 1928
Text: MS Clarke; cited in Lawrence–Gelder 186.

Hotel Beau Rivage. Bandol. Var.

19 Dec 1928

My dear Sister

I had your letter and have ordered you a copy of *Lady Chatterley* from Florence, and also one for Emily. I am writing to her to say she need not cut the pages. – Rhys Davies is here from Nice – brought us a Christmas cake, very nice – and a man Stephensen was here two days – an Australian who publishes expensive books in London – very nicely done, indeed, but I don't think much of the actual contents. But he says that after Christmas he will publish a book of reproductions of my paintings – a large-sized book, to charge ten guineas a copy. Seems to me a bit absurd, but there's this collecting craze nowadays.

It's lovely weather, hot sun again, but the wind rather nippy – makes one a bit chesty, the combination of the two. We linger on here – Friedas daughter Elsa may come with her Teddy just for Christmas week – but I'm not sure. Rhys Davies is staying till Saturday. Anyhow we shall be quiet –

I'm sure you'll have a nice time. I haven't posted Jack's things, because I thought if Elsa came she'd bring them back to London – I'll get them to him somehow.[1] And I enclose 30/- to buy something for Bertie and some trifle for Gertie[2] – I do hope they're all well – so glad the *whoops* went away fairly soon – what a scare, whooping cough in winter!

I wonder when I shall be seeing you – probably before long, one way or another. We must see how things pan out. – I do hope you'll get your copy of *Lady C.* safely. Anyhow have a good time at Christmas, and I shall think of you all.

love. DHL

4825. To Giuseppe Orioli, [19 December 1928]
Text: MS UCLA; Unpublished.

Hotel Beau Rivage. Bandol. Var.

Wed. night

Dear Pino

I enclose Aldous' letter. Will you send Sylvia Beach at once ten copies of the 200-edition. I have told her we charge her 21/- and she sells for 30/- – and

[1] Ada's two sons were John ('Jack') Lawrence Clarke (1915–42) and William Herbert ('Bertie') Clarke (b. 1923).

[2] Gertrude ('Grit' or 'Gertie') Cooper (1885–1942), a childhood friend and neighbour of the Lawrence family; she suffered from tuberculosis and had lived with Ada since 1919.

that she can settle her accounts at the end of every month. She is safe, anyhow.

And I told her to ask you if she wanted any copies of the first edition – that you charge £4. net, and the public price is supposed to be £5..5..0.

Shall we put in a little slip saying:

Two pirated editions of this book, produced[1] in U. S. A., are now on the market, and in some cases are offered to purchasers as being the genuine first edition, even the signature being forged.

Do you think that would be wise?

I have written direct to Sylvia Beach. What shall we do about the Pegasus Press?

Stephensen of the Fanfrolico was here – a go-ahead young man. I think they'll do my pictures. – He might come to Florence and see you.

Sunny weather, but makes my chest a bit sore, with the cold wind.

Love from both   DHL

I have written also to the Pegasus.[2] No word from Pollinger, if he has received his copy.

4826. To P. R. Stephensen, [20 December 1928]
Text: MS Anon; Munro 296–7.

Hotel Beau Rivage. Bandol. Var.

Thursday

Dear Stephensen

I send you three doggerels for the *Aphrodite*, and hope you can make them out.[3] I do so dislike the typewriter. If you want them for the *Aphrodite*, will you, when you get back to London, tell

Miss N. Pearn, of Curtis Brown Ltd. 6 Henrietta St. Covent Garden W.C.2

And you tell her you agreed with me to pay your ordinary rate for poems – whatever it is. And pay her – or rather Curtis B. – when the time comes.

And Curtis Brown's manager, who looks after my things, is a man L.E.

---

[1] produced] are produced   [2] No letters to Pegasus survive.

[3] The enclosure is missing and two of the poems cannot be identified. The third was 'My Naughty Book' (see Letter 4936). The poems were rejected by Jack Lindsay 'for the same reasons [he] did not publish the paintings' (Nehls, iii. 302). Those reasons were: 'I [Lindsay] was not much in sympathy with Lawrence at that time, and his whole outlook and aesthetic ran counter to the positions taken by the Fanfrolico Press, which were based on the ideas of Norman Lindsay ... The feud of Lawrence and Joynson-Hicks was at its height and the police were extremely keen to find ways of taking action against Lawrence ... I therefore felt that to publish Lawrence's paintings would be sure to bring the police down on us; and I still think this idea was correct' (ibid., iii. 300–1).

Pollinger. If you want to fix a contract for the picture-book, go and see him, later on.

I've been thinking hard about the pictures – and alas and alack, you'll hate me for it, but I *don't* like collotype as a means of reproduction, of oil paintings in particular. It's too soft and charcoaly – it's not right – though lovely for reproducing any sort of black-and-white work. I wish you could do them all in colour, just the 3-colour process – or if it's not too dear, the 4-colour. Collotype colour is lovely, but too dear. Why not do them in *good* 3-colour process, as Goldston does his colour-books? But his colour reproductions aren't as nice as German ones of the same sort. Do let me know about this. And after all, there is no terrific hurry about the book, is there? Don't rush it and regret it. Ask Goldston about the colour reproductions – he's used to those things. And if even 3-colour is too dear – but I don't think it is – you could do some of the pictures half-tone black and white, and the rest in colour.

I wish you would ask the printers to send me *their* specimens of collotype, 3-colour, 4-colour, and coloured collotype – I should very much like to see the printer's own specimens. I would send them safely back.

You see, a Turner painting comes out like a Turner etching or one of the *Liber Studiorum* plates.[1] But the Blake doesn't come out like Blake – not a bit – it's something else. I mean, of course, in collotype.

The Germans do such *lovely* colour reproductions. It might be worth while having some done there. There'd be no trouble whatsoever about Customs with the *pictures*, I don't think – and is there any duty on imported prints? Collectors are *much* more likely to buy good colour than collotype, believe me. And with good colour-plates ten guineas is not exorbitant. Do think about this. And I can get German quotations, if you want them. Don't be in a rush, let the mandrake put his roots in firmly, so he won't have to squeal too soon, being uprooted.

If you do a short-long story series, I shall give you one of mine later.

I was glad you came. I was glad to see somebody young with a bit of energy and fearlessness. It's *most* precious. So for god's sake conserve your energy – don't rush in and squander it. It takes such a lot of energy to put a real thing through and often patience is the most concentrated form of energy. Don't drink too much with people like Boris and the rest[2] – it's not your point. They

---

[1] J. M. W. Turner (1775–1851) published seventy plates of his *Liber Studiorum: Illustrative of Landscape Compositions*, 1807–19.

[2] Possibly Boris de Croustchoff, a Russian bibliographer and London bohemian; he claimed to have been the model for Maxim Libidnikov in *Women in Love* (Harry T. Moore, *The Priest of Love*, New York, 1974, p. 286). See *Letters*, ii. 448.

are out to waste themselves – their idea is just to be wasters, since there is nothing they believe in – But I believe one must put one's fist through something much more solid and pernicious than panes of glass. We *must* make a hole in the bourgeois world which is the whole world of consciousness today. If your mandrake is going to grow, let him shove up under the walls of this prison-system, and bust them. But patience, patience all the time, even while one acts most strenuously, somewhere patience. I am determined, like Samson in the temple of Philistia,[1] to pull the house down sooner or later and all I want is men to tug silently and constantly along with me. But you Australians seem to believe in squandering, which is a pity, because squandering, like drink, is only a form of evasion – mere evasion of life. To live one has to live a life-long fight.

D. H. Lawrence

4827. To Juliette Huxley, 20 December 1928
Text: MS Huxley; Unpublished.

Hotel Beau-Rivage. Bandol, Var. France
20 Dec 1928

Dear Juliette

Nearly Christmas! – and snow in the world, though not here. But deep snow at Diablerets. It brings one back to the Beau-Site and Des Aroles.[2]

How are you all? Aldous said you were pretty well. I hope the children are quite quite quite over their whoops. And are you going to have a jolly Christmas there in Highgate?

We are still lingering on this coast – it's been sunny nearly all the time, and very quiet and friendly. The French leave one alone – that's the good thing about them – without being at all disagreeable. I have kept pretty well – getting slowly stronger. At present the combination of hot sun and cold thin wind has made my bronchials sore, as it always does. But I'm pretty well in myself. – It may be Frieda's two daughters will come for Christmas week. It may be we shall go to Spain after Christmas. We are houseless and homeless,

---

[1] Judges xvi. 29–30.

[2] On 23 January 1928 Aldous Huxley wrote from the Chalet des Aroles, Les Diablerets (Vaud), Switzerland: 'We are a very large party here, ourselves, the Julians, and various relations, making up ten souls including three children in this fortunately capacious chalet; with D. H. Lawrence and his wife two minutes away across the snow in another wooden hut [Chalet Beau Site]. So that leisure moments are amusingly filled' (Smith 294). The 'Julians' included (Sir) Julian Sorell Huxley (1887–1975), the eminent biologist; his wife Marie Juliette, née Baillot (1896–   ); her mother Mme Baillot; and their sons Anthony Julian (b. 1920) and Francis John Heathorn (b. 1923). The third child had been Aldous and Maria's son Matthew (b. 1920). See Juliette Huxley, *Leaves of the Tulip Tree* (1986), pp. 115–26.

but since the world is simply crammed with houses and homes that one can rent for modest sums, I feel no anxiety about it. Frieda gets fidgetty, and says she wants a place of her own, and I am perfectly willing. But when I ask her where, she doesn't know, so the castles are in spain and the houses are in the air. Where would you live, if you were free to choose? – Still, if ever I am going to paint again, we shall have to have a house. One can't do much in a hotel bedroom.

I was doing a bunch of scraps of sort of poetry, really my Pensées, which I shall call my pansies. I think they are rather amusing. How has Julian got on with the biology book with Wells?[1] is it nearly done? what a sweat it must have been. By the way did you hear how H.G. liked – or disliked – *Lady C?* It would amuse me to know.

Have you got plans for going up to the snow this year? and where? I don't think we shall go up – certainly not if we go to Spain. But I feel so vague about everything, can't make up my mind: don't know what I want. But I was happy at Diablerets, and if it would all be the same again – or as good – I'd go. We were really a bit above and beyond the weary world, up there, don't you think?

How is your mother in her beloved Neuchatel? Remember me to her. I can still see her whirling away under Beau Site on a little bob-sleigh. And many greetings from us both to you and Julian – and the children.

D. H. Lawrence

4828. To Arthur and Lilian Wilkinson, 20 December 1928
Text: TMSC Sagar; Keith Sagar, 'The Lawrences and the Wilkinsons',
Review of English Literature, iii (October 1962), 73-4.

Hotel Beau Rivage, Bandol.
20.12.28.

We are here in this quite pleasant little hotel by the sea[2] – it's been sunny nearly all the time, and good for my health. Of course I still cough like a brute, but am much stronger ... Frieda says she wants a house – but she doesn't know where, – and you can't have a house nowhere. – Where does one want to live? tell me if you can! – How do you like London? I hear of you giving shows

---

[1] Herbert George Wells (1866–1946), novelist and scientific theorist. DHL had met him in 1909. The 'biology book' was *The Science of Life: A Summary of Contemporary Knowledge about Life and Its Possibilities*, by H. G. Wells, J. S. Huxley and G. P. Wells, 3 volumes (1929–30).

[2] DHL's correspondents were Arthur Gair Wilkinson (1882–1957), watercolourist and puppeteer, and his wife Lilian ('Diddy') (d. 1957); they, with their children Frances ('Bim') and William ('Pino'), and, occasionally, Wilkinson's brother Walter, had been the Lawrences' neighbours at the Villa Mirenda, May 1926–March 1928. See *Letters*, v. 441 n. 1; vi. 128. (The part of the letter printed here was transcribed by Keith Sagar in 1961 from the original which subsequently disappeared.)

at Heal's,[1] and showing A[rthur]'s pictures, and selling them – beato lui![2] So that's all to the good. And I suppose Bim and Pino get more melodious every day! We shall have to see you before long, to see all the strides taken. What a game life is!

This is Happy Christmas to you all – and ricordi cari[3] of last year and the year before – and I hope we shall meet fairly soon, to hear everything.

Tante belle cose![4]   D. H. Lawrence

4829. To Giulia Pini, 20 December 1928
Text: MS UT; Unpublished.

Hotel Beau Rivage. *Bandol.* BANDOL, Var. Francia
20 Decem. 1928

Cara Giulia

Abbiamo ricevuto la tua lettera, e molto contenti che tutto va bene a San Paolo. Qui lo stesso, stiamo bene. Aspettiamo le due figlie della Signora per Natale, col fidanzato della signorina Elsa, la più vecchia: e faremo un poco festa. Abbiamo anche amici qui.

Ma penseremo a voi, e al albero che non possiamo fare quest'anno. Ti mando un'assegna per cinquanta Lire, perche non ho denaro italiano. Tu devi soltanto firmare al dosso – *Giulia Pini* – e alla banca ti daranno il denaro. O il signor Orioli ti lo darà, senza andare alla banca. Compra qualche piccola cosa per Teresina e per Pietro, qualche dolce per la zia, sigari per lo zio, e qualche piccola cosa per il babbo. – Cosi potete fare un poco festa, e rammentarvi di noi.

Intanto molti saluti da noi due, e buona festa.

D. H. Lawrence

Ho messo 60 Lire – Compra qualche piccolo giuocattolo dal quarant'otto per la Dina, e qualche dolce.

DHL

[Dear Giulia

We have received your letter and are very glad that everything's all right at San Paolo. The same here, we are well. We are expecting my wife's daughters for Christmas, and the fiancé of Elsa, the elder; and we'll celebrate a little. We also have friends here.

But we'll think of you, and of the [Christmas] tree that we cannot prepare this year. I'm sending you a cheque for fifty Lire, because I have no Italian

---

[1] *The Times,* 3 December 1928, carried the announcement: 'Heals, Tottenham-Court road, are giving in their theatre on each week-day performances of the Gair Wilkinson puppet-shows . . . until December 22.'

[2] 'happy him!'   [3] 'fond memories'.   [4] 'All the best!'

money. You only have to sign on the back *Giulia Pini* – and they'll give you the money at the bank. Or Mr Orioli will give it to you, without going to the bank. Buy some small things for Teresina[1] and Pietro, some cakes for your aunt, cigars for your uncle, and a small thing for your father. – So that you can celebrate a little, and remember us.

In the meantime, many greetings from us both, and have a good holiday.

D. H. Lawrence

I have written 60 Lire – buy some small toys from the forty-eight for Dina,[2] and some cakes.]

4830. To S. S. Koteliansky, 21 December 1928
Text: MS BL; Postmark, [. . .]; Zytaruk 370.

Hotel Beau Rivage, *Bandol*. Var
21 Dec. 1928

My dear Kot.

Stephensen was here of the Fanfrolico. I *liked* him: not limp at all – been a bit taken in by the 'culture' of the other lot, I fancy. They are starting a new Press in New Year – The Mandrake Press – and are going to publish ordinary books, from 3/6 to 10/6 also – and say they will be glad to do *Fallen Leaves*.[3] He said he'd write you: but if he doesn't, say nothing, and remind *me* to nudge him, when the time comes. He says he'll do my pictures – he's the *man* of the show, and has whatever money they have – and Edward Goldston of Museum St is to back them. He talks of doing my pictures 500 copies at ten guineas. Seems to me very *dear*. But we'll see what actually happens: talks of giving me an advance of £250. Avanti Italiani![4] *don't mention this* – I want to write a foreword. Could you ask any of the booksellers to send me *at once*, with the bill, a copy of Roger Fry's *Cézanne* book.[5] It would make a good starting point for me to write a good peppery foreword *against* all that significant form piffle. And if you can easily lay hands on a cheap copy Tolstoi's *What is Art?* send me that too, *with the bill. I must pay for them.*

Would you care to have a copy of *Lady C's* second edition. I'll give you one for Christmas.

DHL

[1] Giulia's sister.   [2] Dina is unidentified and the remark about her is obscure.

[3] The Mandrake Press published Kot's translation of V. V. Rozanov's *Fallen Leaves* in a limited edn, in November 1929. DHL reviewed it in *Everyman*, 23 January 1930 (Roberts C196; collected in *Phoenix*).

[4] 'Forward Italians!' (Mussolini's rallying call).

[5] Roger Eliot Fry (1866–1934), painter and critic, member of the Bloomsbury group and author of *Cézanne: A Study of His Development* (1927).

4831. To Laurence Pollinger, 21 December 1928
Text: MS UT; Unpublished.

Hotel Beau Rivage, *Bandol.* Var.
21 Dec 1928

Dear Pollinger

You didn't tell me if I was to give you my poems or one of the second edit. *Lady C* – so now I don't know and can't give you either for Christmas. But tell me all the same. You had my letter, didn't you? – And did you get the second copy of *Lady C.* from Orioli?

I think the Fanfrolicos will do my pictures.

Best wishes for Christmas   DHL

4832. To Edward Dahlberg, 22 December 1928
Text: MS UTul; Postmark, Thos. Cook & So[ns] 24 DEC 1928; Moore 1108–9.

Hotel Beau Rivage, *Bandol*, Var
22 Dec 1928

Dear Mr Dahlberg

I have read your MS. At first I didn't like it – the old-fashioned sort of sordid realism done rather in detail. But when it moves to the orphanage it gets into stride and has the myopic vision and exaggerated sensitiveness and exaggerated *insensitiveness* on the other hand, of the sort of substratum, *gamin* life you are dealing with. It seems to me you have hit that layer of American consciousness very well, *got it*: the blindness of it, the extreme sensitiveness over a small, immediately personal field, and then the dumb, slummy unconsciousness to[1] all the rest of the world. I don't know how you carry the book on. As it is, it looks as if it can only continue in the same monotone, the same thing over and over again, even if the scene shifts. But that is the whole point. There are no relationships, no real human connections, therefore no possible development of drama or tragedy or anything like that. The human being is whittled down to a few elementary and almost mechanical reactions. A relationship that amounted to anything would take the book right out of what it is, and put it on another footing, another plane. One feels it would be false, somehow. But that's not for me to say. – The curious street-arab, down-and-out *stoicism*, something very dreary and yet impressive, denuded, like those brown horrid rocks in Central Park, seems to me the real theme. – As far as I can judge, it's a real book, and with a real new note in it. You ought easily to get a publisher, and the thing ought to have a certain success. Is the

---

[1] to] of

book finished? If only we weren't so unsettled, I should have liked to read it all. But I really think we shall leave here next week.

The Viking Press would probably print you in America, and you can say I think it's a worth-while book, if you wish. But no doubt you have your own plans.

I think your style is the natural sort of mode for the stuff you're doing – it conveys the mentality, even nite for night, and all that.

Good luck then   D. H. Lawrence

But stick to your guns – don't weaken and get sentimental or hopeful or despairing – that bony stoicism is the thing.

I'll send the MS back after Christmas Day.

4833. To Laurence Pollinger, 23 December 1928
Text: MS UT; Unpublished.

Hotel Beau Rivage. *Bandol*, Var.

23 Dec 1928

Dear Pollinger

If you wrote me a letter on the 17th., it never came. But I have yours of 20th, also one this morning enclosing the *Boni* letter.[1] What dull swindlers people are! such *stale* dodges! Do let Michael Joseph have the book at two gns., as you say.[2] Privately, I *hate* fancy prices for books. I'm afraid I rile Orioli a bit.

Koteliansky's address is:

5. Acacia Rd. St. Johns Wood. N.W.8

and his telephone is under *Bourse Gazette*, a Russian paper, long dead, for which he was once correspondent. He lives with Michael Farbman, who wrote a book about Russia and who does a European Gazette of some sort.[3]

Orioli has sent you two copies of the 200-edition *Lady C*. He isn't sending any circulars, as he can dispose of the remaining hundred – he has only about a hundred now – direct. But if you like I'll get him to send you half a dozen copies, and if anyone is hard up, whom you know, he can have a copy for a guinea, which is what the booksellers pay us.

By the way I had a letter from a man Quinton asking for a contribution to a British League book, or something like that – asking if I would like St James

---

[1] Alfred Boni of the New York publishers Boni & Liveright had taken over Seltzer's business in 1925.

[2] Michael Joseph (1897–1958), a director and later General Manager of Curtis Brown Ltd. See *Letters*, v. 523 n. 2.

[3] Farbman was manager of Europa Books. DHL read his book, *After Lenin: The New Phase in Russia* (1924): see *Letters*, v. 366 and n. 3.

Palace to write to me for it!¹ What the hell! I'd as leave the Crystal Palace wrote me for a cocoa-nut! Do I send that man anything? – he quotes you as if you were his bosom friend, santo cielo!² Seemed a bit nutty, with his eye-wash.

I'll ask Secker to send over the *Collected Poems*. He says he's contemplating now a cheaper edition in one vol.

Thanks for going after the Boni's and poor Seltzer. The Viking might nip out with the poems before Secker does a cheaper edition.

bonne année³   D. H. Lawrence

4834. To Martin Secker, [23 December 1928]
Text: MS UInd; Secker 113.

Hotel Beau Rivage. *Bandol.* Var
Sunday

Dear Secker

Thanks for yours – glad all seems going well – so you'll have a jolly Bridgefoot Christmas with a turkey and I wish I could be there with you, really. If only there were magic carpets. We shall be alone till Barby comes – about the 28th. We had Rhys Davies here – writes Welsh stories – I liked him. Also P. R. Stephensen of the Fanfrolico press, whom I also really liked. He gave me a number of Fanfrolico books – the inside not worth the outside, alas. Would you like Sir John Haringtons *Metamorphosis of Ajax*? – fairly amusing, and very well produced.⁴ I'll send it if you would. They say they will do a book of my pictures in spring at 10 guineas each – Dio mio!⁵ Orioli doesn't send any *Lady C*'s now without money. The first edit. is £4., but we are selling the little second edit. of 200 at 30/- – one guinea in the trade. Tell me if you want one and *I'll see he sends it*. He's never keen to fulfil orders now – so few left. – You heard there are *two* pirated editions from U.S.A.. – I promised Pollinger a copy of *Collected Poems* for Christmas. Will you please send it him and charge it to me. – I think we shall go to Spain in the first week of the New Year. Frieda wants to go back to Italy, but I feel like a new splash.

¹ Pollinger replied: 'Humphrey Cotton Minchin's remark about St. James's Palace was meant, I imagine, to put the seal of genuineness on the thing. You see some authors rather like to receive note paper bearing the crest of the Prince of Wales' (TMSC UT). Minchin's anthology, *The Legion Book*, in aid of the British Legion, was printed by the Curwen Press, published in September 1929 and dedicated to the Prince of Wales. Contributors included Beerbohm, Belloc, Bennett, Blunden, Bridges, Chesterton, Churchill, Galsworthy, Kipling, Edith Sitwell, Wodehouse; Aldous Huxley contributed a poem.
² 'sacred heaven!'   ³ 'happy new year'.
⁴ Sir John Harington's *Metamorphosis of Ajax* [1596], ed. Peter Warlock and Jack Lindsay (1927). (In this Rabelaisian work, 'Ajax' is a pun on 'a jakes'.)
⁵ 'my God!'

I have made £1000 over *Lady C.*, anyhow – been spending it of course. Thank God I'm sort of better. A good time to you all!

DHL

4835. To Aldous Huxley, [23 December 1928]
Text: Huxley 767–8.

Beau Rivage, Bandol.
Sunday.

Dear Aldous, –

That man Stephensen[1] was here, of the Fanfrolico press. I liked him. They think of starting a new press – with no Lindsay stuff in it – and of splashing out with my pictures reproduced in a book at 10 guineas each! Holy Lord! They want to do most of them in black-and-white collotype, but I don't want it. I want colour at any price – I *hate* collotype reproduction. What do you think? If you hear any interesting news about colour-printing, tell me, because I feel I must keep close after these young men, they don't quite know what's what.

So many thanks to Maria for the blue *Guide*, and you for *Rasputin*.[2] Frieda got wildly thrilled over the latter.[3] I study Spain, and feel like popping off. But now Barbara [Weekley] says she'll come for the fortnight after Christmas – arrive apparently on Thursday – 27th – so that'll keep us here till second week in January. Frieda isn't keen on Spain, but I am, rather. One will have to stay on the Medit. Coast, the inland too bitter cold. But Barcelona, Mallorca, Valencia, Ronda, Malaga are warm.

Stephensen gave me, against my will, about seven massive Fanfrolico books. On the whole, *what* a waste of good printing! Could I perhaps leave some of them in your Suresnes house? And perhaps a couple of African wooden cups or goblets from Upper Congo, which I found here, and like: Maria might like to have them for a time.

---

[1] Here and below Huxley prints 'Stephenson'.

[2] The *Blue Guide* was probably for Spain; *Rasputin* was most likely the book by R. Fueloep-Miller published in German in 1927 and (tr. F. S. Flint and D. F. Tait) as *Rasputin, The Holy Devil* in September 1928.

[3] Rhys Davies recalled:

> At dinner in the full hotel restaurant [DHL] threatened to slap Frieda's face across the soup. He declared she had got herself into a 'mystical' state through reading a German book on Rasputin. He drew a mocking picture of women prostrate and fawning around the dirty scoundrel, their faces gaping up for sensual religious sustenance – 'anything that has no vulgar body!' he jeered. It was true that Frieda, talking of the book at the table, had displayed a rapt interest in the monk. (*Print of a Hare's Foot*, p. 145)

I am telling Pino to send you a copy of the 200 edit. *Lady C.* to Suresnes. Then you'll both have a copy.

I wonder if the address is right, St. Trond.

A cold wind, get my broncs. a bit, I must say – and hotel suddenly full of French people! Merry Xmas to you both!

DHL

4836. To Rolf Gardiner, 23 December 1928
Text: MS Lazarus; Huxley 768–9.

Hotel Beau Rivage. *Bandol.* Var. France
23 Dec 1928

Dear Rolf[1]

I did get your long letter to Port Cros: but only the other day, as it went back to London. We left that island – it wasn't good enough in bad weather. Anyhow I hate poky little islands.

I was glad to hear you had such a good time with the singing[2] – and that Gore is getting on its legs. It'll be good for you to have a place of your own, I should think. It's what I ought to find: somewhere really to live. We've given up the Villa Mirenda, and are once more wanderers in the wide wide world, which alas is all too narrow. Frieda of course wants a house – but even she doesn't know quite where. I believe she secretly hankers after Tuscany, but I set my foot down and say no! – at least for the present. It really was bad for my chest – which has been *so* much better this winter, so far, thank God. And so I haven't felt gloomy at all, quite chirpy and more like myself. This is merely a dull little place on the sea, but it has its own small life, is friendly, and I've felt pretty well here. Still I don't want very much to take a house here – nor does F. I think probably we shall go to Spain – perhaps even at the end of next week. I don't think we shall go up to the snow this spring, if I keep all right. But it would have been nice to see you en passant, like at Diablerets last year. I suppose you'll have another busy year. Myself, I'm afraid I take more and more pleasure in being alone, with just an occasional friend. I think perhaps the nicest thing in the world is to be most of the time alone, then to see a few people with whom one feels a bit of natural sympathy. I'm afraid I'm really not made for groups and gatherings.

[1] Rolf Gardiner (1902–71), pioneer of Land Service Camps for Youth in northern Europe after World War I; founded Springhead Estate (originally Gore Farm) in Dorset. See *Letters,* v. 66 n. 4; W. J. Keith, 'Spirit of Place and Genius *Loci*: D. H. Lawrence and Rolf Gardiner', *DHL Review,* vii (Summer 1974), 127–38.

[2] A possible reference to Gardiner's having taken a German choir to sing in the Great Hall of the new University College, Nottingham, in October 1928 (see *Complete Poems,* ii. 1002).

How is your sister Margaret? I have not seen her after that fleeting visit to Florence – but often think of her.[1] Is she still dabbling with school-teaching? What a horrible thing to dabble in!

No, I don't agree with you about *Lady C.* It's a good book – and if one doesn't smash as one goes, it's no good. This silly White Fox blarney about pure constructive activity is all poppy-cock – nine-tenths at least must be smash – smash! – or else *all* your constructivity turns out feebly destructive. – What about him, by the way – the Kibbo-Kifter?[2]

Amitiés!   D. H. Lawrence

4837. To Charles Lahr, 23 December 1928
Text: MS UNYB; Unpublished.

Hotel Beau Rivage. *Bandol.* Var. France
23 Dec 1928

Dear Lahr

I waited a bit to see if the marked *Lady C.* came from you and Russell Green before writing and sending the dozen signatures. However, here they are – and I hope they'll do. I hope I've not crowded them. If so, tell me, and I'll send others.

Orioli says he's sent out fifty odd of the second edit., according to your list. I do hope they'll all arrive safely.

Davies was here till yesterday evening, and we had a good time. Also P. R. Stephensen came for the night – and I liked him. He seemed alive and straight, I liked him. I think they'll do my picture book.

Davies, and friends, all say they think it would be a great pity to do an expurgated *Lady C.* Perhaps it would. I'm in two minds about it. They say they think there'd be no point to the book if it were expurgated. But that seems to me cutting the point down rather fine.

All good wishes for Christmas.   D. H. Lawrence

4838. To Rhys Davies, [23 December 1928]
Text: MS UT; Postmark, Bandol 24–12 28; Unpublished.

Hotel Beau Rivage. Bandol, Var
Sunday

Dear Davies

A letter from my wife's daughter Barbara to say she will probably start the

---

[1] Margaret Emilia Gardiner (1904–   ) visited DHL at Villa Mirenda probably on 14 April 1928 (see *Letters*, vi. 360 and n. 2).

[2] 'Kibbo-Kift, the Woodcraft Kindred', a visionary right-wing group, founded in 1921 by John Gordon Hargrave (1894–1982). Hargrave assumed the title of 'White Fox, Headman K. K.' (see *Letters*, v. 67–8; *Times* obituary, 25 November 1982).

day after Christmas for here – and stay a fortnight or so. That would mean she'd be here on Thursday[1] morning, which nips Nice again. We might all three come to Nice for New Year. The elder daughter isn't coming out. I'll let you know. Always so uncertain, aren't we!

The hotel is suddenly quite full of people.

I've really finished my pansies, and got the MS. in order, all except the foreword. Don't you really think it's a nice title?

Have you seen Stephensen?

Au revoir!   DHL

4839. To Sylvia Beach, 24 December 1928
Text: MS PU; Postmark, [. . .]; Unpublished.

Hotel Beau Rivage. *Bandol*, Var.
24 Dec. 1928

Dear Miss Beach

Nice of you to write so helpfully. Many thanks for the cheque for £8. – I shall ask Orioli to send you those two copies at once. I hope he has sent the ten of the second edition.

There's no fear about selling this little edition. It was only two hundred, and at once the first hundred were ordered, and a bookseller in London writes that he will take the second hundred, but I don't want them to go like that. I want them to be more distributed.

No, the book has not been banned in England, no action has been taken against it at all, and as far as I know, not one copy has been confiscated in customs. In the U. S. A. also no action has been taken against it, neither Federal nor in any State: it has not been indicted at all. But alas; *customs* have seized quite a lot of copies, so I don't post anything to America. However, as you see, there is nothing illegal in so doing: only the risk.

I can't stop the pirates because, because of the mere 'obscene' words, I can't get copyright.

I wrote to the manager of the Pegasus Press, but have no answer yet.[2] There is hardly time. – I would rather have dealt with someone I know. I suppose you are too busy to take charge of the French edition for me, if I pay the costs of production? You know all the ropes and everything, and I should feel more sure. But of course you may have too much on hand.

The cheque suits me perfectly – so much easier than money orders and those things.

Sincerely   D. H. Lawrence

---

[1] Thursday] Wednesday   [2] The letter to Holroyd-Reece is missing.

4840. To Giuseppe Orioli, [24 December 1928]
Text: MS UCLA; Moore 1107–8.

[Hotel Beau Rivage, Bandol, Var.]
[24 December 1928]

Dear Pino

Please send this man *a copy of the first edition* – Vere H. Collins, he's an old friend, and has helped me with the Oxford University Press, one of whose depts. he manages.[1] Pollinger got both the 1st edit. copies – sold one for 4 gns. and one (as I agreed) for 2 gns. to a man I know who is hard up. – Would you send him six more copies *of the 2nd edition* – if he receives the first two all right. He is a good seller, is Pollinger. And please send *Aldous a copy of the second edition* – it is *a gift* from me to him for Christmas.

Sylvia Beach wrote very friendly, and sent cheque for £8. for two copies of the first edition. There's one in the eye for her, because she *refused* them at £1..14..0 each, now must pay £4. She seems quite anxious to have the ten 2nd. edit. copies, and will pay at end of month. – I've asked her if she would superintend a French edition – if I put up the money. I haven't heard from the Pegasus yet – I haven't heard a word from Enid Hilton. She must be ill again. But another woman whom I know well will store twenty copies of the 1st. edit. for me.

Mrs Brigit Patmore, 4 Milman St. Bedford Row, *London. W.C. 1.*
You could start sending to her, but make sure everything is going through all right, first.

It's a lovely sunny day. I wish you could have been here for Christmas, it would have been jolly. But don't drink too much, it's bad for you. Remember me to Mrs Otway.[2]

We expect Friedas daughter Barbara on Thursday or Friday, for a fortnight. Then we think of going to Spain for a few weeks. I fear Italy is so *cold* – and I have felt so much better here than I did at S. Paolo.

I wonder if the peasants came in bothering you to change their little christmas cheques.

---

[1] DHL wrote to Orioli on the (undated) letter he received from Collins; the letter read:

Dear Lawrence

    Thank you very much. I shall be grateful to have a copy of *Lady Chatterley's Loves* for your kind offer of £2. Please tell me whether I should send you a cheque or a money order; I presume 1/– added will cover postage.

                                                                                        Yours

Vere Henry Gratz Collins (1872–1966) was Educational Books Manager for Oxford University Press in London; he had encouraged DHL to write *Movements in European History* (see *Letters*, ii. 483 n. 1; iii. 261 n. 7).

[2] Eva M. Otway, a friend of Orioli's in Florence and hence a social acquaintance of DHL's.

I hear people say they think Douglas' limericks not good enough. I hope he won't kill his market.

After Christmas I want to chase the people who haven't paid yet. That man Stephensen will help us: seems a good man.

We got Carletto's card. I'll send him one too.

I feel somehow we ought to be getting in the Vingone tram to come into Florence to see you.

DHL

First edition
1. copy Vere H. Collins
2. copies[1] Sylvia Beach, 12 rue de l'Odeon. Paris. 6.

Second edition
1. copy Aldous Huxley
6. copies L. E. Pollinger

4841. To P. R. Stephensen, 24 December 1928
Text: MS Anon; Munro 299.

Hotel Beau Rivage. *Bandol.* Var.

24 Dec 1928

Dear Stephensen

Right-O! I like you too.[2] Come and see us again if you can before you leave the coast. We expect my wife's daughter Barbara on Thursday or Friday, to

[1] 2. copies] 1. copy
[2] DHL was replying to Stephensen's letter (Munro 297–8):

Hotel de Bruxelles, 17 Rue de Belgique, Nice. AM
Friday [21 December 1928]

Dear DHL,

In addressing you thus initially do I convey not a bumptious affectation of impertinent intimacy, but the quite simple cordiality, no affection, which I feel for your heroic loneliness? No not exactly loneliness, with your lady, with our lady of "Lorenzo" there, but simply for your courage, however buttressed, inevitably and eternally buttressed there.

You are one of the very few before whom I don't hesitate to make a fool of myself with a simple declaration of affection "at first sight". Of course all preconceptions were beautifully smashed, you are more than correct in assuming that the tittle-tattle of the bourgeois literary world is particularly vicious in your regard. Without having been unduly prejudiced by this vague chatter, I at least expected that you would have been much more *farouche*, much less tolerant of my inevitable ingenuousness than of course you were.

How could I have expected to find exactly my own succinct hatreds so anticipated? I have tried to hate purposively, not merely to snarl. I blush now to admit that before meeting you I did not realise how integrated your antagonisms are. It is not easy to hate to a plan, to hate synthetically as you do – pardon me, as I do also. We are to destroy the most vile conspiracy which has ever subjugated the human blood; destroy it not merely because it is powerful and

stay a fortnight – so we shall be here for a bit. And I want you to see my
Pansies – my doggerels, with their nice little introduction.[1] And I have begun
the 'Introd. to the paintings', which I am going to make into real serious
essay, but of course on the fantastic toe – I hate heavy-footed seriousness.

Really, I'm very patient with people – my faroucheness lies in the fact that
I rarely want to see them twice, the ordinary lot. But who would!

I feel you and I have something in the spirit in common – or uncommon –

established and everywhere, but because it is vile and a menace to our own pulse. It is too easy,
too much like ordinary envy, to hate the ruling class as a *social* class. We must hate and destroy
it as cancerous; as threatening life, living – I am going to say as threatening all joy. (*Lust* that
wonderful German double entendre). In Nietzsche's phrase: –

I love the great despisers for they are the great adorers, they are the arrows of longing for the
other shore.

I have to explain to you that my respect for Norman Lindsay has always been due to his
capacity for getting under the skin of the citizens with his fat nudes – stressing femininity
(buttocks and bubs) he conditions a wonderful uneasiness in the breast of the paterfamilias.
With all the differences of method and personality this is precisely what you are doing. The
process is to bring sex (balls and all) into consciousness effectively with the distinguishing
subtlety of art – frankness cum delicacy more effective than say pictorial pornography. This is
the first vital attack upon our citizen – to force consciousness of blood upon him – it is enough
to destroy him utterly. The second attack is to pin-prick him into frenzy at a million points of
exposure of his hypocrisy, social, sexual-tribal, political and what-not. This will make him
froth at the mouth and perhaps make him bite you hydrophobically; but actually he is only
destroyed by looking with the mirror of consciousness – blood and balls consciousness – his
whole mechanism being constructed in ignorance of that mirror.

I mustn't go on forever with this theorising but your contact has helped me so much to
clarify for my own purposes. At any rate I see constructive hatred more clearly as a prolegomena to action than ever I did before.

Yes, we shall do your paintings in colour tone process, willingly; but I am not so sure that the
collectors will be pleased. However we may be able to put them on *Japanese vellum* thus
avoiding that wretched art-paper full of chalk. The book will be done well, and to your
satisfaction, rest assured.

I know (or am beginning to know) that energy needs the discipline of patience. I know also,
well enough to be pleased at your reminder, that the drunkenness in vacuo of frustrated men is
not a real gesture other than a gesture of frustration. Believe me I have some work to do yet and
won't let pseudo-"Bohemianism" stop up the pores of my sweating.

The doggerels are quite amusing and we shall certainly use them. Also of course the
long-short story would be ideal for our Autumn list.

Will you let me help you pull that temple down, dear Samson-not-so-agonistes? Just
perhaps to ease the strain, if only momentarily on occasion?

                                                                Yours in that work,

[1] This first draft of the introduction to *Pansies*, written since the letter to Rhys Davies on the
previous day, has been published: see David Farmer, in *Review of English Studies*, xxi (May
1970), 181–4 (Roberts C258). By 5 January when he showed the introduction to Brewster
Ghiselin (Nehls, iii. 289), DHL had written a much longer version, and it was presumably this
which accompanied the poems when he sent them to Pollinger on 7 January (see Letter 4871).
This version was used for the 'definitive edition' (Roberts A47c), which was privately
published, and reprinted in *Phoenix* and *Complete Poems*.

We must work in unison and plan together. I hear those pillars going crack already.[1] Fun!

DHL

4842. To Rhys Davies, 25 December 1928
Text: MS UT; Postmark, Band[ol] 26–1[...]28; Huxley 770.

[Hotel Beau Rivage, Bandol, Var.]
[25 December 1928]

[Frieda Lawrence begins]
Dear Rhys Davies

Do you see Lorenzo in his new dressing-gown?[2] looking not only like one prophet but all the prophets of all times and ages rolled into one – those are his pansies with him. On the top is the sun shining on you and on all your un-born books, this is the brook underneath where we made the daisies float. The flowers, they are *not* welsh, are to enliven your path – I wanted to do some butterflies but they went wrong – Now you know all about it. My daughter Barbara is coming so I dont think we shall come to Nice – as she will be here Wednesday or Thursday. I hope you will have a very nice trip into the hills – Lorenzo will tell you all the other news – I shall love having Barby here and then I suppose it will be Spain – Having to speak Spanish again – The spirit is willing but the flesh is weak –

All good wishes   Frieda Lawrence

[Lawrence begins]
Christmas day. 1928

Dear Davies

The dressing-gown came this morning as I sat in bed at coffee; – very resplendent and I look as if I was just going to utter the unutterable name of God in it. But I'm likely to utter something much more profane to you for spending your money. There do I try to keep you within decent bounds of economy, *knowing* your finances and having lived for years with similar ones, and then you break out into silk dressing-gowns Christmas gifts! It's worse than an expensive tart. I *do* wish you hadn't gone such lengths. I always say I forbid any present dearer than 2/6. But thank you very much and I shall swank my little swank in it; but not cease to be troubled.

I told you Frieda's daughter was coming. If we don't come to Nice you must come again and see us, before we flit.

---

[1] Cf. p. 79 and n. 1.
[2] Frieda's letter is highly decorated, reflecting her remarks which follow.

Tell your man Tchekov is a second-rate writer and a Willy wet-leg.
Lindsay sent me this morning *another* copy of his *Dionysos* book![1]

amitiés   DHL

4843. To Nancy Pearn, 25 December 1928
Text: MS UT; Unpublished.

Hotel Beau Rivage. Bandol, Var
Christmas Day 1928

Dear Nancy Pearn

The *Survey Graphic* of New York asked me for a 2000 word article, say what I like, on New Mexico, payment $100.00.[2] I did the enclosed which I think is quite a beautiful article but maybe too deep for a paper like the *Survey Graphic*. They can cut it if they like. Anyhow will you send it along to New York with explanations – and if Mrs Mabel Luhan. No 1. Fifth Avenue should ask to see the MS., to let her.

We expect my wife's daughter Barbara on Friday for a fortnight, and she can bring back your African table mat – that's all it is – but a big one.

Quiet sunny day here – how quiet this part of Cote d'Azur really is.

Hope you've had a jolly Christmas.

DHL

4844. To Mabel Dodge Luhan, 25 December 1928
Text: MS Brill; Luhan 339–40.

Hotel Beau Rivage. Bandol. Var
25 Dec 1928

Dear Mabel

I wrote what I think is quite a beautiful article on New Mexico – perhaps a bit too deep for the *Survey Graphic*, I don't know. I'm sending it to Curtis Brown London to be typed and they'll send it to Curtis Brown New York to give to the *Graphic*. If the latter think it's not quite suitable for their paper, I don't mind – probably someone else will do it. But I should like you to see it. – Writing it gave me a real longing to be back – and I should like to come in spring even if only to stay the six months allowed by the passport. Brett suggests creeping in unnoticed, but if I feel I have to do that I shall be spitting in everybody's eye. I'm not given to creeping in, and USA isn't paradise anyhow. – My picture show is held off – I think I'm going to have them all

---

[1] Jack Lindsay, *Dionysos: Nietzsche contra Nietzsche*, Fanfrolico Press, November 1928. (The first copy would be one of the 'seven massive' volumes mentioned in Letter 4835.)
[2] Cf. Letter 4820 and n. 2.

reproduced and appear in a book with an essay on painting, to sell at 10 guineas a copy – which is fifty dollars. That's what the Mandrake Press say they want to do – seems to me a fancy price, anyhow. And the exhibition and book appear simultaneously. – I've done such an amusing book of rag poems – pensées – which I call my *pansies* – make them all cross again. But I'm holding it awhile. How are you liking New York. Christmas Day today, and we thought of you at lunch time, and wondered where and with whom you were eating turkey.

Anyhow many greetings   DHL

4845. To Giuseppe Orioli, [26? December 1928]
Text: MS UCLA; Unpublished.

[Hotel Beau Rivage, Bandol, Var.]
[26? December 1928]

Dear Pino

I enclose the telegram from the Pegasus Press[1] – shall we send them a copy of the 2nd edit. – I begrudge it them – the address is

The Pegasus Press, 37. rue Boulard, Paris. XIVe

and the man's name seems to be Holroyd Reece. Of course I want to see what terms the Pegasus offers.

I hope you sent my sisters their copies of the 1st edit.

Did you have a nice Christmas at Vallombrosa? we thought of you in the afternoon.

Do you want one of the Fanfrolico books? – nicely done but contents not exciting.

DHL

I think if I do a Paris edition I shall *not* do an expurgated – would you?[2]

---

[1] The telegram is missing.

[2] DHL's letter is written on one from Charles Lahr to him:

December 22nd 1928.

Dear Mr. Lawrence,

Russell Green is now busy reading and marking a pirated copy of Lady C. As soon as he is finished I'll send it to you.

To-day some more copies arrived. People are clamouring for them and I'll sell them as fast as they come. As many are going direct to customers I will get paid after Christmas for them and will pay the money into your bank and send you the receipt.

Davies wrote me from Bandol that he has been to see you with Stephensen. I hope you fixed things up satisfactorily.

The enclosed cutting from last Sunday's "Weekly Dispatch" might interest you.

Yours sincerely,

4846. To Maria Chambers, 28 December 1928
Text: MS StaU; cited in Schorer 64.

Bandol. Var. France.
28 Dec. 1928

Dear Mrs Chambers

I'm glad you got the poems – one day I'll write in them for you. And I'm glad you had a good time working for Al. Smith[1] – though probably you went pop! after. But never mind. – And I hope you got the other two copies of *Lady C.* that were sent in exchange for those $40. which I *wish* you hadn't sent me: they were yours. – And I hope Dorothy Brett wrote to you – she is in New York now. If she didn't, write to

Mrs Mabel Luhan, No. 1. Fifth Avenue. New York

– and go and see her. She has houses in Taos and is married to an Indian[2] and I'm sure she'd like to see you if you said I told you. – And we are still fidgetting about – can't make up our minds what to do – Still think of coming to America, if only for six months – to summer at the ranch. But there are so many difficulties. – We may go to Spain in a fortnight – and come to America perhaps in March. I wish I felt more sure. I'm a little afraid of U. S. authorities being hostile to me on account of *Lady C.*.

I'm really a good deal better – and I hope you are, now. And I hope you'll have a good satisfying year in 1929.

D. H. Lawrence

4847. To Giuseppe Orioli, 28 December 1928
Text: MS UCLA; Unpublished.

Hotel Beau Rivage. *Bandol.* Var
28 Dec 1928

Dear Pino

Your letter and list of copies of 2nd. edition sent out. Alas that they are gone so soon! – what fools we were not to print 1000!

1. *Don't send Lahr any more (yet).*

The cutting reads:
  Piracy de Luxe.
  As soon as a bannable book appears, the book pirates get ready. Latterly, they have carried their piracy to the realms of art.
    Mr. D. H. Lawrence's last book, which was privately printed, is being pirated in superb style.
    The pirated edition is a photographic replica of the original, and three hundred and fifty copies only are to be published on each side of the Atlantic.
    So that it is a still more limited edition than the first, of which a thousand copies were printed, and moreover the price is double subscription rates of the autographed original.
¹ Unidentified.
² She married Antonio ('Tony') Luhan (d. 1963), a Taos Pueblo Indian, in 1923.

2. Send Aldous a copy, and *Koteliansky* a copy (both gifts for Christmas) 2nd edit.

3. Have you sent a copy to the Pegasus? I'm still waiting to hear more from them.

4. I enclose letter to *Holliday* – will you read it and please post it.[1] *Put the address on.* – Cheats!

5. Will you put this cheque to my account – fancy that swine Holliday! There must be several pirated editions out, signed and unsigned.

6. I have not heard from either of my sisters if they received their copies – *I do hope you sent them.* And yesterday I had a note from Charles Wilson, but no mention of his receiving his copy.

7. I hope you sent Sylvia Beach her two copies first edition – *they are paid.*

8. I enclose the letter from the San Francisco man, which you forwarded to me registered.[2] – Had you sent him his second copy by Express, as I asked? I

[1] Among the accounts relating to *Lady Chatterley's Lover* in DHL's 'Memoranda' (MS NWU) is the following, dated 28 December: 'Returned to Terence B. Holliday. $135.00 for 15 copies refused to him'.

[2] Frank A. Curtin, a lawyer from Fresno, California, had paid for two copies of *Lady Chatterley's Lover*, one in June and one in August (DHL's 'Memoranda'); one copy was sent to him but it was seized by Customs at San Francisco (see *Letters*, vi. 531 n. 1). His letter, 6 December 1928, reads as follows:

My dear Mr. Lawrence:

Your welcome and treasured letter of August 30th I received in due time and you must not think my failure to reply before now is due to any lack of interest or appreciation. Desirous of bothering you as little as possible with any correspondence I have purposely delayed writing until such time as I could feel sure there was no hope of "Lady Chatterley's Lover" being delivered to me after I had written to you. I have never received any word whatsoever other than your letter regarding the second book.

First and above all else I want you to clearly understand that I do not expect and I do not want you to return to me any money. If you are sure both books were sent to me by the publishers the fact that I have received neither is due to no fault of yours or of theirs, but solely to my dear old hair-brained Uncle Sam. And in this connection, hoping that it may be of interest to you, I intend enclosing herewith carbon copies of all the correspondence I have had in connection with the first copy. The letters I trust will in a measure explain themselves, letter No. 1 being explained by letter No. 2. (I thought it would be great fun under the circumstances should I be able to obtain the book through the assistance of our local Chief of Police. Its a kick when one can use the services of one public official to offset the officiousness of another. About a year ago when Ludwig Lewisohn's "The Case of Mr. Crump" was taboo in this country it gave me no little pleasure to have a copy brought to me from Paris by our local Deputy United States Marshal returning from a world tour.)

I am hoping that some day before long you will have brought out in this country a similar strictly limited and autographed edition of your book and that I may hear of it far enough in advance to be successful in obtaining a copy. I am told that already there is a bootleg edition out in New York which purports to be limited and numbered but not autographed and which sells for $10.00. I ordered a copy several weeks ago through my local book seller but he in his careful conservative way ordered it indirectly and thus far it has not arrived.

Thanking you very much for the generous and courteous spirit you have shown in this matter, I remain, with most cordial greetings of the approaching holiday season,

Sincerely,

DHL's reply to Curtin is missing.

am writing to him to say that I will hold him a copy of the first edition, but no
good sending it to U.S.A.

That's all the *Lady C.* news. Yes, I love her, and it grieves me to have her
gone. But we must do something else.

Frieda's daughter arrives on the 2nd – so we shall be here another fortnight
anyhow.

Do you think Sylvia Beach would cheat me if I let her look after an edition in
Paris? – No, don't send her any first editions in deposit. Let her order and pay.

Aldous and Maria are coming to Florence in about three weeks time.

Do you want a Fanfrolico book? nice get-up, but poor stuff inside!! alas
they've got my name in.

love.   DHL

Keep him [Curtin] one of the unnumbered copies, perhaps – You see he's
paid *twice*! I don't enclose the correspondance, it's only dull. But lay him a
copy aside.[1]

4848. To Charles Wilson, 28 December 1928
Text: MS Lazarus; Huxley 770–2.

Hotel Beau Rivage. Bandol. Var.
28 Dec 1928

Dear Charles Wilson

Many thanks for the calendar and the greetings. Here are three scraps of
a sort of poetry, which will perhaps do as a 'message.'[2] I've done a book of
such poems – really they are *pensées* – which I shall publish later – but you
may as well start in with these three bits.

I hope you got your copy of *Lady Chatterley.* It was finally sent from
Florence, so if it doesn't arrive it is lost.

I wonder when we shall come to England. I read with shame of the miners'
'hampers' and the 'fund.'[3] It's a nice thing to make men live on charity and
crumbs of cake, when what they want is manly independence. The whole

---

[1] DHL's postscript was written on Curtin's letter.
[2] The number of poems was increased to six, with an additional prose piece. All the poems (with
some changes of title and textual variants not noted here) appeared in the definitive edn of
Pansies (August 1929) (Roberts A47c). Two poems – 'My naughty book' and 'An old acquaintance' (in *Pansies* called 'The Little Wowser') – were omitted from Secker's expurgated edn
(July 1929) (Roberts A47a and b).
[3] On 2 April 1928 the Lord Mayors of London, Cardiff and Newcastle-on-Tyne launched a
fund to assist 'women and children who are suffering on account of the continued depression in
the coalmining industry' and to assist boys 'for whom employment can be found' outside the
depressed areas. Food-hampers were one way of providing assistance.

scheme of things is unjust and rotten, and money is just a disease upon
humanity. It's time there was an *enormous* revolution – not to instal soviets,
but to give life itself a chance. What's the good of an industrial system piling
up rubbish, while nobody lives. We want a revolution not in the name of
money or work or any of that, but of life – and let money and work be as
casual in human life as they are in a bird's life, damn it all. Oh it's time the
whole thing was changed, absolutely. And the men will have to do it –
You've got to smash money and this beastly *possessive* spirit. I get more
revolutionary every minute, but for *life's* sake. The dead materialism of Marx
socialism and soviets seems to me no better than what we've got. What we
want is life, and *trust*: men trusting men, and making living a free thing, not a
thing to be *earned*. But if men trusted men, we could soon have a new world,
and send this one to the devil.

There's more message – perhaps too strong for you. But the beastliness of
the show, the *injustice* – just see the rich English down here on the Riviera,
thousands of them – nauseates me. Men can't stand injustice.

Happy New Year   DHL

New Years Greetings to the Willington Men – for 1929

———

For God's Sake –

For God's sake, let us be men
not monkeys minding machines,
or sitting with our tails curled
while the machine amuses us, radio or film or gramophone –

Monkeys with a bland grin on our faces!

———

O! start a revolution!

O! start a revolution, somebody!
not to get the money
but to lose it all for ever!

O! start a revolution, somebody!
not to instal the working classes
but to abolish the working classes for ever
and have a world of men.

———

It's either you fight or you die –

It's either you fight or you die
young gents, you've got no option.
No good asking the reason why,
it's either you fight or you die
die, die, lily-liveredly die
or fight and make the splinters fly
bust up the holy apple pie:
you've got no option.

Don't say you can't, start in and try.
give nice hypocrisy the lie
and tackle the blowsy, big blow-fly
of money; do it, or die,
You've got no option.

––––––––

My naughty book

They say I wrote a naughty book
With perfectly awful things in it,
putting in all the impossible words
like b— and f— and sh—.

Most of my friends were deeply hurt
and haven't forgiven me yet;
I'd loaded the camel already with dirt
they couldn't quite forget.

But now, no really! the final straw
was words like sh— and f—.
The camel's righteous back went crack
under the load of muck.

Then out of nowhere rushed John Bull
that ancient hound, good doggie!
squeakily bellowing for all he was worth
old bull-dog, slavering and soggy.

He couldn't bite, he was much too old,
but he made a pool of dribblings;

while[1] the ship of the desert[2] heaved her sides
with moans and hollow bibblings.

he[3] did his best,[4] the good old dog
to support her,[5] the hysterical camel,
and everyone listened and loved it, the
ridiculous bimmel-bammel.

But of course one has no right to take
the old dog's greenest bones
that he's buried now for centuries
under England's garden stones –

And of course one has no right to lay
such words to the camel's charge,
when she prefers to have them kept
in the W.C., writ large.

Poor ancient words, I must give you back
to the she-camel and the dog,
for her to mumble and him to crack[6]
in secret, great golliwog!

And hereby I apologise
to all my foes and friends
for using words they privately keep
for their own immortal ends.

And henceforth I will never use
more than the chaste, pure dash.
So do forgive me! I sprinkle my hair
with grey, repentant ash.

An old acquaintance

There is a little wowser
    John Thomas by name,
and for every bloomin' mortal thing
    that little blighter's to blame.

---

[1] while] ⟨and⟩ in   [2] the ship of the desert] where the she-camel
[3] he] ⟨He⟩ and he
[4] did his best,] kept it up   [5] to support her,] and you […]   [6] crack] gnaw

It was 'im as made the great mistake
    of puttin' us in the world,
shovin' us out of the unawake
    where we were quietly curled

into this hole – but you do your best,
    an' just as you begin
to feel all right, this bleeder busts in
    with: Hello boy! show us your sin!

An' then he leads you by the nose
    after a lot o' women
as strips you stark as a monkey-nut
    an' leaves you never a trimmin'

till somebody has to marry you
    to put him through his paces,
then when John Thomas don't worry you
    it's a[1] wife, with 'er airs and graces.

I think of all the little brutes
    as ever was invented
this little cod's the holy worst.
    I've chucked 'im! I've repented.

———

Character in a novel.

I read a novel by a friend of mine
in which one of the characters was me,
the novel it sure was mighty fine
but the funniest thing that could be

was me, or what was supposed for me,
for I had to recognise
a few of the touches, like the low-born jake,
but the rest was a real surprise.

Well damn my eyes! I said to myself.
Well damn my little eyes!
If this is what Archibald thinks I am
he sure thinks a lot of lies.

[1] a] your

> Well think o' that now, think o' that!
> That's what he sees in me!
> I'm about as much like a Persian cat
> or a dog with a harrowing[1] flea.
>
> My God, a man's friends' ideas of him
> would stock a menagerie
> with a marvellous outfit! How did Archie see
> such a funny cuss in me?

to all men who are men:

———

Be men, be individual men, grounded in your own manhood! Don't believe in the 'working man' or the 'average man' or the 'good man'. Let every man stand by his own manhood, not be squashed into any sort of mass, nor made to any sort of pattern.

And get clear of the money hysteria. Money is the devil that twists all our tails: twists the rich man, who has more than he needs, and twists the poor man, who is threatened with starvation. Yet money is nothing more than the bogey of fear and greed, inside us.

Men, alert men, should neither live nor work for money. Men must work to produce the food, warmth and shelter we all need: but that should soon be done. The rest is the great game of living.

But now, everything is work, it is all slavery. Most men are wage-slaves. Under bolshevism, it is pretty much the same: they are still slaves, machine-slaves, party-slaves.

Work should be comparatively a trivial element in a man's life, and money need not exist. Men must provide food, warmth and shelter for themselves and for all human beings: for every human being should have warmth, food, shelter, free and without question, whether he works for it and 'deserves' it or not. – But this would not be a very tedious or difficult matter. At least seven-tenths of the work of today is waste work: done just because people do not know what to do with themselves: and to get money. It is a form of idiocy.

The real activity of life is the great activity of the *developing consciousness*, physical, mental, intuitional, religious – all-round consciousness. This is the real business of life, and is the great game of grown men. All that other affair, of work and money, should be settled and subordinated to this, the great game of real living, of developing ourselves physically, in subtlety of

---

[1] harrowing] frisky

movement, and grace and beauty of bodily awareness, and of deepening and widening our whole consciousness, so that we really become men, instead of remaining the poor, cramped, limited slaves we are.

But we must first wring the neck of the money bird, and settle the simple question of food, warmth, and shelter.

D. H. Lawrence

4849. To Juliette Huxley, 28 December 1928
Text: MS Huxley; Unpublished.

Hotel Beau Rivage, *Bandol.* Var.
28 Dec 1928

Dear Juliette

How nice if we see you and Julian quite soon. We shall be staying on anyhow till Jan 10th, because Frieda's daughter Barbara arrives on the 2nd to stay at least a week. After that we still think of Spain. But why don't you stop on your way to Grasse?[1] We are between Marseille and Toulon, about 8 miles from Toulon. But it is a long way from Nice – train takes between three and four hours.

It was a warm day with a hot sun this morning and a west wind. I'm afraid it's all over with your snow!

But come down here and stop off at Bandol – either at Marseille or Toulon, as the little train best fits, you can change. Let us know, and we'll have rooms ready. Are you bringing the children.

Many greetings to you all, and to your mother surely, and au revoir.

DHL

4850. To Earl, Achsah and Harwood Brewster, 28 December 1928
Text: MS UT; Brewster 190.

Hotel Beau Rivage, *Bandol.* Var
28 Dec 1928

Dear Earl and Achsah and Harwood

The scarves and letters came yesterday, and the books today, and all perfectly beautiful, and a thousand thanks. And here we sit, neither of the daughters turned up! – Barby arrives *next* Wednesday. My, what a world! Frieda gets most awfully fidgetty in an hotel – wants a house – but not here. – Achsah we have got your African basket – but not the one *I* was going to buy – Frieda chose this – and it's for a work-basket – with a saucer to put over it

[1] The Huxleys were on their way to visit H. G. Wells, who lived with Odette Keun, outside Grasse, near Nice.

for a lid, or to use as a little tray – and Earl I have got you a *nice* silk hanky – but simply we faint before the parcel post here. Harwood gets a quid, which, thank God, is easy to put in a letter. – Earl, I was so glad you liked *Lady C.* I am at my wits end as all sorts of pirated editions seem to be coming out in America and selling at prices varying from $6. to $20 or even $30. I am trying to get out quickly a Paris edition at about 100 frs. to put on the market and nip them if I can. But it's so difficult finding anyone to take charge, and I can't sit in Paris to do it.

The weather has been sunny nearly all the time – practically no rain, but a cold little wind. Now it's warmer and gone cloudy. But this seems to me a good climate.

We just had a letter from Frau Trachsl of the Kesselmatte,[1] very sweet, she says they are in deep snow, but very *good* snow, and 100 English people in your hotel and Bären, enjoying themselves. Achsah dear, aren't you pining to be there?

Well I'm glad you're festivating among friends and fidelities, and I suppose we shall meet again soon – and till then *leb' wohl!*[2] all of you.

DHL

4851. To Lady Ottoline Morrell, 28 December 1928
Text: MS UT; Postmark, Bandol 29–12 28; Huxley 722–4.

Hotel Beau Rivage. *Bandol,* Var. France
28 Dec 1928

My dear Ottoline

I was glad to hear from you again, and very glad to know you are better. Aldous also wrote that you were really wonderfully well, after that bad time. As for me, it's poco a poco,[3] but I'm really getting better all the time.

We have been down on this coast since October, and I must say it has suited me well, it's a good winter climate. I didn't know Katharine had been here – wonder where she stayed.[4] – But I think in a fortnight we shall move on to Spain. From here it's not so very far. We've got to find somewhere to live, now we've given up the Florence house. Frieda gets fidgetty, being without a house. But she doesn't really know *where* she wants one. Where does one want to live, finally?

---

[1] 9 July–18 September 1928 the Lawrences had lived at the Chalet Kesselmatte, Gsteig bei Gstaad, Switzerland, with the Brewsters in the nearby Hotel Viktoria. Frau Käthe Trachsl owned Kesselmatte; she and her daughter acted as servants to the Lawrences.
[2] 'farewell!'   [3] 'little by little'.
[4] Katherine Mansfield (1888–1923) and Middleton Murry rented the Villa Pauline in Bandol, December 1915–April 1916 (see *Letters*, i. 507 n. 3; ii. 465 n. 2).

About *Lady C.* – you mustn't think I advocate perpetual sex. Far from it. Nothing nauseates me more than promiscuous sex in and out of season. But I want, with *Lady C*, to make an *adjustment in consciousness* to the basic physical realities. I realise that one of the reasons why the common people often keep – or kept the good *natural glow* of life, just warm life, longer than educated people, was because it was still possible for them to say shit! or fuck without either a shudder or a sensation. If a man had been able to say to you when you were young and in love: an' if tha shits, an' if tha pisses, I'm glad, I shouldna want a woman who couldna shit nor piss – surely it would have been a liberation to you, and it would have helped to keep your heart warm. Think of poor Swift's insane *But* of horror at the end of every verse of that poem to Celia – But Celia shits![1] – You see the very fact that it should horrify him, and simply devastate his consciousness, is all wrong, and a bitter shame to poor Celia. It's just the awful and truly unnecessary *recoil* from these things that I would like to break. It's a question of conscious acceptance and adjustment – only that. God forbid that I should be taken as urging loose sex activity. There is a brief time for sex, and a long time when sex is out of place. But when it is out of place as an activity there still should be the large and quiet space in the consciousness where it lives quiescent. Old people can have a lovely quiescent sort of sex, like apples, leaving the young quite free for *their* sort.

It's such a pity preachers have always dinned in: Go thou and do likewise![2] – That's not the point. The point is: It is so, let it be so, with a generous heart.

Well forgive all this – but I don't want you to misunderstand me, because I always count on your sympathy somewhere.

Frieda sends her love – and one day I hope we'll have a few quiet chats and laughs together – there's time still for that.

D. H. Lawrence

---

[1] The line to which DHL refers – 'Oh! Celia, Celia, Celia shits!' – occurs in two of Swift's poems: 'The Lady's Dressing Room' (1732), l. 118 and 'Cassinus and Peter: A Tragical Elegy' (1734), l. 118. DHL could not have seen the complete line in print; it was first printed in Swift's *Poetical Works*, ed. Herbert Davis (Oxford, 1967); but it may well have formed a topic of conversation with Aldous Huxley. Huxley himself quoted the offending line (minus 'the monosyllabic verb') in his essay on Swift which was probably already written and was included in his volume *Do What You Will* (October 1929). (He associated the line with 'Cassinus and Peter'.) In neither of Swift's poems is there an 'insane *But* of horror at the end of every verse', nor is either poem addressed 'to Celia'. (See also DHL's 'Introduction' to *Pansies*, in *Complete Poems*, i. 419–20.)

[2] Luke x. 37 ['Go, and do thou likewise'].

4852. To Ada Clarke, 29 December 1928
Text: MS Clarke; Postmark, Ba[ndol] [. . .]; cited in Lawrence–Gelder 187.

Hotel Beau Rivage. *Bandol,* Var.
29 Dec 1928

My dear Sister

Just a note to say the four silk hankies arrived safely and are very pretty indeed, I like them very much. Of course I had to pay 29 frs. duty on them – 5/- – but one knows it.

We had a quiet time – Rhys Davies left the day before Christmas – and then the hotel filled up with strangers – mostly French from Marseilles. Barby Weekley is coming for a week – arrives on Jan 2nd – has been rather ill for some time, so they say. Julian and Juliette Huxley will call and see us too, first week in January, and Aldous and Maria want to join us on 20th – then we motor to Italy with them. But I don't want to go to Italy and I *hate* motoring and I want to go to Spain. I have been so much better this winter than last. I really feel Italy isn't good for me just now – and here is – and Spain would be. Somehow here there isn't enough *to it* to make one want to live – the country is a bit no-how, and the French mess up their sea-side coast worse than anybody – fearful hotchpotch of villas, almost as bad as a slum. Otherwise one might have found a house here. But somehow I'd like to go to Spain before we settle on anything.

I suppose you got your copy of *Lady C.* – as Emily had hers. I was thinking, if I want to store the last twenty copies and keep them for a time, would you store them for me in your house – Orioli would send them by post.

I expect you had a lively Christmas. Poor Pamela sounded a wee bit dull – Frieda was disappointed to have no feast for her, but I say if the sun shines and one feels well that's feast enough – I don't like festivating anyhow.

Love and all the good wishes for the New Year.   DHL
Barby W. will bring Jack's things – I shall send you some books I have here.

4853. To George Conway, 29 December 1928
Text: MS Moore; Postmark, [. . .]; Unpublished.

c/o[1] Pino Orioli. 6 Lungarno Corsini, Florence
29 Dec 1928

Dear Conway[2]

I am most distressed to learn that your copies of *Lady Chatterley's Lover* have not turned up. They were sent by registered book post *long* ago – and surely the Mexican govt. would not confiscate them, as the U.S.A. customs do! I will ask Orioli to send you the registration counterfoil, to see if you can trace them. If not you must have others, if any remain. Orioli has very few, I know – they may be all ordered. But one at least I'll rescue for you. But we must find out what became of the others. The book is selling at $50. in U.S.A. – and anything over £5. here in Europe – so you see it is quite a loss.

Your Christmas card came this morning too – and how pretty it is! – and I had a little book from you which I thought was charming.

We have given up the Villa Mirenda, and are at a bit of a loose end, wondering where to go and where to live next. I think in about a fortnight we shall go to Spain, and try that. But we might go to New Mexico for the summer, so if ever you are passing, make sure first if we are there and *do stop* and see us if we are. – I was ill last year but am much better now and getting to be myself again. Some people were much scandalised by *Lady C.* but many took it in the right spirit, and remain staunch to me. I do hope you'll get your copies, and will read it and not be shocked – Mrs Conway too. We have lived too long to be shocked by *words* any more.

How are you both? I think of you often, and quake sometimes for you, seeing the Mexican news.[3] But you'll go on for ever, I feel, running those trams and deciphering Spanish MS.

– Very many greetings from us both   D. H. Lawrence

---

[1] c/o] Hotel Beau Rivage *Bandol.* Var c/o

[2] George Robert Graham Conway (1873–1951) and his wife Anne Elizabeth (1881–1962) were among the English friends DHL had made in Mexico City in 1925. Conway was an engineer specialising in electric railways; President of the Mexican Light and Power Co. and Mexican Tramways Co.; and an avid collector of Spanish colonial documents. See *Letters*, v. 228 n.

[3] Possibly a reference to the severe earthquakes in Oaxaca, 6 August, and Mexico City, 9 October 1928, as well as to the general instability of the country (witness the assassination of General Obregon on 17 July and the frequent outbreaks of revolutionary activity).

4854. To Aldous Huxley, [30 December 1928]
Text: Huxley 774–5.

Hôtel Beau Rivage, Bandol.
Sat., 30 Dec.

Dear Aldous, –

Many thanks for your information about *offset*.[1] I had a telegram from the Pegasus Press man – apparently called Holroyd Reece – saying he would be in Paris in 10 days' time and would answer my letter fully, and would we meantime send a copy of *Lady C.* to him to Paris. So much for *him*. Sylvia Beach wrote very friendly about the other books – edits., I mean – and sent cheque for £8 for 2 copies of the first. That's one on her: because at the beginning she ordered *three* copies, and then, when she heard that discount was only 15%, demanded back the money for two copies and bought only one: she might have had all the three for £5. Now she's paid £9..14: nearly double. But she acted up so friendly now I did ask her if she would take charge of a Paris edition if I paid for it. But she hasn't answered yet. I suppose she's smoking a pipe on it. Orioli says he has only 25 of the second edit., left, alas! – and they are ordered, but I tell him to hold some. – I'll have to wait, I suppose, till I hear from Beach and Pegasus – I don't incline very warmly to either, yet *must* have someone.

About plans – Frieda's daughter Barby arrives on 2nd to stay a week or so: then we can go. You wouldn't arrive till 20th, would you? Juliette said she and Julian would come, before then, on their way to Grasse to H. G. Wells. Now what are we going to do? I don't really want to go back to Italy. I am *so* much better this winter than I was last, I can *feel* that this place is so much better for me than Italy – something bleeds me a bit, emotionally, in Italy. I really want to go to Spain – I feel I should be well there, too. I think it's a man's country. But Frieda hangs back. She terribly wants a house – doesn't know where – feels Spain is far. But it isn't. It's no further than Florence. I would like to see you both. But these little *en passant* glimpses like Lavendou or Chexbres don't amount to much, do they? If we were going to meet it ought to be after you've done your business in Florence. Wouldn't you like to come to Spain? – to a warm place, Tarragon or Valencia or Malaga – not Malaga, though? But with a car it *is* a long way, I do agree. Unless a ship brought you from Livorno, which isn't so very dear, I think.

Anyhow, that's how it all stands at present. It's been a lovely warm day, like spring. I lie in bed and look at the dawn, and the sort of mountains opposite across the gulf go quite translucent red like hot iron – very lovely dawns – almost like Taormina, where we had it the same. Now it is tea-time

---

[1] Possibly resulting from Huxley's enquiry to Charles Prentice: see p. 62 n. 1.

and just a bit pinky and primrosy and touches of frail grey cloud. This place is nothing much in itself – but I seem to be happy here, sitting on the tiny port and watching the 'life' – chiefly dogs – or wandering out on the jetty. I find I can be very happy quite by myself just wandering or sitting on a stone – if the sun shines. Yes, one needs the sun. If anything, one needs[1] to go farther south than here, rather than further north. But it is *wonderful* how sunny it is here – really one can thank heaven for so shining. And of course we're quite as far south as Florence.

Ottoline wrote very sweetly – very sweetly – but still coughing *a little* over *Lady C.*

I have done my *Pansies*, nice and peppery. I altered Maria's a bit – she must say if she doesn't want it in. I don't know if she had it even. But I changed it to Dear Clarinda.[2] There, Maria! get a new nickname, be a new maid.[3] Now you're Clarinda, my dear!

What's the French for Belgium, I wonder.

DHL

4855. To Charles Lahr, 31 December 1928
Text: MS UNYB; Postmark, Bandol 31–12 28; Unpublished.

Hotel Beau Rivage, *Bandol*, Var
31 Dec 1928

Dear Lahr

Many thanks for yours with the two receipts total £42. I heard from Orioli he has only twenty-five copies left of 2nd and he wants to keep some in Florence. So don't count on many more.

I am trying to arrange a Paris edition, perhaps photographed – offset. I am waiting to hear if Sylvia Beach will help – and the terms of the Pegasus Press. They are very slow. I wish I knew some good, quick, reliable person in Paris – but I don't. Do you?

I agree with you about an expurgated edition. Damn the others. Of course they don't like the *class* analysis and conclusion: too anti-middle-class etc. –

I'm glad you are Clifford Mellors:[4] hope you've got the spunk of the one and the money of the other: how nice!

About the poems – so called – the *Pansies* I call them – I am sort of

---

[1] Huxley's text reads 'need'.
[2] See Letter 4809 and n. 1. 'To Clarinda' opens: 'Thank you, dear Clarinda/ for helping with Lady C.' (*Complete Poems*, i. 550–1).
[3] Cf. *The Tempest*, II. ii. 189 ('Has a new master. Get a new man.').
[4] A conflation of Sir Clifford Chatterley and Oliver Mellors, Lady Chatterley's husband and lover.

undecided. They are very anti middle-class 'How beastly the bourgeois is!'[1] –
I should like them done as you say. But I have all my obligations to Secker
and Knopf, and I have my agents to deal with – they'll be dead against you.
And so[2] far I have kept the MS. and sent it to nobody. But I'll have to rouse
up and send it out – and I'll let you know how things go. I've got to go gently,
warily about it – shall rouse hostility anyhow. – But thanks for your offer,
and probably we'll arrange something, when the others have revealed themselves.

I am waiting for the marked copy of *Lady C*.[3]

Sincerely   D. H. Lawrence

4856. To Laurence Pollinger, 31 December 1928
Text: MS UT; Unpublished.

Hotel Beau Rivage. *Bandol*, Var.
31 Dec.[4] 1928

Dear Pollinger

Thanks for yours with the Seltzer statement. Do keep that cheque and go
after them about the rest.

I see that six of the books are out of print. I suppose there is the usual
clause that if they stay out of print the rights revert to me? Can't we now
claim back the rights to these six books, now – it includes *Birds Beasts and
Flowers* which we want for the Viking. And I should like to recover the
copyright for my books over there. If only one knew how many copies they
had of the other books, one could buy them out and recover the copyright,
because I don't think Boni will reprint them, do you? – Can we do something
about this?

And would you please ask Crosby Gaige to return the MS of *The Escaped
Cock*, if he has not already done so.[5] I shall print it myself.

I shall send you directly the MS. of a new book of poems – sort of poems –
really pensées, I call them *Pansies*!! You won't like them – some.

New Year tomorrow. Many good wishes – what about that Quinton man?[6]

D. H. Lawrence

---

[1] *Complete Poems*, i. 430–1.   [2] MS reads 'so so'.   [3] See p. 95 n. 2.
[4] Dec.] Jan.
[5] Crosby Gaige (1883–1949), American theatrical producer, publisher of fine edns and book
collector; he had been interested in publishing *The Escaped Cock* since at least March 1928 (see
Letters, vi. 326).
[6] See Letter 4833 and p. 85 n. 1.

4857. To Giuseppe Orioli, 31 December 1928
Text: MS UCLA; Unpublished.

Hotel Beau Rivage. *Bandol*, Var.
31 Dec. 1928

Dear Pino

Keep the last twenty copies of the second edition for a while – we may want them.

Lahr has paid in to my bank in London altogether forty guineas, for forty copies.

Don't sent any copies *yet* to Mrs Brigit Patmore. I am thinking it may be better to send them to my sister.

This is merely a note to say keep the last twenty copies, and don't send the six to Pollinger, if you've not sent them. Lahr could have those six.

I hope you sent out the copies of the first edition, as I asked.

Yes, we must try and collect the money owing *now*, in the New Year.

All sorts of good wishes for the New Year – in haste –

DHL

4858. To Edward Dahlberg, 31 December 1928
Text: MS UTul; Postmark, Bandol 31–12 28; Unpublished.

Hotel Beau Rivage. Bandol, Var.
31 Dec 1928

Dear Mr Dahlberg

I'm glad you like *Lady C.* you can get a copy for 1 guinea from
Signor G. Orioli. 6 Lungarno Corsini, Florence
if you tell him I said so. It is second edition, very few of them indeed, selling anywhere over 30/-.

What are you doing about your novel? Would you like to give it to my agents, Curtis Brown Ltd. 6 Henrietta St. Covent Garden? If so I'll write a letter about it to the manager. Or if you'd like to send it direct to the Viking Press, I'll send you a letter to George Oppenheim.[1] If it's done, better try to place it – you might help your financial difficulties that way.

Sincerely   D. H. Lawrence

[1] George Oppenheimer of the Viking Press.

4859. To Dr Anton Kippenberg, 31 December 1928
Text: MS SVerlag; Unpublished.

Hotel Beau Rivage, *Bandol.* Var. France.
31 Dec 1928

Dear Dr Kippenberg

My wife is preparing, with the help of a friend, a German author,[1] a translation of my novel *Lady Chatterley's Lover.* This book, as you know, I published privately in Florence – and my edition is all sold, – with the exception of a very few copies – the price being now doubled. My agent Curtis Brown does not have charge of th[at][2] book. But I understand from him that the contract between you and me will probably be renewed. Therefore I want to tell you that I am planning to bring out a private edition in German as I did in English, limited to a thousand copies, of *Lady Chatterley*, and I want to ask you if you have any desire to publish the book in that way, before I make other negotiations. I understand that since the war you do not print limited editions for collectors, so no doubt you will care nothing about this.

Lady Chatterley is a book that will be very difficult to translate, and I must keep the translation under my supervision. Anything else would be too risky.

Will you please let me have a word on the matter, as I want to go ahead. I am preparing also an edition to be published in Paris, so that the book may be properly circulated.

With all good wishes to you and to Frau Kippenberg for the New Year.
Yours Sincerely   D. H. Lawrence

4860. To Max Mohr, 31 December 1928
Text: MS HMohr; Mohr 33.

Hotel Beau Rivage. *Bandol*, Var.
31 Decem 1928

Dear Max Mohr

I think it is a good idea to publish a limited edition of *Lady C.* for[3] Germany, at perhaps 40 Mark. My first edition now sells officially at 105 M. – but the booksellers often ask 200 M. – and in America the price is $50. – none of which comes to me, alas!

I have written to Kippenberg to ask if he wishes to publish an edition of 1000 copies privately, for subscribers. If not, I shall make other arrangements, I told him.

I said to him also that my wife was preparing a translation with the help of

---

[1] See letter following.   [2] MS damaged.   [3] for] in

a friend, a German author, under my supervision. So even if he *does* decide to publish a limited edition, he must accept our translation.

Thank you very much for saying you will translate the book. I believe you could do it, and keep the tenderness and the freshness. But O! the dialect! I am sure the Kippenbergs will hate the *class* inference, and the industrial analysis. They are more bourgeois than a bidet.

The best will be if you will translate a chapter, and then send your translation to us, and we will go over it and say what we think. In that way, chapter by chapter we could get the thing ship-shape.

And of course you would have to have a proper share of the money: it will be a lot of work for you. But that we can arrange later.

Sunny here, and warm, with just a little cold wind. Many many good wishes for the New Year!

Sincerely   D. H. Lawrence

4861. To Julian and Juliette Huxley, [1 January 1929]
Text: MS Huxley; Unpublished.

[Hotel Beau Rivage, Bandol, Var.]
Tuesday evening.

Dear Julian and Juliette[1]

We are so pleased you are coming, but won't sit up, as you'll be tired and won't want to talk. I hope the taxi finds you all right.

We have coffee in bed, and get up any time after – though usually rather dawdly. Send us word how you are and what time you're going to be out and about. Frieda's room is 12 and mine is 12.B.

What fun to see you! – But what a stormy day! – by far the wildest we've had on this coast. Hope it clears up. – Do hope you'll be comfortable – the hotel is rather full.

till tomorrow   DHL

[1] According to Lady Huxley this note was left in the Huxleys' hotel room in Bandol.

4862. To Harry Crosby, 2 January 1929
Text: MS SIU; Postmark, Bandol 3–1 29; Huxley 776–7.

Hotel Beau Rivage, *Bandol.* Var.

2 Jan 1929

Dear Harry Crosby[1]

I was glad to hear from you again and to know you had a good time in America: but you didn't stay very long.

We have been sitting here the last two months, and I must say, it has been amazingly sunny. I have watched him rise nearly every morning from the surprised sea, as I lay in bed luxuriously, and I must say I was grateful to him every day for coming up so triumphant. This is a dull little place, apart from the sun, but I have liked it. Now before long I think we shall go to Spain. My wifes daughter is with us for a week or so still – after then we shall think of departure. I don't suppose I shall come north unless I have to come to Paris to arrange about an edition of *Lady C.* I want to do a stock edition at about 100 frs – something like Joyce's *Ulysses* or *The Well of Loneliness*[2] – but the difficulty is to get someone to see to it for me. I asked Sylvia Beach if she'd look after it if I paid for the production, but she hasn't answered. The man of the Pegasus Press will answer this week – at least, so he promised by telegraph. I suppose you don't know of any reliable bookseller in Paris – or publisher – who would take charge of the thing for me? I should like to do it quickly, to hit back at those pirated editions which have appeared in U.S.A. – But I'm sure I don't know why I bother you.

Many thanks for the book which arrived from Brentano's this morning.[3] It looks rather massive, but I've no doubt it has good things in it. Your poems are slow coming out. No, I've seen nothing of yours.

How long will you stay in Paris now? till the summer?

I did a book of sort of poems – really little pensées – but you won't care for them except perhaps one or two.

---

[1] Henry Grew ('Harry') Crosby (1898–1929), a rich American playboy, poet and publisher; with his wife Mary, whom he called Caresse (1892–1970), he had published DHL's *Sun* on their Black Sun Press in Paris, October 1928. They had recently returned, after a visit to America, to their new home, the Moulin du Soleil, Ermenonville, near Paris. Crosby had by this time published five books of his poems, the most recent being *Chariot of the Sun* (the second edn of which, 1931, contained DHL's introduction) and *Transit of Venus*, both 1928. See *Letters*, vi. 300 n. 4; Geoffrey Wolff, *Black Sun: The Brief Transit and Violent Eclipse of Harry Crosby* (New York, 1976).

[2] *The Well of Loneliness* by Marguerite Radclyffe Hall (1886–1943). The book (with a commentary by Havelock Ellis) was published in New York and London, 1928; the English edn, July 1928, was withdrawn on 22 August; it was then reprinted in Paris (1928) from stereos of the type.

[3] Brentano's is a bookstore in both New York and Paris. The book is unidentified.

How did Caresse Crosby like her native country too? – if it is her native country, it may not be.

I have been much better in health this winter, and so felt quite chirpy. I should like to paint, but in an hotel bedroom, how can one! We *must* take a house somewhere.

Well, welcome back to Europe, to both of you, and all good wishes for the new year.

D. H. Lawrence

4863. To Rhys Davies, 2 January 1929
Text: TMSC NWU; Unpublished.

Hotel Beau Rivage, *Bandol*, Var.
2 Jan. 1929.

Dear Davies,

My wife's daughter delayed her coming, of course – but is here now – and seems rather to like the idea of coming to Nice – it might possibly be this week-end, or next week. The Julian Huxleys were here for a day – gone on to H. G. Wells' place near Grasse. We should see them too.

What kind of Christmas and New Year did you have? Did you do your walk in the hills? I hope you got back before yesterday. What a wind to blow the New Year in! We went to a pastorelle – a sort of semi-Christmas play, in dialect – very amusing – wish you had been able to come too.

The hotel has been *packed* with French people, till today. Now it's thinning, thank goodness!

I haven't yet walked down the plage in my new dressing-gown declaiming like the prophet Jonah and looking for a whale to swallow me – but no doubt I shall do so.[1] I feel so terrifically prophetic when I wear it.

Well we shall see you soon – I'll let you know. We've got more yellow and white narcissus, but no marigolds – but the room smells as it did last time, of little jonquils.

Amitiés   DHL

4864. To P. R. Stephensen, [2 January 1929]
Text: MS Anon; Munro 299.

Hotel Beau Rivage. *Bandol*, Var.
2 Jan 1928

Dear Stephensen

Well where are you now and what are you doing? I am expecting to hear

[1] Cf. Letter 4842.

that you are coming this way and coming to see us. Let me know, because we *may* come to Nice for a few days, perhaps end of this week, or in next week. My wife's daughter Barbara Weekley is with us for a little while – and today Julian Huxley was here with his wife for the day – gone on to H. G.Wells' near Grasse.

Have you got any news? I have painted two water-colours which I like – one with two men and one a Leda.[1] But they are really studies for larger oils – if I only had room to paint. But I think we shall go to Spain when my wife's daughter returns to England.

Julian Huxley & Co. are starting a new non-fiction magazine – but alas, it's going to be more eye-wash and talking down to a penny-in-the-slot public.[2] I do hope you've got your dander up.

Jack Lindsay sent me his *Helen*[3] and *Dionysos* – but oh! if you Australians didn't do it all so easy! It's as if you could eat a thousand dinners without ever swallowing one of them or having anything on your stomachs: everything just tasty.

I have done two-thirds of my painting introd. – one of the best things I've done – corpses in it like currants in cake, Mr Clive Bell etc.[4]

Well turn up when you can – don't slip past!

DHL

4865. To Nancy Pearn, [5 January 1929]
Text: MS UT; Unpublished.

Hotel Beau Rivage, *Bandol*, Var.
Sat 5 Jan 1928

Dear Nancy Pearn

I will keep in mind the squibbs and the articles for the *Daily News*, and send you some soon. They may amuse me.

I will add on the 650 words to 'Do Women Change', and send direct to Rich.[5]

[1] *Renascence of Men* and *Leda*, in *The Paintings of D. H. Lawrence* (1929), plates 22 and 21.
[2] *The Realist: A Journal of Scientific Humanism*, ed. Archibald Church and Gerald Heard, an intellectual review which ran from April 1929–?January 1930. It included writings by Bertrand Russell, Richard Gregory, Herbert Read, Arnold Bennett, Rebecca West among others.
[3] *Helen Comes of Age* (1927), three verse plays by Jack Lindsay. (For *Dionysos*, see Letter 4842 and p. 94 n. 1.)
[4] Arthur Clive Heward Bell (1881–1964), Bloomsbury art-critic. When writing the 'Introduction to These Paintings' DHL particularly had in mind Bell's *Art* (1914). See *Letters*, ii. 435 n. 5.
[5] DHL sent 'Do Women Change?', originally intended for the *Evening News*, to Nancy Pearn on 8 November 1928 (*Letters*, vi. 610 and n. 3). A longer version appeared, as 'Women Don't

Did you get the article on 'New Mexico' which I posted you just before
Christmas – unregistered? If it is lost, it is my only copy – and such a good
article, ordered by the New York *Survey Graphic*. I *hope* it's not lost.

I want to send the poems today.

My wife's daughter is with us – and we had deep snow – but it is already
gone, and sunny again – but jolly cold for here!

Bonne année   D. H. Lawrence

Did you tell Powys Evans I wasn't near enough to draw? – I never heard of
him.[1]

4866. To Aldous Huxley, 6 January 1929
Text: Huxley 777.

Hôtel Beau Rivage, Bandol, Var.
Sunday, 6 Jan., 1929.

Dear Aldous, –

F[rieda]'s daughter, Barbara, is here, probably till next Saturday – 12th –
so if you are coming soon we shall wait for you, as it would be good to talk
things over, and if it's fine you may like to stay a few days peacefully. Let me
know, will you, and about reserving rooms – if you like two little ones or one
big, etc., etc. It actually snowed, and is beastly cold, but I think it's calming
down. Julian and Juliette called just for the day, and we had a quite jolly few
hours.

Barby got herself into a very depressed state in London. Really, the young
make me feel really low in spirits. I sort of want to go away to the farthest
corner of the earth and never say another word. A young man appeared from
California[2] – to admire me – and you know what a depressing effect admirers
have on me – I want to die. But yet he is really nice and is staying at the other
hotel – and is leaving in a day or two.

I haven't heard a sound from Sylvia Beach nor the Pegasus about *Lady C.* –
though Pino sent the Pegasus a copy of the book. So the Paris edition is still at

Change' in the *Sunday Dispatch*, 28 April 1929. Rich placed it with *Vanity Fair* (New York)
which also published the article in April (Roberts C185). Cf. Letter 4949.
[1] Powys Arthur Lenthall Evans (1889–), portrait painter; cartoonist ('Quiz') on *Saturday
Review*. (Nancy Pearn reported on 9 January (TMSC UT): 'we told Powys Evans that you
were too far away'.)
[2] Brewster Ghiselin (1903–), American poet and academic; he had just completed his MA at
Berkeley, California and was now a graduate student at Oxford. For his account of his visit to
DHL see Nehls, iii. 285–98. Ghiselin also wrote two other articles on DHL: 'D. H. Lawrence
and a New World', *Western Review*, xi (Spring 1947), 150–9 and 'D. H. Lawrence and the
Peacocks of Atrani', *Michigan Quarterly Review*, xiv (Spring 1975), 119–34. m. 1929, Olive
Franks.

a standstill – or rather, nothing done. But at the moment I feel limp, feel I only want to fly away and disappear from it all.

But come soon and let us at least have a few practical days here, before we start dashing off.

The cold here is so nasty – what must the north be like? No, Maria dear, one *must* live in the South.

DHL

4867. To Caresse Crosby, 7 January 1929
Text: MS SIU; Postmark, Ba[ndol] 7 1 29; Huxley 779.

Hotel Beau Rivage. Bandol, Var.
Monday 7 Jan 1929.

Dear Caresse Crosby

I only got your letter and the cheque for *Sun* – 4000 frs – this morning – seems to me quite a large sum, and I do hope you didn't swindle *yourselves*, which I feel is what happens. I do think it made a thrilling little book to look at: and if one gets a bit of fun out of a thing, that's what matters most.

I wrote to Harry Crosby when I got his letter from the ship – hope he had it – though there was nothing in it to interest you, except here we all are again in France!

I'm still waiting to see if I can find some decent bookseller or publisher to take charge of a Paris edition of my *Lady Chatterley*. I think I should like it done by the photography process – offset – as it saves all the bother of type. But I don't care. Tell me if you think of anybody, will you. I would pay for the production myself.

We had snow, and bitter cold, horrid – now it blows and is rather cold and rather horrid. I think we shall go to Spain in about a fortnight's time. What is your Black Sun going to bring forth now?

Sincerely   D. H. Lawrence

4868. To Juliette Huxley, 7 January 1929
Text: MS Huxley; Unpublished.

Hotel Beau Rivage. Bandol. Var.
7 Jan 1929 Monday

Dear Juliette

Sweet of you to send those apricots – how luscious they look! – You sound a bit désœuvrée[1] up there in Grasse – my, what a clicking of writing-machines – ugh! – We've decided not to come this week, because Barbara Weekley, my

---

[1] 'at a loose end'.

wife's daughter, is here, and leaves next Saturday – and it's only an added cold journey for her – so if we come it'll be next week, when we are alone again. When you are in London I wish you'd see Barbara sometimes – she's got into a real muddle with those studio blighters, and I'd like her to get a bit of a new connection – her address is

49 Harvard Road. Chiswick – W.

There is here too a very good-looking young man – Californian – studying at Oxford – and come to admire me. But admiration rather wilts me – that spiritual sort. Also today Stephensen comes, the man who will print my pictures – pity you aren't here, I think you'd like them – the young men, I mean – the second is Australian, from a big cattle-ranch.

Tell Madame Odette[1] there are no more big vases like yours,[2] but a couple of small ones for about 60 frs each – quite nice. If you want to give her a trifling gift, I'll give them you for her. I *shan't* give her my own one.

Frieda has gone out this very minute to buy the linen for your etruscan embroidery, and I shall draw it at once, and send it or bring it.

This is a poem I included in my *Pansies*, with the name quite safe – but if you don't like it I shan't send it to be printed.[3]

au revoir, then.   DHL

4869. To Charles Lahr, 7 January 1929
Text: MS UNYB; Postmark, Bandol 7–1 29; Unpublished.

Hotel Beau Rivage. Bandol. Var.
7 Jan. 1929

Dear Lahr

Just a word to thank you for the receipt for the *Lady C's*. Orioli says he's sent you 112 copies – and he's only about 16 left in Florence – which I told him to keep a while, as we *may* need them –

I've not got any further with my Paris edition, damn 'em all!

Today I'm sending my *Pansies* – pensées, those poems – to Curtis Brown – and telling them to let me have them back at once if there is any queasy

---

[1] Wells's mistress (cf. p. 104 n. 1).
[2] Lady Huxley remembered: 'These were West African "vases" with carving of heads & geometrical designs, in black ebony. DHL gave me one' (note accompanying DHL's letter). Ghiselin recalled: 'In a bookshop kept by a Frenchman who had lived in Africa, Lawrence had bought a ceremonial cup of dark wood embossed with a few Negro faces, the work of a Congo tribe, the Bakuba' (Nehls, iii. 293). See also Letter 4835, and 'Cups' and 'Bowls' in *Pansies* (*Complete Poems*, i. 427).
[3] 'Henriette' was published in *Pansies* (*Complete Poems*, i. 557). See Letter 4884 and Juliette Huxley, *Leaves of the Tulip Tree*, pp. 122–4.

feeling. I'm sick of peoples queasy feelings. I liked the *Natal Verses*,[1] as a Christmassy sort of thing. I often wonder if it wouldn't be possible to publish two or three poems on a sheet of paper and sell them for 2d or 3d. We might have done some of my *Pansies* that way – still might – those that have a sort of public or popular note. But frail poetry needs to be safe-guarded between covers. If I get into a wicked vein, I'll do something.

No, don't make money – it's the ruin of a man. I think the *New Coterie* was a bit sort of precious, else you wouldn't have lost on it.[2]

My, won't I have a time putting fig-leaves on Connie and Mellors!

Sincerely   D. H. Lawrence

I'll get Brigit Patmore to bring you some copies of *Lady C.* 1st edit. which Orioli sent her to store.

4870. To Curtis Brown, 7 January 1929
Text: MS UT; Huxley 778.

Hotel Beau Rivage. *Bandol.* Var.

7 Jan 1929

Dear C[urtis] B[rown]

All right, let the Gaige people do the first part of *Escaped Cock* if they want to, but the second half of the story is the best. So please put in a clause that I can re-print their half in six months time, because I shall put out the whole story, because I know it is good and I believe in it. If I let the first half go now alone, it is because it has already appeared, and it will make way for the second. So send me along the contract when you are ready – or if Mr Wells feels he would rather not have this story, I don't mind a bit.[3]

Sincerely   D. H. Lawrence

[1] To celebrate the birth of Lahr's daughter, Sheila, in March 1927, the novelist and biographer, Rupert Croft-Cooke (1903–79) wrote his (seriously intended but by no means solemn) *Natal Verses for Sheila*; 55 copies of the small booklet, dated 1927, were printed under the imprint of Lahr's wife, 'E. Archer, 68 Red Lion Square, W.C. 1'.
[2] Lahr edited and published the *New Coterie*, Summer 1925–Autumn 1927; 'a quarterly of literature and art', it ran for six numbers. DHL's *Sun* was first published in it, Autumn 1926 (Roberts C145).
[3] Donald Wells, a member of Curtis Brown's London office staff (see *Letters*, v. 348 and n. 1). Pollinger annotated Letter 4871 with a request referring to *The Escaped Cock*: 'C[urtis] B[rown] Will you ask Wells for this?'

4871. To Laurence Pollinger, 7 January 1929
Text: MS UT; Huxley 778–9.

Hotel Beau Rivage. *Bandol.* Var.

7 Jan 1929

Dear Pollinger

Today I am sending you a couple of MSS. of the poems: *Pansies.* They may displease you, so be prepared. If you offer them to Secker, and he doesn't care for them, I don't mind a bit if he doesn't publish them. I shall write him about it.

Did you get the six copies of the paper-bound *Lady C.*? If you did, and Secker sends round for two of them, please let him have them. Orioli wouldn't send them.

Heaven knows how I can write a 'story' of a thousand words or so, for that *Legion* book.[1] My stories won't come so small – and I have nothing to hand. Won't a couple of the *Pansies* do? Let me know, will you?

Hope we can get those books from the beastly little Boni.

Do get me the MS. of the *Escaped Cock* anyhow. It's one of my best stories. And Church doctrine teaches the resurrection of the body: and if that doesn't mean the whole man, what does it mean? and if man is whole without a woman – even Jesus – then I'm damned. No, you are wrong.

I'm not particularly anxious to publish a book of small prose pieces just now.[2] Surely it's not necessary!

We had snow here – and it's been bitter cold – now blowing black and horrid: what a way to start a year! Perhaps London is basking in sun and radiance. Let's hope so.

Sincerely   D. H. Lawrence

4872. To Martin Secker, 7 January 1929
Text: MS UInd; Postmark, Ba[ndol] 7–1 29; Secker 114.

Hotel Beau Rivage. Bandol. Var.

7 Jan 1929

Dear Secker

Today I am sending to Pollinger the MS. of my new book of poems *Pansies* – really pensées. They are more thoughts than poems, and very modern, written for the young, and quite free-spoken. You may just dislike them as you disliked *Lady C.* If so, don't hesitate to say so. I should hate you to

[1] Cf. Letter 4833 and p. 85 n. 1. DHL did not contribute to the *Legion Book*; poems from *Pansies*, in any case, would have been out of tune with other contributions.
[2] The first reference to what became *Assorted Articles*, published posthumously in April 1930 (Roberts A53). See also Letters 5468 and 5477.

publish them if you didn't like them. – If you did publish them, I should like just a limited edition of 500 or so, signed at a guinea or thereabouts, then a quite cheap edition, say 2/6, because I should like them to be easily accessible to poorer people. – But as I say, don't touch them if you don't like them.

The second edit. of *Lady C.* is sold, but I asked Orioli to send six copies to Pollinger to hold, and if Pollinger has them, he will let you have a couple – I asked him – if you will please *send* for them.

Barby here since last Wed. – not in a very good state. She's got herself rather into a mess with those studio blighters. It's rather for her and the young like her that I did the pansies. She stays, I think, till next Sat. – and then Maria and Aldous Huxley will probably be here for a week or so – so I expect we are held for another fortnight. Then really I want to go to Spain –

Frieda says thanks for *Grisha* – it is almost a good book – but there is a certain mealy-mouthedness about modern Germans, which I don't like – a certain falseness.[1]

I am sending you Harington's *Ajax* – quite amusing, really – and very nicely done, I think.[2] But if you do the pansies, I wish you would do a fat little book with real black print – I am so tired of big sprawling books, rather pale, like the Fanfrolicos and most of these editions de luxe.

We had snow here – lasted two days on the hills – and bitter cold and horrid – it's rather horrid even now, windy and grey, but getting warmer. No luck for Barby.

DHL

4873. To Nancy Pearn, 11 January 1929
Text: MS UT; Huxley 780.

Hotel Beau Rivage. *Bandol.* Var
Friday 11. Jan 1929

Dear Nancy Pearn

Herewith I return the article on myself.[3] It seems all right – clever girl! – I sent Pollinger two MSS. of the *Pansies*. When you read them you will see how they are the same as this article. Pazienza!

Haven't you received the MS. of the article on 'New Mexico', sent two weeks ago? Alas, if it's lost![4]

[1] *The Case of Sergeant Grischa* by Arnold Zweig, published by Secker in November 1928.
[2] Cf. Letter 4834 and n. 4. The book was inscribed by DHL: 'to Martin Secker from D. H. Lawrence. New Year 1929'.
[3] Cf. Letter 4810 and p. 65 n. 1. According to a note probably by Nancy Pearn's assistant on the MS, DHL was returning 'proofs' of the article.
[4] Another annotation reads: 'Crossed ours of 9th.'

I've been so busy doing a long introduc. to my vol. of pictures, I've had no time to think of articles – but hope to be clear in a day or two. – Meanwhile don't take fright at the *Pansies* – they're an all right.

Ever   DHL

4874. To Giuseppe Orioli, 11 January 1929
Text: MS UCLA; Unpublished.

Hotel Beau Rivage. Bandol. Var. France.

11 Jan 1929

Dear Pino

I've been a long time writing, but we've had various people here – Barbara and the Julian Huxleys and a young Californian man from Oxford. Barbara leaves tomorrow for London – the Californian goes next week – and then I think Maria and Aldous come: – so I expect we'll be here at least another two weeks. – Then Stephensen of the Fanfrolico came – and I think they'll publish my pictures at ten guineas a time – quite soon – March.

I did a black-and-white frontispiece for *Venus in the Kitchen,*[1] and will send it along, but I can't make up my mind if I like it – so if you have any doubts, *please* just burn it. I'll send it along inside a Fanfrolico book.

About *Lady C.* – Lahr has paid into my bank ninety guineas for ninety copies of the 2nd Edit – I shall ask Mrs Patmore to let him have *her* copies of the 1st edition, to hold. *How many copies have you sent her?*

V. H. Collins sent the cheque for his copy – and my sisters have theirs safely. But I have no word from Chas Wilson (Willington) – and you said you sent his copy (of 2nd) on Dec 17 – also Pollinger apparently has not received his six copies of the 2nd – as he writes asking me for three copies. He has sold the first two. – *Did you send those six?* I want to keep track of everything: I especially want to know if anything goes lost.

Did you send out invoices to people who have not paid? Particularly there is *Miller & Gill seven* copies: *Mrs Varda – 6? – Davis. 6   Glaisher 2.*[2] – Do let me know if you have written them – because Enid would go to some, and Stephensen will tackle Miller & Gill, and Kot. will go to others. I want to make them all pay. Why let them cheat us?

[1] *Venus in the Kitchen* was a collection of supposedly aphrodisiac recipes by Norman Douglas. It was published by Heinemann in 1952 (Roberts B56), with the frontispiece DHL had produced in colour when he wrote Letter 4885.

[2] Miller & Gill were London booksellers; Mrs Varda, a friend of Orioli, operated the Varda Bookshop (*Letters*, vi. 512); J. I. Davis was Orioli's partner at 30 Museum Street, London; probably Henry J. Glaisher, 55 Wigmore Street, London W1, whose cheque for £3.8.0 appears in DHL's 'Memoranda' (MS NWU) for 19 January 1929. Glaisher, presumably a bookseller, was also listed in the *English Catalogue of Books* (1929) as a publisher.

I have no word from Sylvia Beach at all! – has she acknowledged receipt of copies? And I have no word from the Pegasus Press either – damn them both. We had beastly weather here – but it's better. Hope all goes well. I'll send the Venus tossing the pancake!

DHL

4875. To S. S. Koteliansky, 11 January 1929
Text: MS BL; Postmark, Ban[dol] 12–1[...]; Moore 1117–18.

Hotel Beau Rivage – *Bandol.* Var
Friday 11 Jan 1929

My dear Kot

Pollinger says he wants more copies of the first edition – will you let him have whatever he wants – and if you like, Orioli will always send you further copies to make up your twenty-five. He sent some to Mrs Patmore – Brigit – but I don't know if she's very stable – may go away anywhere – so I think I'll ask her to let Lahr have them to hold. They are only about ten. Then I'll get my sister to have twenty. I had to send them the book at last. Ada – in Ripley – has read it, and says she feels I've always hidden part of myself from her. If people refuse to see, what can one do?

Lahr has paid into my bank ninety guineas for 90 copies of the second edit. I think Orioli sent him in all 112 – but O. is a bit vague. There are only 18 copies or so left – and I want to keep a few.

Stephensen was here again – of the Fanfrolico and he seems to be going ahead with my pictures. He is combining with Edward Goldston. There will be no Lindsay – either father or son – in the Mandrake Press. – I have written the introduction – about 10,000 words – slain Clive Bell. I got Fry's *Cézanne* and Bell's *Art* from Bumpus, but no invoice.[1] I wish they'd send it at once, before we leave. What a fool Clive Bell is!

Did you see Pollinger, and what did you think of him?

Barbara Weekley leaves tomorrow for London. She's got herself into a nasty state with those messy second-rate Studio crowd really spoilt herself. Wish she'd get out of it.

I expect we shall stay here another two weeks, as Aldous and Maria are probably coming for a bit, on their way to Italy. – But there's no news. – I forgot to mention Rozanov to Stephensen – but he's only just got back to London – so let him get started with his Mandrake – he'd do it in that press.[2]

DHL

---

[1] Cf. Letters 4830 and n. 5, 4864 and n. 4. J. & E. Bumpus Ltd was a well-known bookseller–publisher in Oxford Street, London.
[2] Cf. Letter 4830 and n. 3.

4876. To Brigit Patmore, 11 January 1929
Text: MS SIU; Moore, *Intelligent Heart* 397.

Hotel Beau Rivage. *Bandol.* Var. France

11 Jan 1929

Dear Brigit

Not heard from you for ages – have you evanesced? Not a Christmas word, not a New Year's note was heard from you![1] Perhaps you were too busy festivating. Anyhow I hope that's it.

We are still here. My wife's daughter Barbara leaves tomorrow for Paris – by your 7.0 a.m. train – do you remember? She has got herself into a very nasty state with those 2nd rate studio-arty people, and now can't get out of it. Damn bohemia, it always gets itself on the brain!

We were in Toulon yesterday – very sunny on the port, same as ever – very cold in the back streets – but we found a *good* tea-room, take you there next time you're in.

Orioli said he'd started sending you copies of *Lady C.* I hope they've arrived safely. I told him not to send more than a dozen. Now a bookseller wants to take them over – Charles Lahr, of 68 Red Lion Street. Holborn. If I tell him to fetch them from you next week, will you give them him. I think he's a nice man.

No news here – except my pictures are probably going to be reproduced in a book at ten guineas a time. I hear you whistle!

It was a very sunny day, and we went out this afternoon on the sea in a motor-boat! When we were getting way out beyond the lighthouse, I made the man turn round, because I knew we should see the spectre of Port Cros in the distance.

Brigit, where art thou?[2]

DHL

4877. To Ada Clarke, 11 January 1929
Text: MS Clarke: Postmark, B[andol] [...] –1 29; cited in Lawrence–Gelder 187–8.

Hotel Beau Rivage, *Bandol.* Var

11 Jan 1929

My dear Sister

Here we still are – Barby Weekley has been here about ten days – she leaves tomorrow, going home. She has got herself into a nasty state of nerves and self-consciousness in that second-rate arty crowd of hers – just got herself on

[1] Cf. 'Not a drum was heard, not a funeral note ...', Charles Wolfe (1791–1823), *The Burial of Sir John Moore at Corunna* (1817), l. 1.
[2] Cf. 'Alice, where art thou?', song by Alfred Bunn (1796?–1860).

the brain, and now can't get free of herself – though she'd very much like to.[1] The beastly selfish *self-consciousness* of the young – makes them no fun to have around. I hope she'll get out of it. You say you think I've hidden some part of myself from you. Not at all. I am always the same. But there is something you just refuse to see and refuse to accept in me. You insisted on a certain idealisation, and there it was. – It's just the same thing makes you thankful Peggy isn't going to read *Lady C.* Little prigs like Peg, at her age ought to be made to read *Lady C* aloud and in company – make them get over some of their priggishness and self-conceit. And if they are going to have miscarriages, like Sarah-Ann's girl,[2] at least they'll have them more open-mindedly. All this hush-hush! stuff is just filthy. Do you think people don't *have* any private thoughts? Of course they do. Much better the thing should be open. – I havent yet heard if Orioli has started to send you any copies to hold – I didn't tell him definitely. But I will, if it is the same to you. – We shall stay a bit longer here because the Huxleys will probably be staying with us, on their way to Italy. – We have a young man, Californian, staying now – nice young fellow. – Look out in next week's *Sunday Despatch* for an article on how I feel about myself.[3] I feel much more strongly, really. – We had snow and frost – horrid – but now it's sunny and warm again, though the mountains behind are all covered deep in snow. We went quite a long way out on the sea in a motor-boat this afternoon – bright, but a chill little wind. I'll really send some books.

love   DHL

I shall send Jack's African music by the Californian – he's safer.

4878. To Emily King, 11 January 1929

Text: MS Lazarus; Postmark, [Ban]dol 11–1 29; Moore 1116.

Hotel Beau Rivage. Bandol. Var, France
11 Jan 1929

My dear Pamela

We've been full up lately with friends coming and going. Barby Weekley has been here ten days – leaves tomorrow for Paris. She's got herself into a disagreeable half-hysterical state messing around at those studio parties in London and having all her own way with everything, and now she can't get out of it. No joke, I tell you. However, she's not really my responsibility. – Then we have a young Californian, studying at Oxford, staying till next week. Then I think the Huxleys come on their way to Italy, so we shall be kept here

---

[1] to.] too.
[2] Sarah Ann Wrath (1882–1972), Sam King's sister. Her daughter was Dorothy Atkin (b. 1905).
[3] Cf. p. 65 n. 1.

for a bit. I don't mind, it is sunny and pleasant, if not exciting – but I don't want excitement. – New Year came in with a crash of storm, then we had snow and ice, unheard of here – and the mountains behind are still white with snow, the wind bites. But the sun blazes and is warm all day. I lie in bed and watch him rise red from the sea, and I must say I think the sun is more important than most things, particularly casual people. – Yesterday we went to Toulon in the bus – a port, all sailors and cats and queer people – not unattractive: and this afternoon we went out on the sea in a motor-boat, the four of us – a blue sea, bright sun, but a cold little tiny wind – and I had no idea the mountains behind us were so deep in snow, a long low range of white. – Stephensen was here again about my pictures – I think they will reproduce them all in a biggish book at ten guineas each, and hold the exhibition exactly when the book comes out, in March. They will print only 500 copies at 10 guineas a copy. But of course I shall give you one. I shan't make a great deal out of it myself.

We had a letter from Frau Trachsel, and she says they are deep in snow, and about fifty English people in Gsteig, in the hotels, for ski-ing.

Has Sam taken stock yet? and how is it?

love!   DHL

4879. To Rhys Davies, 11 January 1929
Text: TMSC NWU; Huxley 780–1.

Hotel Beau Rivage, Bandol, Var.
11 Jan. 1929.

Dear Davies,

Barbara wouldn't come to Nice after all – just wouldn't – said it was too far. She leaves tomorrow for Paris. Sometime next week I expect the Huxleys will appear – Aldous and wife. Stephensen came, and stirred us all up as usual. But I thought he seemed a bit more down-hearted than the first time. He is rushing back to London to work. I think they'll do my pictures all right – and he liked the *Pansies*, was pining to take a pamphlet or broadside from them, for the working-classes. He told me you were doing a Swan story.[1] You must show it me – and I can tell Curtis Brown's people if I think it's a good one for *limited edition* publication. And how's the novel going?

We were in Toulon yesterday – drank coffee and rum on the port the same, and went to the same tea-place after – thought of you.

I'll let you know if plans mature at all. We've a young Californian friend staying here now – all a bit of a whirl; not the peaceful Bandol of before

---

[1] 'Interlude'. See Letter 4906.

Christmas at all. We went way out on the sea on a motor-boat this afternoon
– warm sun, cold wind – such snowy mountains at the back.

Regards from us both.   DHL

4880. To Edward Dahlberg, 11 January 1929
Text: MS UTul; Postmark, [Band]ol [. . .]; Moore 1115–16.

Hotel Beau Rivage, Bandol. Var. France.

11 Jan 1929

Dear Dahlberg

I enclose a letter to George Oppenheimer of the Viking Press,[1] and if you
send it him and your MS. he'll anyhow read the thing properly: your book I
mean.

If you feel you'll go on writing, and producing things, then an agent is
useful – so think twice. I give you a card to L. E. Pollinger of Curtis Brown
Ltd. 6 Henrietta St. Covent Garden – and he'll give you an appointment if
you send it.[2] He manages novels, with special attention to the American
side.

What you will do in your private life, I don't know. But if you are going to
write, manage the business end of it as sensibly as you can. Many young men
make their real mess there. What I like about your novel is that it does not
whine and doesn't look to other people for help. The individuals remain on
their own, and that is so much the best. It's up to you to use your wits and
your energies *not* to go hungry. I have lived myself on next to nothing, for
years, yet I never went hungry, because I had something better to do with
myself. And it's very bad to get relying on other people.

None of this, of course, refers to your novel – there one does need letters of
introduction and all that, because there's such a mechanism of publishing.
But don't get vague and wishy-washy about your private affairs – it's so
weakening.

Sincerely   D. H. Lawrence

---

[1] Enclosure missing.
[2] The card survives at UTul; it is inscribed (above and below DHL's printed name): 'To Mr.
L. E. Pollinger Curtis Brown Ltd., W.C.2.   to introduce Mr Edward Dahlberg'.

4881. To Curtis Brown, 12 January 1929
Text: MS UT; Unpublished.

Hotel Beau Rivage, *Bandol.* Var. France
12 Jan. 1929

Dear C[urtis] B[rown]

The agreement for the *Escaped Cock* just come. I want to make one little stipulation – that is, that on the title page they shall print:

'*The Escaped Cock*
Part One.'

and at the end they shall put:

'*End of Part One of The Escaped Cock*'

That makes my way clear for later on. That is only fair all round. – Let me know, and I'll send contract.

Today I have the bomb-letter about the income tax. Well, if they're going to back-charge at the rate of £125 a year, this child will have to go bankrupt or to prison or heaven or somewhere. Meanwhile the only thing to do is to become a citizen of the Republic of Liberia.

Yrs   DHL

4882. To Laurence Pollinger, 12 January 1929
Text: MS UT; Unpublished.

Hotel Beau Rivage. *Bandol*, Var.
12 Jan 1929

Dear Pollinger

I enclose letter from Viking Press. Meanwhile I have heard nothing from Seltzer about rights of *Birds Beasts and Flowers* and the Kennerley business – but I suppose Rich is attending to that.[1] – I suppose I need not reply to this man Best?[2]

P. R. Stephensen, of the Fanfrolico Press, was here again arranging about my pictures. He is starting a new press – Mandrake – with Edward Goldston – and he wants to reproduce all my pictures in colour, and bring out 500 copies *Paintings of D.H.L.* – at ten guineas a time – give me 10% – and £250 down. That was his scheme. I think they'll do it. I have written an introduction about 10,000 words – so it makes it a book. They say they will go ahead at once, and produce the book in March – have exhibition at same time. I am thinking, they might pay the £250 down for rights to reproduce the pictures – and then give me 5% royalty. So I escape paying the govt. tax on

---

[1] See Letter 4856.
[2] Marshall Ayres Best (1901–) joined Viking Press in 1925; he became director and company secretary in 1927, later general manager and president. His letter to DHL is missing.

the money for the pictures – which is in no way a royalty. Dont forget, later. I shall send you the MS. of the introduction next week, and you can then deal with Stephensen when he's ready. He's an Australian – and I like him – he's got energy, and he seems to me straight – though people say Fanfrolico paid dilatorily.

I wrote Koteliansky about the copies of *Lady C.* – Orioli is supposed to have sent you six of the paper-bound edition – God knows if he did. Anyhow he's only got about twenty left. – Thanks so much for getting the books home – Every bullet has its billet.[1] – Do I understand you sold the three copies Koteliansky left you, and for 12 gns? – that is, after Michael Joseph's copy? Tell me please, because I have to give Orioli his share.

Wonder how you'll like the *Pansies*. They'll go all right. The world is moving that way. Look at the article N[ancy] P[earn] has put over the *Sunday Despatch* for next week – they'd never have published it a year ago – there is something happening internally about financial policy and political policy.

ever DHL

4883. To Sylvia Beach, 12 January 1929
Text: MS PU; Postmark, Bandol 12–1 29; Unpublished.

Hotel Beau Rivage, *Bandol*. Var
Saturday 12 Jan. 1929

Dear Miss Beach

Your card just come. Didn't you get my letter of Decem. 24th – in which I acknowledged your cheque? – Orioli sent you two copies of the first edition a day or two after sending the others – that must be two weeks ago, nearly. It is most queer if they are lost, as they were registered – and they will be the *only* copies that have been lost in Europe. Will you please let Orioli know at once, so that he can make enquiries. – About the paper-covered copies, I am afraid there are none left – or not more than fifteen, and I need to keep one or two. England ordered at once more than we could supply.

In my letter of Decem. 24 I asked you if you would attend to the issuing and distributing of a Paris edition, if I paid for the production. As you did not answer, I concluded you had no inclination to do so – but in case you did not get my letter, I repeat what I said there. – I should like to bring out an edition of 3000 or so, printed in France, preferably by the photographic process – 'offset.' The production would be at my charge – but I do want a reliable bookseller or publisher. – The book has not been suppressed either in England or U.S.A. – and so far, in England I have not lost a copy – all the copies

---

[1] English proverb (see *Oxford Book of English Proverbs*, ed. F. P. Wilson, 3rd edn, 1970, p. 90).

of the second edition, and ten of the first, went in quite safely since Christmas. Only in U. S. A. customs officials seize copies – so I send none there.

For the copies of the 2nd edit., pay me or Orioli, just as you like. And let me have a line, will you please – If you don't want to be bothered handling the book, I shall understand perfectly.

Yours Sincerely   D. H. Lawrence

4884. To Juliette Huxley, [12 January 1929]
Text: MS Huxley; Unpublished.

Hotel Beau Rivage, Bandol, Var
Saturday

Dear Juliette

Just got your letter – I doubt we shan't get to Nice by Monday – Barbara has gone off, and we are taking breath. Why don't you stop off a night here on your way back, since you are going so soon? – Maria says she and Aldous may arrive on 17th., to stay a little while – that's next Thursday. But probably they'll be a bit later. You'd better stop off here, it looks as if we shan't get to Nice. – The African vases were two little ones 100 frs each and a bigger one 150 frs – so I got the bigger one, though it has no faces on it. And a friend who is here – young Californian man – bought the two little ones. – I'll send all on Monday – that is vase and embroidery – no time for post now. – I enclose the poem anyhow. – No, I've never been to those dead hill-top villages – I find the half-dead half-way-down ones like Bormes bad enough – depressing.[1] – I like Odette for tackling Jix[2] – what a pity she couldn't actually drop him down a nice little well of loneliness – miserable mongrel he is! It would have to be a dirty well that would accept him.

Belle cose!   DHL

Henriette

Oh Henriette
I remember yet
how cross you were

[1] H. G. Wells had taken the Huxleys from Grasse to the famous ruined hill-town of Les Baux (Juliette Huxley, *Leaves of the Tulip Tree*, p. 113); Bormes is 14 miles e.n.e. of Hyères.

[2] Sir William Joynson Hicks ('Jix') (1865–1932), Home Secretary 1924–9, 1st Viscount Brentford 1929, was a religious zealot who waged a campaign against what he considered pornography. *The Times*, 16 October 1928, reported him as saying: 'It may possibly be in the near future I shall have to deal with immoral and disgusting books ... There must be some limit to the freedom of what a man may write or speak in this great country of ours.' The titles of books which came into this category and, if published abroad, were seized on entry to the country, were never declared; DHL clearly suspected that *The Well of Loneliness* was among them. The letter following reveals comparable anxieties about *Lady Chatterley's Lover*.

over Lady C.,
how you hated her
and detested me.

But now you see
you don't mind a bit,
you've got used to it
and you feel more free.

And now you know
how good we were
up there in the snow
with Lady C.,
though you hated her
at the first go.

Yet now you can see
how she set us free
to laugh and to be
ourselves, and we
were happy, weren't we,
up there in the snow
with the world below.

So now, when you say
your prayers at night
you should softly pray:
Dear Lord of delight
may I be Jane
tonight, profane
but sweet in your sight,
though last night I was Mary.

You said I might
dear Lord of right
be so contrary.
So may I be Jane
tonight, and refrain
from being Mary?

4885. To Giuseppe Orioli, 14 January 1929
Text: MS UCLA; Unpublished.

Hotel Beau Rivage. *Bandol.* Var

14 Jan 1929

Dear Pino

Your letter this morning – I also am feeling very worried about *Lady C.* in England. Also Sylvia Beach says she has *not* received her two copies of the 1st. edition – whereas she received all the copies of the 2nd edition, and has sold them. I have not heard from Wilson, I have not heard from Mrs Patmore, and when Pollinger wrote he had not received the six copies of 2nd edit. – I have also heard nothing new from Lahr, since I wrote you. – And I have heard nothing from the Pegasus. So altogether it looks a bit black. – I am sorry Douglas posted those limericks – that will bring the hounds down on all Florence books – because of course everybody in London knows about the limericks and where they were done. Douglas should have kept them out of the post. Now I'm afraid they'll stop us. – I had a letter from Kot and he did not mention his copy of 2nd edit – so fear he hasn't got it.

I should take no further notice of that F. S. Ross – the old fool.[1]

I had a note from the post-office here about the money, but nothing paid yet. Perhaps I shall see the names of senders when they bring the money and the papers to sign.

Send me Davis' address in New York, I must write and thank him, I suppose. Did you see the article he put in the *N. York Sun* about your shop etc – and the two photos of me?[2] Yes, do keep the photographs till I want them (!)

I will send you the *Venus* today – I changed her and did her at the oven, just taking out the pie. I used two colours, grey and red, but probably the thing would come out all right in one colour – just black and white.[3]

Barbara has gone back to London. – We are expecting Aldous and Maria this week-end, to stay perhaps a week. Then we shall prepare to move.

I send you the list of unpaid. They are not very many – but they should pay.

If London is stopping all copies, we must send no more. What a curse! But lucky it didn't happen sooner!

---

[1] Unidentified.

[2] Robert Hobart Davis (1869–1942), American writer, editor and photographer. Although he was a member of the executive board of the *New York Sun* and a world correspondent and columnist for that paper, the piece DHL refers to appeared in the *New York Times Book Review*, 23 December 1928 (see Nehls, iii. 209–12). One of the photographs is reproduced in *Letters*, vi.

[3] Cf. Letter 4874 and n. 1.

Did you hear that *Jackson* – our friend Jackson – has got to smuggle the ten copies in to Holliday.[1] I hope *they* get stolen.

love from both.   DHL

4886. To P. R. Stephensen, 14 January 1929
Text: MS Anon; Munro 300.

Hotel Beau Rivage, *Bandol.* Var, France
14 Jan 1929

Dear Stephensen

Thanks for yours and the cheque – glad you are happily busy, and in good hopes – shall look forward to *proofs.* Am sending you here a design for title-page – use it or not, just as you like – it seems to me rather amusing, but Ghiselin, the Californian whom you saw here, doesn't care for it.[2] I am also sending MS. of 'Introduction' today to Curtis Brown to be typed. Have you shown *Leda* and the other paintings to Dorothy Warren?[3] – have you traced all the complete 24 – or was it 25? – no, 24. – And are you *sure* you want to print *Leda* and *Dandelions?* I don't mind if you leave them out.[4]

No cry as yet from my agents over *Pansies* – nor outcry either. – Barbara is back in London – Ghiselin leaves Wed. – Huxleys due to arrive Thursday – meanwhile a *cold* wind!!

D. H. Lawrence

Regards to Lindsay.[5]

---

[1] Cf. Letter 4773 and n. 2.
[2] With reference to 11 January 1929 Ghiselin recalled that DHL

> showed me a black and white drawing he had been doing of a nude man and woman in a kind of complicated electric field, a drawing now reproduced in his book of paintings. In it he had tried to show the special rhythms of the different parts of the body, the head, the breast, the belly, the loins, as they subsisted in themselves and in a pattern of relations. (Nehls, iii. 295–6)

> Stephensen used this drawing as an end-piece above the colophon, rather than on the title page.

[3] When Stephensen returned to England he had taken through customs *Accident in a Mine, Leda* and *Renascence of Men.*
[4] Stephensen omitted *Dandelions*; it was first reproduced in Keith Sagar, 'Six Paintings by D. H. Lawrence', *Words International,* i (November 1987), 30.
[5] The list of pictures was enclosed with this letter; it provided Stephensen with a checklist of the paintings he should have traced by 14 January. After DHL's signature Stephensen added the names of three paintings, two of which were brought to England by Ada Clarke on 22 February: *Spring* and *Summer Dawn*; the third was *Singing of Swans.*

Pictures sent to Dorothy Warren
large oils.   1. *Boccaccio Story*
                 2. *A Holy Family*
                 3. *Red Willow Trees*
                 4. *Fight with an Amazon*
                 5. *Resurrection*
                 6. *Flight back into Paradise*
                 7. *Fauns and Nymphs*
smaller oils.   1. *Family on a Verandah*
                 2. *Close-up (kiss)*
                 3. *Finding of Moses*
                 4. *Dance-Sketch*
                 5. *Rape of the Sabine Women*
                 6. *Contadini*
                 7. *North Sea*
                 8. *Accident in a Mine* (given to Stephensen)
water colours 1. *Throwing back the apple*
                 2. *Mango Tree*
                 3. *The Lizard*
                 4. *Fire-dance*
                 5. *Under the Hay-stack*
                 6. *Yawning*
                 7. *Dandelions*
                 8. *Leda* (given to Stephensen)
                 9. *Renascence of men* ("   "   ")

                                               D. H. Lawrence

4887. To Laurence Pollinger, 14 January 1929
Text: MS UT; Unpublished.

                                Hotel Beau Rivage, *Bandol.* Var. France
                                                      14 Jan 1929.
Dear Pollinger

I am sending you MS. of my 'Introduction to the Paintings'. Will you please have it typed, two copies, and please send me the typescript to revise, and give Miss Pearn the orig. MS. to keep for me along with the others.

I hope you got the *Pansies* all right. And also that you got the six copies of the paper-cover edition of *Lady C.* which Orioli *did* send off some little time ago. Am a bit anxious about these last.

Don't please collect a book of my short stories this spring – not good enough.

                                                      DHL

4888. To Giuseppe Orioli, [15? January 1929]
Text: MS UCLA; Unpublished.

[Hotel Beau Rivage, Bandol, Var.]
[15? January 1929]

Dear Pino

Will you please answer this man and tell him if his copy was sent off – if it was sent to him to U.S.A. and is lost, then it's his funeral.[1]

DHL

I just got a guinea from that man Charles Wilson (Durham). – he did receive his copy of the 2nd edit.

4889. To Hon. Dorothy Brett, 16 January 1929
Text: MS UCin; Postmark, Bandol 16[...]29; Peter L. Irvine and Anne Kiley, eds., 'D. H. Lawrence and Frieda Lawrence: Letters to Dorothy Brett', *DHL Review*, ix (Spring 1976), 91–3.

Hotel Beau Rivage. Bandol, Var
16 Jan. 1929

Dear Brett

I'm glad you have seen Mrs Chambers – I can just imagine what she's like, Spanish and Indian. I'm afraid she burns herself up, not conserving herself. The husband I imagine a bit like most men connected with literature, but not in themselves artists. Still, I don't know, of course.

We are still here – Barby Weekley has just gone back to London – and a nice young Californian – man – just gone back to Oxford. Now we are expecting Aldous and Maria, on their way to Italy. – I may be kept in France a bit, because I want to produce another and cheaper edition of *Lady C.* here –

---

[1] P. Beaumont Wadsworth (later to edit DHL's *Prelude*, Roberts A85) wrote from Berlin; his undated letter reads as follows:

Dear Mr. Lawrence: –

I hate to trouble you, but I am afraid that I cannot do otherwise in this matter.

Last year, while living in New York, I got one of the small prospectuses referring to "Lady Chatterley's Lover", which came to me via Miss Low and Miss Dorothy Richardson. On May 17th. I sent an international money order from the Post Office of Stapleton, Staten Island, New York. U.S.A., for $10 addressed to you care of the man in Florence. Since that day I have not heard a word of the matter. While I was in New York I decided that the book was a long time being published, but on returning to England this winter I find otherwise.

Could you let me know whether the money order was ever received. If not I must make a claim in New York. Or was the book sent to me. As I am quite poor I cannot face the loss of two pounds, with the possibility of even selling the book at a higher rate, at the moment. Also, I want to read the book having been one of your most ardent admirers since 1917. The number of the money order is 11711.

I should be awfully glad if you can give me some information about the whole matter.

Yours very sincerely,

at about 100 frs – or 16/6 – or four dollars. I could sell a lot, if only I could find someone to take charge of it: which I can't.

Thrilling to see the little notice of your picture-show – that must be fun – and I do hope you'll sell some.[1] I wonder what prices you are putting on. I shall put mine pretty stiff £500. – $2,500 – for the big ones. – Mine are going to be reproduced, all in colour, in a book – 24 of them – as well done as possible, pretty *de luxe*: and 500 copies only, at £10. or $50.00 a copy. There'll be 250 copies for America – sounds rather thrilling, don't you think. They want to have the book out in March, and the show in Dorothy Warren's gallery simultaneous. I have written a long essay on painting for a foreword, and I think it's good. – Now the difficulty again will be the customs. They *ought* not to consider any of the paintings improper, even the U. S. Customs ought not to consider them improper. But of course my reputation is so bad, they'll probably act mean as usual. I wish there was some way of getting that arranged. If the customs people don't act mean, they can let the book straight in – and if only one could get hold of the right person, and know the ropes, it could be arranged all right. You might talk to Stieglitz and O'Keefe about it – and to Maria Cristina Chambers. Because of course if that book gets confiscated it's a great loss – a ten guinea book – which will cost even two or three guineas to produce, each copy. – Of course I am not paying for it – I merely get a ten per-cent royalty. But I must do what I can for it.

I think we really may come to America at[2] end of March – come by a Dollar boat – it would be fun! and Mabel would still be there, and you would have the ranch ready. And though my cough is still tiresome, I myself am really a lot better this winter, you'd almost find me my usual self. Though of course I can't do violent or exhausting things. But it seems to me we none of us get tougher – you don't sound so well, there in New York. It's a trying moment all round.

I had a letter from Bynner, also in New York, and also been ill. He wrote very nicely.[3]

I'm sure you'll be glad to go back to Taos and the ranch, and have the space again, and the horses. Hope you can have Maria Cristina Chambers too, if you get on well together. You won't be so isolated.

---

[1] Brett had written to Johnson, 24 November 1928, to explain that Stieglitz could not accommodate her exhibition: 'my pictures all at Rehr's gallery', the Marie Sterner Gallery (Hignett, *Brett*, p. 201). The notice of her exhibition has not been traced. Brett failed to sell a single painting.

[2] at] in

[3] Harold ('Hal') Witter Bynner (1881–1968), American poet; friend of the Lawrences from the New Mexico years (cf. *Letters*, iv. 316 n. 4). His account of his relationship with DHL was published as *Journey with Genius* (New York, 1951).

Write to me about your show, I very much want to know how it goes. –
And ask Stieglitz about my book of paintings. One has to keep on struggling.

DHL

4890. To Max Mohr, 17 January 1929
Text: MS HMohr; Mohr 34.

Hotel Beau Rivage. *Bandol*, Var. France
17 Jan 1929

Dear Max Mohr

We are still here, and I should have written before, but waited to be sure
when we are leaving. But even now I am not sure – I suppose we shall be here
ten days longer at least, because I am trying to arrange a Paris edition of *Lady
C.* – in English, of course, not translation.

I had a letter from Kippenberg saying the Insel Verlag do *not* wish to
publish a translation of *Lady C.*, because they are afraid of prosecution by the
law – 'in spite of the high literary quality of the book.'[1] – So that's that! We
shall have to find some other publisher, perhaps the Swiss you mentioned.

I expect it is pretty cold now in Wolfsgrube, as even here the mistral wind
is blowing, and is bitter. But the sun is very bright and very warm, the sea all
running with light.

How is your novel? – is it out yet and prospering? I hope anyhow it will
make you good money.

Do you care about American books? If so I will send you a great fat book
called *The American Caravan*, which is a sort of literary year-book.[2] I think it's
pretty awful – and of course it's a *Jewish* selection. It is supposed to represent
Amer. literature for 1927 and 1928.

Many greetings to you all   D. H. Lawrence

---

[1] Kippenberg's last extant letter to DHL, 7 January 1929 (TMSC SVerlag), reads as follows, in
translation:

Dear Mr Lawrence!

Thank you very much for your kind letter of New Year's Eve and for your proposal to have a
private edition of your novel "Lady Chatterley's Lover" appear from the Insel-Verlag. I very
much regret to have to tell you, however, that this is impossible for me. I have read the novel:
but I am firmly convinced that a German edition, the high literary quality of the book
notwithstanding, would be confiscated because of the present German laws and the publisher
would be held responsible. It does not make any difference, for that matter, whether the book is
generally for sale or is only produced and sold as a private edition.

I am very sorry to have to give you this reply, but I do it on the basis of a firm conviction and
after consulting a person who seems to me competent in these matters …

[2] *The Second American Caravan: A Yearbook of American Literature*, ed. Van Wyck Brooks *et al.*
2nd issue (New York, 1928).

4891. To Laurence Pollinger, 18 January 1929
Text: MS UT; Unpublished.

Hotel Beau Rivage. *Bandol,* Var
Friday 18 Jan 1929

Dear Pollinger

You should have the two copies of *Pansies.* They were sent from Bandol on Jan. 7th, as *papiers d'affaires*[1] – registered number 587. If they haven't come, enquire at that end, and I'll enquire at this.

I hope too you had the *MS.* of the 'Introduction to Painting' which I sent some days ago, with a letter.

And I do hope you received the six copies of the 2nd edition which Orioli sent you – if not, the customs have started suppressing them, I am afraid. Let me know.

When you do get the MS. of *Pansies,* would you stick in this poem 'Ships in bottles' after p. 81.[2] – Do hope all arrives safely.

DHL

4892. To Giuseppe Orioli, 18 January 1929
Text: MS UCLA; Unpublished.

Hotel Beau Rivage. *Bandol.* Var
18 Jan. 1929

Dear Pino

The two copies of first edition to Sylvia Beach seem to be definitely lost. She says she has written you. Will you please start enquiries at the post-office. We must trace them.

Lahr has received his 112 copies, and has now paid me 100 guineas, for 100. But I have no word from Pollinger or Brigit Patmore, and Kot. wrote yesterday but made no mention of *his* copy – second edition. Suspense still – I'll let you know when I hear something.

What shall we do about that copy to the Pegasus Press? They do not write, and do not acknowledge it. Shall we demand it shall be returned? – or sent to me here.

Will you anyhow please send me at once a copy of the second edition to this address?

I hope you got my registered letter with the frontispiece drawing[3] – which I hope you like – but if you don't, don't bother about it.

---

[1] 'business papers'.
[2] The poem was inserted after 'Don't look at me!' (which was itself omitted from expurgated edns of *Pansies*).
[3] See Letter 4874 and n. 1.

When you have time, will you count up again exactly how many copies of the first edition you still have, and tell me. If the post is safe, I want to send a number to my sister.

Bitter cold here, but sunny. Hope all goes well at Florence.

Do you know anyone who would write you a good essay on 'The Italian Novelette' of the Renaissance – il Novello nel 5.cento – Italian or English – on Boccaccio, Lasca, Bandello, Aretino[1] and the others – it would make a good introd. to a *series* of stories of which Lasca's could be the first. More blurbs in *John Bull* – against the second edition too![2]

ever DHL

4893. To S. S. Koteliansky, 18 January 1929

Text: MS BL; Postmark, Bandol [...] 29; [Stephen Spender], 'D. H. Lawrence: Letters to S. S. Koteliansky', *Encounter*, i (December 1953), 34–5.

Hotel Beau Rivage. Bandol, Var.
18 Jan. 1929

Dear Kot,

Lahr wrote tonight his plan of having *Lady C.* printed in Berlin or Vienna, and having orders go to Orioli and be forwarded from Florence to Berlin. In some ways it is good, but as you suggest, I want to get the thing *finished* at Florence. Orioli is going to publish a story by Norman Douglas, and a translated cook-book by Faith Mackenzie, and he'd just get into a muddle.[3] So we must leave him out of count. If we were going to print in Berlin, it would, in my opinion, be better to have someone there to receive orders. I have a cousin there married to a German, Max Hunger, who spent most of his younger life in England – he would probably do it – though I am not keen to ask him. And would the English want to send orders to Berlin? I suppose so. Lahr said his friend Ehrenstein would do the despatching of orders.[4] Did you see him? –

---

[1] Giovanni Boccaccio (1313–75) was greatly admired by DHL: see *Movements in European History*, ed. Philip Crumpton (Cambridge, 1989), pp. 164–7. On Lasca and Bandello see Letters 4754 and n. 3 and 4756 and p. 21 n. 1. Pietro Aretino (1492–1556), acerbic satirist in verse and prose.

[2] In the issue of *John Bull* dated 19 January 1929, the attack on *Lady Chatterley's Lover* was renewed. Under the heading, 'FAMOUS AUTHOR'S SCANDALOUS BOOK: Chapter Two of the Shame Epic', readers learned of an American pirated edn and 'the dumping in large quantities of the objectionable book on our hospitable shores'. In consequence, 'the printers of the original work have been commissioned for further copies and a second edition has been run off'. The article concludes with a demand that controls should be tightened 'over the channels of entry into this country of all such trash'.

[3] Cf. Letter 4807 and p. 62 nn. 3 and 4.

[4] Carl Ehrenstein (1892–), Austrian-Jewish expatriate (and later refugee from the Nazis), brother of the Expressionist poet, Albert Ehrenstein (1886–1950), and author of *Klagen eines Knaben* (Leipzig, 1913) and *Bitte um Liebe* (Berlin, 1921). Lahr was his friend and benefactor.

What do you think of the German plan, anyhow? I should like to get out another edition, *as quickly as possible*. Do you think 15/- about right for price?

I wondered once if you'd like to go to Paris and do the thing – and we could arrange it all between us. But probably you wouldn't want to. And perhaps there'd be passport difficulties.

Did you get the copy of the second edition which Orioli sent you, as my Christmas card? You don't mention it – so I hope it's not gone lost. Six copies were also sent to Pollinger, and *he* hasn't acknowledged them. And six copies of the *first edition* were sent to Mrs Brigit Patmore, to hold for me, and though I have written to her, I get no word from her. Would you mind ringing her up, if she is on the telephone – and then if she's got the six copies, perhaps you would call and take them over to Lahr, for him to keep, as it is just near. The address is 4. Milman St. Bedford Row. Did you meet Brigit Patmore in Mecklenburgh Square days?[1] She was rich then, but is quite poor now, has left her husband and is living with her two sons.

I'm a little afraid now of mail difficulties, till I hear that your copy, and Brigit Patmore's and Pollinger's are safely arrived. I hear that the police stopped a copy of Douglas' *Limericks* in the post, and the Chief of Police went to interview the man it was addressed to, somewhere in Sussex. But then I think the limericks are just indecent. Why didn't Douglas keep them out of the post? – so bad for everybody else.

Stephensen is rushing round getting his new thing started. He won't print any ordinary Mandrake books till autumn, but go and see him if you wish – or, when I write to him – he's supposed to be sending me a colour-proof of one of my pictures – I will remind him to see you about Rosanov. I thought it best to let him get going first.

I'm not sending any copies to my sister till I hear the post is really safe. But do, if you can, take those six copies from Brigit – I hope she's got them safely.

Orioli sent 10 copies 2nd edition and 2 copies first edition to Sylvia Beach, Paris, just after Christmas. The first arrived and are sold – but the second have not arrived – they are lost somewhere. I have asked Orioli to start enquiries. I do hope the post won't go wrong.

Bitter cold wind here, hard frosts at night, but sunny days. I hear London is dismal. You might really enjoy going to Paris and taking two rooms and publishing the Paris edition of *Lady C.*

                                                                              DHL

Frieda sent to Barbara Weekley your comments on her!! – which I heartily agree with.

---

[1] DHL had lived at 44 Mecklenburgh Square, c. 20 October–30 November 1917.

I wonder if perhaps the French are getting a bit scared of English 'improper' books printed in their country. Perhaps they are. The MSS. I send from here seem to be held up too. I sent copies of my poems *Pansies* to Pollinger twelve days ago, and they are not there yet. – Perhaps the German idea is best – France getting uneasy.

4894. To Brigit Patmore, 18 January 1929
Text: MS BL; Unpublished.

Hotel Beau Rivage. *Bandol.* Var
18 Jan 1929

Dear Brigit

I don't hear from you, although I wrote. I told you Orioli sent you six copies of the book for you to keep for me – and I do hope you have them all right. If you have, would you give them to Koteliansky – to whom I am sending this note.[1] A bookseller wants them already.

I do hope all is well with you. Send a line, if only to say 'alive!'

D. H. Lawrence

4895. To Charles Lahr, 18 January 1929
Text: MS UNYB; Postmark, Bandol 1[. . .]–1 29; Moore 1118–19.

Hotel Beau Rivage. *Bandol.* Var.
18 Jan. 1929

Dear Lahr

Your two letters to hand. The German plan seems to me good. I think Germany may be a better place than France to produce the book. I believe the French are getting scared of English 'improper' books. Two copies of *Lady C.* sent to Sylvia Beach in Paris have not arrived: and my MSS. sent from here are held up. The MSS of the *Pansies*, sent twelve days ago, to Curtis Brown, have not arrived yet. I suppose some of the gentry are reading them. – So altogether probably the German plan is a good one. But it would be no use sending orders to Orioli – it would be best if they could go direct to Germany. Do you think the whole thing could be done safely from Berlin? I wouldn't want to trouble Orioli. – I hope all the copies sent lately to England have arrived: there are six to Mrs Patmore of the first edition, which I have asked Koteliansky to go and collect and give to you, if they are safely arrived. And there are six others I hear nothing of. I am a little anxious. – A copy of Douglas' *Limericks* was held up, and the Chief of Police went to the man it

---

[1] This 'note' probably never reached Brigit Patmore: it survives in Kot's collection of MSS, together with the (unstamped) envelope addressed by DHL.

was sent to. I suppose those dirty *John Bull* dogs do have a certain effect. – I
haven't seen the review in the *New Adelphi*. Is it Murry?[1]
    As for Russell Green and the 'marked' copy, never mind. He funked, of
course. They are all like that. I must see a little later whether I can trim the
book down to requirements. Most people who write me are dead against an
expurgated edition – but I must really see for myself if I can do it, and if I
really want to. At the moment I have so many other bits of things I must do.
    Do talk the German plan over with Koteliansky. And meanwhile we'll keep
the flag flying.

                                                    Sincerely   D. H. Lawrence

4896. To Maria Chambers, 19 January 1929
Text: MS UT; Unpublished.

                                        Hotel Beau Rivage. *Bandol.* Var. France.
                                                                   19 Jan. 1929
Dear Mrs Chambers
    Your letter this evening – I will do a preface to your stories if you will send
me a set of proofs as soon as they are ready.[2] Send them to me
c/o Curtis Brown Ltd. 6. Henrietta St. Covent Garden, *London. W.C.2.*
that is the quickest. And how long do you want it – about 2000 words? And I
hope it'll do your book good, but I fear more people dislike my name than like
it.
    If we come to America as we intend, it would be just when you suggest, last
week in March or first week in April – perhaps by a Dollar boat from
Marseille. I don't seriously expect any trouble myself – yet once before, at El
Paso we were held up by U.S. authorities and detained till next day – I was
called a liar to my face, when I was speaking plain truth – and kept stripped,
being examined by a down-at-heel fellow who was supposed to be a doctor
but was much more likely to be a liquor-runner – all of which I have not
forgotten and shall never forget.[3] Sheer degrading insult! No, I don't trust
your U.S. 'authorities'.
    I am amused at your flights with Brett. She says you are like a humming-
bird, so I just see you humming loudly down Toby, which is the name of her
trombeta.[4] I think you will like her, also because she is not American altogether.

---

[1] Murry had reviewed *Collected Poems* in *New Adelphi*, xi (December 1928), 165–7; his review of
Lady Chatterley's Lover did not appear in the journal until June 1929 (see R. P. Draper, *D. H.
Lawrence: The Critical Heritage*, 1970, pp. 281–4).
[2] The book was never published.
[3] DHL was recalling the events of late March 1925: see *Letters*, v. 229, 230.
[4] 'ear-trumpet'.

They are still fussing over *Lady C.* in England. By the way, did you ever get the two copies Orioli sent you in exchange for those forty surplus dollars? (of course that was *your* money, not mine). If you didn't get them, the Customs swallowed them too, O ostrich!

The latest excitement is that my pictures are being reproduced in colour in a large (sized) book – 24 pictures – and there will be 500 copies printed, at (I think) fifty dollars a copy. The important part again is to get the 250 for America safely into the U.S.A. The book is really perfectly proper, though all the pictures have nudes, or half-nudes in them – and I have done an introductory essay, quite long, about ten thousand words. If it was anybody else's book probably Customs would pass it without a word: as it is mine, they are almost sure to fuss, just out of spite – and this is too costly a book for the U. S. ostrich to swallow *en passant*. – A friend of mine did a little edition of *Sun* in Paris – and the New York Customs wanted to stop it because it contained the word 'womb'. – Pobrecitos,[1] where *were* they conceived? – in old tins, I suppose. – So there's another nut to crack – to get my book of pictures safely in. Find me a way, and then you can take the first copy that lands, and I will write in it: To Maria Cristina, who kept the gate of the western world ajar! – Anyhow never say die! I did a little book of poems – *Pansies* – pensées – many of them very chirpy and 'wicked'. I sent two[2] copies of the typescript to London, and they have not arrived, so who is sniffing my pansies when they've no right to? What a world of canaille![3] But when they irritate me I have to go one worse, like the old Englishman who says: If you have eaten onion and would hide the fact from those that come anigh you, eat garlic!! –[4]

I hope your book of stories will come along soon, and will make gentlemen cease to prefer blondes, so that they buy it in thousands.[5] But most books make not much money. And from what do you want to rest, rest, rest? – Anyhow I hope we may all meet soon and have good times out there at that ranchito – it's really only a ranchiquito,[6] or smaller even than that. But we might have a good summer out there.

belle cose!   D. H. Lawrence

---

[1] 'Poor little devils'.   [2] two] too   [3] 'scoundrels, rabble'.

[4] See M. P. Tilley, *Dictionary of the Proverbs of England in 16th and 17th Centuries* (1950), S 556.

[5] *Gentlemen Prefer Blondes* (1925), by Anita Loos, was one of the best sellers of the decade (cf. *Letters*, v. 574 and n. 4).

[6] 'little ranch . . . tiny ranch'.

4897. To Mr Kendrigan, 20 January 1929
Text: TMSC UT; Unpublished.

c/o Pino Orioli, 6 Lungarno Corsini, Florence, Italy
20 Jan. 1929

Dear Mr. Kendrigan[1]

I have your letter this morning. There are only a very few copies left now of *Lady Chatterley's Lover* – the first edition – and the price is twenty-five dollars. Orioli does not send out any copies without payment in advance. But if you have any orders and send him the cheque, he will send the books safely by registered mail.

I shall be interested to see the 'Revistas Vanguardistas'.[2] – I spent only one day in Cuba[3] – but I hope I shall come again and that then I shall have the pleasure of seeing you.

Yours Sincerely   D. H. Lawrence

4898. To Giuseppe Orioli, [21 January 1929]
Text: MS UCLA; Unpublished.

[Hotel Beau Rivage, Bandol, Var.]
Monday.

Dear Pino –

So the blow has fallen![4] I haven't heard of Mrs Patmore's fate yet. – Now it is very important to trace Sylvia Beach's two copies. – Aldous and Maria are due tonight – will ask them. No word from Pegasus.

DHL

If you haven't sent that copy to me, don't send it till we are sure.

DHL

---

[1] A bookseller in Havana, Cuba (cf. Letter 5157).
[2] The particular title of what was perhaps a Communist or Nationalist Cuban magazine (the 'Avant-garde Review') has not been traced, though DHL may have been referring to a genre rather than to a specific publication. Cuba produced many journals in this period; one, for example, which ran 1927–30, changed its title on principle each year, and is known as *Revista de Avance*.
[3] 25 November 1923, en route from Vera Cruz to England.
[4] This letter is written on one from Pollinger to DHL dated 19 January 1929:

Dear Lawrence,
     I was surprised to receive a visit from two Scotland Yard officials yesterday afternoon, who told me they had intercepted and seized six copies of "LADY C." sent by mail addressed to me from Italy.
     I told them a) that I had no idea these books were on their way to me until I received a letter from you a few days since, asking whether they had reached my hands, b) that I had not ordered or requested anyone in Italy to dispatch them to me and c) as we are your Literary Agents, I took it that the copies were coming to us in the usual way, i.e. that authors always send us copies of all their material.
     I gathered from the two police officials that Scotland Yard consider "LADY C." as indecent

Do you mind paying Egidi's[1] bill for me, and telling them please to put down my address c/o you –

DHL

4899. To S. S. Koteliansky, 21 January 1929
Text: MS BL; Postmark, Bandol 21–1 29; Zytaruk 376.

Hotel Beau Rivage. Bandol. Var.
21 Jan 1929

Dear Kot

Have you heard that two Scotland Yard fellows called on Pollinger and told him six copies of *Lady C.* had been sent him and making enquiries – and saying all copies of the book sent would be confiscated. So that's that! I am wondering about Mrs P[atmore]'s – expect it's the same there. – Also the two MS. copies of my poems *Pansies*, sent to Pollinger, are being held up. What rights have they over MSS, I should like to know?

I am writing Stephensen and shall mention Rosanov.

DHL

4900. To Charles Lahr, 21 January 1929
Text: MS UNYB; Postmark, Bandol 21[...]29; Moore 1119.

Hotel Beau Rivage, *Bandol*, Var.
21 Jan 1929

Dear Lahr

Thanks for the Curwood book[2] and the pirated *L[ady] C[hatterley]*, both arrived. What a shocking puerile forgery of my signature, like a child of thirteen.

The bad news, which you may have heard, is that the six copies of the second edition sent to Pollinger of Curtis Brown's have been confiscated – and two Scotland Yarders called on him to enquire. – I am still waiting to hear of a few other copies. – Add to this that they must be holding up also my two *MSS* of *Pansies*, also sent to Pollinger. Have they any right over MSS, the swine? How sickening this dirty hypocrisy! More later!

DHL

and any copies found entering this country will be seized and destroyed.
Will you be coming to London to see the exhibition of your pictures, in the near future?
Your sincerely,

[1] A firm of shipping agents in Florence.
[2] Possibly the recently published autobiography of the prolific author, James Oliver Curwood (1878–1927), *The Glory of Living* (October 1928).

4901. To Enid Hilton, 21 January 1929
Text: MS UCLA; Huxley 781.

Hotel Beau Rivage. *Bandol,* Var
21 Jan 1929

Dear Enid

Glad to hear you are better and enjoying life. – good thing we sent you none of the books[1] – just heard from Pollinger that six copies sent him were confiscated, and two Scotland Yard officials called to enquire. So the brutes are putting their ridiculous foot down.

The news about the pictures is that they are going to be reproduced in a book, in colour – expensive – ten guineas a copy – book to appear in March, and exhibition to take place at the same time. I suppose this will really come off.

We are still here. Today the Huxleys – Aldous and Maria – are due to arrive – suppose they'll stay about a week. Then I really think we'll leave for Spain. It's been very cold, but bright – at last it's grey and warmer – rather nice for a change. – Frieda's daughter was here awhile – and another friend. – Frieda was thrilled about vegetable dyes – I suppose she'll be trying them, when we get a house. How do you make them fast? or don't you?

You might call at Lahr's and see if he has any news.

Just a hurried note – affection from both of us, also to Laurence.

DHL

4902. To Curtis Brown, 24 January 1929
Text: MS UT; Huxley 782.

Hotel Beau Rivage, *Bandol,* Var. France
24 Jan. 1929

Dear C[urtis] B[rown]

I'm sorry about the bother about those six copies of *Lady C.* – but no good succumbing under it, after all.

What I *am* concerned about is my Manuscript. There are the two copies of the poems, *Pansies,* sent to Pollinger on Jan. 7th from Bandol, registered, as *papiers d'affaires,* No. 587. There is also the manuscript of my essay on painting, for the introduction to the book of reproductions of my paintings. This was sent to Pollinger as registered letter on Jan 14th. No. 718. – Now these two MSS. we must recover, whoever is interfering in their delivery. The essay on painting is my original Manuscript. I have no copy, I sent it to Pollinger to be typed. It is about 10,000 words – is perfectly 'proper' – and I can't have it

---

[1] See Letter 4786.

lost. Will you please make the proper enquiries at that end, and I will do so at this: in that way at least we shall find out where the MSS. are. Then if Scotland Yard or anyone else continues to detain them, I can take the proper steps, make the proper publicity, and bring an action if necessary. After all, Scotland Yard does not rule the country, and mustn't be allowed to. I'm very sorry to bring trouble on your unoffending head – all my fault, I know. But then in this life somebody has got to put up a fight.

P. R. Stephensen said he would be coming along to your office to make a contract for the book of pictures. I asked Pollinger to arrange for a sum *down*, for the rights to reproduce the pictures – and a small percentage as royalty – Stephensen having suggested £250 down on a 10% royalty basis, I would suggest £250 payment for rights to reproduce pictures, and then a 5% royalty – something like that. But we must recover the MS. of the essay.

Ever   D. H. Lawrence[1]

4903. To P. R. Stephensen, 24 January 1929
Text: MS IEduc; Munro 300.

Hotel Beau Rivage. Bandol, Var, France
24 Jan. 1929

Dear Stephensen

The proofs came this morning – the picture loses a lot in reproduction, alas

---

[1] As yet unknown to DHL, Pollinger had written twice to him the previous day, 23 January; relevant to his questions both about *Pansies* and 'Introduction to These Paintings', the letters read as follows (TMS Hutchinson):

Dear Lawrence,
   I have just had a further visit from the same two officials who came in to see me about those six copies of "Lady C" which were addressed to me apparently, by Orioli.
   Acting under instructions from the Home Office, they have seized the two copies of the "Pansies" manuscript, as they consider these poems obscene and indecent.
   All our letters are apparently being intercepted and read by the Police, but I will send you a detailed statement as to what took place in my office at noon today, by the next mail.
Yours sincerely,

My dear Lawrence,
   Yours of January 14th and the introduction to the paintings is just here. It is quite obvious that notwithstanding the fact that it was a registered parcel, it had been opened and sealed up again.
   When delivering it here, the postman made a rather curious remark to our Reception Clerk. He wanted to know how long I had been here and was considerably surprised to hear that I have been here so long that I am now considered as part of the office equipment. Our Clerk tells me that the postman seemed to doubt this statement.
   I wrote you about an hour ago saying that the "Pansies" had been seized by the police. You will also have got my previous letter saying that the six copies of "Lady Chatterley" are also in their possession.
Yours sincerely,

– but still, enough remains to be interesting.[1] I like the creamy paper best – the mould – for this picture, which has no white in it. Pictures with white in them might come out better on cartridge. As you say, this is a difficult picture. – The result is pretty good, though of course I, who painted the picture, see most plainly the big difference between the original and the reproduction.

If you go to Curtis Browns, I suggested to them in a letter you might pay £250. for the right to reproduce the pictures, and a 5% royalty: which amounts to the same as a 10% royalty with £250 advance.[2] But of course you can arrange to pay part of the £250 later, if necessary.

I have done another oil panel, of the workmen here in blue cotton trousers playing ball – and am doing another of two men going to bathe – panels like the *Accident*.[3] Wonder if it's safe to send them.

Have you heard that the police have descended on *Lady C.* – confiscated six copies I sent to Pollinger of Curtis Brown, and six others – detectives calling to interview Pollinger etc. – The worst of it is they are holding up also the MSS. of *Pansies* – which I sent the day before you came here – and also the MS. of the essay on painting, which I sent in a registered letter on Jan. 14 – to Pollinger, to be typed. Of this essay I have *no copy* – it was my original. So we must certainly recover it, police or no police. It's such a bore that people fall into such a state of funk.

The Huxleys are here – and flourishing.

My poor *Pansies*, pawed even before they are printed. We must do something about it.

DHL

4904. To Giuseppe Orioli, 24 January 1929
Text: MS UCLA; cited in Moore, *Intelligent Heart* 397–8.

Hotel Beau Rivage. *Bandol.* Var
Thursday 24 Jan 1929
Dear Pino

Aldous and Maria are here – Aldous has his copy all right – and I had a letter from the Pegasus, they have their copy. So now we have only to trace the two copies to Sylvia Beach, and those we *must* find out about.

---

[1] Stephensen himself annotated this letter as follows: 'The first picture I had reproduced was *Accident in a Mine*, as this looked like being the most difficult.'
[2] 'The arrangement regarding royalties was a method of dodging income tax.'
[3] 'The two new oils were *Spring* and *Summer Dawn*. He took off the blue trousers in *Spring*.' (Cf. Letters 4886 and n. 5, and 4925.)

Brigit Patmore's six are also confiscated – she is away in Italy – her son[1] wrote me a detective sort of fellow called there too. – Kot. wrote – rather in a funk – perhaps fearing they may call on him. – The really annoying part is that Scotland Yard are apparently holding up also two of my manuscripts, sent to Curtis Brown – these we must recover.

Been raining here. Aldous and Maria will be in Florence next week. – If you haven't sent it, don't send that copy of 2nd edit. I asked for, as Lahr sent me a copy of the pirated edit – very bad one too.

affectly. DHL

4905. To Dorothy Yorke, 24 January 1929
Text: MS ColU; Paul Delany, 'D. H. Lawrence: Twelve Letters', *DHL Review*, ii (Fall 1969), 207–8.

Hotel Beau Rivage. *Bandol*, Var.

24 Jan 1929

Dear Arabella

So you are still in London, and we are still here. Frieda's daughter came – and another friend – and now the Huxleys are here. And still I think we shall leave in about ten days' time.

I think if Dahlberg decides to cut out self-pity and leaning on other people, especially women, he may get quite far. It seems to me he has the spunk of a fighter in him, if he didn't damp it down. He still rather hopes to find himself in somebody else – but of course, unless he finds himself in himself he'll find it nowhere. He should stick to his fighting self. But I liked his last letter, and will answer it.

Brigit hasn't written me either, since before Christmas. I hear from her son that she is travelling in Italy. – I sent her – or Orioli did – six copies of *Lady C.* to hold for me – and just at that moment the police decided to pounce, so they seized the copies in the post, and a detective called on poor Brigit – which is a shame. But that's how the son[2] happens to write to me. He didn't send her address either – so – she is where she is –

I'm glad you got rid of the Malthouse, even if it was a wrench. It was an unlucky little place.[3]

---

[1] Derek Patmore (b. 1908), described by his mother as 'author, journalist, playwright and impressario of art' (Nehls, iii. 668); author of a pamphlet, *D. H. Lawrence and the Dominant Male* (1970).

[2] the son] she

[3] The Lawrences had visited Aldington and Arabella Yorke at Malthouse Cottage, Padworth, near Reading, 6–8 August 1926. Aldington recalled: 'The visit began a little inauspiciously, as Lawrence declared the cottage was "sinister"' (Nehls, iii. 84).

What, by the way, of Joseph? Did he stay on the island?[1]

Frieda still keeps wanting a house – and I think secretly hopes to get me back to Italy. And I don't want to go back to Italy, I still want to go to spain. So there we all are, all at our different loose ends.

Affectionately   DHL

4906. To Rhys Davies, [26 January 1929]
Text: TMS UT; Unpublished.

Hotel Beau Rivage, BANDOL, Var
Saturday

Dear Davies,

The story came all right, and I have read it, and alas, I don't think it's so good as your usual stories. You see it has all the beginnings of romance, without any further development. The young man is entirely limited to himself, and so nothing really happens. The two women don't really exist for him, so it becomes a little vulgar. There must be passion of some sort in somebody, to make a story – and here even the swans turn out to be just trivial. If you feel like it, it would be good to do it again, from about page 13 on, and really work out the swan *motiv*, since you've so obviously got a *motiv* there.

The Huxleys have been here all this week: they leave on Monday. We said once more we'd come to Nice with them, and once more we shan't; it's so cold, and we've all got colds, though not bad. So we shall stay here at least two more weeks, so do come again for a little visit. Write and say when it shall be.

I suppose you have heard the tragedies of the police seizing copies of *Lady C.*, and going threatening people? They have even seized the two copies of the Ms. of the *Pansies*, which I sent to Curtis Brown. That makes me very mad. – I have from Stephensen the proofs of the colour print of the *Accident* picture; not bad, but not very good. Show you when you come. – Am doing this on the type-writer because I wanted to see if the new ribbon goes all right. Now I shall have to type the *Pansies* all over again.

Many greetings from us both. Let me know when you will come. I do hate this typing.

Ever   DHL

'Interlude' is a bad title – interlude to what?

---

[1] Giuseppe Barezzi, the Sicilian servant at La Vigie on Ile de Port-Cros. See *Letters*, vi. 590, 592–3.

4907. To Laurence Pollinger, 27 January 1929
Text: MS UT; Unpublished.

Hotel Beau Rivage. *Bandol.* Var
27 Jan. 1929

Dear Pollinger[1]

Well, I'm very sorry you're having all that fuss over the copies of *Lady C* which Orioli sent you at my request – not your fault at all. But either you have some enemy, or they're concentrating their fuss on you, for an example. – I am making enquiries as to their rights to hold the MSS. of the *Pansies* – these people must not overstep their limits. And I want you to observe if this letter has been tampered with, and keep the envelope if it has.

Let me have a typed copy of the 'Introduction to the Paintings', will you, for revision. I suppose Stephensen will be coming to see you about the agreement.

I have received a package of ten sheets of *Rawdon's Roof* from your office – and notice from the shipping agent that a case of 'pages manuscrit' is on the way. I suppose this case is also the sheets of *Rawdon's Roof*, to sign. But what about this separate package of them? It doesn't mention the signature, on the leaf. Do you want them signed and returned?

Aldous Huxley is here staying a few days with us, and very indignant over the Scotland Yard business.

all my sympathy   D. H. Lawrence

Let me have the statement of what happened, when you can – I want to be fully informed.

4908. To Giuseppe Orioli, 27 January 1929
Text: MS UCLA; Unpublished.

Hotel Beau Rivage. *Bandol.* Var
27 Jan. 1929.

Dear Pino

So glad you found Sylvia Beach's two copies – shall be relieved to hear she has got them.

Brigit's six copies are lost – detective called there too – and five of Lahr's copies. Also they have seized my two MS. copies of *Pansies* – the poems (pensées) which I sent to Curtis Brown. I am finding out if they have any right to do that, and if they have not, I shall make a row.

The man wrote from the Pegasus to say he thought they might do an edition of 2000 copies – sell to trade at 100 frs. – and let trade fix [...] their

---

[1] DHL was replying to parts of three letters from Pollinger: see pp. 146 n. 4, 149 n. 1.

own price. He asked me what I should want of the 100 frs. and I said 40 frs. Do you think that's right?

No, don't sell to Galignani for less than £4. I believe Kot has said the London price to be now £6.6.0. See if you can do anything with that man in Cuba – might be an opening there.[1] I told him the price was $25.

Aldous and Maria leave tomorrow – so I suppose you will see them soon. I think they'll stay at the *Moderno*. – I bought such a nice book with coloured engravings of birds and fish and animals in Toulon – *Dictionnaire universel d'[2]Histoire Naturelle* – Charles D'Orbigny – *Atlas* – 3 vols complete for 175 frs. – pub. in Paris 1861.[3] The coloured engravings are charming. Do you know it?

So cold here – but sunny.

DHL

4909. To Charles Lahr, 27 January 1929
Text: MS UNYB; Postmark, Bandol 28–1 29; Unpublished.

Hotel Beau Rivage. *Bandol*. Var
27 Jan. 1929

Dear Lahr

Have your letter – what a joyful business! They seem to be persecuting C[urtis] B[rown]'s office a bit – something to make an example of, I suppose. But they admit they have kept my two copies of *Pansies* – MS. – so I'm finding out if they're within their rights there. They had to let the letter with the 'Introd. to the Paintings' through. – We must see about it. Can't sit down to it.

I had a letter from the Pegasus Press – suggesting they do an edition of 2000, to sell to trade at 100 frs. – and let trade fix its price. They asked me what I should want of the 100 frs. and I said 40 frs. – What do you think? I'm awaiting their further reply. I suppose if they agree, and want to, we might as well let them go ahead. I stipulated 2000 numbered. But of course it is no real check on them – and I believe they are real slippery.

I am expecting Davies either this week or next – then I think we shall leave here.

I'll let you know about Pegasus.

DHL

[1] Cf. Letter 4897.   [2] d'] de
[3] *Dictionnaire Universel d'Histoire Naturelle*, ed. Charles Dessalines d'Orbigny (1805–76), published in 13 volumes (Paris, 1861); the *Atlas* (with coloured plates) occupied three extra vols.

Yes, I had that receipt.

I don't think we ought to raise the price of the first edit – as Orioli is still selling to trade at £4. But he will now only sell to Paris and Italy – so do as you think best.

DHL

4910. To Earl and Achsah Brewster, 27 January 1929
Text: MS UT; Brewster 193–4.

Hotel Beau Rivage. *Bandol.* Var
27 Jan 1929

Dear Earl and Achsah

What has become of you this long while? we haven't heard from you since Christmas. Did you get my letter, and the hundred Lire for Harwood? – or did it go astray? – We are still here, as you see – Frieda's daughter came – and all messed up with the wrong sort of studio love-affairs. Now she is back in London. – At the moment Aldous and Maria Huxley are here – on their way to Florence to sell their Italian car. We seem to have had someone off and on all the time since Christmas – and still don't make up our minds about leaving. I want to go to Spain, to try Majorca – but Frieda somehow funks it – doesn't want to go so far. But at present she's got a cold – perhaps that's it. She wants to go back to Italy and find a house – perhaps near Massa-Carrara[1] – it is feasible, but I just don't want to go back to Italy at present. So it's the knees of the gods, always an uncomfortable place. I expect ultimately we shall just try Majorca – might as well, it's not far.

In our world there's no news, except that the police have started seizing any copies of *Lady C* that go into England, and seem to threaten a little campaign against me. I shall try to give 'em one back. – My pictures are going to be reproduced in a big book at ten guineas a copy – in colour. I had a proof of that panel I did in Kesselmatte – *Accident in a Mine* – but I think I did it after you had left – but you saw it. It came out fairly well, but lost a lot. I have done a long foreword to the book, on painting – quite interesting, I think. I have painted a bit here too – used up all the panels Earl brought me. And I have finished the *Pansies* poems. – Brett writes that her exhibition is over – and she *thinks* she has sold four pictures. I hope she has. But she doesn't sound very happy. Nobody does – so I hope you are. As for me, I just peg along. I've kept pretty well, but have a cold now, from the *bitter* mistral wind. It's an awful wind, really – but mostly sunny with it. But it's got my broncs. – We often think of you and talk of you – glad to think of you safe in Anacapri.

[1] 25 miles n.w. of Pisa.

We shall be here anyhow a fortnight, so do write. If we don't like Spain we'll come and *settle* in Italy – D.V. I'm not really keen on travelling.

Love from us both to all three   DHL

4911. To Martin Secker, 27 January 1929
Text: MS UInd; Secker 115.

Hotel Beau Rivage. *Bandol.* Var.
27 Jan. 1929

Dear Secker

Thanks for your letter, and for the papers, which arrive duly. I suppose you have heard of all the fuss of Scotland Yard seizing Pollinger's copies of *Lady C* – and even my two MS copies of *Pansies.* I am finding out if that is within their rights – am not going to sit down to it. Anyhow I'll send you another copy just now.

Aldous Huxley and Maria are here – going to Italy. It's very cold, but sunny. They are disgusted over this Scotland Yard business, naturally.

Would you send me a copy of *The Woman Who Rode Away* here, please. And would you send to my cousin –

Herrn. Max Hunger, 11. Niebuhrstr. *Berlin – Charlottenburg*

a copy of *The Plumed Serpent* and of *The Lost Girl.*

We are at a bit of a deadlock – I want to go to Spain for a while, and Frieda for some reason funks it, and wants to go back to Italy – where I refuse to go, just now. So what will be the result of this diversity? Oh husbands and wives!

They are going to reproduce my pictures, all in colour, in a book at ten guineas a time! I have a proof of the first picture – not bad – done by a new process.

The mistral is an even nastier wind than the tramontana or the maestrale, which is saying a lot. We've all more or less got chesty colds from it. Do hope you are all well.

DHL

4912. To Edward Dahlberg, 27 January 1929
Text: MS UTul; Postmark, Bandol 28–1 29; Moore 1120–1.

Hotel Beau Rivage. Bandol. Var.
27 Jan. 1929

Dear Dahlberg

I got the 25 francs, am rather impatient that you fuss about them – anyhow the postage was not so much, so I send back the surplus.

If you'll send me a complete proof of your novel as soon as it is possible, I'll have a shot at doing a short critical foreword, and Putnams can settle with Curtis Brown. We may be moving from here, but in that case I'll let you know. I am always on the point of going, then somebody comes to stay.

I'm glad you've got some work – and hope the novel will be a success. As you say, the literary London sets are all just effete. If a man's really going to work, these days, he's got to work alone.

Sincerely D. H. Lawrence

4913. To Brewster Ghiselin, 27 January 1929
Text: MS Ghiselin; Postmark, Bandol 29–1 29; Nehls, iii. 305.

Hotel Beau Rivage. *Bandol.* Var
27 Jan 1929
Dear Bruce

I had your letter – we are still here, as you see. The Huxleys also are here – Aldous has a chill and is staying in bed a day or two – will leave when it's better. Frieda too has a chill and stayed in bed since lunch – so Maria and I went down to dinner alone. Of course the old waiter wouldn't believe that Frieda was ill, while I survived. – It's the wind, which has been bitterer than ever, I never knew such a nasty wind, worse than maestrale or tramontana, by a long chalk. It's got my bronchials too – but that's inevitable.

The only news is that the police have started seizing copies of *Lady C* that enter England, and they have even seized the two MS. copies of the *Pansies*, which I sent to my agent – they say they are obscene and indecent. I must get back at them some way about that – must, must. They even held up the *only* existing MS. of the 'Introd. to Painting', and I trembled with rage. But they've let that go! That's what it is to write for a civilised world.

Stephensen sent a proof in colour of that picture – *Accident in a Mine* – Not bad, but oh, it loses a lot. I've nearly done that panel of which I made the sketch the night before you left – rather nice – and part done another,[1] of bathers. Now I'm having to type the *Pansies* again, to rub salt into my sore against Scotland Yard and such gentry. Attendons!

I read *The American Caravan*, and I wonder it's not called the ambulance Van instead, they are all so sick. Why they don't all quietly take hemlock I don't know. But of course they wouldn't be able to wail any more print across any more pages. The wailers! Edward Dahlberg has asked me if I'll write a foreword to his novel which Putnams are publishing, and I've said probably. Nothing like asking.

---

[1] Both sketches became water-colours: the first, *Spring* (see Letter 5402); the second, *Summer Dawn*. See *Paintings*, plates [16] and [17].

I'm really hoping we'll get away to Spain by 10th Feb. – away from the wind. Such a lot of fusses through the post to attend to. – I hope you're bearing up at Oxford and being a good little, good little boy.[1]

Regards from both   DHL

4914. To Lady Ottoline Morrrell, 30 January 1929

Text: MS ColU; PC v. Côte d'Azur – Bandol-sur-Mer, Terrasse de l'Hôtel Beau-Rivage; Postmark, Bandol 30 1 29; Delany, *DHL Review*, ii. 209.

Bandol.
30 jan 1929

Had another little reunion with Aldous and Maria, wish you were here this warm sunny day, so still with coming spring. I want to write you a letter now.

DHL
Aldous
Maria
Frieda

4915. To Laurence Pollinger, 31 January 1929

Text: MS UT; Unpublished.

Hotel Beau Rivage, *Bandol.* Var.
31 Jan. 1929

Dear Pollinger

I have yours about Cape's American edition of *Twilight in Italy*. I don't mind if he publishes the book over there, but 5% is a very tiny royalty, almost as good as nothing. Do you think it's worth it?

Are you sending me a typescript copy of the 'Introd. to the Paintings', for my revision? – or have you handed it over to Stephensen?

The case of *pages manuscrit* has not arrived – let me know what you want me to do with the small package of sheets of *Rawdon's Roof* – if I'm to sign and number them.

Sincerely   D. H. Lawrence

---

[1] Ghiselin may have seen, or heard the substance of, DHL's essay, written in November 1928, which was published as 'The Manufacture of Good Little Boys' in *Vanity Fair*, September 1929: cf. Letter 4764 and n. 2.

4916. To Giuseppe Orioli, [1 February 1929]
Text: MS UCLA; Unpublished.

Hotel Beau Rivage. *Bandol.* Var

31 jan 1929[1]

Dear Pino

Aldous and Maria left this morning, both of them rather ill, I thought. Try to make Maria take care of herself – she's not at all well – tell her I say she must eat more, too. They are motoring, coming to Florence to sell their car – Frieda says she wants to come to Florence to fetch the trunks, but I am not sure if she will do so. She may. Myself I want to go to Spain, to the warm parts. I do so want to go somewhere new, after all these bothers.

The Pegasus man wrote he has not yet found out details for a Paris edition – he says the pirated edition is selling normally at 200 frs to the trade, 300 frs. to the public – but that lately they have sold to the trade for 150 and even 100 frs. Of course I don't know if it's true. He says if they do an edition to sell to trade at 100 frs. they will give me 40 frs. – if they do a thousand copies. I shall accept, if they go ahead – but how keep a check on them?

I am trying to get a man to go to Philadelphia this summer, to see if they are swindling me also over *Reflections on the Death of a Porcupine.* I'll see if we can't trace some of those nineteen addresses.[2]

If the Pegasus are doing a Paris edition, we might as well sell out the second edition – only keep me a couple of copies. Sylvia Beach wanted some. I suppose you have about sixteen. You could let Brentano's have a few.

The post-office has paid me one vaglia, for 92 Liras – so I suppose it is the man who wrote that he was sending a second five dollars.[3] Did you say there were others coming? The post-office is *very* slow in France.

I should so much like a blue coat like the one I got in Via Tornabuoni last summer – this is all faded – and I like it so much. But Maria and Aldous say it would take *weeks* to send it parcel post. I wonder if anyone might bring it.

I do hope it's warmer now – it is here –

ever DHL

Maria says Haskards are not to be trusted – that they make mistakes in the accounts. Do you think it's true?

DHL

---

[1] The contents of letters dated 1 February 1929 by DHL himself confirm his error here.
[2] The 'man' is unidentified. About the 'addresses' see Letter 4756 and p. 20 n. 3. As for the charge that Mason swindled DHL over *Reflections* with the inference that sales of the book were brisk, in fact there were unsold copies still in the Centaur Book Shop as late as 1938 when Mason left to become Manager of the Philadelphia Academy of Music (information from the Mason family).
[3] Cf. Letter 4819 and n. 3.

4917. To Edward Dahlberg, 1 February 1929
Text: MS UTul; Postmark, [. . .]; Unpublished.

Hotel Beau Rivage. Bandol. Var.

1 Feb 1929

Dear Dahlberg

Orioli has sent me your letter and the hundred Liras. Perhaps you know that customs are now seizing all copies of *Lady C.* that come into England – they have even seized two of my MSS, and apparently destroyed them – so it would be no use posting your copy to London. Let me know if there is any address in Paris or elsewhere where you would like it sent – and if not, I will return you the hundred Liras. All a great nuisance and very irritating, but I suppose one must expect these mean little persecutions.

Don't bother about that introd. to your novel – I don't mind doing it if I have the proof fairly soon. I am pining to go away to Spain now, when I can get loose from these various bothers. I think you are right to think of returning to U.S.A.

Sincerely   D. H. Lawrence

4918. To Juliette Huxley, 1 February 1929
Text: MS Huxley; Unpublished.

Hotel Beau Rivage, *Bandol*, Var

1 Feb 1929

Dear Juliette

Had your letter today – you shouldn't have bothered with those francs. So Odette did receive the vase? – she didn't acknowledge it.

Aldous and Maria left this morning in the car – a lovely morning indeed, still and sunny. But they are neither of them very well – Aldous liverish and run down, Maria very thin and not sound, somehow. They worry me a bit. Poor Aldous was in bed two days with his liver[1] – and Frieda in bed with a cold – now I've got it, and feel rather wretched – but am not yet in bed.

Have you heard that the police have suddenly started seizing all copies of *Lady C* and have even seized two MS. copies of my poems *Pansies.* I want to make a row: can't sit down to it. All too exasperating.

Wonder if you've started your embroidery. Would you like me to send you the photograph I drew it from?

I have got a proof of one of my pictures, in colour, for the book. It's not bad, but it loses a lot. Anyhow they seem to be going ahead with the book.

I am pining now to get away, but am held here by these vexations through

---

[1] liver] life

the post. I want to go to Spain – to Majorca. My heavens, I understand your
wanting a park – just to be alone in – to have a little space around you. – I long
to get away from everything, especially everything connected with literature.
How one is tangled in it all. – I wish we were all in Diablerets – we were
remote there. This time last year we were there.

My regards to Julian.   DHL

4919. To Charles Lahr, 1 February 1929
Text: MS UNYB; Postmark, Bandol 2–2 29; Unpublished.

Hotel Beau Rivage. *Bandol.* Var.

1 Feby 1929

Dear Lahr

The Pegasus wrote he would give me the 40 frs. – but he says pirates, who
sell to trade normally at 200 frs. – public price 300 frs. – have lately been
selling to trade at 150 frs. and even 100 frs. – and that that would necessitate
coming lower. I don't know if this is true, but have to take him at his word.
His suggestion is 1000 copies at 100 frs to the trade: and if he did 2000 copies,
to give me only 30 frs. on the second thousand. I'm waiting to hear further.

Aldous Huxley was here – and wrote to a friend Jack Hutchinson, who is
standing Liberal at the next election, about the MSS. of the *Pansies.*[1] Hutchinson is a friend of that man Moseley, who is socialist, and would no doubt
put a question in the House too – *if the retaining of the MSS. is illegal.*[2] No
good if the brutes are within their legal rights. But you might speak to your
Durham man.[3]

I wonder why Scotland Yard should be so down on Curtis Brown's office?
– seems to me there must be something more than just those six copies of
Lady C. – they wouldn't persecute a whole office for that.

Have you any news of the pirates in England? – they seem rather brisk in
Paris.

And do you know the Centaur Bookshop in Philadelphia – Harold T.
Mason? I somehow feel very doubtful about them. They ordered nineteen
copies to various addresses, unpaid, in Philadelphia – not one arrived. At the

---

[1] St John ('Jack') Hutchinson (1884–1942), barrister, whom DHL had known (and at least
initially had disliked) since 1916 (see *Letters*, ii. 591 n. 1; also iii. 175 n. 1); he later defended
Dorothy Warren when DHL's exhibition in her gallery was closed by the police. He un-
successfully contested the Isle of Wight constituency in 1929. m. 1910, Mary Barnes.

[2] Sir Oswald Ernald Moseley Bt (1896–1980), Labour MP for Smethwick, 1926–31. In 1932 he
founded the British Union of Fascists. He did not participate in the Commons debate, 28
February 1929, on the seizure of DHL's MSS (see Nehls, iii. 308–12).

[3] Perhaps the Labour MP for Durham, Joshua Ritson (1874–1955); he did not take part in the
debate on 28 February.

same time, copies sent by the same mail to other addresses were delivered in Philadelphia. And in that town, apparently, the first pirated edition appeared, almost immediately after mine was out. Douglas – Norman – says the Centaur are swindling him also, deliberately. – There is something wrong in that quarter – and some connection with it in England. I should like to know.

Meanwhile I am typing my poems again – not very brisk, as I've got a bit of flu. But I've done about a third. When I've done half I think I shall send them to Law.[1]

I wanted Davies to come over for a few days, but he says he daren't leave his novel. I'm afraid I offended him a bit by not liking his swan story. But what would be the good of lying! The young man in it is so full of himself that he's no more aware of the two young women than if they were two chamber-pots – and uses them more or less as such. – It's a pity he can't see himself in relation to another person – woman or man. But the young are like that.

                                                          ever.   DHL

Many thanks for the *Adelphi* – poor Murry![2]

4920. To S. S. Koteliansky, 1 February 1929
Text: MS BL; Postmark, Bandol 1–2 29; Moore 1122.
                                          Hotel Beau Rivage. *Bandol.* Var
                                                          1 Feb. 1929
Dear Kot

There is no real news here – except that the man of the Pegasus Press wrote this morning saying he hadn't got the information yet from his distributing agents, but that he agreed to give me 40 frs. per copy if they do an edition of a thousand to sell to trade at 100 frs: – but if they do 2000, then on the second thousand I am to have only 30 frs. I shall write it will be better to do 1000 only. But *how am I to keep a check on him?* – Nothing of course is settled yet, but he says the pirated edition is selling in Paris normally at 300 frs – price to the trade 200 frs – but that lately the pirates have delivered copies to the trade at 150 frs and even at 100 frs. – and he talks as if we would have to come lower. But of course I am not sure that his figures are correct.

Aldous and Maria left this morning – both rather seedy, I thought – Aldous very sympathetic. He wrote to Jack Hutchinson about the MSS. of the *Pansies* – and Jack will talk it over with Moseley, the Socialist with whom

---

[1] Unidentified.
[2] A reference to his review of *Collected Poems* (Letter 4895 and p. 144 n. 1). See also Letter 4922 and p. 166 n.1.

he is great friends, and who can ask questions in the House if necessary. I will let you know results.

When I have got things settled up, I want to go to Majorca. I feel like moving on. But there are various things to do.

Did you see Murry's effusion over me in his *Adelphi*? Semper idem![1]

You might perhaps have a talk with C[harles] L[ahr] about the Pegasus. Curtis Browns have a sort of connection agency in Paris, but I don't know if one could use them to make an agreement – or if they are much good.

Aldous and Maria brought us both bad colds – but the weather's nice.

DHL

4921. To Laurence Pollinger, 5 February 1929
Text: MS UT; Unpublished.

Hotel Beau Rivage. Bandol, Var.
5 Feb. 1929

Dear Pollinger

I had both your letters – on time, but the seals all broken.

I am returning the MS. of the 'Introd. to Paintings' by this mail. I made just a few corrections.

I shall send you also in a day or two all the poems which are quite unimpeachable: the big bulk.

The case of Elkin Mathews sheets has still not come, though sent last week from Paris by the agents. It is this railway. – When they are signed, we shall probably pack up and leave here – shall let you know.

Secker, of course, is even more like a mouse than a rabbit. But mice always reappear. – By the way, I asked him some time ago to send me a copy of *The Woman Who Rode Away*. He hasn't done so – nor referred to it. Can you perhaps tell me why?

Do send me that statement of the two visits when you can – I want to see it.[2]

If you think it is any use, then please do ask Field Roscoe & Co.[3] to apply to the Home Secretary, in my name, to ask for the return or the delivery of the two MS. copies of *Pansies*. I would rather they were returned to me c/o your office, as I shall be travelling. Let me know if I should write direct to Mr Medley – and of course the charges will be made to me.

---

[1] 'Always the same!' [2] See p. 149 n. 1.
[3] Solicitors of 36 Lincoln's Inn Fields (in 1932 they acted for Frieda Lawrence in the action for probate on DHL's will: see Nehls, iii. 477–8). Charles Douglas Medley was a senior partner in the firm.

I am glad you are not quailing. Imagine being at the mercy of *John Bull* and his pups! Pazienza! chi va piano va lontano.[1]

D. H. Lawrence

The terms with Stephensen for the picture book sound quite all right – do go ahead with the contract.

DHL

4922. To Lady Ottoline Morrell, 5 February 1929
Text: MS UT; Postmark, Band[ol] 6–2 29; Huxley 783–5.

Hotel Beau Rivage. *Bandol*, Var.

5 Feby 1929

My dear Ottoline

Aldous and Maria were here for ten days or so – neither of them very well, run down, Aldous with liver, and Maria going very thin and not eating enough. I think the *Counter-Point* book sort of got between them – she found it hard to forgive the death of the child – which one can well understand.[2] But as I say, there's more than one self to everybody, and the Aldous that writes those novels is only one little Aldous among others – probably much nicer – that don't write novels: I mean it's only one of his little selves that writes the book and makes the child die, it's not *all* himself. – No, I don't like his books: even if I admire a sort of desperate courage of repulsion and repudiation in them. But again, I feel only half a man writes the books – a sort of precocious adolescent. There is surely much more of a man in the actual Aldous. – They went on in the car to Italy – and yesterday came a desperate post-card saying they had broken down at Albenga, near Savona, and having to stay in a very bad hotel, very cold, and the wind bitter. I hope they're out of it by now. Today was a beautiful, beautiful day – all bright royal sunshine, and no wind, so one just sat out and felt the brightness. But mostly there has been a very cold wind. It's a cold winter here too, but nearly always clear.

I'm so sad you have such bad health. Aldous thought you so much better. But if you have those blinding head-aches, my word I sympathise. I never really had head-aches till I was ill eighteen months ago – but now I have a holy terror of them. Thank goodness mine are better now. What do you think yours come from? I believe they often arise from a condition of weakness, that one doesn't take sufficient count of. Are you sure you eat enough? Do you drink a little burgundy? Since I am here, and can eat, and drink wine again, I

---

[1] 'Patience! he who goes softly goes far.'

[2] Chapter xxxv of *Point Counter Point* describes the painful and long-drawn-out death of a little boy from meningitis; the child was sufficiently like Matthew Huxley to cause distress (cf. Bedford, *Aldous Huxley*, i. 207).

am surprised how the headaches don't come. One just has to build up resistance – that seems to me the only way.

And I agree with you, people are most exhausting. I like them all right at a little distance, if they will leave me alone – but I don't want to talk to them any more. I find I can sit still on a bench and be quite happy, just seeing the sea twinkle and the fisher people potter with their lobster pots. What is there to say any more, to ordinary people at least? It is lovely to be alone, especially when the sun shines. I think you should winter abroad, in some quiet place like this where you see the sun rise behind the sea at dawn, and every day different, and every day, somehow, the spangle and the glitter of the sea is a different spangle and glitter. I watch the dawn every day as I lie in bed. And now the sun has moved such a long way, and rises behind the queer, tressy, shaking eucalyptus tree.

But I want to go soon, now. Frieda has not been contented here in an hotel – she wanted a house. But I liked the hotel, warm and no effort. Then lately they have been making a great fuss over *Lady C.* – Scotland Yard holding it up – visiting my agents – sort of threatening criminal proceedings – and holding up my mail – and actually confiscating two copies, MS. copies of my poems *Pansies* which I sent to my agent Curtis Brown – saying the poems were indecent and obscene – which they're not – and putting me to a lot of trouble. I don't mind when I'm well, but one gets run down. And those dirty canaille to be calling one obscene! Really, why does one write! – or why does one write the things I write? I suppose it's destiny, but on the whole, an unkind one. Those precious young people who are supposed to admire one so much never stand up and give one a bit of backing. I believe they'd see me thrown into prison for life, and never lift a finger. What a spunkless world!

I was glad to hear of Bertie Russell. Perhaps he and his Dora do something, after all – better than his donning away in Cambridge.[1]

I had such a silly, funny little letter from E. M. Forster, telling me à propos of nothing that he admires me but doesn't read me.[2] Do you ever see him?

Did I tell you my pictures are going to be reproduced and put in a book – in colour – at 10 guineas a copy. I wrote a long foreword on painting in relation to life – good, I think, really.

Don't you think it's nonsense when Murry says that my world is not the

[1] Bertrand Arthur William Russell (1931, 3rd Earl Russell) (1872–1970), distinguished mathematician and philosopher; Fellow of Trinity College, Cambridge. Lady Ottoline had brought Russell (then her lover) and DHL together in 1915 (see *Letters*, ii. 273 n. 2; iv. 190 n. 2). m. 1921, Dora Winifred Black; in 1927 they founded Beacon Hill, a progressive school.

[2] Edward Morgan Forster (1879–1970), novelist and critic, had known DHL since 1915 (see *Letters*, ii. 262 and n. 2). He was to describe DHL, after his death, as 'the greatest imaginative novelist of our generation' (*Nation and Athenæum*, 23 March 1930).

ordinary man's world and that I am a sort of animal with a sixth sense.[1] Seems to me more likely he's[2] a sort of animal with only four senses – the real sense of touch missing. They all seem determined to make a freak of me – to save their own short-fallings, and make them 'normal.'

I wanted to go to Spain, but now it's upset – and Frieda doesn't want me to go. So I don't know what we shall do. I can even be arrested if I come to England – under the Post Office laws – O là là! – I feel like wandering away somewhere – south – south – perhaps to Africa. But I shall let you know.

I do most sincerely hope you'll be better, for I know so well what it is to fight with pain and struggle on from day to day. What I feel is that you are physically too weak, you need building up, you need to build up resistance. I'm sure you are in some way exhausted, and can't recuperate. Tell the doctors to find a way of nourishing you and fortifying you.

Remember me to Philip – Aldous says he is busy editing memoirs for a book, which I'm sure he'll like doing.[3]

We have got a copy of *Sergeant Grisha* – good in its way, but so depressing and – sort of Jewish: not quite true.[4]

I do hope you'll be better and feel stronger.

love from us both   D. H. Lawrence

4923. To Laurence Pollinger, [6 February 1929]
Text: MS UT; Unpublished.

Bandol. Var.
6 Feb.

Dear Pollinger
    The enclosed from Seltzer[5] – he was a long time answering – now writes in

---

[1] Murry remarked in his review of *Collected Poems*: ' ... Mr Lawrence himself is beyond us ... He is like a creature of another kind than ours, some lovely unknown animal with the gift of speech. With a strange sixth sense he explores this world of ours ... '
[2] he's] is
[3] Lady Ottoline's husband, Philip Edward Morrell (1870–1943). In November 1929 he published an abridged edn of the Greville diary. Cf. Letter 5484.
[4] See Letter 4872 and n. 1.
[5] In reply to DHL's letter, 3 December 1928, Seltzer had written on 21 January 1929 (TMS UT):

Dear Lawrence:
    Yes, of course, you may include *Birds, Beasts and Flowers* in a collected edition of your poems, and also *Tortoises* which I published separately. If I did not owe you any money, I'd let you have the rights free, but as I am in debt to you, and God knows when I shall be able to pay, I had better act on your suggestion and charge, say, $2.00, to be deducted from the amount I owe you. This sum seems to be about right, but if you think otherwise, name the figure and it shall be as you say ...

a very funny way – is the $2.00 touch heavy irony? I suppose his permission is valid. What are the Vikings doing about the poems? – got cold feet?

                                                                              DHL

4924. To S. S. Koteliansky, [7 February 1929]
Text: MS BL; Postmark, Ba[ndol] 9–[. . .]29; Moore 1127–8.

                                              Hotel Beau Rivage. Bandol. Var.
                                                                    7 Jan. 1929
My dear Kot.

I suppose you haven't seen Pollinger – I wish you saw him and had a talk with him. – The men from the Yard admitted that they had the MSS. of *Pansies* and they consider them indecent and obscene – which is a lie. Apparently by law, *if* the things are so considered, they are in the right. But I am having C[urtis] B[rown]'s solicitors apply for the release of these MS. – I haven't heard anything from Jack H[utchinson] – and there is nothing further. Mail seems to go through normally, even to CB's office – on which the Yard seems to have concentrated all its efforts. C[harles] L[ahr] thinks they suspect CB's of having handled the whole edit. – but I doubt it. I wonder if old CB has his finger in other pies –

The Pegasus have not written anything further, so things are where they were. I haven't Nancy Cunard's address – have you? If you sent it me I'd write her myself. Aldous and Maria evidently are quite out of touch with her.[1]

They, Aldous and Maria, left a week ago for Florence, where they want to sell the car. On Saturday they broke down at Albenga near Savona and I've not heard a word since. They both seemed rather seedy and run down, I thought. Aldous is really nicer – getting older and a bit more aware of other people's existence.

Spain seems really rather upset[2] – anyhow a great deal of police-watching going on – so I think we'll not go there just yet. I want to move from here soon – though it's on the whole sunny and pleasant – but perhaps go to Italy and find some little house – and then go to Spain later – or somewhere else. – I shall soon have finished typing out the pansies again and correcting them.

---

[1] Nancy Cunard (1896–1965), poet, biographer, rebel and hedonist; owner of the Hours Press. Huxley fell desperately in love with her in 1922; their affair ended, after six to nine months, as abruptly as it began. See *Nancy Cunard: Brave Poet, Indomitable Rebel*, ed. Hugh Ford, 1968; Bedford, *Aldous Huxley*, i. 132–44.
[2] On 30 January 1929 *The Times* reported 'Revolt in Spain'; several units of the Artillery Corps attempted to seize control of garrison towns; most attempts failed immediately, others were quelled within a few days.

Yes, it would be a good thing if someone were in Paris whom one could trust, to do an edition and keep it going.

Ottoline writes very friendly – says she has such a lot of pain nowadays. We've both had a bit of flu – not bad – but it gets at my chest of course. I had a typescript copy of the 'Introd. to the Paintings' from Pollinger, and returned it corrected. They are to give me £250 down, for the pictures, and a royalty of 5% – quite decent.

How are you and what are you doing?

DHL

4925. To P. R. Stephensen, 7 February 1929
Text: MS IEduc; cited in Munro 301.

Hotel Beau Rivage. *Bandol.* Var
7 Feb. 1929

Dear Stephensen

I had the typescript of the 'Introd. to the Paintings', and returned it to Pollinger with a few corrections – hope he has it safely by now. The corrections are not important, anyhow. Did you read it? and did you like it? Ask Jack Lindsay if he knows if my few facts are sound – about Elizabeth's eyebrows and James I's inherited pox-effects, etc.[1] I read them somewhere. I think it's a good essay –

Pollinger told me the terms – sounds very good. How are you getting on with the rest of the work? I don't suppose there'll be any more bother with the John Hops[2] and suppressing – I believe it was a flutter more owing to the pirated editions coming in, than anything. Let me see a copy[3] when you have the proof of the little advertisement sheet – and keep me posted, I want to do some American propaganda. A good way to sound the customs will be to send a set of proofs of the pictures to Alfred Stieglitz, he is an influential figure in the New York art world, and will, I believe, help me a lot. There are other people too.

Shall you keep the plates of the pictures – and the type – for a cheaper edition later on? It seems a shame to destroy them – But the type could be scattered, and a cheaper type used, to make a totally different edition – that wouldn't be much expense. How many pictures can you print from one plate?

---

[1] 'Elizabeth had no eyebrows ... [James I] had brought [the pox] into the world with him, from that fool Darnley' ('Introduction to These Paintings', *Phoenix* 553). The source of DHL's information is unknown.

[2] DHL's character Richard Somers 'knew that Johnny Hop was Australian for policeman', *Kangaroo*, chap. XVI.

[3] see a copy] know

I am typing the pansies out again – nearly done – what a job! But never say die.

Spain looks a bit upset, and too much police business I expect, just now. We may go back to Italy soon – I rather want to get a move on. Been here about long enough.

Anyhow keep me posted as regards all developments.

ever   D. H. Lawrence

When do you now think the book will be ready?

I've got those two panels finished. They're rather lovely. I took off the blue trousers (of course) they were too stuffy – and called it *Spring* – rather lovely and a tiny bit Frenchy old-fashioned. The other one *Summer Dawn* very different, but I like it very much. I can't make up my mind about sending them.

4926. To Earl and Achsah Brewster, 7 February 1929
Text: MS UT; Brewster 194–6.

Hotel Beau Rivage. Bandol. Var.

7 Feb. 1929[1]

Dear Earl and Achsah

Achsah, your second letter came tonight – glad you're full of song and firelight, anyhow. This hotel, thank goodness, is always pleasant and warm: and the place is practically always sunny, though the wind can be devilish. I don't think Frieda should have been discontented – but discontent is a state of mind. Now that I am beginning to come to the end of Bandol and the sojourn here, she's beginning to like it, and I expect her, as soon as I'm ready to go, to refuse to leave its paradisal strand. La donna è mobile.[2] But I'm grateful to the place, it's been very kind to me – and though I've had a bit of flu now, I've not had to stay in bed at all, and have eaten my meals and thanked the gods. I'm really a lot stronger, even with a bit of flu on me.

The Huxleys left a week ago – we heard from them that on the Saturday they broke down at Albenga, near Savona – this side Genoa – and were in an icy hotel in a piercing wind waiting. Since then not a sound. I'm a bit worried, as they were neither of them well. He was run down and livery, and if she doesn't watch out, her lungs are going to give her trouble again. People live the wrong way of their nerves, and of course it destroys them. She minded *Point-Counter-Point* – his killing the child – it was all too life-like and horrible – and the love-affair with the Lucy was Aldous' affair with Nancy Cunard – I think Maria hardly forgives it. And perhaps now he's sorry he did it. But it

---

[1] 1929] 1928   [2] 'Woman is fickle.'

has made them money, and Maria wants money – says so. Yes, she wants to buy a new car in Paris. – But I say there are many men in a man, and the Aldous that wrote the *CounterPoint* and killed the child is only one of the Aldouses, and perhaps by no means the best or most important. I think he's really nicer – realising the things one mustn't do, if one is to live.

My pictures are being done by young men who have been running an edition de luxe press – The Fanfrolico Press – but now it is to change, and be the Mandrake Press – and behind it is a Jew bookseller – Edward Goldston. I think they are all right. Brett is still *hoping* to sell, or have sold, a picture. She sounds excited again, but a bit potty. I dont see how she can help it. I think Mabel is being a trifle mean to her just now – les femmes –

I have nearly re-typed my *Pansies* and made them better. I think you'll like them. For stories and things, I've not done much. There's one – 'Mother and Daughter' – in the next *Criterion* – if anybody lends you that expensive and stewed T.S.Eliot quarterly.[1] The book of pictures will come later in the spring. I wonder how many copies they'll give me – and if I can give you one! Perhaps get a set of proofs.

No, Majorca is by no means a desert isle – like Capri, only bigger. But now there is this revolt business, and police everywhere wanting to look at people's papers – so we may put Spain off again, especially as Frieda doesn't want to go, and come to Italy for a bit, and perhaps take a smallish house somewhere. If we come to Italy I shall come to Capri to see you.

I feel rather like wandering – going to Spain – Morocco – Tunis – anywhere south. I want to go south again, to the southern Mediterranean. I wouldn't mind even going later to India for a spell, to see if I could do an Indian novel – novel with the Indian setting. It tempts me. If one could be fairly sure of not getting ill. Do you hear from Mukerji?[2] Has he gone back? I was thinking of him several times lately.

Is there still the house at Anacapri that Earl mentioned, available?

Poor old Brooks![3] but how nice to be taken on a yacht to Greece, if it doesn't *blow* as it mostly does here!

Tiresome, I've lost Earl's letter with the address of your show in New York. Send it me at once, and I'll get Stieglitz to go and see it, and a few of those people, and perhaps they'll give it a write-up. I do wish you could make a few thousand dollars.

---

[1] The story, written before 7 June 1928 (*Letters*, vi. 421), was published in *Criterion*, viii (April 1929), 394–419 (Roberts C184). T. S. Eliot edited the journal 1922–39.

[2] Dhana-Gopàla Mukhopàdhyaya (Mukerji) (1890–1936), Indian writer and friend of the Brewsters who introduced him to DHL at Gsteig in July 1928 (see *Letters*, vi. 485).

[3] John Ellingham Brooks (1863–1929), expatriate and Hellenist, resident for many years on Capri where DHL had met him in 1920 (see *Letters*, iii. 443 n. 2).

No Achsah, you are wrong. If one is a man, one must fight, and slap back at one's enemies, because they are the enemies of life – And if one can't slap the life-enemies in the eye, one must try to kick their behinds – a sacred duty. We are passive when we are dead. Life is given us to act with.

Tonight is the Bandol philharmonic concert, so of course we've got to go – and Madame[1] says we shall be enchanté, so let's hope so. I only hope we shan't be enrhumé[2] into the bargain.

Well, I suppose we'll turn up one day. Somehow I don't feel very far away.

As for Harwood – vogue la galère.[3] Awful if the galère never puts to sea: storms or not!

DHL

4927. To Martin Secker, [9 February 1929]
Text: MS UInd; Postmark, Bandol 9–2 29; Secker 116.

Hotel Beau Rivage, *Bandol*, Var
Saturday

Dear Secker

Things are going ahead – I've got C[urtis] B[rown]'s solicitors to apply to Home Office for return of MSS – and several M P.'s ready to stand up in the House – and perhaps Ramsay himself would put the question, if necessary.[4] We'll see how it all goes.

Did you send Max Hunger a copy of *Lost Girl* and *Plumed Serpent*. And would you send me a copy of *Woman Who Rode Away* here, please, as I've promised it.

I don't think it would be wise at the moment to send a copy of the novel to you. Orioli is away – Florence is so icy cold – but I'm afraid he's sold that little second edition out. But I have one or two copies of the first edition in London, only the price is four guineas – to the public, five. If you wish, I could have a copy sent to Bridgefoot.

The Huxleys broke down in *Albenga* and had to stay two days – nearly frozen to death. They say Florence is colder than it's ever been before. Seems to me this is still the best and warmest place, as things go[5] – nearly always sunny, only cold winds.

I believe the upset in Spain, too, is fairly serious – anyhow a lot of policing

---

[1] Madame Douillet, owner of the Hotel Beau Rivage, Bandol.   [2] 'given a cold'.
[3] 'Let's chance it' (literally: 'push the boat out').
[4] James Ramsay MacDonald (1866–1937), Leader of the Labour Opposition, who would begin his second term as Prime Minister in June 1929. For an account of the debate in the Commons, 28 February (in which MacDonald did participate), see Introduction pp. 5–6.
[5] MS reads 'so'.

all over the place, and examining people's papers. So *that*'s off for the moment. I suppose we shall go back to Italy when it warms up a bit. Frieda wants Lago di Garda – which I like, but it's pretty cold. We'll see. And for the moment, one is well off here.

Shall send the poems to London again next week.

DHL

4928. To Charles Lahr, [9 February 1929]
Text: MS Lazarus; Postmark, Bandol 9–2 29; Moore 1128–9.

Hotel Beau Rivage, *Bandol.* Var
Saturday.

Dear Lahr

Many thanks for yours and for the receipt. Here things seem much the same. Pollinger said would I tell him to instruct their lawyer to apply to the Home Office for the return of the two MSS, and I said yes. St John Hutchinson said he had several members willing to move, and they might even get Ramsay to do it. We'll see what happens.

The man of the Pegasus said his company felt they must have a council of war to see whether they could undertake this book, owing to 'rumours in the press.' So they are hanging fire still. I'll remember your points if they come to the scratch.

The poems are almost finished typing. Jack Hutchinson wants a copy for these belligerent 'Members' to read. I shall send him the old duplicate on Monday – and as soon as I hear he has it, send you a new dup. – revised – from the new typing.

I do hope Davies isn't going to be hard up. I'll write to him again, and he'll stay a bit here on his way through.

Glad – or rather sad – to hear about Harold T. Mason. I met him and his wife[1] and he seemed so friendly. But now I know why he said he never sold any copies of *Reflections on the Death of a Porcupine* – or so few. I think he has paid altogether $400 on that book. Did you ever see it, by the way? Americans who come over vow he must have sold a good number. Ask him for a copy, let's see what he's doing. I'll pay for it.

D. H. Lawrence

[1] Anne Brakely Mason (1892–1963).

4929. To Rhys Davies, [9 February 1929]
Text: TMSC NWU; Huxley 785–6.

Hotel Beau Rivage, *Bandol*, Var.
Saturday.

Dear Davies,

Well I was sorry about the story, especially as Lahr says you look like being hard up. But if only your novel is done, you can soon do the story up a bit, and we can place it.

When *will* your novel be done? And when will you be coming along? Let me know, as we can have a room for you. The hotel gets very full nowadays. And it is possible my sister will be coming for a fortnight.[1] I am waiting to hear from her. So if she comes you will see her.

The Huxleys say Italy is icy cold, colder than it's ever been. On the whole, we seem to be pretty well off here.

Don't for goodness sake wear yourself out over that book. I've *nearly* re-typed all the *Pansies*, which has been a fair sweat, as I do so hate typing, and am bad at it. Then we both had a bit of flu – but not bad.

Send a line then to say when you'll come, and au revoir from us both.

D. H. Lawrence

4930. To Marianne Moore, 11 February 1929
Text: MS UT; Postmark, Bandol 12–2 29; cited in Marianne Moore, *Predilections* (New York, 1955), p. 107.

c/o Signor G. Orioli, 6 Lungarno Corsini, *Florence*, Italy
11 Feb 1929

Dear Marianne Moore[2]

Mabel Lujan asked me to send you a copy of my poems, *Pansies* – so today I have done so, by registered mail. Will you please let me know at once if they arrive. Perhaps you may like one or two of them for the *Dial*, but if they don't seem to you suitable, don't bother about them a bit. Only would you mind handing on the MS. to Edwin Rich of Curtis Brown Ltd. – as I suppose he will arrange for publication – everything of mine goes through their hands.

Mabel Lujan said you were displeased that I never wrote personally to the *Dial* – but surely I answered any letter nicely and friendlily – and then I never

---

[1] Ada Clarke arrived on 12 February.

[2] Marianne Craig Moore (1887–1972), American poet; in 1925 she succeeded Scofield Thayer as editor of the *Dial*, a magazine to which DHL had often contributed. (See Nicholas Joost and Alvin Sullivan, *D. H. Lawrence and 'The Dial'*, Carbondale, 1970; see also *Letters*, vi. 46 and n. 4.) She selected 'When I went to the Circus' from the *Pansies* MS and published it in *Dial*, lxxxvi (May 1929), 383–4 (Roberts C186); in July 1929 she published ten more poems from *Pansies* (Roberts C189). See Letter 5055 and n. 3.

think people want to be bothered. I *nearly* met Schofield Thayer once – and sorry I didn't – Where is he now? – I should have liked to see you in New York – but how was I to know you would like to see me! – many people don't.

I want to come to New York, to go to Taos – but really, I don't trust the authorities – and now they have started fussing in London, about my novel – and have even held up the MS. of the poems I sent there, saying *they* are indecent – which is surely a lie. What is one to do, nowadays, between policemen and prudes and swindlers. The *Dial* sounds a quiet haven – but even the *Dial* doesn't like me much.[1] – We are staying here in Bandol near Marseille a little longer, then going back to Italy – so would you write me there, if you get the poems. And many greetings – and all my admiration for steering the *Dial* along so bravely and so long – and more or less alone, too!

D. H. Lawrence[2]

4931. To Mabel Dodge Luhan, 11 February 1929
Text: MS Brill; Luhan 340–1.

Bandol. Var. France.
11 february 1929

Dear Mabel

Today I have sent to Marianne Moore a copy of the *Pansies*. It hasn't got my name on, or anything, because the police started a fuss in London over *Lady C.* and even confiscated two MS. copies of the *Pansies* – said they were obscene – a *lie* – I am suing for the return of the MS. – But don't mention it in New York, please – not to anybody – it'll only start the smut-hounds bellowing again. But do let me know if the *Pansies* arrive safely at the *Dial* office – perhaps they might have a typescript copy made, and charge it to me. – Then I want Marianne Moore to send the MS. over to Curtis Brown, they'll have to place it. The Viking Press talked of doing my *Collected Poems* in New York – if they really did so, I suppose I'd offer them the *Pansies* – otherwise Knopf. –

I got the cheque for $100.00 from the *Graphic* – many thanks – it should have gone Via Curtis Brown, they get 10%. Glad you liked the article.

About coming – we really want to come, if only for the summer. But are you sure it's quite safe for me – won't somebody or other begin doing one dirt? If I were quite sure we'd come in all right and peacefully, and have a

---

[1] A great deal of critical attention had been given, in the *Dial*, to DHL's publications, and some of it was inevitably censorious (see Joost and Sullivan, *Lawrence and 'The Dial'*, pp. 178ff).

[2] In her version of the text of this letter Moore included the following: 'Regarding my statement about the Pensées: there are lines in the book, that are the outcome of certain hurts and I am not saying that in every case the lines themselves leave no shadow of hurt' (Moore, *Predilections*, p. 107). This passage is not in DHL's MS; the words are Moore's own: see Letter 5055 and n. 3.

decent summer, I'd say we would definitely sail towards end of March. But even if we come, don't wait in New York longer than you wish. It's New Mexico I want to go to, really.

My pictures are being reproduced in colour to be done in a book, at fifty – or sixty dollars a time. I'm going to send over proofs when they are ready.

I suppose Gurdjeff is as you say an imaginary incarnation of Lucifer[1] – but I doubt he'll never strike much of a light.[2] All so *would-be* – and oh, so much talk.

I hope we'll come, really.

DHL

Write to me
c/o Signor G. Orioli, 6 Lungarno Corsini, *Florence*, Italy.
I expect we shall soon go back to Italy.

4932. To Elkin Mathews, 12 February 1929
Text: MS YU; Postmark, Ba[ndol] 12 2 29; Unpublished.

Hotel Beau Rivage. *Bandol, Var*, France
12 Feb. 1929

Dear Sir

I received the case of sheets of *Rawdon's Roof* on Saturday evening – 9th. – after a good deal of delay on the railway and enquiry at the station. They are now signed – 531. sheets signed – and packed up again, and I am sending them today to Davies, Turner & Cocquyt – 23 rue Baudin. Paris IXe – by *grande vitesse*, for them to forward to you. I am not paying the railway charge, because they never deliver once the freight is paid – witness the ten days which this package took to get from Paris here – and but for constant nagging at the station I should never have got it. Curtis Browns asked me to have the case sent direct to you, for speed – so will you please tackle the agents – Davies, Turner & Cocquyt – if there is any more delay.

I hope the 33 Conduit St address is right – there is no address of yours anywhere in or outside the package.

Yours truly   D. H. Lawrence

<hr>

[1] Georgei Ivanovitch Gurdjieff (1874?–1949), Russian occultist of Greek parentage. In 1922 he established the Gurdjieff Institute at Fontainebleau, where Katherine Mansfield died in 1923. See James Moore, *Gurdjieff and Mansfield* (1980). For DHL's view of the Institute, see *Letters*, v. 422 n. 2.
[2] DHL is punning on 'lucifer' as slang for 'match'.

4933. To Maria Huxley, [13 February 1929]
Text: Moore 1130–1.

Hôtel Beau Rivage, Bandol
Wednesday

Dear Maria:

Yours this morning – so sorry you aren't well – do listen to me and think carefully about nourishing yourself – you don't take enough proper nourishment – do think about it – and have Ovaltine or Horlicks or something.

Bitter cold again here – water-pipes frozen, no water in the hotel – and crammed full of people! My sister arrived yesterday – 3 hours late in Toulon, and no heat in train all the way from Paris – frozen! I was about frozen waiting: – a *vile* Toulon day – but today is sunny but icy. We shall stay here till something improves: my sister leaves on the 22nd. I wish you could have brought me a blue coat – the measure is 15½ inches across the back – between the sleeves. Bring it if there's time – but of course, don't bother about it.

Jack Hutchinson wrote very nicely and very willing to help. I have posted him the 3rd copy of *Pansies* – but I've typed them all out afresh – and revised many, of course. No news from anybody lately. – My sister seemed sad – the Midlands must be just gruesome now. – We might go to Corsica – one can cross to Livorno if one doesn't like it. But we shall be here till end of month. – I do hope you've sold that heavy old brute of a car. The flower book sounds lovely[1] – I took the blue trousers off my men in the picture and it's rather lovely now.

Love to both from both.

4934. To Terence Holliday, [15 February 1929]
Text: David A. Randall, *Antiquarian Bookman*, 4 March 1954.

[Hotel Beau Rivage, Bandol, Var.]
[15 February 1929]

many thanks for the cheque.[2] I realize it is a sheer gift, as far as business goes. I feel the coals of fire of the booksellers singeing my scalp. I ought really to have your cheque mounted on gold and framed, so that I can stand it on my

---

[1] The 'flower book' is unidentified.

[2] DHL was replying to the following letter from Holliday (see also letter following and n. 3):

Since I had at least thirty advance orders which had been solicited and accepted by us in good faith, as we had no idea that there would be any difficulty about importing the book, when difficulties developed our customers demanded copies, and by the time the American edition came along we were fairly certain that the Florentine edition could not be obtained, although we had sent you our check for thirty-five copies. We filled our orders with the only edition available. It was either that or deprive my customers of the privilege of reading what to my

table wherever I go, and look on it, as on the brazen serpent,[1] everytime I'm swindled.

4935. To Giuseppe Orioli, 15 February 1929
Text: MS UCLA; Unpublished.

Hotel Beau Rivage. *Bandol.* Var.

Friday 15 Feb 1929

Dear Pino

Your registered letter this morning – with Sylvia Beach; two Holliday Bookshops, and one Frank Curtin[2] – was that all you sent? – I enclose them all. Nice of the Holliday to send $180 on the pirated copies.[3] I have written him.

Did you send on any other *vaglie*[4] besides the one for Liras 92. – which I received?

Lahr has paid one hundred and eleven guineas for his 111 copies of 2nd edit.

---

mind was a supremely great and fine book. I am a bookseller. My business is to fill the orders I receive from clients who have been guided by my admiration and respect for your work. I could not help it that you had written a book which made so many difficulties.

[1] Cf. Numbers xxi. 9.

[2] The Californian lawyer Curtin wrote as follows on 18 January 1929:

My dear D. H. Lawrence:

I am glad and grateful because of your promise to have a copy of Lady Chatterley saved for me—supremely so now that at last I have read the book and found it so splendid. My bookseller got me a bootleg edition. It cost him $10 and me $15—a sloppy piece of work mechanically as such things often are, but this even more than usual, seriously marred by the many typographical errors.

Now I am more anxious than ever to possess the genuine book, for to me the work seems a perfect piece of fine art, a gem finely proportioned, perfectly cut and flawless. If as they whose word is law say, the book is grossly "obscene" "lewd" and "filthy", then I am grossly obscene, lewd and filthy, and my prayer instead of being one of contrition is a prayer of thanks.

I am very hopeful and fairly confident that it is simply a matter of time, though possibly months before I shall have a friend in Paris to whom I can entrust the book, so please hang on to one copy. And by the way, when I get the name and address of that friend shall I write to you or to Davis & Orioli? In conformance with your December 28th letter I am sending this letter "c/o Pino Orioli, 6 Lungarno Corsini, Florence, Italy". But the address on the postcard acknowledging receipt of my original order is "Davis & Orioli, 16 Lungarno Acciaioli, Florence, Italy". Which should I use?

Gratefully,

DHL added in the margin opposite the end of Curtin's first paragraph: '– I'm afraid these are in the original too!!' and, after Curtin's signature at the end of his letter: 'I'm sending him a note – so you needn't bother. DHL' (DHL's 'note' is unlocated.)

[3] Among DHL's 'Memoranda' (MS NWU) is the note: 'Terence Holliday – 5th Aven. Bank N.Y. royalties on 30 pirated copies $180 – Jan 31st'.

[4] 'money orders'.

I shall add up and pay you your percentage very soon now – I wanted to have all the second edition paid for first: quite a lot!

My sister is here, so she will take the poems back to London. I want them to be published *cheap*, for the public.

Very swank, your notice of *Nerinda*.[1] I look forward to having a copy.

P. R. Stephensen, Fanfrolico Press. 5 Bloomsbury Square, W.C. 1.

asked me if he could get a list of subscribers to *Lady C.* Would it be a great nuisance for you to send [2] him the names you think worth while? – he has the bookshops, I imagine. He expects to have the book out in April – 500 copies at ten guineas each – we must get him to give you a copy. – If you make him a list, don't put any mention of me or of *Lady C.* or anything on it.

Here also it has been so cold, that all the water froze up. Today is warmer – but the air cold still.

Will Aldous and Maria bring me a blue coat?

For two days the train did not come from Paris – snow and ice-bound! Horrible!

Tell Maria, Frieda has finished her pyjamas – sulphur yellow, with pink – so she'll look a sneezer.[3] We'll send them to Paris.

Yes, we'll wait here till the world warms up a bit – no use moving. But we'll come to Italy in the spring.

love from both   DHL

Could you send to

Herrn Dr. Max Mohr, 'Wolfsgrube', *Rottach-am-Tegernsee*, Oberbayern, Germania

a copy of the 2nd edit. for German publishers to read? He is trying to arrange a German translation. I shall get the copy back.

The Pegasus were almost going to do an edition, when the great English scare frightened them – so I've heard no more.

DHL

4936. To P. R. Stephensen, 15 February 1929
Text: MS Anon; Munro 301–3.

Hotel Beau Rivage. *Bandol.* Var
15 Feb 1929

Dear Stephensen

So sorry you have flu – I think one ought to mind whom one kisses – its mushy, anyhow. Flu is certainly plague – and moreover, it is the disease of the

---

[1] Cf Letter 4807 and n. 4.   [2] MS reads 'you send'.
[3] I.e. 'exceptionally smart or striking'.

changing psyche – when mankind is in for one of the great psychic changes, as before the Renaissance and after the Cromwell period – then plague marks the change in the physical constitution – it is the whole chemical and dynamic condition of the blood and body undergoing a change. So take care and be aware, and be ready to change.

You make quite a dash at me – poor Pommy[1] with a beard! Brotherliness is all right – but *defenceless* brotherliness, that will let itself be dragged into a war, fooled, despised, made bankrupt and as good as exterminated – won't do. At the present moment you've got to have your brotherliness armed to the teeth, and to know your enemies. Brotherliness isn't something you can just have, like jam for tea – it's something you have to fight like hell for, to re-instate it. I am only capable of a fighting brotherliness – the easy sort isn't in me, I have had to struggle so hard to keep what I am. The bourgeois, the machine civilisation, *and* the 'Worker' (as such) all want to destroy real humanness. If Bolshevism is going to classify me as a Worker or a non-worker, I am against it. – I *hate* our civilisation, our ideals, our money, our machines, our intellectuals, our upper classes. But I hate them because I've tried them and given them a long chance – and they're rotten. If a man has not 'risen in the world' he'll be *forced* to admit there is something 'above him.' – Many ladies nowadays, very many, have love affairs with their chauffeurs – the chauffeur is the favorite fucker. But the chauffeur stays where he is – and is a *machine à plaisir* – and the lady stays where *she* is – and nothing is altered in the least. If Mellors had never *found out* the upper classes, by being one of them, Connie would just have had him and put him down again – elle m'a planté là![2] – No, it's all much more difficult than you imagine. The Working man is not much of a British Bulldog any more[3] – he's rather a shivering cur – one has to try slowly to rouse the old spirit in him – and *definitely* disillusion him about the 'upperness.' – You see you yourself are really much more *impressed* by the 'upper' gentleman – even by Aldous – than ever Mellors is. You are impressed, you can't help it. And that makes you squirm. And you'll be impressed until you know all their tricks – then you won't squirm any more. It's all very well being a bush-whacker, but when the business-men and intellectuals are going to whack the bushwhacker into limbo – which is rapidly happening – why, you'd better do something else than whack bush.[4] – It's all so difficult – and such a struggle – and will take so

[1] 'Englishman'.   [2] 'she jilted me!'

[3] The February 1929 issue of *London Aphrodite* which Stephensen had sent to DHL contained his poem 'Barrel-Organ Rhapsody'; in it he praised the unemployed workers as the new 'Bulldog breed' (Munro, *Wild Man of Letters*, p. 78).

[4] The Mandrake Press was soon to publish Stephensen's *The Bushwhackers: Sketches of Life in the Australian Outback* (June 1929) (see Munro, ibid., p. 79).

long. And you Australians want it quick and easy, and think that fiddling about with girls will do it. My God, if it would! Meanwhile you'll merely be shoved aside, you Australians. You don't *bite on* hard enough. All that silly twiddling with girls! – it isn't even really sex. – I have the *Aphrodite* – and it's very much that twiddling business – sticky and feeble. Did you think it better not to print 'My Naughty Book' etc? Perhaps just as well.

No, I won't do a cheaper edition if you don't want it. The plates are *yours*, so how could I? But I would have liked, if possible, to bring out the pictures quite cheap, later, so that anybody who wanted could get them. And the text too. But after a year, if you wish. I *can't* see how a little cheap edition affects collectors of first editions. But you can put a *year* stipulation in the contract if you wish.

My sister is here, and will bring *Spring* and *Summer Dawn* – and have them delivered to Dorothy Warren.

The page of proof is very handsome print but it'll need a pretty big page to carry it off.

I have asked Orioli to send you a list of such subscribers as he thinks would be of use.

Do print – *Moses* in the prospectus. – I want very much to see a proof of a *pale* picture – like the *Boccaccio*.[1]

Am so glad your flu is better – but be careful – and *be wary* – in England, *always* be wary. It is not Australia, where none of the animals bite.

———

Oh my dear chap, brotherliness is real, God knows it is – but if it isn't armed to the teeth, it'll soon cease to exist.

We shall be here for a while longer. Been *bitterly* cold. – all water frozen.

My sister makes me feel *very* down about the Miners and the Midlands; she is herself terribly depressed – like an illness – *curse* the industrial world.

DHL[2]

4937. To Brewster Ghiselin, 16 February 1929
Text: MS Ghiselin; Nehls, iii. 307.

Hotel Beau Rivage. *Bandol*. Var.
16 Feby 1929

Dear Bruce
    I have not heard again from you – I suppose you had my letter in answer to

---

[1] *The Finding of Moses* was used for the prospectus of the Mandrake *Paintings*. The *Boccaccio* is *Boccaccio Story* (*Paintings*, plate [9]).

[2] Following the text of this letter in Munro 303, a list of '*Pictures sent to Dorothy Warren*' is printed; it does not form part of the MS of the letter: see Letter 4886.

yours. We are still here – it's been so cold that the railway stopped running, so did all the water in the hotel – now it's warmer. We both had flu, but fairly mildly – hope you haven't got it, it seems universal.

My sister is here staying a while with us – when she leaves we shall go, I really think. I was rather surprised when she told me you had not sent that little African musical instrument to her boy – and he on tenterhooks to get it, poor lad. Would you send it him please, if it's not too much trouble:

Master Jack Clarke, 'Torestin', Broadway, *Ripley near Derby*.

The Huxleys were here for ten days – both rather seedy. Now they are freezing in Florence, where there are 50,000 cases of influenza, and ice over the Arno!

How are you bearing up against Oxford? – I hope it's not doing deadly things to you.

We sat out on the end of the jetty this afternoon – where you swam. It was just warm enough to sit for an hour, but colder than that time. A palish octopus kept rising and sinking in the water, pale green like a streak of slime. You wouldn't have bathed today.

Do let us know how you are, and many regards from us both.

D. H. Lawrence

4938. To Laurence Pollinger, 16 February 1929
Text: MS UT; Unpublished.

Hotel Beau Rivage, *Bandol*, Var
16 Feby 1929

Dear Pollinger

So sorry you have flu – hope it's not bad. We've had it too – but mildly, thank heaven. I hear in Florence there are 50,000 cases!

The Elkin Mathews sheets are gone off – owing to the P[aris-] L[yon-] M[arseille] being stopped with snow and ice, they didn't actually leave till yesterday, from the station. I sent them grande vitesse, paid as far as Paris – to the agent who forwarded them to me

Davies, Turner & Cocquyt, 23 rue Baudin. Paris, IXe

they ought certainly to be in Paris by Monday. They are addressed to:

for Messrs Elkin Mathews. 33 Conduit St. *London W. 1.*

I don't know if that is right – but you said send them direct. And I wrote Elkin Mathews of what I had done. So now I hope they come all right, and quickly.

I heard from Stephensen you received the corrected MS. of the 'Introd. to the Paintings' – I was wondering about it. – And did you get the letter from Thomas Seltzer, which I forwarded, giving me the rights to *BirdsBeasts and*

Flowers in America? I wish I knew what the Viking Press intend doing about the *Collected Poems*.[1] And I hope you have Seltzer's letter.

I do trust you'll get over this flu quickly.

Sincerely   D. H. Lawrence

I could only pay for the sheets as far as Paris – but I did that.

4939. To Edward Dahlberg, 17 February 1929
Text: MS UTul; Postmark, Bandol 17–2 29; Moore 1131.

Hotel Beau Rivage, *Bandol*, Var.

17 Feby 1929

Dear Dahlberg

So sorry you've had that appendicitis – for heaven's sake, *leave off being unlucky* – you seem to ask for it. Do go back to America and be quiet for a bit, and get strong.

Putnam's wrote me they were sending me the first batch of your novel in galleys, but it's not here yet. They say you think of 'Hot-dogs'! for a title – but it's surely[2] too cheap. Better 'Cold Feet' – they've all got cold feet all the time. Or else a proper phrase: 'It's Cold on the Bed-rock!'. – I think the second is better.

It wouldn't be any use sending you the novel to U. S. A. either, it would only be confiscated in customs. So I am sending you the money back – and the surplus postage you sent me – and the trifle more which you will please spend on eating the right food – and don't thank me, because I hate all this kind of business. If you care for what I say, take care, get well, and be in condition to put up the right kind of fight in life. Life needs to be fought for, by men.

If you go back to New York I will give you a letter to a couple of people – but leave off being a down-and-outer – you've got other things to do.

Putnams will give you the money for the cheque.

D. H. Lawrence

Call it, if you like 'O! the Down-and-outer!' a title with a bit of jump. – And then don't bother me.

4940. To Maria Huxley, 18 February 1929
Text: Huxley 786–7.

Hôtel Beau Rivage, Bandol, Var.

Monday, 18 Feb., 1929.

Dear Maria, –

Your letter this evening. I'm a bit worried about your health, so please be a

---

[1] Cf. Letter 4812 and p. 66 n 1.   [2] MS reads 'it's surely it's'.

good child and *really* take care for a while – don't bother about *anything* else. Now do as you're bidden, and don't go squiffing about any more, but keep still and warm and well fed: and don't buy a car just yet. Just be without one for six weeks, really. You need a rest from driving.

I wrote you to Haskard's, but perhaps you didn't get it. Alas, my blue coat is an illusion! – My sister is here, arrived a week ago: and I am fond of her, but she fills me with tortures of angry depression. I feel all those Midlands behind her, with their sort of despair. I want to put my pansies in the fire, and myself with them – oh, dear! But this afternoon Frieda and she have gone to Toulon – and it was a lovely warm day, the loveliest – so you should have had a good journey – O the blue sea! But *all the palm trees and eucalyptus trees of Bandol are dead* – frozen dead. They look funny and dry and whitish, desiccated – but I can't believe they'll not put forth. But Madame says the gardeners say no, they are all killed. I feel as if half the town had died. Then these wonderful blue tinkling days so still and fair!

We had a bit of 'flu – I had – but not bad. Every single body in the hotel had it – but mostly mildish.

I have no news from London. I sent Jack Hutchinson a copy of the *Pansies* a week ago – want very much to know if he's got them.

We now think of Corsica. Frieda has read it up in Baedeker, and is thrilled! So I expect we'll go – perhaps even end of next week. It sounds rather nice – and wonderful for motoring in – and all sorts of climate – Ajaccio warm like here, then the mountains for summer. Anyhow, it's only a night from Nice or Marseilles, and only six hours from Livorno. So one easily gets out. If we don't like it, we'll just cross to Florence – where it's warmer – and get our things and perhaps go to the ranch for the summer. No good trying to take Frieda even to Mallorca.

I wonder if Aldous would put Paulhan's address on this letter – look at it – Joseph Barezzi is the famous Sicilian man-servant of Port-Cros – and the letter finds me instead of Paulhan – who as you know is editor of the *Nouvelle Revue Française*.

Well, let us know you are safely arrived, and safely in bed, and warm and well fed. I shall fidget till I know.

DHL

Could you get me Nancy Cunard's address? I'll ask her if *she* will do *Lady C*.

The Pegasus makes no more show.

4941. To St John Hutchinson, 19 February 1929
Text: MS Hutchinson; Unpublished.

Hotel Beau Rivage, *Bandol*. Var.
Tuesday. 19 Feb. 1929

Dear Hutchinson

I sent you the MS. of the poems identical with those confiscated, last Tuesday – a week today. If you have not got them they too have been seized. But do let me know. They were sent registered letter mail. – I suppose you had my letter, anyhow?[1] This sort of persecution is a bit thick.

ever   D. H. Lawrence

4942. To Giuseppe Orioli, [19 February 1929]
Text: MS UCLA; Unpublished.

Bandol.
Tuesday

Dear Pino

Do please send this man another copy of the first edition, using the label enclosed.[2] And *please* send him the registration receipt of his first two copies, because then he can find out where they went astray, if the U. S. stole them – and we can claim the money for them. Conway is quite an influential person in Mexico – about the most influential Englishman – so it's well to have him do these things.

My sister leaves on Friday, and next week I think we shall go to *Corsica* – look round there. That isn't far from Florence – we can sail from Bastia to Livorno in five or six hours. And if we stay in Corsica you can come and see us.

No other news – it is warm again here, but all the beautiful palm trees and eucalyptus frozen dead – such a pity.

You put Bardol on your letters – and it is *Bandol*.

Love   DHL

P.S. Don't charge Conway for this third copy.

---

[1] The letter is unlocated.

[2] DHL had assured Conway, on 29 December 1928, that a copy of *Lady Chatterley's Lover*, first edn, would be 'rescued' for him from the few remaining (Letter 4853). This letter to Orioli was written at the end of Conway's to DHL; only p. 2 of the latter survived and it reads:

She is 19 and is continuing her education in French, Spanish, stenography, golf, riding, etc. Nan is as busy and as energetic as usual. She goes to England in July to spend the summer with the children there.

I am going to try to prepare a serious book on the Sixteenth Century Englishmen in Mexico, using the voluminous material I have in an attempt to make it readable for the average person.

I hope you will continue well. Please give our kindest regards to Mrs Lawrence.

With best wishes   Yours very sincerely

When Brentanos pay for their copies I shall send you your money, because then all the 2nd edition will be paid for – and I shall owe you about £25.

4943. To Rhys Davies, [19 February 1929]
Text: MS UT; PC v. La Cote d'Azur. Bandol (Var). – Boulevard Victor-Hugo; Postmark, Bandol 19–2 29; Unpublished.

[Hotel Beau Rivage, Bandol, Var.]
Tuesday.

– My sister leaves on Friday – and next week we may leave for Corsica – but if so, we shall come to Nice and sail from there – and so shall see you. Otherwise we shall expect you here on March 4th – I shall let you know. – Nothing new in our world, except all Bandol's palm trees are frozen dead – so Madame says – which grieves me. – Would you mind asking Cooks about boats to Corsica from Nice, and letting me know? Then I'll fix up our departure.

DHL

4944. To Nancy Pearn, [19 February 1929]
Text: MS Lazarus; PC v. La Côte d'Azur – Bandol: Plage; Postmark, Bandol 20–2 29; Unpublished.

[Hotel Beau Rivage, Bandol, Var.]
19 Feb

Received[1] proofs of 'Mother and Daughter' this evening – shall send them registered tomorrow, but there are no alterations of any account. I sent you these corrected proofs long ago. – so where are they? Do use anything of mine you like, for your Rotary magazine.[2]

DHL

4945. To Nancy Pearn, 19 February 1929
Text: MS UT; Unpublished.

Hotel Beau Rivage. *Bandol*, Var
19 Feby 1929

Dear Nancy Pearn
Here are the proofs of 'Mother and Daughter' – which I got only this evening. I doubt you won't have them back by the 21st. – you should, of course, have had them ten days ago, if the mail had not been interfered with.

[1] MS reads 'Receive'.
[2] In a letter of 13 February (TMSC UT) Nancy Pearn had asked DHL for permission to include extracts from 'Flowery Tuscany' in a Soroptimist monthly magazine for which she was responsible. (No copies of this magazine have survived in the society's archives.)

I enclose also a letter from America – would you or Pollinger answer it or not answer it, as you think best.[1]

I sent you a p.c. saying use anything you like for your Rotary magazine. I do hope Pollinger is better from his influenza.

Salutations   D. H. Lawrence

4946. To Giuseppe Orioli, [21 February 1929]

Text: MS UCLA; PC v. La Cote D'Azur – Bandol: La Jetée Vue Du Fort; Postmark, Ba[ndol] 21–2 29; Unpublished.

[Hotel Beau Rivage, Bandol, Var.]
Thursday

– I have notice of another vaglia from Florence – forwarded from Rutherford, America – and I think only for five dollars. I have made arrangements for it to be paid to the proprietor of the hotel here, as I expect we shall have left before it arrives. Do tell me if there are more of the beastly things on the way. – If you have not sent the list of subscribers to Stephensen, *don't* send it – send it to me. I believe the police are opening the letters – a great hunt after the 'naughty' books. – We want to leave for Corsica next week. Send a line.

DHL

4947. To Ada Clarke, [22 February 1929]

Text: MS Clarke; Lawrence–Gelder 201–3.

Hotel Beau Rivage, *Bandol* – Var.
Friday

My dear Sister

I felt awfully unhappy after you had left this afternoon – chiefly because you seem miserable, and I don't know what to say or do. But don't be miserable – or if you must be, at least realise that it's because of a change that is happening inside us, a change in feeling, a whole change in what we find worth while and not worth while. The things that seemed to make up one's life die into insignificance, and the whole state is wretched. I've been through it these last three years – and suffered, I tell you. But now I feel I'm coming through, to some other kind of happiness. It's a different kind of happiness we've got to come through to – but while the old sort is dying, and nothing new has appeared, it's really torture. But be patient, and realise it's a process that has to be gone through – and it's taken me three years to get even so far. But we shall come through, and be really peaceful and happy and in touch. You will see, the future will bring big changes – and I hope one day we may

---

[1] The enclosure is missing.

all live in touch with one another, away from business and all that sort of world, and really have a *new* sort of happiness together. You'll see – it will come – gradually – and before not so very many years. This is the slow winding up of an old way of life. Patience – and we'll begin another, somewhere in the sun.

love. DHL

4948. To Emily King, [22 February 1929]
Text: MS Lazarus; Unpublished.

Hotel Beau Rivage. *Bandol.* Var.
Friday evening

My dear Pamela

Ada left this afternoon – Frieda has gone with her to Toulon. I felt very unhappy after she had left – she doesn't seem her old jolly self any more, and that distresses me. But I suppose we are all changing in our feelings and our outlook, and a time of change is always painful. Let's hope we can come through to something better and more peaceful. I didn't go to Toulon today having got a bit of a sore chest – but it's nothing. I wish I felt more happy about you all. The only thing is to be patient and wait for a new release.

I want to leave here now in about a week's time, if it keeps fairly warm – and go perhaps to Corsica. I should like to find a place where I felt I could take a house and settle and make a life, and you could all come out and stay much longer than these few days. I wish I could find a place this spring. Corsica isn't so very far, if we really like it. And it's really much better for you to come out into the sun, than for me to come to gloomy England –

I haven't thanked you for the hankies, which I like very much. I like coloured ones so much better – I always use yours you gave me – though some of them have gone into holes, with much use. I didn't send presents – somehow I don't like this exchanging of presents business. Yet I like my hankies very much. But you know what I mean.

There doesn't seem any news – and I'm feeling depressed about Ada – but I shall write next week again and tell you all the plans.

With love   DHL

4949. To Nancy Pearn, [23 February 1929]
Text: MS UT; Unpublished.

Hotel Beau Rivage. Bandol. Var.
Sat. 22 Feby 1929

Dear Nancy Pearn

Herewith the extended article 'Do Women Change'.[1] The extension came a bit too poetical, a bit too lovely. I had already added a chunk, an even bigger chunk, to this same article, for *Vanity Fair*, and they gave me $50 extra. So perhaps you would rather get the *Vanity Fair* version from Rich – though I found they'd bowdlerised some of my phrases in the first half, and I don't want them to have any more of my things – bowdlerising without asking me. Anyhow do as you wish – use this version or get the American one, which is a good bit longer.

I enclose also another article, more or less stating my position, and you can offer it the *Sunday Despatch*, but I don't mind a bit if they don't want it.[2]

The man did write me – Bernard Falk,[3] is it – quite nicely. But I shan't accept that sketch of me, because it might as well be the man in the moon. He suggested some articles – titles – and I'll do them when the mood comes – but I never promise to supply anything. I'll write him tomorrow.

I think we shall definitely leave here end of next week.

Hope you had those proofs – and that all goes well.

D. H. Lawrence[4]

---

[1] See Letter 4865 and n. 5. Nancy Pearn had written to DHL on 18 February 1929 (TMSC UT): 'If you feel like elaborating your 'DO WOMEN CHANGE' article to fill six typewritten pages, the "*Sunday Dispatch*" will take this at the Twenty-five guineas rate. The editor says he would naturally want to use it as a leading article, and for that purpose it is a bit short as it stands.'

[2] According to a note probably by Nancy Pearn's assistant, on the MS, the article was 'The State of Funk'; its first publication was in *Assorted Articles* (1930).

[3] Bernard Falk (1882–1960), editor of the *Sunday Dispatch*, 1918–31. For 'that sketch' see the letter following.

[4] Nancy Pearn acknowledged the arrival of 'Mother and Daughter' proofs and the extended article, on 26 February (TMSC UT). She added:

I also have the article on THE STATE OF FUNK and am thinking over the way to use this, which will be to your greatest advantage. It may be best to wait a week until the legal side is clarified . . . As you may already have heard we are in close touch with Mr St. John Hutchinson with a view to deciding on a course of action.

That man Falk promised not to bombard you with tiresome suggestions but merely to make his little personal offering. But there, what can you expect of Fleet Street and its undertakings.

4950. To Bernard Falk, 24 February 1929
Text: MS YU; Moore 1132.

Hotel Beau Rivage: *Bandol.* Var, France
24 Feby. 1929

Dear Mr Falk

Many thanks for your letter and for offering me the sketch of myself.[1] But don't give it me, it will only worry me: I hate photographs and things of myself, which are never me, and I wonder all the time who it can be. Look at this passport photograph I had taken two days ago, some sweet fellow with a black beard which I haven't got. But do thank Mr Simpson for not making me satanic for once. Even his tragic brow that he gave me was better than the smirking Satanismus I am so used to.

I'll do some articles along the lines you suggest, when the wind blows me that way. It's no good my promising anything definitely, it's sure not to come off. But I'll do some articles, and when you have something you really *want*, tell me, I can always do things better if I know they're actually wanted. I sent Miss Pearn an article yesterday, to show you, putting 'very delicately' on tip-toe like Agag,[2] my position with regards to my naughty book etc. If it's not suitable for the *Dispatch*, I don't mind at all. I really don't know much about the Sunday morning public: or any other.

But I'd rather write for the *Sunday Dispatch* than for the high-brow papers and magazines. Though the thought of the godless Sabbath public makes me shiver a bit, I still believe it has more spunk than the 'refined' public. It comes back with *some* sort of response, even if it gives one goose-flesh. – I too am beginning to receive letters from boys whom I went to school with, thirty years ago, and have never heard of since. They pat me half-approvingly, half reprovingly on the back – and luckily, can't see me bristle.

Sincerely   D. H. Lawrence

---

[1] Nancy Pearn had written to DHL, 20 February 1929 (TMSC UT): 'The editor of the "*Sunday Dispatch*" . . . wants to give himself the pleasure of offering to present you with the original of that drawing which appeared in the "Dispatch" on Sunday, of which I have already sent you a copy . . . They are growingly keen on your articles down at the "Sunday Dispatch".' The 'Portrait Study' by Joseph Simpson, showing a gentle and rather sad DHL ('*The Most-Discussed Novelist of the Day*'), appeared in the *Sunday Dispatch*, 17 February 1929; it accompanied 'Myself Revealed' (cf. Letter 4810 and n. 1).

[2] 1 Samuel xv. 32–3: 'Then said Samuel, Bring ye hither to me Agag the king of the Amalekites. And Agag came unto him delicately. And Agag said, Surely the bitterness of death is past . . . And Samuel hewed Agag in pieces . . . '

4951. To Maria Huxley, [24 February 1929]
Text: Moore 1133–4.

Hôtel Beau Rivage, Bandol
[24 February 1929]

Dear Maria:

The coat came last night, and very many thanks. It's a bit small, considerably smaller than the other – which looks pale grey beside it – but I shall let down the sleeves a bit, and keep it, and if it looks a bit of a blue monkey jacket, that's rather my style. I sent the pale flannel trousers to be cleaned, so shall emerge with the spring a new blossom. I enclose cheque for thirty bob – the last one cost 125, so if they charged you more for this one tell me, the swine – no, send me the price ticket, or I shall never believe you either. I'm sorry if your sister feels done out of it – but she won't.[1] This must be the very coat I tried on last May and found too small and ordered another, and sent Carletto in haste across to say I didn't want the buttons *in oro*.[2]

Well my sister left on Friday, and left me feeling battered. How one's family can wrack one! Of course she wanted – secretly – the moon: to abandon all the life she's so deliberately built up there in the Midlands, and have a new one – 'away from it all.' – But as you make your bed so you must lie, and if you don't want to, then don't make an elaborate and four-posted bed.

Jack Hutchinson writes he has got the copy of *Pansies* and likes them, and they have written to the Yard demanding the other copies back. So we'll see what happens. He writes very nicely – his mother has been ill – fancy a man that size and experience has still a mother.

We plan to leave here next Saturday for Nice, and sail from there on the following Friday for Ajaccio. You will disapprove of the insular move, but it's not a long swim. We think to go to Piana, on the west coast, sounds nice and has one good hotel.

The photograph of you and the boy and the flying machine is very amusing – you look so much as if you wanted to be snatched up and swept to realms on high, and the boy looks so perky, ready for it all. Glad you are settled and cosy. Now for heaven's sake stay so.

You didn't send me Nancy Cunard's address – could you get it? And nothing is done about a Paris edition of *Lady C.* – Funny it should be so difficult.

There was a circus on the beach here on Friday, but I didn't go as my sister had just left and I felt a rag. But Frieda went and there just behind her in all his glory sat our negro waiter with the pretty governess of the little boy with fringe whom you couldn't stand. They were alone and glorious – but other

---

[1] Most probably Maria's youngest sister, Rose Nys (cf. *Letters*, vi. 120).   [2] 'in gold'.

guests sat across – and since then there is a low temperature in the hotel, the nigger is in a stubborn tantrum, the girl pale and wan, and altogether the Beau Rivage a bit peaked. Time to go. –

With love to you both.

4952. To Rhys Davies, [24 February 1929]
Text: MS UT; Postmark, Bandol 25–2 29; Unpublished.

Bandol.
Sunday

Dear Davies

We want to leave here next Saturday, and arrive in Nice at 2.25. in the afternoon. Would you tell me again which hotel you suggest – one more or less like this – and perhaps not too far off from everywhere.

Many thanks for the Corsica news. We'll sail – D. V. – for Ajaccio on the following Friday.

See you soon, then.

D. H. Lawrence

Not heard for long from Lahr – anything happened?

4953. To Jean Watson, 24 February 1929
Text: MS UT; Unpublished.

Bandol. Var.
24 Feby 1929

Dear Miss Watson

Look at me like an *ass* beginning to alter this agreement, having the alteration of the other in my eye. I hope it doesn't matter.

Thanks for your sympathy – of course I get so mad I almost burst – that one can't go with a thick stick and crack them on the head! hard!

We leave here on *Saturday* – will send an address.

Sincerely.   D. H. Lawrence

4954. To Nancy Pearn, 24 February 1929
Text: MS UT; Unpublished.

Bandol. Var.
24 Feb. 1929

Dear Nancy Pearn

Here is the Foreword for the Dahlberg novel for *Putnams Sons Ltd.*[1] Will you deal with them – or Pollinger.

[1] Cf. p. 65 n. 3.

And would you give Miss Watson this signed agreement.

And I will send you an *expurgated* copy of the *Pansies* this week. Meanwhile you could take copies from Mr. Hutchinsons MS. – which is identical with those confiscated – of anything you wanted to use for periodicals.[1] – But I typed the whole thing afresh and revised many of the poems very much, and I want you to use my revised version – especially for a book. For the magazines or papers it doesn't matter.

We have decided to leave here next Saturday, for Nice, then probably Corsica and Italy – Do tell all the other depts, will you.

belle cose!   D. H. Lawrence

4955. To G. P. Putnam's Sons, 25 February 1929
Text: MS UT; Unpublished.

Hotel Beau Rivage. Bandol. Var
25 Feby 1929

Dear Sir

The proofs of the novel came and I read them at once – and have just finished the introduction, which I shall send to Curtis Brown. As you say, it's not an easy novel for the public to take up. But it should have a certain sale. For a title, you might have 'Underdogs.' Or really a phrase would suit this book better: 'Underpups become Underdogs.' – Or a question: 'What about the bed-rock?' – which is pertinent – or 'Would you bark, you underdog?' Go a bit out of the way for a title – use that last one. It's right.

I hope the English will understand American money well enough – I mean *bits* and *dimes* and bucks and so on. It's necessary, in that getting lodgings.

And Plattdeutsch[2] is spoken in north Germany, not south.

Anyhow I hope I shall have been of some use.

Yours Sincerely   D. H. Lawrence

We're leaving here next Saturday – will you address me c/o Curtis Brown.

4956. To Ada Clarke, [27 February 1929]
Text: MS Clarke; Unpublished.

Hotel Beau Rivage. Bandol. Var.
Wed.

My dear Sister

Your letter today – what a home-coming! and Pamela says it snowed all Sunday! It's a mercy the poor old chap has gone[3] – that dismal life in that

---

[1] periodicals.] serials –   [2] 'Low German dialect'.
[3] Ada's father-in-law William Clarke (1856?–1929); he had a tailor's shop. Cf. Letter 4982.

kitchen was no good. But it's upsetting and pathetic, no matter – and a shock. You had the funeral today – here it is a spring day with a softish wind and some clouds – but the soft days make the trees deader. – I hope you had a decent day too, for Eastwood cemetery.

I am sending you the fifty quid towards the money you paid for Mountain Cottage – I don't remember what the rent was there – was it sixty?[1] Anyhow I have always intended to give it you back when the right moment came – and I feel this is the moment, now when you'll want some ready cash. If you'd like to borrow £100 or more from me, tell me, and I'll send it at once. My money only lies there in the bank producing nothing, so if it would be of any use to Eddie, just have it, and pay me back any time – it makes not the slightest difference to me. As for this fifty, please take it and say nothing, it is your own – or Eddie's – and you'll only fidget me if you talk about it.

I think you weren't very anxious to see Fritz – perhaps you didn't want to go to Beckenham very badly.[2]

We are staying here till next Wednesday, and Rhys Davies will come to us. I think we shall go to Spain after all – myself, it would interest me more – and it is only 24 hours from Paris – We should go from Marseille.

Well I do hope things aren't in a great tangle, and that you're feeling all right.

love   DHL

4957. To Edwin Clarke, 27 February 1929
Text: MS Clarke; Unpublished.

Hotel Beau Rivage. *Bandol*, Var.
27 Feby 1929

Dear Eddie

So the poor old chap has slipped off quietly at last – it's a mercy too, but I know it upset you – it's no joke, when people die. But anyhow you needn't think of him any more half starving himself, wilfully, in that unhappy house – and tangling himself and everybody else up in more debts. I'm glad Ada got home to be with you – she must have had an instinct.

Now you'll have all the worry of winding up his business. Please don't say anything about the debt I'm re-paying – or partly re-paying – to Ada. I've owed it you all these years. And I know you gave it freely. That's why I didn't

---

[1] Ada had paid the rent of Mountain Cottage, Middleton-by-Wirksworth, Derbyshire, during DHL's tenancy, May 1918–April 1919.
[2] Fritz Johann Heinrich Krenkow (1872–1953), the husband of DHL's maternal aunt Ada Rose (1868–1944), left Beckenham in 1929 to become Professor of Islamic Studies, Muslim University, Aligarh. See *Letters*, i. 77 n. 1.

say anything sooner. But now I feel it's the right time to pay it back. – And if you want any ready money, do let me lend it you. I've got plenty of money at the moment, and it all just lies in current account in the bank, doing no good. So do have it if it's any use to you.

It was so nice seeing Ada – and I was glad we were all so nice together. We get older and sadder, perhaps, but perhaps a bit wiser. Anyhow one can live through the surface frictions and stick to what is the real relationship underneath. Patience is a great thing –

Frieda sends her affection and her sympathy, with mine too.

DHL

4958. To Rhys Davies, [27 February 1929]
Text: MS UT; Postmark, Bandol 28–2 29; Unpublished.

Hotel Beau Rivage, *Bandol*. Var.
Wednesday

Dear Davies

We really are impossible. Once more we've decided not to come to Nice – nor to go to Corsica – but to go to Spain, as I always wanted. So we shall stay here till next Wednesday – at least – and shall expect you on Monday by the 4.30 train, unless we hear to the contrary.

I'm really awfully sorry to be so changeable and probably upset your plans. But do come along and let's have a final talk.

ever   D. H. Lawrence

I suppose you had my last letter saying we *were* coming on Sat.

4959. To Aldous Huxley, [28 February 1929]
Text: Moore 1134.

Hôtel Beau Rivage, Bandol
Thursday

Dear Aldous:

Here I am bothering you again – you see the Pegasus has got string-halt.[1] I have written to Mr Moulder[2] – is the name auspicious or inauspicious? – and we'll see what he says. Where I'm bothering you is that I've asked Holroyd Reece – the Pegasus man – to send the copy of *Lady C.* he had from me, to you, for you to hold for me – and I told Mr Moulder, if he wanted same copy,

---

[1] An infection causing the hind legs of a horse to jerk spasmodically. Pegasus was the winged horse of the Muses.

[2] On the staff of Galignani. Huxley had recommended this 'Dickensian gentleman' as a possible publisher of a Paris edition of *Lady Chatterley's Lover* (cf. Letter 4974). DHL's letter to him is unlocated.

you would hand it him. Don't mind, please, my making this bit of use of you. – The Jixy business seems to be moving a bit. Anyhow Jack H[utchinson] got my *Pansies*. We are once more wobbling about Corsica, and thinking it shall be Barcelona. Seems not much point in Corsica. If it is Spain, we shall wait till about next Wednesday – instead of leaving this Saturday – shall write you. I wish now we either had a house or made up our minds to have one. Am tempted to go to the ranch for the summer. – You never saw such awful devastation as among the trees and plants here – corpses, corpses everywhere – a dreadful battlefield. Seems to me ill-omened. – I want to get a new suit in Toulon: my sister liked my overcoat – she arrived home midnight Saturday night, so her father-in-law died in her arms on Sunday morning. She seems fated to have people die in her arms, but I won't oblige if I can help it. The Governess is still under cloud. Mr Scott[1] showed me his water-colours this morning – mostly Indian – if only these good Englishmen put a bit of shit in their pictures, they'd achieve creation. *Such* careful work – and real feeling too – but pure as soap-powder – it's a tragedy. It's sort of Spring, but the land is ravaged dead. I hear Corsica is the same. Be patient with me.

4960. To Martin Secker, [28 February 1929]
Text: MS UInd; Secker 115.

Hotel Beau Rivage, *Bandol*, Var.
Thursday

Dear Secker

I am sending you today the *expurgated* MS. of my *Pansies*, keeping back all those that might – falsely – be considered improper. I wish you'd wire me 'received', when you have it – and I'll send the missing pages by hand – also the other thing I will have delivered by hand.

We are fixed to leave next Wednesday for Barcelona. Perhaps I ought to have gone to Italy to finish the Etruscans – but all this jixing has spoilt my temper and made me too angry. Perhaps in another country, in Spain, I might do a little book for Autumn. Meanwhile the *Pansies* will sell, if you get them out.

Do hand over the MS. to Miss Pearn when you've read it: and ask her to show you her copy of the *original* one – I expect she's had a copy made by

[1] Unidentified.

now – to see which introd. you prefer.[1] I prefer the original.
Thanks for the papers. Remember us to Rina.

DHL

4961. To Rhys Davies, [28 February 1929]
Text: MS UT; Postmarks, Marseille 1 3 29 and Nice II-III 1929; Unpublished.

Bandol. Var.
Thursday evening

Dear Davies
    Your letter this evening – you will have had mine, saying we are heading for Spain instead of Corsica – going via Marseille. and wanting to leave here about Wednesday. I wonder if you will turn up on Monday? I shall be in Toulon and shall come home with the 4.15 train, so shall look out for you. You might come with us to Marseille, and stay a couple of days there. If we leave here Wednesday, I expect we should leave Marseille on Friday or Saturday. – Anyhow do come if you can. It's colder again, but I don't think it'll last. We must have a last talk over things –

DHL

4962. To the Play Committee, P.E.N., [March? 1929]
Text: P.E.N. News, April 1929, p. 5; PC.

[Hotel Beau Rivage, Bandol, Var.]
[March? 1929]

All my good wishes to the P.E.N.[2] Even if I'm the black sheep amongst members, yet I feel that wherever I go P.E.N. would accept me and be kind to me if I'd let them – all over the face of the earth – which is somehow comforting.

---

[1] The introduction sent to Secker, the third version (Roberts E302g), had been written by 11 February when DHL sent a copy to Marianne Moore. Realising that Secker would not publish the second version (which DHL here calls 'the *original*'), with its reference to the arse as God and the quotation of Swift's 'Celia, Celia, Celia shits', DHL replaced the whole of the second half, on obscene words, with several paragraphs on the mass versus the minority and the individual, and on bolshevism and fascism. See Letter 5043. (The third version of the introduction was published as *Foreword to Pansies*, intro. Keith Sagar, Libanus Press, 1988.)

[2] The P.E.N. (International Association of Poets, Playwrights, Editors, Essayists and Novelists) was founded by Amy Dawson Scott in 1921. DHL joined on 4 August 1924 (see *Letters*, v. 88 and n. 1). On 12 April 1929 P.E.N. staged a matinée of Hermon Ould's play *The Moon Rides High*, to raise funds. Prominent members were invited to send messages of support, and a selection of these was printed in the April *P.E.N. News*. DHL's postcard may have been addressed to Amy Dawson Scott (as were his three surviving letters to P.E.N.), or to the Hon. Sec., Anne Radcliffe, or to Henrietta Leslie, the organiser of the event.

4963. To S. S. Koteliansky, 1 March 1929
Text: MS BL.; Postmark, Bandol [. . .] 3 29; Zytaruk 380.

Bandol.
1 March 1929

My dear Kot

We had intended to leave tomorrow, but are staying on a few more days – probably till Wednesday – then I think we shall really go to Spain – probably stay in Palma – Majorca – for a while. Frieda wants to find a house – we might do so there – who knows! I would rather like to go to America for the summer, to sell the ranch and settle up there – but don't know really if I'm well enough.

The fuss about the *Pansies* and the rest seems to go on. I get bored even by the thought of it. It is all so artificial and stale, and they are all so feeble. But let us hope they can fix Jix up a bit – it's too childishly silly.

My sister was here about two weeks – seems changed – a good deal sadder, but I doubt not much wiser. Perhaps sadness and wiseness no longer go together. But of course those mining districts *are* depressing now, trade all gone to pieces, and no real hope.

Secker wants me to go back to Italy to finish my Etruscan sketches, but I don't want to. He very much wants me to give him a book for the autumn – but I've got none, and all this jixing business has put me out of temper for writing. I wonder if you could take him round a little parcel that he keeps asking for.[1] He is a funny chap – quite perky now he has made money with the German translations.[2]

I am correcting the Foreword to my paintings – proofs. I think Stephensen is having a bit of a struggle. – It's gone a bit colder again here – time now that spring began to come – all plants and flowers and most trees frozen dead down here – a great loss, and very sad.

DHL

4964. To Charles Lahr, 1 March 1929
Text: MS UNYB; Unpublished.

[Hotel Beau Rivage, Bandol, Var.]
1 March 1929

Dear Lahr

I have been amused by the various cuttings which you sent on – and your

---

[1] DHL meant Kot to take Secker a copy of *Lady Chatterley's Lover*, which he would not mention by name in a letter, but Kot apparently did not understand. See Letter 4977.

[2] DHL probably had in mind Secker's commercially successful publication of Lion Feuchtwanger's novel, *Jew Süss* (November 1926), tr. Willa and Edwin Muir (*Letters*, v. 388, 655). DHL had advised against publication; Secker's financial success rankled with him (cf. ibid., vi. 173).

letter. What a nice windfall of an old Kipling book![1] You'll feel lordly. Davies says you have been nearly frozen in your little shop – and I can believe it. Even here all the plants are dead – all their market flowers – and even the big trees and the palms. Really tragic! – I do want to know why 'Low' in the *Evening Standard* didn't give me an 'inspiration' along with all the rest. Did he think my rage was my inspiring fount, so I didn't get a female? It was an amusing drawing.[2]

We want to leave here next Wednesday, and go to Spain. I am expecting Davies on Monday – hope he'll turn up.

I want Kot. to take a book over to Secker – wonder if he will –

That *Dispatch* article is too small to print alone. It existed in a longer form – probably Miss Pearn of C[urtis] B[rown]'s has it. I'll ask her to let me see it, and see if it would make a booklet.[3] Wait a bit.

Shall send you an address as soon as I have one.

At the moment am feeling sort of fed-up. – Stephensen is having quite a job getting the printers to make the plates of the pictures. – Too boring – too much of a muchness.

                                                                                   DHL

4965. To P. R. Stephensen, 1 March 1929
Text: MS Anon; Munro 303–4.

                                                                   Hotel Beau Rivage. Bandol, Var
                                                                                   1 March 1929

Dear Stephensen

Here are the proofs back. I never intended the heading to be 'Introduction to Painting' – Have made it now: 'Introduction to These Paintings'. But there's no need to put this title at the head of every page, is there? – I give people too much for their money. Most men would make two vols. out of the stuff there is in this essay. Am afraid I give it 'em too condensed.

So the printers now are fussing – damn all their eyes, I'm sick of 'em, it's a world of Willy Wet-legs. I feel I don't care what you leave out or what you put in – or if you don't do the thing at all. Why slave offering things to Willy Wet-legs! Perhaps it's a pity to do the book at all. What's wrong with *The Mango Tree*, – the scurvy mongrels. It's one of the best. Some people like it

---

[1] Which book by Rudyard Kipling (1865–1936) is not known.

[2] One of the cuttings Lahr had sent was the Low cartoon entitled 'Jix, the Self-Appointed Chucker-Out' from the *Evening Standard*, 26 February 1929. See Illustrations; see also Letter 4973.

[3] 'Myself Revealed'. The longer version to which DHL alludes may be '[Return to Bestwood]' first published in *Phoenix II: Uncollected, Unpublished and Other Prose Works by D. H. Lawrence*, ed. Warren Roberts and Harry T. Moore (1968).

best of all. But I don't care. Leave it out if you like. Leave 'em all out if you like, and print blank pages with the titles at the bottom – You ought to do that anyhow – put a blank page *Dandelions* and a blank page *Mango Tree* and give 'em what they ask for. *Do that*! a bit of blague for the guinea-pigs, wee-wee-wee! Ten-guinea pigs too. – My sister took the two panels – *Spring* and *Summer Dawn* – to England – and wrote to me from her home that she was sending them by post – I presume to Dorothy Warren.[1] You might find out if they've come, as Miss Warren is a perpetual dumb Crambo as far as I'm concerned.[2] I've not heard a word from her for six months. – We are leaving – D. V. next Wednesday for Spain – I'll send an address from there. – But perhaps I shall get the prospectus proof before I leave – I want to see it. I don't think it matters if *Moses* is full size, though one hates giving them anything for nothing. – Do write your book about how the bush hit back. But don't forget to put a sketch 'The Bush in 1960' – and a concluding one: 'The Bush in 2500'. – And see who gives whom the death-blow. Whack-whack-whack! Do you know 'Low' the caricaturist who did the *Evening Standard* cartoon of Jix turning the authors out of hyde park? Quite amusing, but I demand my 'inspiration'. – What a slush-mush humanity!

DHL

Keep the book as plain as you can – no frills. – I wish you'd please send me a duplicate set of these proofs, to show to a friend.

If ever you go to Miller & Gills' place, you might ask them why they refuse to pay for the seven copies of the novel, which they had. – They could even pay the money to you.

---

[1] Among the Stephensen MSS there is, in DHL's hand, a list of paintings sent to Dorothy Warren which updated the list enclosed with Letter 4886. It must be dated after 22 February 1929 because it includes *Spring* and *Summer Dawn* which were sent with Ada Clarke on that date, and before 4 March when *Singing of Swans* was painted and would have been listed. The list was, therefore, almost certainly sent with the present letter. It has additional importance since it includes – though their titles are deleted – two small oils mentioned nowhere else in the *Letters*, *Fire in the Sands* and *Pietà*, each described as a 'very small panel – Gsteig'. Both these paintings were auctioned at Sotheby's 10 December 1968, as 'from the collection of Lady Ottoline Morrell'. The size of *Pietà* is given as 240mm. by 190mm. and of *Fire in the Sands* 190mm. by 240mm. *Pietà* was auctioned again at Sotheby's 16 July 1984, and was reproduced in the catalogue. The present location of these paintings is unknown.

In May 1928 DHL had reopened his correspondence with Lady Ottoline after a lapse of many years. He may have sent these paintings to her, or to her niece Dorothy Warren to pass on to her. Since they were to be neither exhibited nor reproduced, they were of no concern to Stephensen.

[2] Dumb Crambo, a game in which words are mimed.

4966. To John Middleton Murry, 1 March 1929
Text: MS NYPL; cited in John Middleton Murry, 'Reminiscences of D. H. Lawrence, VII',
New Adelphi, iii (March 1931), 461.

Hotel Beau Rivage, Bandol. Var.
1 March 1929

Dear Jack
    I didn't know your handwriting any more, it seems to have gone so small and sort of invisible.[1] How are you? I'm pretty well, but a scratchy chest and cough as ever – sickening – but pretty well in spite of all. – I believe Katharine once stayed here, so perhaps you know the place. – We gave up the Florence house, and are houseless. We think to leave here next Wednesday, and go to Majorca, perhaps take a villa there. I haven't any great hunch as to where I want to live – only, for the moment, not Italy.
    I haven't got a copy of the *Rainbow*, to Save my life. My copy was stolen from me long ago – as every single first-edit. copy of my own books has been – just 'lifted' by one kindly visitor or another. But the man can get the American edition from Galignani, for a dollar. I'll write and tell him.[2]
    And how are you? and how is your wife?[3] I heard she was ill, but do hope she's better. Do you live in Hants now, and not Dorset?
    Frieda is about the same – but not quite so energetic as she used to be. I begin to realise that we *do* get older, and that it *does* make a great difference – in some ways, it's pleasanter – I like being older – if only my chest didn't scratch so much.
    I'll send you a line when we get an address – otherwise you must write me c/o Curtis Brown.

tanti ricordi![4]   DHL

4967. To Nancy Pearn, 1 March 1929
Text: MS UT; Unpublished.

Hotel Beau Rivage, *Bandol*, Var
1 March 1929

Dear Nancy Pearn
    I hope you got the three things I sent you lately:
1. The proofs of 'Mother and Daughter' registered
2. The article for the *Sunday Dispatch*, which I lengthened – and with it another article: 'The State of Funk'.

---

[1] DHL and Murry had not corresponded since July 1926.
[2] See Letter 4968 and n. 2.
[3] In 1924 Murry married Violet le Maistre; in July 1927 she was diagnosed as suffering from incurable tuberculosis; she died in 1931 (cf. *Letters*, vi. 41 n. 3, 47 n. 1, 445 n. 2).
[4] 'so many memories!'

3. The MS. of the Foreword to the novel by Edward Dahlberg, for Putnam & Sons – sent unregistered.

I wrote Bernard Falk of the *Sunday Dispatch* very nicely.

We stay here till next Wednesday, and then I want to start for Spain. If there is anything special you might wire me before we go – but there won't be.

Tell Pollinger I have corrected proofs of the Introd. essay to the book of paintings. – And I hope his flu is better.

And would you tell the American side that the *Survey Graphic* sent me $100. direct for that article on New Mexico,[1] – I don't know why – so the N. York office can charge the $10 percentage against me.

Am feeling fed up.

D. H. Lawrence

4968. To G. B. Edwards, 1 March 1929
Text: John Wilson Catalogue (March 1981).

Hotel Beau Rivage, Bandol, France
1 March 1929

Murry told me you were writing a book about me[2] – which of course makes me bristle a bit – I'm sorry I haven't a copy of *The Rainbow* in the world – people always steal my books – I mean my own copies of my own works. But you can get a copy of the American Edition in the *Modern Library* $1.00 – from Galignani – 224 rue de Rivoli ... it's only one page different from the English edition – what's the odds! The omitted page is one near the end where Ursula is in a hotel in London with the young man – very harmless, I believe.[3]
[The two-page letter concludes with Lawrence's future travel plans.]

4969. To Giuseppe Orioli, 2 March 1929
Text: MS UCLA; Lacy, *Escaped Cock* 71.

Hotel Beau Rivage. *Bandol*, Var
Sat. 2 March 1929

Dear Pino

We are staying here a day or two longer – no use hurrying away from this warm hotel, while the cold weather lasts – it has come back a bit, but not so

[1] Cf. Letter 4820 and n. 2.
[2] Nothing is known of DHL's correspondent except that he lived in Switzerland and later reviewed Stephen Potter's *D. H. Lawrence: A First Study* (1930), in Murry's *New Adelphi*, iii (June–August 1930), 310–16. His own projected work never appeared.
[3] The omissions in the American edn had made DHL 'sad and angry' at the time (*Letters*, ii. 480). For the omission he seems to have in mind here, see *The Rainbow*, ed. Mark Kinkead-Weekes (Cambridge, 1989), 421:21–422:2. For full details of the thirteen omissions from the American edn, see ibid., p. xliv n. 34.

bad. But I think we shall go on Wednesday to Marseilles, and then to Spain. I think spain would be more fun than Corsica, at least for a while – and it's really not far from here.

I'm glad those two copies to Conway of Mexico City were not lost. The Mexican mail should be quite safe – has nothing to do with U. S. A. Have you sent them off now? – and the one to the man in Germany?[1] I hear Lahr has sold one or two copies – five or six, really – of the first edition, but he's not paid in the money yet. What a pity he hasn't got more! I wish Brentanos would pay for those ten, then the second edit. is all paid, and I could send you your share.

I suppose you have heard of all the fuss with Jix. I don't know if there is any result yet. Did you see this cartoon from the *Evening Standard?* I'm getting very bored with the whole silly show.

The Crosby Gaige man drew up a contract for the first half of *Escaped Cock* – in which I promise not to issue the second half till 1930. But I wrote back saying he must put in a clause: that the title must be *The Escaped Cock. Part One* – and that at the end he must put: *Here ends the First Part of the Escaped Cock.* – That puts salt on *his* tail. He's hanging fire – not answered yet. If he backs out, I don't care – then we'll do the whole thing for Easter 1930 – it would just make a nice book for you to do, about sixty pages. And next year let us hope we can post again to England pretty freely. – The Pegasus Press turned down the *Lady C.* proposition: now I have written to Mr. Moulder of Galignani. I hear the pirated edit. is on sale in Nice at 400 frs! Shame that no one would tackle a Paris edit. – I got the blue coat from Maria – it's the very same I tried on last year in the shop, a bit *small*, with the golden buttons – but it will do. – I wonder where we shall ultimately settle! At the moment I feel very undecided about everything. I shall send an address as soon as I have one – then write me.

                                                Love from us both   DHL

4970. To Charles Wilson, 2 March 1929
Text: MS IEduc; Unpublished.

                                        Hotel Beau Rivage. Bandol, Var.
                                                        2 March 1929
Dear Charles Wilson

    I received your poems safely[2] – and yes, I had the guinea in the other letter, for the copy of *Lady C.* – which copy you can already sell for more than double, if you wish.

---

[1] Max Mohr (Letter 4935).
[2] It is not known which verse Wilson had sent; he is not credited with having published any after 1916.

The poems have a certain charm – sometimes there is a real simplicity which I like very much. But often there are worn-out phrases – Far from the madding crowd – rosebud sweet as May – days of yore – accents mild – a loving kiss so sweet – the happy throng – etc. They are all rather dead echoes from other poetry, no longer really natural to us, and certainly stale. And surely there are too many sighs and tears for the dead! you are too young to be bothering about the dead. – Still, I got some pleasure from the poems, and I'm sure you did.

We are leaving here next Wednesday, going to Spain for a while. I shall send you an address as soon as we settle – I don't know where it will be.

I suppose you saw all the fuss about my Poems – *Pansies* – There are some good ones there for your colliers, that I hope you'll read to them one day.

Yours ever   D. H. Lawrence

4971. To Mabel Dodge Luhan, 2 March 1929
Text: MS Brill; Luhan 341–3.

Hotel Beau Rivage. Bandol. Var
2 March 1929

Dear Mabel

It's no good, I really don't think I'm well enough, with this cough, to come to America and stand the racket of journeys and seeing people. It makes me very mad. I *am* better – I am really quite well and quite myself so long as I stay fairly quiet. But as soon as I begin taking journeys, even going to Toulon and doing a bit of shopping and running round, I feel rather rotten and cough more. So it's no good – I shall have to give up again for this year. It is maddening – nothing is so wearisome as prolonged ill-health. Not that I'm an invalid or anything like that. I've not been in bed a day all winter, and I eat just as well as I ever did – though that's only since I am here in Bandol. But the minute I start[1] walking at all far, especially uphill, and running round, especially in a town, I go all queer. It's partly psychological, of[2] course. Some connection with the *current* world broke in me two years ago, and now I have to be different. I feel my inside energy just about the same. It's my outside energy I can't manage. And so I'm afraid of the long journey and all the people – and possible unpleasantnesses with authorities or public.

And I'm thinking, really, we ought to sell that ranch, so that perhaps we could be more free when we do come. It is a bit remote and strenuous when one is not well. Yet I should be sorry to think we couldn't go there and have it for our own any more – so would Frieda. While Brett stays, I suppose it's safe

---

[1] start] shall   [2] MS reads 'off'.

204 2 March 1929

enough. But if ever she left it, it would soon get smashed up by Mexicans and roughs. Last year when the Taos bank asked me to sell, Brett said she would buy it. What do you think? You see there are many MSS. there – some that are, and will be, really valuable – they may easily be all lost or stolen. What should one do? Don't say anything to Brett to hurt her feelings. Would you suggest putting the MSS. and things we value in some safe deposit place? I've lost so many MSS already – Seltzer has some – Mountsier[1] – some have disappeared unaccountably – and it seems a shame. – As soon as I feel well enough and *confident* I shall come. But now I feel unsure and a bit shaky – and Frieda isn't very well either – no longer so strong. – Tell Maria Cristina – yes, I like her too, I like the feeling one has of her. But don't say anything particular to Brett. I would hate to hurt her feelings.

Did you get the *Pansies* – or did Marianne Moore? Have you heard the row in London about them – seized by Scotland Yard, and now questions being asked about them in Parliament? It's just March lunacy – those poor bits of *Pansies*. Everybody is of course quaking, at the same time they are getting the wind up against that imbecile Jix, the Home Secretary. – And the colour-printers are frightened too, and refusing to reproduce some of the pictures – perfectly harmless pictures. But the people are going ahead – and I suppose they'll get the book out about May: 500 copies at ten guineas each: I'll get them to send you prospectuses with the reproduction of *Finding of Moses* in colour, and you may get a few subscribers. I don't think the pictures will have any difficulty passing through customs – they certainly wouldn't, but for my bad name.

We are leaving here on Wednesday, I think to go to Majorca – Spain – where we *might* take a house for six months or a year. It remains to be seen.

I wonder how Tony will stand New York. I find big cities are just too much for me now: or at least, all wrong.

And do give Maria Cristina all my news, and tell her I will write.

And you write to me c/o G. Orioli, 6 Lungarno Corsini. Florence. – I think that will be as quick as any other way.

Why can't one make oneself *tough*!

DHL

---

[1] Robert Mountsier (1888–1972), American journalist known to DHL since 1915; acted as DHL's agent in USA, 1920–3. See *Letters*, iii. 24 n. 4.

4972. To Hon. Dorothy Brett, 2 March 1929
Text: MS UCin; Postmark, Bandol 4–3 29; Moore 1135–7.

Bandol. Var. France.

2 March 1929

Dear Brett

It's no good, I'm not really well enough to come over this summer. I went to Toulon on Wed. and felt so shoddy after it – and such a beastly cough – I knew it was no good. I am *really* much better – you'd think me[1] just the same as ever, here quietly in Bandol – plenty of inside energy. But as soon as I begin going about, especially in towns, I give out. I can't do much walking, and no climbing, and not much seeing people. So what's the good coming to America? – where they might even begin fussing about letting me in. If I were *there*, in Taos, I'd probably be all right – though I'm not sure of the high altitude. But there's getting there. And they hate you so if you cough – particularly on ships – and cough I do. Yet I'm not *ill*. I've not been a day in bed all winter, I eat all my meals good enough – I can work away. Yet strange people, and effort in cities especially, just does me in. So there you are! I'll have to leave it for another year. – Mind you, I'm a lot better than last year. So next year, let's hope to God I'll be tough enough to stand the world.

I worry sometimes a bit about the ranch. Do you think we ought to deposit the MSS. in some safe place? They are getting valuable now, they may come in so handy some rainy day. And so many have already been stolen from me. All the early ones are gone, for good. I ought to look after these.

Sometimes I think it would be best to sell the ranch. You said we ought to offer it to you: and I agree. But you'd never be able to pay anything for it to Frieda, would you now?[2] The bank at Taos wrote last year offering two thousand dollars – but surely it's worth more than that, with horses and all and what furniture there is. We don't really want to sell it – how sad to think we couldn't come any more! – but if we can *never* get back, it seems useless to hang on. If only I were really well! But I've been saying that for two years now.

We leave here next Wednesday – D. V. – and go to Majorca, the island off Barcelona, Spain. We might possibly take a house there for six months or a year – God knows – I don't care very much.

I suppose you've heard of all the Scotland Yard fuss over *Lady C*. and the MS. of my poems *Pansies*. What a lot of hypocritical rot! makes me so tired. The world is a dirty place.

---

[1] me] the
[2] Frieda was the owner of the Kiowa ranch which she had acquired from Mabel Luhan in exchange for the MS of *Sons and Lovers* (*Letters*, v. 65).

They are going ahead with the reproduction of my pictures, but since the scandal of Jix (the Home Secretary Joynson Hicks) and the *Pansies*, the colour-printers refuse to reproduce some of them. What dirty snivelling cant. But I suppose the book will come out about May, with 24 of the pictures. – I don't care about showing them in New York – don't care about selling them anyhow – the book should make me close on £500, and I'd just as leave keep the pictures. I suppose Dorothy Warren will show in London if she's not frightened. I don't care. Anyhow I have enough to live on. *And let me know* if there are any ranch expenses, and I'll send you the money. Am fed up with a good many things. – *Did you* yet sell any pictures? How *mean* people are! they enjoy *not* buying – gives them a sense of power. Well, they shan't have it with me.

You are right to quit Nina[1] – what's the good of mere *probing* a sore soul. Beastly! All that talk is *no good*, none at all – whether it's Leo Stein or Orage[2] or Gurdjeff or any other chuffing jinx. Damn them all. If there could be a little nice friendly *living* and less unfriendly talking we'd be all right.

Seems to me about time you left New York. You must be about ruined, more ways than one.[3] It doesn't look as if I'd get out, and I'm sorry. But patience is best: though I *curse* this cough of mine. Let me know about the ranch and all. – Murry wrote the other day – a bit feeble.

DHL

4973. To Nancy Pearn, 2 March 1929
Text: MS UT; Keith Sagar, *The Life of D. H. Lawrence* (1980), p. 232.

Bandol, where the *Pansies* were born
2 March 1929

[Lawrence returned to Nancy Pearn the Low Cartoon he had received from her.[4] Low's caption below his cartoon reads: 'A "FRANK" WOMAN NOVELIST, SHAKESPERE, SHAW, WELLS, BENNETT, ALDOUS HUXLEY, D. H. LAWRENCE, JAMES JOYCE. EACH IS ACCOMPANIED BY HIS LITERARY INSPIRATION'. DHL added his message]: except me, so I suppose I've got none!

D. H. Lawrence

[1] See Letter 4762 and n. 6.
[2] Leo Stein (1872–1947), American expatriate and art-collector (brother of Gertrude Stein), whom DHL had met in Settignano in 1919; Alfred Richard Orage (1873–1934), journalist, author and editor of *New Age* (see *Letters*, ii. 366 n. 3).
[3] Brett was short of money; she was staying at the Shelton Hotel, Lexington Avenue.
[4] Nancy Pearn sent the cartoon with her letter dated 26 February 1929 (TMSC UT), to which she added a postscript the following day; it read: ' . . . I expect several people will be sending you this priceless cartoon from last night's *Evening Standard*. Do be a dear and sign it and let me have it for historical records.'

4974. To Aldous and Maria Huxley, [4 March 1929]
Text: Huxley 787–8.

Bandol.
Monday, Feb., 1929.

Dear Aldous, –
Well, here is your *Dickensian Gentleman*[1] – suggestions, but not much help.
I have written to Mr. Groves and told him to let me know at once,[2] as if there
is anything doing I will come to Paris to see to it: which I will. I would do a
good bit to get this thing going. And it would be fun to see you in your house.
But if it is once more 'unfortunately we can't!' then we'll leave here for
Marseilles on Thursday, and go to Spain. Am feeling fed-uppish.
    The weather has been coldish and now it's raining a bit. I'm afraid this
winter is going to be one of the long-drawn-out miseries of linked vileness. –
Yes, Jix won't have a long run for his money – the English won't stand for
that rant – fools if they did. – Rhys Davies comes this afternoon – and I've got
to go to Toulon to get my new suit – grey – 750 frs. – I believe it will look nice
– shall buy some nutty[3] shirts and new shoes and see if I can't come out a
butterfly for once – I want a metamorphosis or metempsychosis or both – a
reincarnation into a dashing body that doesn't cough. – A few daffodils in the
shops, little wild ones, and I think of those in the woods near you, that were
out when you came from Diablerets. Damn all American women with insist-
ent voices! The sound of the hammer in those voices of theirs almost kills me.
– The printers, terrified of Jix, are refusing to reproduce some of my pictures,
so Stephensen writes: the *Mango Tree*, for one – that water-colour of which
Maria said she couldn't hang it up in her bedroom when the boy was about –
so I shall give it her, to hang in the servant's room. – Am doing a lovely one –
water – of fighting men and singing swans.[4]
    Do you think 'Groves' sounds better or worse than 'Moulder'?

DHL

Dear Maria –
    The governess is engaged to the negro waiter and they walk arm in arm on
Sundays like two birds of Paradise, but she looks none the less *diminished* –
and I disapprove.
    Did you see the cartoon of us all in the *Evening Standard?* – got you by the hair! –

DHL

[1] See Letter 4959 and n. 2.
[2] Frank A. Groves, of the Paris bookshop, Groves & Michaux. DHL's letter is missing.
[3] I.e. smart.
[4] *Singing of Swans* was to be included in *Paintings of D. H. Lawrence* and in the Warren Gallery
exhibition.

4975. To Aldous and Maria Huxley, [7? March 1929]
Text: Huxley 789.

Bandol, Var.
[7? March 1929]

Dear Aldous and Maria, –

Well, though I've not heard from Mr. Groves, I've decided to come to Paris to see about an edit. of *Lady C.* – else I'll feel *minchione*,[1] with all those other pirates. So expect to arrive Paris at 10.0 on Tuesday night. Frieda says she wants to go straight to Baden-Baden – by Lyon, Besançon, Strasburg – and join me in ten days or so. If you have a nice handy hotel to suggest, send me a line, I expect I'd get it – otherwise I shall probably go to the little Hôtel de Versailles, Bvd. Montparnasse – near the *gare*.[2] But I'd send you a line.

Rhys Davies will probably be coming up at the same time, so I'd have company.

So see you soon – and hope it'll be nice weather and can have some lovely meetings.

DHL

4976. To Aldous Huxley, 8 March 1929
Text: Moore 1137.

Hôtel Beau Rivage, Bandol
8 March 1929

Dear Aldous:

I have a letter from Frank A. Groves of the Librairie du Palais Royal – Groves and Michaux – to say they will help me with an edit. of *Lady C.* and do the distributing. So it's good I am coming up – shall arrive Tuesday night, as I said – and if I don't see you sooner, perhaps we could meet at Galignani's bookshop, 224 rue de Rivoli, ar. 11.0 on Wednesday morning. I wrote to the admirable Mr Moulder asking him when he would see me and give me his sage advice in the matter of printing etc. – so he may send me a letter c/o you. I don't know why I feel rather thrilled at getting out this new edit. – a little fat book that will go in your pocket and cost only 50 frs. or 75. – It is exactly a year since I left Diablerets and went to Florence to get *Lady C.* launched and on[3] her first voyage – now she must make her second splash. I feel she's been quite effectual, in the twelve months. But she must go further – I shan't be able to have her photographed if I want a *pocket* size. Proofs again!

Frieda will go straight to Baden. Rhys Davies will come up with me. He is

[1] 'gullible'.
[2] 'railway station'. DHL stayed at the Hotel de Versailles 21–5 February 1924.
[3] Moore prints: '[on?]'.

by no means thrilling or dazzling. I expect you and Maria will think him unspeakably pedestrian – but he's no fool, really, and one can be quiet with him – he's not nervy or nerve-racking. I expect we'll stay in some quiet little hotel on the left bank.

I shall bloom out in my new grey suit and even a pair of Toulon gloves, most fetching – and let's hope the weather will be decent and my cough in *abeyance* – and I do hope those wild daffodils will come out and we can go and see them – and I'm glad you've not got a motor-car, I always feel it a strain on Maria, and one can take a taxi.

– *Au revoir* then.

4977. To S. S. Koteliansky, [8 March 1929]
Text: MS BL; Postmark, Bandol 8–3 29; Zytaruk 382.

Bandol.
Friday 8 March

My dear Kot

We are still here – leave on Monday – Frieda for Baden, I for Paris, to attend to a new edit. of my novel – which I shall probably produce myself, but which will be distributed and put on the market by the Librairie du Palais Royal – Groves & Michaux. I have a letter from Mr Groves – sounds all right – but I'd better see to it personally. Shall try to do a pocket edition, to sell to trade at 50 frs. Galignani's wrote me, they are now selling a *German* reprint – pirated![1] Must stop that.

I only wanted you to send a copy of my book round to Secker, and deliver it into his hands. He seems to want one very particularly.

Shall send an address from Paris – or c/o Aldous – 3 rue du Bac. Suresnes (Seine) will do.

Yrs   DHL

4978. To Emily King, 8 March 1929
Text: MS Lazarus; Postmark, Bandol 9–3 29; Unpublished.

Bandol. Var.
8 March 1929.

My dear Pamela

You see we are still here – but definitely leaving next Monday – I am going to Paris, Frieda will go direct to Baden to see her mother. I have to go to Paris

---

[1] Perhaps the piracy which 'came to light in Paris in 1928 . . . marked "Imprimé en Allemagne"' (Roberts 109). See photolithographed piracy 1.10, in Jay A. Gertzman, 'The Piracies of "Lady Chatterley's Lover": 1928–1950', *DHL Review*, xix (Fall 1987), 286–7.

now to arrange about publishing a cheap edition of *Lady C* there. – There are now three pirated editions, two produced in U.S.A. and a new one, apparently done in Germany: all making money on my work. If I can bring out an edition myself, and sell it cheaper than theirs, I can cut them out once and for all, at any rate on the Continent. And now I have got a big book shop in Paris to handle it all for me: I think the people are all right: so I'll go and see to it, and get the thing done as quickly as possible. Frieda will go straight from Marseille to Strassburg, she won't come to Paris: but Rhys Davies is coming up to Paris with me, and we shall no doubt stay in the same hotel, so I shan't be alone. And Davies is really very nice: rather poor, struggling along.

Then of course the Huxleys are in their house at Suresnes, only a few miles out, so I shall have them too. I'll send you the address – probably the Hotel de Versailles. Bvd Montparnasse – where we stayed before.

There seems a little turn to real spring here – the air has gone softer, and I saw two white butterflies fluttering along the edge of the sea. Yesterday we went a drive into the country – quite lovely, it was, with a soft blue sky: but what a havoc that awful cold has made, everything dead. The people who grow flowers are in despair – but fortunately the vines are all right, and that's the chief crop.

I don't think I shall come over to England just now – unless something special brings me. In a day or two I expect you'll get a prospectus of my book of pictures, with one of the reproductions in colour: hope you'll like it.

I do hope Joan is better – the flu seems to have gone again here, so perhaps it has also with you. Now we need the *real* spring. We'd all do with a bit of tittivating up.

Love from us both to you all.   DHL

4979. To Gertrude Cooper, 8 March 1929
Text: MS Clarke; Unpublished.

Hotel Beau Rivage. *Bandol*, Var.
8 March 1929

Dear G[ertie]
Your letter came on all right – glad you are safely in Bournemouth and having a bit of sun. It's been cold enough even here: but now there seems to be a bit of a turn towards spring.

We were glad to see Ada, but she seemed changed, not so cheerful and easy as she used to be. I suppose as time goes on things weigh on her more, especially with trade so bad in Ripley. I think everybody gets fed up, and feels as if they'd like to go right away and leave it all for good.

We are leaving on Monday – I am going to Paris, and Frieda to her Mother in BadenBaden. I'm not very keen on going north – Paris will be cold still, I'm afraid – but I have a bit of business to arrange there, and I suppose I shall only stay a fortnight or so: then Frieda will join me, and we'll come south again. – But perhaps Frieda might run over to England while she's so near – to see her elder daughter, Elsa, who is getting married on April 6th.[1] – and is not coming to see us till later. Anyhow I have friends in Paris, shan't be alone. It's a pity you can't winter in a sunny place. But the journey here would be so bad for you – and then the food and all so different, you wouldn't really like it. You'd never feel at home and quiet. But I think Ada really liked it. She seemed for the first time in her life to be happy being alone and quite still, sitting in the sun and seeing the easy, drifting life of the place. That's how I am happiest nowadays – just sitting still, quite alone, with a little friendly life to watch.

I do hope you're feeling pretty well, and eating better. Thank God I can eat again with pleasure: it's *so* important, it makes all life different.

With love from us both.   DHL

4980. To Ada Clarke, [8 March 1929]
Text: MS Clarke; PC v. La Cote D'Azur – Bandol: La Jetée Vue Du Fort; Postmark, Bandol 8–3 29; Lawrence–Gelder 170–1.

[Hotel Beau Rivage, Bandol, Var.]
Friday

Had your letters – you mustn't refuse what I sent. – We are leaving Monday – I must go to Paris for a bit – business – and Frieda will go to Baden. But Rhys Davies will be coming along with me, so I shan't be alone. He was here this week – and yesterday we drove in the carriage to le Beausset and le Castelet[2] – a lovely day – pity you weren't there – but the country still absolutely bare with frost, only a few almond trees in blossom. Shall send address in Paris – hope all goes well –

love   DHL

4981. To Nancy Pearn, [8 March 1929]
Text: MS UT; Unpublished.

Bandol.
Friday 8 March

Dear Nancy Pearn
We've not gone yet – but leaving Monday, for Paris. I shall have to go there for a couple of weeks, to attend to a new small edit. of my book, which I want

[1] See Letter 4817 and n. 2.   [2] 5 miles n.e. Bandol.

to get out – by small I mean small in size, cheap. Am not sure which hotel I'll stay at, but will send an address on Wed. – My wife is going to see her mother in BadenBaden.

Just had proofs of the prospectus for my book of pictures – disappointing how *dim* the first picture comes out – loses such a lot – smudged! – Would you tell Pollinger, by the way, if they do ten signed copies at fifty guineas each – awful thought! – they must give me more than 5% royalty, or even 10%, on that little lot. How I hate these high-power editions!

Ever.   DHL

4982. To Ada Clarke, [9 March 1929]
Text: MS Clarke; Unpublished.

[Frieda Lawrence begins]

Bandol
Tuesday

Dear Ada,

We are still here as you see – Rhys Davies is also here, we have just been to the top and we talked about your visit – He looks different & *well*, how handsome all the English would become if they got a bit of sun-shine into their blood – I still dont know what will happen – Lawrence may go to Paris, as there are 3 pirate editions out of Lady C, people getting really rich – it is *so* annoying – But politically the cat is jumping our way – He may get out (Lawr not the cat) another edition of Lady C – He is doing another picture at this moment[1] – Elsa very excited about marriage, she is *not* coming before – You must have had a time with poor old Mr Clarke[2] – He is past all scheming now, but I hope there will be a demand for some clothes in heaven & he gets some orders! A letter from the Nottingham Guardian inviting L to a luncheon & for him to lecture!! Your letter just come, you seem to have a good busy time! Anyhow would'nt you like to borrow the 50£ or *more* if it would be convenient? Rhys Davies is really a nice young man – I hope Elsa has written to you she seems in a frenzy about her wedding – L may go to Paris, I am not keen for him to go – but we may come to England then! But nothing is sure – To-day a lovely spring day – So glad the children were pleased with their things –

Hope you will have a little peace soon –

Love   Frieda

---

[1] Cf. Letter 4974 and n. 4.   [2] Cf. Letter 4956 and n. 3.

[Lawrence begins]

Saturday[1]

The address in Paris will be:
        Hotel de Versailles, Bvd. Montparnasse, *Paris*
And I shall be there on Tuesday, all being well.

love   DHL

4983. To Earl and Achsah Brewster, [9 March 1929]
Text: MS UT; Brewster 197–9.

Hotel Beau Rivage. Bandol. Var.
Sat. 10 March 1929

Dear Earl and Achsah

We are leaving finally on Monday – I for Paris, of all places, Frieda for BadenBaden. I must go to Paris to settle about a cheap edition of *Lady C.* – which the Librairie du Palais Royal will publish for me. But I want to go and look after it, do it quickly: make a little fat book you can put in your pocket, to sell at 50 frs. or 75 frs. I don't know how long I shall have to stay – possibly three weeks – and I've no idea where we shall go afterwards. It was so hard to get Frieda to move to Spain, that I never did move her. So what we shall do after Easter remains to be seen. Really, if I was stronger, and didn't cough so much, I'd go to the ranch for the summer. But I'm afraid I'm not up to America, just yet at least. – We almost went to Corsica, but people arrived from there looking still frozen, having been snowed up – so we cooled off. And the P[aris] L[yon] M[arseille] buses raging round and round all the time with tourists must be very trying: and the food supplies very bad, and the good hotels very expensive. – But perhaps when spring really begins to look in, one will get definitely drawn somewhere. – The air has gone milder and more springlike these last few days, but the land is inert and desert, all the plants are dead. Luckily the vines are all right. – I've got a bit of a sore throat and don't feel particularly bright – but nothing bad. It's been very pleasant here, I feel we shall easily get something worse.

There's no particular news. My sister was here a fortnight – and depressed me very much – she too has sort of gone all out of gear, with her life – and she always seemed to enjoy it so much. Of course the mining districts are terribly depressing, and if you are in trade, there *is* no trade, so that is partly it. But like all women, she has turned forty and more or less turned against all she has lived for up till now: business, house, family, garden even – doesn't want them any more. It is something organic in women, and not to be argued with.

---

[1] DHL completed the letter (begun on the 5th) on 9 March.

Largely it's the result of having been too 'pure' and unphysical, unsensual. The organism itself reacts at last, and makes havoc. – I am speaking of my younger sister, Ada.

They have been fussing about the seizure of my poems, *Pansies* – asking questions in Parliament, and so on: but I'm afraid without getting anywhere. They are a lot of muffs and ninnies – and now I am past caring. – I haven't done much in the way of work – two oils on those panels you bought in Paris[1] – and three water-colours on Harwood's block – which still says 'with love to Uncle David' – three nice waters – *Leda*, and *Renascence of Men*, and *Singing Swans*. I expect you will see them in my book of pictures, which is going slowly ahead. I'll get them to send you the prospectus with reprod. of *Finding of Moses*[2] – full size reprod. – What about Achsah's exhibition in New York? It seems very hard to get anybody to move. Brett hasn't sold a thing, after all the fuss. – My show still hangs fire, they are afraid of the police. But if it doesn't come off, I don't care one iota. Sick of 'em all. Fed up. – The only thing I *really* wish is that I didn't always cough and have either a sore chest or a sore throat as well as a sore spirit. Why should the gods keep me always so sore inside? I get so tired of it. But even that doesn't help.

– I'll send you the Paris address in a day or two.

Love. DHL

4984. To Giuseppe Orioli, [10 March 1929]
Text: MS UCLA; Moore, *Intelligent Heart* 402.

Bandol.
Sunday

Dear Pino

We leave in the morning. The address in Paris is:

Hotel de Versailles, Bvd. Montparnasse, *Paris*

Send me a line there.

Of course I've got a sore throat, to travel with.

Mr Groves, of Groves & Michaux, Librairie du Palais-Royal, says he will collaborate with me in any way, in getting out an edition. I think I shall print it myself, and let them do the publishing and distributing – and so keep the thing in my own hands. The idea now is to bring out a little fat book that will go in a man's pocket, and sell it about 60 frs. Then people could easily carry them. What do you think? I shall try to get everything done as quick as possible.

Seems a long time since I heard from you – how are you?

---

[1] *Spring* and *Summer Dawn*.   [2] *Moses* –] *Moses* not –

I heard the Gotham bookshop did the pirating.[1]

Wish I weren't suddenly feeling rather seedy. Frieda is going to Baden-Baden direct, for a fortnight –

love   DHL

They say there's now a German pirated edition.

4985. To Martin Secker, [10 March 1929]
Text: MS UInd; Postmark, B[andol] 11 –3 29; Secker 116–17.

Bandol
Sunday

Dear Secker

After all I sent you the missing pp. of the Poems, or had them sent by post, as it seems all right now. Hope you received them safely, in London. – Hope by now also you have a copy of the novel delivered to you.

We are leaving tomorrow, I am going to Paris, Frieda to BadenBaden. I must go for about a fortnight to do an[2] edition of my book there, cheap – at about 50 frs to the trade. There is now, I am told, a German reprint on the market. I must stop it. I have a good man of the Librairie du Palais-Royal to do the publishing and distributing, but I think I shall print the thing myself.

The address in Paris will be –

Hotel de Versailles, Boulevard Montparnasse, *Paris*

Send me a line there to tell me if you have the complete MS. of the poems, and if you have arranged it properly – the pages are numbered – and what you think of it, and what are the plans. – I shan't send my final copy to London till I hear you have yours.

Of course I've got a sore throat to travel with – hope it will go off. – Frieda may come to England. – My picture-book is going ahead.

Send me a line.

DHL

4986. To P. R. Stephensen, [10 March 1929]
Text: Charles Hamilton Catalogue, 14 November 1974, item 202.

Bandol
Sunday

Dear Stephensen

[Lawrence gives his Paris address.] . . . my wife is going to Baden Baden –

---

[1] Frances Stellof of the Gotham Book Mart in New York was an admirer of DHL; there is no evidence to link Gotham with a piracy of *Lady Chatterley's Lover*.

[2] MS reads 'and'.

Davies is coming along with me. Of course I've got a sore throat like anything, to add to the joys of travelling ... Hope you got the *Singing Swan* picture. Let me know.

D. H. Lawrence

4987. To Nancy Pearn, [12 March 1929]
Text: MS UT; Unpublished.

[Grand Hotel de Versailles, 60. Boulevard Montparnasse, Paris]
Tuesday

Dear Nancy Pearn
Here is the address[1] – *not* 'grand',[2] but quite nice, if ever you want it. Send me all the news and give the address to the other depts – have just got here – so tired.

D. H. Lawrence

4988. To Harry and Caresse Crosby, 13 March 1929
Text: MS SIU; Postmark, Paris 13.III 1929; Unpublished.

Hotel de Versailles, 60 Boulevard Montparnasse
13 March 1929

Dear Harry and Caresse Crosby
I am here for a little while seeing about *Lady C.* – my wife is in Baden Baden. Send me a word if you are at home, and if we shall meet. I may be going out to stay with Aldous Huxley at Suresnes – not far –. So cold here – and the south was so sunny. – Your poor horse Sunstroke won't have been stroked lately. How is he?[3]

D. H. Lawrence

4989. To Emily King, [13 March 1929]
Text: MS Lazarus; Unpublished.

[Grand Hotel de Versailles, 60. Boulevard Montparnasse, Paris]
Wednesday

My dear Pamela
Just a line to say I'm here all right, a bit tired, but not so much as you might expect. Seems very dark and grey in Paris after Bandol, but the hotel is nice.

love   DHL

---

[1] MS reads 'addess'.
[2] DHL struck through the word 'Grand' in the hotel's headed notepaper.
[3] Sunstroke was a yearling ('terribly cunning and young and fiery') Crosby had bought on 15 August 1928. His mixed fortunes are recorded in Crosby's diaries, *Shadows of the Sun* (ed. E. Germain). On 31 March Crosby was to drive DHL to Chantilly to look at Sunstroke and Gin Cocktail (ibid., p. 244).

4990. To Harry Crosby, [14 March 1929]
Text: MS SIU; Postmark, Paris 14.III 1929; Unpublished.

Hotel de Versailles
Thursday

Dear Harry Crosby

Found your note this evening – shall be pleased to come to lunch tomorrow at 1.0.[1] The Huxleys are living out at Suresnes, and I'm going to stay a few days with them next week – so if you'd like to meet them, we'll arrange something.

hasta la vista[2]   D. H. Lawrence

4991. To Harry Crosby, [16? March 1929]
Text: MS SIU; Unpublished.

[Grand Hotel de Versailles, 60 Boulevard Montparnasse, Paris]
[16? March 1929]

I'd have liked to come very much, but am engaged till about 6.0 – so sorry – perhaps another time.

D. H. Lawrence

4992. To Edward Dahlberg, [16 March 1929]
Text: MS UTul; Unpublished.

Hotel de Versailles, 60 Bvd Montparnasse
Sat night

Dear Dahlberg

Sorry I was out when you called – and tomorrow I am busy, and on Monday morning going out into the country to stay a while with friends. Shall let you know when I come back to Paris.

[1] Crosby recorded in his diary for 15 March 1929:

D. H. Lawrence for luncheon and we disagreed on everything. I am a visionary I like to soar he is all engrossed in the body and in the mushroom quality of the earth and the body and in the complexities of psychology. He is indirect. I am direct. He admits of defeat. I do not. *He is commonplace. I am not. He is unthoroughbred. I am thoroughbred. He was "seedy" looking how I hate the word "seedy".* I guess he is a sick man I forgive him a great deal because of The Plumed Serpent *but I can see no excuse for writing* Lady Chatterley's Lover. *That is why* he is here in Paris to try to get someone to publish *Lady Chatterley's Lover.* There have already been several pirated editions both in France and in America where Lawrence doesn't get one cent of benefice. An editor who can do that is a skunk. Lawrence stayed until four attacking my visionary attitude but my fort withstood the bombardment and I marshalled my troops and sallied out to counter-attack all of which took time so that I was not able to go out to the opening of the flat races at Maisons Laffite where I wanted to see the Lady of the Gold Horse [Constance, Comtesse of Jumilhac] and watch The Arrow win at seven to one I had a thousand on her to win. (*Shadows of the Sun*, p. 241)

[2] 'until we meet'.

I enclose a letter from Pollinger.[1] Very mean of Putnams – you must have an agent, as they say you should.

Sincerely   D. H. Lawrence

4993. To Laurence Pollinger, [18 March 1929]
Text: MS UT; Unpublished.

c/o Aldous Huxley, 3 rue du Bac. Suresnes (Seine)

Monday

Dear Pollinger

I have all your letters. Damn mean of Putnams! – I saw Dahlberg in Paris and gave him your message – he's a poor under-dog.

About the *Pansies* – I really wanted a cheaper edition – but I'll see about that later. What I want to know is *exactly* what poems Secker is leaving out – please let me know this precisely. I might have some of them done as a broadside at 2d., for the election.[2] – If Secker leaves out too many, I won't have him do the book at all, voilà tout![3] So don't do anything without me.

I don't want Dahlberg to *possess* that introd. – that is, I want the right to reprint it. Cape has asked me for a book of my literary criticisms and introductory essays, and it would make a good book, and I'll soon have enough.

Stephensen is going ahead with the pictures – but they come out very dim. I expect he delays signing because of paying. – I suppose you saw I said I wont have 5% merely on the fifty guinea copies – what has he arranged there? – Answer all the rest tomorrow.

Ever   D. H. Lawrence

4994. To Giuseppe Orioli, 18 March 1929
Text: MS (Photocopy) HU; cited in Moore, *Intelligent Heart* 402.

c/o Aldous Huxley, 3 rue du Bac, Suresnes (Seine)

18 March 1929

Dear Pino

Am staying with Aldous and Maria a few days, in their little house – very nice. Frieda comes on 28th. – but I think I shall go back to Paris on Saturday. I had your letter, and cheque from Toronto,[4] and bordereau – shall make up

---

[1] The enclosure is missing.

[2] A general election had been called for 30 May. Pollinger wrote on the MS alongside DHL's remark: 'He's crazy!'

[3] 'that's all!'

[4] DHL recorded in his 'Memoranda' (MS NWU) the receipt of £1.14.0, by cheque (dated 10 March 1929) from Toronto; it came from Roy Britnell (1900–83), owner of the city's largest bookstore (cf. *Letters*, vi. 574 n. 1). See Letters 5110 and 5125.

the accounts when I go back to Paris, as I haven't got the book here, and send you your share. Meanwhile do add up the postage, and let us get that square. I enclose a letter about the Hollidays[1] – also Lawrence Gomme – nice people, I must say! such lies! I have to answer Ted Gillett, as he is a friend, and a decent fellow[2] – but I feel very sharp about it. I suppose they must have their original price of $8.50.

I haven't done any more about a cheap edition – it seems so difficult. But the man Groves, of Groves & Michaux, the Librairie du Palais Royal, is apparently responsible for putting on the market the European pirated edition, printed in Germany – which Galignani is selling at 300 frs and Castiglione at 400 frs. – they get it from Groves at 100 frs. a copy. But Groves has burnt his fingers – the Amer. booksellers sell the Amer. pirated edition, and the others won't properly sell the 'printed in Germany' one: Sylvia Beach won't touch it. So now he wants me to *authorise* his edition – print a little slip in front authorising it – and he will give me 20% on the whole edition of 1500, on the selling price of 100 francs a copy to the trade. I am almost inclined to do this. What do you say? Afterwards we could get out a cheap edition at 60 frs. What do you think. Did I tell you this before?

It is very quiet and sunny – Suresnes a quiet little place, nice by the river, but nothing otherwise.

I am not sure if we shall go to Spain – I want to, but Frieda doesn't want to very much. So perhaps we shall have to compromise, and come back to Italy.

Tell me what you think about Groves – it seems rather bad, taking up with a pirate. But they are *all* pirates.

How is Carletto – must send him a trifle with yours, for Easter.

DHL

4995. To Jean Watson, 18 March 1929
Text: MS UT; Unpublished.

c/o Aldous Huxley. 3 rue du Bac, Suresnes. (Seine)
Monday 18 March 1929

Dear Miss Watson

I always wonder if it is worth while letting Tauchnitz have books at £25.

---

[1] The enclosure is missing.
[2] Frederick ('Ted') W. Gillete, husband of Bobbie née Hawk, the younger of the girls from Del Monte Ranch in New Mexico. Gillete, a wealthy young man whom DHL had known in Taos, was sent one of the earliest copies of *Lady Chatterley's Lover* (*Letters*, vi. 448).

each – it's so insignificant. Yet if you think it worth while, then go ahead with *Sons and Lovers* and *Woman Who Rode*[1] – if there's really any point in it.

Yours Sincerely   D. H. Lawrence

4996. To Rhys Davies, [20 March 1929]

Text: TMSC NWU; Huxley 790–1.

3, rue du Bac, Suresnes, Seine.
Wed.

Dear Davies,

I arrived here with a bit of flu or something – felt very cheap – but they are really very nice and kind to me, and look after me so nicely.

I am coming back to the hotel on Monday, after lunch – will you tell the man? And I expect my wife on the Wed. following – perhaps with her nephew.[2] You might tell him that, without *fixing* it, because I'm not quite sure.

Would you come to tea tomorrow, come a bit early, and we can walk in the Bois by the river. I won't say lunch, because there are always people here, and you'd only be bored – the people bore me a bit.

Could you bring me, out of my trunk, the wooden African vase, with it's lid? I shall leave it here. It is at the bottom of the trunk, which I think I did not lock. You can lift out the tray of the trunk – it's under that.

Do come, I shall be glad to see you and hear your news.

DHL

4997. To Harry and Caresse Crosby, [20 March 1929]

Text: MS SIU; Postmark, Sur[esnes] 20[...]; Unpublished.

ch. Aldous Huxley, 3 rue du Bac, Suresnes, Seine
Wednesday

Dear Harry and Caresse Crosby

We are so full up here with engagements all this week – every moment – so silly! But I shall go back to Hotel de Versailles on Monday or Tuesday, and I think my wife will come, and perhaps we can all meet somewhere next week. Shall it be so?

D. H. Lawrence

---

[1] *The Woman Who Rode Away and Other Stories* was published in the Tauchnitz series on 4 May 1929, *Sons and Lovers* on 8 June 1929 (William B. Todd and Ann Bowden, *Tauchnitz International Editions in English 1841–1955*, New York, 1988, Nos. 4877 and 4879A). The Tauchnitz *England, My England* had appeared in 1928 (*Letters*, vi. 262 and n. 3).

[2] Friedrich ('Friedel') Jaffe (b. 1903), eldest son of Frieda's sister Else. He had visited the Lawrences at Kiowa ranch, May–July 1925.

4998. To Ada Clarke, [20 March 1929]
Text: MS Clarke; Postmark, Sur[esnes] 20 –3 29; cited in Lawrence–Gelder 189–90.

c/o Aldous Huxley. 3 rue du Bac, *Suresnes*, Seine
Wed.
My dear Sister

I should have written you before – but one feels so scattered and a bit bewildered in these towns – so much talk and fuss, and nothing very real. Am staying with the Huxleys till next Monday, and they are very nice to me. Have got a bit of chest, with dirty Paris air. Frieda says she is happy in Baden, and is coming to Paris next Wednesday – we shall be in

Hotel de Versailles. 60 Bvd Montparnasse, Paris. 15me

I suppose we'll stay till after Easter – then go somewhere, I don't know quite where, to find a house – perhaps to the Lago di Garda – feel I don't much care. Secker is going ahead to do an expurgated edition of the *Pansies* – leave out a few poems. Stephensen sent me the reprod. of another of my pictures – also very dim and vague and disappointing. I am sad about them. But of course other people don't know them as I do. – Paris at the moment is very sunny and warm, but there is not a flower anywhere, except in the shops – in all the Bois – like Hyde Park – not a spark of anything. A very dreary spring. I do hope you are all well – can't write letters here –

love DHL

4999. To Laurence Pollinger, [20 March 1929]
Text: MS UT; Unpublished.

c/o Aldous Huxley. 3 rue du Bac, *Suresnes* (Seine)
Wed.
Dear Pollinger

I told Secker the original introduction, of Jack Hutchinson's MS., pleased *me* more than the second one, of Secker's MS. But I doubt he won't print the first one.[1]

As you think best about a lawsuit for the *Pansies*[2] – but Jix needs a thorough showing up. He opened my sealed registered letter, and that should be fixed on him, absolutely.

I'm disgusted with the Viking Press. They knew all about the laws of copyright and importation all along – then why did they insist that I should offer the book to them in the beginning, especially as Jonathan Cape was making an offer? What about Cape now?

---

[1] See Letter 4960 and n. 1.   [2] Pollinger annotated here: 'Glory be!'

I shall have to leave the Seltzer-Boni affair entirely to you, as I don't know what any of them are worth.

Do send me Mr Bradley's address, and tell me where he could help me.[1]

ever DHL

5000. To P. R. Stephensen, [20 March 1929]
Text: MS Anon; Munro 304–5.

c/o Aldous Huxley. 3 rue du Bac, *Suresnes*, Seine

20 March

Dear Stephensen

Thanks for the *Prospectus* with *Moses* – Oh dear, *Moses* is dim! They get them so *smudgy*. Can't they get *anything* clear – that yellow light at the back! Oh dear, how sad. – So you are sending out the prospectus *without* the picture? – just as well. You *can't* fold the picture, it cracks it raw. Be sure to send several prospectuses to

Alfred Stieglitz, The Shelton Hotel, Lexington Avenue, New York City

and several to

Herbert J. Seligman, 245 East 36th. St. New York

And several to

Mrs Mabel Luhan[2], No. 1. Fifth Avenue. New York.

You asked me to come to England – but the detecs. at Curtis Brown's office said if I came to England I should be at once arrested. Voilà! – My wife may come for the show, if Dorothy W[arren] will bring it off. Do you expect her to, really? – and when? – Secker is going to do the *Pansies*, but of course, expurgated. Conversation overheard here from my window –

votre chat, Madame, est il un mâle?

Oui Madame, mais il a été arrangé – n'ayez pas de peur pour votre 'pussy'. –

C'est comme ça –[3] all been jixed, fixed, arrangé.

DHL

---

[1] William Aspenwall Bradley, a literary agent in Paris.   [2] Luhan] Lujan
[3] 'your cat, Madam, is it a male? Yes Madam, but he has been fixed – have no fear for your "pussy." – It is like that –'.

5001. To Daniel Halévy, 22 March 1929
Text: MS Halévy; Unpublished.

3 rue du Bac, Suresnes, Seine
22 March 1929

Dear Monsieur Halévy[1]

Many thanks for your letter. Aldous Huxley and I will come then at 5.0 tomorrow, and I shall be very glad to see you, and M. Marcel,[2] and Mlle Clairouin whose letters I have received,[3] and Mme Duclaux whose work I know a little.[4]

Yours Sincerely   D. H. Lawrence

5002. To Glenn Hughes, [22 March 1929]
Text: MS UT; Unpublished.

3 rue du Bac, Suresnes, Seine
Friday

Dear Mr Hughes[5]

Will you come to tea here next Monday at about 4.15, please. It is three minutes from the Suresnes bridge.

Yours Sincerely   D. H. Lawrence

[1] Daniel Halévy (1872–1962), distinguished French historian, author of studies of Nietzsche, Péguy, Michelet, Proudhon, of the workers' movement in France (1910), etc. 1921–30 director of the Gasset collection 'Les cahiers verts', which published the first works of Montherlant, Mauriac, Giraudoux, Malraux; a close friend of Charles Péguy and George Moore, his salon was attended by the leading figures of the Paris literary and intellectual world.

[2] Gabriel Marcel (1889–1973), French philosopher and dramatist. His plays include *La Coeur des Autres* (1921), and *Un Homme de Dieu* (1925). He published his *Journal Métaphysique* in 1927, converted to Roman Catholicism in 1929, fashioned an existential philosophical system in Roman Catholic terms and published *Etre et Avoir* (1935), *Le Mystère de l'Etre* (1951), etc. His favourable review of the Paris edition of *Lady Chatterley's Lover* in *La Nouvelle Revue Française*, xxxii (1929), 729–31, described DHL as 'one of the most powerful and original personalities of European literature ... there is no other novelist nowadays to whom we can render such homage'. Marcel continued to write perceptively about DHL, particularly on his last poems. See James C. Cowan, *D. H. Lawrence: An Annotated Bibliography of Writings about Him* (De Kalb, Illinois, 1982), i. 197–8.

[3] Denyse Clairouin translated *England, My England* (1930) and *The Plumed Serpent* (1931); she developed literary exchanges between the French and English speaking countries; she died in Mauthausen extermination camp in 1945.

[4] Mary Duclaux (1857–1944), née Robinson, critic, biographer and poet. m. (1) 1888, Professor James Darmesteter (d. 1894); (2) 1901, Professor Emile Duclaux, director of the Pasteur Institute (d. 1904). Author of *La Vie de Renan* (1893), *Froissart* (1894), etc. Her reviews in *The Times Literary Supplement* introduced many important new French writers to English readers. (See obituary, *The Times*, 22 April 1944.)

[5] Glenn Arthur Hughes (1894–1964), Professor of English Literature and Director of the School of Drama at the University of Washington. In 1929 he was in Europe on a Guggenheim Fellowship researching for his book *Imagism and the Imagists* (Stanford, 1931); in it he cites a conversation with DHL in May 1929, during which DHL 'declared there never had been such a thing as imagism. It was all an illusion of Ezra Pound's, ... and was nonsense' (pp. 169–70).

5003. To Edward Dahlberg, [23 March 1929]
Text: MS UTul; Postmark, Suresnes 23 –3 29; Unpublished.

3 rue du Bac, Suresnes, Seine
Sat.

Dear Dahlberg

Shall be back in Paris Wednesday – expect my wife will arrive in the evening – have got the copy of *Lady C.*[1] – very dirty, the swine – will bring it for you, and we'll meet in town and have tea one day, if you like –

D. H. Lawrence

5004. To Earl and Achsah Brewster, [23 March 1929]
Text: MS UT; Brewster 199.

3 rue du Bac, Suresnes, Seine
Sat

Dear Earl and Achsah

Just a line to say I am here – staying at the moment with the Huxleys – Frieda in Baden, joins me next Wed. – and I go in to Paris.

Hotel de Versailles, 60 Bvd Montparnasse, Paris. XV.

Got a cold – feel sort of feverish – don't like Paris – but think I shall manage to do an edition of *Lady C.* pretty cheap – to sell about 60 frs – so that's what I came for. Otherwise no news and no wits and feel very tired of seeing people and wish I was on a desert island or in Bandol or even Capri. We'll leave next week – after Easter – D. V. – but I don't know where for – shall let you know. Has Achsah sold any pictures? – Brett not sold a thing – mine are being reproduced, but very unsatisfactory – Towns are dirty and horrid, and I wish I was well away.

DHL

5005. To Genevieve Taggard, 23 March 1929
Text: MS Lazarus; Unpublished.

c/o Aldous Huxley, 3 rue du Bac, Suresnes. Seine
23 March 1929

Dear Genevieve Taggard[2]

I had your letter here – never mind about the review – most things go wrong in print, the devil invented it. As for my seized poems, I only hope they bit the Seizers.

Sincerely   D. H. Lawrence

[1] From the Pegasus Press (see Letter 5015).
[2] Genevieve Taggard (1894–1948), American poet. Ed. *The Measure: a Journal of Verse,* 1920–6, and *Circumference. Varieties of Metaphysical Verse, 1459–1928* (New York, 1929); *Collected Poems, 1918–38* (1938). She reviewed *Mornings in Mexico* very favourably in *New York Herald Tribune Books,* 7 August 1927.

5006. To Emily King, [23 March 1929]
Text: MS Lazarus; Unpublished.

c/o Aldous Huxley, 3 rue du Bac. Suresnes, Seine
Saturday

My dear Sister

Such a sort of fuddle here I never got your birthday letter written[1] – I hadn't forgot it, only there are *always* people here. Send you a little money. – I am staying here till Wednesday, then back to Hotel de Versailles – expect Frieda will[2] arrive in the evening with her nephew Friedel. – I got a cold in Paris, of course – dirty place, filthy air, don't like it – but don't know where we shall go after – I suppose we shall stay till after Easter. It's been very warm muggy weather. Now I've got to go to some French literary people down in the cité – I do hate it. The Huxleys are very nice and look after me very well – but I don't feel nearly so well as in Bandol. – Well I'm sorry my letter is late – and such a shabby dull letter – but I can't write here –

love to you   DHL

5007. To Laurence Pollinger, 24 March 1929
Text: MS UT; Unpublished.

3 rue du Bac, Suresnes, Seine
24 March 1929

Dear Pollinger

Herewith the agreement for the picture book. – And would you please answer the man about the poem.[3]

Many thanks for Mr Bradleys address. I shall telephone him tomorrow, about an arrangement I am making with a Mr Titus.[4]

I went to a French literary tea yesterday – with Mauriac[5] and a few more – ye gods, how literary – the Lord made Adam out of printers ink, in Paris.

Am going back to Hotel de Versailles on Tuesday – had a bit of grippe, of course, from the filthy city air!

DHL

---

[1] Emily's birthday had been 21 March.   [2] will] with   [3] Unidentified.

[4] Edward W. Titus (1880–   ), wealthy American owner of a bookshop at 4 rue Delambre, Paris 14; editor of *This Quarter*. First husband of cosmetician Helena Rubinstein (d. 1965). He was to print and distribute the 'Popular Edition' of *Lady Chatterley's Lover*, published in Paris in May 1929 (Roberts A42c).

[5] François Mauriac (1885–1970), French novelist, playwright and journalist. Author of *Genetrix* (1924), *Le Désert de L'Amour* (1925), *Thérèse Desqueyroux* (1927), *Asmodée* (1938), etc. Like Marcel, converted to Roman Catholicism in 1929. Awarded the Nobel Prize for Literature in 1952.

5008. To Edward Dahlberg, [25 March 1929]
Text: MS UTul; Postmark, Suresnes 25–3 29; Moore 1138.

3 rue du Bac. *Suresnes*. Seine
Monday

Dear Dahlberg

I was sorry I couldn't ask you in last evening, but the house isn't mine, and I don't like to interfere in the social arrangements.

Do leave out of that introduction anything that you wish – I wrote it, as one must write, without thinking of persons. But I entirely sympathise with you in your desire not to hurt your mother.

As for writing pariah literature, a man has to write what is in him, and what he *can* write: and better by far have genuine pariah literature than sentimentalities on a 'higher' level.

I'll bring you that copy of *Lady C.* – it's rather dirty – and I'll give it you on Thursday – perhaps we might meet somewhere for tea – I'll send a line to Cooks.

Yrs   D. H. Lawrence

I don't want you to pay for that *Lady C.* – the people who had it made it so dirty, anyhow.

5009. To Frederick (?) King, 25 March 1929
Text: MS UTul; Postmark, Suresnes 25–3 29; Unpublished.

3 rue du Bac, *Suresnes*, Seine
25 March 1929

Dear Mr King[1]

It is very kind of you to offer to take those books to America, but I really wouldn't trouble you, – and besides, I don't exactly know when they'll be ready.

I'm sorry too that I missed you in Paris. But when you are coming back to Italy, write to me c/o Pino Orioli, because I might possibly be in Capri, and then we could meet.

Yours Sincerely   D. H. Lawrence

---

[1] DHL's correspondent may have been Frederick Allen King (1865–1939), American, the Literary Editor of *Literary Digest* (New York), 1909–33. The letter was addressed to F. A. King in Naples.

5010. To St John Hutchinson, [25 March 1929]
Text: MS Hutchinson; Unpublished.

3 rue du Bac. Suresnes

Monday

Dear Hutchinson

Very good of you to take so much trouble over those *Pansies*. I'm never keen on law, and Jix says 'my magistrates' – so what's the good of going to *his* magistrates against *him*. But I *do* wish it could be shown in the House that he is a *liar*, and he did open my sealed and registered *letter*.[1] Oh do make Moseley expose the old skunk as a liar.

I liked so much meeting Mary Hutchinson and your girl here.[2] Mary is one of the few women left on earth who really listen to a man – no men do – and it's quite stimulating. And your daughter is so nice and young and charming, and even doesn't seem bored. Very nice.

A warm still day – still like October – pity you aren't all here so we could gas away a bit.

belle cose!   D. H. Lawrence

5011. To Juliette Huxley, 25 March 1929
Text: MS Huxley; Unpublished.

3 rue du Bac, *Suresnes*, Seine

25 March 1929

My dear Juliette

Your note found me here – where I came two weeks ago, to arrange for the publication of a cheap edition of *Lady C.* – which I think will come off all right – Aldous helped me. Frieda is in Baden, but comes tonight. Of course I got a bit of flu with the *dirty* air of this town, so Maria looked after me, and it's about all right. Plans are very vague – perhaps we'll go to Holland to sit in a village and drink milk and be looked after by a doctor Maria believes in – but I'm not sure. Anyhow we shan't stay long in Paris, because it doesn't suit me – but wait a bit, and I'll tell you where we go. It is very nice of Julian to offer me the book, I shall be pleased to have it, as soon as I have an address – and I know I shall learn a lot.[3] – I have that etruscan photograph in my bag for you – but you'll not think of silks if you've got no maid – oh what a curse! Still, the

---

[1] DHL's anger and frustration were conveyed by the unusually vigorous underlining of the three italicised words in this sentence.

[2] The Hutchinsons' daughter Barbara (b. 1912).

[3] Possibly a copy of Huxley's *Essays in Popular Science* (1926) which was re-issued in March 1929.

weather is better – and I hope you're all feeling cheerful, in spite of trials.

Sempre.[1] DHL

5012. To Herbert Seligmann, 25 March 1929
Text: MS PM; Unpublished.

Paris.

25 March 1929

Dear Seligman

Your letter reached me here – I have told the man responsible for my book of paintings to send you the small prospectus. If it doesn't come, write to him: P. R. Stephensen. 5 Bloomsbury Square, *London W.C. 1.*

They are printing 500 copies at ten guineas – and ten at fifty guineas – prices that make me feel ill. Of course I get the usual ten per cent. The reproductions are all in colour: but oh dear, they lose a lot: so dim and smudgy.

Perhaps the best way to get the books hot from the press would be to ask L. E. Pollinger of Curtis Brown's London office to send them you. He's a nice man and does things very willingly for me. – Secker is supposed to be printing those 'seized' *Pansies* now. That bit of idiocy was purely Joynson Hicks, the Home Sec. – the Postmaster General[2] said *he* saw nothing alarming in them, and would have passed them on, but that bobby fool Jix wouldn't let him.

Damn them all, anyhow.

Yours Sincerely   D. H. Lawrence

5013. To Jean Watson, 26 March 1929
Text: MS UT; Unpublished.

Hotel de Versailles, 60 Bvd Montparnasse, Paris XV.

26 March 1929

Dear Miss Watson

Herewith the two Tauchnitz agreements.

I went to a French literary tea on Saturday – terribly literary – and saw Mlle Clairouin, who said she had been very severely drubbed for writing to me about that chapter of *Plumed Serpent* for the *Nouvelle Revue Française* – but let her go ahead with it. – The French are as slow in life as in letters – so slow! but quite nice.

Sincerely   D. H. Lawrence

---

[1] 'Always.'   [2] Sir W. Mitchell-Thomson, MP for Croydon South.

5014. To William Bradley, 26 March 1929
Text: MS UT; Unpublished.

Hotel de Versailles, 60 Bvd Montparnasse. XVme
26 March 1929

Dear Mr Bradley

Mr Pollinger of Curtis Brown's said you'd advise me about printing my novel *Lady Chatterley's Lover* in Paris. – I went today to Mr Titus, who has a bookshop behind the Dôme just near here. He said he could get the book produced by offset – the photographic method – printing to cost about 3 frs. a copy, paper 3 frs., other items, binding and *paper* cover, about 4 frs. – making a cost of 10 frs. a copy for 3,000 copies. It was suggested he should put down 1500 frs and I the same, and we sell the book to trade at 40 frs. (or a little less) published price 60 frs. If cost of book is 10 frs., then profit would be 30 frs. – (as a matter of fact, a little less) – then we divide the profits of this hypothetical 30 frs. in the proportion 16 frs to me and 14 to Mr Titus. He will distribute the book as Miss Beach does *Ulysses*, to every bookseller, French or not, who will take a few copies.

Would you tell me if that seems all right to you? I would come and see you if you aren't busy, only I must go slow, as *of course* Paris gave me a bit of grippe, not very bad, but enfeebling. I would like to leave the noisy and dirty city at the week-end – but I should be glad to meet you, and hear your opinion, if you feel like it. – Titus suggests a little peppery foreword[1] – and I wish I had an exact description of the various pirated editions, to put in it – Also Titus suggests I write him a letter and he confirm it, for all necessary 'agreement'.

I feel it's too bad rushing at you with all this, which probably bores you. But I'm not very sure how to proceed.

Sincerely   D. H. Lawrence

I hate the bald way I try to make use of you.

5015. To Giuseppe Orioli, 26 March 1929
Text: MS (Photocopy) HU; cited in Moore, *Poste Restante* 99.

Hotel de Versailles, 60 Bvd. Montparnasse, Paris. XV.
26 March 1929.

Dear Pino

I came back here yesterday, and Frieda arrived last night. Have got a bit of grippe – don't feel very well – must be x-rayed again – and we shall leave

---

[1] The title-page published by Titus (Roberts A42c) declared that the edn included 'My Skirmish with Jolly Roger' 'Written Especially and Exclusively as an Introduction to this Popular Edition'.

Paris if possible at the end of the week, perhaps for Holland, where there is a doctor I think I shall try. I wish I was really well – Bandol did me good, Paris does me harm.

I have been arranging with Titus the Bookseller here about an edition of *Lady C.* He says it will cost about 30,000 frs. to produce 3000 paper-bound copies: seems to me rather dear. He will put down 1500 frs. and I 1,500. We sell to trade at 40 frs – published price 60. – the profits will be about 30 frs. (or less) – which we divide 16 frs. for me, 14 frs. for him – he do the distributing. He will print the book by offset – photographic process – and will therefore need two clean copies. Could you please send two copies of the 2nd edition to Aldous for me – even if you have to send me two of the copies you were keeping – because the one returned by the Pegasus is so *dirty.* I want Titus to go ahead at once – he seems fairly all right.

I made up the accounts, and the gross profits, up to today, come to £126..9..0 – including the $180. which Holliday *gave* me on the pirated editions. So your per-centage is £23..19..0. I enclose cheque for £25 – will you please give Carletto £1., leaves you £24. – This makes your receipt in all £126. – and Carletto £8.[1] – Do tell me if this is right. I always hoped you would get £150. – perhaps you will, by the end.

And do tell me what the *postage* is. – Did that American King buy a copy?

You didn't answer my last letter – but as you forwarded others to Suresnes, you must have got it. Write to me here – even if I am gone, they will forward it. I do hope you are well and happy.

DHL

---

[1] This statement is unintentionally misleading; DHL's 'Memoranda' (MS NWU) make the financial position clearer:

Paris. March. 26. 1929.

Total money received	in English cheques, to date	£1224 .. 5 .. 3
.. .. ..	in cash	£ 136 .. 17 .. 0
.. .. ..	in dollar cheques	£ 268 .. 4 .. 0
	Gross receipts. Mar. 26. 1929	£1629 .. 6 .. 3
	Gross profits to date =	£1264 .. 16 .. 3

10% of gross profits = 126 .. 9 .. 0
already paid to Pino = 102 .. 10 .. 0
due to Pino = 23 .. 19 .. 0

Paid to Pino Orioli as 10% discount   £24.   March 26. 1929
to Carletto   £ 1
To Pino and Carletto   £25   March 26./29

final gross profit £1239 .. 16 .. 3.   March 26. 1929

Paid in all to Orioli for percentage £126. – to Carletto £8. – March 26 1929

Tell me if my reckoning agrees with yours – I think I have put every item down.

Send the books to Aldous at once, if you can. – Happy Easter.

5016. To Harry and Caresse Crosby, [27? March 1929]
Text: MS SIU; Unpublished.

[19 rue de Lille, Paris]
[27? March 1929]

called with my wife[1] – was afraid you might be out – had a bit of grippe, Paris not good for me – we shall probably leave Sunday or Monday, either for few days in the country, or for Spain – So sorry not to see you – you are going to your mill – am returning now to 60 Bvd Montparnasse.

D. H. Lawrence

5017. To Edward Dahlberg, [27 March 1929]
Text: MS UTul; Postmark, Montparnasse 27 –3 29; Unpublished.

Hotel de Versailles, 60 Bvd Montparnasse
Wednesday

Dear Dahlberg

Would you care to call tomorrow evening about half past eight, like the other time, and we can have a little talk and I can give you the copy of *Lady C.* My wife is here. We want to leave Paris for Spain on Saturday – it doesn't suit me here, not at all – bit of grippe all the time – I think you are wise to go to America.

D. H. Lawrence

5018. To Laurence Pollinger, [28 March 1929]
Text: MS UT; Unpublished.

Hotel de Versailles, 60 Bvd Montparnas
Thursday

Dear Pollinger

I had a telegram[2] from Boni – we are going out of town tomorrow, but shall be back after the week-end – see him next week: he said he would be here next week – shall leave him a letter here, don't know his Paris address – will be nice to him.

Yes, let me know as soon as you can what Pansies Secker wants to omit.

No, I didn't *promise* Cape that book of literary essays. It was he who wrote

---

[1] The note was left at the Crosbys' town house, 19 rue de Lille, in Paris.

[2] telegram] letter

me about them, and I said it was too soon to talk about it, we could talk when
the time came. I suppose you'd want Secker to have it. Anyhow no hurry.

This dirty noisy town full of grippe gave me a touch – so I felt like dying
for choice – but am feeling better. These great cities are nothing but vast
death-traps. I shall get out as quick as I can – next week.

I think I shall do my business of a cheap edition with a Mr. Titus, an
American bookseller here – seems all right – shall settle next week –
paper-cover edition to sell at 60 frs. to the public. I wrote your Mr Bradley,
but have as yet no answer.

Would you please have the copies of *Rawdon's Roof* mailed according
to enclosed list. Do take one if you'd like one – Hope you'll have a nice
Easter.

D. H. Lawrence

6 copies of *Rawdon's Roof*

please mail as follows:

1. copy. Mrs L. A. Clarke, Broadway, Ripley nr. *Derby*
1. copy. Mrs S. King, 16 Brooklands Rd, Sneinton Hill. *Nottingham*
1. copy. Miss Dorothy Yorke, 4 Holland Place Chambers. *Church St. W. 8*
1. copy Madame Caresse Crosby, 19 rue de Lille, *Paris*
1 copy Pollinger, if he wants it
1 copy please keep for me

5019. To Mabel Dodge Luhan, 30 March 1929
Text: MS Brill; Unpublished.

Paris.
30 March 1929

Dear Mabel

This is to introduce Mr Edward Dahlberg, who has written a book for
which I did an introduction – and is just coming back to New York and will
call on you – Hope you'll have an interesting chat. – Wish I was coming too. –
Am writing a proper letter.

D. H. Lawrence

5020. To Aldous and Maria Huxley, [1 April 1929]
Text: Moore 1138.

Hôtel de Versailles, 60 Bvd Montparnasse, Paris
Monday

Dear Aldous and Maria:

We are just back – it was nice out there, but I don't like the north, so dreary even when rather beautiful.[1]

When shall we see you? Tomorrow we are lunching along with a little fellow[2] – and going out ½ hour into the country to the villa of the hotel, *to tea*. Frieda's nephew Friedel is here. Rhys Davies *et famille* leaves tomorrow morning. I am continually warned against Titus – but what's the odds. If you are in town tomorrow come and lunch along with us just near here – else let us meet Wednesday with the Crosbys 19 rue de Lille – near quai Voltaire – and you are invited if you can come.[3] I want to get away Thursday if possible.

I *must* go south – I hate it here and hate the mouldering dead north altogether. Did Orioli send me two copies *Lady C.* c/o you? I want them for Titus – if it is to be Titus. Will you ring up about tomorrow.

5021. To Charles Lahr, 1 April 1929
Text: TMSC ULon; Unpublished.

Paris.
Monday 1 April 1929

Dear Lahr

I am giving the complete Ms. of the poems to Davies for you. Please keep it for me safely. Secker is boggling and wanting to leave out about a dozen – too many – am fed up about it – shall be glad to know your opinion.

I hear that Pollinger of Curtis Brown has still three copies of my novel – no doubt he'd be glad to be relieved of them – wonder if you could get them for me, and perhaps hand one to Secker – Ask Kot, will you.

I somehow *can't* authorise that pirated edition – it goes so against my grain. I think I shall do a 60 frs. edition with a man Titus – Davies will tell you.

Are you *sure* Harold Mason did the first pirated edition? Was it facsimile? –

---

[1] The Lawrences had spent the weekend, 29 March–1 April, at le Moulin du Soleil, the mill at Ermenonville, 30 miles n. of Paris, which the Crosbys had rented from Armand de la Rochfoucault in July 1928. (Rousseau and Cagliostro had both lived there.) For Harry Crosby's account of the weekend see *Shadows of the Sun*, p. 244; for Caresse's account see her *The Passionate Years* (1955), pp. 230–2.

[2] Possibly Eldridge Adams; see Letter 5023.

[3] Crosby recorded in his diary:

April 3. Exhausting day. D. H. Lawrence appears to be sculpted by Caresse. Frieda appears with Aldous Huxley and the typewritten sheets of The Escaped Cock and there is a discussion about Joyce. C and I pro-Joyce Lawrence and Huxley anti-Joyce and I proclaim the Word itself the Word is a talent of gold but it is a friendly discussion this time (no need to call out my shock-troops) and there was tea and glasses of sherry and then C and I rushed off to the lawyers on the Place Vendôme where we met Joyce and drew up the contract for us three to sign … Afterwards Joyce went with C to the Black Sun Press (he didn't want to meet Lawrence – said his eye hurt him – he is very timid). (*Shadows of the Sun*, p. 245)

signed or unsigned? – I saw another Amer. copy – bound in black cloth, with page elongated, and beastly vignette of American Eagle triumphant on the title page[1] – But I believe there's still a fourth.

I must say I don't like Paris. – Davies sad at coming to London, and I don't wonder – it's no place to live in. – So you got a pound a day for a year out of Rudyard![2] good for you!

DHL

5022. To Lady Ottoline Morrell, 3 April 1929
Text: MS UT; Postmark, Paris 4 IV 1929; Moore 1139–40.

Hotel de Versailles, 60 Bvd Montparnasse, Paris. XV

3 April 1929

My dear Ottoline

Your letter finds me here, where I came just three weeks ago to arrange a cheap edition of *Lady Chatterley*, to try to stop the pirated editions selling. There are three, perhaps even four pirated editions produced in U.S.A., and there is another edition pirated over here – with the legend *imprimé en Allemagne.*[3] They none of them sell less than 300 frs a copy – so I am arranging for an edition, smaller, paper bound, at 60 frs., so that anybody can get it. People must already have made two or three thousand pounds out of pirated editions – and I am left with nothing. However, I hope my own little venture will be a success. I have written a nice introduction telling them all what I think of them – one can't do more.[4]

I don't a bit like Paris. It is nowadays incredibly crowded, incredibly noisy, the air is dirty and simply stinks of petrol, and all the life has gone out of the people. They seem so tired. The mills of God grind on, and will grind these great cities exceeding small:[5] in weariness and effort. I want to get away on Saturday, moving south by stages to Spain – to Barcelona first, then I'm not sure. If I like it, I want to stay there – perhaps even a year. I have never been to Spain, I hope I shall like it. I very much want to find a place to stay in.

I stayed a week with Aldous and Maria in Suresnes, while Frieda was with her mother in Baden Baden. I had a bit of grippe, from this dirty city, and they were very good to me, tended me so kindly. I am really very much attached to them, humanly. There is that other side of them, the sort of

---

[1] Perhaps the photolithographed piracy, 1.7, in Gertzman, *DHL Review,* xix. 285–6.
[2] Cf. Letter 4964.
[3] 'printed in Germany' (cf. Letter 4977 and n. 1).   [4] See Letter 5014 and n. 1.
[5] 'Though the mills of God grind slowly, yet they grind exceeding small', from 'Retribution' by Henry Wadsworth Longfellow (1807–92) ('Poetic Aphorisms' from the 'Sinngedichte' of Friederich von Logau).

mental and nervous friction and destructiveness which I can't bear, but they leave that out with me. As I grow older I dread more and more that frictional nervousness which makes people always react *against* one another, in discord, instead of together in harmony. It is so nice to feel peaceful and quiet with people one likes and can trust. Only a few friends to be at peace with, that is all I ask. I want no excitements or exaltations or extravagancies. I don't want anybody even to *love* me – it is so possessive. But a few people to be really fond of me, and for me to be fond of, that I would like indeed. And of course I have a few. – I wish we lived nearer to one another, you and Philip and us, I feel we might be friends now really and with that stillness in friendship which is the best.

I'm glad you like the poems – there is a lot of my very life in them. The young, of course, are too hasty and too much afraid of real feeling, to care much about them. I find the young so strangely afraid of having genuine feelings, and especially any feeling of attachment, of warm affection. They want to be so detached, like bits of glass. But I think the gentle flow of affection is really wonderful.

Yes, I remember your coming to Sussex – stepping out of an old four-wheeler in all your pearls, and a purple velvet frock – and going across the meadows to the other cottages at Greatham.[1] It is a pity something came across it all and prevented us keeping a nice harmony.[2] But life does queer things to us, and it takes us a long time to come to our real steady self.

I wonder where you will go when you do leave England? I too should like to go to Greece, but it is a long journey, and can be very trying.

For the present, I put my hopes in Spain. And for the future, I leave it to the Lord.

Have you seen the prospectus for my book of pictures? I think the book will be ready early in May, and I expect Dorothy Warren will hold the exhibition at the same time. Do go and look at the pictures, because some of them you will surely like – there is a suggestion of Blake sometimes.

I haven't been well in Paris. Sometimes one feels as if one were drifting out of life altogether – and not terribly sorry to go. These big cities take away my real will to live – or at least my present desire to live. One so dreadfully wants something better.

But we are leaving on Saturday, and if nothing goes wrong, I know I shall feel better in the south. I shall send you an address when we have one.

Love from us both, and remember me to Philip.

D. H. Lawrence

---

[1] The Lawrences lived at Greatham, Pulborough, Sussex, January–July 1915. Lady Ottoline visited them there on 8 and 23–4 February.

[2] What had 'come across it all' was Lady Ottoline's recognition of herself in the unflattering character of Hermione Roddice in *Women in Love* (cf. *Letters*, vi. 82 and n. 4).

5023. To Laurence Pollinger, 3 April 1929
Text: MS UT; Huxley 791–2.

Hotel de Versailles, 60 Bvd. Montparnasse, Paris XV.

3 April 1929

Dear Pollinger

Albert Boni called last evening, and we talked things over – and though he is not the publisher I should exactly choose, I think it would be a good thing if he could have all my books and publish them in a uniform edition, as he seems quite keen to do. In that case, he wants the poems, so we shall have to decide quickly in order to ask Cape to release his claim to these, before he goes any further. And then there is Alfred Knopf; Boni suggests I write him saying I was hurt by his refusal to print the poems, and now should be glad if he would release me from my contract with him. Shall I do that? – We talked about money, but very indefinite. Boni said I ought to get more than 20% of Seltzers debt, and that whether I went over to him, Boni, or not, he would give me £200. on the debt – that being, as far as I remember, just about 20%. He asked me if I was in need of money, as he had a cheque in his pocket and would be glad to write it out for me. I said, thank God I was not in need of money, and would prefer he settled with you. Very distasteful, having people hand one a cheque across the table, and expecting you to receive it as if it were the body of God. – Rather repulsive.

There came also the man Adams of the former Crosby Gaige concern,[1] with something of the same story, offering me money if I was 'in need,' and asking about the *Escaped Cock*. I said I would not let him print the first half of that story as a complete thing, without indicating that it was only a part. I hear he let James Joyce down badly in the same way.[2] He kept repeating over *900 dollars* till I almost told him nine hundred shits. I said I *might* prepare for him a little novel – about 25,000 words – which I did two years ago but which wants doing over. I might – when I settle somewhere. The MS. is in Florence.[3]

I wish you would please ask for the MS. of *The Escaped Cock* to be posted *at once*, and complete, to

Mrs. Harry Crosby – 19 rue de Lille. Paris. –

There will be no danger of the mail, and I shall know the MS. lies safely and *privately* with a friend.

---

[1] Eldridge Adams.
[2] In October 1928 Crosby Gaige had published *Anna Livia Plurabelle* (a chapter from *Finnegans Wake*) in a de luxe edition of 850 copies.
[3] *The Virgin and the Gipsy.*

My cold is a good bit better, and we want to leave on Saturday, going south in stages to Spain. I shan't have an address for about a week.

Those three books of mine you wrote me about, if a man calls for them with a pencil note from me, will you just hand them over to him.[1] I note your account of the others. – I suppose you paid them all into the bank. And many thanks.

D. H. Lawrence

5024. To Martin Secker, 3 April 1929
Text: MS UInd; Secker 117.

Hotel de Versailles, 60 Bvd. Montparnasse, *Paris* XV

3 April 1929

Dear Secker

Don't go and be too squeamish about the *Pansies*.[2] Myself I dont see anything in 'Be a Demon' or the other one to the Young Girl, to be alarmed about. Would you mind copying out the bits you fear, and letting me see. And tell me, of the others, exactly what you want to omit. When I sent the so-called 'expurgated' MS. I expurgated very radically and roughly, for the post. But I'm sure there are not many poems you need really omit. Probably a word or two altered or blanked would be enough. Anyhow let me know exactly and in detail, what you want to do.

---

[1] Charles Lahr. See Letter 5021.
[2] Pollinger had passed on to Secker DHL's question about '*exactly* what poems Secker is leaving out' (Letter 4993). Secker had replied on 27 March (Secker Letter-Book, UIll):

Dear Pollinger,
   We have your letter about "Pansies", and Lawrence's question is quite simply answered. In the 102 page typescript [Roberts E302f?] referred to by you as the "MS received by Secker", which was the subject of our conversation the other day on which you wrote to Lawrence, we should propose to omit two poems, "Be a Demon" and "The Jeune Fille" on pages 100 and 101 respectively. These two poems, it appears to us, might more logically have been removed and placed with the small group of poems which Lawrence himself removed and of which type-script has reached us separately. On the other hand, there seem to be about a dozen poems in this latter MS. which could be included in the book, if Lawrence cared for us to use our discretion. The introduction we have would stand perfectly well with the omission of the top paragraph on the second page regarding the "obscene words", which, as we pointed out to you, would be irrelevant to the poems as printed. Without seeing the "original introduction" to which you refer we can't express an opinion as to which would be preferable. The publication we would propose would be an original (unlimited) edition at 10/6, with 150 signed copies at Two Guineas and a subsequent edition, within a year, at 3/6d.
   We should of course be delighted to bring out a book of Lawrence's literary criticisms and introductory essays, but we note that the material at present does not exist. When it does, we shall hope to be given the opportunity of equalling Cape's terms. We have, of course, the introduction to the "Foreign Legion", which would help considerably in making up the contents of such a book.
                                                                        Yours

I think I have made a satisfactory arrangement here for a cheap edition of my novel. – to sell at 60 frs. – I don't like Paris so terribly noisy and full of traffic and stench of petrol. I stayed a week with Aldous and Maria, and they were very nice, but Suresnes, where they live, seems to me a dismal place. But then I had a bit of grippe. – But I do hate these huge noisy cities – and Paris is no longer gay – no élan – too strained.

We plan to leave on Saturday, to go south by stages to Spain, first Barcelona, and then Majorca or Valencia or Granada. I long to go south again.

Albert Boni was here, talking of doing all my books in uniform edition in U.S.A. – don't know if we can arrange it. He wants to do the *Collected Poems* this autumn. If he does, it would be better not to come out with a cheap edition in England until spring of next year.

I get so sick of cities – Hope all is well –

DHL

5025. To St John Hutchinson, 3 April 1929
Text: MS Hutchinson; Unpublished.

Hotel de Versailles, 60 Bvd Montparnasse, Paris XV.

3 April 1929

Dear Hutchinson

It was nice seeing you and your daughter that Saturday: you seemed to be having such a lark with Paris. We are leaving the day after tomorrow, going gradually south, to Spain – and I hope to God I shall like it there. I don't like Paris a bit, and feel seedy all the time.

When you have done with that MS. of the *Pansies*, I wish you would send it to my sister –

Mrs. W. E. Clarke, 'Torestin', Broadway, *Ripley nr Derby*

It is the only MS. I have got, of the poems and the introduction in their original form, and I should like to keep it, for comparison.

I didn't hear any result of Moseley's questions in the House. Perhaps there was none. But many thanks all the same for the trouble you took.

Sincerely   D. H. Lawrence

5026. To Maria and Aldous Huxley, [3 April 1929]
Text: Huxley 790.

60, Boulevard Montparnasse.

Wed. Evening.

Dear Maria and Aldous, –

We won't come to lunch to-morrow, it's so far, and an effort – and crowning glory, that man [of the Crosby Gaige Concern][1] will turn up at your house directly after lunch – and I don't want to see him twice. He called here – was most honoured by having had an interview with Jix – so I told him he'd be [raping little girls] before ten years are out – don't think he wants to see me twice – hope not – says you are 'a bright fellow' – I said 'Quite!' (Aldous, that's you.)

I think we'll get off Saturday, for more quiet travelling. I don't want to go north, don't want to *be* North, shan't have any peace till I see the Mediterranean again, all the rest hell! Think we'll go in little stages to Mallorca. The North has all gone *evil* – I can't help feeling it morally or ethically. I mean anti-life.

We'll see you though – ring-up.

DHL

5027. To Harry and Caresse Crosby, 4 April 1929
Text: MS SIU; Postmark, Paris 5–IV 1929; Lacy, *Escaped Cock* 72.

60 Bvd Montparnasse. Paris
4 April 1929

Dear Harry and Caresse

I was sorry I couldn't come in yesterday – a set of complications – but I know, Caresse, you were so busy anyhow, you'd be glad to escape me.

I got the enclosed leaflet from Philadelphia. These people must be pirating *your* edition of *Sun*.[2] But since the story is copyright in my vol of short stories *The Woman Who Rode Away* (Alfred Knopf 1928) we can prosecute them and get them into prison. I must do this, or they'll pirate my very beard. Only I'm wondering how best to set about it. I don't have a New York lawyer.

We must make very sure of the copyright of *The Escaped Cock*. The first part of the story was printed in the *Forum*, New York in the spring of 1928.[3] Does that secure permanent copyright? We must find out. If not we must have a small edition of the first part printed in New York – say about 50 copies at 2 dollars each – and get the copyright on *that*. If you have read the story, and like it, and still want to print it, you might think about this, and perhaps speak of it to your man Marks (your New York bookseller). For the whole story, I think, if you copyright it in France, under the Berne Conven-

---

[1] Huxley – who published and thus preserved this and some other texts for which no MS survives – deleted certain words and personal names. Occasionally (as here and 3 lines below) Catherine Carswell's annotated copy of Huxley supplies the missing words or name; for the use of her marginalia the editors are indebted to John Carswell. (It is interesting to note that here and elsewhere her reconstructions coincided with the text of the uncorrected proofs of Huxley's *Letters*.)
[2] See Roberts Appendix II (I).   [3] *Forum*, lxxix (February 1928), 286–96.

tion, it holds good for England. We will make sure – I *must* protect myself from pirates. You see another 1500 edit. of *Lady C.* at 15 dollars – over $20,000 for a new lot of rogues – I am sick of it.

Please don't lose that little leaflet. We must trace that pirate.

My grippe came back on me a bit – but I am getting tickets to leave for Spain on *Sunday* morning. Hope you are not inundated by family feeling.[1]

All good luck

Affectionately   D. H. Lawrence

5028. To David Lederhandler, 5 April 1929
Text: MS Rosenbach and UT; Postmark, Paris 5 IV 1929; Huxley 792.

c/o Signor G. Orioli, 6 Lungarno Corsini, *Florence*, Italy
5 April 1929

Dear Mr Lederhandler[2]

Many thanks for sending me that leaflet. As you surmise, *Sun* is included in *The Woman Who Rode Away*, so I shall be able to prosecute those pirates, which I must do, as it is becoming intolerable. But I presume they have pirated the little unexpurgated edit. of 150. copies of the unexpurgated form of the story – only slightly different from the Knopf version – which was printed over here in *Paris* by the Black Sun Press and sold in New York by Harry F. Marks, 31 W. 47th St. – I wish you'd ask him about it.

And still *another* – the fifth – pirated edition of *Lady Chatterley*!! Makes one ill! I was very upset when I *heard* that Harold T. Mason of the Centaur Bookshop in Phila. was back of the *first* pirated edition of *Lady Chatterley*. He is a personal friend – so I hated to hear such a thing, and am loath to believe it. Do you think there is anything in it? Do tell me. A certain circumstance makes me suspicious.

No, alas, all my early first editions have been stolen from me. But G. Orioli has one or two of my MSS. of stories – how much do you want to pay?[3]

In any case, many thanks for sending me that leaflet.

Yours Sincerely   D. H. Lawrence

<hr/>

[1] Crosby's father, Stephen Van Rensselaer Crosby, arrived in Paris from USA on 5 April (Crosby, *Shadows of the Sun*, p. 245).
[2] David V. Lederhandler (1900–59), American businessman; in the retail clothing industry in Philadelphia and later in the handkerchief manufacturing business in New York. Travelled extensively in Europe and lived in Italy for a year.
[3] See Letter 5109 and n. 1.

5029. To Emily King, 5 April 1929
Text: MS Lazarus; Unpublished.

Hotel De Versailles, 60 Bvd Montparnasse, Paris XV
5 April 1929

My dear Sister

Well we have almost left Paris. We depart on Sunday morning, stop a night at Lyons, and again in the South of France by the sea, then go on to Spain. I am so anxious to go. I hate these great cities – the traffic and noise are fearful. I will never stay long in one again, they are so bad for my health. But I've settled my business and done what I came for, so now I can go. I am longing for the south again, the Mediterranean, the clear sky, the people not so worried. The people in the north all seem worried to death.

We were away for four days at Easter in the country with rich American friends – lovely forest, and an old mill – but the French country seems to me very melancholy and dead. – Frieda's nephew Friedel is here – none too happy either, I wonder why he stays. He has a job now in the Town Hall in BadenBaden.

The weather is rather cold and trying to rain, but the trees and bushes in the Bois de Boulogne are all coming out green and bright. How lovely the Bois was in the days of horses and carriages! now it is obscene with motorcars. No, these great cities have gone absolutely wrong, since electricity and petrol came into use.

Frieda's daughter Elsa gets married tomorrow – a great splash of a 'white wedding'. I don't envy her the show. But perhaps she'll be happy with the man.[1]

I shall write you as soon as I have an address. I wish we could *all* go south and live in the sun. But I can't come to England – Paris even lays me low.

My love to you all   DHL

5030. To Martin Secker, 5 April 1929
Text: MS UInd; Postmark, Paris 6·IV 1929; Secker 118.

Hotel de Versailles, 60 Bvd. Montparnasse. Paris XV.
5 April 1929

Dear Secker

Your note this evening. I specially don't want you to make just a little bourgeois book of the *Pansies*. I want you to put in *all* the poems that won't expose you to Jix. And before I sign an agreement I want to know exactly what you are omitting from the *complete* MS. So will you send me a list. I

[1] Cf. Letter 4817 and n. 2.

know the twenty poems I sent in the second batch can most of them be included. I simply don't want to come out with a bourgeois 'inoffensive' *Pansies*. I want every poem included that is not definitely open to legal attack. And in such poems as might be, I can make slight modifications. So will you write me an exact list of contents to

c/o Thomas Cook & Sons, Calle Fontanella 19, *Barcelona*, Spain

We leave on Sunday morning – take the journey in stages, because I've still got a bit of this Paris grippe. I've settled all the business for a cheap *Lady C*, except the final signing, which I do tonight. I shall be glad to get away from Paris.

I'm sorry you haven't got the copy of the novel. I'll insist on it once more, and see if there's a result.

Poor Elsa getting married tomorrow – a wedding must be an ordeal! But she'll probably be happy with her Teddy, since she's the sort that will at least make a try.

DHL

5031. To Laurence Pollinger, 5 April 1929
Text: MS UT; Unpublished.

Hotel de Versailles, 60 Bvd. Montparnasse, Paris. XV

5 April 1929

Dear Pollinger

I'm sorry I haven't got any photographs whatsoever of myself – hate them. But a man called R. H. Davies,[1] of the *New York Sun* did two of me, not bad, and I know he'd let Cape or anybody have a copy.

I wrote Secker asking him to let me know exactly what poems he is omitting from *Pansies*. He replies with one of his usual white-rat evasions. I can see he wants to make a nice null bourgeois book of it. He's not going to. He must put in *all* the poems that run him no real risk, and he must let me know in detail what he's leaving out, or I will sign no contract with him. I asked him to write me

c/o Thomas Cook, 19 Calle Fontanella, *Barcelona*. Spain

We leave on Sunday morning – and shall be in Barcelona by Thursday or Friday, I hope.

You will have had my letter all about Boni and the rest. – Tonight I sign finally for the cheap edition of my novel – at 60 frs. – So *that* will be settled.

A man from Philadelphia sent me a notice today announcing still another edition of *Lady C*. over there – of 1500 – and also an edition of 500 of *Sun*.

---

[1] Cf. Letter 4885 and n. 2.

Now this short story is included in Knopf's *The Woman Who Rode Away*, so these unknown people are pirating a copyright story. If I can I *must* get after them and prosecute them. It must be done – and we can get damages. As you know, the Black Sun Press in Paris did a little edition of 150 copies of this story in its unexpurgated form, only slightly different from the Knopf version – which was the first published, anyhow. – I'm sure we could lay hold of these pirates, anyhow.

I still feel my grippe, and am longing to get away. Paris is all rattle and noise and nervous people.

Secker agrees not to publish a cheap version of *Collected Poems* this autumn, if Cape or Boni does them in U.S.A.

I'm a bit disappointed with the two reproductions of the pictures I've seen – so dim, so smudgy. They'd have been so much better done in Germany, or even here.

ever DHL

5032. To P. R. Stephensen, [5 April 1929]
Text: MS BucU; Munro 305–6.

Paris.
Friday

Dear Stephensen

Thanks for yours and for the other announcements of the book. I think *Moses* is suitable to represent the pictures, but oh, I *do* think the reproduction is smudgy. Paris booksellers complain the same – it is too smudgy, too indistinct, doesn't look good enough. I am convinced the English don't properly know how to handle the process. If only you'd spent the same money in Germany, or even here in Paris, you'd have seen different results. But let's hope they'll get better as they go on. I am anxious to see a pale picture reproduced.

Probably the orders will be slow till the book is actually in existence – it was so with *Lady C.* – Will you send a prospectus to

David V. Lederhandler, 1627 Chestnut St. Philadelphia, Pa.

I am settling up finally tonight for the cheap edition of *Lady C.* – to sell at 60 frs. And on Sunday morning we leave for Spain. Write me

c/o Thomas Cook & Son, 19 Calle Fontanella, Barcelona. Spain

Did you get the list of addresses sent by Orioli?

I've still got a bit of grippe on me, and feel feeble. These great cities are awful – just lay one out.

Booksellers here say you'll sell your edition all right.

DHL

5033. To Edward Titus, 5 April 1929
Text: TMSC UT; Unpublished.

Hotel de Versailles, 60 Boulevard Montparnasse, Paris.

April 5th, 1929

Dear Mr Titus,

Referring to our several interviews on the subject of publishing a Paris edition of *Lady Chatterley's Lover*, I wish to confirm our understanding as follows:—

You agree to publish an edition of three thousand copies of the book. The cost price of this edition shall not exceed twelve francs (12 frs) a copy. The cost of production shall be divided equally between you and me. All invoices for plates, printing, paper, binding etc shall be made in duplicate and a copy sent to me. You may call on me for my share in the cost of production should the necessity arise. The retail price of the book is to be sixty francs (60 frs) a copy. This price to be printed on the cover. The discount to the trade shall be one third the retail price. Profits are to be divided between us in the proportion of eight francs (8 frs) to me, seven francs (7 frs) to you. Statement to be rendered and settlement made every three months.

You will of course allow me or my representative to go over with you all accounts concerning the book.

For any reprint after the three thousand (3000) copies of this edition are sold, a new agreement shall be made. In case this edition of three thousand (3000) copies is not sold out at the expiration of two years from the date of publication, this agreement may be dissolved at the will of either party, and an arrangement made for the purchase of plates and remaining copies by me.

If at the expiration of this agreement either party decides to dissolve the connection[1] in this concern, the property in the plates is to pass to me, on condition that I pay you your half of the cost of their production.

Yours sincerely,[2]

[1] connection] partnership (DHL initialled the alteration).
[2] Titus's typed draft (dated 4 April 1929) of this agreement was mostly rewritten by DHL, with some deletions and revisions of the wording (UT); this version was typed and is reproduced above. Another typing including DHL's handwritten change (see footnote above) and with a few small variants (e.g. ll. 12–13 read 'Statements ... settlements') is located at SIU, as is a TMSC of Titus's letter of acceptance, dated 6 April.

5034. To Max Mohr, [6? April 1929]
Text: MS HMohr; Mohr 34–5.

Hotel de Versailles, 60 Bvd Montparnasse, Paris XV.

5 April 1929[1]

Dear Max Mohr

I wonder what has become of you, and if there is anything doing. I have been here a month, and at last have arranged for a cheap edition of *Lady C*. – in English – produced here – and to sell at 60 frs (10 M.) – Paris gave me grippe and I was miserable: the town is too depressing. Tomorrow we leave, going south to Lyon, Avignon, Perpignan, and so to Spain. I shall send you an address. How are your affairs? Have you found a publisher for your book? or for a German translation of *Lady C*. – I do hope you are well, and sufficiently prosperous. If you need any help I can give you – a little money etc – only tell me. I shall write in about a week's time.

Yrs   D. H. Lawrence

5035. To William Bradley, 6 April 1929
Text: MS UT; Unpublished.

Hotel de Versailles, 60 Bvd Montparnasse

6 April 1929

Dear Mr Bradley

I didn't know you were a literary agent, or I'd have come to you long ago. When I did know, it was rather too late, as I'd settled so much with Titus I couldn't suddenly have sprung an agent on him without offending him. But I think it will be all right with him –

About the other matter, – I have no agreement with any French publisher for the translation rights of *Lady Chatterley's Lover*, and should be glad for you to act as my agent here, for this book, if you would care to, and if you will tell me your terms. – But Curtis Brown's have some sort of fuddled and unsatisfactory arrangement with Kra[2] for the publishing of some of my other books in translation. Anyhow nothing happens. If you could come to some satisfactory arrangement with the publisher you mentioned, no doubt Curtis Brown would find some way of squaring with Kra. – But *Lady Chatterley's Lover* is entirely in my hands, and as I say, I shall be glad for you to handle the translation rights here in Paris.

We are leaving on Sunday morning, for Spain – so it leaves me no time to

---

[1] DHL knew on 5 April 1929 that he would leave Paris on Sunday 7th; thus his remark, 'Tomorrow we leave' suggests that this letter was written on 6 April.
[2] The Parisian publishing house of which Philippe Soupault (1897–) was the *directeur littéraire*. See *Letters*, vi. 430 and n. 2.

call on you, I'm sorry to say – And I've still got a bit of Paris grippe, I must get away. If there is anything to communicate, you might write me
c/o Thomas Cook & Son, 19. Calle Fontanella. Barcelona, Spain.
Yours sincerely   D. H. Lawrence

5036. To Giuseppe Orioli, [6 April 1929]
Text: MS UCLA; cited in Moore, *Intelligent Heart* 403.

Paris.
6 April

Dear Pino
Thanks for sending the two copies of *Lady C.* – I have settled up with Titus, and we leave tomorrow morning for Spain. I am longing to get away from Paris, so noisy, dirty and nervous – not a bit gay any more. Write to me
c/o Thomas Cook & Son, Calle Fontanella 19, *Barcelona*, Spain
Don't trouble about sending a copy of *Lady C.* to Else – Frieda's sister – as I am giving her the pirated copy.
But I *do* hope you sent the two copies to Conway, Mexico City – and also to that man Curtin – to Tiajuana – also Mexico.
Aldous is coming down to Spain for a fortnight – without Maria – They too are very *nervoso.*[1]
How slow *Nerinda* is, coming out!
Perhaps you too will come to Spain, if we stay there.
I shall write again.

DHL

5037. To Harry Crosby, [6 April 1929]
Text: MS SIU; Postmark, Paris 8.IV 1929; Huxley 793.

Paris.
6 April

Dear Harry
The packet of sweets just come – awfully nice of you and Caresse. We've thought of you a lot, these two pregnant days. But keep a little sun-spot of insouciance somewhere inside you. I'm sure one of the great secrets of the sun is a strong insouciance, in the middle of him, where no-one breaks in on him.
We leave in the morning – via Orléans and Toulouse. I do hope we shall like Spain, and perhaps find a place a bit like your mill, with sun in the courtyard, and very still.

[1] 'nervy'.

I shall write you as soon as we really arrive anywhere – meanwhile
Thomas Cook & Son, Calle Fontanella, Barcelona
will find us.

Pax, then! the sunny sort.   DHL

5038. To Ada Clarke, [10 April 1929]

Text: MS Clarke; PC v. La Cité de Carcassonne: Vue générale de l'Ouest – Les deux Ponts
sur l'Aude; Postmark, [. . .]; Unpublished.

[Hôtel de la Cité, Cité de Carcassonne]
[10]¹ April.

– Got so far on our [j]ourney – lovely to be south again [in] the warmth and
the clear light – I never want to go north any more. We aren't far from [the]
Mediterranean – go tomorrow to Perpignan, then to Barcelona. Write me
    c/o Thomas Cook & Son, Calle Fontanella 19, *Barcelona*, Spain
Hope you are all going gaily.

DHL

5039. To Charles Lahr, 10 April 1929

Text: MS UNYB; Postmark, Carcassonne 11-4 29; cited in Moore, *Poste Restante* 99.

[Hôtel de la Cité, Cité de Carcassonne.]²
10 Avril 1929

Dear Lahr

I didn't have any word from you or Davies before I left Paris – and Davies
gave me no address. Hope he doesn't find London gloomy. I am so thankful
to be south again – near the Mediterranean – there is already the light in the
air, and tomorrow I hope we shall get to Perpignan – doing the journey in
stages. By the week-end we should be at Barcelona.
    c/o Thomas Cook & Son, Calle Fontanella 19. *Barcelona*, Spain
Write to me there, and tell Davies. This is rather a marvellous place, but
perfectly kept in camphor for the tourist – a day is enough.

Hope all goes well.

DHL

¹ MS extensively damaged.
² Here and for Letter 5042 DHL used the hotel's headed notepaper.

5040. To Baroness Anna von Richthofen, [10 April 1929]
Text: MS UT; PC v. La Cité de Carcassonne – Vue générale du Nord; Postmark,
Carcassonne 11 IV[...]; Unpublished.

[Hotel de la Cité, Cité de Carcassonne]
Mitwoch

Wir sind so weit gekommen – nicht weit vom Mittelmeer, und es freut mich
furchtbar, wieder im Süden sein und das helles Licht zu fühlen – die
Frieda ist auch seelig. Morgen fahren wir nach Perpignan – dann Spain. Du
kannst schreiben:
    bei Thomas Cook & Son, Calle Fontanella. 19, *Barcelona*, Spanien
Wir werden Samstag dort ankommen.
Geht es dir gut? –

DHL

[*Wednesday*
We've got this far – not far from the Mediterranean, and I'm fearfully happy
to be in the south again and to experience the bright light – Frieda is also
blissfully happy. Tomorrow we're going to Perpignan – then Spain. You can
write:
    to Thomas Cook & Son, Calle Fontanella. 19, *Barcelona*, Spain
We shall arrive there on Saturday.
Are you well? –

DHL]

5041. To Lady Ottoline Morrell, [10 April 1929]
Text: MS UT; PC v. La Cité de Carcassonne. La Côte d'Aude; Postmark, Carcassonne 11 IV
29; Robert Gathorne-Hardy, *Ottoline at Garsington* (1974), p. 137.

[Hôtel de la Cité, Cité de Carcassonne]
10 April.

Had your letter just on leaving Paris – was so glad to leave that city of
dreadful night.[1] Here it's rather lovely – very touristy, of course, but silvery
spring and the first leaves and lilacs in flower – after all, leaves are so much
more interesting than fortresses. We go on tomorrow to Perpignan – then to
Barcelona. Shall write from there.

DHL

---

[1] Cf. the poem by James Thomson (1834–82), 'The City of Dreadful Night' (1874).

5042. To Nancy Pearn, 10 April 1929
Text: MS UT; Unpublished.

[Hôtel de la Cité, Cité de Carcassonne.]
10 April 1929

Dear Nancy Pearn

This is to say we have got so far on our journey, and the address will be c/o Thomas Cook & Son, Calle Fontenella 19, *Barcelona*, Spain.

I expect we shall be there by the week-end. I hope the other depts have the address.

I heard that *The Studio* wanted me to do an article on my pictures – I'll do it as soon as I sit still – this week-end if possible.[1]

Nothing but tourists here – but still a curiously interesting place – and summer coming so fast there is no spring, lilacs in full bloom and no primroses, cherryblossom dying and blackthorn bursting full out – out of order, out of order. But a lovely silvery day.

DHL

5043. To Martin Secker, 14 April 1929
Text: MS UInd; Postmark, Barcelona 14 ABR 29; Secker 119.

c/o Thomas Cook & Son. 19 Calle Fontanella, *Barcelona*.
14 April 1929

Dear Secker

We are indeed at cross purposes regarding the poems. My 'expurgation' was merely for the post. Do you imagine I would haul down my flag to such an extent in front of the public, for all the Jixes in Christendom? Not I. – If you and the respectable booksellers can't stand the word cat-piss, then put two plain dashes for the two monstrous syllables. And if – 'To pee in the eye of a policeman' is beyond all bearing, then put 'To — in the eye etc.'[2] But would you scrap that good sarcastic little poem for the mere three letters 'pee'. That's outjixing jix. It is quite simple. Where the word merely is offensive, put a dash. If there is any poem whose *content* is alarming, just tell me exactly which it is. – And if this isn't agreeable to you, let us not bother about the matter any further. I can look for another publisher, without being in the least offended. – But make the *Pansies* into a good, 'innocuous', bourgeois little book I will not, and you shall not. – Also we must scrap that

---

[1] DHL sent 'Making Pictures' to Nancy Pearn on 15 April (Letter 5045). It appeared in *Studio*, accompanied by a reproduction of *The Finding of Moses*, and its American counterpart, *Creative Art*, in July 1929, and in *Vanity Fair*, August 1929 (Roberts C188). The autograph version of the essay was written on notepaper from the Hôtel de la Cité.

[2] 'my-eye' was substituted for 'cat-piss' in DHL's poem, 'The Saddest Day', and 'whizz' for 'pee' in 'True Democracy', in Secker's edn of *Pansies*, pp. 146 and 24.

introduction and I will write another, briefer, and more to the point.[1] – Let me know at once how you feel about this. If you want to go on, send me a list of the poems you think unsafe for printing, exact: or if it is just a verse, send me the verse. For mere words you can substitute, as I say, the plain dash – But I am determined to omit as *little* as possible.

This is a queer place, rougher than I expected, very 'proletariat' in feeling. We want to go over to Majorca on Tuesday, a night's crossing, and I hope to settle there a bit. Shall let you know. Meanwhile Cooks will forward letters. That wedding sounds pretty awful. – Lovely flowers in the street here, but weather not so very warm.

DHL

5044. To Earl and Achsah Brewster, 15 April 1929
Text: MS UT; Brewster 200–1.

c/o Thomas Cook & Son, Calle Fontanella 19, *Barcelona*, Spain
15 April 1929

Dear Earl and Achsah

I have been thinking of you these last few days – was upset to hear from your last letter that poor Anna di Chiara had been so ill – my regards to her – and that you in consequence will be houseless again. I do wonder where you will go.[2] Achsah, my dear, do one of two things – find yourself a permanent little place on Capri – or go back, volontieri,[3] to America. Don't be turned loose into the wide wide world. It's as wide as ever, but so much fuller and more peaceless than ever before. So stay in quiet hermitage on Capri – or go to America and bear it. You must let Earl do as he wishes, if he wants anything different.

We have got so far – and tomorrow night we cross to Palma, Majorca. It is queer, Barcelona – so modern, and yet not, so full of wealth, yet so proletariat. At first one recoils – but I think I really like it. The people are self-contained and calm, they don't gibber like most moderns. The air seems good and alive and a bit tonicky, bracing – rather cold too. And the flowers in the street are marvellous, so are the vegetables and fish in the market – a certain rich splendour and abundance which I had not expected. But as a place, I doubt you wouldn't like it – and I'm sure Earl wouldn't – too much of the old reserve and a certain callousness to other people, the very reverse of those

---

[1] See Letters 4960 and n. 1, and 5065.
[2] The Brewsters had been staying in the di Chiaras' house, the Villa Giulia, in Anacapri. When the di Chiaras were obliged, by Anna's ill-health, to return to it, the Brewsters moved to the Pensione Bella Vista (letter from the late Harwood Picard to eds, 20 November 1982).
[3] 'willingly'.

soft, gibbering Hindus. I think it may be really good for my health – a tonic. So if we like Majorca, we shall contrive to stay, find a house if possible. Unfortunately everything is rather dear, especially hotels. But if one could have a little house, I think it would work out like Italy. I shall write to you from Majorca and tell you. – Meanwhile do let me know what you are doing. When does sister Lola come?[1] How is Harwood? Do let her go to America. – I feel better here than in Paris. Wish I felt you were settled. It's no good for you, Achsah, to be distracted – not your line.

Love from us both.   DHL

5045. To Nancy Pearn, [15 April 1929]
Text: MS UT; Unpublished.

Hotel Oriente, Barcelona
Monday 15 April

Dear Nancy Pearn

Had yours forwarded from Paris today – have utterly forgotten what 'Enslaved by Civilisation' is about. But I wanted to write a word to Rebecca West – could you forward it to her.[2] – I enclose article for the *Studio* on 'Making Pictures.' Hope you can make it out – and will you let them have it – and will you ask them to put in the name of the Japanese artist who is in vogue in Paris and does pencilly nudes – I can't remember names.[3] – Queer place, Barcelona, throngs of sort of proletariat people, but not unsympathetic – and lovely flowers in the street. We are going over tomorrow night to Majorca – I hope we shall stay there some time – if we like it. The address will be:

Hotel Royal, *Palma de Mallorca*, Spain

I'll write some articles – must make some money – this life very dear, and pesetas, francs, or Liras, it's pay and be damned.

D. H. Lawrence

That hotel in Carcassonne is the most swindling I've ever been in – 400 frs. the night – with dinner.

[1] Lola Derby, Achsah's sister, came from USA with her daughter Rachel to visit the Brewsters in Capri (letter from the late Harwood Picard).

[2] DHL had sent this essay to Nancy Pearn, 24 November 1928 (see Letter 4764 and n. 2). She had told him on 18 March 1929: '"*Vanity Fair*" are getting terribly attached to you! They have now bought "ENSLAVED BY CIVILISATION" at a Hundred dollars ... ' (TMSC UT). More recently, on 8 April 1929, she wrote: 'The "*Sunday Dispatch*" are glad to have "ENSLAVED BY CIVILISATION", at Twenty-Five Guineas, and intend to get Rebecca West to reply to it, so things are beginning to blossom out again' (TMSC UT). The *Dispatch* appears not to have proceeded with this plan but the information reached DHL when he wished to address Rebecca West on another subject (see letter following).

[3] DHL refers to ' ... the Japanese Ito with his wish-wash nudes with pearl-button eyes', in 'Making Pictures' (*Phoenix II*, ed. Roberts and Moore, p. 602).

5046. To Rebecca West, 15 April 1929
Text: MS UTul; Unpublished.

c/o Thomas Cook & Son, Calle Fontanella 19, *Barcelona*, Spain
15 April 1929

Dear Rebecca West[1]

Somebody sent me *Time and Tide* and I wanted to write and thank you for shaking your fist at Jix and Joynson. I always like you when you are on the war-path, a real good squaw for scalps. But somehow I thought you were a bit disheartened – in your article. Don't be downhearted; there's such a lot of scalps ripe for taking, and so many would rejoice to hear that a good tomahawk was down and out. Don't let these dishearten your [   ][2] No good, the battle is here – below, and it's too soon for us to look on from the heavenly balconies. So I am once more spitting on my hands – so no doubt are you. Then a war-whoop.

But don't be alarmed at a few naughty words, either. The words are all right. It's the attitude towards them that is so fishy – stale fishy. So perhaps if we bring the words into the open and clean them up, it'll help to clean up the stale-fishy condition of the vulgar mind. That's my idea.

Anyhow I hope you are renewing your energy like the eagle. We are going over to Majorca, to see if my cough will calm down a bit there. Jix would say it's my sins – I say it's his. –

Sincerely   D. H. Lawrence

5047. To Giuseppe Orioli, 18 April 1929
Text: MS UCLA; Moore, *Intelligent Heart* 403–4.

[Hotel Royal, Palma de Mallorca, Baleares, España][3]
18 April 1929

Dear Pino

Had yours in Barcelona – and the two you forwarded. Am sure you will be glad to get away for a bit, after the rush with *Nerinda*. Do keep my copy for me. – Secker is doing the poems in expurgated form, and I may have a small edition done in England, *privately*, of the unexpurgated. I don't want you *yet*

---

[1] Rebecca West, pseudonym of Cecily Isabel Fairfield (1892–1983), novelist, critic and journalist. She met DHL in Florence in 1921 (*Letters*, iii. 709). She reviewed several of his works, including *The Trespasser* and *Women in Love*, and *Paintings* in *Bookman* (New York), September 1929. Her 'Elegy' for DHL (which referred to this letter), first published in the special number of the *New Adelphi* (Summer 1930), was issued as a small book, *D. H. Lawrence* (1930); it is reprinted in Nehls, ii. 61–6. The essay to which DHL referred here is 'A Jixless Errand', *Time and Tide*, x (15 March 1929), 282, 284–6.

[2] MS stained and illegible.

[3] Here and for Letters 5052–5, 5057 DHL used the hotel's headed notepaper.

to do anything that will get your press into discredit with the Puritans. Keep pure for a while, till you are well going, then I'll give you something. The Fanfrolico Press has more or less dissolved. The *working* partner was always P. R. Stephensen – Lindsay was the literary side of it. Stephensen has joined with Edward Goldston the Jew bookseller of Museum St, to make the Mandrake Press, of which my pictures are the first thing done. – The reproduction of *Moses* seemed very dim to me.

This island – Majorca – is rather like Sicily, but not so beautiful, and much more asleep. But it has that southern sea quality, out of the world, in another world. I like that – and the sleep is good for me. Perhaps we shall stay a month or two – and come to Italy to find a house for the winter. Frieda will never take to Spain, and she won't even try to speak Spanish – So I expect we'll be back in Italy in autumn. But I like this sleep there is here – so still, and the people don't have any nerves at all – not nervosa, anybody.

I do hope you kept the price of your last sale of Our Lady,[1] to pay the postage. I should like us to be quite square now, on each side. So let me know. You said you sold a copy, and I don't think you sent the bordereau, so that would be part. And did you keep two copies of the guinea edition for yourself? Let's get quite square now then we shall have settled all the bulk of it. Write to me here. I wonder if you'll go to Capri. Remember me to N[orman] D[ouglas] and to Reggie[2] – I'll see them in autumn.

DHL

5048. To Else Jaffe, 18 April 1929
Text: Frieda Lawrence, *Nur Der Wind* . . ., (Berlin, 1936), p. 327; PC.

Palma da Mallorca,
18. April 1929

Hier sind wir wieder am Meer, es erinnert etwas an Sizilien, aber nicht annähernd so schön wie Taormina, nur viel ruhiger, der ruhigste Ort, den ich je gekannt habe, scheint eher langweilig, aber mir gefällt es und sicher ist es bekömmlich. Wir werden wohl eine Weile bleiben. Natürlich traf ich einen Freund auf der Straße, so sind wir bereits nicht allein auf der Insel. Das Hotel ist deutsch, sehr nett. Wie hat Dir *Lady Chatterley* gefallen. Frage M., was er dazu sagt.

DHL

[Here we are, by the sea again, it's a bit reminiscent of Sicily, but not nearly so

---

[1] The affectionate title by which DHL often referred to *Lady Chatterley's Lover.*
[2] Reginald ('Reggie') Turner (1869–1938), novelist and journalist; a resident of Florence (where DHL had met him in 1920) and companion of Norman Douglas (see *Letters,* iii. 594 n. 4).

beautiful as Taormina, just much quieter, the quietest place I've ever known, seems rather boring, but I like it and it certainly is good for my health. We'll certainly stay for a while. Of course I met a friend in the street,[1] so already we're not alone on the island. The hotel is German, very nice. How did you like *Lady Chatterley*. Ask M.,[2] what he thinks of it.

DHL]

5049. To Lady Ottoline Morrell, [18 April 1929]
Text: MS UT; PC v. El Puig en Pollensa, Mca.; Postmark, Palma 18 ABR 29; Unpublished.

Hotel Royal. Palma de Mallorca
Thursday.

Here we are on an island again – reminds me of Sicily, in the blue southern light, so strong – but this place isn't lovely like Taormina – only much calmer – the calmest place I know – I believe it will do one good – we shall stay a while I think. Met Robert Nicholls in the street – still a bit scattered.

Do hope you are well.

DHL

5050. To Emily King, [18 April 1929]
Text: MS Sagar; PC v. Bellver. Mca; Postmark, Palma 18 ABR 29; Unpublished.

Hotel Royal, Palma de Mallorca, Spain
Thursday

Here we are on Majorca – very warm and sunny, and a bit like our old Taormina in Sicily, but not so beautiful. But I like it, and think we shall stay awhile. Already met a friend in the street – English – going to see them this afternoon.

love   DHL

5051. To John Clarke, [18 April 1929]
Text: Lawrence–Gelder 191–2; PC v. [Peasant's house].

Hotel Royal, Palma de Mallorca, Spain
1929.

Well here we are on an Island again – Majorca this time. It reminds me of Sicily, warm and brilliant in the sun – but it's not so beautiful. I think we shall stay awhile – perhaps all summer. Already met some friends here – going to see them this afternoon. How do you like this peasant's house?

[1] The 'friend' was the English poet, Robert Malise Bowyer Nichols (1893–1944); DHL first met him in 1915 when Nichols was in hospital suffering from shell-shock (see *Letters*, ii. 442 and n. 2). m. 1922, Norah Denny.

[2] Unidentified.

5052. To Harry and Caresse Crosby, 18 April 1929
Text: MS SIU; Postmark, [Palma] 18 ABR 29; Lacy, *Escaped Cock* 73.

[Hotel Royal, Palma de Mallorca, Baleares, España]
18 April 1929

Dear Harry and Caresse

Well here we are on Majorca – and those brilliant incandescent blue mornings of the Southern Mediterranean that I know so well from Sicily – something eternally new and dawn-like. But this island, at least here, doesn't seem *beautiful* like Sicily – It has a certain forever asleepness which is also utterly dull, but which has too the charm of the sleep trance. I think we shall stay a while, and I think it will do me good, body and soul – sleep, the sweet sleep! – and the trance of islands that lie in the sun, and cannot be ravished out of the sun.

I wonder how you got along with your father,[1] and how Berlin affected you. I should think it was nervous excitation and exasperation all the while – the reverse of here, where the people still haven't reached the stage of having nerves, and where, at first, one is exasperated by the sheer absence of nervous tension. It is almost like falling down a clear, calm hole: and landing on sheer dulness. But not really dull, as the little boats go out past the mole, so white in the asleep afternoon: and somehow uplifted.

Curtis Brown's said they were sending you the other copy of *Escaped Cock*: so you will keep it safe for me. I discovered the MS. of the first part in my bag – and I know where the MS. of the second part is, in London. If you are the first to print the thing, then you must have the MSS. too. But I won't send them now to Florence to be bound – safer not risk too much postage.

I do hope you are feeling easy and not all upset.

Many greetings from us both   DHL

5053. To Charles Lahr, 18 April 1929
Text: MS StaU; Postmark, Palma 18 ABR 29; Moore 1143–4.

[Hotel Royal, Palma de Mallorca, Baleares, España]
18 April 1929

Dear Lahr

Had your letter in Barcelona – it had been opened, and no doubt read, by all Cook's office – as they have a clerk Mr Lawrence, and you put no initials. – I really don't think my mail is interfered with *at all* – but you could still write to my wife –

Secker is trying to leave out about 20% of the poems – but I am making

---

[1] See p. 240 n. 1.

him include some, and put just a blank when a *word* is improper. I won't have him issue a perfect hymn-book. I should like you to do a little edit, say 250,[1] with all the words in complete – but not with that introduction you've got, which is modified, but with the original introduction which I'll have sent to you: and perhaps an added word from me: Let me know your full idea. Would you like to do the whole MS. complete with all the words? – or only just those poems Secker has omitted or put blanks in? The former would be more worth having: and I can make Secker agree.

I don't mind a bit if your friend does 500 of Our Lady.[2] He can give me 15% on his selling price, that being the usual. Let me know.

Wait a bit till I see exactly what Secker is omitting, before we send to the *Sunday Worker*.[3] And I have no MS. here now from which to choose an election broadside. But *you* choose one, and let me know, and we can go ahead with that.

I should like you to do 250 of the *complete* poems, exactly as in M.S., but with the *original* foreword, not the one you've got, the one the jixers seized. Or would that clash too much with Secker's edition, as he wants to do a small signed edition also of his expurgated *Pansies*? What do you think? I should very much like to see the book in its complete form.

We may stay some time on this island – seems very quiet and congenial.

I don't agree that T. F. Powys[4] is a better writer than Hardy. His[5] is a wooden Noah's-Ark world, all Noah's Ark. But amusing as such.

Not had a sound from Davies – and we've wondered about him so much.

You can write to my wife
                    Frau Frieda Lawrence, geb. von Richthofen
if that pleases you more.

                                                                   DHL
          Hotel Royal, *Palma de Mallorca*, Spain.

---

[1] 250] 200
[2] This seems to be the first mention of the third edition of *Lady Chatterley's Lover* published in 1930 by Lahr and Stephensen. See Letter 5075 and Craig Munro, '*Lady Chatterley* in London: The Secret Third Edition', in *D. H. Lawrence's 'Lady'*, ed. Michael Squires and Dennis Jackson (Athens, Georgia, 1985), pp. 222–35.
[3] A radical paper which ran 15 March 1925–1 December 1929.
[4] Theodore Francis Powys (1875–1953), novelist and short-story writer, who, like Hardy, lived in Dorset. His best-known novel is the allegorical *Mr Weston's Good Wine* (1927).
[5] His] He

5054. To Laurence Pollinger, 18 April 1929
Text: MS UT; Unpublished.

[Hotel Royal, Palma de Mallorca, Baleares, España] Spain
18 April 1929

Dear Pollinger

I believe I had all yours. – I'll leave you to deal with Boni and Cape – and keep mum. – You are right, neither Field Roscoe nor Jack Hutchinson got any further than was already got – curse the law, and those who have it at their disposal. – we'll drop it now,[1] the *Pansies* business, for it's clearly no good struggling with a machine when the mechanic is against you. Wait! Aspettiamo! Esperamos![2]

I'm waiting to hear from Secker – don't want him to run any risks – but this is a black sheep that refuses to be whitewashed all over – must at least be piebald.

Funny place this – so curiously calm – and sunny and Mediterranean and before the birth of nerves – rather like Sicily, but not so lovely – but calmer and more outside the world – think we may stay a bit.

DHL

Hotel Royal, Palma de Mallorca, Spain

5055. To Marianne Moore, 18 April 1929
Text: MS UT; Postmark, Palma 18. ABR. 29; M. Moore, *Predilections*, pp. 107–8.

[Hotel Royal, Palma de Mallorca, Baleares, España]
18 April 1929

Dear Marianne Moore

Too late to cable you anything – so its all right to print the 'Circus' poem as you put it.[3]

---

[1] Pollinger's evident relief at DHL's decision is signalled by his marginal note to Nancy Pearn: 'Glory be!' He added a further note at the end of the letter:

Dear Pearnie
    I'm conceited enough to say that I believe I know how to handle D.H.L. wilful & childish as he may be

L.E.

    – glad I've got babies!!!
[2] 'Wait! Wait! Let's hope!'
[3] DHL's letter was in answer to Moore's, March 1929 (Joost and Sullivan, *Lawrence and 'The Dial'*, pp. 110–11):

Dear Mr. Lawrence:
    By reason of the delay of one and another, it is only now that we have found that we may have the following poems:
    WHEN I WENT TO THE CIRCUS
    TO LET GO OR TO HOLD ON
    THINGS MEN HAVE MADE

I like the little group you chose – some of my favourites – but you'd better keep in touch with Curtis Brown's office to see what arrangement they make for book publication. Anyhow I think I shall withdraw that introduction from the book form – so you just keep any part of it you wish, and use it with your group of poems, as you wish. But you'll want to come out *before* the book appears, won't you?

I knew some of the poems would offend you. But then some part of life must offend you too, and even beauty has its thorns and its nettle-stings and its poppy-poison. Nothing is without offence, and nothing should be: if it is part of life, and not merely abstraction.

We may stay on this island a while, but my address is best c/o G. Orioli.

All good wishes   D. H. Lawrence

WHATEVER MAN MAKES
WORK
NOVEMBER BY THE SEA
SEAWEED
WHAT WOULD YOU FIGHT FOR?
LIZARDS
CENSORS
ATTILA

Next week we shall send a cheque for one hundred and sixty dollars ($160) to Miss Rowe Wright of Curtis Brown. Although it precludes our sending you proofs of WHEN I WENT TO THE CIRCUS, we have embodied this poem in the May issue (withdrawing something to make room for it) and are asking your permission to regard the enclosed typescript as proof. There is not even time, however, for it to be returned to us and should anything be amiss, please cable at our expense. Dialpubco, New York is the address. If for instance there ought to be space before the line beginning, "The elephants," the one word "space" would be sufficient; and if you objected to the title's being set in capitals, the word "low" would indicate the change. If, however, by April 15th, we have not had a cablegram from you we shall know we may proceed without changes. The other poems we should, as we think, like to publish as a group in November; they would appear about the middle of October, but we could publish them sooner if it were to your interest that we should.

We admire exceedingly the sentences:

Pensées, like pansies, have their roots in the earth, and in the perfume there stirs still the faint grim scent of under-earth. Certainly in pansy-scent and in violet scent it is so: the blue of the morning mingled with the corrosive [s]moulder of the ground.

Should the Foreword not have been published before we have brought out this group, might you accord us the privilege of prefixing these two sentences to our group?

One can hardly express the enjoyment given by poems in this book, as feeling and as form of expression, and that we should have for The Dial what we have selected, is an eager delight. I admit, there are lines in the book, that are the outcome of certain hurts, and am not saying that in every case the lines themselves leave no shadow of hurt; one asks for the high beauty that you conceive, inviolateness from reprisal. But taken as a whole, there is an infection of beauty. Wishing you always the best,

Yours sincerely,

For publication see p. 173 n. 2.

5056. To Barbara Weekley, [post 18 April 1929]
Text: Nehls, iii. 284.

[Hotel Royal, Palma de Mallorca, Baleares, España]
[post 18 April 1929][1]

I think that your headaches may be due to a deep change in the psyche, and you will just have to lie low and bear the change. Don't make too many efforts, especially efforts with people, and don't try to paint at present. Later on you might be really worthwhile.

5057. To Edward Titus, 19 April 1929
Text: MS UT; Unpublished.

[Hotel Royal, Palma de Mallorca, Baleares, España]
19 April 1929

Dear Mr Titus

We have got so far south – probably we shall stay a while on this island, Majorca, so the address will be good. It is sunny and brilliant as the southern Mediterranean should be, but the breeze is quite cool, at evening almost cold. I like it here, though, and think it'll suit my health.

How are you getting on with Our Lady, as we call her? Let me know what progress, and I hope not too many hitches.

I'm thinking about my article for your magazine, but am too unsettled for the moment. I shan't forget, though.[2]

Hope you are well.

sincerely   D. H. Lawrence

5058. To Ada Clarke, [22 April 1929]
Text: MS Clarke; PC v. Puerto Santany Mca.; Postmark, [. . .] 22 ABR 29; Unpublished.

Hotel Principe Alfonso, Palma de Mallorca
Monday.

We have changed hotels – much nicer here – but the weather pretty rough. I haven't had any word from you at all – but heard from Emily and Peg, so suppose you are all right. Wonder if you got the MS. of those poems – they should have been sent to you. The pictures are going ahead rather slowly – a long job. Love to all. Is Gerty back?

DHL

---

[1] Barbara Barr believed this letter was written from Mallorca (Nehls, iii. 284).
[2] 'Pornography and Obscenity' appeared in *This Quarter*, ii (July–September 1929), 17–27 (Roberts C190).

5059. To Rhys Davies, 25 April 1929
Text: TMSC NWU; Huxley 793–4.

Hotel Principe Alfonso, *Palma de Mallorca*, Spain.
25 April 1929.

Dear Davies,

How fortunate I needn't ecstasise to you! – everybody seems to think I ought to be in ecstasies over this place, even including Frieda – Majorca is one of her oldest dreams – and I don't really care for it. True, the sea is usually a most heavenly blue, and the old town lies round the bay, pale, phantom in the strong light, all a funny heapy-heap of buff and white – and the flowers are nice – and I like this hotel. But there is a cold little wind, and some days it is all funny and grey and clammy, scirocco, and they give one far too much food to eat, quite good food here, but *too much* – and my bill last week was over eleven pounds, merely the hotel – and the Spanish wine, my God, it is foul, cat-piss is champagne compared, this is the sulphureous urination of some aged horse – and a bottle of Julien, the cheapest claret, costs 9 pesetas – over six shillings – and worst of all, the place gets on my nerves all the time, the people are dead and staring, I can't bear their Spanishy faces, dead unpleasant masks, a bit like city English – and my malaria came back, and my teeth chattered like castanets – and that's the only truly Spanish thing I've done. We nearly took a house – and I must say, in some ways it was very nice, but thank God my malaria came on in time to save us from deciding on it. And that's about all the news – except that we ran into Robert Nichols in the street the second day we came here, and saw quite a lot of him and his wife, and we liked them very much. They had been here three months, and just got fed up, and had booked their berths, so they sailed off to Marseilles on Tuesday morning, and at that moment I wished I was sailing too. But in the morning when it is lovely and sunny and blue and fresh, I am reconciled again, for a time. We may stay another twelve days – we *might* stop a month – but I think, by June surely we shall be sailing also to Marseille, and going either to Lago di Garda or somewhere like that. I don't want to take a house here, to stay. I think, all in all, Italy is best when it comes to living, and France next. *Triumphat Frieda!* I don't feel as if I should work here – Nichols couldn't – I feel somehow *peeved*, a state I do dislike, in myself even worse than others. Yet I do like the sea and the sunshine, and the pink convolvulus flowers all on the rocks. And we know some rather nice people, residents, who invite us to lunch and dinner, quite social.

No news of the world. I'm sorry Stephensen is getting vaguer and vaguer. Will he pop like a bubble – even before he's through with my book of pictures? Frieda's daughter is

Miss Barbara Weekley, 49 Harvard Rd., Chiswick. W.

The other one is honeymooning – we had very grand photos. of the wedding. So very glad you've got clear of Brentanos – and am sure Chattos will look after you well. That's good news, and all luck! I am still having wibble-wobbles with Secker over *Pansies* – and damn all publishers, and all the trade.

Remember us warmly to your mother and sister. If ever you want a week-end, and there are cheap tickets to Derby or Ambergate or Whatstand-well or Nottingham, go and stay a few days with my sister, she'd be so pleased (truly) and you'd like her and her husband too. Only tell her I told you.

Mrs. W.E.Clarke, 'Torestin', Broadway, *Ripley nr. Derby*

She knows all about you, of course. They'd no doubt be able to fetch you from some near station in the car, though week-end is their busy time. But go and see them.

Many regards from us both – and I hope you hate the thought of Spain and Majorca, sufficiently.

DHL

5060. To William Bradley, 25 April 1929
Text: MS UT; Unpublished.

Hotel Principe Alfonso, *Palma de Mallorca*, Spain
25 April 1929

Dear Mr Bradley

You will be wondering where I've got to – not so far, either.

I like the idea of Gallimard's doing me in translation, they are a bit more go-ahead than some, and I hope they will make a proper offer.[1] If they do, then ask Curtis Brown to let you deal with them for me, as it is useless, I can see, trying to handle French publishers from London.

I hope Titus will soon have out the cheap edition of *Lady Chatterley*, so you can get one. The only other way is to get one from the Librairie du Palais Royal, who sell their pirated edition at 100 frs., direct – so I am told. The booksellers put it up to 300 and 400 frs.

Very dry and quiet on this island – everybody leaving, visitors I mean – but I don't think it will be too hot till June. It's quite cool now.

Sincerely   D. H. Lawrence

---

[1] Gallimard was to publish Roger-Cornaz's translation of *Lady Chatterley's Lover* (with a preface by André Malraux) in 1932 (Roberts D44).

5061. To Emily King, 27 April 1929
Text: MS Lazarus; Postmark, Palma 28 ABR[. . .]; Unpublished.

Hotel Principe Alfonso, *Palma de Mallorca*, Spain
27 April 1929

My dear Pamela

We had Peg's letter this morning – so that jewel of a Joan has gone in for mumps. Tell her I'll send a list of all possible childish ailments, for her to pick and choose.

But I needn't talk. To my disgust, I had a little whack of malaria the other evening – teeth chattering like a sewing-machine. They say there's no malaria on the island, but I suppose the coming suddenly so far south, and the hot, moist, clammy day, off the sea, just brought it out. We were on the point of taking a house, but I thought I'd better beware. If I'm in the shaking zone, I'd better not stay, at any rate permanently.

We've changed hotels, and this is very nice, over the sea with big gardens and lots of room. People are bathing, but it's very cool for the time of the year, almost chilly. And here too there's a great lack of water, the island is very dry. It's very nice, very quiet, not so beautiful by far as Sicily, and somehow duller. But I suppose that's good for us, more restful. Frieda has gone off to Palma to a concert, with friends – and a mosquito has just sailed in from my balcony.

The pictures are steadily being photographed in colour, and plates made. It's rather a long and slow process, as there is only one firm in England that can do it. I have seen reproductions of two of the pictures, and am disappointed. They are smudgy, and the colour is not true. That's because the English don't know how to do this work. If only it could have been done in Germany! – They don't want to start the exhibition till the book is ready – so that both can launch off together. Now they say May – but you never know what more delays there will be.

Elsa's wedding apparently went off in great style, a great success – and the happy couple are at present in Turin, with Lady Becker, his aunt.[1] I think they are quite happy.

I haven't heard from Ada – suppose she is busy. I do hope Joan is better – and that spring is co-o-oming, as we used to sing.

Love to all   DHL

[1] Lady Delphine Therese Becker, widow of Sir Walter Frederick Becker (1855–1927), lived at Val Salice, near Turin. DHL had stayed two nights with the Beckers in November 1919; they were the originals of Sir William and Lady Franks in *Aaron's Rod*. See *Letters*, iii. 417 n. 1.

5062. To Hon. Dorothy Brett, 27 April 1929
Text: MS UCin; Postmark, [. . .]28 ABR 29; Huxley 795–6.

Hotel Principe Alfonso. *Palma de Mallorca*. Spain
27 April 1929

Dear Brett,

So you are safely back in Taos, but not yet been up to the ranch. I had your letter today. And Mabel has dropped the Dude Ranch idea,[1] but the Dude Rancheress isn't so easy to drop. I can imagine the horror of it, the crass paint and the dyed curtains and the built-in sleeping porches. Mabel should never have entertained the idea at all. – And perhaps it will be better if you have a separate studio, off the estate, so to speak.

We have been here ten days. It's quite nice, southern and Mediterranean and a bit like Capri – only much more island and much fewer people. One could live quite lonely if one wanted. We nearly took a house – but then an attack of malaria came on, and my teeth chattered, and I thought I'd better beware. There isn't malaria on the island – so they swear – but it's evident I'm in the malarial tremble-zone. Still we'll stay a while, and see. It's a very pleasant hotel, and practically no people at all.

I wish, somehow, the mysterious bars would lift that keep us from coming back to the ranch – a sort of fear, a sort of instinct. Now I am in a Spanish-speaking country, I have New Mexico before my eyes every moment. After all, it's so much bigger and lovelier than this is: Europe remains a bit poky, wherever you go. Yet I feel the stars are against my crossing the Atlantic just now. – But we shan't make any move about selling the ranch. – Only, when you get back up there, I do wish you would carefully collect all my MSS. and make[2] me a list, and have Mabel check it, and send it me, and put the MSS. in safe-deposit in Taos bank. I'll send a cheque for the costs. Also let me know what the horses have cost, feeding – and the taxes. – Somebody said you were trying to sell some of the MSS., but I expect you were only dangling bait, to see what sort of fish would rise. – My pictures are busily being reproduced – I've seen proofs of two of them – very disappointing and smudgy. The exhibition should be ready in May, when the book comes. – I can't paint in these hotels, and am a bit at a loose end. Perhaps the Gods will move. – Anyhow I hope you'll have a nice summer, and get good things done. – Wonder if the cellar *did* fall in!

DHL

---

[1] 'Mabel considered turning her homestead into a ranch resort. She opened the main house briefly in the spring of 1929 to serve meals, but closed it to the public after a short time' (Lois P. Rudnick, *Mabel Dodge Luhan*, Albuquerque, 1984, p. 233).
[2] make] send

5063. To Brewster Ghiselin, 27 April 1929
Text: MS Ghiselin; Postmark, Barcelona 28 ABR 29; Nehls, iii. 320–1.
Hotel Principe Alfonso, *Palma de Mallorca*, Spain.
27 April 1929

Dear Bruce
Your letter came on to Paris, but your telegram took eight days to wander here to us – and by that time I was afraid you would have left Naples: moreover Spain was too much off your map. Did you have a nice trip, I wonder, or were you only the more disillusioned after it? I think one shouldn't ask too much from the outside world, especially if one is not interested at all in the tradition, as you are not. You rather dislike the tradition, really, and any manifestations of it – so perhaps it is a mistake travelling to look at old countries.

The island is very pleasant, very quiet, very Mediterranean, and very dull. I quite like it, but don't contemplate ending my days here. Still, for the time being it is soothing and calm, so I think we shall stay till it gets too hot. The trouble is that I had a whack of malaria, and shook in my skin – I suppose that's with coming so far south – and it was a muggy clammy day. But I mistrust a place where malaria comes back.

You haven't much longer to endure Oxford and Europe. I shall be quite relieved to think of you safely returned to California, and comparatively happy there.

Frieda has gone off to a concert in Palma, but she'd send her greetings, with mine.

Yrs   D. H. Lawrence

5064. To Charles Lahr, 27 April 1929
Text: MS StaU; Postmark, Barcelona 28 ABR 29; Unpublished.
Hotel Principe Alfonso, *Palma de Mallorca*, Spain
Sat. 27 April 1929

Dear L[ahr]
These are the poems Secker is omitting:
'Ego-bound woman'
'There is no way out'.
'My naughty book'.
'The little wowser'
'The young and their moral guardians'
'What does she want?'
'Don't look at me'.
'To Clarinda'

'Demon justice'.
'The noble Englishman'
'Women want fighters'

Other poems I modified, and all suggestions of improper words are removed. –

Secker wants to do a regular edit. at 10/6, with 150 signed copies at two guineas – and later a 3/6 edit. – I am stipulating that I have the right to print a small private edition of the *complete* MS. – not exceeding 250 copies. – Now let me know your idea. – I suppose you had my last letter.

Everything perfectly quiet and serene on this island, though somebody said there was a revolution in Barcelona. Hard to believe it could mean anything.[1]

I thought the last *London Aphrodite* took the biscuit for silliness.[2]

DHL

5065. To Laurence Pollinger, 27 April 1929
Text: MS UT; Unpublished.

Hotel Principe Alfonso, *Palma de Mallorca*, Spain
27 April 1929

Dear Pollinger

I have your two letters, and the contracts.

All right, I will do nothing with regard to Boni – I haven't heard from him at all, nor written him, since I saw him that evening in Paris. But it seems to me he will have a right to complain that we have treated him shabbily – and I doubt if ever he'll release the books he has, to Cape. Question is, whether he leaves them out of print long enough to lose the rights to them. But I doubt Jonathan will never do the uniform edition – even if Knopf and Seltzer-Boni would let him have the books they own – another doubtful point. And I should have liked to see my books rescued in U.S.A. from the sort of scrap-heap where they now lie.

Concerning the agreement for *Twilight in Italy*, why should the royalty be

---

[1] *The Times* shared DHL's view; except in early edns on 20 April it ignored the 'revolution'.

[2] The April issue of the *London Aphrodite* included a story ('A Pig in a Poke') by Rhys Davies, prose by Norman Douglas, verse by Jack Lindsay and Edgell Rickword, an article on Douglas by Lindsay and a Nietzschean essay by Stephensen called 'The Whirled Around: Reflections upon Methuselah, Ichthyphallos, Wheels and Dionysos' which was intended for public debate with DHL (in the essay DHL is described as 'a modern Luddite rioter . . . singing swan songs aloofly'). The issue to follow in July was announced as 'positively the last', after which readers would be abandoned to 'the Squire–MacCarthy–Eliot–Lewis–Transition sort of thing in literary journalism' (p. 400).

only five per-cent? It is almost as good as nothing – five cents on every copy sold in U.S.A.: and 2½ cents on every copy sold in Canada. It seems to me merely ridiculous. I want to hear from you about it, before I sign such a contract. Why not say I should pay 5% to Cape for the honour of appearing in his dollar museum! – As for the $60 advance, I care nothing about it. I can get that for any little article for a newspaper.

Concerning the agreement for *Collected Poems*, why should the ten per-cent royalty continue up to *ten thousand* copies sold? It seems to me that even after two thousand copies sold, Cape should be able to give me the normal and surely sufficiently-small fifteen per-cent. Why are the publishers allowed these huge margins, and the author whittled down? I wish to God I had published my *Collected Poems* myself. *Then* I should have made some money. I begin to feel more and more it is useless to write books, which cost one one's life and bring practically no return. I get so sick of these mean agreements and five per-cent beggaries; I know I shall never start another novel for the publishers. I can live by casual work better. – Let me know about that 10,000.

About the *Pansies* and Martin Secker: who, of course, always manages to irritate one with his small little ways – and whose honesty I do not trust. I wish I could feel that even the statements he renders are correct.

But with regard to *Pansies*: in the first place, I agree entirely that the New York edition should be identical with the London edition – so that Knopf had better wait for Secker's galleys.

With regard to the contract, however:

1. I must reserve myself the right to do a small private edition of the *Pansies*, not exceeding 250 copies, including all the poems in the MS. as they stand. This small edition will not affect either Secker or Knopf, especially as the little private edition would be subsequent to the public editions.

2. Does Secker want to call the book 'Pensées' – as he puts it in the agreement? But my title is *Pansies*, and that is much better, and he must keep to that. He can say

Pansies
(Pensées)

if he likes.

3. He can leave out the poems in his list – but let him print 'Worm either way' and I can re-write the last verse on the proofs:[1] as I have now no MS. by me at all.

4. On my own account I shall make little or no proof-alterations, and if the

---

[1] Secker included 'Worm either way' in his edn of *Pansies* (pp. 22–3); the final stanza shows one variant from the definitive edn (Roberts A47c): 'Have one with me!' replaced 'What? cat-piss?'

alterations made to please Secker exceed the 5/- for 32 pp. – I will not be charged for them. They are none of my wish.

5. Again, on a book selling at 10/6 and costing very little to produce, why should my royalty be only ten per-cent? why not a regular fifteen? why this beautiful margin *always* for the publisher? *Pansies* will cost to produce not more than half the cost of a novel. Yet my royalty is down to 10%. I won't agree to it.

6. For signing the 150 copies we will follow the same plan as in *Collected Poems*, and I will be paid a *sum down* for my signature. In that case I had one-third the profits accruing *merely* from the signing – which was one-third of £100, for 100 signatures. We will do the same here, and I'll have £50 for 150 signatures – and on this £50. I needn't pay government tax. Then the 150 signed copies are counted as ordinary copies and I get the royalty on them as on the unsigned copies. The £50. I get simply for my signatures.

7. I will send a new little introduction tomorrow – perfectly proper.

If Secker agrees to my stipulations he can go ahead and I'll make the slight alterations on the agreement and sign and send them.

You'll think I'm getting difficult – and so I am. I feel it's not good enough – and really, I've lost all my desire to publish any more books. It's merely not worth it.

This island is very quiet, and mostly sunny – the sea very blue. I'm not sure I'd like to live here always – there is a certain deadness, inertia, in the atmosphere – but for the time I like it, and this hotel is very pleasant indeed, for ten shillings a day. – You'll see we've changed from the Royal. – It's a pity you can't take a couple of months here. They say there is a revolution in Barcelona: there'll never be one here: there's nothing to revolve. – Ask C[urtis] B[rown] to send that MS. to Mrs Crosby. – I begin to get good-tempered again as soon as I leave off thinking about publishers.

DHL

I enclose the new foreword to *Pansies*.[1]

5066. To Enid Hilton, [27 April 1929]

Text: MS UCLA; PC v. Andraitx; Postmark, Barcelona 28 ABR 2[. . .]; Unpublished.

Hotel Principe Alfonso. Palma de Mallorca.

[27 April 1929]

Had your letter today – sorry it sounds a bit woe-begone. – We have been here a fortnight – very pleasant, very calm and quiet and Mediterranean – weather rather cool and often overcast. On the whole, we like it, and I think we shall stay till it gets hot. But I had a touch of malaria suddenly – so if that

---

[1] This is the 'Foreword', dated 'Palma de Mallorca. April 1929' which Secker used and dated 'Bandol, March 1929'. It survives with the letter.

returns, *we shan't* stay. Otherwise all well. They are getting on with the pictures, and as soon as the book is ready the show comes off.

                                                                Ever   DHL

5067. To Nancy Pearn, [29 April 1929]

Text: MS UT; Unpublished.

                              Hotel Principe Alfonso, *Palma de Mallorca*, Spain
                                                                      Monday
Dear Nancy Pearn
    This article is done for a man
                Edward W. Titus, Bookseller, 4 rue Delambre, *Paris XIVe*
He is starting a new magazine in Paris in July – international sort of thing – and I promised him this article[1] – so will you please type it and let him have it as soon as possible. I dont suppose he can pay much. But he is doing the cheap edition of my novel in Paris – I hope it'll soon be ready – so I do this for him.
    You see we've changed hotels – nice here – but a stormy wind today.

                                                                D. H. Lawrence

5068. To Edward Titus, 29 April 1929

Text: MS UT; Postmark, Palma 29·ABR·29; Unpublished.

                              Hotel Principe Alfonso, *Palma de Mallorca*, Spain
                                                                 29 April 1929
Dear Titus
    Thanks for yours – now I hope Our Lady is photographed down to her last dot, and on the point of reappearing in this dark world. Tell me how she is.
    Today I sent the MS of the article on 'Pornography and Obscenity' to
            Miss N. Pearn, Curtis Brown Ltd. 6 Henrietta St. Covent Garden,
                                    London W.C.2.
with instructions to type and send it to you at once – and I forgot to say that you don't want them to offer it to anybody else, either in England or America – so you say that to them from me. – You see I have to let all my stuff go through their hands, except Our Lady.
    Majorcan climate rather queasy – scirocco – gave me a slap of malaria – but am better – and the other grippe business quite gone. Today it blows the sea to bits, fresh I must say, and whistles round the hotel like ten errand boys. Talk about climates!

                                                                D. H. Lawrence
    Tell me if you'd like the article altered anyhow.

[1] Cf. Letter 5057 and n.2.

5069. To Nancy Pearn, 1 May 1929
Text: MS UT; Unpublished.

Hotel Principe Alfonso, *Palma de Mallorca*, Spain
1 May 1929

Dear Nancy Pearn

The editor of the *Architectural Review*:
H. de C. Hastings, 9 Queen Anne's Gate. Westminster S. W. 1.
asked me for an article on artists and decoration, so will you let him see the enclosed.[1] I don't know whether it is the kind of thing he wants – if not, no matter. – But if he doesn't want it, probably some other 'decorative' magazine would take it – and I should think America might like it, too.

I sent you yesterday an article for Edward W. Titus on 'Obscenity and Pornography' – hope it has come to hand. He won't be able to pay much.

Just have yours about £10. for the *Studio* article. I suppose these little papers really can't pay more – and if they can't, I don't mind.[2]

Brilliant sunny May Day here, but wind cool – everything very sparkling.
D. H. Lawrence

5070. To P. R. Stephensen, 1 May 1929
Text: MS Anon; Munro 306.

Hotel Principe Alfonso, Palma de Mallorca, Spain
1 May 1929

Dear Stephensen

Had your letter and *London Aphrodite* last week – No, I don't think I inspired you to a brilliant article – not even very estimable – but it might have been worse, like the one on poor Douglas.[3] *Caramba!*[4] (since we're in Spain).

You said you were sending more proofs of the pictures. They haven't come yet – did you send them? I am very anxious indeed to see them, as I have told you before. How many have you got done? When do you think the book will be ready? I'm sorry it is not ready now, because of the exhibition – it will be a great pity to delay it after May, because everybody begins to go away in June. I must write again to Dorothy Warren about it. She might hold the exhibition anyhow, if we are uncertain of the date of the book's appearance.

[1] 'Pictures on the Wall' appeared in *Architectural Review*, February 1930, and as 'Dead Pictures on the Wall' in *Vanity Fair*, iii (December 1929), 88, 108, 140. Collected in *Assorted Articles* as 'Pictures on the Wall' (Roberts C195). Hubert de Cronin Hastings (1902–?73) edited the *Architectural Review* 1927–73.
[2] Nancy Pearn had told DHL, 25 April 1929 (TMS UT): 'Ten guineas is as high as we could get the "*Studio*" to rise for your "MAKING PICTURES" article: this being above their usual rate.'
[3] See Letter 5064 and n. 2.   [4] 'Good gracious!'

Thanks for the booklet on the Indian sculpture.[1] It interested me very much – I like Indian art extremely – But the man who wrote the essay knew a bit too much, and didn't come through to his reader as well as if he'd known less.

We've changed the hotel – very nice here. We think we may stay till end of May. So please send me what proofs you have, and let me know when you hope to get the book out.

Hope you are getting on with your novel.[2]

Sincerely   D. H. Lawrence

5071. To P. R. Stephensen, 3 May 1929
Text: MS ULon; Moore 1145–6.

Hotel Principe Alfonso, *Palma de Mallorca*, Spain.

3 May 1929

Dear Stephensen

The proofs have come today, and I am very much relieved. It is as I hoped, the paler ones come out better. Sometimes the reproduction succeeds well as a whole, even when it doesn't follow the original very exactly. – But I enclose a list of suggestions for each picture.

Do you think you ought to put the *size* of each picture, under the title?

Do send me the other proofs as soon as you possibly can, so that I can make my suggestions.

I think after all it will be a lovely book, and am very anxious about it, and want to see the whole set of proofs.

DHL

Eight Proofs of Pictures
suggestions for improvement

Contadini (pretty good this) the man's *back* has lost its modelling – put a little more light on it, if possible – – and the patch of yellow near the doorstep is wrong. The tiny bit of green door by the second man (back) too dark.

Leda and the Swan: (quite good too) – greens are wrong, her bit of hair quite wrong, and please try to make the black foot of the swan distinct, and make the bird's thigh just above it whiter, colder, a little more modelled, so that we know what it is.

A Holy Family (not bad) woman's hair rather grey – man's halo gone thin – child's hand wrong colour, a mere smudge.

[1] Most likely *An Introduction to the Study of Mediaeval Indian Sculpture* by K. de B. Codrington, published by Edward Goldston in May 1929.
[2] Stephensen was not then writing a novel; DHL was presumably referring to *The Bushwhackers*.

Resurrection – (poor – the worst of all) – please try to get back the luminosity, especially on to the Christ – he is all blackish inky – his arm, his knee, his breast should all be luminous – and the old woman's arm is very flat and dead – and sky all wrong – please try to get this better, the *quality* is all lost.

Throwing Back the Apple: (not very like, yet pretty good in itself) – floor should be more ruddy and alive with leaves and fruit – the old man's hair nasty and pink, his skirt too much like the tree, too green, the tree itself too pale green all over, and the gateway wrong.

Renascence of Men (not bad, but a few corrections very necessary) – Please attend to the land behind the seated man's waist, it is very wrong, and kills his shape. Try to get a little glow on to the far sea, and the lip of the near sea more vivid – this near sea is bad, blackened and dead. Please rescue the *feet* of the man a little.

Flight Back into Paradise (rather thin – colour lost) – Please try to put the *glow* into the showery yellow, and make the sea with its white lip look like a sea – and make the houses a little less *black*, blackish – more olive green – if that blackish look could be avoided –

Summer Dawn (not very good) – Again too much mere *black*, especially under the man's buttocks – Try to put the light along the man's back, to restore the modelling – The bodies of both should be lifted a little paler to differentiate them from the background. It's too much of a smudge, the different *luminous* places are lost, sunk in. It's not a question of edge, but of the local glow. Blue sky is all wrong, orange sky too all-of-a-piece – same with the sea.

DHL

5072. To Edward Dahlberg, 7 May 1929
Text: MS UTul; Postmark, Palma 8 MAY·29; Moore 1147.
[Principe Alfonso (Hotel), Palma de Mallorca, (Baleares)] Spain[1]
7 May 1929

Dear Dahlberg

Thanks for yours, and the news of the pirates. Those babe-faced pussy-footing thieves make one very tired.

I went ahead with Titus after all – he seemed no worse than anyone else – and the book is now being printed. You see I simply *can't* make an expurgated edition – and that is all Gollancz is good for.

---

[1] Here and for Letters 5073 and 5079 DHL used headed notepaper, twice adding 'Spain' to the printed address.

Sorry you feel a bit irritated by my preface to your book. But it's quite simple to suppress it altogether in U.S.A. – make no mention of it, and it doesn't exist. – It won't hurt *English* Sales, as Putnam knows, even if it is a bad Sales-letter in America. – I can't help it, anyhow – I had to write what I felt.

Very quiet here on this island. – I don't know how long we shall stay – but not after the real hot weather sets in. – Hope you are feeling well in New York.

Sincerely   D. H. Lawrence

5073. To Laurence Pollinger, 7 May 1929
Text: MS UT; Unpublished.

[Principe Alfonso (Hotel), Palma de Mallorca, (Baleares)] Spain
7 May 1929

Dear Pollinger

I said plainly to the man Adams I would *not* let the first half of *Escaped Cock* be done alone – and he said then let it rest. Tell him to wait for the short novel: or do the story 'Mother and Daughter' from the *Criterion*, if he wants it.

I'll send Secker's agreement. – I know it will be dear, setting up the poems in U.S.A., yet still I think Cape should raise the royalty before *10,000* – That's too much.

That poem 'Mountain Lion' first appeared in Thomas Seltzer's edition of *BirdsBeasts and Flowers* I think in 1924.[1]

The *Criterion* sent me direct a cheque for £17..16..0, for the story in their current number – I suppose 'Mother and Daughter'. – I don't quite know whether they've taken off your discount or not – I think Miss Pearn said £20. Anyhow will you tell her please, and if I owe you the ten per-cent charge it to me.

Nothing new on this island – all asleep.

Yrs   D. H. Lawrence

Ask Secker to let me know plainly what words or phrases he wants altered on the proofs. I enclose both copies of the agreement – will you send me mine back with Secker's initials.

Your man William Aspenwall Bradley wrote me he has an offer from Gallimard – the *Nouvelle Revue Française* people – *publishers* – to do all my works in translation – and really go ahead with them. I rather believe in Gallimard. – But apparently your foreign dept. is negotiating with another

---

[1] The volume was published in 1923.

Paris firm – unknown. – Miss Watson has been struggling in vain, for two years, to get a French publisher who would live up to his word and agreement – they are very difficult. I doubt if she'll have any better success with the one (unknown) she's struggling with now. I wish you would have a bit of a talk with her about it, and see if we couldn't come to some sort of agreement to have Bradley handle the matter in Paris. He's on the spot and knows them – and they are so difficult – French publishers. – And I think the French are just about ready for me, really: better really than the Germans.

DHL

5074. To William Bradley, 7 May 1929
Text: MS UT; Unpublished.

Hotel Principe Alfonso, *Palma de Mallorca*, Spain
7 May 1929

Dear Mr Bradley

I'm sorry there's that scotch with Curtis Brown's people negotiating with another firm. Miss Watson has been negotiating and negotiating in vain, for the last three years, with Paris. So I have written to Pollinger to ask him can't we come to some arrangement to put the matter in your hands. I hope they'll find a way to do it, for I completely doubt their power ever to manage the thing properly from London – they seem to put the French people's backs up so completely. I'm afraid Miss Watson's manner is not good with foreigners – so of course, she is in charge of the foreign dept. However, we'll see what happens.

Sincerely   D. H. Lawrence

5075. To Giuseppe Orioli, [9 May 1929]
Text: MS UCLA; Moore, *Intelligent Heart* 404–5.

Hotel Principe Alfonso, *Palma de Mallorca*, Spain
Ascensión

Dear Pino

I wonder if you are back – I haven't heard from you at all. We are still here – quite pleasant, and cool rather than hot. But I have no desire at all to live on this island, the people are sort of dead, and it has a rather dead atmosphere. I much prefer Italy – and of course, so does Frieda. I think we shall stay here till about the end of the month, then make a little tour in Spain – to Alicante and Granada and Sevilla and Madrid – and then, I think, come to Italy to see about a house. Frieda suggests Lago di Garda, and that might be good. But I feel I'd like to be in sight of the sea. Maria and Aldous wanted us to look for a house behind Massa-Carrara, on the mountain looking to the sea. I think I should like that, so we might go to Forte and motor from there, to see if there was a house.[1] If you hear of anything, make a note of it. I should like a *house* – not just half a house, as at the Mirenda – not too big, and with a garden. If I found a place I liked, I would take it for some years, and furnish it, and perhaps put in central heating. If you happen to go to Forte, do take a motor and look round for me, and I will pay the expenses. – Or if you hear of a nice place in the hills round Florence, let me know. I want to find a place, if possible, which we can keep. There are plenty of suitable houses here – but I don't want them.

The only news of Our Lady is that I got a cheque for $68 from Lawrence Gomme, for eight copies. So cross him out. Now if we could make Miller & Gill pay up – and Davies – we shouldn't have done so badly. Titus has got the plates made, in Paris, and I think this week they start printing. So that should not take long. He sent me a specimen page, reduced – and it looked quite well. A man in London talks of doing an Edition of 500 there – printing it himself in London, right under Jix's nose. Don't know if this will come off. – Secker is doing the *Pansies*, omitting about a dozen poems. – Stephensen has sent me proofs of nine of the pictures. Some of them are not bad, but some very smudgy and thin. You'll hardly recognise them. Still, I think they'll make a fine book. You must try and make him give you a copy – and if he won't, I'll give you one of mine. But try and get one out of him. He must have had your list of addresses, as I hear from people who have received his circular, whose names he could not possibly have known, except through you.

That's all the news, for the moment.

Let me hear how you are, and if you have sold *Nerinda*, and how is Carletto. It will soon be a year since I saw you – I left Florence in June. And that Mrs Humes[2] who saw us off at Florence station, along with Nelly Morrison, suddenly turned up here, and is in Palma now. Do you remember her? She went to America, and it has quite broken her down.

Do you ever see any of the Pini, or the Salvestrini?[3]

love from both.   DHL

Remember me to Douglas – how did he like that blurb in the *London Aphrodite?* What news of Reggie? – and Miss Moller – and Gino?

[1] Forte dei Marmi, on the coast n.w. of Florence; the Lawrences had often been there when the Huxleys were staying in a house owned by friends (cf. *Letters*, vi. 246 n. 1).

[2] Probably the mother of Elizabeth Humes, an American girl living in Rome whom DHL had known since 1921 (see *Letters*, iii. 687 and n. 1).

[3] Peasant families living on the Villa Mirenda estate (see Letter 5256).

5076. To Maria and Aldous Huxley, [9 May 1929]
Text: Huxley 796–7.

Hôtel Principe Alfonso, Palma de Mallorca.
Ascension Day.

Dear Maria and Aldous, –

I had your letter, Maria, but no post card from Cook's, Barcelona – and not a sound from Aldous – which made me wonder where he was. However, I suppose you are both in London now, though I don't know where, so will send this to Suresnes.

We are still on the island – but changed the hotel. This is very nice, on the edge of the sea, good food but too much of it – ten shillings a day. We are only four people in the place, so have it to ourselves. The weather continues dry, the island parched, the sun hot, the wind often rather chill. The air itself is cold rather than hot – anyhow, cool. The exchange went down to thirty-seven.

Yesterday we motored to Valdemosa, where Chopin was so happy and George Sand hated it.[1] – It was lovely looking out from the monastery, into the dimness of the plain below, and the great loose roses of the monastery gardens so brilliant and spreading themselves out – then inside, the cloisters so white and silent. We picnicked on the north coast high above the sea, mountainous, and the bluest, bluest sea I ever saw – not hard like peacocks and jewels, but soft like blue feathers of the tit – really very lovely – and no people – olives and a few goats – and the big blueness shimmering so far[2] off, north – lovely. Then we went on to Soller, and the smell of orange-blossom so strong and sweet in all the air, one felt like a bee. – Coming back over the mountains we stopped in an old Moorish garden, with round shadowy pools under palm trees, and big bright roses in the sun, and the yellow jasmine had shed so many flowers the ground was brilliant yellow – and nightingales singing powerfully, ringing in the curious stillness. There is a queer stillness where the Moors have been, like ghosts – a bit *morne*,[3] yet lovely for the time – like a pause in life. – It's queer, there is a certain loveliness about the island, yet a certain underneath ugliness, unalive. The people seem to me rather dead, and they are ugly, and they have those non-existent bodies that English people often have, which I thought was impossible on the Mediterranean. But they say there is a large Jewish admixture. Dead-bodied people with rather ugly faces and a certain staleness. Curious! But it makes one have no

---

[1] Frédéric François Chopin (1810–49), Polish composer and pianist, lived with the French novelist George Sand (1804–76), at the monastery in Valdemosa, 1838–9.
[2] Huxley prints 'to far'.
[3] 'gloomy'.

desire to live here. The Spaniards, I believe, have refused life so long that life now refuses them, and they are rancid.

I think we shall stay till towards the end of the month – about a fortnight more – then I want if possible to take a steamer to Alicante or Valencia, and do a trip in Spain – Burgos, Granada, Cordoba, Seville, Madrid. I don't expect to *like* it immensely – that is, sympathetically. Yet it interests me.

Then perhaps we'll go to the Lago di Garda or perhaps for a week to Forte, to see if there is a house there. Since I don't think I want at all to stay permanently in Spain, we'd better cast round for a house before the real hot weather sets in.

And I wonder how you are getting on in England, how it all seems to you. Somehow, I don't want to come. The cistus flowers are out among the rocks, pink and white, and yellow sea-poppies by the sea. The world is lovely if one avoids man – so why not avoid him! Why not! Why not! I am tired of humanity.

But I hope you are having a good time, and remember me to everybody and send a line.

                                                                        DHL

5077. To Mabel Dodge Luhan, [9 May 1929]
Text: MS Brill; Luhan 343–4.

                              Hotel Principe Alfonso, *Palma de Mallorca*, Spain
                                                                  Ascención
Dear Mabel

I think John[1] was right to squash the dude ranch – and you must have been a bit loco to go and do it – after all, you mustn't humiliate your place like that. But I'm glad you've got it back, and sent the woman away, and can wash off the Philistine paint. It was a very 'small' feeling, somehow, to think of your hill as a dude ranch with Jews and Jew-gaws. Better the houses stand empty, than that.

I can understand your feeling about Brett – her complete and destructive insentience round one-half of the circle – and her hideous *persistency*, no longer human, in the other half. But of course to me she showed only her good qualities, and really was, in a way, devoted and helpful, so I feel a bit bad to think of her cut adrift. But it's no good, the most fateful thing of all is this halfness, half awfully good, and half horrible. One has, somehow, to cut clear of it.

I have written to her to get all my MSS. together, and make a list of them,

---

[1] John Ganson Evans (1902–78), Mabel's son by her first marriage.

and bring them to you, so that you can check the list: and then perhaps you could deposit them there in a safe in the Taos bank for me – and the bank will charge it to my account – they have $100 of mine. And perhaps at the same time it would be wise to give the deeds of possession of the ranch into the charge of the bank – what do you think? We left them locked in the iron trunk, but of course Brett has all the keys. I have not mentioned this about the deeds to her, but will do so.

What is her stunt about gold on the place? – she writes very fervently about it, but I put it to her romantic account. I think, after so many nosy prospectors and such have run the place over, it is unlikely Brett shall have lit on a gold mine within the fence.

We have been here on this island – Majorca – two weeks. It is quite pleasant and Mediterranean, but not at all exciting, and less beautiful than Italy. I don't think we shall stay long. I want to do a little tour in Spain towards the end of the month, then go to Italy to see to a few things. – I feel somehow that it isn't quite time yet for me to come to America – my instinct is against it, for the time being – but slowly the fates are working round that way. I am relieved that the dude ranch is quashed. And I feel we've all grown more tolerant, perhaps more whole in ourselves, so things should be easier. Poor Brett is damned forever to her awful halfness, of which she could never even be made aware.

I shall write to Mrs Chambers – but don't in the least know, as yet, where we shall spend the summer. After June, Spain is uncomfortably hot. We may go to Lago di Garda.

Lately I have dreamed of the Indians, and all Tony's songs come back into my head. I wake up with unfamiliar melody running in my consciousness, and it takes me a long time to identify it as one of Tony's or Trinidad's songs[1] – that I had utterly forgotten. Somewhere underneath in myself I feel a very deep sympathy with the Indians – superficially I don't really like them.

I wonder who is going to stay with you this summer? is Ida? I'm sorry she's left stranded, but she *did* let those silly conjugal hysterics get the better of her, when she shouldn't.

tante cose!   DHL

---

[1] Trinidad Archuleta was Tony Luhan's nephew and a famous dancer at the Taos pueblo (see *Letters*, v. 42 n. 6); he had worked for the Lawrences 1924–5. (DHL loved to hear 'a Red Indian singing to the drum', *Letters*, v. 570.)

5078. To Charles Lahr, 14 May 1929
Text: MS UNYB; Postmark, Palma 14 MAY 29; Unpublished.

Hotel Principe Alfonso, *Palma de Mallorca*, Spain
14 May 1929

Dear Lahr

Yes I had yours – waited to hear those estimates – we shan't leave here for another fortnight, I don't suppose – perhaps longer – not till it gets *hot*, which it isn't. – I sent you a list of the Pansies Secker is omitting: eleven: then there are various changes and suppressions in the ones he is printing. – If you would prefer to do just the eleven omitted poems, do so – I don't care – it would be small, cheap and easy. You could put that introduction to the first MS. with it, if you like – but I can't get it out of Jack Hutchinson. Kot. might tackle him and get back the whole MS. – I asked H. to send it to my sister, but he didn't reply – About broadsides, I sort of can't make up my mind – I can't *see* it. Now I suppose it's too late. No matter. – And what of your friend and Our Lady?

I don't think there is any interference really, with my mail.

I have got proofs of nearly all my pictures, from Stephensen – some rather good, some disappointing, but they are doing their best – I suppose it will be a nice book.

Tell Davies to write to me – his story was good, in the *Aphrod*[*ite*] – but how hideous, really![1]

DHL

I enclose a note for Hutchinson,[2] and Kot. can give it him if you want that MS.

5079. To P. R. Stephensen, 14 May 1929
Text: MS ULon; Moore 1149–51.

[Principe Alfonso (Hotel), Palma de Mallorca, (Baleares)]
14 mayo 1929

Dear Stephensen

I have got the twelve proofs – some not bad, some to weep over. Have written what suggestions I can. It isn't always wise to force the man to try to get nearer the original. If he achieves a pleasing result in a reproduction, one has to accept it and not upset it. I'm sorry that *Kiss* is a bit of a failure – it becomes trivial in reproduction: depends on its treatment.

[1] See p. 265 n. 2. In 'A Pig in a Poke' a God-fearing, respectable Welsh collier brings home a wife from London, and lives to regret it.
[2] The enclosure is missing.

Send me proofs of *Moses* and *Accident in a Mine*, will you please, so I have a complete set.

And then from your list you omitted *Rape of the Sabine Women*. I suppose you overlooked it. So that there are to come:

Rape of Sabine Women
Fight with an Amazon
Fauns and Nymphs
Singing of Swans

I'm expecting now to hear from Dorothy Warren. If she has no trouble with the show, you should have none with the book. After all, what is there to find fault with! If only it goes into America all right, you will sell it easily. I'm sure it'll be a book people will want.

Looks like the weather may suddenly be piping up hot here. If so, we shall move next week or week after.

Good luck to your mandrake – hope nobody will ever try to pull it up by the roots.

DHL

Suggestions

Close-Up (Kiss): fairly good – but girl's face too monochrome pink, her *arm* has lost all its life and quality, especially along the bottom of the picture, and the man's shoulder and throat have lost their modelling.

Boccaccio Story: fair – gone very grey, nuns should be silvery lavender, there should be pink trees in background, and grass on which the man lies should be actual grass, not merely a greyness.

Yawning: engraved rather black – the colour-relation is wrong, people too brownish and dark, not *lit up* enough, green too blue and heavy, basin too brown.

North Sea: not bad – nasty flush of pink over the foreground woman – her arm and side: water rather dead.

Mango Tree: lost its glow – the sky gone dead – the man should be more coloured.

Haystack: The man much too black on his body, especially the dark-grey belly – and the piece of land just beyond him is wrong – this reproduction pretty bad.

Fire-dance: try to get the flames a little more subtle, and the bodies more glowing, their high lights more delicate, so that the flesh shows in contrast to the background and fire. The torso of the darker man isn't treated right.

Spring: Colour and modelling of the foreground is wrong – the bits of blue should suggest blue-bells – the bright green isn't in proper relation.

Dance Sketch: the dark patch between the man and woman is a mess – the girl's breast has lost its modelling, so has the man's body.

Willow Trees: this is the most successful reproduction – but too monochrome brown – the green fields should be more emerald, the water more bluey-grey, less *yellow.*

Family on a Verandah: – pick out the high lights on the flesh, so that it glows a little and is not so monochrome and monotone – the man's back and hips are too greenish and background-coloured.

Lizard: – the whole thing is etched very black, and the flesh-quality lost.

5080. To Giulia Pini, 16 May 1929
Text: MS UCLA; Huxley 797–9.

Hotel Principe Alfonso, *Palma de Mallorca*, Spagna

16 maggio 1929

Cara Giulia

Ieri il Signor Orioli mi ha mandato l'indirizzo tuo, posso dunque scrivere una lettera per dire che non vi abbiamo dimenticato, parliamo tanto di te e di tutti gli altri di San Paolo, vogliamo anche sapere come andate voi. Come vi piace il posto nuovo? la terra, come è? il lavoro, è duro, o più liggero che a San Paolo? e il grano e gli ulivi, promessono bene per quest'anno?

Qui siamo proprio al mare; Mallorca è una isola che appartiene alla Spagna, la gente parla spagnuolo: ma tutto ressembra molto à l'Italia: la campagna ha gli ulivi, il vino, grano, iguali alla Toscana. Pero fa un poco più caldo, e più asciutto qui. Non ha piovuto quasi niente, quest'anno, il grano va male, ma gli ulivi fioriscono belli. Già mangiamo ciliege e nespole, le mandorle sono già grosse.

Restiamo ancora un poco qui, perché ci piace. La signora fa i bagni di mare, e abbiamo amici qui, come dappertutto. Ma non vogliamo vivere qui per sempre. Ritorniamo in Italia, forse nel luglio, o in settembre, per cercare una case per vivere. Questa volta vogliamo una casa intera, e non un appartimento di sopra, come alla Mirenda, con una Zaira ed un Tito di basso. Vorremmo una casa non troppo grande, ni troppo piccola, e con un giardino: dove possiamo stare in santa pace, senza queste fastidie della Villa Mirenda. C'è qualche cosa nella tua vicinanza? –

Pero, quando veniamo a Firenze, o quest'estate o nell' autunno, verremo alla Villa Sguanci per vedervi tutti, e per salutarvi. Intanto tu ci scriverai e ci dirai tutto che c'è di nuovo: come state tutti voi; la Teresina, come va lei? – se va sposarsi? e il Pietro, pensa lui anche a sposarsi, e porta la sposa a vivere con voi? il Pierino, va sempre alla scuola? e come gli piace poi la scuola nuova? e il babbo, e la zia, e lo zio, stanno tutti contenti e bene? e la Stellina?

Io vado sempre megliorando, poco a poco. La tosse me da sempre noie, pero di salute sono più forte. La signora sta bene. Sua figlia, la più vecchia, Elsa, che tu non hai vista, si è sposata un mese fa, ed ha passato un tempo col marito in Italia. Ora sono tornati a Londra. – I miei quadri, quelli che ho fatto a San Paolo, e che stavano nella Villa Mirenda, ora sono esposti a Londra in un'esposizione, tutta la gente va a vederli: sono anche riprodotti in un libro, tutti quelli quadri, e alcuni altri, e quando veniamo a Firenze ti farò vedere il libro, e riconoscerai i quadri.

Mi pare che non c'è altro a dirti – dirò dunque *a rivederci*, e molti saluti di me e della signora a tutta la famiglia.

D. H. Lawrence

[Dear Giulia

Yesterday Mr Orioli sent me your address, so I can write a letter to say that we haven't forgotten you all, we speak a lot about you and about all the others at San Paolo, we also want to know how you are. How do you like your new place? the land, what is it like? the work, is it hard or lighter than at San Paolo? and the corn and the olive trees, are they promising this year?

Here we are right on the sea; Mallorca is an island which belongs to Spain: but everything is very much like Italy: the countryside has olive trees, wine and corn, just the same as in Tuscany. But it is a little hotter here, and drier. It has hardly rained this year, and the corn is doing badly, whereas the olive trees are blossoming beautifully. We can already eat cherries and medlars, the almonds are big already.

We are going to stay a little longer here, because we like it. My wife swims in the sea, and we have friends here, as everywhere. But we don't want to live here for ever. We'll return to Italy, perhaps in July or September, to look for a house to live in. This time we want a whole house, and not an upstairs flat, as at the Mirenda, with a Zaira and a Tito downstairs.[1] We would like a house, neither too big nor too small, and with a garden: where we can live in peace, without all those nuisances at the Villa Mirenda. Is there anything near your place? –

But, when we come to Florence, either this summer or in the autumn, we will come to the Villa Sguanci to see you all, and to say hello. In the meantime you will write to us and you'll tell us all the news: how you all are; and Teresina, how is she? is she going to get married? and Pietro, does he also think of getting married, and will he bring his bride to live with you? Pierino, does he still go to school? and if so how does he like his new school? and your father, and aunt, and uncle, are they all happy and well? and Stellina?

[1] Zaira was Raul Mirenda's mistress, Tito her dog (cf. *Letters*, vi. 398).

I am getting better and better, little by little. My cough still bothers me, but my health is stronger. My wife is well. Her daughter, Elsa, the eldest, whom you never saw, got married a month ago, and spent some time with her husband in Italy. Now they've gone back to London. – My paintings, those that I painted at San Paolo, and which were in the Villa Mirenda, are being shown now at an exhibition in London, lots of people go to see them: they are also reproduced in a book, all those paintings, and some others, and when we come to Florence I'll show you the book, and you'll recognise the paintings.

I think I haven't anything else to tell you – so I shall say see you soon, and many greetings from me and from my wife to all your family.

D. H. Lawrence]

5081. To S. S. Koteliansky, 17 May 1929
Text: MS BL; Postmark, Palma 18 MAY 29; Zytaruk 383.

Hotel Principe Alfonso, Palma de Mallorca, Spain
17 May 1929

My dear Kot

So long I haven't written to you – but then you didn't write to me. And we have been on this island a month – very agreeable, so calm and so sunny. But humanly it's a bit dead – I believe all Spain is – so I don't want to live here. We want to leave at end of this month, and can't make up our minds whether to do a trip in Spain – Alicante, Bourgos, Granada, Sevilla, Toledo, Madrid – or whether to take the boat straight to Marseille. Frieda is moaning again for a house – and now it's a year since I left Italy. So I think we shall go back to Italy and look for a house there. All in all, it seems the best place.

What do you think Lahr wants to do about the poems? I can't quite make out. Secker is omitting about a dozen, so he said – but I have no proofs from him yet, so can't verify. I don't mind much what Lahr does, whether the complete MS. or only those left out by Secker. And I feel hesitant about a broadside for electioneering purposes – it's not quite my line. – But do get the original MS. of *Pansies* from Jack Hutchinson if you can, and keep it for me.

I have seen proofs of nearly all the pictures from Stephensen – some very nice, some smudgy. But I believe they'll make a fine book – they have already got orders for 200 or so copies: and *all* the vellum copies at £50 ordered! Now I want to know if Dorothy Warren will really hold her show.

What's your news? none, as usual? Are you staying in the cave all summer?[1] or will you get away a bit? Pity you can't come abroad, it's really better.

Many things!   DHL

[1] Kot's home at 5 Acacia Road, St John's Wood, was known to his friends as 'the cave' or 'cavern'.

5082. To Aldous Huxley, 17 May 1929
Text: Huxley 799.

> Hôtel Principe Alfonso, Palma de Mallorca.
> 17th May 1929.

Dear Aldous, –

Your p.c. on the 7th reached me to-day – don't know why it took ten days. You should put *Spain*. I have sent you a letter and p.c. lately – hope you have them – we came to this address three weeks ago. – We didn't go into that house as I had a shot of malaria and didn't want to risk the climate – but it hasn't come back. It's rather lovely here – so fresh and calm and sunny – but there is a certain something about the atmosphere, a human deadness and a foolish ineffectual sort of resistance, to life, which bores me and makes me not want to stay. With all their tiresomeness I like the Italians much better, and the French too. They are more alive, more frank, more life-generous. The Spaniards seem like boxes of something shut up and gone stale. We want to leave at the end of the month, and hesitate very much whether to take the steamer straight to Marseilles, or whether to get the boat to Alicante, and go to Burgos, Granada, Seville, Cordoba, Toledo and Madrid, then on to Italy. Frieda is again moaning for a house, so I think we'll look in Italy – either Massa or Lago di Garda – we may as well try to get something quite soon, so as not to remain in space. Maria, what do you *really* think about Massa?

When do you leave for Italy? I must say the Mediterranean is a great comfort – and there are stretches of wild coast, and little uninhabited bays on this island, really lovely, like the first day of time – only, queerly enough, a bit *haunted*. I feel old and sullen ghosts on the air, and am rather frightened.

I have seen proofs of most of my pictures – some rather good, some lamentable. But I think it'll be a nice book – and they've already got orders for about £2,500 worth – orders for all the vellum copies – ten – at £50 each. *Figurati.*[1] I doubt Stephensen can't give you a copy, so shall give Maria one of mine.

> DHL

5083. To Earl and Achsah Brewster, 17 May 1929
Text: MS UT; Brewster 201–2.

> Hotel Principe Alfonso, *Palma de Mallorca*, Spain
> 17 May 1929

Dear Earl and Achsah

I keep wondering how you are and what you are doing. I wrote you from

---

[1] 'Just imagine.'

Barcelona, and have kept on expecting an answer, but nothing has come. So now I don't know where you are nor anything.

We have been on this island for a month – very pleasant and sunny, right on the sea, and very peaceful. They call it the island of calm, and indeed it is. Yet there is a certain deadness in the human atmosphere at least, which makes it unattractive in the long run. We went across to the other side of the island. There are lovely lonely little bays with pine trees and sand and no people – and big stretches of a sort of heath-land or moor. One could be a lonely hermit here if one wanted – and the climate seems to me very good, about the best in Europe, I should say. Yet I don't want to stay – and I don't want a house here. I think in about a fortnight's time we shall take the boat to Marseilles and come to Italy and see if we can light on a suitable house. We hesitate whether to take a trip in Spain – to Granada and Sevilla and Madrid – but the railway journeys are so long and tiring, and as I get older I care less and less about merely *seeing* things or places – or people.

There's our plans as far as they go – now write and tell me where and how you are, and perhaps we can meet during the summer.

Love from us both.   DHL

5084. To Caresse Crosby, 17 May 1929
Text: MS UT; Postmark, Palma 18 MAY 1929; Lacy, *Escaped Cock* 74.

Hotel Principe Alfonso, *Palma de Mallorca.* Spain
17 May 1929

Dear Caresse Crosby

Too bad that it's still chilly at the Mill – I like to think of the courtyard flooded with sunshine, and a few bright daffodils sparkling. Here it goes on being sunny, but sometimes the wind is cool almost to chill. It hasn't rained for months.

It's rather nice – but I don't think I want to live here. There's a certain deadness. I think in about a fortnight we'll take the boat to Marseilles, and go to Italy. Frieda is still lamenting for a house, so I suppose we'd better go and look for one. So we shan't be here in July to receive you and your party on a yacht – staggering thought – though perhaps we may see you somewhere else, for I don't expect we shall go very far away. The yacht sounds thrilling – Whose is it?

And how did your race-party go off?[1] – and did you ride the She-ass of the first order? – I hope you've got her. I expect you'll end by having a strange and wonderful collection of asses, striped ones and plain, pale and dark, in the

[1] There was a donkey-track behind the Mill. The latest race-party had been on 11 May.

effort to come at the right article: and they'll get uppish, and rove around like lions.

I think the *Escaped Cock* MS. is all right. Curtis Brown now has it in his safe in London, and says every post he is sending it to you, but hangs on to it in order to prevent my publishing it. He doesn't know I've got a duplicate. In my next I'll tell him to send it *at once*: though I don't divulge any plans. They were at me again to let the Fountain Press, or whatever it is, publish part I. separately, and I again said no! Persistent as the devil they are, to try to prevent one having anything done apart from *them*.

I have had proofs of twenty or so of my pictures – reproductions – some not bad, some to weep over. They talk of getting that book out by the end of the month.

Hope you are both cheerful and calm. Keep us posted as to your plans.

belle cose!   DHL

5085. To P. R. Stephensen, [18 May 1929]
Text: MS StaU; Munro 308–9.

Hotel Principe Alfonso, *Palma de Mallorca*, Spain
Sat. 18 May

Dear Stephensen

I sent back the signed sheets this morning from Palma, by registered book mail, as the parcel was accepted closed up exactly as it was, no ends would be opened, they said – only the English p[ost]-o[ffice] would have the right to look into it in England. But since they open everything, even registered letters, that are of any bulk, and since all your seals had been broken and the parcel looked into – they suspect silk smuggling, of course – it seems to me just the same. One of the unnumbered sheets seemed to me dirty and thumb-marked – the rest intact. Hope they arrive so.

Have you sent me the other five proofs? – and *Moses* and *Accident*? – Do! – The pictures on vellum aren't nearly so nice – too yellow. – I am very excited to see the book.

Ask Goldston what he wants to give me for the MS. of the Introd. If he wants to look at it first, he can – it is in Miss Pearn's charge, at Curtis Brown's office. I think it's a nice clean MS. I never sell MS – practically never – but this one might go to the Mandrake.

Yrs   D. H. Lawrence

5086. To Robert and Norah Nichols, 18 May 1929
Text: TMSC NWU; Huxley 800.

Hotel Principe Alfonso, Palma de Mallorca, Spain
18 May 1929

Dear Nichols and Mrs. Nichols

I was very sorry to hear from Nell[1] that you, Robert, had rather crocked up in Paris and gone on being crocked up in England. That's really too bad. Take it from me, you ought to live in the south, in the sun – not here, I think, but some place like Rapallo, where it's rather lovely, and not too far. I agree this isn't a good place for work. I have tried to paint two pictures – and each time it's been a failure and made me all on edge. So I accept the decree of destiny, and shall make no further attempt to work at all while I am in Spain.[2]

I think we shall leave this day fortnight on the boat for Alicante, and make a little tour of Spain, and then sail Barcelona to Genoa and look for a house in Italy. If we find one, I hope you'll come next winter within reach, that would be fun if we could see one another.

It is brilliant and sunny here, but the wind is still cold if you sit in it. We went to Cala Rajada[3] for a long week-end, with Mrs. Murray and Mrs. Leopold.[4] It is on the N.E. coast, and in some ways rather lovely, lonely clean little bays with pine trees down to the shore. But the queer raw wind caught my chest – yet the sun was amazing, so bright, the sea so pure. Mrs. Murray and Mrs. L. are leaving on Tuesday – we have been just four in the hotel – the tall waiter has gone to Paris. Now we shall be alone with an elderly American man who giggles and is a fool.[5] But not for long.

Send us a line and I do hope you are better. I still duly eat the Bemax for breakfast – 'Begin Breakfast etc. –' and I think of you each time.

Many good wishes from us both.   D. H. Lawrence

5087. To Max Mohr, 18 May 1929
Text: MS HMohr; cited in Mohr 35.

Hotel Principe Alfonso. *Palma de Mallorca*, Spanien[6]
18 May 1929

Dear Max Mohr

It is such a long time since you have written, I wonder if anything has gone wrong. I hope not. How are you all at Wolfsgrube? Why have you never sent a line?

---

[1] Probably William Nell whom DHL (and presumably Nichols) met in Mallorca (see Letter 5121); nothing further is known of him.
[2] DHL was to write at least the first fifty-three poems in *More Pansies* before leaving Mallorca.
[3] Cala Ratjada.   [4] Unidentified.   [5] Unidentified.   [6] Spanien] Spagna

We are here by the sea on Mallorca, and like it very well, but don't want to live here. In July, when it gets hot, we shall come north again. Meanwhile it is very nice here.

Have you done anything about *Lady Chatterley?* I suppose not, or you would have told me. Yesterday I had a letter from a

Dr. Felix Abraham, *Berlin. N. W. 40,* in den Zelten. 9A.

saying he would like to translate the book, and could find a publisher, if I had not made any other arrangement. He says: 'Ich selbst bin Arzt an einem wissenschaftlichen Institut, und auf Sexualwissenschaftlichem gebiete tätig. Der Verlag des Buches wäre mir durch meine Beziehungen wesentlich erleichtert'.[1] – I shall tell him that you thought of undertaking the translation, but that perhaps you have given up the idea. If you still want to do the translation, will you send him a line and so settle the matter?

I expect we shall stay here a week or two longer, so do write and tell me how you are and what are your plans. I am so afraid you may be ill, or something gone wrong.

Yours Sincerely   D. H. Lawrence

5088. To John Young-Hunter, 19 May 1929
Text: MS Anon; Unpublished.

Palma de Mallorca. Spain
19 May 1929

Dear Jack Young Hunter[2]

Your letter came on here. It is rather bitter to sell that ranch, or even think of it, we loved it so much. Yet it seems best. It is so far away, the immigration laws are so tiresome, and individually, I know I belong to Europe, not to U.S.A. – so what's the good hanging on!

But Miss Brett is there – she's looked after the place these three years, and loves it too: and she says *she* wants to buy it, and will give five thousand dollars – which, I admit, seems a highish price. But where is she to get the money? I don't believe she can raise it. And perhaps she isn't quite serious about it. You might write to her:

Hon Dorothy Brett. c/o Del Monte Ranch. *Questa*

and ask her. – And ask her anyhow if she'd let you spend the month of August there – she might like it. As for rent for that month, we don't want any, but

---

[1] 'I am myself a doctor at a scientific institute, and working in the field of the science of sexuality. My connections would considerably simplify the publication of the book'.
[2] John ('Jack') Young-Hunter (1874–1955), Scottish-born portrait painter living in Taos. His land bordered Mabel Luhan's. m. 1921, Eva ('Eve') Renz Schroeer (1894?–1963). (See *Letters,* v. 89 n. 5.)

tell Brett you'll give her something if she wants it – I suppose, if you bought the place, you'd take it as it stands, with what furniture there is, horses, saddles, the old buggy and all. We'd just get our personal things removed, and a few Mexican blankets, things like that. – I had rather nice tools – hope they're still there. We spent a good bit on the place, one way and another.

Well, see Brett about it – or write her – and then let me know the result. We shall be moving around, so write
                    c/o Curtis Brown, 6 Henrietta St. Covent Garden W.C.2.
– I wish so much we could be there again, and ride around in that marvellous country. But the gods seem against it – and one can't lead two lives at once. But it seems like losing one's youth and glamour of freedom, to part with Lobo.[1] But if you had the place, you'd let us come and stay a bit, I know, if ever we were in New Mexico.

Regards to you both from us   D. H. Lawrence

5089. To Hon. Dorothy Brett, 19 May 1929
Text: MS UCin; Postmark, Palma [...] MAY 29; Moore 1153.

Palma de Mallorca. Spain.
19 May 1929

Dear Brett,

We had a letter from Jack Young Hunter asking if we would sell him the ranch, and to name the price, and he would pay cash down. He also said would we *rent* it him for this month of August. – I have written and said that you told me you wanted to buy the place, that you offered five thousand, that I thought it was a rather high price – and would he write to you to know if you are serious about it. Also I told him to ask you if you would care to let him and his wife stay on the ranch for the month of August anyhow, that I didn't want any rent, but he might pay *you* a little if he – and you – wished. So that's that!

Bitter as it is, and like parting with a lovely stretch of one's youth, it seems to me best to sell the ranch. I feel as if destiny didn't intend me to come back, not permanently, at all. And if we only came for a month or two, we could have a house in Taos.

Now let us know about yourself. If you still want the ranch, can you raise the money? You see Young Hunter would pay on the nail, and Frieda would be glad, because we shall have to get a house now, and she could get a nice place and fix it up with the ranch money. We shall go back to Italy and get a place there – D. V. – It seems the only feasible thing to do. So let us know.

---

[1] 'Lobo' (Wolf) was the original name of the ranch on Lobo Mountain which DHL renamed Kiowa after the local tribe of Indians.

We want to leave here in a fortnight or so, take a little tour in Spain if possible – then take a ship to Italy, to Genoa, and find a house in some healthy place. It seems the best thing to do – My health improves, but *very* slowly, and the cough is a great nuisance. I wish it was better. – But still I must be thankful it doesn't get worse.

I feel it's no good trying to go against one's destiny – and I feel my destiny doesn't let me come back to the ranch – and would never let me come there to stay permanently.

If we sell the place we'll just take out our personal things, blankets, best books etc., and leave all the rest. – But it's sad, for all that.

DHL

Did you collect my MSS? – and the deeds?
I'm telling Mabel about Young Hunter's offer.

5090. To Mabel Dodge Luhan, [19 May 1929]
Text: MS Brill; Luhan 345–6.

Palma de Mallorca. Spain.
20 May 1929[1]

Dear Mabel,

Yes, I think I had all your letters safely – and I have written several.

We heard from Jack Young Hunter this morning that he would like to buy the ranch – would like anyhow to rent it for August to try it out. I have asked him to write to Brett about *her* intentions. I have written her also. She said I was to make *her* the first offer, if ever we thought of selling, and she would pay five thousand dollars. That is a good price – perhaps too much. – But could she ever raise the money? It's no good selling her the place if she hasn't a sou. Of course one would only want a fair price from her. What do you consider would be fair? We'd sell right out, horses, saddles, furniture – only take away our personal things. If there is anything of yours, you could reclaim it.

Jack Young Hunter said he would pay cash down, and that would be nice, because we shall have to get a house, and then Frieda could fix it up as she liked, with the ranch money.

It is bitter to sell the ranch, it is like parting with one's youth. Life is cruel, gives one things, then snatches one away and there is that awful bereft feeling. I don't want to talk about it.

We think to leave here in about a fortnight – perhaps make a little tour in Spain – then go to Italy to find a house. We must live in a house. We are tired

---

[1] It is clear from Letters 5088 and 5089 that DHL heard from Young-Hunter on 19 May 1929; since DHL declares that this letter was written on that day, he must have misdated it.

of hotels – My health is about the same – certainly no worse – but nothing to crack about.

If you come to Europe in the winter we might manage a little cruise in the Mediterranean – I should love that – go to Greece, and the isles of Greece, and Crete and Cyprus and perhaps Jerusalem – just move on in short flights.

You see, even if I was really well again, I don't think I should want to come to America to *live* – though I'd dearly love to come to New Mexico for a year or so. But the authorities are so hateful.

Are my MSS. rescued from the ranch, I wonder – and the deeds?

As one gets older, one's choice in life gets limited – one is not free to choose any more.

DHL

5091. To Harry Crosby, 20 May 1929
Text: MS IEduc: Postmark, Palma 21 MAY 29; Lacy, *Escaped Cock* 75–6.

Hotel Principe Alfonso, *Palma de Mallorca*, Spain
20 May 1929

Dear Harry

Yours today – and didn't I give you the *complete* MS. of *Escaped Cock?* – was it only the second half? Curtis Brown, the old devil doesn't forward the full typescript – ask Caresse would she mind writing him as follows – 'Mr Lawrence asked me to take charge of the complete MS. of *Escaped Cock*, and I am a little anxious that it does not turn up. Will you please tell me if you have sent it already, or if you are sending it' – That'll get it out of him. Meanwhile I send you my handwritten MS. of the first part, which I found in my bag, and which I want you to accept from me as a small gift. – Then further I shall have sent to you the written MS. of the second part, which also please accept from me, together with *corrected typescript* of first part.[1] These are in the hands of a reliable friend in London, but she is in S. of France for another week, I believe – then going back.[2] It would be well to print from this corrected typescript – but you can begin from my handwritten script, because only the end is changed just a trifle: that is, if you want. (When I look at the MS. – I find it is rather mixed – I can't remember exactly what I did with it. Of course one could easily get a copy of *The Forum*, containing the story: spring 1928. But the MS will come from London.)

---

[1] After DHL's death Caresse Crosby refused to return these MSS to Frieda on the grounds that they had been a gift to Harry. See *Frieda Lawrence and her Circle*, ed. Harry T. Moore and Dale B. Montague, 1981, pp. 39–41.

[2] The 'reliable friend' was Enid Hilton who sent the MS to Caresse Crosby, 7 June. See letter following and Lacy, *Escaped Cock* 76.

Frederick Carter

Edward Dahlberg, 1932

P. R. Stephensen, 1929

Rhys Davies, from a drawing by William Roberts, 1927

Sylvia Beach, c. 1930

Marianne Moore, c. 1935, from a photograph by Arthur Steiner

Brewster Ghiselin, Autumn 1928

Low cartoon, *Evening Standard*, 26 February 1929

David Lederhandler, c. 1940

Edward Titus

Rebecca West, c. 1932

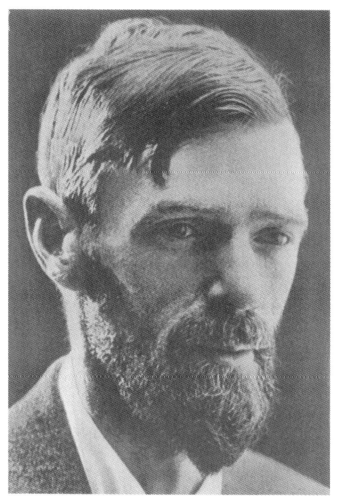

D. H. Lawrence, from a photograph by Ernesto Guardia, at Palma, 1929

Caresse Crosby, at the Moulin du Soleil, Easter 1929, from a
photograph by Lawrence

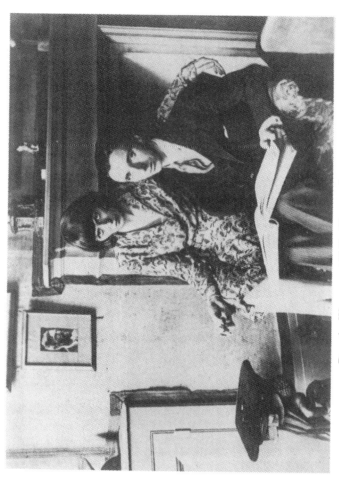

Dorothy Warren and Philip Trotter, August 1929

The Warren Gallery Exhibition, July 1929. The paintings are, l. to r., *Flight Back into Paradise*, *Close-Up [Kiss]*, *Resurrection* and *Red Willow Trees*.

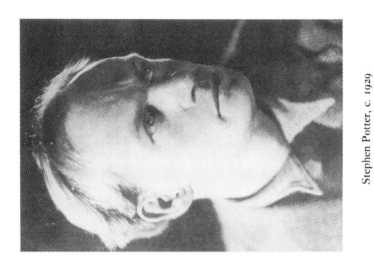

Stephen Potter, c. 1929

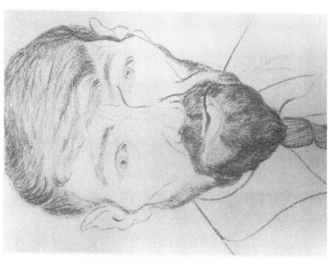

D. H. Lawrence: self-portrait, June 1929

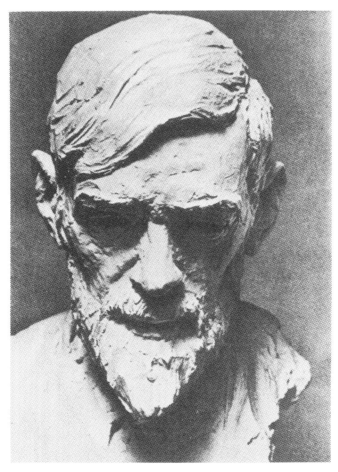

D. H. Lawrence: bust by Jo Davidson, February 1930

D. H. Lawrence's letter to Ada Clarke, 30 January 1930 (see pp. 631–2);
someone (unidentified) added '(Ada)'

I wrote Caresse and hope she had it. I think we shall try and make a little tour in Spain, if my health holds up – it's pretty good here – and then sail Barcelona to Genoa. Frieda does want a house – and in Italy – so we'd better go and find one. But we shan't go far from the sea, so do sail and see us – fun! Good that Constance – la comtesse[1] – has her divorce – but tell her to spend a year in contemplation before she starts marrying again. Marriage is a treacherous stimulant.

It's all summer here, so the restlessness of spring has gone by. I find I can be very successfully lazy – in fact I don't do a thing but eat and sleep and chatter. – Allanah Harper sounded – in letters – so brisk, that I'm surprised she has faded out.[2] As for the four seas, that's too many – get your MS. back and do it *Narcisse*. I hate *all* publishers – and agents.

Hope you are serene – with all the asses and lasses, Narcisse[3] and Caresses.

DHL

Frieda would love a little gramophone, but *no* Joyce,[4] – and please, not till we get a house – don't give us a single thing, not even a book, not a post-card, while we are still living in and out of bags.

DHL

5092. To Enid Hilton, 20 May 1929
Text: MS UCLA; Huxley 802.

Hotel Principe Alfonso, *Palma de Mallorca*, Spain

20 May 1929

Dear Enid

I wonder if you are still there – send me a line if you get this. It was very nice of you to send all the information – have written it down in my book. But it doesn't look as if it would easily get hot. It's lovely and sunny here, but not a bit too hot – very nice, in fact.

---

[1] Constance Crowninshield Coolidge Atherton, Comtesse de Jumilhac. See Wolff, *Black Sun*, p. 214ff.

[2] Allanah Harper (1904–92) founded the magazine *Echanges* (which ran December 1929–December 1931); DHL's introduction to *Chariot of the Sun* appeared in the first issue as 'Chaos in Poetry'.

[3] Narcisse was one of Crosby's whippets.

[4] 'One night [in Paris, April 1929] Frieda sat alone in a corner, listening again and again to Bessie Smith's "Empty Bed Blues", which Lawrence so despised. Finally [he] erupted and smashed the record across Frieda's head. Harry immediately promised to replace the record, and to buy Frieda a phonograph to play it upon. So he did – and Lawrence never forgave the kindness' (Wolff, *Black Sun*, p. 234). In 1928 Crosby had played for DHL 'a recording of James Joyce reading from *Ulysses*, and Lawrence had said of Harry's most revered idol, "Yes, I thought so, a preacher a Jesuit preacher who believes in the cross upsidedown." Earlier, Lawrence had told Harry that Joyce "bores me stiff – too terribly would-be and done-on-purpose, utterly without spontaneity or real life"' (ibid., p. 206).

We think of staying another fortnight, then doing a little tour in Spain, if it won't be too strenuous, and then taking a boat to Genoa. Frieda of course pines for the Mirenda, or something like it – so I think the best we can do is to go to Italy and find ourselves a *proper* house – not a half, like the Mirenda – and fit it up for good and for keeps. I think, all in all, that's the best – and Italy most suitable. We may sell the ranch.

When you go back to London will you please post for me the complete MSS of *The Escaped Cock* – both parts – to

Mrs Harry Crosby, 19 rue de Lille, *Paris. 7e.*

They are rather important, so please register them safely.

And I expect you'll find the exhibition about ready to open. I've had 21 – of the proofs of my pictures – some of the reproductions quite good – I think it will make a stunning book – wish I could give you one, but my poor six copies are all demanded, what with family and obligations.

I do hope you've had a jolly holiday – later on you must come where we are.

regards to both   D. H. Lawrence

5093. To Martin Secker, 20 May 1929
Text: MS UInd; Postmark, [. . .] 21 MAY 29; Secker 119–20.

Hotel Principe Alfonso, *Palma de Mallorca*, Spain
20 May 1929

Dear Secker

I hope you got the agreement via Curtis Brown – I sent it almost two weeks ago – and I hope it's all right. –

I notice your office has forwarded my last letters to Barcelona. Do please use this address, as Thomas Cook is most unreliable.

Would you please send me those poems you are omitting from the *Pansies* book: either those in my typescript MS. or copies. I want to keep copies, and perhaps publish this dozen as a tiny private book, to show what John Hop hops on.

I think we'll stay here another fortnight anyhow – it's very nice – then if my health is good enough, do a little tour in Spain – a bit strenuous. Then we'd take a boat to Genoa, because we both feel that after all Italy is best to *live* in, though these places are very nice for a while. So we'll go and look for a house if possible before the real hot weather comes – a house that we can keep a long time, I hope, and make it nice and buy furniture and all that. Seems to me I'd best have a proper place to live in.

It's splendid weather here, and quite cool – much cooler than you'd expect.

regards   D. H. Lawrence

5094. To Catherine Carswell, 20 May 1929
Text: MS YU; Unpublished.

Hotel Principe Alfonso, *Palma de Mallorca*, Spain
20 May 1929

My dear Catherine[1]

Yours today – Take it for granted everything Maria says is a gross exaggeration, and everything via the Franchettis a misrepresentation.[2] He's going dotty, anyhow. But I did have flu – a low, horrid flu, in Paris – pulls one down. Am much better here. Cough rather a nuisance, so don't walk much, but eat well and sleep well and feel alright in myself. I think I'm a tough and stringy bird.

I want you to finish the Burns book, very much indeed – it's mere desperation when I ejaculate 'she'll never finish it.'[3] I think one has to forego the outer world a good bit, and make peace inside oneself in one's soul. The outside world wears one to a shred. So do be still and *inward* – then you won't get worn.

Am sorry about Don – it's not his line, to be ill. He mustn't be ill, leave it to me, who am more used to it.

I think they'll show my pictures soon, in the Warren Gallery in Maddox St – and I do hope you'll go and see them. The reproductions for the book are nearly all made – colour – some not bad, some disappointing.

It's quite nice here – very sunny – and quite cool still – But I think on the whole I like Italy better – and Frieda is moaning for a house – so I think we'll leave in about a fortnight, and go back to Italy, sail to Genoa, and look for a house. I don't know if we shall come north – not to England, anyhow. The detectives said, over that fuss at Curtis Brown's office about my poems etc – that 'if Lawrence lands in England he will be at once arrested'. So Lawrence had perhaps better continue to give his native land a wide berth.

Am very sorry about Gordon[4] – my God, we're growing old, or something.

DHL

---

[1] Catherine Roxburgh Carswell (1879–1946), novelist, biographer and journalist. She and her husband Donald Carswell (1882–1940), a barrister, had been friends of DHL since 1914. Her enthusiastic review of *The Rainbow* in the *Glasgow Herald*, in 1915, put an end to her work for that paper; her *The Savage Pilgrimage* (1932) was the first full biography of DHL. See *Letters*, ii. 187 n. 5.

[2] Baron Luigi Franchetti, professional pianist, and his wife Yvonne (née Palavicino, and later Mrs Hamish Hamilton); both were close friends of the Aldous Huxleys; Yvonne was Catherine Carswell's cousin. For the background to DHL's assertions see *Letters*, vi. 385–7.

[3] Catherine Carswell's *Life of Robert Burns* was finished by the late summer and published in October 1930 with the dedication: 'Without D. H. Lawrence, my friend, and Donald Carswell, my husband, this book could not have been. I therefore inscribe it to them both.' See *The Savage Pilgrimage* (Cambridge, 1981), pp. xx–xxii.

[4] George Gordon MacFarlane (1885–1949), novelist, Catherine Carswell's younger brother. See *Letters*, iii. 146 n. 4.

5095. To John Middleton Murry, 20 May 1929
Text: MS NYPL; cited in Murry, *New Adelphi*, iii. 461.

Hotel Principe Alfonso, *Palma de Mallorca*, Spain
20 May 1929

Dear Jack

Your letter came on here[1] – I had your other one, too, with photographs of the children – felt so distressed about your wife.

But you see, my dear chap, leaving aside all my impatience and 'don't care,' I know too well that we 'missed it', as you put it. I don't understand you, your workings are beyond me. And you don't get me. You said in your review of my poems: 'this is not life, life is not like that.'[2] And you have the same attitude to the real me. Life is not like that – ergo, there is no such animal. Hence my 'don't care'. I am tired of being told there is no such animal, by animals who are merely different. If I am a giraffe, and the ordinary Englishmen who write about me and say they know me are nice well-behaved dogs, there it is, the animals are different. And the me that you say you love is not me, but an idol of your own imagination. Believe me, you don't love me. The animal that I am you instinctively dislike – just as all the Lynds and Squires and Eliots and Goulds instinctively dislike it[3] – and you all say there's no such animal, and if there is there ought not to be – so why not stick to your position. If I am the only man in your life, it is not because I am I, but merely because I provided the speck of dust on which you formed your crystal of an imaginary man! We don't know one another – if you knew *how* little we know one another! And let's not pretend. By pretending a bit, we had some jolly times, in the past. But we all had to pretend a bit – and we could none of us

---

[1] Extracts from two letters from Murry to Brett (MSS UCin) – the first in 1929 but undated, the second on 26 September 1929, and both torn – illustrate the views to which DHL was replying in this, his last, letter to Murry:

> I toil away; and watch, with a sort of resignation, the high hopes I once had of Lawrence fade away. It can't be helped. L. has his destiny, you yours, I mine ... I hate all this cheap-jack publicity which Lawrence now seems made for. There's something vulgar about this parade of contempt for everybody & everything. But what odds? We must all go our own ways.

> I am sorry for Lawrence's parting from me – that cut me deepe[st?] but it is he & not I who will suffer – now. I have tried to [make] advances to him (because I heard he was ill) but they were rep[ulsed] and there was nothing in me that *cared* any more. To be beyond *caring*: then one begins to learn about love. [   ] Lawrence: I love you. And it doesn't matter one halfpenny w[hat] you think of me.

[2] Murry did not use these words though they sum up one theme in his review of *Collected Poems* (see p. 166 n. 1).

[3] Robert Wilson Lynd (1879–1949); (Sir) John Collings Squire (1884–1958); Thomas Stearns Eliot (1888–1965); and Gerald Gould (1885–1936): all were (among other things) literary editors, poets and reviewers (see Draper, *The Critical Heritage*, pp. 91–2, 275–7, 299–302). For Squire see also *Letters*, vi. 617 and n. 3, and for Gould ibid., 422 and n. 2.

keep it up. Believe me, we belong to different worlds, different ways of consciousness, you and I, and the best we can do is to let one another alone, for
ever and ever. We are a dissonance.

My health is a great nuisance, but by no means as bad as all that, and I have
no idea of passing out. We want to leave next week for a short tour in Spain –
then go north. So don't think of coming to Mallorca.[1] It is no good our
meeting – even when we are immortal spirits, we shall dwell in different
Hades. Why not accept it. But I do hope your wife is getting better and the
children are well and gay.

DHL

5096. To Nancy Pearn, 21 May 1929
Text: MS UT; Unpublished.

Hotel Principe Alfonso, *Palma de Mallorca*, Spain
21 May 1929
Dear Nancy Pearn[2]

That certainly is meagre from Titus: but then he's a meagre person: I gave
him the article because he is doing a cheap edition of my novel for me – or
managing it. So let him go.

The Mr Hastings of the *Architectural Review* wrote that he likes the 'Wall
Pictures' article very much and will pay twenty guineas. Good for him.

I suppose the alarm of my being ill came from Maria Huxley – she is
nothing if not wildly exaggerating. True I had Paris grippe when I stayed
with them – and it has left me coughing a bit extra – but on the whole I'm all
right – not a bloomin' carnation, but there –

Would you ask Pollinger if he had my last letter – written about a fortnight
ago, and enclosing the signed agreements for Secker? Because I've had no
sound from him. And ask him to be sure to see that the book of pictures is
properly copyrighted – it is almost ready – I've got proofs of all the pictures
except two. I hope you'll go and see my show, when Dorothy Warren opens
it, which she should do about 30th of this month.

Somehow this is a place in which I neither want to write nor paint – no
impulse at all – so I just leave it. My wife still moaning for a house – so I

---

[1] Having heard that DHL was terminally ill, Murry offered to visit Mallorca in order to see him
(Murry, *Reminiscences of D. H. Lawrence*, 1933, p. 208).

[2] DHL was replying to Nancy Pearn's letter, 17 May 1929 (TMSC UT):

Edward Titus says that the most he has been counting on having to pay for your article is Five
Guineas. Seems a miserable amount, but I gather from your letter that you weren't expecting
him to pay much.
     What a fright we got over that rumour that you were ill, but it seems from all accounts that
you were never better. I suppose you must have been heard to sneeze one day!
                                                                          Yours ever

suppose we shall go back to Italy before it gets too hot, and look for one. Wonder what'll be the result!

You didn't try any of the *Pansies* poems on the magazines? – The *Dial* has done one, and is doing another batch of ten – I just had proofs and $180. – I also had proofs of the *Studio* article.[1]

Regards. D. H. Lawrence

Have this minute got P's letter with agreement and proofs enclosed – so that's all right.

DHL

I wish you'd tell Pollinger, if he doesn't care to mail the *Escaped Cock* MSS – both parts, please – to Mrs Crosby, please to give it to Koteliansky.

I believe the hotel boy Antonio sometimes loses !! the letters here. Did you get one from my wife?[2]

5097. To Laurence Pollinger, 22 May 1929
Text: MS UT; cited in Huxley 803.

Hotel Principe Alfonso. Palma de Mallorca, Spain
22 May 1929

Dear Pollinger

I refuse to omit the three poems: 'What Matters' (p. 51) 'Be a demon' (p. 65) and 'Jeune Fille' (p. 66), because it seems to me there is absolutely nothing in them that could bring a censor down. *Will you read them and tell me if you don't agree.* I am perfectly willing to be reasonable, but Secker is trying to scotch me.[3]

---

[1] 'Making Pictures'.

[2] Pearn replied on 24 May 1929 (TMSC UT):

> Our latest letters have crossed: yours of May 21st arriving today. I got Mrs D.H.L.'s letter on Tuesday, so don't blame the hotel boy this time ...
> So far I have done nothing about the poems, as it was generally felt it would be better to let the clamour die down first. I have not even seen a copy. I'll get Pollinger to try and get hold of one from Secker.
> Most certainly I am planning to go to your show. And how relieved I am to hear that Maria was so exaggerated. Will you be coming back to Italy, I wonder, in time for me to get a sight of you, if, as perchance may be, I come that way this year?
> Yours ever

[3] Secker had written to Pollinger, 15 May 1929:

> Here are two sets of slip proofs of "Pansies". All that D.H.L. is asked to do is to re-write one stanza of a poem (as already agreed) slip 5, and to make one verbal alteration, as suggested, on slip 6. But I should also like to suggest that three poems should be omitted and included instead in Lawrence's privately printed Florence edition. These three poems are "What Matters" slip 51, "Be a Demon" slip 62 and "Jeune Fille" slip 66. All these three obviously need alteration,

Also, I refuse to sign 250 sheets unless I share equally with Secker in the profits of signing. I made that clear over *Collected Poems*. I will not merely sign money into Martin Secker's pocket. 250 copies at two guineas is 500 guineas: 250 copies at 10/6 each is 125 guineas: therefore the sheer profit from the signatures alone is 375 guineas: for I take it that Secker is just having the ordinary 10/6 edition signed up, as he did in *Collected Poems*. If this is so, then allowing one-third of those profits to the bookseller, then Secker gets also one-third and I one-third, which will be £125 – not pounds, but guineas. Over and above this I get the current 15% royalty on the signed copies. – If Secker is printing a more expensive edition of 250, for signing, then we can again discuss the matter. But I insist on having ⅓ of the gross profits deriving from the signatures, on having this paid me as a fee, free from government tax. – I don't mind if you take 10% of it, if you fix the matter for me. But I won't sign under any other conditions.

I'm fed up with Secker.

I think these corrected galleys ought to go to Knopf.[1] The printer won't take more than a day to correct them.

But I tell you, I have *struck*: I will not be merely made use of by publishers.

I accept Cape's decision about *Twilight in Italy* because it is an old book, but I will never again agree to such terms. I accept too about *Collected Poems*, but I think Cape is *mean* not to raise the royalty to 15% after 3,000. He could do so in all fairness.

I wish you would please send the complete MS. of *The Escaped Cock* Part I and Part II both, to

Mrs Harry Crosby, 19 rue de Lille. Paris.7*e*.

– at once: or, if you do not care to mail this MS., will you please give it to Koteliansky to hold for me. I should prefer it sent to Paris.

I hope Bradley can fix up with Gallimard – It would be a good thing to have a real Paris office, and an active office in Germany.

You didn't attach the letter from Jack Kahane.[2] What was it?

I wish very much it could be found out who is actually back of those pirated editions of *Sun* and *Lady C* in Philadelphia, because I am told once or twice that Harold T. Mason of the Centaur Bookshop, who published my *Bibliography* and *Reflections on the Death of a Porcupine* – and whom I know personally, and who professes the greatest friendship for me, is responsible for both piracies. The Philadelphia bootleg edition of *Lady Chatterley* has a water-marked paper, and I am told the origin of the edition could be traced by

---

and I think it would be much easier and probably more satisfactory from the author's point of view to adopt the course I suggest. (Secker Letter-Book, UIll)
[1] Knopf published the first American edn, 27 September 1929.   [2] Unidentified.

that. I don't know if it is the same with *Sun*. But by hook or crook I must find out, for I could never rest, or let Mason rest, if I thought the Centaur Bookshop was responsible for such Judas blackguardry.

No, I am not going to die just yet, I hope. My bronchials have been acting up and making me swear, these last ten days – but I eat my dinner as usual, and go out to tea and luncheon here and there. How anxious they must be to have me dead, my fellow scribes and countrymen! I won't oblige if I can help.

I hear Stephensen's book of my pictures is nearly ready – and apparently he has orders for half of them – perhaps more by now, this was two weeks ago – and all the ten vellum copies at 50 guineas ordered. Be sure and see the book is properly copyrighted.

We have decided against taking a house here – though it's nice, and would be easy. But my wife likes Italy so much better – and I think I do, really. So probably in a fortnight we shall sail to Marseilles and then to Genoa, and look for a house in one or other of the old Italian haunts. I do want to find a place that we can keep at least for some years.

I enclose the various contracts. Will you please get Secker to initial the alteration along with my initials.

If Secker does *250 signed Pansies*, then I shan't do [. . .] an edition of the whole book – only a little booklet of the dozen omitted poems – that is my intention at the present, anyhow.

Will you get Cape to initial the alteration on the contracts.

Well, I hope we'll smooth out all these little businesses for the moment – but this country makes one feel extra pugnacious and disinclined for compliance.

regards   D. H. Lawrence

You will see I altered the 250 back to 150, for the nonce!

5098. To Martin Secker, [23 May 1929]
Text: MS UInd; PC v. 'Principe Alfonso Hotel' – Palma de Mallorca. *Vista posterior*; Postmark, Barcelona 24 M[AY] 29; Secker 118.

Palma.
Thursday

We shall probably be taking the ship to Marseille on June 4th, so if you want me to sign any sheets, try to send them before then, by book post, with wrapper all ready for return – Frieda wants to find herself a house before the hot weather starts – in Italy somewhere – so we'll have to be moving if we're to do it.

Regards to Rina and the boy.   D. H. Lawrence

Of course you could send the sheets to Marseille.

5099. To Margaret King, [23 May 1929]
Text: MS Sagar; PC v. 'Principe Alfonso Hotel' – Palma de Mallorca. *Vista posterior*;
Postmark, Barcelona 24 MAY 29; Unpublished.

[Hotel Principe Alfonso, Palma de Mallorca, Spain]
Thursday

Thanks for your letter – we had never promised definitely to go back to Kesselmatte – only said we might. I think we shall sail on June 4th to Marseille, because Frieda wants to find herself a house in Italy before the hot weather really starts – so we shall have to move if she's to do it. – I have had proofs of all my pictures except one – so the book will probably be ready about June 1st – and the show ought to open about the same date – I still haven't heard definitely. It will be quite a fine book – shall either have one sent or you can pick it up in London.

All well here: love!   DHL

5100. To Ada Clarke, [23 May 1929]
Text: MS Clarke; PC v. 'Principe Alfonso Hotel' – Palma de Mallorca. *Vista posterior*;
Postmark, Barcel[ona] 24 MAY 29; Lawrence–Gelder 175–6.

[Hotel Principe Alfonso, Palma de Mallorca, Spain]
Thursday

– Had your letter – how nice the greenhouse sounds! Hope you heard nothing of the silly rumour that I am ill – I'm perfectly all right. I expect Maria Huxley started it when she was in London. – We think of taking the ship to Marseille on June 4th – and going on to Italy – Frieda is so keen on finding a house before the hot weather starts, so we shall have to move soon. I think perhaps Italy is best to *live* in. – I've had proofs of all my pictures except one, so the book is nearly ready – promised for June 1st. – and the show ought to open about the same time, though I've had no definite date yet. The book will be rather fine – you can either pick up your copy in London or I'll have it sent. Weather lovely and cool.

Love   DHL

5101. To Enid Hilton, 25 May 1929
Text: MS UCLA; Unpublished.

Hotel Principe Alfonso, *Palma de Mallorca*, Spain
25 May 1929

Dear Enid

Yours today. We think of sailing to Marseille on June 4th., but am not sure.

This is to say that I am going to find out the cheapest price at which I can

buy my book of pictures – I have special terms – and so I shall let you have a
copy and you can pay me when you like or never." So hold on a bit.

We have had such a lovely day on a lonely bay under pine trees – it seems a
shame to go away; and I am so sorry you have to return to London.

DHL

5102. To P. R. Stephensen, [25 May 1929]
Text: MS UT; Munro 309.

Hotel Principe Alfonso. Palma de Mallorca, Spain
25 May

Dear Stephensen

Thanks for the four proofs – *Singing of Swans* and *Accident* are not very
good – but I knew they'd be difficult. But *Rape* and *Amazon* are quite good.
Now send me *Fauns and Nymphs* and *Moses* and it is finished.

When do you think you'll be ready? – did you get the signed sheets safely?
– do you know Dorothy Warren's plans? How many orders have you now?

And will you tell me how much you will charge me if I order one or two
extra copies. I take it you are giving me six mould-made and one vellum copy.
But I shall want to keep one of each kind – and I must give aw[ay]¹ more than
five, alas. Are you going to give the Huxleys a copy? – and Orioli, who sent
you the addresses? If not, I must give them. So tell me how much you'll
charge me per copy.

What about sending to America? Are you going to try the registered mail?
Because I too must send a copy to U.S.A. Let me know, will you?

Sincerely   D. H. Lawrence

I hope you are keeping the plates of the pictures, so we can publish a
cheaper edition later on – for which, if you like, I can write a quite different
introductory essay, more simple, more popular, and referring to the pictures
themselves. That would make quite another book of it.

5103. To Charles Lahr, 25 May 1929
Text: MS StaU; Postmark, [...]; Unpublished.

Hotel Principe Alfonso, *Palma de Mallorca*. Spain
25 May 1929

Dear Lahr

Yours today. I am in a bit of doubt about the poems. I had the proofs from
Secker and returned them a few days ago. He wants to leave out three more
poems: 'What matters'! – 'Be a Demon!' – and 'Jeune Fille'. I said No! – I

¹ MS torn.

would not agree. But if you are doing an edit., perhaps I shall consent. – Then he wants to do 250 signed at 2 guineas. I had agreed to 150, and he shoved in another 100 at the same price. He is an artful dodger of the worst sort, and I begin to think I don't like him very much myself. – But if he agrees to pay the proper sum down for signing the 250, I'll sign them – otherwise I won't. He wants to publish on or about June 30th. – and Knopf is to publish in New York as near to that date as possible. So that will secure the copyright in the two countries. – Now about a Red Lion edition[1] – you see I only stipulated with Secker that I should do on my own an edition of 250 copies, and that it should *follow* his first edition. It would take you more than a month to get yours out, in any case – when you can get your 'Introduction' from Jack Hutchinson. – Of course he, Hutchinson, must yield up that MS. It does not belong to him in any way whatsoever. But of course he'll *try* to hang on to it. – I don't mind whether I do a signed photograph or not – but I haven't got any photograph. I could have one taken in Palma and risk it – sign it and send it if it was good, and if it was no good, sign sheets. I'll get it taken next week, and see. – Meanwhile I'll wait for the next letter from Secker, before I decide whether I do only 250 copies myself – or 500. As for your share, I think if you take all the trouble you should have a bigger share in the profits. Would you like me to pay for the costs – I can easily do so? – If the wholesale price is 42/-, then the bookseller gets 14/- discount, I suppose – and the cost of production 2/- – (seems to me rather low estimate) – leaves 26/-, of which you must have a proper per-centage. It can't all come to me, as you said in your letter, because on the copies you sell to booksellers you won't get the ⅓ discount. You must have at least 6/- per copy besides – and that leaves me 20/-: which is perhaps too much. It is half the *gross* profits – and if you always got the other half, well and good, we share and share alike. But what about when you sell to the trade? – We must arrange this properly. – Then can we do a limited edition without stating the number? and without numbering the copies? It seems hardly fair. I must find a way out of this.

Kot. wrote me that the copies of Our Lady should now be six guineas, but I think it's better to go on at four. Don't you agree? How do you stand in that matter? Secker has never said he got his copy. I must write him about it.

Stephensen has sent me proofs of all the pictures except one – so that's well ahead.

I think we shall take the boat on June 4th. to Marseille. My wife very much wants to find a house in Italy before the hot weather really sets in, so if that is

---

[1] The location of Lahr's 'Progressive Bookshop' in Red Lion Square led to his nickname, 'the Lion', which DHL occasionally used.

to happen we must move soon. Don't write here, then, after June 1st. But I think in Marseille we shall stay in the Hotel du Louvre – will tell you for sure.

all good wishes   DHL

5104. To S. S. Koteliansky, 25 May 1929
Text: MS BL; Postmark, [. . .]29; Zytaruk 384–5.

Hotel Principe Alfonso. *Palma dè Mallorca*, Spain
25 May 1929

My dear Kot

Don't take any notice of my not having written – it was that I had grippe when I stayed with the Huxleys, and felt pretty rotten when I was with them, so lost track of most things for the time. I think one shouldn't stay with people – though they were very kind; – but it is best to keep one's very own atmosphere about one, and not be plunged in other peoples'.

I think Jack Hutchinson must yield up that typescript to you complete. He has no further right to it – he achieved very little – and of course it will have a certain value now, after all the fuss: Not that I care about *that*. Neither do I want the MS. trailing round in Hutchinson's possession.

I am a bit puzzled what to do about the poems. Secker sent me the proofs the other day, and wants to come out with his edition at 10/6 on June 30th or thereabout. He also wants to do 250 copies at two guineas. I had agreed to 150 copies, so he stuck in another 100 copies *at the* same price. Of course I jibbed – and shall not sign 250 unless the price is forthcoming. – But the trouble is, I only stipulated to print myself – that is, the Lion – 250 copies, and I don't like to go back on my word. – Of course Knopf is publishing the book identical with Secker's in U.S.A. – so that the copyright will be secured in both countries. I shall be my own pirate, this time – What do you think?

I think Stephensen will do pretty well with the book of paintings, if there is no interference. The reproductions are rather poor, in some cases – but it is very difficult getting them true.

We think to sail to Marseille on June 4th. Frieda is very anxious now to find a house, and on the whole, I think Italy is the best place. So we shall go there and look round, before the weather gets too hot. It's not at all hot here yet, but very nice – and I am pretty well, save that my cough is a curse and a nuisance.

I can hardly imagine the Cave nowadays it seems so remote. Murry wrote me a loving letter, but I told him it was no good. I think he's about at the end of himself.

I wonder if the election will make any difference? it may.[1]

DHL

I hear the Bibescos are on the island – hope they don't find me out.[2]

5105. To Laurence Pollinger, 25 May 1929
Text: MS UT; Unpublished.

Hotel Principe Alfonso, *Palma de Mallorca*, Spain

25 May 1929

Dear Pollinger

I have been thinking about Secker and his three poems – and if you agree with him that there is reason to leave them out, then be damned to it, leave them out. Don't let *me* make him frightened. – I suppose by now you have received the proofs and the three agreements. As for the number of signed copies, I think he'd better make it 150 as on the agreement at first. We've arranged for that. But if he is bent on 250 signed, then he must pay me properly.

But I think I shall also return to my original idea, and publish a *complete* edition of the poems with the original 'Introduction'. I stipulated that this should come out after Secker's edition – which it will – and be not more than 250 copies, and you said Secker agreed. But it would be much more profitable to me if I could make it 500 copies instead of 250. Do you think there would be any objection? I don't think my private edition of 500 would affect either Secker or Knopf: especially coming after theirs. – When, by the way, do you think Knopf will get the book out?

We want to leave here on June 4th for Marseille, by boat – arriving June 5th. – and I expect we shall stay in the Hotel du Louvre. It will be important for Secker to get the sheets for signing to me *quickly* – by book post, with wrapper inside for return. If he sends them in time I will do them here – otherwise they had best go to Marseille.

My wife is bent on leaving on June 4th. as she is so keen on finding a house in Italy to live in. Otherwise it's quite nice here.

ever   D. H. Lawrence[3]

---

[1] A General Election had been called for 30 May 1929 (it resulted in a defeat of the Conservative party and victory for Labour).

[2] Prince Antoine Bibesco (1878–1951), Romanian diplomat, and his wife Elizabeth (1897–1945). For DHL's attitude to Bibesco see *Letters*, iii. 315–18.

[3] When Pollinger received this he wrote at once to Secker; he in turn replied promptly, on 30 May 1929 (Secker Letter-Book, UIll):

As regards the signing of 250 copies, we agree to [DHL's] fee, provided it is understood that the royalty on these 250 copies is 15% of 10/6, the ordinary edition price. I think he intends this: it was the plan adopted in the case of "Collected Poems". As regards the three poems, we will agree to print them, since the author insists, but I hope he will oblige by altering the words marked.

5106. To Max Mohr, 25 May 1929
Text: MS HMohr; Mohr, Briefe 532–3.

Hotel Principe Alfonso, *Palma de Mallorca*, Spain

Dear Max Mohr   25 May 1929

I was glad to get your letter and to know you were all right. I'm sorry about your novel, that none of the damned publishers will print it. It's a pity they don't every single one go bankrupt, and stay there for evermore. But I am wondering what sort of weird fantasy your book is. When we get to a settled place, do send me the typescript that I can read it. And anyhow you have made money with comedies, and the roof is safe over your heads: thank God. Ist man arm, isst man Judendreck; ist man reich, lässt man Juden weg.[1] – As for *Lady C.*, I'm sorry you have such endless bothers, you must be bored stiff with the affair. Rhein verlag or Sauerverlag, damn all their eyes!

I too had great troubles with the *Police*! In England they seized the MSS. of my new book of poems, and there was a great row, questions in Parliament and so forth. Now the matter has more or less gone quiet – and Martin Secker is publishing the book with twelve poems omitted. I shall send you a copy. – However, I shall get a complete edition done at two guineas, *sub rosa*, in London. One must always fight the police and the censors, and fortunately there are always a few fighters 'under the rose.' Also in about a fortnight my book of paintings will come out – coloured reproductions of 26 paintings, and a long foreword on Modern art – more or less. The reproductions are not very good, I *do* wish they could have been done in Germany. However, they are the best they could manage. The book is to be sold at 10 guineas a copy, with ten copies on vellum – Pergament – at 50 guineas a copy. You know a guinea is 21 Mark. – 21 shillings. Well there were *sixty* orders for the copies at 50 guineas[2] – those on vellum. Of course only ten are printed. But this shows you the insanity of the modern collector of books. And a good author can't even get his work printed. Makes me tired! I hate this expensive edition business.

I think we shall take the boat on June 4th. to Marseille, and go from there to Italy, because my wife wants so badly to find a *house*, and she thinks Italy is best. Perhaps it is. Anyhow we can try. I like this island all right, and have been pretty well here, but the human life is dull. My cough is still a great nuisance, I wish it would get better. Yet I am a bit fatter, and stronger. I can hardly imagine you have still snow – it has been summer so long here.

I'll write again soon – regards to you all.

D. H. Lawrence

Harpers are all right, but rather old-fashioned.

[1] 'If one is poor, one eats Jew-shit; if one is rich, one ignores Jews.
[2] MS reads 'guines'.

5107. To Giuseppe Orioli, [25 May 1929]
Text: MS NWU; PC v. 'Principe Alfonso Hotel' – Palma de Mallorca. *Vista posterior*;
Postmark, [...] 25 MAY 29; Unpublished.

[Hotel Principe Alfonso, Palma de Mallorca, Spain]
Sat

I suppose you had my letter – yours crossed it. We think of taking the boat on
June 4th to Marseille, stay there a day or two, then come to Florence and take
some of our things and see if there is any house we should like. The fattore at
the Mirenda said, in the autumn, that he knew of some nice places which we
should like. But I think one ought to go a bit higher up than San Paolo – even
than Fiesole – perhaps in the Mugello direction.

Anyhow we shall see you soon – what fun!

DHL

5108. To Marianne Moore, 25 May 1929
Text: MS UT; Postmark, Palma 27 MAY 29; Unpublished.

Palma de Mallorca, Spain
25 May 1929

Dear Marianne Moore

Many thanks for sending the copies of the *Dial.* I think my 'Circus' poem
looked all right – and I hear people say they like it.[1]

Secker wants to get the book *Pansies* out on June 30th – and Knopf should
come out as near that date as possible. Secker insists on leaving out a dozen or
more of the poems – so probably there won't be much left for you to object to.
I get very weary of objections and the silly word 'filth' hurled at me – and am
quite thankful to be doing at present no work at all and so provoking no more
insults. – But since all the 'objectionable' (I can't see it though) poems are left
out, I left out the 'Introduction' too, and wrote just a tiny one to have done
with it.

At the end of June the book of reproductions (in colour) of my pictures will
appear – so we can expect a new shower of epithets. Basta la mossa![2]

D. H. Lawrence

5109. To David Lederhandler, 25 May 1929
Text: MSS UT and Rosenbach; Postmark, Palma 28 MAY [...]9; Huxley 803–4.

Palma de Mallorca, Spain
25 May 1929

Dear Mr Lederhandler

I think in Florence I have got some nice little essay or story in MS. that I

[1] Cf. Letter 5055 and n. 3.   [2] 'Any move on my part is enough!'

can send you for your $60. – since that is what you want. But it must wait awhile till I go to Italy, as the MSS. are locked in my private trunks, and I never sell any – I only sold one in my life, really – to a personal friend. Write to me again c/o Orioli to remind me, and I'll tell you what I've got, so you can choose.[1]

And I will give you these two pages of the rough draft of one or two of the *Pansies* poems – due to come out in book form just now. I shall burn the rest of the rough drafts – I hate such stuff about – but as I have nothing else, you can have these two pp. if you want them.[2] I'm sorry I crossed them out, but I did that to all the poems as I got them into shape.

Don't tell anybody I gave you these, or I shall have no peace.

Thanks for the news about the pirates. Perhaps we shall succeed in coming at something more definite, later on.

My book of pictures is ten guineas in English. It is nearly ready – and will be very nice, I think.

Yours Sincerely   D. H. Lawrence

5110. To Roy Britnell, 26 May 1929
Text: MS UN; Unpublished.

Palma de Mallorca. Spain.
26 May 1929

Dear Mr Britnell[3]

I am very sorry Orioli made that mistake and wrote as he did. I make a note

---

[1] On 16 July 1929 Orioli wrote to Lederhandler (MS Rosenbach): 'Mr Lawrence has asked me to send you a MS of him. I have just posted as registered book post. Mr Lawrence hopes you will find it to your taste. Mr Lawrence just left for Germany and his letters will be forwarded from here.' Presumably the MS was 'None of That' (Roberts E275a) for which Lederhandler paid $15.00 (information from the Rosenbach Museum & Library). The other MSS DHL sold previously were *Sun*, 'The Man Who Loved Islands' and some poems, bound up together, to Harry Crosby (see *Letters*, vi. 388–9).

[2] In fact DHL also gave two pages of autograph MS of *Pansies* to Achsah Brewster (Roberts E302b).

[3] See p. 218 n. 4; see also *Letters*, vi. 574 n. 1. DHL was responding to Britnell's letter of 30 April 1929 (MS UCLA):

Dear Mr Lawrence; –

  Some few weeks ago your agent Orioli wrote me that unless I made immediate remittance for a copy of "Lady Chatterley's Lover" that you had sent me he or you were going to complain to the London trade papers and the rest of it.

  My credit is good, and while I had no fear that Orioli could do my name any damage, I remitted in a hurry a cheque on London for £1–14–0. This cheque was made payable to you and is endorsed by you.

  Since remitting this cheque on London, I have had time to trace and find that I remitted, when ordering the book, a cheque on Toronto payable to yourself for $8.50. I now have the of the cheques I endorse,[1] and have both yours down: but of course I don't know what orders are received and fulfilled, so I had no idea one was duplicate. I hasten to return the £1.14.0, and repeat my regrets; and I will ask Orioli to send you a line of apology.

Yours Sincerely   D. H. Lawrence

5111. To Hon. Dorothy Brett, [26 May 1929]
Text: MS UCin; PC v. 'Principe Alfonso Hotel' – Palma de Mallorca. *Vista posterior*; Postmark, Palma 29 MAY 29; Irvine, *DHL Review*, ix. 93.

[Hotel Principe Alfonso, Palma de Mallorca, Spain]
26 May

Just a line to say that my book of pictures will be out in about a fortnight – at ten guineas a copy – but I am going to try to send you a copy. I shall wait however to see if the way is all clear – so if there is a bit of delay you will understand. Very pleasant on this island, and I think it really agrees with me. Hope you are all settled in and safe.

DHL

5112. To Maurice Speiser, 26 May 1929
Text: TMSC NWU; Huxley 804–5.
To Speiser & Speiser.

Palma de Mallorca, Spain.
26 May 1929.

My dear Mr. Speiser,[2]

That is very kind of you, to say you will try to hunt out the pirates of *Lady Chatterley's Lover* and of *Sun*. Perhaps you disapprove of my novel – if you have read it – myself, naturally, I stand by it, through all time. But it would be a service to literature if this unabashed piracy were stopped, or even checked. There have appeared at least three pirated editions of *Lady Chatter-*

cheque in front of me and same bears your endorsement in the same manner as the later cheque and also the endorsement of the Bankers Trust Co., Haskard Casardi & Co., Ltd.,

I shall return the cheques to you if you wish and I must ask you to mail me a refund for $8.50 on Toronto or £1–14–0 on London or failing this mail me another copy of your book.

Please let me hear from you by return.

Sincerely yours,

DHL recorded in 'Memoranda' (MS NWU) that he had returned the money as Britnell 'had paid twice for his copy. Palma. 26 May 1929'.

[1] endorse] sign
[2] The name 'Maurice B. Speiser' has been added in an unknown hand on the typescript; Speiser remains unidentified though he was presumably a member of an American law firm (possibly in Philadelphia and known to Lederhandler).

ley's Lover in U.S.A. – I have seen copies of two. But I have not seen a copy of the first the Philadelphia bootleg edition, though I have a description of it – and I hear Terence B. Holiday sells it steadily. It ought to be more easy to lay hold of the pirates of *Sun*, a short story included in my volume *The Woman Who Rode Away*, published and copyrighted by Alfred A. Knopf last year. Later a little unexpurgated edition of the story was privately printed in Paris – only very slightly different from the Knopf version – and sold in New York by a book-seller called, I think Harry Marks: I dont know him. I asked Edwin Rich to see if he could find out who pirated *Sun* (Rich is manager of Curtis Brown Ltd., my literary agents in New York) – but I don't know what success he had. Also Harry Marks – or Harry B. Marks – said he would try to prosecute the same pirates. But I hear nothing further.

Myself, I write in all honesty and in the sincere belief that the human consciousness needs badly now to have the doors freely opened into the dark chamber of horrors of 'sex' – it is no chamber of horrors really, of course – and I feel the language needs to be freed of various artificial taboos on words and expressions. All those taboos and shut doors only make for social insanity. I do my work, and take the reward of insult, since it is to be expected. But surely all sincere work is worth some bit of protection.

If there is any information I can give you, will you please address me c/o Curtis Brown Ltd. 6 Henrietta St. Covent Garden, London W.C.2. That is quickest. And anyhow many thanks for your sympathy.

And if you can assure me that the Centaur Bookshop is not concerned in any way in pirating my books, I shall be very glad. But tell me if you find it is otherwise. It's hard to know.

Sincerely   D. H. Lawrence

5113. To Rhys Davies, 26 May 1929
Text: TMSC NWU; Huxley 805–6.

Hotel Principe Alfonso, *Palma de Mallorca*, Spain.
26 May 1929.

Dear Davies,

Well I'm very sorry about your not getting your novel published just now. But don't you think of altering it a lot. They'll swallow it in a while, when they've got over their Jixing constipation. My word, I'd give 'em jalap[1] – and I hope the election will. Never you mind. For the time being, *write short stories*, and see about getting one done in a limited edition. And damn all their frightened little eyes.

[1] A purgative (originating in Mexico).

I won't give Jacksons a short story, because they played me a nasty trick over *Lady C.*[1] So tell them to wipe their arse on their own shirt-tails, I'm sending them no paper. But of course if they treat you all right, well and good. But they are methodising shit-bags. Insist on getting £20. And if ever you get right stumped, ask me for money before you ask your honorable begetter.

If you find out when Dorothy Warren's show is coming off, then my sister will come down for it, and if you wrote to her you could meet her then. But go to the Midlands one day. And don't go to Julian Huxleys if you don't want to. Aldous has been suffering acutely from a stiff-neck – stiff-necked and uncircumcised generation.[2] They are leaving for Italy next week, having come to hate that house mortally.

It is really rather lovely here, warm and sunny and blue, and so remote, if one goes a bit away. Of course we know a number of residents – come-to-lunch kind of thing – but nice. Today we motored along the coast to a lonely bay with pine-trees down to the sea, and the Mallorquin servants cooked Spanish rice over a fire in a huge pot, and the others bathed, and I sat under a tree like the ancient of days[3] and drank small beer – microscopic bock – and it was really very lovely, no one in the world but us. This is a wonderful place for doing nothing – the time passes rapidly in a long stretch of nothingness – broken by someone fetching us out in a motor, or somebody else in a donkey-cart. It is very good for my health, I believe. This letter is my most serious contribution to literature these six weeks. There's something I like about the Island – but the people are dullish – and a man pinched Frieda's bottom on the tram – I wasn't there – don't tell her I told you – so she despises every letter in the word Mallorca and is rampant to sail to Italy – to Marseille anyhow – on June 4th. – where her squeamish rear has never been nipped. We *may*. But we mayn't. There is a great fume again about a house. 'I *must* have a house of my own now'. Meanwhile we have this rather large, striped hotel almost to ourselves – and have the run of the establishment. It's very free. The food is very good, but so abundant – 5 courses for lunch, and then a lot of fruit – that I get frightened. The servants eat themselves tight, you never saw such a full-fed lot. Thats Mallorca. I never want to see roast chicken or fried chicken again. The hotel bill comes to about ten quid a week – exactly – and they say I'm fatter. I'm certainly fuller. I still haven't got

---

[1] See Letter 4773 and n. 2. (Huxley omitted this paragraph as well as the later anecdote about Frieda.)

[2] Cf. Acts vii. 51. Cf. *Sons and Lovers*, ed. Helen Baron and Carl Baron (Cambridge, 1992), 16:30.

[3] A scriptural title of the Christian Deity (Daniel vii. 9).

used to the wine, but I have a hollow suspicion that you'd even *like* it. – sugary. – I drink this canary be-pissed beer.

Yes, go to the Zoo. The animals don't care for gin! I didn't see Hendersons stammerings on me, and don't send them unless I shall feel like buttered asparagus (it's all wild here) when I read it.[1]

Remember us very nicely to your mother and sister; tell them to be good and sporting, and trip out to Italy or Spain next year. C'est le premier pas qui coûte[2] – and they took it this spring. Keep up your fine enthusiasm for scrubbing the bedroom floor, and tell me when you're going broke.

Belle cose!   D. H. Lawrence

5114. To Martin Secker, [28 May 1929]
Text: MS UInd; PC v. 'Principe Alfonso Hotel' – Palma de Mallorca. *Vista anterior*; Postmark, Palma 30 MAY 29; Unpublished.

[Hotel Principe Alfonso, Palma de Mallorca, Spain]
28 May

We shan't get the boat on June 4th after all – probably the one a week later – so that gives a bit more time for sheets. – Thanks for typescript received this morning.

DHL

5115. To Nancy Pearn, [29 May 1929]
Text: MS UT; PC v. 'Principe Alfonso Hotel' – Palma de Mallorca. *Vista anterior*; Postmark, Palma 30 MAY 29; Unpublished.

[Hotel Principe Alfonso, Palma de Mallorca, Spain]
29 May.

Had your letter. We can't get next week's boat to Marseilles after all, so shall stay on another week or maybe fortnight. The boat is weekly. But we want to go to Italy soon – must get some summer things out of the trunks. When do you think you'll be there? – in Italy? and where? I expect for the hot weather we shall go up somewhere into the cool. – Tell Pollinger we're not leaving, will you?

DHL

---

[1] Possibly Frank Henderson, a London bookseller (he had made supercilious remarks about *Lady Chatterley's Lover* in October 1928 in the *Sunday Chronicle*: Nehls, iii. 265).

[2] 'It's the first step that counts'.

5116. To Baroness Anna von Richthofen, [30 May 1929]
Text: MS UCB; PC v. 'Principe Alfonso Hotel' – Palma de Mallorca. *Vista posterior*;
Postmark, [Palm]a [...] MAY 29; Unpublished.

Hotel Principe Alfonso
30 Mai –

Wir bleiben noch zehn Tage – wir wollen das Schiff nach Marseille nehmen,
an 11n Juni, um nach Italien zu gehen. Wir brauchen ein Paar Sachen aus den
Köffern, und die Frieda will auch ein Haus suchen. Es ist immer schön hier,
fangt an aber heiss zu werden – morgen und abends kühl.

Wie geht es dir? Wir gehen ein wenig herum, haben Freunde – und sind
faul.

DHL

[We're staying here another ten days – we want to take the boat to Marseilles,
on June 11th, so as to go to Italy. We need a couple of things out of our cases,
and Frieda also wants to look for a house. It's always lovely here, but starts to
get hot – mornings and evenings cool.

How are you? We go about a bit, have friends round – and are lazy.

DHL]

5117. To Harold Mason, 31 May 1929
Text: MS (Photocopy) UT; *The Centaur Letters* (Austin, 1970), p. 36.

Hotel Principe Alfonso. *Palma de Mallorca*. Spain
31 May 1929

Dear Mason

I had your letter today, and am glad to be reassured that the Centaur had
nothing to do with pirating *Lady C.*[1] I know the first pirated edit. was

---

[1] Mason wrote to DHL, 17 May 1929, as follows (TMSC Mason):

Dear Lawrence:

I have been wondering how it is that I have not heard from you for such a great while and I
learned only the other day what is perhaps a possible explanation of your silence. Through a
mutual friend I was shown a letter in which you said that you had heard that the Centaur was
responsible for one of the pirated editions of LADY CHATTERLEY, which have been
flooding the book trade, and that you hoped it was not so, feeling that we were friends.

Let me hasten to assure you at once that there is absolutely no truth in any report of our
having the least thing to do with the publishing of LADY CHATTERLEY. I do not even
know myself who is responsible for any of the varieties of editions which I have seen. I am told
by a fellow-bookseller that one was produced in Philadelphia but I do not know by whom, and
we were approached early last Autumn by a salesman who purported to have "the only
authorised American edition." This salesman was known to us, having represented Longmans,
Green for a number of years in the Philadelphia trade, and his story that a firm had been
organized in New York to print limited editions, of which the first was your book, seemed
plausible and might have been true. Subsequent developments, however, in connection with

produced in Philadelphia – and is now in second edition – and two different sources told me you were back of it – which I was very loth to believe. I expect Lawrence Gomme could tell us, if he would. Anyhow I'm glad to know you're not in it, because the thought of it worried me a good bit.

We are here for a week or two longer, then shall move north, to the cool, probably to Germany. I doubt if we shall be coming to America just now. My health has been pretty bad these last two years, and still is nothing to crack about. And then I would not trust the U. S. authorities not to do me some mean trick, hold me up some way or other, out of spite for *Lady C.* and one thing and another. So I'd better stay where I'm corporally safe, at least. I wanted very much to go back to the ranch for a time – but after certain developments, I give up the idea.

I hope all goes well with the Centaur, and that he is going strong. I haven't heard from McDonald.[1]

Regards from us both to you and Mrs Mason.

Sincerely   D. H. Lawrence

5118. To Laurence Pollinger, 31 May 1929
Text: MS UT; Unpublished.

Hotel Principe Alfonso, *Palma de Mallorca*, Spain
31 May 1929

Dear Pollinger

Rich seems to be damn feeble at making a contract. I have received today the agreement for *Pansies* for Knopf. This contract stipulates that Knopf shall be offered *the next two books of poetry at the same terms.* Now this is nonsense, in view of the fact that we are trying to get clear from Knopf. Anyhow I won't sign it. I wouldn't bind myself to two more books of poetry at the same terms,

another book which he brought in later, the story of which he told us, we found to be absolutely untrue, making me doubt entirely the authorization of his edition of LADY CHATTERLEY although typographically this was by far the most respectable and satisfying form in which I have seen the book.

I hope that I may have a letter from you very soon as I do not like to feel that you may still think that we might have had some responsibility for the unfair stealing of your work, and I wish I might shed some light on the situation myself but I am unable to do so. The mysterious underground methods of such fellows are too much for me and I never know the source from which such productions eminate.

I am hoping that the time may come when we will again see you in this country and perhaps we may have the pleasure of a visit from you and Mrs. Lawrence in Philadelphia. McDonald has been intending to write you for sometime and may have done so but I know if he hasn't he will do so shortly. Meanwhile I shall be glad to hear from you. With kind regards

Sincerely yours,

[1] Edward David McDonald (1883–1977), DHL's bibliographer. See p. 20 n. 3; see also *Letters*, v. 63 n. 2.

not to anybody. I don't want, henceforth, to pledge myself to *any offering of future books*, not to anybody. – I dont care if Knopf doesn't publish *Pansies* – not a straw. I'll find a publisher myself. Agree to bind myself to two more books of poetry I will not, and it's final.

We are staying on here a bit longer – till June 11th at least. But the sun is getting very hot, it may send us off then.

ever   D. H. Lawrence

Doesn't it strike you yourself as feeble, to be working to get away from a publisher, and then bind oneself to *two more future books*? Are we on our knees before Alfred A. Knopf, or what is it?

5119. To Arthur and Lilian Wilkinson, 31 May 1929
Text: MS Schlaefle; cited in V. de S. Pinto, *D. H. Lawrence after Thirty Years 1930–1960* (Nottingham, 1960), p. 47.

Hotel Principe Alfonso. Palma de Mallorca, Spain
31 May 1929

Dear Wilkses

Your letter this morning – as I was sitting in my pyjamas on bedroom floor painting a little picture which you would all thoroughly dislike, I'm sure – so you'll see things are pretty much as usual. You seem to have a busy time – which I suppose is highly admirable – but here on this island it makes one wilt to think of so much doing. This is called *la isla de la calma*,[1] but it should be called worse names than that. It's a marvellous place for doing nothing in – one just doesn't want to do a thing – and even to write a letter costs great efforts. In seven weeks I have painted one small picture and written nothing at all. But I suppose it's good for me. I'm pretty well – so is F[rieda].

The place is curious – very attractive, and quite unattractive. Not beautiful like Italy – nor *vivace* nor *allegro*[2] – people a bit dull, dreary, really. Yet it's all so easy, and so thoroughly indifferent to everything – except perhaps riding along the coast in motor-cars. The people don't seem to care about a thing – and nobody bothers – not even I. One feels, in a sense, one has dodged the 'world of care' and settled down in the world of indifference. The climate is very good – today is a brilliant blue day, beautiful, with white surf running in to the little bay. We are in a rather big, fairly dear hotel on the sea's edge – very good food, and too much of it. We are only six guests, and about ten servants – so very spoiled – and we have the run of the place – are waited on hand and foot, given everything we want, let to do as we like, and altogether

---

[1] 'the island of calm'.   [2] 'nor lively nor merry'.

ruined for life. Sounds about the reverse of your strenuousness – and I'm sure the young ones at least, dont envy us.

When it gets too hot – the sun is wildly hot already, but the breeze fresh and cool – we shall get on the steamer to Marseille, and go probably to Italy to collect a few things, then somewhere cool. Frieda says she wants a house in Italy. I am not sure. Anyhow we can look. We might come back here, to the *isla de la calma*. *Quien sabe!*[1] – which we say now instead of *chi lo sa!*

We hear from Giulia, they like their new podere and new padroni[2] very much, for the present – and the padroni send us an invitation to go and stay in their villa. Florence seems to be the same, very social. The Brewsters are in Capri, but again without a house – and the Court in Boston sent them a notice that a long lost cousin of Achsah's, supposed dead in the San Francisco earthquake twenty years ago, has now turned up and claims the money that Achsah inherited from an uncle – about three-quarters of all they possess.[3] – I'm not going to put my trust in Buddha. – The Huxleys have left Paris this week for Forte dei Marmi – having come to hate that little Paris house of theirs.

I think that's about all our news. Do you have letters from the Nencioni[4] still? What news of the Poggi?[5]

I suppose you'll go and see my pictures when Dorothy Warren shows them, just to renew the acquaintance. Remember me to them.

Now I fizzle out!

                                        Belle cose!   D. H. Lawrence

I'm pining to know the election results, though – and this island has nothing to divulge, so far. So I'll take my siesta, close the balcony doors and nod off, for it's nearly 3.0.

5120. To Charles Lahr, 1 June 1929
Text: MS StaU; Postmark, Palma 3 JUN 29; Unpublished.

[Hotel Principe Alfonso, Palma de Mallorca, Spain]
1st June 1929

Dear Clifford[6]

Had your note of 29th today – I don't believe my mail is tampered with. – I had your other letter too, and replied to it the same day, I believe. I hope you have *my* letter, else we shall have to fear they are interfering with *your* mail.

---

[1] 'Who knows!'   [2] 'new farm and new landlords'.   [3] See Letter 5122 and p. 316 n. 2.
[4] Unidentified.
[5] The Wilkinsons' landlords at the Villa Poggi, adjacent to the Villa Mirenda.
[6] The envelope is jokingly addressed to 'Clifford Mellors Esq., c/o Charles Lahr Esq.' Cf. Letter 4855 and n. 4.

You see I reserved *myself* the right only to do 250 copies, to appear *After* Secker's edition. I wrote to London same time as I wrote you, saying: would there be any objection to my doing 500 copies? – So far I have no answer. I shall let you know at once, when I hear.

I also said your offer to me was too good – I can't take more than £1. per copy – even if so much. – By no means raise the price to three guineas. – About signing sheets, I find I can't get decent photographs here – and I'd prefer to sign the ordinary sheet, I think.

I agreed with Secker he should do only 150 signed copies. He shoved in another 100, on the agreement, at the same price, hoping to catch me. I checked him, and wrote that if he didn't share with me the profits accruing from the signatures, half and half, I would sign only the original 150 copies, at the arranged price. Am awaiting the answer. I would prefer to sign only 150 copies for him.

Cape is doing *Collected Poems* in New York, and Knopf is doing *Pansies*. If we ship 250 signed copies to U.S.A., I suppose I shall have to tell Knopf, as, apparently, he is not coming out with his regular edition till autumn.

We thought to leave here on June 4th, but shall stay at least till 11th. – perhaps longer. It's not at all hot.

The Island papers quote the election returns: Labour 289, Conservative[1] 252, Liberal 44, Independent 5. That means a change of government, anyhow – and with Lloyd George playing balancing-pig.[2] Let's hope things will be better.

I send this sealed.

DHL

Hope you get the 'Introd.' from Hutch[inson] – Here are the 'lines' – and my signature could come underneath them.[3]

This limited edition, issued privately, for subscribers only, is printed with the original introduction from the original manuscript held up by Scotland Yard. This is the book as I intended to offer it to the public. Now I can offer it to a few subscribers only, the public edition being pruned[4] of most of its gaieties.

(then follows my signature)

---

[1] Conservative] Liberal
[2] The final figures were: Labour 289, Conservative 260, Liberal 58, Others 8. On 5 June Ramsay MacDonald became Prime Minister but, in a hung parliament, the Liberals led by David Lloyd George (1863–1945) held the balance of power.
[3] them. This] them. It is my desire to This   [4] pruned] cut down

316 *1 June 1929*

5121. To Edward Titus, 1 June 1929
Text: MS UT; Unpublished.

Hotel Principe Alfonso, *Palma de Mallorca*, Spain
1 June 1929
Dear Titus

This is to introduce my friend, William Nell, who is coming up to Paris
from Mallorca. Please tell him about Our Lady, and how she is getting on;
and when the book is ready, please give him a copy, from me.

I haven't heard from you for a long time, and should be glad of news. You
must have something to tell me, about the book, and also about the Introduction, which I presume has already appeared in New York.[1] Please let me
know.

It still isn't hot here, so we shall stay on for a time, then come north.
Meanwhile I hope all goes well.

Yours Sincerely   D. H. Lawrence

5122. To Earl and Achsah Brewster, 2 June 1929
Text: MS UT; Brewster 202–4.

Hotel Principe Alfonso. *Palma de Mallorca*, Spain
2 June 1929
Dear Earl and Achsah

Well what a budget! – Harwood falling over a cliff and spraining her ankle
(though I want to know *which* precepts of her mother's bore her up from more
serious damage) – and a distant cousin who should be dead coming out of an
earthquake to claim the family inheritance[2] – and no home once more – and
an all-pervading uncertainty – No, it won't do. Achsah, my dear, you must
come to a few decisions *all on your own*, Earl is out of the running *pro tem.*, and
I seriously think Buddha and deep breathing are rather a bane, both of them.
Now Earl will never fit properly into a normal environment, so it's no use
counting on him. – As for Harwood being a doctor – if she *wants* to, let her –
and if she's going to, then it's high time she began some regular work in
preparation, at some regular school or college. If it's not going to be America,
let it be England. But for God's sake do *something* about it – another year has
gone by, she's going to be seventeen, and the muddle only deepens. Achsah, it
is now up to you. This is a question of environment and adaptation to the

---

[1] Random House published *My Skirmish with Jolly Roger*, 15 July 1929 (Roberts A48a). The
Paris edn of *Lady Chatterley's Lover* – with *My Skirmish* as the introduction – for which Titus
was responsible, appeared in May (Roberts A42c); but see Letters 5151 and 5157 n. 1.
[2] DHL's remark was confirmed by Earl Brewster in a letter to his older brother, Ara, on 16 July
1929. (Information from Professor Keith Cushman.)

western world. Earl has more or less destroyed his adaptation and dislocated himself from the western environment, with his deep breathing and Buddha. He doesn't want to adapt. Neither do I, beyond a certain point. But up to a point, one must. And for Harwood the question is vital. If you aren't careful, she'll be a sort of social freak, with no place anywhere. Achsah, this is for you to decide, definitely. Earl is out of the running. Harwood can come back to Buddha and deep breathing later on, if she likes. But first give her her chance in the 'normal' world. Let her be a doctor if she wants to; and in that case, start out at once with some proper schooling in a school, in England or America.[1]

Yes, I like Brewster Ghiselin all right – but I didn't know he called himself my disciple. I certainly don't call myself his master. I know almost nothing of him, and he knows almost nothing of me – and I feel we're as different as chalk and cheese. But people must have their little fancies.

We keep lingering on here. Now we say we will sail to Marseille on June 11th. It is very pleasant here, we know people,[2] the island is extremely calm and lazy, one wastes no energy, and I think it has been good for me. So far, it isn't at all too hot – but one feels it may begin to be so. It's an excellent climate, no rain, practically, and nearly always sunny. If we come to Italy just now, we shall probably go to the Lago di Garda. Frieda has a great idea that that's where she wants to be. I don't feel any particular urge, but I liked it when we were there before. And I certainly think July and August would be too hot here. We could come back in the winter if we wished.

That little book of poetry *Pansies* should be out this month. I will have a copy sent to you.

Yes, Brett writes from Taos. She had some sort of ructions with Mabel during the winter, but I think it is patched up. But anyhow Brett no longer lives on Mabel's place, but has a room in the village.[3] She didn't sell any

---

[1] The late Harwood Brewster Picard wrote to the editors:

In Sept. 1929 I did go to school in England at Dartington Hall in Totnes, Devonshire. I was there for two years. I think Lawrence was worried that I would never get away from my parents – but I don't think that this was the reason for my going to England. We had heard about Dartington even before going to India in 1927. After Dartington and several attempts and finally passing Matriculation, I then went to the London School of Medicine for Women and was there for three years, passing 1st M.B. and 1st part of 2nd M.B.

See also Letter 5345 and n. 1.

[2] Cf. Letter 5151.

[3] Brett was known to the Brewsters from her five-month stay on Capri, November 1925–March 1926. In Taos she had a room 'on top of an adobe house belonging to the Chaplines, a Taos couple, and could only be reached, Pueblo-Indian style, by an outside ladder. Her winter address for some years thereafter became "The Chapline Roof"' (Hignett, *Brett*, p. 202).

pictures in New York. Now she is showing in Buffalo. I expect she has gone up to the ranch now. We think, by the way, we might sell the ranch. It's too far off.

No more news – I do hope Harwood's ankle is better, and that you are all cheerful.

Love from both   DHL

5123. To Ada Clarke, 2 June 1929
Text: MS Clarke; cited in Lawrence–Gelder 192–4.

Hotel Principe Alfonso, Palma de Mallorca. Spain
2 June 1929

My dear Sister

Your letter yesterday – sorry you were worried – those fool newspapers! I always say they are pining to announce one's death. But they're too 'previous.'[1]

The photographs were very nice – the country, as you say, is looking lovely, even in those snaps. If it weren't so far, I should dearly like to see it. But that long journey! – and your garden must be quite a triumph. Lilac was passing when we came here two months ago. They were cutting the corn – it is very dry, and will soon look like autumn. And with you everything is just coming to luxuriance. – I think, when we *do* settle down to a house, gardening will be my hobby too. But here the earth is as dry as dry rock.

We keep putting off our departure. Now we say we will sail on June 11th. to Marseille. If we go to Italy we shall probably go to the Lago di Garda, where it is not too hot. It is the first place we came to, in Italy, and Frieda has a great idea she wants to go there again. If we don't care to stay in Italy, we can come back here for the winter. It's very easy – and there is a weekly boat from Marseille, takes 22 hours.

Jack Hutchinson has been away campaigning in the Isle of Wight, where he was putting up as a Liberal candidate. I don't suppose he's got in.[2] Anyhow I asked Koteliansky to go to his house and get that MS of the poems, as soon as Hutchinson is back in London. So don't you bother about it. – I have corrected proofs for Martin Secker – he has omitted about a dozen poems, with my consent – no use raising a fuss – and he expects to get the book out this month. I will see he sends you a copy. But probably I shall get a small private edition issued, complete and unexpurgated, so that the poems appear just as they were written. – But don't mention this. – I will let you have a copy.

No definite news still, about the pictures – nor the book of them. I have got

---

[1] 'premature' (slang).   [2] Cf. p. 161 n. 1.

proofs of all except one – so I shouldn't be surprised if Stephensen suddenly issues the book, this week or next. You see, since the great scare of Jix and suppression, all publishers are terrified of the police – lest they come in and confiscate a whole edition. That would be a terrible loss, in the case of my book of pictures, as it has cost about £2,000 to produce. But already there are orders for more than half – and the ten copies on vellum at fifty guineas each were ordered six times over. Madness! I think, if you go to London to the show, when the Warren opens it, you could call and ask for your copy of the book – and Emily's –

P. R. Stephensen. The Mandrake Press. 41 Museum St. W.C. 1.

It's just near the Brit. Museum. – Stephensen was at Bandol just before you were. – The first day of the show will probably be by invitation only, so you'd have to write and ask Dorothy Warren for invitation cards. Say how many you want – and don't be too big a party. – You'd also have to write Stephensen, and tell him when you were calling for your book. – You might see Enid Hopkin and Koteliansky and Barbara Weekley, if you liked.

Enid Hilton. 44 Mecklenburgh Square. W.C. 1

S. Koteliansky. 5. Acacia Rd. St John's Wood. N. W. 8

Barbara Weekley, 49 Harvard Rd. Chiswick. W.

What about the summer holidays? Where do you think you'll go?

I suppose Emily would go to London with you.

I must send Bertie a p.c.

DEAR BERTIE YOU WRITE MOST BEAUTIFULLY AND YOU LOOK TWICE AS BIG AS WHEN I SAW YOU.

                    MUCH LOVE   UNCLE BERT.

5124. To S. S. Koteliansky, 5 June 1929

Text: MS BL; Zytaruk 386–7.

Hotel Principe Alfonso, *Palma de Mallorca*, Spain

5 June 1929

Dear Kot

I'm still waiting final news of Secker's *Pansies* – also of Stephensen's book of pictures, also of the Warrens show. Do tell me if you can find out anything about the picture-book and the show. Stephensen is not *too* dependable, either.

I think I shall agree to the lion's 500 of the poems[1] – and we needn't number them. But the price is best two guineas, not three – and I do want

---

[1] See Letter 5103 and n. 1.

him to take a proper percentage. I say if I take £1. a copy that is already huge. I hope he'll choose nice paper. Do overlook him a bit – and what do you really think are his weak points, besides enthusiasm? I do wish you also would take a little per centage, for all the trouble. Say you will.

Knopf wouldn't do my *Collected Poems* – he wouldn't buy back the rights from Huebsch[1] and Seltzer. So I'm going to leave him as soon as I have fulfilled my contract with him. Cape made a pretty mean contract for the *Poems* – but I did want them rescued from the Huebsch-Seltzer-Kennerley scrapheap in U.S.A.

Wonder if you have seen Hutchie. Wonder if he got in! Bet he didn't. If there is any interesting election-govt. news, do tell me. I am interested in it.

Just heard from Curtis B[rown] – Secker is doing 250 *Pansies* – and agrees to my doing 500 if they *follow* his edition. So tell the lion 500 O. K. – but not till after Secker is out – and nothing to America till after Knopf is out too with his edit. Secker fixes June 30th for his date. – Tell the Lion I'll try about a photograph or a drawing – perhaps a drawing by an artist here.[2] Must hurry off to Palma.

                                                                        DHL

tell Lion we stay till 18th.

5125. To Giuseppe Orioli, 5 June 1929
Text: MS UCLA; Unpublished.

                                    Hotel Principe Alfonso, *Palma de Mallorca*, Spain
                                                                     5 June 1929

Dear Pino

– I answered this man[3] and sent him a cheque for £1.14.0. Would you just write him a word of apology for the mistake.

I hear from Lahr he has sold 17 copies of *L[ady] C.* at 4 guineas – but not paid in the money yet. I hope we can get some more copies over to him soon, now we have a different government.

We are still here, as it is very pleasant. Perhaps we shall sail on June 18th to Marseille.

It's a long time since you wrote – and I think you must have had my last letter. Have you seen Aldous and Maria? Tell them we are still here.

---

[1] Benjamin W. Huebsch (1876–1964), New York publisher. He was responsible for the following US edns of DHL's poetry: *Amores* (1916), *Look! We Have Come Through!* (1918) and *New Poems* (1920). The other American publishers mentioned published as follows: Seltzer, *Tortoises* (1921) and *Birds, Beasts and Flowers* (1923); Kennerley, *Love Poems and Others* (1913).

[2] The edn included a self-portrait done in 1929 (cf. Letter 5144).

[3] Roy Britnell. See Letter 5110 and n. 3.

I'm still waiting final news of the pictures – also *Pansies*. Shall send you a copy. Hope all is well – and that we shall see you soon.

DHL

5126. To P. R. Stephensen, 7 June 1929
Text: MS Forster; Munro 309–10.

Hotel Principe Alfonso. Palma de Mallorca. Spain

7 June 1929

Dear Stephensen

I was glad to have your letter – was afraid something had gone wrong. Thrilling news about the book: am so anxious to see a copy. But don't send me more than *one* ordinary copy here: and not that, unless I shall receive it before the 17th., as we plan to take the boat to Marseille on the morning of the 18th.

Makes one sick to think the police might interfere – I don't imagine they will. The best thing is not to announce the book at all. Certainly don't announce it until you've sent out all your orders. Let them imagine it is still to come. Keep as quiet as possible for the first few weeks. And don't send out any review copies – why waste them? The book will sell of itself, once it is out and is *seen*. But go gently – and pretend you've shipped a lot to U.S.A. or Paris. – I'm sorry the copyrighting takes so many – but it's always so – and unless that essay is copyrighted in U.S.A., they'll pirate it at once. There have been four pirated editions of *Lady C.* in America, and one of *Sun*. – As for my six copies, would you please send them out for me. But keep the vellum copy for me, or give it to my sister when she comes to see Dorothy Warren's show: if Dorothy holds it. I put here a list of the people for the other copies.

my sister   1. Mrs. L. A. Clarke. 'Torestin'. Broadway. *Ripley near Derby*

also a sister   2. Mrs S. King. 16 Brooklands Rd. Sneinton Hill. *Nottingham*

    3. Miss Barbara Weekley. 49 Harvard Road. Chiswick. W.

    4. S. Koteliansky. 5. Acacia Rd. St Johns Wood. N.W.8.

    5. Mrs L. Hilton. 44 Mecklenburgh Square. London W.C.1.

    6. Signor G. Orioli. 6. Lungarno Corsini. Florence. Italy.

    7. Aldous Huxley. Il Canneto. *Forte dei Marmi* (Lucca) Italy

With the one you send to me, this makes eight, so I shall owe you eight guineas. But I shall have to order a couple more or so, later. – You can give Kot. and Barbara their copies – also Mrs Hilton, if you send her word to call for it. And if Dorothy is holding the show, my sisters will come down, and you can give them *their* copies – save a lot of post. – Do try and find out something definite for me from Dorothy Warren. If she procrastinates any longer, I must just take the pictures from her. I will do so.

The *Studio* is doing an article on[1] painting by me in the July number, and reproducing one picture.[2] You could get them to put in a notice of the book, if you like.

If you can get the book into America, you can soon sell it.

I think perhaps it is as well you and Jack Lindsay dissolved partnership for a while. He has too strong an influence over you – and while he is clever, he has no strength of character and no underneath power.

I shall be interested to see your *Bushwhackers.* I am puzzled that you should feel you have to conquer or contradict something of me inside yourself. *Kangaroo* was only just what I felt. You may indeed know something much deeper and more vital about Australia and the Australian future. I should be the first to admit it. I should hate to think I ever said the last word, on anything. One says one's say, and leaves someone else to continue and improve on it.

Send me news as soon as possible. – and the plates. I still haven't seen *Fauns and Nymphs.*

DHL

5127. To Harry and Caresse Crosby, 7 June 1929
Text: MS IEduc; Postmark, Palma 7 JUN 29; Lacy, *Escaped Cock* 76–7.
Hotel Principe Alfonso. Palma de Mallorca. Spain
7 June 1929

Dear Harry and Caresse
You see we are still here – keep putting off leaving – now we say we'll catch the boat on the 18th.

I hear you have got the complete MS of *Escaped Cock* from Curtis Brown: and probably by now the original MS. of the second part, from Mrs Hilton. With the latter must be my typescript of the first part, which I did myself, with alterations and additions, from the handwritten MS. of the first part which I sent you.[3] So now you will have all the original MSS. of *Escaped Cock* and I want you to keep them in memory of the Black Sun Press edition. – Curtis Browns want me to publish a book of short stories in September, and

---

[1] on] of   [2] Cf. Letter 5042 and n. 1.
[3] Enid Hilton wrote to Caresse Crosby, 7 June 1929 (MS SIU): 'I have today sent by registered letter post, the manuscript of [DHL's] story "The Escaped Cock". This is in two parts, the first part being in type and the second in manuscript.'

to include in it the first part of *Escaped Cock*. I am inclined to do it, as it secures copyright of at least so much. And a public edition will not hurt our edition: and you might possibly get yours out first. What do you think? – If you copyright the whole thing in Paris, under the Berne Convention law, that covers England but not U. S. A. Tell me how many copies you think of printing – I suppose five hundred. I have a bookseller in London who no doubt would take 150 or 250, if we could get them over to him. He is very reliable. And if Marks takes the others for U.S.A., then there is no advertising or canvassing to be done. – I suppose the price will be ten dollars or two guineas.

So much for business. My book of pictures is just about ready – and will go all right if the police don't start interfering again. I would send you a copy, but I feel perhaps you don't want it. I believe you won't like my pictures. Too concrete, too physical. But I like them. Then the poems *Pansies* are coming out this month, but I shan't send you a copy of the public edition, as a little later I am bringing out a private limited edition (secret) and I shall give you a copy of that, because it is unexpurgated and complete, and I believe you'll like some of the poems. The public edition is expurgated.

How long are you staying now in Paris? Let me know.

I knew that big horse of yours wouldn't run – his flanks are the wrong shape. He's no go. The little one will be better, if you enter him right.[1] Those stable people of course will always tell you lies – a stranger might get a hint of their real opinion from them.

The Moulin must be a god-send now the hot weather is come – the forest so near – and real good donkeys to drive out with, or to ride. That must be fun. And *where* is the swimming pool? – When a man has nothing to do, how hard it is for him to do nothing! You ought, you know, to be a fighter. There's such a lot of things you could go for, tooth and nail, if you would. With life as it is today, the battle is everything. But of course if you don't really believe in anything, there's nothing to fight for. Anyhow Heliogabalus[2] is all bunk – he was so bored he went cracked, out of boredom.

Lovely weather here – and such hot sun – but the air is cool. You'd be cooked as brown as a brioche, on this little beach.

Caresse, write us a line and tell us *your* side of the news. You are dead silent lately. I hope you haven't lost your heart entirely to the Comte – or is it

---

[1] The 'big horse' was 'Gin Cocktail'; 'Sunstroke', the 'little one', was to be no better.

[2] Varius Avitus Bassianus (205–22) adopted the name of the sun-god Elagabalus (or Heliogabalus) for his brief reign as Roman emperor, 218–22.

Vicomte? – at the Mill.[1] You'd never be able to pay his bills. And is he still handsome? (absolutely red-faced and stupid) and virile (fat, and *quite* a lump) and does he respond to Harry's challenging cannon-shot with wild caterwaulings from the château? If not, he ought.

Au revoir, mes chers, soyez deux petits anges.[2]

DHL

5128. To Glenn Hughes, 7 June 1929
Text: MS UT; Unpublished.

Palma de Mallorca.
7 June 1929

Dear Mr Hughes

Jonathan Cape is doing my *Collected Poems* in U.S.A. and now has the rights – you can ask them for the permission[3] –

You can get a photograph of me from R. H. Davis of the *New York Sun*. He took two last year.

I can give you permission from the English side to quote the poems you mention. I'll tell Secker.

This in haste.

Yours Sincerely   D. H. Lawrence

5129. To Charles Lahr, 7 June 1929
Text: MS StaU; Postmark, Palma 7 JUN 29; Moore 1160–1.

Hotel Principe Alfonso. Palma de Mallorca. Spain
7 June 1929

Dear Lahr

I had your letter – I asked Kot. to tell you Secker has no objections to my doing 500 copies of my edition, so we will do 500, but we will not number them. Yes, do leave about a dozen copies for me to give away. And it is a good idea to keep the *Lady C.* money to pay the printer etc. But do choose a nice paper, and have the book as well bound as possible. – Secker fixed his date of publication for June 30th., but I have not yet received any sheets to sign, from him. Then there is that beastly Knopf in New York, who won't come out, probably, till September, with his edition. Pollinger suggested I shouldn't

[1] Armand, Comte de la Rochefoucauld, owner of the chateau at Ermenonville and of the Mill, became one of Caresse's lovers.
[2] 'Goodbye, my dears, be two little angels.'
[3] In addition to thanking DHL personally in his Preface, Hughes acknowledged his indebtedness to Knopf as the holder of the (American) copyright on DHL's poems. Hughes quoted twenty-two poems, whole or in part.

bring out my edition till 'towards Christmas' – but he can whistle, with his Christmas. We'll come out before then. – An artist here is trying to draw me, without much success.[1] I did a drawing myself in sanguine that is really better, though I don't know if you'll like it. But I'll send it in a day or two – when I see what the other man's results are. Then you can choose. We shan't sail from here now till 18th. at the earliest. – I hope you have the 'Introd.' from Hutch[inson]. I was wondering if you'd like to print the little introduction to Secker's edition too? it is quite short, you have almost the whole of it on that leaflet. I could get Secker to send a complete set of proofs to Davies. Original Foreword: Foreword to the Public Edition. – But do as you think best about that, I don't care either way. – About proofs, you needn't really send them to me, if you can revise them carefully yourself. I made a few alterations on Secker's proofs – one or two for expurgation, and those of course you would ignore – but a few I made in the poems. I will get Secker to send Davies a complete set of revised proofs, and then if someone would read the poems aloud to you, from Secker's proofs, you could make the alterations. That would really be best. – The poems that belong to your edition only, I don't want to alter. – Secker is leaving out those three – 'What matters': 'Be a Demon': 'Jeune Fille'. I'll see you have the drawing in a day or two, if I have to slave and do another myself. Alas, drawing my own face is unpleasant to me.

Thanks for sending the Baldwin letter – a bit of cheek, that.[2] Anyhow, for the moment he's out. They say Ramsay has gone to the King at Windsor. Hope they won't be a lot of Willy wet-legs, the Laborites.

I'm not telling anybody about your edit. – Pollinger is very curious, but he can stay so.

How's the man getting on with Our Lady?

DHL

We shall be here – D. V. – till 18th. of this month.

5130. To Martin Secker, 7 June 1929
Text: MS UInd; Postmark, Palma 7–JUN–29; Secker 120–1.

Hotel Principe Alfonso. Palma de Mallorca. Spain.

7 June 1929

Dear Secker.

We are not sailing before Tuesday 18th – so I hope I shall get the sheets to

---

[1] Tom Jones (see Letter 5144).
[2] Stanley Baldwin (1867–1947) – the defeated Prime Minister in the recent General Election – had issued an appeal to the electors in the form of a letter, written on 10 Downing Street notepaper and reproduced in facsimile. The Labour Party took strong exception to the tactic.

sign while I am here. Do send them book post; in easy packages, with paper that I can wrap them up again. – The agreement goes all right now.

I wish you would send at once a set of complete revised proofs to

Rhys Davies, 43 Third Avenue, *Manor Park*, Essex.

He is going away, and I promised him them. We used to read the poems in Bandol.

I told Glenn Hughes he could quote the things. You can say if you have anything to Stipulate.

It is still lovely here. We went motoring yesterday – sun very hot – but the country attractive, it is much wilder, less lived-upon than Italy. I wish it didn't get too hot.

The Renn book was good – one of the best war books I have read.[1] But all war books depress me horribly. Can't imagine why the public likes them so.

Pollinger says you want to do a book of short stories in autumn. Are there really enough? – and is it worth while? I must ask P. for a list of the stories. Seems to me there are not enough – especially as 'Man Who Loved Islands' has appeared in U. S. A.

Let me have those sheets as soon as you can, so they are off my chest – And do send a set of proofs to Davies, please.

ever   DHL

5131. To Emily King, 8 June 1929

Text: MS Lazarus; Postmark, Barcelona 11. JUN 29; Unpublished.

Hotel Principe Alfonso. Palma de Mallorca. Spain
8 June 1929

My dear Pamela

I'm sorry I was so long writing last time – but surely you had a p.c. in the meantime from Cala Ratjada, when we went for a week-end?[2] – One lets the time slip by, and does nothing. This is an extraordinary place for *not* working – I hardly do a thing, except go out to tea and dinner sometimes with people. But I neither want to write nor paint at all – which is very good for me – I am certainly better for my stay here. The weather is fairly hot, but it seems to suit me – one lounges away the morning in pyjamas – or goes down to the little beach. Frieda has just gone to bathe. Soon I shall take a dip too, if my cough holds better. – We went a long motordrive on Thursday with friends, up the east coast – very steep and wild and lovely. But the sun is getting too hot and powerful for motoring – I was nearly blinded: should have worn dark glasses.

---

[1] *War*, by Ludwig Renn (pseudonym of Arnold Friedrich Vieth von Glosenau), tr. Willa and Edwin Muir (Secker, June 1929).

[2] No such postcard has been found.

I hear the book of pictures is being bound up – practically ready. I sent Stephensen your address, to forward you a copy. But I still hear no news of the exhibition. I suppose they are a bit afraid of the police interfering, since this Jix upheaval and Scotland Yard activity. But perhaps now there is a Labour cabinet things will be a little easier.

Of course if I was in England I should vote Labour, without hesitation. I have no sympathy with mealy-mouthed nonentities like Baldwin, and as for a treacherous bug like Lloyd George, we know what he is worth. My sympathies are with Labour. But then of course I don't live in Brooklands Rd.[1]

We keep saying we'll leave, and then staying on. But I'd rather stay while it suits me. I am not keen on going to Germany – and I don't want to go to Switzerland – we may go to the north of Italy, Lago di Garda. It remains to be seen how hot the summer turns out. I shan't mind if I don't go to Germany this summer.

The *Pansies* are due for the end of June – I will see that Secker sends you a copy.

I do so hope this summer will get my chest a bit into order – I've had such a long whack of it. – Glad Joan is well – I hear you are getting new furniture.

Love to all   DHL

5132. To Max Mohr, [8 June 1929]
Text: MS HMohr; PC v. 'Principe Alfonso Hotel' – Palma de Mallorca. *Vista posterior*; Postmark, Palma 11. JUN 29; Mohr 166.

Mallorca.
8 Juni.

Wir sind immer hier – bleiben noch zehn oder fünfzehn Tage – ich habe gern das warmes wetter, es geht mir besser. Wie ist es im Wolfsgrube? – und gibt's etwas neues? Wir sitzen und vegetieren, es ist aber gut für die Gesundheit.

belle cose!   DHL

[We're still here – stay another ten days or a fortnight – I like the warm weather, I'm better. How is it in the Wolfsgrube? – and is there anything new? We sit and vegetate, but it's good for the health.

all the best!   DHL]

[1] Emily King's address in Sneinton Hill, Nottingham. Cf. *Letters*, i. 40 n.2.

5133. To Charles Lahr, 10 June 1929
Text: MS Lazarus; Postmark, Barcelona 11 JUN 29; Unpublished.

Hotel Principe Alfonso. *Palma de Mallorca*. Spain
10 June 1929

Dear Lahr

Knopf is trying to make Secker delay the date of publication for the *Pansies*, and Secker is refusing as far as possible. I hope the result will be that Alfred has to hurry up and come out with the book now, as soon as possible. Then our 500 can also emerge.

I shall send you this week a sketch – perhaps two – of my unhappy self, and a photograph, if it comes out fit to be seen, which is being done by a photographer.[1] I may not be able to send them till end of the week.

We are not fixing the date of leaving. My wife sprained her foot bathing – not bad, but inconvenient – so we'll wait a bit. So write to me here.

Tell Davies I asked Secker to send those proofs to Manor Park – I expect he'll do so at once.

Kot insists on the 3-guinea price, but I think not. – He says you suggest dividing ⅔ to me, ⅓ to you, of the profits. Do do that if you think it's quite fair to you. I shall trust you to take your fair share.

Who is the new Home Secretary, after all?[2]

Yrs   DHL

5134. To Laurence Pollinger, 10 June 1929
Text: MS UT; Unpublished.

Hotel Principe Alfonso. *Palma de Mallorca*. Spain
10 June 1929

Dear Pollinger

I enclose the Knopf agreement with the option clause cancelled. – I think Secker is right to want to come out now with *Pansies*: why waste his advertisements! Let Alfred hurry up, that's all. Let me know result of your cable.

Why doesn't Secker get those sheets over to me, to sign, while I'm here. I wrote him we were staying on. – By the way, you have got *both* agreements for *Pansies* – send me mine when Secker has initialled it – same with Cape's *Collected Poems* agreement.

Stephensen sent me a set of proofs of the pictures – I too wish they could have been seven-colour: but the final result is not bad, all things considered. I

---

[1] Ernesto Guardia of Palma. See Illustrations. Another pose is reproduced in Sagar, *The Art of D. H. Lawrence* (Cambridge, 1966), opp. p. 231.

[2] John Robert Clynes (1869–1949).

like Stephensen, but like all enthusiasts, he's not entirely dependable. – The show of pictures is supposed to be fixed for a fortnight today.

My wife sprained her foot – not bad, only inconvenient – bathing in the bay, so she can't walk much just yet – so shan't fix the date of leaving here.

all good wishes   D. H. Lawrence

5135. To P. R. Stephensen, 12 June 1929
Text: MS Anon; Munro 310–11.

Palma de Mallorca. Spain
12 June 1929

Dear Stephensen

I got the set of plates – many thanks. They are much improved on the proofs. Now I hope the book will arrive this week, because we want to leave next Tuesday – 18th. by the boat to Marseille. My wife wants to come to London to see after the pictures – that wretch, Dorothy Warren! I've heard not a word from her – the pictures must be taken from her as soon as the show is over, and stored somewhere, or given to my sister to keep. I do hope my wife will be intelligent about it.

I want my sister Mrs Clarke to keep my vellum copy for me.

I think I shall go to North Italy – shall write as soon as I have an address.

Ever   D. H. Lawrence

5136. To Nancy Pearn, 12 June 1929
Text: MS UT; Unpublished.

Hotel Principe Alfonso. Palma de Mallorca, Spain
12 June 1929

Dear Nancy Pearn

We are planning really to leave on 18th June – next Tuesday – I hope my wife's sprained foot will be all right. She wants to come to England from Marseille, to see after my pictures. Dorothy Warren is so irresponsible, and I've nobody to look after the thing for me. So my wife will probably be in London next week-end. – I don't know where I shall go – probably to North Italy. The journey to England is so far. – I shall send an address when I have one. Will you please tell *all the departments* not to write till they hear from me again. This hotel is very bad at forwarding letters.

As for my doing any work – this island won't let me.[1] I can't do a thing here. Though it's good for my health. But later I'll see.

DHL

---

[1] The remark was probably in response to Nancy Pearn's enquiry, 6 June 1929 (TMSC UT): 'Are you planning any more travel articles of one kind or another? . . . Now that the Election – to say nothing of the Derby – is over, there are more openings again for general articles.'

5137. To S. S. Koteliansky, 12 June 1929
Text: MS BL; Postmark, Palma 12 JUN 29; Zytaruk 387.

Hotel Principe Alfonso. *Palma de Mallorca*, Spain
12 June 1929

My dear Kot

We want *really* to sail next Tuesday, 18th., to Marseille. Frieda wants to come to England to see about my pictures. Somebody must see about them – Dorothy Warren can't be trusted. I shan't come because of the long journey. Probably I shall go to North Italy and wait there. Tell Lahr not to write here any more. – He will have had my letters saying print the 500 – and I'll send a drawing or photograph this week.

I'll write you as soon as I get somewhere.

DHL

I asked Stephensen to give you a copy of the picture book.

5138. To Ada Clarke, 12 June 1929
Text: MS Clarke; Postmark, Palma 12–JUN–29; Unpublished.

Hotel Principe Alfonso. *Palma de Mallorca.* Spain
Wed. 12 June 1929

My dear Sister

It is nearly your birthday, and I am sending you a little money. I hope you will get it in time.[1]

I hear the private show is to come off tomorrow – Thursday.[2] I do hope you get the notice and invitation in time. The book will be out today. I had a set of the plates – pretty good now, I think. I told Stephensen either to post your copy, and Emily's, or give them you – and also my *vellum* copy, which I want you to keep for me.

I think we shall *really* leave next Tuesday, 18th. And Frieda will probably come to London from Marseille. Dorothy Warren is so irresponsible – somebody must actually see about the disposal of the pictures. So F. had better come. I don't know where I shall go – perhaps to north Italy, where it isn't hot. I'd come to England but for the long journey. – When Frieda comes back, send me one or two pairs of pale thin socks, and two men's combinations, thin ones, made of ordinary underwear cotton fabric. The others you

---

[1] Ada's birthday was on 16 June.

[2] In fact the private view was on Friday, 14 June. This is confirmed by a personal letter from Dorothy Warren to Mary Hutchinson on 13 June (MS Hutchinson) urging her to attend 'Lawrence's private view tomorrow. Do come and bring friends. I know that you will find the show interesting, I myself am thrilled by it, but I anticipate quite a nasty form of attack!'

sent I wear for spring and autumn, half-weight. These I want for hot summer, just white cotton. And a pair of braces. I've got everything else.

At last, thank heaven, it has rained. The island was crackling with dry heat. I'll write as soon as I have an address.

Love DHL

5139. To Emily King, [12 June 1929]

Text: MS Sagar; PC v. 'Principe Alfonso Hotel' – Palma de Mallorca. *Vista posterior*; Postmark, Palma 12 JUN [. . .]9; Unpublished.

[Hotel Principe Alfonso, Palma de Mallorca, Spain]
12 June.

We really want to sail next Tuesday to Marseille, as Frieda wants to come to London to see after my pictures. I hear the private view is to take place tomorrow – hope you will be able to go. And the book is ready today – so either you will get your copy in London, or it will be posted to you. – Frieda sprained her foot, but I think it will be better by next Tuesday. – I think I shall go to North Italy – to the Lakes – shall send an address as soon as I decide.

DHL

5140. To Else Jaffe, 12 June 1929

Text: MS Jeffrey; Frieda Lawrence 286–7.

Hotel Principe Alfonso. *Palma de Mallorca*, Spain
12 June 1929

Dear Else

We want to leave here next Tuesday – 18th. – by the boat to Marseille. Frieda sprained her foot, bathing, but I think it will be better by then – it's not bad. I want her to go and see after my pictures, as the show is supposed to open this week. And the book is ready today – I have a set of the coloured plates – 26 – rather good, although only done in 3-colour process. I hear they have already orders for about 300 copies at 10 guineas, and the ten vellum copies at 50 guineas are all ordered. World of crazes! But I ought to make about £500 out of the book – not bad. I shan't send you a copy – I know you don't care especially about it – and in these things you belong to the opposite direction, so of course don't see much value in work of this sort. You say *Satanisch*. Perhaps you are right; Lucifer is brighter now than tarnished Michael or shabby Gabriel. All things fall in their turn, now Michael goes down, and whispering Gabriel, and the Son of the Morning will laugh at them all. Yes, I am all for Lucifer, who is really the Morning Star. The real principle of Evil is not anti-Christ or anti-Jehovah, but anti-life. I agree with you, in a sense, that I am with the antichrist. Only I am not anti-life.

If Frieda comes to England from Marseille, I shall probably go to North Italy, the Garda, where it won't be too hot. This year I don't want to come very far north – I feel I am better south of the Alps – really. Probably Frieda will come to Baden on her way back from England.

This island is a queer place – so dry – But at last it has rained. We might possibly come back next winter.

I expect the Schwiegermutter will have gone back to the Stift. I was glad she was well enough to come to Heidelberg. It must be summer with you, leafy and lovely. Here it is all dried up, only the bushes of wild thyme in flower on the waste places, and the bougainvilleas in the gardens.

I wonder where you will go for the summer holiday – ? Anyhow we will meet somewhere, if not in Baden.

Greet everybody from me.

DHL

5141. To Enid Hilton, [12 June 1929]
Text: TMSC NWU; PC; Unpublished.

[Hotel Principe Alfonso, Palma de Mallorca, Spain]
12 June.

I ordered you a copy of the picture-book, which is to be ready today – hope you get it all right – it is from me.

We want to leave definitely next Tuesday, by the Marseille boat – Frieda wants to come to England to see after the pictures when the show is over. I think I shall go to North Italy.

DHL

5142. To Harry and Caresse Crosby, 12 June 1929
Text: MS IEduc; Postmark, Palma 12–JUN–29; Unpublished.

Hotel Principe Alfonso. *Palma de Mallorca*, Spain
12 June 1929

Dear Harry and Caresse

I think we shall definitely get the boat to Marseille next Tuesday – so don't write here any more. Frieda wants to go to London to see after my pictures – but I shrink from the long journey, and shall probably go to North Italy from Marseille. When do you go to Cannes?

I expect you have my letters and everything. Shall send you an address as soon as I have one.

Ever   DHL

5143. To Max Mohr, [12 June 1929]
Text: MS HMohr; cited in Mohr 166.

Palma de Mallorca.
12 June

Dear Max Mohr

I wrote this man that you were negotiating in the matter[1] – but I would ask you if you had any result, and would let him know. What do you think of him? We intend to leave here definitely next Tuesday, the 18th, for Marseille. My wife will go to England to see about my pictures, and I shall probably go to North Italy. I will write to you as soon as I have an address.

You can write direct to Leopold Löwenstein if you have anything to say to him.

ever   D. H. Lawrence

5144. To Charles Lahr, 15 June 1929
Text: TMSC ULon; cited in *Letter to Charles Lahr* (1930).

Palma de Mallorca, Spain
15 June 1929

Dear Lahr

My wife will come to London, arrive there probably Saturday, 22nd. We are due to leave on Tuesday for Marseilles. I shall give her the drawings and photographs, you can choose which you like. I like best the big head in red chalk, done by myself – I think it is *basically* like me. But my wife thinks it is awful – chiefly because she doesn't understand – and prefers the seated figure drawings by Tom Jones, which I think rather trivial, and bad in the sticking on of the head. But I don't really care which you choose – use even a photograph if you wish – anyhow if you use one of my sketches, don't say it's by

---

[1] DHL's letter is written on one to him from Leopold, Prince of Löwenstein-Wertheim-Freudenberg (1903–74); see *Letters,* vi. 535 n. 2.

> Blau-rot, London Office and Literary Agency, 31, Soho Square, W. 1
> June 7th 1929.
> Dear Sir,
>   I think our mutual friend Miss Dorothy Warren about a year ago mentioned my name to you in connection with the publication of your works. Unfortunately I could then not secure the German rights of your works for the S. Fischer Verlag whom I represent in this country. About the same time I got a copy of your novel "Lady Chatterley's Lover" and I have pleasure in telling you that I have found a German publisher who wants to translate and publish it.
>   There is, of course, as you will realise, some risk in publishing this book, but nevertheless I think it only fair that you should get some royalty of the German edition.
>   I suggest that you should leave it to me to arrange this matter and I may mention that the firm who wants to undertake the publication of the work, is one of the leading Publishing Houses in Germany. I should be very pleased if you could let me have a word on this subject.
>   Yours sincerely,

me. – Do get a better paper – get quite a good paper, not thick, but white and strong – and I quite like a half-limp sort of paper or parchment cover, creamy, with title in black and red, and covered in a permanent wax-paper. The cover consists only of stiffened good paper and parchment, folded down, with a fly-leaf inside, and covered again in wax-paper. The Black Sun Press in Paris did my *Sun* that way – and will do another story. I'm glad you and Davies will correct proofs. – Thanks for the *Adelphi* – Murry wrote me very emotionally – he understands quite a lot, but I wouldn't trust him for a moment – which is depressing. – As for Max Plowman and *Everyman*, who is Max Plowman and why should *Everyman* be such a cringing mongrel.[1]

I still agree 2 guineas for the price – and whether you number the copies or not, I don't care. Anyhow don't say anything about America.

I'll send you an address next week – Wonder so much how my picture show went – do hope there was no interference.[2]

DHL

The post is very erratic here, for everybody. They say it's the exhibition in Barcelona.[3] – I have signed and returned the 250 sheets for Secker.

5145. To Giuseppe Orioli, [15 June 1929]
Text: MS NWU; PC v. 'Principe Alfonso Hotel' – Palma de Mallorca. *Vista posterior*; Postmark, Palma 15–JUN 29; Unpublished.

[Hotel Principe Alfonso, Palma de Mallorca, Spain]
Sat

Had your letter yesterday – We want to sail Tuesday – Frieda go to England for a bit, I come to Italy meantime – don't quite know where – perhaps Forte, stay in an hotel. If Mrs Chambers writes from Paris, tell her she never sent a

---

[1] Mark ('Max') Plowman (1883–1941), journalist and poet, to whom DHL wrote six times between September 1919 and January 1920 (see *Letters*, iii.); he wrote frequently for *Everyman*. In the issue of 6 June 1929, he contributed a column about DHL; it is rather convoluted in argument and pretentious in manner. Plowman treats DHL as a representative of the age during which women were enfranchised and which therefore led, in novels, to the presentation of female characters not as 'the sweet girl [or] the refined lady' but as 'woman – rebellious, vivid, intelligent and instinctively an Amazon ... Mr. Lawrence is the prophet of this young woman'.

It is difficult to understand DHL's dismissive remark, 'a cringing mongrel': *Everyman* showed a great deal of respect for him. Its front cover on 6 June carried a portrait-drawing of him by Joseph Simpson (different from that in the *Sunday Dispatch*, cf. Letter 4950 and n. 1); on 25 April the editor had expressed sympathy with DHL over the seizure of the *Pansies* MS, and in the same issue a page was devoted to an intelligent 'appreciation' of him by Philip Henderson.

[2] For a full account of the exhibition see Nehls, iii. 326–41.

[3] The huge international exhibition at Barcelona was opened with great pomp by King Alfonso on 19 May 1929; it closed on 6 November; the wide coverage given by *The Times* – in reports, articles, pictures – is indicative of its significance.

Paris address – but I will write her as soon as I have her address. – Hope then to see you soon.

DHL

5146. To Max Mohr, [17 June 1929]
Text: MS HMohr; Mohr 166–7.

Palma de Mallorca
Monday

Dear Max Mohr

Your letter this morning – I hope the Ernst Rowohlt[1] Verlag will not let you down again. Tell Rowohlt I have a letter from Anton Kippenberg saying he does *not* wish to make a translation of *Lady C.* and that he relinquishes his claim to the book. If necessary I will get Kippenberg to confirm this.

Would you mind once more answering Dr Abraham – I don't quite know what to say to him.

I hope you won't be too busy to make a translation of Our Lady. If so, then we must find somebody else. But it will be as well to do it *as quickly as possible* – otherwise somebody will *pirate* it in Germany as it is pirated in France and America, and we lose everything. Did you notice that Loewenstein in his impudent letter said I *ought* to get royalties? – which means he threatens me with a pirated edition.

We leave tomorrow for Marseille, my wife goes to London to see after the pictures, I go to Italy. Write to me

c/o Aldous Huxley, Il Canneto, *Forte dei Marmi*, Lucca. Italy.

I shall send you a set of plates of the pictures, and you can tell me what you think of them. The book of poetry will come later, and will amuse you.

Perhaps later on we shall come to Germany. Then I should come over the Brenner and come to see you. But I will write properly from Italy.

haste. DHL

5147. To Martin Secker, [17 June 1929]
Text: MS UInd; PC v. 'Principe Alfonso Hotel' – Palma de Mallorca. *Vista posterior*; Secker 120.

[Hotel Principe Alfonso, Palma de Mallorca, Spain]
Monday

I sent off the signed sheets on Saturday – hope you have them safely. We leave here early in the morning tomorrow for Marseille – Frieda is coming to

---

[1] Ernst Rowohlt (1887–1960), probably the best-known publisher in Germany during the 1920s and early 1930s.

London, I'm going to Italy. Probably I shall stay a day or two in Forte dei Marmi (Lucca). You could address me there

c/o Aldous Huxley, 'Il Canneto'

We are wondering so much how the show went – now we shan't hear before we leave. Thanks for the *News*es.[1]

DHL

Send you two photographs – you may like to use them some day.

5148. To Laurence Pollinger, 17 June 1929
Text: MS UT; Unpublished.

Palma de Mallorca
Monday 17 June 1929

Dear Pollinger

We leave for Marseille early in the morning. You can address me if necessary

c/o Aldous Huxley, 'Il Canneto', *Forte dei Marmi* (Lucca), Italy.

But I don't expect to be there long.

By the way I found the Cape agreement for *Collected Poems*, but not Secker's for *Pansies*. – I sent Secker the signed sheets on Sat.

I enclose ten photographs – which perhaps will be useful for the press or those that want them – not bad.

ever   D. H. Lawrence

5149. To Charles Lahr, [17 June 1929]
Text: MS UNYB; Postmark, Marseille 19–6 29; Unpublished.

Palma.
Monday. 17 June

Dear Lahr

Your letter of 13th. Have you sent sheets to sign? they haven't come. If they don't come this evening I shan't get them. We leave in the morning, boat sails at 9.0. – You could write me

c/o Aldous Huxley, 'Il Canneto', *Forte dei Marmi* (Lucca), Italy

I shall probably stay a week there. My wife is coming to London – arrive next Saturday, I expect. I am giving her photographs and sketches. –

I would rather the poems were two guineas, not three. – If you want to do fifty on Jap vellum, I don't mind. Do put the Phoenix on the cover – I want it on all my private issues.

---

[1] Secker had sent the *Illustrated London News* (and *Times Literary Supplement*) to DHL with great regularity since at least 1924 (*Letters*, v. 112 n. 3). Cf. ibid., vi. 32, 69, 463. See also Letter 5417.

I am so anxious to hear about the show. Tell me all you know – I mean the pictures at Dorothy Warrens.

Haste   DHL

The parcels haven't come – but Stephensen's book turned up tonight.

5150. To P. R. Stephensen, [17 June 1929]
Text: MS Anon; Munro 311.

Palma.
Monday evening

Dear Stephensen

The book just came – thank goodness, because we leave early tomorrow. It looks very nice indeed – quite handsome, in fact, and nothing that I can see to criticise – only rather dirty and numerous thumb-marks. Is that the post, I wonder? –

I read *Bush-Whackers*, and it's not 'childish', it's that it's too sketchy. You won't be patient enough and go deep enough into your own scene. You always stay at the level of the sketch because of the hurry. If you went deeper you'd get a *real* book out of it. But you haven't the submission.

Frieda is coming to London – arrive probably Saturday. I am going on to Italy – shall call probably at Huxleys

Aldous Huxley. 'Il Canneto', Forte dei Marmi (Lucca), Italy
Do send me a line there and tell me about the show – I'm pining to hear what happened and any further news of the book.

Don't post me my extra copy abroad – many thanks for it – send it to my sister

Mrs Clarke. Broadway. Ripley nr Derby
– to keep for me, with my vellum copy. She is safe. – I wonder if they all came to the show – and got their books.

Tell me if you have tried posting to America – I should like to send a copy of the book to New York – if it is possible.

I hope you and Goldston will help Frieda about the pictures, disposing of them etc. She'll need some help with that Warren; my hat!

DHL

5151. To Edward Titus, [18 June 1929]
Text: MS SIU; Unpublished.

Marseille – train
[18 June 1929]

Dear Titus[1]

Was so glad to hear from Nell that Our Lady of Paris will be out this week.

[1] DHL used the verso of his bill from the Hotel Principe Alfonso for his letter to Titus.

Will you please send a copy to
           Mrs Wm. Nell, S'Ermita, Genova, *Palma de Mallorca*
and one to
           Mr T. Jones, Son Toëllo, Genova, *Palma de Mallorca*
and one to
           E. S. Huelin Esq,[1] San Agustin, Cas Català, *Palma de Mallorca*
and one to me, please
           c/o Aldous Huxley, Il Canneto. *Forte dei Marmi* (Lucca), Italy
My wife will bring you my greetings – do send me word – c/o Aldous H.
                                                        ever   D. H. Lawrence

5152. To Emily King, [23 June 1929]

Text: MS Lazarus; PC; Postmark, Forte dei Marmi 24.6.29; Unpublished.

              Pensione Giuliani, Viale Morin, *Forte dei Marmi* (Lucca), Italy
                                                                    Sunday

Just a p.c. to send you the address and say I got here quite easily after a
pleasant journey – The Huxleys are living just near – also some German
friends – but very few visitors yet. It's very nice on the beach, hot sun but
fresh breeze. – Hope you've been to London and seen Frieda and also the
show. I hear the critics are adverse,[2] but take no notice, they always are, to
me. The show seems to be a success, anyhow –
                                                        Love   DHL

5153. To Ada Clarke, [23 June 1929]

Text: MS Clarke; PC; Postmark, Forte dei Marmi 24.6.29; Unpublished.

              Pensione Giuliani, Viale Morin, *Forte dei Marmi* (Lucca), Italy
                                                                    Sunday

Got here last evening after very nice journey – Aldous and Maria here –
and other friends – It's not too hot, very pleasant on the beach – but I
don't like Italy so much as I used. – Hope you have been to London and
seen Frieda – she will be there now – also the show. I hear it's a success,
but press adverse as usual – One just expects it. – I suppose I shall stay
here about two weeks. Do hope Eddie is all right again – make him take
bitter tonics.
                                                        love   DHL

[1] See Letter 5204 and n. 1.   [2] See Letter 5164 and n. 3.

5154. To Harry and Caresse Crosby, 23 June 1929
Text: MS IEduc; Postmark, Forte dei Marmi 24.6.29; Unpublished.

c/o Aldous Huxley. 'Il Canneto', *Forte dei Marmi*. (Lucca), Italy
23 June 1929

Dear Harry and Caresse

I wondered very much if you were in Cannes, the other day when I went through. Let me know where you are, and if you might come here in your *boat* before long – it is just north of Viareggio, south of Carrara – and if so I shall stay on for you – if not I shan't stay long. Frieda is in England. – This is on the sea, of course – but no harbour.

Don't decide to print only 250 of the *Cock*, because my English bookseller might want 250 also. I'll ask him as soon as I know when you think it'll be ready – about.

The Huxleys send their greetings, with mine.

DHL

Have you ever been to Corsica?

5155. To Giuseppe Orioli, [23 June 1929]
Text: MS NWU; cited in Moore, *Intelligent Heart* 407.

Pensione Giuliani. Viale Morin, Forte dei Marmi
Sunday.

Dear Pino

I got here last night – Frieda is in England. Do come down and be my guest in this little pensione – nice and cool, we eat out of doors under a big plane-tree. Forte is not at all hot. Aldous and Maria are very well indeed, very healthy – and I'm a lot better, though still coughing.

If you are coming this week, will you bring me some money from Haskard – I enclose the cheque. But if you can't come, please ask the bank to *post* me the money here to this pensione, as I have only a hundred Liras.

Glad you have the picture-book – I ordered it for you – do you like it? I hear the show is a success, but the critics hostile – some pictures sold, I don't yet know how many.

Titus is bringing out Our Lady of Paris this week.

I still don't love Forte – but it is quiet, very few people, and cool and pleasant. I shall probably stay two weeks.

Come down any day you like – tomorrow if you wish – there is always a room here in this pensione. I shall be glad to see you, and we can have our meals together under the plane tree and talk about everything.

Poor Reggie, burying his friends! Did you hear that Brooks died in Capri? – did you know him? Douglas did.

Remember me to Carletto – and a rivederci

D. H. Lawrence

5156. To Charles Lahr, [23 June 1929]
Text: MS UNYB; Unpublished.

Pensione Giuliani, Viale Morin, *Forte dei Marmi.* (Lucca), Italy

Sunday 23 June.

Dear Lahr

Yours just now – I think I shall be here two weeks – if you send the sheets by book post, registered – you can send them to Aldous Huxley, 'Il Canneto' (here) if you like – they ought not to take more than four or five days at most. Parcel post takes up to twenty days. – I shall sign and return at once. – *Don't* take my drawing unless you like it – my wife doesn't. Ask my wife for the copy of *Kay Boyles* stories for style of binding,[1] then decide if Phoenix is better on the back or the front – and if in red or in black.[2] It all depends on the spacing of your front cover. Glad you have a better paper. Do the book nicely. Don't be over-ruled by Kot. – if you like to include the Secker preface, then so do I. What are K's reasons against? And I am opposed to the three guinea price – too high.

Do send me any criticisms of the pictures that you come across. I hear they are hostile, but one expects it. – I received enclosed telegram last night – don't know from whom, or what it means altogether – or what or whom I'm to reply to.[3] It is reply paid: but why? You might find out from Stephensen – or perhaps its Dorothy Warren.

Send sheets by *Printed Matter* post, parcels not too big, and easy for me to post back to you.

Ever   DHL

---

[1] Kay Boyle's *Short Stories* was published by Crosby in a Black Sun Press edn (Paris, 1929).
[2] The phoenix was printed on the back cover of *Pansies*, in black for the edn of 500 copies (at 40s) and in gold for the special edn of 50 copies (Roberts A47c and d).
[3] Cf. Letter 5160.

5157. To Edward Titus, 23 June 1929
Text: MS UT; Postmark, Forte dei Marmi 24.6.29; Unpublished.

c/o Aldous Huxley. 'Il Canneto', *Forte de Marmi*, Lucca.

23 June 1929

Dear Titus

Your letter and prospectus today.[1] Sorry you have been worried – but what else can you expect, in this world? One wins out in the end, nevertheless.

I had written Aldous about your magazine – really, he shouldn't have promised. He works with a good deal of difficulty – and of course your prices are not high – so there you are! The younger generation! – though he's only ten years – only eight years, I believe – younger than I am – the younger generation doesn't mind promising.

Please charge the three copies to Majorca to me – in fact, if ever I order a copy sent, charge it to me of course. By the way,

Robert Paraf, 'Le Coin de Nice', 2 rue Maccarani. *Nice* – a bookseller – used to worry me terribly in the winter for copies of Our Lady – so he might like some now. And a bookseller in Cuba whose name

---

[1] Letter 5151 was delivered to Titus by Frieda Lawrence; it prompted the following (incomplete and partly illegible) response dated 21 June 1929 (TMSC SIU) to which DHL was replying:

Dear Mr Lawrence,

I have had the pleasant surprise of your wife's visit this morning. She delivered your note to me. I explained the situation to her and she took away a copy of the book. I am sending you two more copies under separate cover, – one of which if it is not too much trouble and would ask you to inscribe it to me personally and return.

The sale of the book has begun. Small orders have gone this day to Venice and Florence. Brentano gave me an order; also Smith & Son. For reasons which Mrs. Lawrence will explain to you I am proceeding very warily. Have had to take counsel's advice as the pirates have tried to intimidate me. One of the European book salesmen took the book along on tour and he is placing it in Berlin, The Hague, and other centres, in a small way of course. But unless I am mistaken I may be able to do quite a bit with the good Paris English bookshops who received the proposition favorably, but thought it was a mistake to sell the book at so low a price.

I have not purposely written to you before because I did not wish to disturb you unnecessarily. To tell the truth I was considerably worried for a while. The swine kept on telephoning me friendly (?) advice, etc., etc. I apprehended my nervousness might betray me in my letters to you and might unnecessarily disquiet you. I would have liked so much to have talked things over with Mr. Huxley, but was unable to get in touch with him. I wrote to him twice on the subject of my Review ostensibly, intending to put before him Our Lady's situation had it been possible for me to see him or to speak to him. My letters remain unanswered. – The American end of the business has [ ] do it with much trepidation.

I would be obliged to you if you would tell me whether the three copies you wish us to send to Majorca are to be charged to you or am I to ask those persons for a remittance.

You may tell Mr. Huxley from me that I am very angry and disappointed that he left me in the lurch with the first issue of my quarterly [*This Quarter*] which will be out the end month. If you dont mind I will send you a copy.

Yours very sincerely

I've lost – in Havana.[1] But you might do a fair sale in Havana: given a proper man.

I shall be here a fortnight, anyhow, I suppose – So shall look forward to a copy of your magazine. I'll send you back your copy of Our Lady. Let me know all the news.

ever   D. H. Lawrence

5158. To Hon. Dorothy Brett, 23 June 1929
Text: MS UCin; Postmark, Forte dei Marmi 24.6 29; Huxley 807–8.

Forte dei Marmi. Italy
23 June 1929

Dear Brett,

I want to write you just about my manuscripts. You know I keep them as a sort of nest-egg. One day I shall need them. So I depend on them for my reserve. For this reason I don't sell them. I've only sold one manuscript in all my life, and that is the complete version of *Sun*, which Harry Crosby printed unexpurgated in Paris, and he gave me a hundred gold dollars. Beyond that, nothing. Yet I am always hearing of MSS. of mine for sale in dealers' catalogues – things that have been sneaked from me by various people – friends and otherwise. And it's very unpleasant.[2]

So now I want you to get straight for me the MS. I left at the ranch. Will you please make me a list of them, and let Mabel and Mr Read,[3] of the Taos

---

[1] Kendrigan (cf. Letter 4897).

[2] Not until late September 1929 was DHL convinced that Brett had not been guilty of disposing of his MSS other than some he had given her (see Letters 5335 and 5355). On 14 August (MS PM) she turned for help to Seligmann:

> Someone – God knows who – has written Lawrence I am selling his manuscripts. You know he left some up at the Ranch. And the poor man is *fussing*. I have told him repeatedly, that they are safe – then fresh news reaches him that manuscripts of his are for sale in New York – those same ones we heard of, I suppose, last winter.
>
> Now – can you prospect. Will you search out these manuscripts as if you were a possible buyer & get the names of them. Then write Lawrence – tell him I have told you the whole story – that I am supposed to have stolen them and sold them – and asked you to get the names of the manuscripts for sale in New York & send the names to him.
>
> When a careless man like Lawrence becomes careful – & has no track of his carelessness – he is apt to fly off the handle –
>
> I have had two Hymns of Hate from Frieda – terrible letters – insane & vulgar!! But I want Lawrence's mind put at rest – so will you help . . .
>
> Everett Marcy looking for a copy of "Twilight in Italy" walked down 59th Street – just East of Park Ave on the North Side in a second hand shop the man told him he had one or two of Lawrence's manuscripts & one of them was Sea & Sardinia. Will you try & find this shop – the man was selling them between 250 & 500 dollars.

[3] James B. Read, manager of the First State Bank of Taos (cf. *Letters*, vi. 443).

Bank, check[1] the list: then take a safe-deposit *in my name* in the Taos bank, put the manuscripts in it, and give the key to Mr Read to hold for me. – At the same time will you give the deeds of the Ranch, all the papers connected with the property, which we left in the iron trunk, to Mr Frayne,[2] the lawyer – I suppose he is still there – for him to see if the holding is properly recorded in Court; and then give these papers to Mr Read to put in the safe-deposit with the rest.

I trust you to do this faithfully, and as soon as possible after you receive this letter.

Then I want you to tell me exactly what manuscripts I gave to you: and which exactly you sold to Mrs Hare:[3] and how much she paid – Also if you have sold any others elsewhere. You will see that I need to keep track of my manuscripts, sold or unsold, and I need to know the price they went at, in fairness to any possible future purchaser. So please answer me quite plainly and definitely, or I shan't know what to think.

We left Majorca last Tuesday – it was too hot. Frieda has gone to England to see her children and see about the pictures. The show began on June 14th and I've heard no definite news – a long incomprehensible telegram here – saying show great success – press critique bored or scurrilous – and apparently some pictures sold, but I can't make out quite what. – The book is out – a very handsome volume – it has sold over 300 at ten guineas, and all the 50 guinea ones (ten). I am keeping you a copy, it is very swanky – but not sending it till I know how to get it through. Anyhow there has been no interference, so far, in England: so perhaps U. S. A. will not kick.

I am staying here in a pensione for a fortnight or so – Aldous and Maria have a little house – then I shall probably go to Switzerland to meet Frieda. I hear Maria Cristina is in Europe, but where, I don't know. – I wonder what is happening about the sale of the ranch. I think almost certainly we shall come over this autumn to settle up – or if I don't come, then Frieda will come alone. We must get it wound up now, it's no use dragging on.

I shall trust your loyalty to do the things I ask you to do, in this letter.

DHL

c/o Curtis Brown Ltd, 6 Henrietta St, Covent Garden, London. W.C. 2.

---

[1] check] cheque

[2] A lawyer, probably in Taos, whose services about taxes on the Kiowa Ranch DHL had used before (though he did not greatly trust Frayne): see *Letters*, v. 70, 187, etc.

[3] Elizabeth ('Betty') Hare (1878–1948), wealthy American patron of the arts, especially painting: see *Letters*, v. 304 and n. 1. In order to cover her expenses in New York, November–December 1928, Brett had sold to Mrs Hare one of the MSS DHL gave her (Hignett, *Brett*, p. 203).

5159. To Mabel Dodge Luhan, 23 June 1929
Text: MS Brill; Unpublished.

Forte dei Marmi. Italy.
c/o Curtis Brown, 6 Henrietta St, Covent Garden, *London. W.C. 2.*
23 June 1929

Dear Mabel

Yes, altogether it is *very* tiresome about the Brett. But now we must firmly and *quietly* get things out of her hands. We mustn't alarm her – if she feels she's being put out, God knows what she'll do – . I have written her today asking her to collect all my MSS. – to take a safe-deposit in *my name* in the Taos bank – to have you and Mr Read check the list of MSS. – put them in the safe-deposit and give the key to Mr Read. – Also to take the deeds and papers of the ranch to Mr Frayne, for him to see if they are in order – and then deposit these in the safe-deposit too. I call on her loudly-professed loyalty to do this faithfully and punctually. I am writing to Mr Read – and perhaps you will speak to him and to Mr Frayne. I have paid Brett money for the taxes and horses feed each year – so hope this is straight.

She said in her last letter she had sold some MSS. to Mrs Hare. I don't remember ever giving her any of my manuscripts for herself. I used to give her the MS. to type, and she was supposed to hold the MS. for me. However, let that go. I may have given her some, and forgotten. – Now I have asked her to let me know exactly what I gave her, and exactly what she has sold, and for how much. You see I very much want to keep track of my MSS. – so many have been stolen from me already. I *don't want* them sold at present. And I *don't want* them on the market. I shall write a note to Mrs Hare – wonder where she is.

Maria Cristina wrote she was sailing, but gave no address in Europe, so I can't write to her. But she can get me via Orioli. – Frieda has gone to England – we left Spain, it was too hot. I am here on the sea with the Huxleys for a fortnight or so, then shall probably meet F. in Switzerland for the summer. Italy rather bores me, after Spain. – My picture-show began on June 14th – goes on another ten days or so. I have no definite news yet – except a long telegram here, undecipherable which says show great success – pictures sold – but I can't make out the number – press critique adverse, as usual. – The picture-book also is out – very handsome indeed. I am keeping a copy for you – though I have to pay for it, they wouldn't give me above my six, which of course have to go to the family etc. I hear they had sold over 300 of the ten-guinea copies, and all the ten 50-guinea copies. I expect they will soon sell out – only 500 printed. I don't think any have been sent to America – unless smuggled in by booksellers. So I daren't send you your copy till I know *how* to send it: no more trusting the post and the customs of St Louis Mo. etc. You must tell me if you have a bright idea for shipping it.

Yes, I should like to get everything out of Brett's hands, and get clear of her. Her hints of my having 'betrayed' her are pure calumny – but then she is in that hysterical-exalté state when she fabricates her own truth to the disaster of everybody else. I'm awfully sorry you are let in for her dangerous vagaries. But let us go gently and take the ranch and all its possessions out of her hands – and she will leave Taos. Frieda and I will try and come in Sept. to get everything settled – and if I don't think it would be safe for me to come, Frieda may come alone. – Get Ida to help you about Brett – she won't get so upset. The thing to do is to get the ranch and all my property out of Brett's hands, and then she will not stay in Taos. But don't put her on the defensive – use her own famous loyalty as the lever against her. We must all get clear of her, I can see that. – Yes, Ida is better than Andrew. There is something a bit deficient in Andrew, makes him mean. His ferocity is the filling up of a deficiency. I do hope Ida doesn't fret any more. – I'm sorry about your heart. You are probably under too great a nervous strain. Perhaps really you have done your work in Taos, and now it damages you, holding on. But you know best.

DHL

5160. To Dorothy Warren, 24 June 1929
Text: MS UN; Nehls, iii. 324-5.

Pensione Giuliani. Viale Morin, *Forte dei Marmi*. (Lucca), Italy.

24 June 1929

Dear Dorothy

I received the enclosed telegram Saturday night – had it repeated this morning – am not much further. I still don't know who wrote it – did you? – and what I am to reply to – there is a reply paid. Anyhow I am glad the show is a success: though whether you sold 17 paintings or 17 *painting-books* I still don't know. If you haven't already sold *Boccaccio Story* and *Red Willow Trees* and *A Holy Family*, please don't sell them, I very much want to keep them. Stephensen said they would buy *Boccaccio Story*, but I shall tell him I want to keep it.[1] – I am sure you have worked heroically, and are worn out: I do hope you feel it's been worth it.

---

[1] Philip Trotter records the sale of only three paintings, all on 4 July: *The Finding of Moses* to a Cambridge undergraduate for 50 guineas, *Boccaccio Story* to 'a high officer of the crown' and *Leda* to a Scottish collector. The last two were seized in the police raid the next day, and the purchases cancelled (Nehls, iii. 342).

I suppose by now you will have seen Frieda, and heard whatever she has to say. But send me a line of definite news –

Ever.   D. H. Lawrence

5161. To Frieda Lawrence, 24 June 1929
Text: MS UN; Nehls, iii. 325.

Pensione Giuliani. Viale Morin, *Forte dei Marmi* (Lucca)
24 June 1929

Your letter from Paris today – sorry you didn't feel well – it's the change – guess you are better now. Damn Billy Nell and all wash-outs. As for Titus, the copies of Our Lady of Paris haven't come yet.

I want very much to have *real* news of the show – have written the Warren today please to keep *Boccaccio*, *Red Willow Trees*, and *Holy Family*, if they are not already sold. – Hope you've been to see Lahr, taken him the drawings etc. I particularly *don't* want him to print mine of me unless they (in general) like it. – And Rhys Davies wrote anxiously about seeing you – and Kot. Of course you must see Kot.

Don't butt in heavily about my money affairs with Pollinger – I don't wish it – and it is no good.

Probably you'll see my sisters this week – find out how they are, and all.

Great stews of Brett and Mabel, Georgia O'K[eefe] and my manuscripts and the Taos bank!!

Buy a packet of *Carter's Little Liver Pills* for me.

My little pensione is very nice – eat out of doors under a big plane tree – with a little cat – and a bedroom rather like my Mirenda one. Go to Il Canneto to tea – and see them on the beach. They are very well indeed, nice to me – but a bit queer together. Maria still tangled up in a way I dislike extremely with Costanza – Poor Peterich lots of spots on him –[1]

Am going to dinner with the old Baronessa Franchetti tomorrow night – common old thing, but anyhow not dead.[2] Weather a bit scirocco, but not so bad – not so hot as Palma. I expect Pino down this week – he'll be my guest

---

[1] Costanza Petterich, née Fasola (1906–1954?), had been a close friend of Maria Huxley's since they were adolescents. Sybille Bedford writes of her at Forte in 1927:

She would come swinging into the house early of a morning, sit down on Aldous' bed and tell him – all ears – about everybody's love affairs including her own . . . Costanza was now married . . . had finally accepted one of the boys of the *petite bande* of their youth, his name was Ecki Petterich and he was a German intellectual, very German, in a sugary artistic way, with Greek ideals. (The marriage fizzled out after some years.) The Huxleys did not like him much. In a certain way – says [Maria's sister] Jeanne, who knew it all so well – Costanza belonged to them. (*Aldous Huxley*, pp. 184–5)

[2] The mother of Baron Luigi Franchetti.

here. – I somehow am not pining for a house here – or anywhere – – we must leave it till it happens – what's the odds! People who do have houses only leave them.

I'm quite comfortable and quite all right, so don't bother about me – but mind your *foot*, and have a good time in London, and stay while you feel like it, and write to your mother, and if she wants you to go there now, perhaps best do so. –

Love to Barby, and all   Lorenzo non santo.[1]

5162. To Martin Secker, 24 June 1929
Text: MS UInd; Postmark, Forte dei Marmi 25 6.29; Secker 121.

Pensione Giuliani. Viale Morin, Forte dei Marmi. (Lucca)
24 June 1929

Dear Secker

Yours today – glad *Pansies* is not postponed – what about Knopf?

The picture show seems to have been a success, but I have still no definite news. Frieda will be in England now, and will send it me.

Send me a copy of *Pansies* here, will you please, and the other five to these addresses:

1. Mrs L. A. Clarke. Broadway. Ripley nr. Derby.
2. Mrs S. King. 16. Brooklands Rd. Sneinton Hill. Nottingham.
3. Mrs Julian Huxley. 31. Hillway. Highgate N. 6.
4. Miss M. Beveridge. 20 Rossetti Garden Mansions. Chelsea S.W.3.[2]
5. Miss Mabel Harrison. 49 Bvd. Montparnasse. Paris.[3]

I shall send you a copy of the unexpurgated edition when it comes out.

I don't like Italy so much nowadays – don't know if I want to live here. – It isn't too hot at Forte yet, but it will be soon. I suppose I shall join Frieda further north – Lago di Garda or somewhere. –

Aldous and Maria are very well indeed, and they like it here – they stay all summer. Where are you going this year?

Are you still wanting to do a book of Short Stories this autumn? I'm not very keen, if you aren't.

ever   DHL

---

[1] 'not saintly'.
[2] Anne Millicent Beveridge (1871–1955), Scottish painter whom DHL had met in Sicily in 1921. See *Letters*, iii. 671 n. 2.
[3] Mabel Harrison was a friend of Millicent Beveridge and a fellow artist; they – with Mary Beveridge – lived in Villa La Massa, close to Villa Mirenda, from late February to early May 1927 (*Letters*, v. 643–6; vi. 39 and n. 1).

5163. To Giuseppe Orioli, [26 June 1929]
Text: MS NWU; PC; Postmark, Forte dei Marmi 27.6.29; cited in Moore, *Intelligent Heart*
407.

Pensione Giuliani. Viale Morin, Forte dei Marmi.

Wed. 25 June

Thanks for yours – shall be pleased to see you for the week-end – let me know
what time you will come. I suppose you will take the tramvia from Viareggio
– it passes the door here – at least the garden gate. We are about a mile from
Forte piazza.

Will you please bring me half a pound of Ridgways tea and a box of
chocolates for Maria. – Many thanks for the money, which came today. – I
have written to Maria Cristina Chambers – perhaps she will come here.

It is rather scirocco weather, trying to rain. I wish it would rain, everything
is very dry.

allora à bientôt.[1]   DHL

six pictures sold – but 3,500 people went to see the show the first week.

5164. To Laurence Pollinger, 26 June 1929
Text: MS UT; Unpublished.

Pensione Giuliani. Viale Morin, *Forte dei Marmi* (Lucca), Italy

26 June 1929

Dear Pollinger

Yes, tell Harold Munro he can have the six poems for his anthology:[2] and
try the four guineas apiece on him – see if he'll pay it – bet he won't – but he
must pay something. I'll write him.

Feeble, that rot from the *Daily Express*![3]

Will you tell Miss Pearn and the Accounts dept. that *The Studio* sent me
direct the ten guineas for the article on 'Making Pictures', so I forwarded the
cheque to the bank.

---

[1] 'soon then.'

[2] Harold Edward Monro (1879–1932), poet and editor; proprietor of Poetry Bookshop; editor of
Poetry and Drama to which DHL contributed in 1914 (*Letters*, ii. 53 and nn. 2,3). In the event,
five poems by DHL ('Humming-Bird', 'Love on the Farm', 'Noise of Battle', 'Renascence' and
'Street-Walkers', i.e. 'Piccadilly Circus at Night: Street-Walkers') were included in Monro's
anthology, *Twentieth Century Poetry* (Chatto & Windus, November 1929).

[3] Presumably DHL was referring to the item in the *Daily Express*, 17 June 1929, headed: 'D. H.
Lawrence as Painter   Censored Novelist's Pictures Intimate Nudes'. The tone of the article is
conveyed by the single sentence: 'The ugly composition, colouring, and drawing of these works
makes them repellent enough, but the subjects of some of them will compel most spectators to
recoil with horror' (Nehls, iii. 388). Philip Trotter recalled that on 17 June 'the rooms filled
rapidly with a crowd of visitors new to any picture gallery, mostly carrying the current issue of
the *Daily Express*' (ibid.).

Did you get the photographs of me which I sent you a week ago – ?

Alfred is a bore – and as a publisher he's on the wane.[1]

My wife is in London, and probably you have seen her by now. She still complains of that ankle. I guess you'll be amused by her ideas of business.

ever   D. H. Lawrence

Enclose the *Studio* receipt for the sake of your accounts.

5165. To Harold Monro, 26 June 1929

Text: MS UCin; Postmark, Forte dei Marmi 27.6.29; Unpublished.

c/o Aldous Huxley, 'Il Canneto', *Forte dei Marmi* (Lucca), Italy
26 June 1929

Dear Munro

Pollinger sent me on your letter – yes, I like those six poems all right – perhaps I should choose a little differently – but then nobody in the world has less notion of what will please the public, than I have. It's quite wrong, to please the public, anyhow.

How are you now? I was so sorry to hear of you so ill, and do hope you are better. As for me, I'm pretty much the same – which is not very good, neither desperate.

My wife is in London, perhaps you will see her. And if you see Hilda Aldington, do ask her where I am to write to her.[2]

Poetry seems not quite so dead as she is reported – in fact perhaps there is a young phœnix stirring among the ashes.

all good wishes   D. H. Lawrence

5166. To Max Mohr, 26 June 1929

Text: MS HMohr; PC; Postmark, Forte dei Marmi 27.6.29; Mohr 167.

Pensione Giuliani. Viale Morin, *Forte dei Marmi* (Lucca)
26 Juni 1929

Ich bin hier seit Samstag – meine Frau ist in London wegen die Ausstellung meiner Bildern. Es gehen viele Leute in die Austellung – und machen Skandal – sehr dumm. Alles auf der Welt is nur Dummheit. – Ich bleibe noch zehn Tage hier – denn treffe ich meine Frau, oder in Mailand oder in Deutschland. Ich habe Italien nicht mehr so gern – es ist mir nicht mehr sehr sympatisch. – Wie ist es jetzt im Wolfsgrube?

DHL

---

[1] Nancy Pearn annotated the letter at this point about Knopf: 'I agree! N.P.'

[2] Hilda Doolittle ('H.D.') (1886–1961), a poet closely associated with Imagism, was married to Richard Aldington (cf. p. 17 n. 3) when DHL first met them in 1914, but they separated in 1919 and divorced in 1938. See *Letters*, ii. 203 n. 3.

[I've been here since Saturday – my wife is in London because of the exhibition of my pictures. Lots of people are going to the exhibition – and making a fuss – very stupid. Everything in the world is simply stupidity. – I'm staying another ten days here – then I meet my wife, either in Milan or in Germany. I don't like Italy so much any more – it isn't sympathetic to me any longer. – How is it at present in the Wolfsgrube?

DHL]

5167. To Laurence Pollinger, [28 June 1929]
Text: MS UT; Unpublished.

Forte dei Marmi
Friday

Dear Pollinger

If you had to put up with as many little meannesses from Secker as I have, through the years, you'd be more than tired.[1] His little dodge is *entirely* typical. His cunning letters are inevitable. And *watch close* that he doesn't dodge the *Pansies* contract. He will find some trick to get back at me for making him pay for those signatures. – As for Harold Munro – he's rather another – I knew he'd have no money. I don't care one hollow straw whether I go into Chattos anthology or not. But poor Munro has been so ill, don't worry him too much. – I wrote him a note, but didn't mention any paying. Am weary of little people. – I'd have signed one of the photographs if I'd thought you wanted it – send it along. – Yes, we can pay all right for that copy of Stephensen's book for U.S.A. – wonder if it'll get in. – Wonder if you've seen my wife – she won't cheer you about Martin!

DHL

---

[1] Perhaps related to news of Secker's response, 14 June 1929, to Monro's request for permission to include DHL's poems in his anthology, *Twentieth Century Poetry*. Secker gave permission but stipulated a fee of one guinea for each poem, adding: 'we have no authority to deal with any of Lawrence's rights outside English book-publication. Mr Pollinger of Curtis Brown's will arrange this for you' (Secker Letter-Book, UIll). On 26 June Secker wrote again to Monro expressing annoyance at 'the muddle [he had] made over the Lawrence poems'. Monro had assumed that the one guinea fee covered Pollinger's fee as well as Secker's. Secker therefore revoked his permission: 'you must now start again ab ovo, and negotiate the matter direct with Pollinger, who is empowered to grant permissions both on the author's behalf and on our behalf'. Cf. Letter 5171.

5168. To Maria Chambers, [1 July 1929]
Text: MS StaU; Schorer 64.

[Pensione Giuliani, Forte dei Marmi]
[1 July 1929]¹

There are all sorts of rules and regulations for this beach – which I don't understand – Maria H[uxley] said the bagnino² woman had asked her to tell you please to undress in the little hut – the bathing-hut – belonging to Maria – though since you don't undress at all, I dont understand. But Maria H. *never* gets to the beach before 10.0 – usually never before 11.0 – and the door of the hut is open – so you could just go in and leave your mackintosh and towel there. – If you don't want to, ask the signora downstairs here – or the bagnino woman – what the rule is: the patrona here must know. – All so stupid. The feathers are lovely³ – and the orange juice – anyhow have a good dip!

DHL

5169. To Emily King, [1 July 1929]
Text: MS Lazarus; PC; Postmark, Forte dei Marmi 2.7.29; Unpublished.

Forte
Monday.

Had your letter – glad you liked the show. I am very well – Wonder if Frieda is coming up to see you this week? She wants me to come to England now – but it is such a long journey, and though one part of me would like very much indeed to come, another part shrinks from it perhaps even more. I shall write Frieda definitely tomorrow, to the Kingsley. And then I will write about your holidays too – It is fairly hot here – I shall leave anyhow next Saturday, or Monday. One needs to bathe if one stays in these flat, hot places, which get very breathless in the afternoon. I think I shall go to Florence, just for two or three days, to pick up some thin things – then come north to Milan. I wish it were not so awfully far, to England. If I don't come, I suppose Frieda will meet me either in Milan or Como – unless she wants to go to Germany straight away – then I'd join her there. But I'll write properly to say:

love! DHL

¹ Maria Chambers was in the Pensione Giuliani; this note was sent to her by hand on the second day of her stay. When she arrived, Orioli, who had come for the weekend, was still there; she had therefore probably arrived on Sunday 30 June. Hence the conjectural date of this letter. (For a full account of the visit see Maria Cristina Chambers, 'Afternoons in Italy with D. H. Lawrence', *Texas Quarterly*, vii, Winter 1964, 114–20.)
² 'bathing attendant'.
³ Maria Chambers had made a 'feather cape' and taken it for Frieda.

5170. To Ada Clarke, [1 July 1929]
Text: MS Clarke; PC; Postmark, Forte dei Marmi 2 7.29; Lawrence–Gelder 163–4.

Forte
– Monday

Still only a postcard – but I'll write a letter in a day or two, and send a photograph that Emily asked for – one of each sort, I'll send. – – I shall be leaving here on Saturday, or Monday at latest – go to Florence for just a day or two. c/o G. Orioli, 6 Lungarno Corsini. – I was tempted to come to England – but the long journey – then the things they say about the pictures put me off terribly. You'll have to come and see me. I wonder if Frieda is coming to see you this week – I expect so. If she doesn't want to go to Germany, I suppose we'll meet in Milan on the 11th or 12th – have written her to the Kingsley. Luckily it's not too hot here – but it may be any day – so I'm prepared to leave. – Expect you have got a copy of the *Pansies* – I have.

Love to you all   DHL

5171. To Laurence Pollinger, 1 July 1929
Text: MS UT; Unpublished.

Pensione Giuliani. *Forte dei Marmi.* (Lucca), Italy
1 July 1929

Dear Pollinger

Thanks for the Secker agreement. There's one thing doesn't hold. It says I am to get £50. down for signing 150 copies, whereas I signed 250 copies and stipulated that I got one-third of the profits due to signing alone = which is:

$$\frac{250 \times 1\frac{1}{2} \text{ guineas}}{3} = 125 \text{ gs.}$$

So please watch that Secker pays this *for signing alone* – he agreed to it by letter: 125 guineas for signing 250 copies.[1]

About Harold Munro, you must do as you think well – I don't really care – sort of feel 'poor old Munro' – but perhaps I'm wrong.[2]

I suppose you've seen my wife – She wants me to come to England – or says she does – but I'm not keen. It is *such* a long journey – and I'm just getting really to feel better – why knock myself up! – Besides why expose myself to the tender mercies of my fellow countrymen! The things they say about my paintings don't attract me to them one bit.

---

[1] Cf. Letter 5097.   [2] Cf. p. 350 n.

I expect to leave here next Saturday or Monday for a day or two in Florence, to pick up some things, then go north, to the Lakes. It can be pretty hot here already, and since I don't bathe, no place for me.[1] So dont use this address after Thursday – and please tell the other depts. – am sorry to be so shifty.

Ever   D. H. Lawrence

I shall be

      c/o Sig. G. Orioli, 6 Lungarno Corsini. Florence.

for a few days after the 6th.

5172. To P. R. Stephensen, 1 July 1929
Text: MS Anon; Munro 311.

Forte dei Marmi.
Monday 1 July 1929

Dear Stephensen

I was very tempted by your letter – if it weren't for the long long journey – then the thought of *Dover* – and Victoria Station! – If I could have flown straight to the cottage[2] – But my spirit simply shrinks away from the thought of the actual coming. I'm so sorry; and you are so kind.

I expect I shall leave here on Saturday – go to Florence for two or three days –

      c/o G. Orioli. 6 Lungarno Corsini.

– What, by the way, about the entry of the book into America? Any results yet? There is a woman here, Mrs Chambers, sailing back to New York from France on July 27th. – and anxious to take some copies in. What about it?

Wish I was more satisfactory. – Orioli wants to buy *Dandelions* for £20.

DHL

5173. To Charles Lahr, 1 July 1929
Text: MS UNYB; Postmark, Forte dei Marmi 2.7.29; Unpublished.

Forte dei Marmi.
1 July 1929

Dear Lahr

No luck with these sheets. Of course they won't let them pass plain. You have to print something on them – because a *parcel* may take a month or six weeks. Why not recover the sheets and print on them: 'This limited edition is

---

[1] DHL blamed his sea-bathing at Forte in June 1927 for his subsequent haemorrhages (see *Letters*, vi. 97–8, 107).

[2] Stephensen had invited DHL to stay at his cottage, 'Treesby', Knockholt, Kent. In the event Frieda stayed there (Munro, *Wild Man of Letters*, p. 85).

printed complete, following the original manuscript, according to my wish.'[1]
– Then I can sign, and surely nobody can take alarm. – If you also print:
Signed _____ : and a *line* on which I can sign, the post will understand, also
here in Italy. But anything that looks like simple paper they won't accept here
either.

I shall leave here next Saturday, or Monday 8th. – and shall be a day or
two[2] in Florence. You can send the sheets to G. Orioli if you like – without
my name – and a note to him saying they are for me. He will forward if I've
left.

I was almost tempted to come to England – but I can't. The things they say
about the pictures repel me also from Albion's shore. No good, my spirit can't
come to England – something holds it back.

Sorry about the sheets.

D. H. Lawrence

5174. To Giuseppe Orioli, [2 July 1929]
Text: MS NWU; PC; Postmark, Forte dei Marmi 3.7.29; Unpublished.

[Pensione Giuliani, Forte dei Marmi]
Tuesday

Dear Pino –

The signorina of the pensione says the falegname could certainly mend the
baulo,[3] so if you have not sent the new one, don't trouble. But if you have, I
hope it will arrive soon, then I will pack it and we will come to Florence on
Saturday, arrive by that train about one o'clock. Mrs Chambers will stay in
the Moderno – and afterwards she will go to Venice. I think I shall meet
Frieda in Milan on Thursday, 11th. – and perhaps go to Lake Como, it is
easier than Garda. I hope all is well with you – a little friction between the
ladies here!

DHL

5175. To Max Mohr, 2 July 1929
Text: MS HMohr; Mohr 167–8.

Forte dei Marmi (Lucca)
2 July 1929

Dear Max Mohr

I had both your letters here – it seems to be going all right with Rowohlt,
but why is he fussing about a translator? Why do people make so many fusses,

[1] following . . . wish.'] according to my wish, following the original manuscript.
[2] MS reads 'to'.
[3] 'joiner (falegname) . . . trunk'.

anyhow? But I hope you will do the translation. I have not received any letter from Rowohlt, forwarded from Palma. Do you think he really wrote to me there? – However, I will write to him.

It is rather hot here, I am going to Florence on Saturday, just for a day or two – the address

c/o G. Orioli. 6 Lungarno Corsini. Florence.

– Then on the 10th. I shall go to Milan, probably meet my wife there, and we may stay a week or two on Lago di Como. I don't think it will be too hot. Later we shall come to Germany, and if you are doing the translation, it would be a good thing to meet in Bavaria in September. I should like that. Meantime let me know if there is any further development from Rowohlt.

What is this Fieber[1] you say you are all suffering from? I hope it is nothing serious, and that you are all better. It must be lovely summer now at the Wolfsgrube.

The Paris edition of *Lady C.* is out – at 60 francs – quite nice. Would you like me to send you a copy? I hear some German bookshops have ordered copies.

I do hope you are well, and having a good summer.

Many greetings.   D. H. Lawrence

Ich habe keine Adresse für den Rowohlt – bitte schicken Sie ihm meinen Brief – Sie werden lesen was ich sage.[2] –

DHL

5176. To Giuseppe Orioli, [3 July 1929]

Text: MS UCLA; Moore, *Intelligent Heart* 407–8.

Pensione Giuliani, Forte dei Marmi. (Lucca)
Wednesday[3]

Dear Pino

Thank you for sending the trunk. It hasn't come yet, but I hope the *corriere*[4] will bring it today.

Maria Cristina wears me out rather – so she is going to Pisa tomorrow, to stay the night there, and come on to Florence on Friday.[5] She will arrive at 13.15, but I don't think there is any need for you to meet her, if you will just engage her a room at the *Moderno* for Friday at 1.15, she can drive there in a vettura.[6]

---

[1] 'fever'.
[2] 'I have no address for Rowohlt – please forward him my letter – Do read what I say.'
[3] Wednesday] Thursday   [4] 'carrier'.   [5] Friday.] Sat   [6] 'tram'.

I expect I shall come on Saturday, by the same train. Shall I really stay with you in your flat? I should like to. But don't meet me either at the station, it is so easy to drive to you.

Sorry the dinner was dull. Here Maria and Yvonne Franchetti were very *cattive*[1] with M.C. – but suddenly Maria changed, and became patronisingly sweet. They are still wondering when you are going to Montecatini with Aldous. A few more people on the beach – all so terribly aware of *themselves* and their beastly bodies.[2] Well I shall be glad to escape an atmosphere of women, women, women, and see you again.

DHL

5177. To Giuseppe Orioli, [4 July 1929]
Text: MS NWU; PC; Postmark, Forte dei Marmi 6.7.29; Unpublished.

Forte.
Thursday

Dear Pino

– It has been very hot today, a fierce hot wind. We have decided that I had better come on Saturday *night*, to be cooler. Maria says she will drive me to Pisa (the night train is so slow – I'll take the 17.40 at Pisa –)[3] and I will come to Florence by the train that arrives about 7.15 (seven fifteen)[4] o'clock at night – I'll look it up – the diretto.[5]

Maria Cristina will stay on here, and I will try to get Aldous to see that the bank here cashes her cheques.

The trunk is not here yet, but we have the avviso,[6] so tonight no doubt they will bring it.

Frieda leaves London on Saturday, for BadenBaden.

Hasta muy pronto![7]   DHL

---

[1] 'ill-natured, harsh'.
[2] See 'Forte dei Marmi' and 'Sea-Bathers' (*Complete Poems*, ii. 625).
[3] (the night ... Pisa –)] – we have dinner there –   [4] 7.15 (seven fifteen)] eleven
[5] 'through train'.
[6] 'advice note'.   [7] 'See you very soon!'

5178. To Maria Chambers, [5 July 1929]
Text: MS StaU; Schorer 64–5.

[Pensione Giuliani, Forte dei Marmi]
[5 July 1929]¹

I've written in the poems already² – shall be on the beach about 6.o, Maria is
going to Viareggio, so won't be there – I am tea-ing with Aldous.³

5179. To Giuseppe Orioli, [5 July 1929]
Text: MS NWU; PC; Postmark, Forte dei Marmi 6.7.29; cited in Moore, *Poste Restante* 100.

[Pensione Giuliani, Forte dei Marmi]
Friday tea-time.

Dear Pino

I shall arrive tomorrow evening, as I said, at 7.12 (19.12) by the quick train.
The wretches still have not brought the baule from Querceta. Mrs Chambers
has changed her money at the bank here, so does not need any.

DHL

5180. To Maria Chambers, [6 July 1929]
Text: MS StaU; cited in Chambers 117–18.

[Pensione Giuliani, Forte dei Marmi]
[6 July 1929]

Many thanks for juice and plums – the new trunk is about half as big as the
old one – so some diminishing feat will have to be performed.

Perhaps everybody wants to turn over a new sweet leaf, decorated with
pansies and forgetmenots. Quanto a me, non capisco niente – la donna è
mobile ecc. ecc.⁴

The party was all right – talk –

---

¹ DHL most probably wrote this note on the last day that Maria Cristina Chambers spent with
  him: 5 July 1929.
² DHL's note was in reply to, and written on the verso of, a note from Maria Cristina:

  Señor Lawrence, I am going to let you rest now. I'll see you this evening. Maria Cristina. Send
  me the *poems* if you have written something in them! –
³ Later Maria Cristina recalled:

  He had been 'teaing' with the Huxleys, and when he returned he was in a strange mood, very
  silent, lost in some wretched depression. All through dinner he was remote. Something told me
  he would be pleased if I too kept silent. I risked a polite inquiry about 'teaing' with the
  Huxleys.
      'Talk, talk, talk,' he said finally. 'Words, words, words! They kill the flow of life.' (Chambers
  117)
⁴ 'As for me, I understand nothing – woman is fickle etc. etc.'

I shall pack my trunk a bit later on, and call for you when I get stuck.[1]

It may be two friends from Florence will call this morning – a Miss Morrison and Signor Sensani.[2] I think you might like them.

I'll give you a photograph I had taken in Palma – Mallorca.

DHL

5181. To Laurence Pollinger, 6 July 1929
Text: MS UT; Unpublished.

Forte dei Marmi
6 July 1929

Dear Pollinger

Will you please answer this woman.[3]

I will send the Secker agreement signed when I know he is paying O. K. for the 250, and not 150 signatures – viz £125. and not £50.

Am leaving this afternoon for Florence. Getting pretty hot –

D. H. Lawrence

5182. To Maria Chambers, [7 July 1929]
Text: MS StaU; cited in Schorer 65.

Firenze.
Sunday

Dear Maria Cristina

Had a very pleasant and easy journey here, not at all too hot. Florence is a bit hotter than Forte, though, so if you are afraid of the heat, beware a little.

Pino says he'll probably be going to Montecatini for his cure next Saturday – or else Monday – and he's so sorry he won't be here to see you. But his cure is an annual institution, really.

I do hope you are having a nice time. I want to leave on Tuesday or Wednesday – the address

c/o Frau Baronin von Richthofen, Ludwig-Wilhelmstift, *Baden Baden*, Germania.

Had a letter from my mother-in-law this morning, she wants us all to go up into the mountains near Baden next Saturday.

---

[1] Later, anxious about DHL's physical condition, Maria Cristina Chambers went to his room. 'There was Lawrence, bending over a huge trunk. He looked tired, breathing painfully from the asthma. But he was pleased to see me. When I told him I was going to finish his packing, he sat on the bed with a grateful smile and told me to go ahead' (Chambers 118).

[2] Nellie Morrison; unidentified.   [3] Unidentified; enclosure is missing.

I shall send you a letter for Edwin Rich before I leave here. Do hope you are having a nice time.

tante belle cose! D. H. Lawrence

Italian proverb: Due Marie insieme non anderanno mai bene.[1]

5183. To Frieda Lawrence, [7 July 1929]
Text: MS UCB; Frieda Lawrence 288–9.

6 Lungarno Corsini. *Florence*
Sunday. 7 July

Maria drove me to Pisa yesterday afternoon – very scirocco and overcast, but not hot, not at all uncomfortable. Unfortunately my inside is upset – either I must have eaten something or it came from drinking ice-water very cold on Thursday when it was hot. Anyhow my lower man hurts and it makes my chest sore – which is a pity, because I was so well. Now I'm rather limp. But I've kept still all day in Pino's flat, and he looks after me well[2] – so I hope by tomorrow or Tuesday it will be all right. Luigino Franchetti said he'd got ptomaine poisoning, on Friday at Forte – but I think it was an upset too, nothing serious. I think mine is going off. Pino's flat gets a bit hot just at evening, but in the night and most part of the day it is pleasant and cool – it's not really a hot year. Carletto has gone off for a day's tramp in the hills beyond Fiesole. Pino and I will have a cup of tea now, then perhaps take a carriage-drive for an hour.

I had your mother's letter this morning – she says you are all going up to Plässig[3] or somewhere on the 13th – which is next Saturday. What is it like there? Probably I shall arrive in Baden by then – depends a bit on the innards. I wanted to look at the Lake of Como to see if we'd like a house there – but am not sure if I shall want to make the effort. And I was so well before.

Maria Cristina is staying on in Forte, thank God – till about 15th. She must be in Paris by 23rd. – sails on 27th – thank heaven. She's a mixture of the worst side of Arabella – turns up her eyes in that awful indecent fashion – and of Ivy Low[4] – humble, cringing, yet impudent, with an eternal and ceaseless self-preoccupation, tangled up in her own ego till it's shameful – and one is socially ashamed of her – gutter-snipe, thinking all and only of herself.

---

[1] 'Two Marias will never get on well together.'
[2] Orioli had been so distressed by DHL's appearance on his arrival in Florence that he had him brought by car to his own flat; Orioli then telegraphed Frieda to come at once. He later told her 'how scared he had been, when he had seen Lawrence, his head and arms hanging over the side of the bed, like one dead' (Frieda Lawrence 213: cf. Nehls, iii. 353).
[3] Kurhaus Plättig, bei Buhl, Baden-Baden.
[4] Ivy Teresa Litvinov, née Low (1889–1977), novelist: DHL had known her since 1914. m. 1916, Maxim Litvinov (1876–1951), Soviet diplomat. See *Letters*, ii. 160 n. 3.

Ugh, she's awful. At the same time, she's a poor pathetic thing. – She has sent you a feather thing that she says is for a little cape – pretty – but I shall leave it behind in the trunk. I am leaving this trunk here also – the money they cost in transport and fachinaggio[1] is awful, pure waste – and the bother.

Well, I've not had a coherent or sensible letter from you since you left Paris – so I suppose you were gone overhead – and then it's no use saying anything. However, emerge quickly – and we'll see if we can settle this problem of a house.

Had a letter from Barby – but it wasn't somehow very nice – same cattiveria[2] as Maria, underneath – or so it seemed. – I suppose you didn't go and see my sisters. Hope Else is better. – Aldous was very well, I've never seen him so well. – Am seeing nobody here. – No sound from Brett about MSS. or ranch. – Think I shall come by night to Milano – but hate sharing a berth with some stranger. Hope you are nice and peaceful in Baden.

L

I really think Italy is not good for my health – the country is much *slacker*, all going deflated – and a lot of poverty again, so they say. But everybody is very *nice*, much softer once more, and sort of subdued.

5184. To Frieda Lawrence, [8 July 1929]
Text: MS UCB; Frieda Lawrence 290.

Florence.
Monday night

The pains were a chill – have been in bed all day today – damn! – Pino very nice, but oh the noise of traffic! – I'm a lot better. I want to get up tomorrow, and leave if possible on Wednesday night for Milan. I might arrive Baden on Thursday night – otherwise Friday – all being well. Hot internal cold I've got, real Italian. I hate this country like poison, sure it would kill me.

I should rather like an apartment for six weeks or so – Ebersteinburg, Baden – anywhere – where I can lie in bed all day if I want to – and where I needn't see people. But don't at all know what you feel like, since you have not written lately.

Rained a bit today – quite cool. Pino and Carletto gone out into town.

DHL

Shall wire – suppose you had all my letters addressed to the Kingsley.

---

[1] 'porterage'.   [2] 'nastiness'.

5185. To Dorothy Warren, 9 July 1929
Text: MS UN; Nehls, iii. 342.

c/o G. Orioli. 6 Lungarno Corsini. Florence
9 July 1929

Dear Dorothy

Well there's a go! – even the *Boccaccio Story* and 'Eve'[1] shut up in prison now, with only Mr Mead to look at them.[2] Hope he'll get his meed. But send me news. If only one could shoot a few of the old fungoids!

I've written to Frieda to the Kingsley – is she still there? – I hear nothing from her.[3]

5186. To Charles Lahr, [9 July 1929]
Text: MS UNYB; Postmark, Firenze 9. VII.29; cited in Moore, *Intelligent Heart* 414.

c/o G. Orioli. 6 Lungarno Corsini, Florence.
Tuesday. 9 July

Dear L[ahr]

The parcels of sheets came today, safely. I will address them to Rhys Davies, *4 Fitzroy Square* – by registered printed-matter mail. If I seal them letter-post they hold them and make more fuss, asking if they contain contraband.

Bit of a blow about the pictures – Hear my wife is staying on – is she at the Kingsley?

Thanks for the cuttings – You might get somebody to write to *Daily News* and ask if Sylvia Lynd made this mis-quotation on purpose

Don't make it in ghastly seriousness
– (Don't) do it because you hate people

---

[1] With reference to this letter and the police raid on the Warren Gallery on 5 July 1929, Philip Trotter remarked: 'This is a mistake. "*Eve*" was not seized. D. H. L is quite clearly referring to *Flight Back into Paradise*, by far the biggest picture in the exhibition. He would never have singled out a water-colour [*Throwing Back the Apple*]. Of course neither of these was seized' (Nehls, iii. 717 n. 211). Trotter however believed that *Boccaccio Story* (together with *Fight with an Amazon*) 'may fairly be assumed to have precipitated the crisis' (ibid., iii. 354).

[2] Frederick Mead (1847–1945), the magistrate on whose authority the police raid was made and before whom the case of DHL's paintings was heard on 8 August at the Court of Summary Jurisdiction, Metropolitan Police District, Marlborough Street Magistrates' Court, London.

[3] The complimentary close and signature, if they existed, were torn off.

the *Don't* omitted from her quot. – which gives an ugly face to the thing.[1]
That's the way they do me harm all the time.

Shall send parcels today or tomorrow.

                                                                              L.

5187. To Martin Secker, 9 July 1929
Text: MS UInd; Postmark, Firenze 10.VII.29; Secker 122.

                                          c/o G. Orioli. 6 Lungarno Corsini. Firenze.
                                                                      9 July 1929.
Dear Secker

So now I hear they've put my pictures in prison – che festa![2]

I saw the *Times Sup.*[3] and Sylvia Lynd on the *Pansies* – feeble – and she ought to be pulled up for that misquotation: *Do it because you hate people*: instead of *Don't do it because etc*. As if deliberately they tried to make a nasty impression. – The book is attractive, I think; tell me how it goes. – By the way, Orioli says he ordered one 2 guinea copy and one ½ guinea, but you havent sent them!

Would you send a copy to Frieda's sister

                 Frau Dr Else Jaffe. Bismarckstr. 17. *Heidelberg*

unless you have sent one already. And a copy to:

                 Mr and Mrs E. Brewster. Casa Surya. *Anacapri*. Napoli.

I was at Forte dei Marmi two weeks – not bad, but a place I should never love. Italy seems a bit *flat* to me, deflated – like a flat tyre. I don't like it much. I shall come north to meet Frieda, probably in Germany, when she is ready to leave London – but I haven't heard from her for some time.

Luckily it's not very hot here – rained today – a bit muggy. And of course

---

[1] Lines 2 and 5 of DHL's poem, 'A Sane Revolution' (*Complete Poems*, i. 517); l.5 was misquoted in the review of *Pansies* (Secker edn) by Sylvia Lynd (1888–1952), poet and novelist, printed in the *Daily News*, 4 July 1929. The gist of her review is that DHL 'does not appreciate the beauty of anonymity . . . we are distracted by what seems to us an over-aggressive, undignified and conceited presence' of the poet himself. She accuses DHL of 'sneering bad temper' but admits that 'he is not dull. There is the stir of his vivid personality behind even the most unnecessary of these scribblings.'

[2] 'what an entertainment!'

[3] The unsigned review of *Pansies* in *The Times Literary Supplement*, 4 July 1929, was not unappreciative: '[The poems] fix with an unusual precision a particular set of opinions and memorialize disgust of our civilization as few treatises by social reformers could hope to do . . . And, while there is much modern poetry which does not seem to express anything that the poet greatly wished to say, there is scarcely a line of Mr. Lawrence's verses which does not sound like a piece of the author's mind, in both the obvious and the idiomatic sense of the phrase' (Draper, *The Critical Heritage*, pp. 310–11). The reviewer was Alan Clutton-Brock (1904–76), subsequently art-critic for *The Times*, 1945–55, and Slade Professor of Fine Art at Cambridge, 1955–8.

it's given me one of my Italian colds, all hot and feverish inside. I seem only to get them in Italy. And the *noise* of Florence is real torture, when one feels a bit feverish. Poveri noi – !¹ Edward Hutton turned very Catholic, forever on his knees.² Douglas pain in his shoulder and numbness in his hand – and very frightened lest it might be paralysis coming. Hope it's not. Everybody seems a lot older in a year.

Where are you going for the holiday? I expect we shall be somewhere in Germany. Wish I was a bit stronger in health, to fight the decayed masses of muffs.

Hope all's well!   DHL

5188. To Maria Huxley, [10 July 1929]
Text: Huxley 808.

Florence,
Wed. 10.vii.29.

You have heard of the catastrophe, of course – 13 pictures seized and in gaol – yours among them³ – and threatened to be burnt – *auto-da-fé*⁴ – you have no luck in that picture. Frieda is staying on in London, don't know how long – had a telegram, nothing else. Arrived with a nasty cold, in bed two days – *miseria* – guess I got it sitting too late on the beach on Friday, as it was all in my legs and lower man – better now – out this evening for the first time. Shall leave Sunday or Monday, I think for Bavaria – not at all hot here, by good luck – more anon.

DHL

5189. To Maria Chambers, [10 July 1929]
Text: MS StaU; PC; Postmark, Firenze 10.VII.29; Unpublished.

Firenze
– Wed.

Thanks for sending on the letter – suppose you have heard by now that the police raided the picture show in London and seized thirteen of the pictures, which now lie in gaol with threat of being burnt! Bella fortuna!⁵ – My wife staying on in London awhile – I shall stay here till the week-end, then go to Germany when Pino goes to Montecatini. Fortunately it is not hot in Flor-

---

¹ 'Poor us – !'
² Edward Hutton (1875–1969), author of many books on Italian history, literature and art; he was a founder-member of the British Institute of Florence and had lived in Settignano. (Obituary, *Times*, 23 August 1969.)
³ *North Sea* (see Letter 5200).   ⁴ The public burning of a heretic by the Inquisition.
⁵ 'Good luck!'

ence, quite comfortable – and if there were not so many motor-horns, quite nice. I do suffer from the noise. – Hope you are having a good time and not getting nearly drowned daily.

                                                                                    DHL

Many thanks for the list.

5190. To Emily King, [10 July 1929]
Text: MS Lazarus; PC; Postmark, Firenze 10 VII 29; Unpublished.

Florence.
10 July

More catastrophes – it really is too ridiculous – as if any of them really believed in the nonsense – makes one tired. I hear Frieda is staying on in London, don't know how long – but I think I shall leave Florence at the week-end as it may get unpleasantly hot any day now   it's quite cool because of thunder showers, which is lucky. I had a nasty cold, the week-end – so stayed in bed in Orioli's flat – it came on suddenly Friday evening – must have been their beastliness in London reaching out to me. Of course it is partly the *Pansies* makes them attack me again. – I seem so unsettled, can't get to writing letters. Hope you are all well.

                                                                        love.   DHL

5191. To Ada Clarke, [10 July 1929]
Text: MS Clarke; Postmark, Fi[renze] 10 VII.29; cited in Lawrence–Gelder 194.

6 Lungarno Corsini. Florence.
Wed. 10 July.

My dear Sister
    Yes, one feels very sick about the pictures – I suppose they won't let them burn them!
    Funny, but I got a bad cold on Friday afternoon – like a shot in the back – so have stayed in bed here in Florence in Orioli's flat – now it's a lot better – think I shall go out a bit. Orioli has to go away on Sat. or Monday to take a liver cure – I suppose I could stay on here alone with his servant, but don't much want to, as it may get very hot any day. Luckily it's cool now. Perhaps I shall go to Bavaria, to Max Mohr – as I don't know when Frieda intends to come – she never writes – and her mother is going away from Baden for a fortnight – besides I don't want to go there.
    Well, it's an unpleasant world – but I shan't let it worry me more than it need – and don't you either. The dirty swine would like to think they made you weep.

                                                                        love!   DHL

5192. To Charles Lahr, 10 July 1929
Text: MS UNYB and Forster; Postmark, Firenze 10.VII.29; Unpublished.

6 Lungarno Corsini. Firenze.
10 July 1929

Dear Lahr

I sent off two packages of sheets today, signed – to Davies at Fitzroy Sq. Hope they arrive safely. The third parcel I shall send, the same address, tomorrow. I signed 56 of the vellum, and about 514 of the ordinary. I numbered them all, as it seems useless to say 'limited' without putting the limit. You can add: Edition of 500 copies – if you wish.

I like the drawing – so does Orioli. But the phœnix is really too small – nothing but a button. You might have sent me a sample of the cover, in a letter.

Well I am very sick about the pictures and all.

DHL

5193. To Max Mohr, 10 July 1929
Text: MS HMohr; Mohr, Briefe 533.

6 Lungarno Corsini. Firenze.
10 July 1929

Dear Mohr

Well now the police have raided my picture show in London, and carried off[1] 13 pictures, and have them locked up, and want to burn them? Auto da fé. My wife is staying on in London, I don't know how long.

I think I should like to come to the Tegernsee. If my wife does not make some other plan, I think I shall take the train on Sunday or Monday to München from here, and then come to Rottach. Perhaps you can find me a room in a Gasthaus, not so very far away.

I am *not sure* that I can come – it depends on Frieda – but I should like to, and I shall send you a telegram at the week-end.

auf Wiedersehen. D. H. Lawrence

5194. To Max Mohr, [13 July 1929]
Text: MS HMohr; Mohr 168.

Florence.
Sunday

Dear Max Mohr

My wife came here suddenly – and she wants to go *first* to BadenBaden to

[1] MS reads 'of'.

her mother, and come later on to Bavaria, perhaps September. I'm not very keen on Baden – but if I don't like it I shan't stay. Anyhow we shall not come to Rottach just now – and I'm sorry, really –

ever   D. H. Lawrence

5195. To Ada Clarke, [13 July 1929]
Text: MS Clarke; Postmark, Firenze 13.VII.29; Unpublished.

Florence –
Sat.

My dear Sister

Frieda arrived all right Thursday night – not very tired – but of course wrenched her foot again on Milan station, and it's very swollen.

Still waiting to hear fate of pictures – fed up.

Expect we shall leave early next week – Tuesday – for BadenBaden. Send you five pounds for the children's holiday – hope they'll have a good time.

love   DHL

lovely socks! – and the braces.

5196. To Emily King, [13 July 1929]
Text: MS Lazarus; Postmark, Firenze 13.VII.29; Unpublished.

Florence.
Sat.

My dear Pamela

Frieda arrived suddenly on Thursday night – seems very well – but wrenched her foot again and it's very much swollen up again – a great nuisance. Otherwise she's very well – and my cold is a lot better – still sore inside.

We shall leave for BadenBaden next Tuesday, all being well – it's getting hot, but not yet too hot here.

I enclose £10. for the holidays – give Peg some of it.

I am still awaiting a wire, to know the fate of the pictures. Very fed up.

love   DHL

5197. To Maria Chambers, [13 July 1929]
Text: MS UT; Unpublished.

Florence –
Saturday

Dear Maria Cristina

Your letter this morning. – No, I would just avoid the Moros de la Costa, if

I were you. All no good.[1]

My pictures lie in prison and *may* be burnt.

The picture-books[2] are all sold – the last 50 bought up as a speculation by a rich American,[3] so there is now nothing to send to New York – many thanks all the same.

I am better – but inside a little sore still – expect to leave on *Monday* for Baden. Orioli sends greetings.

DHL

5198. To Dorothy Warren, [13 July 1929]
Text: MS UN; Nehls, iii. 357–8.

Florence.
Sat. night

Dear Dorothy

Frieda came all right – but wrenched her foot again, and limps – otherwise is blooming, and all sorts of fine feathers making her a fine bird – She says she had a coruscating fortnight. – I had a nasty chill in my inside – special Italian sort, Forte beach, Forte water etcetc. – but it's passing. No need for poor F. to rush here.

Your telegram come – but you don't say if you've got the pictures out of prison – and I'm so anxious about that. The letter has not come – Victor Cunard wired about it. I will answer at once when it does.[4] – You know

---

[1] In a note on a TMSC of this letter at UT, Maria Chambers explained:

The reference to Moros de la Costa is to Aldous and Maria Huxley. It was in answer to my letter asking him if I may not be a little more sociable with the Huxleys, now that he had gone away, because the Huxleys had been nice to me, as far as I could see. Lawrence, however was very set in my having nothing to do with them. I had told Lawrence a little Spanish story. How after the Moors invaded Spain, the natives had a saying to warn people of unpleasant and intruding persons. The saying being: 'Moros en la Costa and gatos en la azotea.' (Moors on the coast and cats on the roof). Lawrence always called the Huxleys the 'Moros de la Costa' because, as he said, they were always intruding in his affairs.

[2] DHL initially wrote 'books' and then inserted 'picture-books' without deleting his first choice, so MS reads 'picture-books books'.

[3] Unidentified.

[4] Dorothy Warren had written 'a long and bracing letter' to DHL 'lest Frieda should infect him with the submissive overtones' of a compromise proposed by Percy Robinson, the solicitor appointed to watch DHL's interests in the legal battle. Robinson proposed that – in order to recover the pictures intact from the police – Dorothy Warren's counsel, St John Hutchinson, should give an undertaking in court that the pictures would never be exhibited again in England. Warren and her husband opposed the compromise: 'this might mean the ignominious return of the pictures as undesirable objects not worth a bonfire, in complete vindication of the filthy [newspaper] campaign. [Warren's] letter was taken by Victor Cunard to be posted from Rome, where he was special Correspondent of *The Times*. He was to telephone Lawrence on his arrival' (Nehls, iii. 357).

Alinari's have a shop in London, near Brit. Museum – but I'll hunt here on Monday.

I'm sure you are worn out. But do get me all my pictures back safely – I am so anxious about that. And don't sell any more of them at those prices – I'd rather keep them: why sell them at all?

Very many thanks for the lovely jade box – but I had to drop a tear in it when I thought of my *Boccaccio* in gaol.

Waiting your letter – and thank you both for being so nice to Frieda. She'll write too – but now her limp is an occupation!

                                                                 DHL

5199. To Laurence Pollinger, 13 July 1929
Text: MS UT; Unpublished.

                                                                 Florence.
                                                        Sat. 13 July 1929
Dear Pollinger

I was waiting the original of your letter, but see it was sent to Baden.

I wired *Islands Accept* yesterday. Sounds quite good.[1]

No definite news still of the paintings, only a long long flowery incomprehensible telegram from Dorothy Warren, and she doesn't say if she's got the thirteen out of prison. Am most anxious about that – and Dorothy is not very definite, to trust – wish I had the pictures all back safe, whether I get any money from her or not. Too much of a hullabaloo – too much sensation – I don't like it – wish I had my pictures safe back here, and damn everybody.

I've tried once or twice to cut *Lady C*. and *couldn't*. I may try once more.

We want to leave for Baden on Tuesday or Wednesday – fun to see you there. It's still quite pleasant here – not too hot – Shall write properly from Baden –

                                                        haste!   DHL

      Percy James Hall Robinson (b.1870?) was the senior partner in Percy Robinson & Co., 15 Great Marlborough Street.
      Victor Cunard (d. 1960), 'a man of culture and tolerance, of wit and distinction ... between the two wars he worked at Rome and in Paris as a correspondent of *The Times*' (*Times*, 1 September 1960, p. 12).

[1] Heinemann had offered an advance of £300 on a limited edition of 'The Man Who Loved Islands' (which had appeared in the American, but not the English, edition of *The Woman Who Rode Away and Other Stories*; cf. *Letters*, vi. 69 n. 1). The edn never appeared.

5200. To Dorothy Warren, 14 July 1929
Text: MS UN and Nehls, iii. 359–60; cited in Moore, *Intelligent Heart* 409.

Hotel Porta Rossa. Florence

14 July 1929

Dear Dorothy

Your long and very interesting letter this morning.[1] – Lord, what a go! But I think it's a mistake to want to go to High Court – what to do? prove that the pictures are not obscene? but they are not, so how prove it? And if they go against you there – then more is lost than will be got back in years. No no, I want you to accept the compromise. I do not want my pictures to be burned, under any circumstance or[2] for any cause. The law, of course, must be altered – it is blatantly obvious. Why burn my pictures to prove it? There is something sacred to me about my pictures, and I will not have them burnt, for all the liberty of England. I am an Englishman, and I do my bit for the liberty of England. But I am most of all a man, and my first creed is that my manhood and my sincere utterance shall be inviolate and beyond nationality or any other limitation. To admit that my pictures should be burned, in order to change an English[3] law, would be to admit that sacrifice of life to circumstance which I most strongly disbelieve in. No, at all costs or any cost, I don't want my pictures burnt. No more crucifixions, no more martyrdoms, no more autos da fé, as long as time lasts, if I can prevent it. Every crucifixion starts a most deadly chain of karma,[4] every martyr is a Laocöon snake to tangle up the human family.[5] Away with such things.

I want you to get my pictures back. If you have to promise never to show them again in England, I do not care. England can change its mind later if it wants to – it can never call back a burnt picture. If the things *are* burnt, I shall not break my heart. But I shall certainly have much less hope of England, and much less interest in it.

If you want to arrange a show in Germany, and can, I don't mind, but I am not keen that you should do it. I should like you soon to wind up the show altogether – sell the pictures at much better prices, if there are purchasers. If there are no purchasers, I am just as well content, I have no need and no desire to sell. You can have *Contadini* for £20, if that is the one you want – it is

---

[1] Cf. Letter 5198 and n. 4.   [2] or] and   [3] an English] a
[4] I.e. inevitable consequences (a Buddhist conception).
[5] Laocöon (in post-Homeric epic) tried to prevent the Trojans opening their gates to the Trojan horse. He and his two sons were strangled by sea-serpents. The event is depicted in a famous statue now in the Vatican Museum. See *Letters*, i. 136–7; ii.137 and n. 2.

a favorite of mine.[1] I want you to give *North Sea* (of course, if you recover them) to St John H[utchinson] for Maria Huxley, according to long promise.[2] Orioli wants to buy *Dandelions* for £20.[3] About the disposal of the others I will write you in detail when you are ready to close the show. But we want to take a house in France or Italy this autumn, and I shall have most of the pictures back to hang in the rooms, as at the Mirenda. – I am very grateful for all you and Philip Trotter have done – but now it is about enough, and anything else will be in the nature of an anti-climax.

tante belle cose!   D. H. Lawrence

We leave here Tuesday for BadenBaden.

c/o Frau von Richthofen, Ludwig-Wilhelmstift

[Frieda Lawrence begins][4]

Dear Dorothy,

Your long letter to Lawrence only came this morning. So you got an adjournment we guess.[5] There is a lot to be said for your fight to the finish plan. But Lawrence and I who have been up against it so often, know what can be done at one go. If you overdo our side the Soloman's baby i.e. pictures will be burnt. That would be a feather in *their* cap. You have won so far with showing the pictures at all, and it's all been a great advertisement for us all round. One has got the thin end of the wedge in, a new way of looking at things started. Let's go slow and sure and with a *far* vision. Keep some of your fighting spirit for future occasions, keep some in reserve. I have so enjoyed these London days and you and Philip. I am glad to be with Lawrence, we are so *sure* of ourselves in the long run. Don't take it too seriously!

Love   F.

---

[1] Philip Trotter remarked: 'This fine painting disappeared with several others from a half-way house between our London home and the wartime sanctuary of Thomas Agnew & Sons' (Nehls, iii. 715 n. 185). It has never reappeared.

[2] The picture was destroyed in the fire at the Huxley home in 1961.

[3] Now in the possession of Melissa Partridge.

[4] The text of Frieda's letter comes from Nehls, iii. 359–60.

[5] An adjournment of the hearing from 12 to 18 July had been secured by Percy Robinson; it was almost at once extended by the police to 8 August (Nehls, iii. 369).

5201. To St John Hutchinson, 14 July 1929
Text: MS Hutchinson; Unpublished.

Hotel Porta Rossa. Florence
14 July 1929

Dear Hutchinson

I have no definite news about the seized pictures – I should think there is an adjournment. For my part, I wish Dorothy Warren to accept the compromise she mentions, if that is possible. I see very little good in taking the case to High Court, anyhow – if you lose it, it is a general disaster for the cause: and if you can only win it at the expense of burning my pictures, then for my part, it can remain unwon. The censorship law should most obviously be altered. Why burn my pictures to prove it? I do not believe in sacrifice, it is false doctrine anyhow. And to burn my pictures just to get a sensational case, seems to me a crime. Alter your laws without burning anything or anybody – there's my creed.

I'm afraid Dorothy gets very worked up and excited. I think myself it would now be as well to close the show altogether, and have done with it. I have asked her to do so, and to let me have the pictures back. I don't want her to sell any more at those low prices – I'd *far* rather keep them. But I have asked her to give you *North Sea* (if recovered) for Maria Huxley, according to long promise – and if there is any one that you or Mary would like, you can have it at your own price.[1] – I do hope I shall be able to wind this thing up satisfactorily with Dorothy Warren – she has so many ideas and schemes, and leaves me rather powerless.

Many thanks again for your help – you will soon be the real St. George of the censorship battle.

We leave on Tuesday for BadenBaden –
c/o Frau von Richthofen. Ludwig-Wilhelmstift –
Send me a line there, please, I can get nothing definite out of Dorothy Warren.

With many regards to you and Mary, also to Mademoiselle – does she still wear her blue frock?

D. H. Lawrence

---

[1] Lord Jeremy Hutchinson believes that his parents never acquired a painting by DHL.

5202. To Enid Hilton, [14 July 1929]
Text: MS UCLA; Unpublished.

Florence.

Sunday

Dear Enid

Dorothy Warren very vague – do send us news to Baden Baden, if there is any. We leave Tuesday

c/o Frau v. Richthofen, *Ludwig Wilhelmstift*

Could you tell me, did you give Miller & Gill any copies of my novel – I have them down for seven – (4 + 3) – but they have never paid.[1] Did they return them.

Perhaps I'll let you keep a picture for me when the show is really over – house it for me. Which one would you like?[2]

DHL.

5203. To Juliette Huxley, [15 July 1929]
Text: MS Huxley; PC v. Firenze, Chiesa di S. Maria Novella; Postmark, Firenze 15.VII.29; Unpublished.

Florence

15 July

– Your letter came on here – glad you liked the *Pansies* and your own particular viola![3] We leave tomorrow for BadenBaden –

c/o Frau v. Richthofen. Ludwig-Wilhelmstift

– don't know how long we shall stay, but the address is good. – Awful fuss about the pictures – shall burst with rage if they burn them. We may meet in Switzerland or Germany – Baden is very near – Thrilling for Julian, all good wishes for his trip[4] – and au revoir!

DHL

---

[1] Presumably DHL had forgotten that, as recorded in his 'Memoranda' (MS NWU), Miller & Gill paid £5.5.0 on 27 April 1929.

[2] Enid Hilton bought *Fire-Dance* (now in the possession of Marshall Flaum).

[3] See Letter 4868 and n. 3.

[4] In August 1929 Julian was to go to Uganda for three months to study gorillas.

5204. To Edward Huelin, 15 July 1929
Text: MS Huelin; Unpublished.

Hotel Porta Rossa, Florence.

15 July 1929

Dear Huelin[1]

Yes, they've got 13 of my pictures in gaol, and want to burn them – don't suppose they'll dare – dirty hypocrisy. The worst of it is, Dorothy Warren, who runs the show, *loves* the sensation and wants to heighten it. – But those pictures did get beneath the English skin – some people simply dithered with rage – the place was black with peering parsons – a church conference was on in London[2] – and some days over 1000 people went through the little gallery. But damn them all.

My wife had the time of her life, fêted and champagned and made a fuss of[3] – however, she appeared suddenly here on Thursday night, so I suppose she had enough. She wrenched her foot again and limps as bad as ever – after having paid twelve pounds in London to have it rubbed by a 'specialist' –

Italy has suddenly slumped down into a funny deflated condition – all the tension gone. It is very easy, very amiable, not inspiring – but in its way, quite

---

[1] Edward Scotton Huelin (1888–1967) aspired to be a writer, but was obliged after the war to work at a succession of boring jobs in London. In 1928 he went with his wife Hilda and son David for a holiday in Mallorca (where his brother-in-law Ivan Lake was British Vice-Consul). While there he inherited a legacy which enabled him to give up his job and remain in Mallorca (in the village of San Agustin) for three years. There he met DHL whose work he had long admired, and they became friends.

[2] Probably the Church [of England's] Assembly which met in Church House, Westminster, 17–21 June 1929.

[3] Frieda confirmed this and provided other information in a letter to Mrs Huelin (MS Huelin; undated but shortly after she and DHL left Florence, and before 8 August):

Dear Mrs Huelin!

When we had left Mallorca I had qualms, that I had let you bother about the scent, knowing what a reliable person you are & bothering in the heat, thank you very much, let me know what you spent. Barby will rejoice – You must see them the old address when you go to London – I had a terrific time there, feeling no end of an important person, it was all *very* interesting, the condemnation of the pictures & all – They are still in a cellar at Marlborough police station, on the 8th of August they will be *released* or *burnt*!! Also if it amuses you go & see Dorothy at the Warren galleries, 39 Maddox Street at[?] Bond Street, she'll tell you all about things – It's a fight I suppose & *fun*! We also travelled from Florence with a niece of yours!! I had rushed there because Lawr was'nt well! he was so cross but has recovered & does'nt like it a bit in the north. We did love it at Mallorca & shant forget the jolly times, we had with you! Lawr is writing poems called "Nettles"! But the fun is that all this fuss means lots more money for Lawr's work – I am determined about it! Have you been *very* hot? I fear it – I loved Florence again – You must go there one day – Please greet your husband & your son from me & let us hear from you sometimes –

All good wishes to you!   Frieda Lawrence

Lawr is not very well. Where are the Jones?

pleasant. Suddenly, from your letter, I see what a rest it is, after Mallorca –
none of that resistance which one has to bear up against, on the island.
We leave tomorrow night for Milan, en route to BadenBaden. The address
c/o Frau Baronin von Richthofen, Ludwig-Wilhelmstift, *BadenBaden*,
Germany
I expect we shall spend August and September in the north, then come south
– perhaps to Mallorca, some time in the winter. Who knows!
Sorry San Augustin is vulgarised – pazienza, they'll go away again.

Regards to you all three   D. H. Lawrence

5205. To Max Mohr, [16 July 1929]

Text: MS HMohr; Mohr 169.

Florence.
Dienstag

Lieber Mohr
Es thut mir so Leid, dass wir nicht nach Rottach kommen. Aber meine
Frau will nach Baden gehen, wegen 77n Geburtstag der Schwiegermutter,
am 19n – Donnerstag. So fahren wir heute Abend ab. – Schreibe mir
per. Adr Frau v. Richthofen – Ludwig Wilhelmstift.
Ich höre nichts von Rowohlt. Meine Frau sagt, der Leopold Loewenstein
hat ihr in London gesagt, der Kippenberg will absolut *Lady Chatterley* aus-
geben – Wenn es so ist, werden die anderen Verlegern zurückstehen. Aber
ich fürchte mich, sie werden das Buch piratieren – Pirate – wie sagt man auf
Deutch? Ich höre es kommt noch ein Pirated Edition in Amerika, *illustrierte.*
– Gott!
Meine Bilder sind noch *sub judice* in London, und können noch gebrannt
werden – ein Prozess wird gemacht. –
Ich möchte wirklich nach Bayern kommen – wenn nicht früher, denn Ende
August. – Ich fühle mich irriziert und *ennuyé*, troppe fastidie!

DHL

[Tuesday
Dear Mohr
I'm so sorry that we're not coming to Rottach. But my wife wants to go to
Baden, because of the 77th birthday of the Schwiegermutter on the 19th –
Thursday.[1] So we're leaving tonight. – Write to me
at Frau v. Richthofen – Ludwig Wilhelmstift.
I hear nothing from Rowohlt. My wife says, Leopold Loewenstein told her

---

[1] In fact it was her 78th birthday and 19 July 1929 was a Friday.

in London that Kippenberg really wants to publish *Lady Chatterley* – If that is so, the other publishers will have to give it up. But I'm really afraid, they will pirate the book – pirate – how does one say it in German? I hear yet another pirated edition is coming out in America, *illustrated.* – God!

My pictures are still *sub judice* in London, and may still be burned – there will be a court case. –

I would really like to come to Bavaria – if not earlier, then at the end of August. – I feel irritated and *fed up*, too many things upsetting me!

DHL]

5206. To Charles Lahr, [16 July 1929]
Text: TMSC ULon; PC v. Cenotaph; Unpublished.

[Hotel Porta Rossa, Florence]
17 July.

– Your letter today – we leave tonight for Baden-Baden¹ – you have the address there –

c/o Frau v. Richthofen, Ludwig-Wilhelmstift

– I will write from there – send me two copies – or even four – do as you like about the other drawing – but would that mean you use both drawings in the vellum?

L.

5207. To Laurence Pollinger, [16 July 1929]
Text: MS UT; Unpublished.

Florence.
17 July 1929

Dear Pollinger

Cheek of Boni² – tête de veau truffée.³ – Robert Mountsier kept all my Seltzer contracts, and he is supposed to have turned them over to Barmby⁴ – they *ought* to be in the New York office.

More requests for photographs – will you send to this man if you think fit.⁵ These Swiss do articles on me from time to time – what difference it makes, God alone knows.

---

¹ DHL left Florence 16 July. This and the following letter were both misdated 17.
² See Letters 5280 and 5283 and subsequent references to Boni.
³ 'calf's head stuffed with truffles'.   ⁴ See pp. 27 n. 4, 204 n.
⁵ The 'man' is unidentified. DHL's letter was annotated with reference to the request, in Curtis Brown's office, first by Pollinger to Jean Watson: 'I have photo to spare if you don't think it will be *wasted*'; then her response: 'I don't think the enquiry is serious – let's forget it!' The only Swiss article known prior to this date is a review of *The Boy in the Bush* in 1920.

We leave tonight for BadenBaden, so address me there. Getting hot here – but not unpleasant. – Douglas not at all well – Am so bored by all that fuss over the pictures – pity you don't have hot sunny summers when people go quiet. – But I hear that dirty dog J. C. Squire gave the final blow to my pictures in his dish-rag *Mercury*.[1] I must find a way of knifing him – tell me if ever you see a chance.

DHL

In the same line, did you, or did I ever agree to that man Richards taking the poem 'Piano' for his beastly book *Practical Criticism?* I received a copy of the second edition from the publishers the other day – Kegan Paul was it? – and was a bit riled.[2] The Cambridge don had chosen that poem just to do me harm in the eyes of students and public – as it is obviously the one really sentimental thing out of the two vols. – But I bet Secker got money there too.[3]

DHL

5208. To Charles Lahr, [16 July 1929]
Text: MS UNYB; cited in Moore, *Poste Restante* 101.

Florence.
Tuesday evening

Dear Lahr

On second thoughts, *don't* put two sketches in the vellum copy – the second would have to go among the text, which I dislike. Do only the one sketch the same, as frontispiece.[4]

When they are ready, send two copies to Orioli, one for him and one for Douglas.

[1] Lahr (cf. letter following) appears to have told DHL of Squire's comments on the paintings in the July *London Mercury*, and to have sent him a copy. In his 'Editorial Notes' Squire expressed surprise that the exhibition had so far gone 'scot-free': 'we never felt more embarrassed than when we stood surrounded by those walls of pink and palpitating flesh quivering with lust ... the animals themselves do not attempt the fierce frenzies of Mr. Lawrence. It is one thing to revolt against conventionality and hypocrisy; it is another thing to run naked through the streets.' For DHL's response see Letter 5225 and n. 5; 'London Mercury' in particular was aimed at Squire.
[2] I[vor] A[rmstrong] Richards (1893–1979), *Practical Criticism: A Study of Literary Judgment* (Kegan Paul, 1929). The book was first published in June; there was no second edn or impression in the same year.
[3] DHL cannot have read the pages on 'Piano' very carefully, since Richards' main point is that only a grossly inadequate reader could dismiss as sentimental a poem which is in fact a critique of sentimentality. Secker waived the normal charge for quoting the poem since Richards' purpose was 'critical and explanatory' (Secker Letter-Book, UIll, 3 October 1928).
[4] DHL's self-portrait in red crayon appeared as the frontispiece in both edns.

We are off just now – *Mercury* not come yet – must find some way of getting back at Squire – think of a revenge for me.

L.

5209. To Baroness Anna von Richthofen, [17 July 1929]
Text: MS IEduc; PC v. Basel – Hotel Continental; Postmark, Basel 17·VII 1929; Unpublished.

Basel
Mitwoch.

Wir sind schon so nah! – trinken Thee bei dir um 5. Uhr morgen.

DHL

[*Wednesday.*

We're already this near! – will be having tea with you at 5 o'clock tomorrow.

DHL]

5210. To Dr David Eder, [July 1929]
Text: J. B. Hobman, ed., *David Eder: Memoirs of a Modern Pioneer* (1945), p. 123.

[Hotel Löwen, Lichtenthal, bei Baden-Baden]
[July 1929]

['The last request was made a year before Lawrence died, when this time he wanted the Eders to join him at Wiesbaden.'[1]]

5211. To Maria Chambers, [19 July 1929]
Text: MS StaU; PC v. Baden-Baden – Gruss vom alten Schloß; Postmark, Baden-Baden 19 7 29; Unpublished.

BadenBaden
– Friday

I wonder if this will catch you before you leave – pretty hot even here, so am afraid you will have it strong. Am writing you a letter to Gt. Neck and enclosing one for Rich.[2] Frieda loves the feathery cape – says she will write you. Hope everything has gone off nicely.

DHL

---

[1] Dr Montagu David Eder (1865–1936), an early Freudian psychoanalyst, socialist and Zionist, and his wife Edith, née Low. DHL had met the Eders early in 1915 through Edith's niece Ivy Low. (See *Letters*, ii. 258 n. 2.) In 1917 he had tried to recruit them for an ideal community (Rananim) in the Andes (see *Letters*, iii. 173), and in 1919 had asked Eder about the practicability of Palestine (see *Letters*, iii. 316). It is presumed that DHL sent his invitation to the Eders early in his (final) visit to Germany.

[2] See Letter 5221.

5212. To Emily King, [19 July 1929]
Text: MS Sagar; PC v. Baden-Baden Paradies; Postmark, Baden-Baden 19 7 29;
Unpublished.

[Hotel Löwen, Lichtenthal, bei Baden-Baden]
Friday

– hot weather everywhere – but better here than Italy and Switzerland –
Next week they want to go up to the Plättig, a mt. near here, to stay – altitude
about 3000 ft – will be cooler – Have no news from London.

love DHL

5213. To Ada Clarke, [19 July 1929]
Text: MS Clarke; PC v. Baden-Baden. Das alte Schloß; Postmark, Baden-Baden 19 7 29;
Lawrence–Gelder 194.

[Hotel Löwen, Lichtenthal, bei Baden-Baden]
Friday

– pretty hot here too, but not like Italy – the others want to go up higher next
week – not far from here – about 3000 ft. – No further news from London.

love DHL

5214. To Earl, Achsah and Harwood Brewster, [19 July 1929]
Text: MS UT; Brewster 204–6.

Hotel Löwen, Lichtenthal, bei BadenBaden
Friday July 19

Dear Earl and Achsah and Harwood

– You see where we are – and I have Achsah's rooms, Frieda has Earl's,
and the Schwiegermutter has one of ours.[1] It's pretty hot, but the garden cool
and still, rather lovely – In the Kurpark flowers everywhere, millions of roses
– We eat in the garden – and Germany seems very quiet and easy. But the
women want to go next week up to the Plättig, about an hour's drive, 3000 ft.
It may be nice – but the high places are all pretty crowded, whereas Baden is
rather empty still.

If Achsah and Harwood come this way, we really must contrive to meet
and have a confab. Harwood, I had your poem, and one side of my face was
laughing at you, and the other was touched.[2] – If you really want to be a

---

[1] The Brewsters had stayed at the Hotel Löwen with the Lawrences and Baroness von
Richthofen, 18 September–1 October 1928.
[2] Harwood had written a poem (the only one she ever wrote) for a paper she and the Reynolds
girls brought out (information from the late Harwood Picard):

D.H.L.

Oh red bearded man in coat of bright blue,
How often have I heard thee tell

doctor, do insist now on a school, and start in – really don't delay any longer. – Achsah, I'm sorry you were not well – it's these wearing indecisions. I still think the best is for you either to go to America or to find yourself a house on Capri, even if it's only a little bit of a place. – I liked Mallorca, but I'm not sure I should like to *live* there, and I'm certain you wouldn't. I like very much the French coast between Toulon and Marseilles – Bandol, Cassis – but Frieda didn't care for it, and I'm sure you'd think it ugly. Better a small place on Capri where you *know* you like it – and then stop fretting about anywhere else. – Frieda of course is still pining for her Florence district – I was there a day or two, and it seemed so familiar and friendly. We *might* try the Impruneta – it is fairly high.[1] Italy seemed to me gone very flat, the short while I was there – but not unpleasant, really nicer. But gone deflated, like a deflated tyre.

I suppose you heard my picture show was raided in London – after over 12,000 people had been to it – and the police seized 13 pictures as being obscene – which pictures now lie in gaol under threat of being *burnt*. England my England![2] Did ever you know such hypocrisy. That *Accident in a Mine* which I did in Gsteig seized for obscene – it is too crassly stupid. But now the police hate me – for *Pansies* too – I suppose you have your copy now – expurgated perforce.

My mother-in-law sends greetings and wants to thank you for your book.[3] Write to the Ludwig-Wilhelmstift, BadenBaden, as we may leave here next Tuesday or Wednesday. I suppose, now we are here, we shall spend the summer in Germany – perhaps go to Bavaria in August. But write me all your news.

love! DHL

Of mother, father, aunt and uncle too
Of childhood thou rememberest well.

On Swiss hills overgrown with dark pine rims,
In chalet filled with smell of cow,
In train winding its way fast, singing hymns,
I do so long to hear thee now.

I see thee poet and I hear thee tell,
Now gentle and tender, then fierce,
With words that speak not of heaven and hell
But through man and the earth do pierce.

[1] About 12 km. s. of Florence at an altitude of 275 metres.
[2] Embittered use of famous words from the refrain to W. E. Henley's patriotic poem 'England' (1900): 'What have I done for you,/ England, my England?'
[3] According to the late Harwood Picard, this was probably *L'oeuvre de E. H. Brewster et Achsah Barlow Brewster; 32 reproductions en phototypie précédées d'essais autobiographiques* (Rome, 1923).

5215. To Giuseppe Orioli, [20 July 1929]
Text: MS NWU; PC v. Baden-Baden – Gönneranlagen; Postmark, Baden-Baden 20 7 29;
cited in Moore, *Poste Restante* 101.

BadenBaden.
Saturday

Had quite an easy journey here – but very hot. Baden very green and very
pink, with roses everywhere – not many visitors. We had a great thunderstorm last night so today is very fresh and cool. Wish you were here to go into
the Kurhaus with me now: sure you'd like it. The women want to go up to the
Plättig, about 3000 ft. up, next week – it's only an hour from here.

No news of pictures or anything – write to the Stift –

DHL

5216. To Charles Lahr, 20 July 1929
Text: MS UNYB; Postmark, Baden-Baden 20 7 29; Unpublished.

Ludwig-Wilhelmstift, *Baden Baden*, Germany
20 July 1929

Dear Lahr

I had a letter a day or two ago from Secker saying his signed edition *was not
yet ready*, although sold out: and he had sold 1500 of the ordinary copies. I
don't know what he's up to – but before you let out your edition, make sure
that Secker's 250-signed are out and gone. It is a stipulation.

Here are a few addresses for gift copies – out of series – I can sign them
when I turn up – Kot, Davies, Stephensen, Pollinger, Mrs Hilton,
Aldous Huxley, 'Il Canneto', Forte dei Marmi (Lucca)
my sister Mrs L. A.Clarke. Broadway. Ripley – Derby
Dr. Max Mohr. Wolfsgrube. Rottach-am-Tegernsee, Oberbayern
Miss Barbara Low, 13 Guilford St. W.C. 1.[1]
Miss Barbara Weekley. 49 Harvard Rd. Chiswick. W.
Dorothy Warren (Mrs Philip Trotter.)
The ones you are sending to me you can address direct to my mother-in-law,
if you like, Frau v. Richthofen. I suppose you will deliver by hand all possible
– not use the post.

No further news – was very hot, but a good thunderstorm last night cooled
it off. We think we shall all go up to the Plättig next week – about an hour
from here, 3000 feet up. The women are pining for altitude.

Hope all goes well.

L.

---

[1] Barbara Low (1877–1955) was an old friend of DHL, sister-in-law to David Eder and a
pioneer in psychoanalysis (see *Letters*, ii. 279 n. 6).

5217. To Laurence Pollinger, 20 July 1929
Text: MS UT; Huxley 809.

Hotel Goldner Löwen. Lichtenthal/ BadenBaden
20 July 1929.

Dear Pollinger

Well here we are, all right – it was so hot yesterday, we just did nothing, but last night a long and lurid thunderstorm poured out endless white electricity and set us free – now it's delicious and cool and fresh.[1]

I find your fat letter here – but not much left to answer. I had a letter from Secker last week saying his signed edition was *not yet ready* – Orioli had ordered copies – and that he had sold 1500 ordinary copies. Seems very queer. I must find out if he has yet sent out his signed 250, because the unexpurgated edition is about ready to come out, and there seems no reason for holding it back, once Secker's is gone.

You know, we weren't quite cute enough over that £250 fee from Stephensen – it should have been guineas, since the book sells in guineas.

I suppose you had the wire from Florence about 'Man Who Loved Islands'.[2] I must get a copy of Romer Wilson's *Hill of Cloves* – she is not such a fool as her critics try to make out.[3] – I'm sure Mackenzie still has a finger in the Secker pie, so we'll put in as few plums as possible, for him to pull out.[4] And what about Howe?[5] His eyes aren't right, either – I mean they don't have the right look.

I told that man Barnet B. Ruder that I didn't want to bargain with him for the MS. of *Lady C.*[6] – and since I shan't be in London, I shan't bother to answer his cable about seeing him there.

No further news of the pictures – am so bored by the idiocy and falsity of all that fuss – it *is* so false. But once we[7] get the pictures together again, you must help me to rescue them from Dorothy Warren, she is a very evasive and uncertain bird.

I hear there is *another* edition (pirated) of *Lady C.* about to appear in

---

[1] See DHL's poems written at this time: 'Trees in the Garden' and 'Storm in the Black Forest' (*Complete Poems*, ii. 646–7).
[2] See Letter 5199 and n. 1.
[3] Florence Roma Muir Wilson (1891–1930), *The Hill of Cloves: A Tract on True Love, with a Digression upon an Invention of the Devil* (October 1929).
[4] Compton Mackenzie was published by and personally associated with Secker's firm. DHL had to some extent based 'The Man Who Loved Islands' on him; Mackenzie's threat of legal action was to prevent the proposed publication of the story by Heinemann.
[5] Percival Presland Howe (1887–1944), biographer and critic and, since 1918, Secker's partner. See *Letters*, v. 638 and n. 5.
[6] American dealer in MSS and rare books.   [7] we] you

Philadelphia, *illustrated* this time. My hat! What will it be like. If only I could hash that novel up into sausage-meat for Mr Mead.

This is a nice old gasthaus, quiet rooms on the garden, 9 Mark a day pension. Lichtenthal is about 1½ miles from Baden, but it joins on now and is incorporated – and there is the tram. Even I can remember when it was a separate village. The tram only takes a few minutes – or you can walk along the Lichtenthaler-Allee, under the trees by the Oos, all the way. Baden itself is incurably 1850, with the romance and the pathos and the bathos of Turgenev rather than Dostoevsky. Just now the trees are very green, the roses very pink and very numerous, the fountains very white, the visitors not many, and the music also a little pathetic. It would amuse you for a little while. – But my wife and her mother want us to go on Wednesday up to the Plättig – about 3000 feet up – only an hour or so drive from here. Everybody is crazy for altitude – except me, and I don't like it very much. But I think every hill-top in Germany over 2000 ft. must be crowded with Germans, stepping heavenward. That's why Baden is comparatively empty. – I don't know if you'd like to come to the Plättig – have never been there myself – and I don't know how long we shall stay. I'll tell you, and perhaps if it's nice you'll come. Or come here when we descend again. I'm sure you'd like the Löwen, and BadenBaden, for a bit. Germany seems to me, here, very quiet, prosperous, cheaper, and not so shoving or assertive any more. – You must come for a week or so, either to the Plättig or to here. – Better write to the Ludwig-Wilhelmstift.

ever   D. H. Lawrence

5218. To Jean Watson, 20 July 1929
Text: MS UT; Unpublished.

Ludwig-Wilhelmstift. *Baden Baden.* Germany
20 July 1929
Dear Miss Watson

The French royalties on *Lady C.* are not royal, are they! truly rather paltry. But if they'll translate the book well and present it well, that is a great deal – so I suppose we shall have to accept: though where, in France, they are going to find a man of 'highest literary standing and most un-impeachable moral authority', I ask you. Will it be M. Gide?[1] or M. Mauriac?

---

[1] André Gide (1869–1951), French novelist and critic. His homosexuality, outspokenness and belief in the absolute freedom of the individual brought him into conflict with conventional morality. Author of *The Immoralist* (1902), *Strait is the Gate* (1909), etc.

or M. Maurois even?[1] Mon dieu! I suppose it will come down to little Marcel![2]

As for old Kippenberg, he is an old twister. I have a letter from him saying he does not wish to publish *Lady C.* and waives all his claim to the book. This being so, I arrange with a German author, a friend, to do the translation and get a good publisher – all is nicely settled, with Rowohlt of Berlin, when in steps old cunctator Kippenberg again, to spoil other people's plans. – I'm not going to stand it. There is now no contract with the Insel Verlag – I have signed none. Either that old greybeard of Leipsig deals a bit straighter and sounder and is less pontifical, or I have done with him. *I don't really want him* to do *Lady C.* I would rather Rowohlt had done it. I don't like the Insel Verlag. So if the old man tries any more of his tricks, I'll have done with him. Let me know just how you stand with regard to *Lady C.* – and if there is any doubt with old K., I will forward you Rowohlt's letter.

I was arranging personally for the publication in Germany of *Lady C.* because I thought your firm wanted to be free from all connection with the book, after the fuss with Scotland Yard in February.

I hope you'll have a nice time in America–

Yours Sincerely   D. H. Lawrence

5219. To Giuseppe Orioli, [22 July 1929]
Text: MS UCLA; Huxley 810–12.

write to: Hotel Plättig. Badischer Schwarzwald,[3] Germania
Monday

Dear Pino

Suddenly I have the bright idea that the *first* version of *Lady C.* may be the right one for Knopf and Secker.[4] I believe it has hardly any fucks or shits, and no address to the penis, in fact hardly any of the root of the matter at all. You remember the first version is the one you had bound for Frieda, and it is in your flat. I wish you would just glance through the so-called hot parts, and tell me how hot they are. I'm sure they are hardly warm. And I'm sure I could expurgate the few flies out of that virgin ointment – whereas *our Lady C.* I cannot, absolutely *cannot* even begin to expurgate.

---

[1] André Maurois (Émile Herzog, 1885–1967), French biographer, novelist and critic. An Anglophile who had served in the British army in the war, and had written biographies of Shelley and Disraeli.

[2] Gabriel Marcel. See Letter 5001 n. 2. For the French translation see Letter 5060 and n.

[3] Hotel Plättig. Badischer Schwarzwald] Ludwig-Wilhelmstift. *BadenBaden*

[4] Written in the autumn of 1926, *The First Lady Chatterley* was eventually published in 1944. It differs considerably from the final version, and does not contain any so-called obscene words or sexual explicitness.

If you think we can go ahead with the first version for the public edition, then perhaps you had better send me the MS. along. I suppose I shall have to have it all typed out, since the whole thing will be different from *our Lady*. Perhaps I can find a typist here in Germany. I shall not risk sending the MS. to England.

It's been pretty hot here – especially in the afternoon. But the evening and night and morning are cool. The hotel is very pleasant – an old Gasthaus with a garden and trees, where we sit out all day and drink beer and do nothing. But the women want to go up to a higher altitude, either the Plättig – about an hour from here – or Herrenalb, a bit further.[1] Frieda is going to look at the Plättig this morning.

She is very well, and as usual, pretends to love it here, and as usual, secretly rather hates it. The Germans are most curious. They love things just because they think they have a sentimental reason for loving them – das Heimatland, der Tannenbaum, das Brünnele, das Bächlein[2] – the very words send a German into a swoon of love, which is as often as not entirely false. They make up their feelings in their heads, while their *real* feelings all go wrong. That's why Germans come out with such startling and really, silly bursts of hatred. It's the result of never living from their *real* feelings, always from the feelings they invent in their heads. And that's why, as a bourgeois crowd, they are so monstrously ugly. My God, how ugly they can be! And it's because they *never* live direct from their spontaneous feeling; except in the matter of eating and drinking, God help us!

I wish you were here to laugh at them with me. I daren't say much to Frieda – she really hates them worse than I do, and flies into a state. My God, why are people *never* straightforward!

But the Garden is so pleasant and still and green, the food is good, my mother-in-law is 78, and quiet now. I go by myself to the Kurhaus, and sit under the trees listening to the orchestra and looking at the amazing grotesques of people. But I should go much oftener if you were here to go with me. – The world is fantastic.

I do hope you are not killing yourself in that hole of a Montecatini. Don't die of heart-failure to cure your liver. – I do so wonder if Aldous is with you. – Don't forget the Impruneta –

DHL

How is Douglas?

---

[1] Plättig is 10 miles s. of Baden-Baden, Herrenalb 15 miles e.n.e.
[2] 'the homeland, the fir-tree, the little fountain, the rivulet'.

5220. To Hon. Dorothy Brett, 22 July 1929
Text: MS UCin: Postmark, Baden-Baden [. . .] 7.29; Irvine, *DHL Review*, ix. 93–4.

BadenBaden.
22 July. 1929

Dear Brett

Just a word in answer to yours. – If you could *really* buy the ranch, and pay for it, I should be glad. But Frieda is against it.

And if you will please send all my Manuscripts to
Edwin G. Rich. Curtis Brown. Ltd. 116 West. 39th St. *New York City*
that, I think is the best. They have a safe for my particular use already.

I shall be glad when these vexed questions are settled. So wearisome, this nagging.[1]

I ordered you a copy of my *Collected Poems* – American edit. Hope they arrive – Have forgotten if I ordered you the English edit. or not.

I suppose you have heard the police seized thirteen of my pictures – and have them in gaol, and threaten to *burn* them. The case is tried on August 8th – Of this also I am extremely weary. – I can't send you the book of pictures – The show in London was a succès de scandale – Dorothy Warren had over 12,000 people – and took over £500. in shillings – none of which comes to me – and my sales scanty, but she didn't want to sell them – neither did I, really.

DHL

5221. To Maria Chambers, 22 July 1929
Text: MS StaU; cited in Schorer 65.

Ludwig-Wilhelmstift. *Baden Baden*, Germany
22 July 1929

Dear Maria Cristina

I am sending this to Paris to the address you gave. I do hope Forte didn't become insufferably hot. Pretty hot, even here.

I enclose a letter to Edwin Rich,[2] which I hope will say all that is necessary. But please don't make any great efforts – why wear yourself out.

---

[1] Frieda made her contribution to the 'nagging' in a letter to Brett on 29 July 1929 (MS UCin):

It was a final blow to Lawr, Brett, you selling his manuscripts. I never thought much of you or your "love", for anybody, but to do that is more than I expected you to do . . . What did you sell of the Mss?, do you not know how *dishonest* that was without telling Lawr – criminal, you know, did *no*body ever teach you honesty? Put those Mss into the bank *at once* & send a list of the Mss in that little cupboard of L's or it will be put into the hands of Curtis Brown's lawyers, you dont want *that* humiliation, I hope – I dont want to sell the ranch – You can "look after it", you cant do it much harm – . . .

[2] Enclosure is missing.

Titus, who publishes the cheap *Lady C*, is in the rue Delambre, just behind the *Dôme* café, where the Bvd Raspail crosses the Bvd Montparnasse.

Frieda still hasn't written to thank you for the feathers – she is bad at letters – but she says she will do so.

I do hope you'll have a pleasant voyage, and everything easy –

hasta otra vez!   D. H. Lawrence

5222. To Jean Watson, 22 July 1929
Text: MS UT; Unpublished.

Ludwig-Wilhelmstift, *Baden Baden*
22 July 1929

Dear Miss Watson

So after a whole year, Fratelli Treves have managed to raise five pounds![1] beati loro![2] It is a year since I 'arranged' about these two stories with Carlo Linati, who has done the translating. – But there, nobody reads books in Italy – Guido da Verona, that's all.[3] So even five pounds, as you say, is five pounds beyond expectation.

I should like to know pretty quick about Kippenberg and *Lady Chatterley*, Because if there is any hesitation on the part of the Insel Verlag, I want to strike a bargain with Rowohlt, and have Max Mohr do the translation. – And if Kippenberg is going to do a translation, he should do it quickly. And tell him, for this book I must really supervise the translation – will he send me the typescript, preferably two or three chapters at a time, as it is done, for me to go over.

Aren't you gone yet to America, then?

D. H. Lawrence

5223. To Laurence Pollinger, [23 July 1929]
Text: MS UT; Unpublished.

Lichtenthal.
23 July

Dear Pollinger

I return the Heinemann agreement. Don't forget that this 'Islands' story is included in Knopf's *Woman Who Rode Away*. The agreement stipulates the

---

[1] Treves Brothers of Milan published the translation of 'The Fox' and 'The Ladybird' in 1929 (Roberts D112), by Carlo Linati (1878–1949), the Italian critic. Cf. *Letters*, v. 90 and n. 2; vi. 516.

[2] 'lucky them!'

[3] Guido da Verona (1881–1938), Italian novelist and poet, very well-known after World War I; his novels, with their mixture of erotic and decadent elements in ornate language, proved highly popular.

story shall not have appeared before in book form. If this applies to America, then you must not give them the agreement as it stands.[1]

I am anxious to see what Cape's *Collected Poems* look like, and to see if Secker has printed *The Rainbow* entire.[2] You might send me the two books to Hotel Plättig, Badischer Schwarzwald.

We are going up there this afternoon – I dont know the actual address, but that will find it easily.

It is very hot – will be cooler up there. I find this moist heat of the north much more difficult to stand than the dry heat south. Mallorca was hotter, but didn't affect me. Here my bronchials are already acting up, and making me feel limp and raggy. I'll try the Plättig – about 2600 ft. – and if that doesn't suit me better, shall move again to drier air. Perpetuum mobile![3]

Has Secker got his 250 edition of *Pansies* out yet?

DHL

Collected Poems of D.H.L. Cape edition

1. copy D. H. Lawrence. Hotel Plättig. Schwarzwald. bei *Baden Baden*.
1. copy Hon. Dorothy Brett. Box 215. *Taos*, New Mexico. U.S.A.
1. copy. Willard Johnson. *Taos*. New Mexico.
1. copy Mrs Mabel Luhan. *Taos*. New Mexico.
1. copy Witter Bynner. 342 Buena Vista Rd. *Santa Fe*. New Mexico
1. copy. Alice Corbin Henderson. *Santa Fe*, New Mexico

I had already sent the list to Rich, asking him please to forward the books – so if you happen to be writing, do tell him.

DHL

5224. To Max Mohr, 24 July 1929
Text: MS HMohr; Mohr, *Briefe* 533–4.

Kurhaus Plättig, *bei Bühl*, Baden
24 Juli 1929

Lieber Mohr

Sehen Sie wo ich bin! – unter 150 Kurgäste, 750m. hoch im heiss-geliebten Schwarzwald! – um 11 Mark am Tag! – mit Frau und Schwiegermutter von 78 Jahren! Es ist natürlich furchtbar – nur oben in meinem Zimmer hab' ich es gern. Der Tannenwald ist ganz herum – ganz im Wald, Friedele, merkst du! im grossen, wunderbaren Tannenwald! nein! und die Luft! – und die

---

[1] Cf. pp. 368 n. 1 and 381 n. 4.
[2] Secker's pocket edition of *The Rainbow*, published in June 1929, did not fulfil his promise to DHL to print it some day 'without the alteration of a single word' (Roberts 22).
[3] 'Perpetual motion!'

nette Leut' die so freundlich mit mir reden! – ach, *wir* haben's gut, *wir* sollen dankbar sein! Wenn ich denke an Männer die in Kohlengruben arbeiten – in grossen Fabriken – !!!! – Natürlich hasse ich jeden Tannenbaum mit giftigen Hassen, so schwarz und hart und steif-haarige. Warum können sie nicht Blätter haben!

Wir bleiben nicht sehr lang – vielleicht bis 3. August. – O Gott! Dann will ich *nicht* in BadenBaden sitzen, um die alten Damen zu amüsieren – ich amusiere sie überhaupt nicht, bin sehr bös. Wenn einen Englischen Freund nicht kommt, dann fahren wir um 5n (ungefähr) weg. Wenn er kommt, bleiben wir bis 10n (vielleicht): O Gott mein Gott, und ich bin so ungern hier! – Sollen wir nach Rottach kommen? und was finden wir für Wohnung? – wird's sehr voll sein?

Vielen Dank für den Brief. Ich hoffe die Hand geht besser – sind Sie einer unglücklicher!!

Hier ist das Wetter noch gut – Vorgestern abends hat es furchtbar gewittert und geregnet – ist noch wolkig, sieht aus wie Regen, aber regnet nicht.

Schicken Sie mir nichts – ich kann nicht lesen, kaum leben – und ich kann nimmer gehen – ja, ich bin der Unglücklicher, diesmal.

Grüsse   DHL

[Dear Mohr

Look where I am! together with 150 people at a spa, 750m. up in the much beloved Black Forest! – at 11 Marks a day! – with wife and 78-year-old Schwiegermutter! It is of course dreadful – I only like it up in my room. The pine-forest is all around – really in the forest, my little Frieda, do you realise? in the great, wonderful pine-forest! ah! and the air! – and the nice people who so kindly chat with me! – ah, aren't *we* lucky, shouldn't *we* be grateful! When I think of men working in coal-mines – in great factories – !!!! – Naturally I hate with poisonous hatred every pine-tree, so black and hard and stiff-haired. Why can't they have leaves!

We're not staying very long – perhaps till the 3rd August. – O God! I do *not* want to sit around then in BadenBaden so as to amuse the old ladies – I won't amuse them at all, I'm very angry. If an English friend doesn't come, then we leave about the 5th. If he does come, we'll stay on till the 10th (perhaps): O God my God, and I dislike so much being here! – Should we come to Rottach? and what kind of place would we find to stay in? – will it be very crowded?

Many thanks for the letter. I hope your hand is better – aren't you an unlucky one!!

The weather here is still fine – the evening before last there was a fearful thunderstorm and rain – it's still cloudy, looks like rain, but doesn't rain.

Don't send me anything – I can't read, can hardly live – and can't walk any more – yes, I'm the unlucky one, this time.

Greetings DHL]

5225. To Charles Lahr, 25 July 1929

Text: MS UNYB; Postmark, Bühlerhöhe 26.7.29; Moore 1168–9.

Kurhaus Plättig – *bei Bühl*, Baden
25 Juli 1929

Dear Lahr

Here we sit, wife, Schwiegermutter und ich, 750 m. hoch im Schwarzwald, among 150 Kurgäste um 11 mark am Tag[1] – and I really hate it. I hate Kurhäuser – I hate Tannenwald – I hate Sommerfrischler[2] – and we're due to stay at least till August 5th. Then we'll go down – and I shall *not* stay in Baden to amuse the old Stiftsdamen.[3]

But this is really a note to say, perhaps not send out or let out any *Pansies* till the business of the Meade and the Trotter has been heard on August 8th – don't you think it would be better? If anything went wrong, everything would be much worse all round. – I hope Stephensen & Co. won't *talk*. It is talk that starts the *John Bull* pups yapping.

I feel too bored and irritated by this last business to write anything serious against the squirearchies[4] and noahsarkies. I can only let off a few Pansies – Nettles, rather[5] – against them – and I do that – but I can't take them prosily.

Am pining, of course, to see *Pansies* all abloom! Send me here – or when you do send – only two copies. I do hope all will be well.

L.

---

[1] 'mother-in-law and I, 750 m. up in the Black Forest, among 150 health-resort patients at 11 Marks a day'.
[2] 'I hate health-resort assembly rooms – I hate pine-woods – I hate summer holiday-makers'.
[3] 'women who live in Homes'.   [4] A reference to Squire, editor of the *London Mercury*.
[5] The poems in question were, e.g., 'London Mercury', 'My Little Critics', 'Editorial Office' and '13,000 People' (*Complete Poems*, ii. 581, 582, 577–9). They were included in *Nettles* (Faber & Faber, March 1930). Cf. Letter 5281.

5226. To Laurence Pollinger, 25 July 1929
Text: MS UT; cited in Huxley 810.

Kurhaus Plättig. *bei Bühl* (Baden)
25 July 1929

Dear Pollinger

Pardon me if I write on the back of your letter – no paper down here, and my room three flights up.[1]

First about the Random Press and *Jolly Roger* business[2] – When I wrote the Introd. to the Paris edition of *Lady C.* I asked Edward Titus to get it printed and published in New York, to secure the copyright – and suggested he should get someone to print 200 copies at two dollars each, and he should give me fifty dollars. I've asked him several times about this, and he's always evaded a reply – and not paid me the $50. So would you now tackle him and see if you can't get a proper sum out of him. Treat him politely, he's a nasty fellow when nasty, but perhaps he'll be all right with me. I've not gone far enough with him yet, to know. – I didn't say anything to you about the Paris *Lady C.* at the time, because of all the fuss with Scotland Yard. But if you do settle at last to have Bradley managing your Paris side, I wish you'd take over this Titus business for me. He must sell that edition pretty fast. Have you seen a copy? – quite nice, small, 60 francs.

[1] Pollinger had written on 23 July (TMS UT):

My dear Lawrence,

Elbridge Adams says when he saw you in Paris in April you spoke to him about a long story or novel which you were writing and which, as he remembers it, you had almost finished. His understanding was that you were to let him see the manuscript as soon as you had put the finishing touches to it with a view to making you an offer on a special limited edition.

Now, you must not let Adams use this story until Nancy Pearn has had an opportunity of selling it to one of the Magazines here.

I wrote Adams several weeks ago suggesting that he should use "Mother and Daughter" instead of "The Escaped Cock", but up to the time of writing, have not received any word from him about this.

In addition to this short story, it occurs to me that perhaps we could get Adams to issue a small volume of some new poems, if you had 'em available ...

As you know, the hearing before Mr. Mead was adjourned. As soon as this has taken place I will trot along and see Dorothy Warren. Meanwhile please let me know where we are to send the pictures as soon as we can get them together again.

Please do make another attempt to cut "Lady C." She should be worth anything from £200 to £500 advance in abbreviated attire. If miserable Martin [Secker] won't rise to at least £300 I think we ought to see what we can obtain elsewhere...

By the bye, what is the meaning of the attached Random House advertisement. Is it something that you fixed up direct with them ...

P.S. Do you want to make any alterations in the text of "THE MAN WHO LOVED ISLANDS" ...

[2] See Letter 5121 and n. 1. Though the statement of limitation specified 600 copies, Random House printed 700 and sold them for $3.50.

As for Eldridge Adams, I didn't like him and shan't give him that short novel even if I *do* do it over and get it ready to publish.[1] He offered me about 1000 dollars – and Heinemann gives me £300 for a short story. – No, I haven't any poems for a book now –

No, I don't want to alter the 'Man Who Loved Islands' – let it stand as it appeared. – But you remember, once more, Knopf has it printed in the *Woman Who Rode Away* book. And I remember you said in one letter that Howe (Secker) told you that Compton Mackenzie would certainly take proceedings for libel, if this story were published in a book.[2] Was that just bluff?

I had the bright idea that perhaps we might print the *first* version of *Lady C.* as it stands. In my usual way, I wrote the whole novel, complete, three times. The first time is almost quite proper – but very much tamer than the second and third time – and a good deal different – *quite* a different gamekeeper, for example – a little man of the people, merely of the people – I glanced at the MS. when I was in Florence – it is there, bound up complete. I could have it sent here and go over it – and could, I believe, easily make it passable. But shall I? shall I print a crude first version? – I *cannot* expurgate the real one – physical impossibility.

Quite cool up here – had a huge storm – it's the usual Kurhaus with 150 people – and I am rather unhappy and wish I was back in the south, and could see the olive trees and the Mediterranean. I hate these great black pine forests – and this heavy, though good food. I should pine away quite soon if I had to stay – fortunately I haven't.

If you were coming to Baden I should descend willingly to the Löwen again. Else we shall soon go to Bavaria and then over the Brenner to the Garda. I hate the north.

DHL

Edward W. Titus. 4 rue Delambre. Paris XIV
(I think that's right – Miss Pearn knows).

5227. To Edward Titus, 25 July 1929
Text: MS UT; Unpublished.

Kurhaus Plättig. *bei Bühl* (Baden), Allemagne
25 July 1929

Dear Titus

Would you please send me a copy of *Lady C.* here! They are worrying me and worrying me to do a public expurgated edition – but I *can't* expurgate her – physically can't. – Only I wondered if I might print the first version – I

---

[1] See Letter 5023.
[2] In a guarded way Howe conveyed this information in his letter to Pollinger, 1 July 1929 (Secker Letter-Book, UIll).

wrote the book three times, complete – and the first version is mild – but very different – and I should like to have a copy of the true version – the third – to compare.

Then I see that Random House is doing 600 copies of the *Skirmish with Jolly Roger*, at four dollars. Why didn't you tell me? That's all different from our arrangement, so I suppose we'll make new terms. I asked Curtis Brown to write to you about it – they handle everything of mine – and they may as well look after Her Ladyship a bit.

I expect we shall be in Germany till September – then go south – perhaps over Paris – when I hope I shall see you. How does Our Lady go? – I hear wild accounts from Berlin – but apparently no bookseller in Heidelberg has her – which is a mistake, as there are lots of Americans.

My wife is here – she duly reported all your communications to me – fancies herself quite a business-woman.

Send me a line, then. – And I never saw a copy of your quarterly – did you ever send me one?

Sincerely   D. H. Lawrence[1]

[1] Titus replied on 27 July 1929 (TMSC SIU):

Dear Mr Lawrence,

I am sending you a copy of Lady C. as requested. If I also may venture an opinion it would be a great débâcle of principle to expurgate. I doubt whether it would be a paying enterprise even if you agreed to do so, for the simple reason that the reading public would, and justly so, think they would not be getting full value in purchasing an expurgated book. On the other hand you will find that in the long run you would have earn[ed] on the existing edition, without the ignominy of a compromise, as much as an expurgated edition would yield you . . .

As to Random House, – I have been in communication with them by cable repeatedly . . . Your news that they are bringing out or have already brought out the Skirmish, is the first definite news that I myself have had in the matter . . . However, you need feel no uneasiness in the matter and you have my assurance, that you will receive not the $50.00 which was the amount originally agreed upon, but as much more as will represent fifty per cent of what I shall receive from them, – minus of course the $50.00. I am taking care of your interests, and neither you nor Curtis Brown can do more than that . . .

Now as to the distribution of the Lady in Germany, – it has been difficult to cover the whole ground . . . I therefore hired a traveler, – a man who travels for a number of London publishers . . . I pay him ten per cent on the wholesale price. Something had to be done and this mode was the only one I could see. Now this man has not as yet succeded in penetrating all of Germany. On the other hand the book is having some sale in Holland, Italy and Spain; Berlin has been covered, Cologne a little. Baden, Heidelberg, should of course be taken care of, and I am immediately getting in touch with the traveler on that point . . .

On the subject of his commission of ten per cent which I mentioned I must make it clear that legally speaking I cannot perhaps ask you to share in this expense, and I am in this respect totally in your hands. If you do not agree to it, I will pocket the loss myself and say [n]othing further about it . . .

I have had several enquiries for translation right for French of Lady C. and I gave your address. Have any propositions been made? . . .

My magazine will be out next week, and of course the first copy will go out to you.

I take note that you will be in Baden till September . . .

I have a promise of an article from Rebecca West "in praise of D. H. Lawrence", – which of course will give [me] great pleasure in paying for and publishing . . .

5228. To Ada Clarke, [28 July 1929]
Text: MS Clarke: PC v. Blick ins Bühlertal mit Höhenkurorten; Postmark, [Bühlerh]öhe 28.7.29; Lawrence–Gelder 195.

Kurhaus Plättig. bei Bühl (Baden)
[28 July 1929]

Had your letter and snaps yesterday – I suppose it will be cooler now – here it has thundered and rained so much, it is really cold, and we hug ourselves inside our overcoats. We are in this hotel about 2,600 ft. up – Frieda and her mother and I – and I think we shall stay about another week – then go down to Baden and perhaps on to Bavaria. I must say I don't like the north – something depressing about it – long for olive trees and the sight of the Mediterranean. But I suppose this is good for one. How nice, your garden – ! and soon you'll be off to the sea!

Love. DHL

5229. To Emily King, [28 July 1929]
Text: MS Sagar; PC v. Der Peter von Herrenwies; Postmark, Bühlerhöhe 28.7.29; Unpublished.

Kurhaus Plättig, bei Bühl (Baden)
[28 July 1929]

Had your letter – so you are off to Skegness – I hope the weather hasn't broken – here it has thundered and rained tremendously, and is now so cold, we hug ourselves in overcoats. But we are nearly 3000 ft. above the sea. I am here with Frieda and her mother. Shall stay about another week, I suppose, then down to Baden again – and probably to Bavaria. This place is on the top of a mountain, all in the great forest – and though it's supposed to be good for me, I really hate it – hate the dark forest and the north altogether. I do hope you'll have a nice time at the sea.

love! DHL

5230. To Giuseppe Orioli, [28 July 1929]
Text: MS UCLA; PC v. Mummelsee; Postmark, [Bühler]höhe 28.7.29; Unpublished.

Kurhaus Plättig, bei *Bühl.* (Baden)
[28 July 1929]

So you are in Montecatini with Aldous – and boiling hot!! I am here on the top of a mountain with Frieda and her mother, and it has thundered and rained terribly, and is now so cold, I just shiver in the wind. I suppose we shall stay another week – then go down to Baden. I just hate altitude – and the great cold pine forest, and everything. – Do let me know about the first version of *Lady C.* and send me the MS. if you think it well. They go on worrying me about the expurgated edition. – I have started the *Seconda Cena* of Lasca – and when we settle a bit, I will do Lorenzo.[1] But not here – I want to go to Bavaria and to the Garda.

DHL

5231. To Enid Hilton, [28 July 1919]

Text: MS UCLA; PC v. Höhenluftkurort Herrenwies, nördl. bad Schwarzwald. 764 m ü.d.M. mit Kurhaus Herrenwies; Postmark, Bühlerhöhe 28.7.29; Unpublished.

Kurhaus Plättig. bei Bühl (Baden)
[28 July 1929]

Many thanks for your letter and reassurances – no, I *hate* the whole fuss, and wish to God I had kept the pictures in Italy. No more shows in England for me, while I live. If only I can get the pictures back, and stop the whole hullabloo, I shall be relieved. Swine those Miller & Gill – I wish you'd ask Stephensen about tackling them – he knows them, and said he'd go for them, if I wished. – We are here about 2700 feet up, and it has thundered and rained and turned bitter cold. I really hate it, and long for the Mediterranean again, but suppose we shall stay about another week here. Was so relieved to hear from L[ahr], sanely; get long raving screeds from Dorothy. If only it were all over! How weary to death I am of the Brit. public. Thanks for all the help.

DHL

5232. To John Cournos, 28 July 1929

Text: Moore 1169–70.

Kurhaus Plättig, Baden
28 July 1929

Dear Cournos:[2]

Your letter came today. No, I never got *O'Flaherty the Great* – expect somebody else did. Life is more or less serving a sentence anywhere in the thick of the 'civilized' world today. I am rather hating it here just now – don't come to Germany.

Where we shall be by end of August I don't know – probably somewhere south of the Alps again. As the rather doddering Ford observes, I prefer the

[1] DHL's translation (MS Lazarus) of the first story of the *Second Supper* by A. F. Grazzini (called Il Lasca) was published in the *Telegraph Sunday Magazine*, 25 October 1981. DHL did not translate any Lorenzo di Medici.
[2] John Cournos (1881–1966), Russian-born author, editor and autobiographer whom DHL knew from 1915. m. 1924, Helen Satterthwaite. His novel, *O'Flaherty the Great*, was published (by Knopf) in June 1927. See *Letters*, iv. 296 n. 1 and v. 410 n. 1.

Mediterranean.[1] I hadn't seen that review – thanks for sending it – rather impotent and elderly. Why do poets in particular go so soon elderly and impotent? Is it poetry, or lack of it? Poor John Gould is always talking about being buried in Arkansas – well, if Arkansas is willing, why not?[2] I will send you a copy of *Lady C.* to Paris – the little Paris edition pub. at 60 francs for me by Edward Titus in his shop behind the Dôme Café, *rue* Delambre. I'll put an inscription in it – if I forget remind me. But c/o Curtis Brown, 6 Henrietta St, Covent Garden, W. C.1. is safer for forwarding than Secker. No, I haven't got away from Alfred A. [Knopf] yet, but I want to, and shall as soon as I can clear my contract. He refused to take up *Collected Poems* so I've done with him. But am afraid just for the sake of being nasty he'd figure me at more than $150, so I'll go a bit slow and get cheaper. I suppose you saw the police raided my picture show. I am so infinitely bored by a world of *crasses*,[3] I am neither writing nor painting, but letting the clock go round – and my health, as ever, is merely so-so. I have decided that the human race is a mistake – one of evolution's mistakes, since God can't make 'em – but don't let it worry me overmuch. Don't you leave your wife if you don't want to, is my advice to any man. – Well I hope this will catch you before you leave the land of hope and glory, and probably we'll meet in the course of the winter, though don't expect to get golden truths out of me.

5233. To Giuseppe Orioli, 29 July 1929
Text: MS UCLA; Moore, *Intelligent Heart* 410–11.

Kurhaus Plättig, bei *Bühl.* (Baden)
Monday 29 July 1929

Dear Pino

I have corrected the proofs[4] and am sending them back at once. Will you just glance through them.

Yes, I had Dorothy's long and senseless letter:[5] but only one card, from Aldous, none from you. – I can't be bothered with the Victor Cunard nonsense of telephones.[6] The case of the pictures is postponed until August 8th,

[1] Probably Ford Madox Ford (formerly Hueffer) (1873–1939), novelist and editor; DHL had known him since 1909. See *Letters*, i. 138 and n. 1.
[2] John Gould Fletcher (1886–1950), b. Arkansas, Imagist poet, had reviewed DHL's *Collected Poems* in the *New York Herald Tribune Books*, 14 July 1929, describing DHL as 'a fanatic, nonconformist puritan in his creed of orgiastic liberalism' and claiming that he had 'steadily declined as an artist'. In 1917 Cournos introduced Fletcher to DHL who liked him (*Letters*, iii. 190 and n. 2).
[3] 'scum'.   [4] Of *The Story of Doctor Manente*.
[5] The letter may have included information about an announcement in *The Times* on 28 July, 'More Paintings by D. H. Lawrence': ten of DHL's early paintings had been supplied by Ada Clarke to fill the gaps on the gallery walls resulting from the police raid (Nehls, iii. 371).
[6] Cf. Letter 5198 and n. 4.

so nothing to do till then. Fancy, Secker could not supply all his orders for that swindling 250 edition – over-subscribed. He is now selling the third thousand of the ordinary 10/6 edit. – good for poetry.

Don't bother to send on the *Dials*.[1] By the way, those are the last numbers, it is now dead.

I shall send you Jonathan Cape's *Collected Poems* of mine, for you to keep for me with my books. – Heinemann is doing 'The Man Who Loved Islands' in an expensive edition, and giving me £300. down. – The Random Press doing that Introduction to the Paris *Lady C* at $4. a copy: swindle, such a little thing! – Lahr will have his *Pansies* ready this week, but I ask him not to let them out till after August 8th when the pictures will be tried – they are still in prison. Dorothy continues the show – foolishly –

It rains and rains here, and is bitter cold. I have to lie under the great feather bolster on my bed, to be warm. I have got a cold, and I simply hate it here. We shall go down in a day or two – and perhaps to Bavaria – or perhaps to Como. I wish I was in Florence, it is so cold and awful here.

Titus doesn't want me to do an expurgated *Lady C*. – everybody else does. Send me all the news.

ever   DHL

5234. To Edward Titus, 29 July 1929
Text: MS UT; Unpublished.

Kurhaus Plättig. bei *Bühl* (*Baden*)
29 July 1929

Dear Titus

Your letter today.[2] Random House were certainly very slow letting you know anything, since they have the thing advertised large all over the place, and my agents and others writing to me: What about it? – But if Curtis Browns write to you, do fix the terms with them, as you tell me now – and pay them in due course – then I don't have to think about it. Don't worry, Random House won't ruin themselves –

I am sure you are quite right to get a travelling agent, and of course we share the expenses of him. You know best what is necessary for distribution, and I leave it to you, and pay my share of the costs.

Gallimard is supposed to be doing a translation of *Lady C*. with no omissions – great palaver, and very paltry terms, of course. But they say they want to get the very best translator (the man who translated *Ulysses*, I forget his

---

[1] See pp. 173 n. 2 and 257 n. 3.   [2] See p. 392 n. 1.

name)[1] and put in a preface by a man of 'the highest literary and moral reputation' – so that there shall be no *cri de scandale* – and altogether be most pi-pi. I suppose it is all to the good. I ought to get their signed contract this week. – But how slow they will be getting the translation out, none can foretell. However, it will probably ease your end of the affair. – I know Gabriel Marcel, the man who did the N.R.F. notice of the book[2] – he was giddily pleased to have me sign the book for him – and thrilled by it like six old maids – so of course, comes out with an O aunty! article like that. If only I had the patience to bother with him, I'd slap him for it.

No, Good Lord, we shan't be here till end of September: but round and about in Germany: and

c/o Frau Baronin v. Richthofen, Ludwig-Wilhelmstift, BadenBaden

will always get me.

Here it rains and is very cold and I hate it.

ever   D. H. Lawrence

5235. To Ada Clarke, 2 August 1929
Text: MS Clarke; Postmark, Bü[hlerhöhe] -2.8.29; cited in Lawrence–Gelder 196.

Kurhaus Plättig
2 Aug. 1929

My dear Sister

The underthings came last night[3] – they are awfully nice, so soft and light. But why will you always send more than I say – I only wanted two pairs, not four.[4] My things last me for years, anyhow. But these are so nice!

You will be off to the seaside this week-end, I suppose.[5] I hope to heaven it is better weather than here. We are stuck on the top of a mountain looking across the Rhine to the Vosges, and I simply hate it – rainy and bitter cold all the time, cuts my chest, the wind – and a big hotel with 150 fat guests, weigh on one's soul – and Frieda's mother really rather awful now. She's 78, and suddenly is in an awful state, thinking her time to die may be coming on. So she fights in the ugliest fashion, greedy and horrible, to get everything that will keep her alive – food, high air, pine-trees, Frieda or me, *nothing* exists but just for the purpose of giving her a horrible strength to hang on a few more

[1] *Ulysse* had been published by Adrienne Monnier in February 1929, trans. Auguste Morel.
[2] In his article (*Nouvelle Revue Française*, xxxii. 729–31) Marcel had said that, strictly speaking, *Lady Chatterley's Lover* is undoubtedly a pornographic novel; but he had gone on to remark: 'the absence of libertinism and perversity is so complete that this book disarms more than it intimidates' and 'there is no other novelist nowadays to whom we can render such homage' (Cowan, *An Annotated Bibliography*, i. 98).
[3] MS reads 'nice'.   [4] Cf. Letter 5138.
[5] Ada Clarke and her family were on holiday at Bridlington.

years.[1] She simply *hates* me because I insist on going down tomorrow to Baden. We've been here twelve days, I've been seedy all the time, kept in my room most of the time, yet that old woman would see me die by inches and yards rather than relinquish her 'mountain air'. She stands in the road and gulps the air in greedy gulps – and says – 'it does me so much good! it gives me strength, strength!' Yet she won't stay here for a day alone, though she is perfectly well and perfectly looked after. No, she must have Frieda or me there. It's the most ghastly state of almost insane selfishness I ever saw – and all comes of her hideous terror of having to die. At the age of seventy-eight! May god preserve me from ever sinking so low. I never felt so cruelly humiliated.

We shall be at the:

Hotel Löwen, Lichtental, bei BadenBaden

for about a week, I suppose. Frieda suffers here almost as much as I do, but fortunately it doesn't make her ill, as it does me. Her foot gets better slowly – she still limps.

I think after a week or so we shall go south again to Lake Como – I don't believe it will be hot. I can't stand much more Germany, this trip. And then as soon as possible we shall begin looking for a house – I think in Italy – and make it nice, and you can come and stay with us in the winter, better than an hotel.

I do hope you'll have decent weather – was poor Pem at Skegness this week? I hope it wasn't as it has been here. Glad Jack is becoming such a prize lad at school! – not that I think much of schools and their prizes.

love! DHL

5236. To Harry and Caresse Crosby, 2 August 1929
Text: MS UT; Postmark, [. . .]; Huxley 813.

Hotel Löwen, Lichtental, *bei BadenBaden*, Allemagne
2 August 1929

Dear Harry and Caresse

It is a long time since I heard from you, you have answered none of my letters. I have been thinking perhaps you got cold feet about *The Escaped Cock*, since the ridiculous fuss over my pictures again, and since your Harry Marks came to Paris – if he came. And I want to tell you not to bother for a moment about the thing, if you don't want to. If circumstances have so worked that it makes it inconvenient for you to publish the story, will you only please let me have back the MSS – you have all my copies – so that I can

[1] See 'Old Men' and 'Death' (*Complete Poems*, ii. 662–3).

make other arrangements. Believe me, I shall understand perfectly, if you tell me your plans are changed.

We are here for another week or so, then I think we shall go down to Lake Como. It is rather cold and rather rainy, and I don't like Germany this year. I want to go away. And as soon as it gets cool enough, we shall go to Italy and look for a house to live in.

Meanwhile I hope you are having a nice time and not too many complications. You are due to be in Cannes, but I suppose you're elsewhere.

You, Caresse, please answer my letter if Harry is otherwise involved, and tell me how you are and how things are, and let me know about the story.

Sincerely   D. H. Lawrence

5237. To Giuseppe Orioli, 2 August 1929
Text: MS (Photocopy) HU; Moore, *Intelligent Heart* 412–13.

Kurhaus Plättig. Baden.
Friday 2 Aug. 1929

Dear Pino

The MS. of *Lady C* came yesterday – many thanks for sending it. Of course I still don't want to make a castrato public edition, and doubt if I shall bring myself to do it. If the dirty public haven't the guts to get hold of the existing edition, let them do without. Why should I trim myself down to make it easy for the swine! I loathe the gobbling public anyhow. – I shall not in any case send this MS. to England – shall send it back to you. Now I am sending the Amer. *Collected Poems* for you to keep for me.

It has rained and been bitter cold all the time we have been up here on this beastly mountain, and I have hated it, and only stayed because my mother-in-law got into a frenzy at the thought of going down, because she says it does her so much good here and gives her so much strength – es gibt mir Kraft, Kraft![1] – She is 78, and is in a mad terror for fear she might die; and she would see me or anyone else die ten times over, to give her a bit more strength to drag on a few more meaningless years. It is so ugly and so awful, I nearly faint. I have never felt so down, so depressed and ill, as I have here, these ten days: awful! What with that terrible old woman, the icy wind, the beastly black forest, and all the other depressing and fat guests – really, one wonders that *anyone* should be so keen to live, under such circumstances. I know I'm not.

But tomorrow we are going down, and it will be better. We shall stay a week or so in the:

Hotel Löwen, Lichtenthal, bei Baden Baden.

[1] 'It gives me strength, strength!'

It is better there – I can sit in the Gaststube where the men come in from the village to drink their beer and smoke their pipes, and I can escape a bit this awful atmosphere of old women who devour the life of everything around them. Truly old and elderly women are ghastly, ghastly, eating up all life with hoggish greed, to keep themselves alive. They don't mind who else dies. I know my mother-in-law would secretly gloat, if I died at 43 and she lived on at 78. She would feel an ugly triumph. It is this kind of thing which does kill one.

I think we shall stay in the *Löwen* about a week, then come south again to Lake Como. I feel I can't stand much more Germany. It's given me a bad blow this time. – Take care of Mumsey, I believe she kills one's life too.[1]

Don't send me Lorenzo di Medici till I get somewhere where I am more at ease and cheerful. At present I can do *nothing*: except write a few stinging 'Pansies' which this time are 'Nettles'. I shall call them nettles.

Do see what there is at Impruneta. And the fattore[2] at the Villa Mirenda told Frieda last autumn that he knew of lots of nice villas she would like. He seemed a decent man. Carlo could get his name and address from the Salvestrini.

DHL

If it's nice on Como, you might come and join us there! – Still rainy and cold here.

5238. To Laurence Pollinger, 2 August 1929
Text: MS UT; Unpublished.

Hotel Löwen. Lichtental, bei Baden Baden
2 August 1929

Dear Pollinger

We are going down to the Löwen again tomorrow, thank God! – been icy cold up here, and very bad for me. In fact I think Germany doesn't suit me this time – or the weather is acting up extra mean. But I suppose we shall stay a week anyhow in the Löwen – and if you were coming for a long week-end, next week-end, of course we'd stay on. You must come if you can get away.

I have been thinking if Secker wants a book of 'articles' and short pieces for the late autumn or spring, I'm sure there are plenty. I can think of a good many that are not on Miss Pearn's list, when I start thinking – all those that the *Adelphi* printed, for example. Murry will have track of those.[3] And then, did you ever see that book which the Centaur Press published at $4., I think –

---

[1] Perhaps Orioli's mother. See Letter 5255.   [2] 'bailiff'.
[3] Only two *Adelphi* pieces were included in *Assorted Articles*: 'On Being a Man' (March 1924) and 'On Human Destiny' (September 1924).

Reflections on the Death of a Porcupine. It was never circulated in England, and very little in U. S. A., if I am to believe Harold Mason, of the Centaur Bookshop in Philadelphia. But I find he's a very very untrustworthy person – and he seemed such a friend of mine – we know him personally. Some of the essays from the *Porcupine* would go very well – some I might revise a bit. Secker has a copy of the book – I'll ask him what he thinks of it. And if you say you want a book of collected pieces, I will rake over my memory – and perhaps somebody would look through my bibliography, of which you have a copy, for the essays and pieces prior to 1924.

I have the MS. of the first *Lady C*. It is just the handwritten MS. I read bits of it – but have a strong reluctance to letting out the book in popular edition, different from the existing edition. I doubt if I shall do it: though it would be much more feasible with this MS. But I don't want to do it.

Titus wrote me that Random House had gone ahead without ever letting him know direct facts – and that he was going to give me half of what he gets from them. I told him I was asking you to write to him. *Go gently with him* – he is a nasty fellow if he cuts up rough, and so far, I believe he piques himself on the fact that he is dealing with me direct, and so he is going to deal *very* straight. He seems to have been afraid the Paris authorities would come down on him – but if Gallimard's are really doing a French translation in full that will calm his fears. Write then!

DHL

5239. To Nancy Pearn, 2 August 1929
Text: MS UT; Huxley 812–13.

Kurhaus Plättig
2 August 1929

Dear Nancy Pearn

I am sending you the article which *Everyman* asked me to write for their series – 'A Religion for the Young'.[1] This is my idea of a religion for the young – don't know if they'll print it – and don't care very much, for I have a rather poor opinion of *Everyman* – and I'm sure they can pay nothing. But it's a nice article, much too good for them, so take care of it for me, and please read the beginning and correct my quotations where wrong.[2]

---

[1] The essay enclosed, 'The Risen Lord', appeared in *Everyman*, 3 October 1929 (Roberts C192).
[2] Against the quotations in the third sentence of the essay, DHL wrote: 'Dear Nancy Pearn – Do correct these if they are not right – so long since I went to church'. She annotated the MS in her turn: 'J.S. Passed to you. My dear – this awe-ful responsibility!! N.P.'
    In DHL's MS the sentence read: 'The Litany [revised from 'Creed'] says: Was crucified, dead, and buried, and rose again on the third day – and the Creed says: I believe in the resurrection of the flesh –.' In the published version this became: 'The Creed says: "Was

And no good asking me to do stories or anything else just now[1] – I'm quite out of mood – I hate it here – it's bitter cold, rainy, pine woods black as hell, and 150 Kurgäste in this hotel, somehow weighs on my spirits horribly. I don't feel 'good' in germany this time. However, we are going down from this *beastly* mountain tomorrow – we are here for my mother-in-law's sake, she is 78, and insanely only thinks of clutching at life to live till she's 100. It's too awful. But tomorrow we go down to more normal life –

Hotel Löwen. Lichtenthal, bei Baden Baden.

Be so good as to tell the other depts., will you – though I think we shall stay only about a week – then go south probably to Lake Como, for I feel no good at all here: don't feel well: icy wind has cut my chest, after we had stewed in heat down in the valley. Ye gods!

I was thinking of those articles – essays – of mine which Murry printed in the *Adelphi* – four or five – a few years ago. I wonder if you have copies of them. They would come in handy for a book. I have no copies of them – but Murry would have. And I expect he'd tell you exactly what articles of mine he ever printed. There must be *lots* that are not on your list.[2] There must be quite enough for a book, really.

I've got a little novel – but I want to re-write it – if ever I get into the mood. It's about 30,000 words I suppose.[3]

DHL

5240. To Martin Secker, 2 August 1929
Text: MS UInd; Postmark, Bühlerhöhe -3.8.29; Secker 122–3.

Hotel Löwen, Lichtental, b/BadenBaden

2 Aug 1929

Dear Secker

Tell me how the *Pansies* are really doing, will you? – because if they sell well at 10/6, I do hope you'll bring out a cheap edition soon. I should like that. – And then I will do another volume, of *Nettles* this time, for the spring, and get a bit more of my own back.

And Pollinger has been asking me several times about a book of collected

crucified, dead, and buried ... the third day He rose again from the dead." And again, "I believe in the resurrection of the body ..."' (*Phoenix II*, ed. Roberts and Moore, p. 571).

[1] Nancy Pearn had written to DHL on 22 July 1929 (TMSC UT):

> There are rumours I hear of a new story? ... It would be splendid to have some short stories for offer right away I think; some like those loves of mine in some of the early collections. That love, I may add, still continues.
>
> The editor of 'Travel' is asking whether you have any more travel articles like those Flowery Tuscany ones for instance. Couldn't you be tempted to do some about Majorca?

[2] See Letter 5278 and n. 1.   [3] *The Virgin and the Gipsy*.

pieces – articles. I'm sure there are plenty of articles to make a book, if we cared to hunt them all together – and a good many of them are, or were pretty popular when they appeared. Then there is that book *Reflections on the Death of a Porcupine*. That has never been circulated at all in England, and I think the essays of the second half of the book – not those that appeared in the *Signature*[1] – are really good, and with a bit of revision would go down very well now. Let me know what you think – You have a copy of the *Porcupine* – and I really think people are more interested in my articles than in my stories.

The unexpurgated *Pansies* will come out shortly, and I shall send you a copy. For that last copy of *Lady C.* that you had, will you put it to my credit and subtract what I owe you for books ordered – and let me know how it stands. I have to square accounts with Orioli.

They keep worrying me to do an expurgated *Lady C.* for the public, but my feeling is all against it.

We are at present at the Plättig on top of a mountain in the Schwarzwald – bitter cold and rainy it's been these last ten days, and not suiting my health *at all*. Tomorrow thank God we go down to Lichtental – where it will be warmer, and an inn, not this great Kurhaus, which I hate. I find Germany a bit depressing this year. Shall go south as soon as possible.

I wonder if you are going away for a holiday – it seems to have become one of the modern compulsions, another task, and a great bugbear. When I get a house where I *can* stay at home for August, I shall stay at home.

Frieda still limps with her foot – and isn't very happy here either. She never is in Germany. – Greetings to Rina and the boy.

Yrs.   DHL

5241. To Enid Hilton, [2 August 1929]
Text: MS UCLA; PC v. Herrenwies 764 m Ü.d.M.; Postmark, Bühlerhöhe -3 8.29; Unpublished.

Hotel Löwen. Lichtental, bei BadenBaden
[2 August 1929]

Thanks for your letter – we are going down to the Löwen tomorrow, stay about a week. Here has been very cold, didn't suit me at all. Am wondering what Miller & G[ill] have to say[2] – it is no mistake on their part. Dorothy

---

[1] *Reflections on the Death of a Porcupine* begins with 'The Crown'. An earlier version of the first three parts of this six-part essay had appeared in *The Signature*, 4 and 18 October and 1 November 1915 (Roberts C39, C40 and C41). For both versions see *Reflections on the Death of a Porcupine*, ed. Herbert, pp. 247–306, 469–79.

[2] Cf. Letters 4874 and 5202.

telegraphed 'glowing love' and said she is writing 'marvellous news'. What a woman! Wish it was all over.

DHL

5242. To Charles Lahr, [2 August 1929]
Text: MS UNYB; PC v. Kurhaus Plättig b. Baden-Baden, 800 M. ü. d. M; Postmark, Bühlerhöhe -3.8.29; Unpublished.

Hotel Löwen. Lichtental, Baden Baden
Friday.

We are going down to the Löwen tomorrow – expect we shall stay there about a week – been horribly cold and unpleasant here, not agreeing with me at all. – The two books have not come, you said you were sending them on Tuesday. – I think for the vellum I prefer green, if it's a really nice green.[1] – Your photograph made you and Mrs Lahr *very* plain – but the child charming. Send me any news.

L.

5243. To Laurence Pollinger, [4 August 1929]
Text: MS UT; Unpublished.

Hotel Löwen. Lichtental, *BadenBaden*
Sunday

Dear Pollinger

Thank God we are down from that cold mountain. It is quite nice here, warm, but so far, not too hot. I hope it'll stay like it.

If you can get away this week-end for your long week-end, do come and be my guest here in the Löwen for the days that you can stay. I think you'd like it all right, but it's quite simple. So come if you can.

As for Titus, I more or less gave him that *Jolly Roger* to secure American copyright, so go easy with him.

Perhaps you'll come then?

DHL

5244. To Nancy Pearn, 5 August 1929
Text: MS UT; Unpublished.

Hotel Löwen, Lichtenthal / BadenBaden
5 Aug. 1929

Dear Nancy Pearn,

Here is your photograph, signed and I hope all right – photographs are so horrid to write on.

---

[1] Ten special copies of Lahr's *Pansies* were bound in green vellum (Roberts A48d(3)).

There is an article for the *Star Review* – and their letter – they may say my article isn't their line – I don't care.[1] I'll try and do a freedom one – but feel a bit out of temper with England and her freedom.[2]

We feel better down again from that mountain – but this morning it rained all morning – wonder how England bankholidayed it. Hateful Bankholiday! – Now it's tea-time, sunny and warm, so tea in the garden. – Wonder if Pollinger will come!

D. H. Lawrence

5245. To Harry and Caresse Crosby, [5 August 1929]
Text: TMSC NWU; Unpublished.

Hotel Löwen, Lichtenthal, BadenBaden
5 Aug.

Dear Harry and Caresse

A rushed word to catch post – have your wire. Wherever did the Italian letters go? Where did you send them? No sign or sound of them. Send proofs here, we shall be here two weeks – and write all the news. Didn't you go to Cannes? How are you? – hope nice and sunny. I was afraid you were all tangled up.

It rains – but yellow sun shines through and the leaves sparkle. Good omen!

DHL

---

[1] Emily Lutyens, editor of the (London) *Star Review* had written on 10 July 1929:

Dear Mr. Lawrence,
  We are proposing in this Review to have a series of articles dealing with various aspects of life under modern conditions. The sequence will run as follows.

The Individual	Literature
Men and Women	Science
The Child	Industry
Nationality and Internationality	Philosophy and Religion
The Arts	Civilisation

Would you be willing to contribute an article of about four thousand words on the subject of Men and Women for which I should have much pleasure in offering you an honorarium of £20.

DHL's article (sent to Nancy Pearn) was entitled 'Men and Women'; it appeared in the *Star Review*, ii (November 1929), 614–26; it was collected in *Assorted Articles* as 'Men Must Work and Women as Well' (Roberts C193).

[2] The invitation to write an article on freedom had come from Ernest E. Williams of the Freedom Association. (Williams, 1866–1935, was a barrister and prolific author of works on political as well as legal matters.)

5246. To Charles Lahr, 5 August 1929

Text: MS UNYB; Postmark, Baden-Baden 6 8 29; Unpublished.

Hotel Löwen. Lichtenthal / Baden Baden
5 Aug 1929

Dear Lahr

The book came today. I like the cover and I don't really mind the wiggly title-page, but why oh why were you so economical over the paper? There should have been at least four blank pages at the beginning. And then the pages themselves – it looks as if the one idea had been to economise paper. That awful little top margin! – and all so crowded, some pages look like a Hansard's report.[1] You should have used about a third more paper. – It's all in a lifetime, but I hope the purchasers wont grumble – and poor Stephensen, with his fancy name[2] – or his name for fancy books. However, we'll manage better next time. Another important thing is, that in starring the poems omitted from the Secker edition, they have starred only about *half*. There are ten stars, and there are at least eighteen poems here that Secker omitted: 'Jeune Fille', 'What Matters' – quite a lot.[3] I haven't a copy of Secker's edition here, or I'd go through the list. Would it be a great trouble for you to do it, and put a little cross in ink against the poems that should be starred? One should either star all or none. – Anyhow the book will remain as a curiosity, and I'm glad it's done entire.

Don't send me any more copies till I ask for them. – I suppose you had a list of names I sent you, to give copies to. I do hope everything will go quietly, and you can dispose of the 500 soon.

This is just a rushed note, in haste. We shall be here two weeks more, I expect.

Anyhow I'm glad the book is *there*! – But what will 'nice' collectors say!

L.

5247. To Laurence Pollinger, [5 August 1929]

Text: MS UT; PC v. Hotel Goldener Löwe, Baden-Baden, Lichtental; Postmark, Baden-Baden 6 8 29; Unpublished.

[Hotel Löwen, Lichtenthal, bei Baden-Baden]
Montag

Your letter this evening – try to come – the case is on Thursday at Marl-

---

[1] I.e. like the official report of parliamentary debates.

[2] P. R. Stephensen allowed his name (instead of Lahr's) to appear as the printer in the 'definitive edition' of *Pansies*.

[3] Lahr's edition contained fourteen poems omitted by Secker, of which Lahr had starred eleven, missing 'Be a Demon' in addition to 'The Jeune Fille' and 'What Matters'.

borough Rd[1] – it rains again, alas, – the Löwen looks much less imposing in reality, come and see.

DHL

5248. To Aldous and Maria Huxley, 6 August 1929
Text: Huxley 814–15.

Hôtel Löwen, Lichtenthal, Baden-Baden
6 Aug., 1929.

Dear Aldous and Maria, –

We had both your letters – up on that beastly Plättig that I loathed so much, and where I nearly perished of cold if I put my nose out of doors – the hotel being heated up. Horrible! Save me from *Höheluftkurorte*.[2] It is quite nice here – an old inn, we sit in the garden and eat fat red plums – and the weather is just right, sunny and just pleasant for meals out of doors.

Aldous, I didn't know Frieda had been turning her heavy artillery on you. She only confessed very proud of herself, after I had your letter. Anyhow, let's hope it'll be another shot in the bows of the old buffers, your article.[3]

I haven't any news – the case is supposed to be on Thursday – I expect, anyhow, they'll burn the four books just to show that they can burn something[4] – their own fingers also, I hope. Am exceedingly bored by it all, and wish I had never had a show. Never again. But one does forget what they are like, the swine people.

The *Pansies* unexpurgated are ready and will be sent to you this week, I expect. I must say they've made rather an awful book of it, filled up the pages like a cheap printed report, and paper absolutely scarce. I pity the poor devils who pay £2 a copy – but I can't help it. Stephensen lent his name as printer, but he'll look down his nose when he sees how badly the book is planned and executed. I'm disappointed – but I can't help it.

I wonder how you are feeling up in your mountains. I felt rotten here – I hope you won't also get cold and rain. I am seeing a doctor, so we shall

---

[1] See p. 361 n. 2.   [2] 'high-altitude health resorts'.

[3] Probably 'After the Fireworks' (collected in *Brief Candles*, 1930), in which Huxley made use of his recent visit to Montecatini with Orioli which in many ways paralleled DHL's experience at Plättig. On 2 August 1929 Huxley had written to Robert Nichols:

> Have you ever been to a spa? If not, go. It's the most grotesque vision imaginable – all the obese, the bilious, the gluttonous, the constipated, the red-nosed, the yellow-eyed, standing about in a pump-room, that looks like ancient Rome through the eyes of Alma Tadema, and drinking, to classical music and at 8.0 A.M. glass after glass of salt water. Really fascinating. (Smith 316)

[4] The police took four copies of *The Paintings of D. H. Lawrence* when they raided the Warren Gallery.

probably be two more weeks here at least. After that, I don't know. I felt
incapable of a plan. Only this autumn I *want* to find a house, either in Italy or
Marseilles. I think Italy for preference. – I hear the Crosbys sent Frieda a
gramophone to Italy – I hope not c/o you, or you'll have all the fuss. I so
carefully asked him, *please* to send *nothing* till we had a house – but there you
are! People! They are still in Paris.

I feel very *piano*[1] here in Germany and incapable of much. A *Gesängverein*[2]
is just arriving with oak-wreaths round their heads and red ribbons – so we
shall have music wherever we go, like the Lady of Banbury Cross.[3] People do
make efforts to keep it up.

                                                                      DHL

5249. To Max Mohr, 6 August 1929
Text: MS HMohr; Mohr 170–1.

                                            Hotel Löwen. Lichtenthal/BadenBaden.
                                                                  6 August 1929
Lieber Mohr

Gott sei dank, wir sind unter von jenem kalten Berg, wieder in der Wärme.
Hier ist es ganz angenehm, ein altes Gasthaus, wirklich, und beinah keine
Leute. Wir sitzen still und warm im Garten, und leben noch. Meine
Schwiegermutter ist still dabei – zieht aber morgen ins Stift wieder. Heute ist
auch hier die ältere Schwester meiner Frau, Frau Dr. Else Jaffé: und zum
Thee kommt heute der Professor Alfred Weber, im Auto, und sie fahren
heut' abend weiter. Sie wissen, die Else und der Alfred Weber sind schon 25
Jahren Freunde, mehr wie heiratet. Sie gehen nach Irschenhausen, wo wir
waren, bei Ebenhausen im Isartal, wo Sie zu uns gekommen sind, mit dem
riesengrossen Blumenstrauch, erinnern Sie, vor zwei Jahren? Vielleicht wird
die Else ein Besuch nach Wolfsgrube machen – der Alfred ist[4] letzen Jahr ein
Auto als Geschenk bekommen, zum 60n Geburtstag – von einem Zurichern
Bankman – Banquier – Gott weiss warum, sicher nicht für seine *beaux yeux*.
Solche geschenke sind nur für Professoren und Geheimräthle. Aber das Auto
haben sie, und 4000 M. im Jahr um Chauffeur u. s. w. zu zahlen. So können
sie ganz leicht nach Rottach kommen. Aber man weiss nicht ob der Alfred
kommen will. Er ist furchtbar nervös geworden, ein nervenkranker Mensch,
auch mit Angstgefühl, und man weiss nimmer was er machen wird. Als
Mann war er einmal ganz nett, nimmer sehr fein oder von der Natur gescheit.

---

[1] 'flat'.   [2] 'choral society'.
[3] Nursery song: 'Ride a cock horse to Banbury Cross/To see a fine lady upon a white horse./
    Rings on her fingers and bells on her toes,/She shall have music wherever she goes.'
[4] ist] ward

Als Professor war er immer furchtbar: eine Wortenquelle. Was er jetzt ist, ist unbeschreiblich: aber ein krankes Ding.

Und wir, wir sitzen noch 15. Tage hier, meine Frau will *massage* haben für ihre Gelenke – ich habe Ihnen schon gesagt, dass sie den Fuss umgetauscht hat, nicht wahr? – und ich gehe auch an den Arzt. Und dann, nachher, hängt es auf dem Wetter. Wenn es regenisch und kalt is, werden wir nicht nach Bayern kommen, ich habe den Plättig so gehasst. Aber wenn es wirklich warm wird, und sonnig, dann wäre es schön. Ich bin aber nicht sehr glücklich in Deutschland. Etwas druckt, man wird deprimiert. Und ich habe gar keine Lust zur Arbeit: und spazieren kann ich nicht.

Gut dass Ihr Roman endlich herauskommt. Es wird mich sehr interessieren. Und wann wird die Komödie fertig sein? – Man braucht Komödien zu schreiben, man ist so voller Gift, heutzutage. Ich höre nichts weite von Curtis Brown über *Lady C.* – der Kippenberg ist ein altes Schlange, lässt die andern es nicht machen, und thut es selber nicht.

Aber man wird müde, und kann nicht mehr kämpfen.

Alles Gutes.   DHL

[Dear Mohr
Thank God, we're down from that cold mountain, in the warmth again. Here it's very nice, an old inn really, and almost no one about. We sit quiet and warm in the garden, and are still alive. My Schwiegermutter is still with us – but will move back into the Stift tomorrow. Today my wife's elder sister, Dr Else Jaffé, is here too: and Professor Alfred Weber comes to tea today, by car, and they will drive on tonight.[1] You know Else and Alfred Weber have been friends, more like a married couple, for the last 25 years. They are going to Irschenhausen, where we were, near Ebenhausen in the Isar valley, where you visited us with the enormous bunch of flowers, do you remember, two years ago? Perhaps Else will pay a visit to Wolfsgrube – last year Alfred was given a car as a present for his 60th birthday – by a Zurich bank-man – banker – God knows why, certainly not for his *beautiful eyes*. Such presents are only for Professors and little Privy Councillors. But the car they have, and 4000 Marks a year to pay for a chauffeur etc. So they can get to Rottach quite easily. But one doesn't know whether Alfred wants to come. He's grown terribly jumpy, a man suffering from a nervous disease, and suffering angst too, and one never knows what he will be up to next. As a man he was once quite nice, never very refined or naturally intelligent. As a professor he was

---

[1] Dr Alfred Weber (1868–1958), Professor of Sociology and Political Science at the University of Heidelberg, and Else Jaffe's lover. Cf. *Letters*, i. 413.

always dreadful: words just spilling over. What he is now, is indescribable: a sick thing, though.

And us, we're stuck here for another fortnight, my wife wants to have *massage* for her joints – I already told you, didn't I, that she turned her foot over? – and I'm going to the doctor too. And then, after that, it depends on the weather. If it's rainy and cold, we shan't come to Bavaria, I hated the Plättig so much. But if it turns really warm, and sunny, then it would be lovely. But I'm not very happy in Germany. Something bears down on one, one gets depressed. And I really don't want to work: and I can't go for walks.

Good that your novel will come out at last. It will interest me a great deal. And when will the comedy be ready? – One needs to write comedies, one is so full of poison nowadays. I hear nothing more from Curtis Brown about *Lady C.* – Kippenberg is an old serpent, won't let the others do it and doesn't do it himself.

But one gets tired, and can't fight any more.

All the best.   DHL]

5250. To Giuseppe Orioli, 7 August 1929
Text: MS UCLA; Moore 1174–5.

Hotel Löwen, Lichtenthal / BadenBaden
7 Aug 1929

Dear Pino

I am returning the Lasca proofs at once – it will be a good thing when it is all printed and you can go ahead as you please.

We are down here, much nicer than up that mountain. It is warm, but not a bit hot, we sit in the garden most of the day. Frieda still cannot walk much – she is having massage for her foot. I am going to the doctor also – he says the lung is better, but the asthma is bad: all of which I know myself: and that I ought to live in the south near the sea, and not go up high mountains – which I also know. And still I feel rather feeble, and my bronchials are the devil. But I suppose we shall stay two more weeks here to finish the doctoring. I *don't* think we shall go to Bavaria. We'll come south over the Gotthard, and if Florence is hot, we'll stay a bit on Lake Como, and you can come and see us there. I like Lake Como. And then we can all go back to Florence together.

It will be great fun if we can find a house and have ducks and goats. I've never tried my hand at pigs, but why not? They must be nicer than human ones. We might even make bacon, and hang a long flitch against the wall. My father always said that was the beautifullest picture on a wall – a flitch of bacon! – and *Boccaccio* could hang opposite – all the carnal sins together.

I've done some nice stinging nettles, and let's hope they'll sting the arses of all the Meads and Persians of slimy London.[1] I shall read them to you. – Also I have got a copy of Lahr's *Pansies*, and I must say, it's rather awful – he didn't supply enough paper, and the print almost bursts out of the pages, it is so crowded. I must say, I had a bad ten minutes when I saw it. But it's not my fault. Lahr didn't buy enough paper. But how can he have been so stupid as to let the pages be crammed up as they are! The man can have no eye at all. Lamentable!

The case is tomorrow. I expect they'll burn the four books anyhow. I really come to hate the hypocritical swine.

Poor Miss Mollar – when you were teasing her at Pasquale's about becoming a baroness, she said: It's all very well his talking about a baroness, but I'm a barren woman anyhow.[2] Sh! don't tell him! – – True enough – but it would be worse if she had a set of children living on top of the Lungarno Acciaioli, as well. Most women should be barren.

Did Aldous promise to do Machiavelli? I haven't the energy to do a thing, here – no go at all.

Tell me all about Vingone and the Salvestrini – that will interest me. I'm sure Florence is better than Vallombrosa.

Wiedersehen! DHL

The man Barnet B. Ruder now offers 3000 dollars for MS of *Lady C*. – but I shall not sell. – Also I shall *not* make an expurgated edition at all – shall send the MS back to you.

5251. To Caresse Crosby, [8 August 1929]
Text: MS UT; Postmark, Baden-Baden 8.8.29; Huxley 755–6.

Hotel Löwen, Lichtenthal, *Baden Baden*
Thursday

Dear Caresse

The proofs came at lunch time – I have already done head-piece and little tail-piece for Part I – shall have a go at the others tomorrow and forward to you as quickly as possible. – I wish you would send me *two* more sets of proofs, for my use – at your leisure. And tell me what terms you have arranged with Marks, because he must not sell this too *cheap* – I should say $10. since Random House charges $4. for that foreword to the Paris *Lady C*. – And on the cover will you please print my phoenix, quite small – nest and flames might be red and bird black. – I think under my name.

No sign or sound of any gramophone –

---

[1] Cf. Daniel vi. 8: 'the law of the Medes and Persians, which altereth not'. See also p. 361 n. 2.
[2] Cf. Letter 4772 and n. 2.

Harry's loves – just like his whiskies, to excite his head and die away dead! nothing.

I like the look of the book very much. – Send me the fifty sheets to sign.[1]

love from both   DHL

5252. To Charles Lahr, 8 August 1929
Text: MS StaU; Postmark, Baden-Baden 9.8.29; Lacy, *Escaped Cock* 78–9.

Hotel Löwen, Lichtenthal / Baden Baden
8 Aug. 1929

Dear Lahr

The poems in the case came today – but how did you send them, because my wife had to go to Zollamt[2] for them, and they asked if it was anything political. Asses! I like the case all right – and I'm glad you can insert that page, it makes the copy that came today much better. But the crowding of the pages is still rather a grief to me – though I don't want to seem ungrateful, you've been awfully good doing all the work, and I'm so glad to see the book in existence. – Will you mark the other non-Secker poems?

About the green vellum – if I choose a green it will sure to be one that doesn't exist in vellum. Could you perhaps send me one or two patterns? I can send them all back if necessary.

Pouring with rain – and Thursday evening, the fate of the pictures should be decided by now. A sad sort of evening. I don't feel very happy in Germany.

Don't send me any more copies of the poems – you've sent me now No 13 and No 15. Perhaps you can send the other gift copies 'out of series' and unnumbered. You could write inside: *Out of Series – for Max Mohr* – and so on: *Out of Series: for Enid Hilton.* Then you would have all the numbered copies for sale.

I do hope there'll be no fuss – I am so tired of the nonsense.

The Black Sun Press in Paris – you had one of their books – is doing a story of mine for the autumn – *The Escaped Cock* – an important story. They are doing 450 copies and 50 on vellum, and are sending them all to New York: none to England. I shall send you a set of proofs. Perhaps we might do that next, for England. It is a longish story: I care a good deal about it: about 100 pp. I am doing water-colour decorations for this Paris edition. What do you think of it? It is no use for public editions – but nothing terrible.

Well, now we must wait and see if all goes well with the heartsease.[3] Next year my nettles.

---

[1] For the special autographed copies on Japanese vellum (Roberts A50b).
[2] 'Customs House'.
[3] Heartsease is a common name for pansy.

I shall ask Secker to send review copies to the *Sunday Worker*[1] – little snob. But you'll see, the socialists will hate me most of all. I should like to see real Labour or Socialist or red reviews of *Pansies*: of which, by the way, I am asking Secker to bring out a cheap edition – but it depends also on that damned slow Knopf. He wont want to be undersold. Secker wants to do a 7/6 *Collected Poems*, but Cape is still selling at $5. – so impossible yet.

Well – you know I'm really grateful to you for doing the book for me –

DHL

5253. To Laurence Pollinger, 9 August 1929
Text: MS UT; Unpublished.

Hotel Löwen, Lichtental, Baden Baden
9 Aug 1929

Dear Pollinger

I had your wire, and so sorry you can't come. I thought you might manage it. But I must say these last two days have been rainy. What about next week?

I enclose Seltzer's account – don't know why it came to me. Also Barnet B Ruders letter – well, it couldn't possibly be Barnet B. Politer! – what a painful tone! It doesn't seem any use my answering – will you do as you think best.

As to the Secker short story scheme, it seems so complicated, let it wait a bit.[2]

I hear the pictures are to be returned, the books burned.[3] Ma questi Inglesi sono scimmie, bruciano il proprio gallo che non canti più. Ebbene, non farà

---

[1] Cf. Letter 5053 and n. 3. No review of *Pansies* in the *Sunday Worker* is known.

[2] P. P. Howe – on Secker's behalf – wrote to Pollinger on 31 July 1929 (Secker Letter-Book, UIll):

... as the whole point of the "Collected Short Stories" is to make it a big-value book, this would hardly be achieved by limiting it to the three volumes of the short stories proper, and excluding the long-shorts, as without these it could not possibly make more than 900 pages. Our own view is that it should include all Lawrence's fiction to date short of novel length (making "St Mawr" the dividing line), and this would mean the contents of the three short story volumes ("The Prussian Officer", "England, My England" and "The Woman Who Rode Away"), "The Ladybird" trio, and "The Princess" from "St Mawr". Possibly Lawrence would care to drop two or three of the weaker magazine stories from "England", for example; at all events, there would be scope for this. The resulting volume would be one which we could present as containing first-class value.

[3] The magistrate's decision at the Marlborough Street court was: 'The case to be adjourned *sine die*, the pictures released and restored to their owners, and the four books of reproductions destroyed. In consideration of this latter clause, Mr Mead awarded £5.5.0 costs against the Warren Gallery' (Nehls, iii. 387).

nemmeno alba laggiù. Paese di scimmie senze palli, che finisca nel fango! Basta!¹

DHL

I have decided also; and finally, that I cannot make an expurgated edition of *Lady C* – cannot and will not – so there's the end of that.

Would you be so good as to send Rich the little list of addresses for the 6 copies of Knopf *Pansies* – then they needn't trail to England. Do you know Knopf's date for bringing them out?²

DHL

Copies of *Pansies* from Alfred A. Knopf
please send to the following addresses:
1. Mrs Mabel Luhan. *Taos*. New Mexico
1. Hon. Dorothy Brett. Box 215. *Taos*. New Mexico
1. Willard Johnson Esq. *Taos*. New Mexico
1. Mrs Christine Hughes. *Santa Fe*. New Mexico³
1. Mrs Alice Corbin Henderson. *Santa Fe*. New Mex.⁴
1. D. H. Lawrence, c/o Sig. G. Orioli, 6 Lungarno Corsini, *Florence*. Italy.

5254. To Hilda Aldington, 10 August 1929
Text: MS UNYB; Moore, *Intelligent Heart* 414–15.

Hotel Löwen. Lichtental / *Baden Baden*, Germany
10 Aug. 1929

Dear Hilda

Your note this morning – here are a few bits – the typed poems crossed out in red ink are omitted from Secker's *Pansies* – these bits I have written out from some oddments.⁵ I have changed a word or two in the typed poems, to

¹ 'But these English are apes, they burn their own cock so that it crows no more. Well, there won't even be dawn over there. Country of apes without balls, that will end up in the mud! Enough!'
² 27 September 1929.
³ DHL had known Christine Hughes and her daughter Mary Christine (1908?–) in New Mexico; their acquaintance was renewed in December 1926 when the Hughes were in Rome (see *Letters*, vi. 38 n. 2). His horrified fascination as he showed them round Florence is reflected in the sketch 'Laura Philippine'.
⁴ Alice Corbin Henderson (1881–1949), American poet who helped to found and edit the *Poetry* magazine. m. 1905, William Penhallen Henderson. See *Letters*, iv. 290 n. 4.
⁵ DHL enclosed six poems in autograph ('True love at last!', 'Lucifer', 'Sphinx', 'Intimates', 'Image-making love' and 'Ultimate Reality'; all subsequently published in *Last Poems*, Florence, 1932), and eleven 'Pansies' in corrected carbon typescript (see Roberts E319.1). Hilda Aldington used the autograph poems in the 1930 *Imagist Anthology* (New York; Roberts B27).

make them possible. Now do as you like – take or leave what you like. – You won't really like any of 'em, but you can't get blood out of a stone.

We are here for another ten days or so, I expect, then really I must go south. My cough is a great nuisance, and it is very damp and steamy here in Baden – not good weather.

Where we shall be in the autumn I don't know – but probably somewhere in Italy. – But now it's more than ten years since we met, and what should we have to say? God knows! nothing, really. It's no use saying anything. That's my last conviction. Least said, soonest mended: which assumes that the breakage has already happened.

Douglas is in Austria, not very well and not happy. Arabella I hear is in Paris – also not in a good way at all, poor Arabella.

                                                              DHL[1]

5255. To Giuseppe Orioli, 10 August 1929
Text: MS (Photocopy) HU; Moore 1176.

Hotel Löwen, Lichtental / Baden Baden
10 August 1929

Dear Pino

Here are the last proofs of Lasca – I hope you had the others, I sent them off at once. – About the notes – if you will send me a complete set of page proofs, with the lines numbered, I will do them. I have your list, and the Fornaciari book, and the Biagi.[2] – About the lines – I am afraid they may run up clumsily into thousands and thousands. Perhaps the best would be to number each page afresh – it would be very simple – then in the notes we could put p. 12. line 15 or whatever it is – and the numbering will be very easy. But as you like –

I had telegrams to say: Pictures to be returned, books to be burned. – Let them burn their own balls, the fools. This has given me a great sickener of England. I begin to loathe my 'nice' fellow-countrymen, especially their niceness.[3]

Here it isn't hot – and it rains – at least it rained yesterday and Thursday, and today is all grey and gloomy – the Black Forest is as black as its name, my cough is a great nuisance, and I am miserable. – I go to the doctor – he says

[1] This letter is written on a spare leaf from those DHL had signed for the special copies of Secker's *Pansies*.
[2] Raffaello Fornaciari (1837–1917) provided introduction and notes to *Scritti Scelti de A. F. Grazzini in Prosa e in Poesia* (Florence, 1911); Guido Biagi (1855–1925) contributed a study of Grazzini to *Grazzini . . . Le Novelle* (Milan, 1915), pp. 9–24; he also published *The Private Life of the Renaissance Florentines* (Florence, 1896), etc.
[3] Cf. 'The English Are So Nice!' (*Complete Poems*, ii. 659–60).

my lung is healed, but my bronchials and asthma only a little better – and I ought to live by the sea. I can hardly believe it is hot in Florence – here seems so grey and like the beginning of winter. I want to come south soon – in ten days time – to Lugano, and then Bellagio or somewhere on Como where you can join us: if it's not very hot. Anyhow a little heat seems to be better for me than this damp.

Frieda of course is pining to rush away to Impruneta – she is never happy in Germany.

Don't stay long under Mumsie's wing – that must be more stifling than Florence, even.

ciau!   DHL

5256. To Giuseppe Orioli, 12 August 1929
Text: MS UCLA; cited in Moore, *Intelligent Heart* 415.

Hotel Löwen, Lichtental. Baden Baden.
Monday 12 Aug 1929

Dear Pino

I think Lasca will make a very nice book – I like the title-page *particularly*, and the old boy himself. Now if you send me the proofs with the lines numbered, I will do the notes and it is finished.

I believe Aldous will do Machiavelli – he can't afford to sneeze at £300. – And I was thinking you might ask Aldington to do a vol. – preferably of poetry. You might even ask him to do Lorenzo de' Medici, I shall have my hands full of Lasca, and I believe we shall need to keep our promise and put out the other two suppers. You could write him:

Malthouse Cottage. *Padworth nr. Reading*, Berks. England.
though I believe he is in Paris: and tell him I told you.

I am glad you saw the Salvestrini – I believe if we had known them better we should have found them very good people. I shall send them a card from here – Of course the Pini always did everything for us, so the Salvestrini were jealous. – I wish you would speak to the fattore – I never knew him – you remember we had that old scoundrel in brown most of the time we were there. But this man is much more a gentleman, and if you ask him he will call at your shop and you can have a chat – much better than I can write to him – and if we give him trouble to no final purpose, then of course we'll give him 20 Liras or 30 or whatever you think well, for his pains.

By the way, Miller & Gill, being tackled by Enid Hilton and Goldston, said they had now sent off a cheque to you. Have you got it? The liars made excuse that they had received no invoice, and didn't know whom to pay nor what to pay.

I suppose you have seen the papers about the pictures – the nasty insolence makes me simply ill. They may well leave the culture of the country to such canaille.

Maria wrote – only telling Frieda that they cared more about me than my pictures, and Lawrence dead would be good for no pictures, no books, and nothing. The Goose that lays the coloured Easter eggs.[1] How they do all like to dwell on the thought of my being dead! but everybody alike. They have determined I shall die. So of course I shall live a hundred years, and put wreaths on all their graves. – Maria says Aldous isn't very well, and they are not happy on that mountain. – Also she says he takes his paints to the top of the mountain at evening – so I suppose he does the landscape in the setting sun. At Forte he used to draw Maria in the nude – lying on the bed. I know because she used to complain how cold she got. So we can expect Ingres at least, and Turner.[2]

It is quite nice weather here, sunny but not hot. Last night Frieda celebrated her 50th birthday – a party of nine, and Bowle,[3] Trout, Duck – Very good. But she is never in a good temper in Germany, so Maria had better look out!

DHL

5257. To Caresse Crosby, 12 August 1929
Text: MS SIU; Lacy, *Escaped Cock* 79.

Hotel Löwen. Lichtental. Baden Baden
12 Aug 1929

Dear Caresse

I have done the four small bits of decoration for the *Cock*, and have nearly finished the frontispiece – shall send them along soon.[4] But I was wondering about your edition. Why don't you print 750? – and let Marks have 500, and keep 250 to dispose of this side? I don't see why Marks should have the monopoly. And do please tell me what price he is going to charge – it should be at least $10 – and what terms does he make with you? He ought, of course, to pay you $6.65 for each $10.-copy – and no bookseller would take more than 40% – which means he would give you $6. on a $10 copy. What are his terms? Have you already fixed them? This is a book that will soon be snapped up –

---

[1] DHL added this sentence marginally as an afterthought.

[2] An allusion to the sensual nudes by the French painter, Jean Auguste Dominique Ingres (1780–1867), and the landscape paintings (especially the mountain scenes) of Joseph Mallord William Turner (1775–1851).

[3] 'punch'.

[4] The original decorations, used for Crosby's edn, are lost. The frontispiece is reproduced on the cover of Lacy's edn of *The Escaped Cock*.

why give it away to Harry Marks? Then I suppose you halve profits with me – was that your intention? Write me a business letter with all details, we may as well have it all square. What I don't see, is why all copies should go to New York. Why should not some be sold in Europe?

Anyhow let me know and I will send proofs and decorations. We shall be here some time still.

I heard from Forte from Maria Huxley – no sign so far of any gramophone. How is Harry?

DHL

5258. To Emily King, [12 August 1929]

Text: MS Sagar; PC v. Baden-Baden – Kapelle Stourdza; Postmark, Baden-Baden 12 8 29; Unpublished.

[Hotel Löwen, Lichtenthal, bei Baden-Baden]
Monday

Had your letter from Ripley – did Joan stay on with Gertie? – I hear also from Ada, she is visiting all the old places. – We are much better down here – haven't you got this address:

Hotel Löwen, Lichtental, Baden Baden.

There is a quiet garden with old trees, where one can sit out all day long. Yesterday we celebrated Frieda's 50th birthday – champagne and trout and ducks – nine people – very nice . – I went to the doctor, he says my lung is very much better, healed, only the bronchials and the asthma are still bad. – Frieda still having massage for her foot – it takes a long time. Weather has been good – but now is cloudy again.

Love to you all.   DHL

5259. To Catherine Carswell, 12 August 1929

Text: MS YU; Postmark, [. . .]; cited in Carswell, *The Savage Pilgrimage*, pp. 284, 286, 287.

Hotel Löwen, Lichtental / Baden Baden
12 Aug 1929

Dear Catherine

I was glad to have your letter today and to know you really do like the pictures. It pleases me very much when people genuinely respond to them: and you know, the peasants loved them, at the Mirenda: and the proprietress of the hotel at Bandol loved the four I did there – and the post-man, an intelligent young Swiss, used to stand and stare and stare at those I painted in Gsteig. It never occurred to any of them to be shocked. Yet people who called themselves my dear friends were not only shocked but *mortally offended* by them. But they were just bourgeois. I could see my sister Ada genuinely loved them. There seems to be no middle line.

The police case business bores and disgusts me, and makes me feel I never want to send another inch of work to England, either paint or pen. Why are those morons and canaille allowed to insult one ad lib. while one is defenceless. England is a lily-livered country, when it comes to purity.

Your Whitman joke is amusing, but alas, it would only be played once more at my expense. These people are nastier than you imagine, and it only needs a little more to start them putting pressure on the French or Italian govts. to prosecute me for producing and issuing obscenity. I do not want to find myself in gaol, as a final insult – with a little vague sympathy in the far distance. No, for God's sake leave my unfortunate name alone just now.[1]

I am glad you are out of the Studio and having a rest from housework, and getting along with Burns. What a thrill when the book is finally done.

We shall stay here a little longer – then begin to move south. We want to go to Italy to find a house – it's becoming imperative to have some sort of a place of our own – Meanwhile it's really very nice here – an old inn with garden quiet and shady, where one can sit all day if one likes.

No, the trouble is, once the police attack you, you are entirely at their mercy – so there it is.

ever. DHL

The poem is delightful[2] – but I don't understand all the words.

5260. To Maria Huxley, 12 August 1929
Text: Huxley 815–16.

Hotel Löwen, Lichtenthal, Baden-Baden.

12 Aug., 1929.

Dear Maria, –

Sorry your mountain is no better than ours – though it certainly is not worse. We are much better down here – an old inn, with old garden with such nice trees, and I have a room with a balcony among the leaves, might be a sparrow. The weather has been very nice again, sunny and warm with a touch of autumn. I like it, really – but the atmosphere of Germany itself somehow

---

[1] Catherine Carswell explained: 'His post was again being tampered with, and I had suggested that it might be good if the police were tempted to seize as obscene some extracts from Whitman's *Leaves of Grass* in his handwriting, just as they had at first seized some of Blake's drawings at the Warren Gallery. But he would have none of it' (*The Savage Pilgrimage*, p. 287).

[2] If Huxley's note (p. 817) to this remark – 'A love dialogue by Dunbar' – is accurate, then the poem would probably be either 'The Tretis of the Twa Mariit Wemen and the Wedow' or 'The Merle and the Nychtingall', by the Scottish mediaeval poet, William Dunbar (1460?–1513?).

makes one irritable. Frieda is really very irritable – but then she always is, in her native land. She never feels free, yet seems to hug the thing she isn't free of, and altogether I just leave her alone. She has massage for her foot, and all sorts of baths at the *Kuranstalt*,[1] and takes it out that way. Yesterday, evening, we celebrated her 50th birthday – we were nine people, five of whom were over seventy, and we drank *Pfirsich Bowle* with 2 *Flaschen Sekt*[2] in it, and ate trout and ducks – very nice. It was quite nice – but the Germans themselves are very depressed, and they leave me hollow. There are lovely roses on the table, and I dread the effect on Frieda of four large boxes of chocolates.

I have been going to the old *Medizinabrat*[3] who examined me two years ago. He says the place on the lung very much healed, the bronchial condition better but not very much better, and the asthma no better. I needn't bother about the lung – but must look after the broncs and asthma – must *not* go to high altitudes, not even 3,000 feet – and am best living near the sea – and otherwise there's not much to be done, except avoid damp, sudden changes, and *dust:* keep as even temperature as possible, and not try to walk or climb much, as I should never exert the asthma to make me pant. – I knew it all. Meanwhile another *Medizinabrat* gives me a little treatment for my ear, and life is a jest and all things show it, and my name's Mr. Gay.

Don't ask me what we shall do in Sept. While we stay in Germany I am sort of paralysed – can't come to any conclusion – and Frieda is worse. But we shall look for a house. I suppose you have seen about the pictures. I merely had two telegrams, they both say: 'Writing,' but not a word has appeared yet. At the moment I despise and detest the very name Englishman. They are *minchioni*,[4] the best of them, and foully 'pure,' white as lepers. Pah!

Well, that's about all. We shall be here ten more days, anyhow, I suppose. Remember me to Costanza and Ekkie, if they are still there.[5]

                                                                        DHL

I'm sorry Aldous isn't well – hope he's not in for one of those long psychological-organic changes that men get, like the change of life in women.

---

[1] 'health institute'.   [2] 'peach punch with 2 Bottles of champagne'.
[3] 'adviser against medicine'. (DHL used here, and in Letter 5308, a joking variant on 'Medizinalrat', a 'medical officer', the term which occurs in Letters 5305 and 5315.)
[4] 'idiots'.
[5] Costanza and Eckart ('Ekkie') Petterich, close friends of the Huxleys; the Lawrences spent Christmas Day 1927 at their house in Florence (see *Letters*, vi. 246 and n. 1).

5261. To Ada Clarke, 12 August 1929

Text: MS Clarke; cited in Lawrence-Gelder 196–7.

Hotel Löwen. Lichtental / Baden Baden

12 Aug 1929

My dear Sister

I'm glad you are having a good time – how well I remember that cold Flamborough, which I loved, and Robin Hood's Bay, which I thought so beautiful![1] – Here too the weather has been delicious, and we've both felt much better – and Frieda's mother, when she saw finally she couldn't have all things her own way, became her old self again, and is nice. Only Frieda's foot still hampers her – it is so slow. She has massage, and doesn't use it much – but now she frets about it and gets depressed. She always gets depressed and nervous in Germany – yet she doesn't seem to want to go away – seems afraid of the next step – I don't quite know why. I have been to the doctor too, the one who examined me two years ago. He says my lung is much better, much healed up, and the bronchial condition better, but still bad – and asthma bad. He now says not to go to altitudes – before, he said up to 3000 feet. Now he says the sea – and I know that's best – the Mediterranean, that is – not those cold seas.

We had telegrams from Dorothy and from the lawyer,[2] but so far, not a single letter about the case. It seems curious. I have seen two English newspapers – disgusting, how one is insulted! I shall not forgive it easily, to my white-livered nation. What a white-livered lot! Thank God I needn't live amongst them, even to hear their beastly mingy British voices. Of course it makes us both very angry – but Frieda is more off her balance. She thought she sailed along so gaily and triumphantly in London, and this shows what it was all worth. A lot of rats with long tails! However, the best will be to forget it as soon as possible. Then there is getting the pictures out of Dorothy – she is so uncertain. No, I don't want to sell them. I hope you will store some of them for me – especially the big ones. Can you do that? Let me know, and I will tell Dorothy. I want to know they are safe. Then when we have a house we will hang the others on the walls again.

I suppose we shall stay on here for a while. I shall be glad when I can go south again.

If you get a copy of the private edition of the *Pansies*, don't talk about it.

Frieda had her 50th birthday yesterday – we were nine people, her old friends, and her mother's – and we had champagne Bowle and trout and

[1] The Lawrence family holidays had been spent at Robin Hood's Bay, near Whitby, in August 1907, and at Flamborough, also on the Yorkshire coast, the following August.

[2] Percy Robinson.

ducks, very good, and everybody seemed very pleased. But I must say, today Frieda is in a bad mood – I don't know what's the matter with her. Hope she'll soon chirp up.

Love to you all.   DHL

5262. To Else Jaffe, 13 August 1929
Text: MS Jeffrey; Frieda Lawrence 291–2.

Hotel Löwen, Lichtenthal
13 Aug 1929.

Dear Else

Hans[1] says it rains in Bavaria, and Max Mohr says it rains in Bavaria, so I suppose it does. Only now I hope it has left off. Here it is quite decent, sunny mornings, cloudy afternoons, and quite pleasant. The Schwiegermutter is here, but says she will go back to the Stift on Thursday. On Friday her 'heissgeliebte Anita'[2] is due to arrive, with the nichtsoheissgeliebter – aberdochgeliebter Hinke:[3] they will stay a while here in the Löwen. I have never met the Hinke, so I have a joy in store.

We had the 50n Geburtstagfeier[4] on Sunday evening, very noble, Bowle, trout, ducks, and nine people – 3 Halms, 2 Schweikharts, 1 Kugler[5] – and they all *seemed* very happy and we all kept it up very bravely. But alas, next day Frieda was in one of the worst moods I have ever seen her in! – a seelenkater,[6] or however you spell it.

You hear the pictures are to be returned to me, on condition they are never shown again in England, but sent away to me on the Continent, that they may never pollute that island of lily-livered angels again. What hypocrisy and poltroonery, and how I detest and despise my England. I had rather be a German or anything than belong to such a nation of craven, cowardly hypocrites. My curse on them! They will burn my four picture books, will they? So it is decreed. But they shall burn through the thread of their own existence as a nation, at the same time. Delenda est Cartago![7] – but she will destroy herself, amply. Che muoia![8]

---

[1] Hans Jaffe (b. 1909), Else's youngest child.
[2] 'dearly-beloved Anita'. Anita von Hinke, née Schreibershofen (b. 1901), daughter of Frieda's younger sister Johanna.
[3] 'not-so-dearly-beloved – but-still-beloved Hinke'. Ernest von Hinke whom Anita had married in 1922. Cf. *Letters*, iv. 76 and n. 2.
[4] 'birthday celebration'.
[5] Unidentified friends of Frieda's mother. Cf. *Letters*, vi. 207, 398.
[6] 'spiritual hangover'.
[7] 'Carthage must be destroyed!', Plutarch's *Life of Marcus Cato*, xxvii [' . . . Carthago'].
[8] 'May she drop dead!'

Your mother says we are to stay here till middle September. I hope not. We have been here a month on Thursday, and when the heissgeliebte Annie is here we shall surely be a superfluity. I should like to move in another week or ten days. Shall we come to Bavaria, to Rottach, do you think? or best go south to Lugano?

I wonder if Hans is setting off across the mountains!

We are going to tea with some Taormina friends, Americans,[1] who are staying in the Stephanie. Your mother says: Du wirst was schönes sehen, das Stephanie![2] – It is all I can do not to make some really rude remark. I am so sick of all those old lies. It is terrible to be old, one becomes a bottle of old, but *never* mellow *lies* – lies, lies, lies! everything. Weisheit der Alten![3] – 19th Century lies.

Well I hope it's pleasant in Irschenhausen. Only today I threw away the flowers you gathered when you were here – and the Toadflax (wilde Löwenmäule)[4] were still fresh.

Ever DHL

Remember me to Alfred, and Hans – and is Marianne[5] better?

5263. To Earl Brewster, 13 August 1929
Text: MS UT; Brewster 207–8.

Hotel Löwen, Lichtental, Baden Baden.

13 Aug 1929

Dear Earl

We are back here – went for a while up to the Plättig – a mountain near here – and I nearly froze to death and simply hated it. But it is very nice down here – warm, but not hot, and very few people, we mostly have the garden to ourselves. So it is not so bad – though I really don't like northern countries, and shall be glad when we can come south again.

I haven't heard from Achsah at all – I wonder where she is by now. If she is in England she will have come in for all the scandal of the pictures; how hideous, indecent, obscene and horrible they are, and how they ought to be burnt, and me along with them. However, they haven't quite dared to burn them; but having kept them for a month locked up in Marlborough Street gaol, they are returning them to me on condition they shall not be exhibited in any way again. What canaille!! – what a country! and the papers reeking with

---

[1] Unidentified   [2] 'You will see something beautiful, the Stephanie!'
[3] 'Wisdom of the aged!'
[4] 'wild snapdragon'.   [5] Else's daughter (b. 1905).

'obscene' and 'indecent', and suggesting that I am a degenerate horror.[1] Nice country to do work for, I must say. I am humiliated at the very thought of being an Englishman: but my spirit spurns the craven, white-livered, hypocritical country. Thank God I need never set foot on the degraded island again.

I'm glad you like the *Pansies*. In the spring I expect they will bring out a cheap edition, at 3/6. Meanwhile they want to go on selling at 10/6. – I am sure Ghandi is right for India[2] – and I'm sure every race and nation will have to fight, and fight hard, to survive the machine. But I am European, and my fight is in Europe.

I haven't done much work lately – a few 'Nettles' to follow my *Pansies*. 'The Flying Fish' remains where it was.[3] All this persecution and insult, and most of all, the white-livered poltroonery of the so-called 'free' young people in England puts me off work. Why should one produce things, in such a dirty world! If one leaves them to themselves they will accomplish their own destruction so much the quicker. Far be it from me to hinder them.

We don't have many plans. In September we want to come to Italy and look for a house – or to the French coast. The doctor says I should live by the sea, and I know it is right. But when exactly we shall leave here, I don't know.

Frieda celebrated her 50th birthday on Sunday – with trout and ducks and champagne, and we were nine people. She doesn't seem any the happier for the event. We think of the birthdays in Gsteig last year – and yours here.

I wonder what you are doing and where we shall meet. I have a feeling we shall see each other this autumn – you will come at least some way north, won't you? I am not in a good mood, and feel churlish – but I hope soon it will change. – We are going to tea with some Americans in the Stephanie – that is sure to do it!

a rivederci   DHL

[1] For the views of the *Daily Express* see Letter 5164 and n. 3. The paintings were described in the *Morning Post*, on 18 June, as 'indecent' and in the *Daily Telegraph*, on 27th, as 'gross and obscene' (see Nehls, iii. 338–9, 716–17 n. 204).

[2] Mahatma (Mohandas Karamchand) Gandhi (1869–1948) pursued a non-violent policy of opposition to British rule in India; the policy included the fostering of home industries such as handweaving and spinning.

[3] 'The Flying-Fish' is an incomplete story which DHL began on his way from Mexico in March 1925; he read it to the Brewsters in summer 1928 and they asked 'at various times' if he had finished it. DHL replied: 'I've an intuition I shall not finish that novel' (Brewster 288). See *St. Mawr and Other Stories*, ed. Brian Finney (Cambridge, 1983), pp. xxxiv–vi, 205–25.

5264. To Dorothy Warren, 14 August 1929
Text: MS UN; Nehls, iii. 389–90.

Hotel Löwen, Lichtental / Baden Baden
14 August 1929.

Dear Dorothy

We haven't received any letter from you, after the telegram when the case was settled. Today only Percy Robinson's letter arrived, written on the ninth. Why it should have been five days on the way, when ordinary letters take two days, I don't know.

He, however, insists that the pictures which are to be returned to me should be packed up at once and sent to me, out of England. Of course there are those that are sold – and then *North Sea* to go to Maria Huxley, either via Hutchinson or direct to Paris: then there is one promised to Enid Hilton, and the *Dance Sketch* was promised to Frieda's daughter Elsa, and *Renascence of Men* to Monty:[1] and you were having one – *Contadini* – and Mary Hutchinson one. It won't leave many to be sent back. – But I don't know if you are free to dispose even of these. Anyhow I will send you a definite Florence address in a day or two, that you can forward those returning ones to me as soon as they are packed up.

Then I wish you would close the show altogether. My sister Mrs Clarke will take care of all the big pictures you still have hanging in the gallery, and I will write you about the disposal of the smaller ones. I must think out carefully, which they are.

Well Dorothy, there is the end of my first, and probably my last picture-show in England. I must say it leaves me feeling depressed and nauseated – so many insults, such silly extravagance of insults, and a meek or gloating public. Heaven helps him who helps himself, and really, the English seem as if they can't help themselves. A lily-livered lot: that's where all their purity lies. Alas, that they should be a nation of poltroons, in the face of life! But that's what they are: bossed by the witless canaille and off-sweepings of a dead 19th century.

Well, I'm sure you feel a bit weary and depressed and bitter also. The sooner we wind the whole thing up, the better. Take the *Contadini* then for love, for money is a weariness too. Mañana es otro dia![2] We'll come back in triumph one day – you see. But at the moment, I'm sick.

My regards to Philip   D. H. Lawrence

[1] Frieda's son, Charles Montague ('Monty') Weekley (1900–82), Assistant in the Department of Circulation, Victoria and Albert Museum. According to his letter to the eds, 17 April 1961, Weekley knew nothing of any such promise: 'I did not receive *Renascence of Men* and have never heard that Lawrence proposed to give it to me.'
[2] 'Tomorrow is another day!'

5265. To Caresse Crosby, 15 August 1929
Text: MS SIU; Lacy, *Escaped Cock* 80.

Hotel Löwen.[1] Lichtental. Baden Baden.

15 Aug 1929

Dear Caresse

Here are the décors for the *Cock*, and the corrected proofs go off by the same mail, but as imprimés. I hope you'll like the decorations – I almost wish I had done the frontispiece in two colours only, it will be so tiresome to reproduce. You might ask the colour-printers how it would come out, in the same green and red as the other things. – For the little tail-pieces, choose whatever you like and the things will reduce to proportion. The little round head-pieces will need to be reduced to about the size of the ring I drew at the head of Part I.

What about the copyright? It is really important to secure it, or this story will be at once pirated, in U.S.A. anyhow. Do you think it would be any good to print on it: Part I: This story has appeared in the American *Forum*?

For getting the thing in to America, that also might help. – Or you might try sending in sheets – and if they go through, then the bindings and the frontispiece, and let the book be bound up in N. York. Are you going to have those cases again? they don't seem very necessary to me.

And don't let Marks sell to the public under $10. a copy, really. You see the other things I bring out privately are that price. – And don't let him rook you. I am so used to being rooked by booksellers et al., that I'm sick of it, and on the defensive.

Well anyhow I hope you'll like the decorations. Let me know. And I hope things are going smoothly.

No sound of gramophone, or anything, from Italy. Pazienza!

I like the look of the book very much – think you've made a nice thing of it.

Love from both to both   DHL

It is MariasHimmelfahrt – Maria's Ascension to heaven – today: the bells are ringing for her departure. I say *bon voyage* – but not *au revoir*. Goodbye dear, but don't come back!

5266. To Harwood Brewster, 15 August 1929
Text: MS Holt; Brewster 209–10.

Hotel Löwen, Lichtental, BadenBaden

15 Aug 1929

Dear Harwood

Here we are – I'm back in your room,[2] and the sun is shining in almost hot,

---

[1] Hotel Löwen.] Hotel Lichtental.
[2] Cf. Letter 5314 and p. 378 n. 1.

the garden is very green and pretty, it's almost tea-time, and we're just off to Geroldsan to tea – that village where we walked, do you remember, and came back in the bus. So now you see the whole picture. Frieda's bunch of birthday roses stands on my table and the pink petals fall on your letter – it was a lovely bunch of roses. We thought of you on your birthday, last year at Gsteig: and we thought of you again on Frieda's 50th on Sunday. Not once have I seen Achsah's white wings fluttering down the Lichtenthaler Allee this year, nor up the steps to the Trinkhalle: though almost I see her ghost sitting at a little table in the corner sipping the hot water at a penny a time, and feeling so good after it: though I declare it is indigestible. Baden is very green and leafy this year, and the geraniums are very red, and the people are very fat, and the frocks are very weird, some with flouncing flat tails like beavers, some with pointed raggledy-taggledies all getting mixed up with their legs. I suppose you sport the latter sort. We don't go much to the Musik – I'm rather worse at walking, than better – though the doctor says, as far as lung goes, I am very much healed up, but my asthma, which seems to go to my legs, is not much better. So I cough, to the general annoyance or cold commiseration of a nervous universe. And I suppose, cough I shall – though perhaps one day I shall leave it behind, I suppose.

We had quite a party on Sunday night – peach Bowle made with champagne and Gauwinkelheimer,[1] large blue trout, ducks, and fat mér-ingues. But I forget, perhaps you still think with horror of the fleshpots.

I suppose you have seen in the newspapers what a dreadful man I am and what fearsome pictures I paint. When the magistrate said that perhaps even children had seen them, I half hoped you would rise up and chirp: Yes Sir! Please Sir! And I thought them so pretty! – But alas, you weren't in court to bear witness.

Well my dear, so now you're seventeen and going to be a doctor, so[2] hurry up and cure my asthma, for you've only got half an Uncle David instead of a whole one. And I send you a quid, since it seems your fate to receive a paltry quid. And write me about your school, and your plans, and the future.

love. DHL

We shall be here another week or perhaps more – then we want to go to Italy to find a house to live in. Achsah, what are your plans? – I wrote to Earl.

---

[1] A white wine of distinctive quality.   [2] so] and

5267. To Giulia Pini, [16 August 1929]
Text: MS UT; PC v. Baden-Baden – Josefinenbrunnen in der Gönneranlage; Postmark,
Baden-Baden 17[. . .]29; Unpublished.

Baden Baden
−16 Agosto.

Siamo qui in Germania con la madre della signora – ora la suocera ha 78 anni,
e sta sempre bene. Vogliamo tornare in Settembre a Firenze, per cercare una
casa, e verremo a troverte. Spero che state tutti bene. Molti saluti a tutta la
famiglia, da noi due.

D. H. Lawrence

[We are here in Germany with my wife's mother – my mother-in-law is now
78, and is always well. We want to return to Florence in September, to look
for a house, and we shall come and see you. I hope you are all well. Many
greetings to all the family, from us both.

D. H. Lawrence]

5268. To Edward Titus, 16 August 1929
Text: MS UT; Lacy, *Escaped Cock* 81.

Hotel Löwen, Lichtental / BadenBaden
16 Aug 1929

Dear Titus

Your letter this morning, and the cheque for francs 3810 – which as you
say, is not so bad. Who was it, by the way, let you down in the first place? I like
to know who is reliable and who isn't. The Gotham Book Mart, by the way,
tried hard to let me down over *Lady C.*[1] – I hope Random House or somebody will send me a copy of the *Skirmish* – surely I am due to have a copy. It
seems to me they figure very low when they expect their profits to be only
$200 or $300, selling out the whole 600 copies. If it is so, they've chucked
money away rarely on production.

There is no Paris *Pansies* as far as I know. You are aware, of course, that
Secker's public edition has been out in London a month – and sold about
3000 copies at 10/6, last time I heard – so the pirates would hardly tackle that.
But what there is – and I wanted it kept secret – is a little edition of 500,
printed and produced in London – coming out in London just now. It is
printed unexpurgated and complete from the original confiscated MS. – and
is to sell at £2. I believe it is all ordered. But I shall try to send you a copy. I
have to keep quiet about it as the police are getting fierce because I defy them.

[1] Cf. Letter 4984 and n. 1.

– Another thing that is coming in Paris is a long short story – about 100 pp. – which the Crosbys are doing on their Black Sun Press – 500 copies. But I believe they are shipping the whole 500 *en bloc* to New York, which seems a pity. Why not have some to sell in Europe! – I arranged this with them before I knew you, so it can't be a *casus belli*.[1]

I haven't a word from Curtis Brown's office lately, most of them are away holidaying. But I will write and ask about the Gallimard contract, and let you know.

I haven't thanked you for the copy of *Lady C.* and *This Quarter*, safely received.

We are staying on here, as it is very pleasant. Hope you'll have a nice[2] change (can't write, people talking to me all the time).

Sincerely   D. H. Lawrence[3]

5269. To Laurence Pollinger, 16 August 1929
Text: MS UT; Unpublished.

Hotel Löwen. Lichtental, Baden Baden
16 Aug 1929

Dear Pollinger

I have received today a cheque for francs 3810. from Titus, as my half of the $300. which Random House paid him for the *Skirmish with Jolly Roger*

---

[1] 'justification for war'.   [2] nice] pleasant
[3] Titus replied to DHL's letter on 17 August 1929 (TMSC SIU):

Dear Mr Lawrence,

I am sending you a copy of the Skirmish received from New York. I received two copies, but, frankly, I am ashamed of it, – which really I should not be because I am not responsible for its make-up. To me it seems a dreadful piece of book making; the title page is a night-mare. And they seem proud of it!!

I am enclosing, as an humble gift, a copy of a booklet I have just issued, but not yet released, The Legend of Ermengarde, which will not take over a half hour to read, and I want you to read it. It is very amusing and they are all sold out except a few which I keep for my special friends.

A man by name of Fred. Carter, an etcher, called on me to-day. He said you had stopped at his house for a couple of days some time back. He came with a message from Chas. Lahr – underground messages in booklegging are extraordinary – to say I may have a few copies of Pansies if I wanted any, at Two Guineas. They are apparently not all sold out. Is that the genuine one in question?

Was it oversight or deliberate that you did not answer the last point in my letter, to wit: a second printing of Lady C.? I would be glad to have your decision by return of post, if possible. I do not wish to rush you, but it would be just as well to be prepared in case an unexpected rush should find us at the end of our tether suddenly. Wholesale orders this week amount to about 400 copies. If this performance should be repeated more or less, – we shall stand empty-handed, – and after all the trouble and expense I have had I would not like to find myself in an unpleasant predicament. The expense I am referring to is a quite particular and personal one, which does not enter into our accounts, but it bears on our mutual venture, and I would naturally expect to recoup myself in the long run. I explained this superficially to your wife

pamphlet. So that is settled, and if you haven't already written to him, don't do so.

I haven't heard from you for a long time – is there any reason?

If you see Miss Chapter[1] of the Foreign Dept. would you ask her if there is any news of Gallimard and the contract for the translation of the novel, which was to be drawn up at once.

Lovely weather now – Send me a line.

DHL

5270. To Max Mohr, [17 August 1929]
Text: MS HMohr; Mohr, Briefe 534–5.

Hotel Löwen. Lichtental – BadenBaden
Samstag

Lieber Mohr

Wir möchten wirklich nächste Woche kommen – am 24n oder 25n weg von hier – und wahrscheinlich müssen wir in München ubernachten. So kommen wir – wenn Gott will – am Sonntag oder Montag, 25n oder 26n an Rottach. Meine Schwägerin wird vielleicht uns von München nach Rottach bringen, aber man weiss nicht.

Was wir hätten sehr gern wäre eine kleine Wohnung nicht zu weit vom Dorf und Läden. Sie wissen, meine Frau henkt noch mit dem Fuss, und ich kann nimmer weit gehen. Es ärgert mich, dass ich nicht gehen kann, aber da ist es. Husten ist auch noch schlecht – der Artzt sagt aber es ist Asthma und Bronchien, die Lungen sind besser – der Asthma aber ist schlecht. So wenn wir eine Wohnung oder Häuschen für uns hätten, mit einem Mädchen die am Morgen kommen könnte, und am Nachmittag weg gehen, wäre es schön. – Aber wenn das schwer ist, werden wir ganz zufrieden sein mit zwei Zimmer in einem Gasthaus oder Bauernhaus. Wir wollen drei Wochen oder einen Monat bleiben, dann nach Italien ziehen. Wenn Sie etwas finden können, wird es nett sein. Aber geben Sie sich nicht viele Schwierigkeiten dazu. Sie wissen wie es war in Diablerets – so mögen wir es haben.

Ich habe genug von Baden: nur diese Gasthaus ist ganz nett. Aber die Schwiegermutter ist immer dabei, und ihre 78 Jahren, und ihre Ideen vom when she was here. – However, it would be very convenient to have your decision. I told you when I first met you that I am looking forward to a long stretch of amicable and pleasant relationship with you, based on mutual confidence. I am looking forward to the day when I shall be able frankly and without apprehension to put my imprint on Lady C., and not only on Lady C., but also on other books by you.

Yours sincerely,

[1] Sonia K. Chapter had been assistant manager (to Nancy Pearn) of Curtis Brown's Periodicals Department: see *Letters*, v. 110 n. 2.

19n Jahhundert liegen schwer auf meinem Leben. Ich kann es wirklich nicht viel länger aushalten. Ich muss weg.

Ist die Heuernte schon wieder angefangen! Ach, dass ich kann nicht hilfen! – ich war einmal so gut. Aber jetzt bin ich kaput.

Schreiben Sie mir denn, und alle Grüsse.

D. H. Lawrence

[Saturday

Dear Mohr

We really would like to come next week – leaving here the 24th or 25th – and very probably we'll have to spend the night in Munich. So we're arriving in Rottach – God willing – on Sunday or Monday, 25th or 26th. Perhaps my sister-in-law will bring us from Munich to Rottach, but one can't be sure.

What we would very much like would be a small flat not too far from the village and shops. You know, my wife is still limping with her foot, and I can no longer walk far. It annoys me that I can't walk, but there it is. Cough is still bad, too – but the doctor says it is asthma and bronchials, the lungs are better – the asthma however is bad. So if we had a flat or little house to ourselves, with a girl who could come in the morning and leave in the afternoon, it would be fine. – But if that is difficult, we will be perfectly happy with two rooms in an inn or farmhouse. We want to stay three weeks or a month, then go on to Italy. If you can find something, it will be nice. But don't put yourself to much trouble over it. You know what it was like in Diablerets – that's how we would like to have it.

I've had enough of Baden: just this inn is very nice. But the Schwiegermutter is always around, with her 78 years and her 19th century ideas lying heavily on my life. I really can't stand it much longer. I've got to leave.

So the hay-harvest has already begun again! Ah, that I can't help! – I was once so good at it. But now I'm kaput.

So write to me, and all greetings.

D. H. Lawrence]

5271. To Edward Titus, 19 August 1929
Text: MS UT; cited in E. W. Titus, *Times Literary Supplement*, 16 July 1931, p. 564.

Hotel Löwen. Lichtental. BadenBaden
19 Aug 1929

Dear Titus

Thanks for the copy of the *Skirmish* and of *Ermengarde*.[1] As you say, the

[1] See p. 429 n. 3 for the letter to which DHL was replying. *The Legend of Ermengarde*, which Titus had published, was translated (allegedly from the Provençal of the troubadour Uc Saine) by Homer Rignault. (No other translations by this pseudonymous writer are known.)

title-page of the *Skirmish* is pretty bad, and I don't like the lining paper. – *Ermengarde* looks very amusing, from the glance I've taken, and the man a good translator – and a clever craftsman at verse – a smart bit of work – but your paper is too hard.

Is Fred Carter in Paris? If you see him tell him to send me a line.[1] – Yes, that is the *Pansies* I mentioned – also, in my opinion, a sad example of book-making.

I forgot to mention the second printing of *Lady C.* – partly because I assumed you would go ahead anyhow. It was 3000 you printed, wasn't it? or fewer? Anyhow do go ahead with a second printing – and tell me how many it will be. – You mustn't expect my wife ever to remember any of the really business matters in business – she remembers only the romantic incidents, no more. So if you were thinking that she will have given me a solid report of what you told her, disillusion yourself.

I told you I have decided against any expurgated edition of *Lady C.* That's final.

yrs   D. H. Lawrence

5272. To Giuseppe Orioli, 19 August 1929
Text: MS UCLA; Unpublished.

Hotel Löwen. Lichtental. Baden Baden
Monday 19 Aug 1929

Dear Pino

Here then are the notes, and the proofs once more revised. I hope Franceschini has not started to print off,[2] as there are a few corrections I should like to have made.

I wish you would go through the notes and see that they are all correct. I have just taken them from Fornaciari and Biagi.[3] I am not sure of distances – if the Mugello villa would be more than ten miles from Florence.

I am thinking, if you cannot get an old map, just use the government survey maps and make one that will include Florence, Camaldoli, La Vernia, Mugello, and if possible show the Poggio Villa at Poggio a Caiano, and the Careggi – and

---

[1] Frederick Carter (1883–1967), artist and astrologer, had written to DHL in 1922 about his ideas on the Apocalypse. The following year he sent DHL a manuscript entitled *Dragon of the Alchemists*, and in January 1924 DHL visited him in Shropshire. See *Letters*, iv. 365 and n. 3; Nehls, iii. 728 n. 380; and Leonora Woodman, '"The Big Old Pagan Vision": The Letters of D. H. Lawrence to Frederick Carter', *Library Chronicle of the University of Texas at Austin*, n.s. xxxiv (1986), 38–51 (this also carries reproductions of several Carter drawings).

[2] L. Franceschini was the printer for *The Story of Doctor Manente* (as well as for *Lady Chatterley's Lover*).

[3] Cf. Letter 5255 and n. 2.

perhaps Pieve a S. Stefano.[1] You could leave out most of the other places. This is quite easy to do, when they make a plate. – Then when you announce the book you can say: with notes and map, especially suitable for college use. – I am sending you also a little book Titus gave me. Keep it for me. I think the man is a very good translator, you might get hold of him for Berni.[2] I wouldn't do all Lorenzo's: amore, amore sono io il fattore.[3] – Somebody more lively.

I am tired of being here, and on Saturday we want to leave, go to Bavaria for a bit, then come south. It rains again and is almost cold. How horrible a winter would be here!

Those Crosbys sent Frieda a gramophone, c/o Aldous at Forte.[4] I want him to pass it on to you, for you to keep for us.

Lahr seems to have sold most of his *Pansies*. He is sending out the presentation copies last. I hope there'll be no fuss, but Stephensen seems rather to invite it.[5]

Titus has sold already the first 3000 *Lady C.*

I am so sick of being here – so sick of nothing but women on top of me – old women.

DHL

5273. To Else Jaffe, [19 August 1929]
Text: MS Jeffrey; Frieda Lawrence 294.

Hotel Löwen
Monday

Dear Else

Just a line to say we expect to leave here for München next Saturday – I have written to Max Mohr to say we shall arrive in Rottach either on Sunday or Monday. I suppose we shall stay one night in München. What is the name of the hotel where we stayed last time? at the station?

Marianne sounded quite sad in her letter to Frieda. I'm so sorry, and do hope she's feeling better.

The Hinkes arrived on Saturday, both very nice. They are staying in the Löwen here – your mother too – she would not go back to the Stift. But Hinke returns to Völklingen today, and Annie and your mother return to the Stift on Thursday – so we want to depart on Saturday. I want to go – I get really depressed here – and you know it isn't usual for me to get depressed. But here I get spells of hopeless feeling, heavy, and I hate it. What is it? I

[1] A map was provided; it included Florence and places as far west as Camàldoli.
[2] Presumably the Italian poet Francesco Berni (1497?–1535).
[3] 'love, love it is I who am the creator'.
[4] Cf. Letter 5091 and n. 4.   [5] Cf. Letter 5283.

never have them in other countries. Is it Germany? or your mother, who is now so afraid of death? Anyhow I hate it, and want to go away.

So I expect we shall see you in Bavaria – perhaps even in München. I'm so glad you are having a good time – I can just see the yellow Pfifferlinge[1] in the woods.

Regards to Alfred and to Marianne. – It has begun to rain again here!

DHL

5274. To Charles Lahr, [19 August 1929]
Text: MS UNYB; Postmark, Baden-Baden 19 8 29; Unpublished.

Hotel Löwen
Monday

Dear L[ahr]

I have your letter – and the press notices and receipt. Good that all goes so well. I hope it will finish without any fuss. Step[hensen] sounds as if he would like to figure in a 'case' – but I don't think they'll rise to him.

The samples of green cloth – it was just cotton cloth gummed up – were all hideous. If you can't get a real vellum, parchment, of a good green colour, then perhaps best stick to cream. – Or make a 'board' cover bound in some nice greyish or buff paper, with a black-and-white label. – Anyhow send me samples.

Forty[2] shillings a copy is fairly high – but I suppose charges must be more than normal. – At the end you'll send me a statement of accounts, I suppose.

We want to leave on Saturday, go to Bavaria for a bit, to see a friend there. But no doubt I shall write you before then.

Is Davies back in town? I must write him. And how is Kot. I haven't written him because I felt that correspondence made him uneasy, during the fuss.

Raining here, after a fine week.

DHL

Thrilling getting the book off!

5275. To Maria and Aldous Huxley, 20 August 1929
Text: Huxley 817–18.

Löwen, Lichtenthal, Baden-Baden.
20 Aug., 1929.

Dear Maria and Aldous, –

Glad you are down again in the proper warm – it's rather cold here, and we

---

[1] 'chanterelle mushrooms'.
[2] MS reads 'Four'. (Lahr printed 500 ordinary copies of his definitive edn at 40/-; this compared with Secker's 2,600 copies of his expurgated edn at 10/6.)

have arranged to leave on Saturday and go to Bavaria, where I'm afraid it will be colder. Seems a funny summer, started so hot and then left off. Everything here so intensely green, it quite hurts. Yet there is a chill autumn feeling in the air. I feel more and more one should never go far from the Mediterranean!

I suppose that you know by now that the pictures are safe – Dorothy has them back, and she will give Hutchinson the *North Sea* for you. I'm sure you will like it. But they burnt four of the picture books, including one of the vellum copies, and somehow it makes me very mad. Why can't they burn some of their own idiocy, and leave things alone they don't understand.

A bore that gramophone! Could you somehow deposit it with Pino? Perhaps you will be going to Florence? Or even Costanza might kindly take it. I'm so sorry you are troubled with it, but really it's not my fault.

I hear most of the new *Pansies* are sold, but they haven't sent out the gift copies yet – some delay or other getting them from the printers.

Titus has sold the first 3,000 *Lady C.* and is printing again.

I don't think we shall come to Forte. If we go to Bavaria we shall stay till mid September, then come south by way of Garda. Frieda still limps, but her foot is much better. I'm not in a good mood at all – can't do anything and am altogether disagreeable. I want to move from here – have had enough of Germany and relatives and family relations are *always* bad for one, and should be taken in the smallest doses possible. These five weeks here were two too many.

The photographs were very jolly, I'm sure the boy has a good time. Poor Jehanne, I often think of her.[1] Her shawl is so much admired – and she's so down on her luck. And once one goes down it's so hard to come up – my health has taught me that. – I shall send a post card with new address.

DHL

5276. To Else Jaffe, 21 August 1929
Text: MS Jeffrey; Frieda Lawrence 293.

Löwen, Lichtental. BadenBaden
21 Aug 1929

Dear Else

Frieda says she wants to stay till Sunday, to have her bath and her masseuse once more. She is still troubled about the foot, though it is much better. – So I suppose we shall arrive in München on Sunday evening. – Max Mohr says he will meet us at Rottach station with a Wagen – and he knows of a nice little house for us. So it sounds quite good, if only it will not rain.

[1] See Letter 5392 and n. 5.

Your mother is going back into the Stift today – very sad – and Annie is going to her tomorrow – there was no room for Anita till tomorrow. I am very fed up with here, and shall be glad to be gone too.

So – we shall see you one of the days in Bavaria!

DHL

5277. To Emily King, 21 August 1929
Text: MS Lazarus; Baden-Baden 21. 8[...]; Unpublished.

Hotel Löwen, Lichtental, Baden Baden
21 Aug 1929

Dear Pamela

We are leaving here on Sunday, going for a while to Bavaria, where we shall see Frieda's sister Else and some other friends. I am not sure of the address, but shall write you a post-card. – We have been here five weeks tomorrow, and it is about enough. Frieda's mother has been with us all the time here in the hotel – she is going back into the Stift this afternoon – and though she is wonderful for her age, still I find her seventy-eight years weigh on me and become oppressive. I get depressed here – which is not usual for me, I am very rarely depressed. The last few days have been grey and rather cold – Bavaria, being in the mountains, may be even colder, but I hope not. Anyhow September is supposed to be the best month there.

I hear from Dorothy Warren she has got the pictures safely back, and that she will shut the show altogether on the 31st August. I shall be glad when it is all over, for I feel very angry at all the false hypocritical fuss – and the burning of the books too. However, I'll have my own back one of these days.

Achsah Brewster and Harwood are in England, at Stratford-on-Avon with some friends. Harwood is going to school in Devonshire – starting at the tender age of seventeen. She now wants to be a doctor – but I'm afraid she'll have to forge ahead if ever she is to get there. – Earl is still in Capri. They want us to go and live there – in Capri – but it is too small. – Boshi, the Hindu who was at Gsteig,[1] has gone back to India, so of course Earl is pining to join him. If I wanted anything as much as Earl seems to want to go to India – why, I'd damn well have it.

I'm glad you liked Skegness – my God, how I should have hated it. The Huxleys want us to go to Forte for Sept. – it is a flat coast like Skegness – but I don't want to. If it is fine we will stay in Bavaria.

There is a touch of autumn already in the air – it seems very early – and the

[1] Boshi Sen, a scientist whom the Brewsters met in Calcutta in 1926; he gave DHL massage when he visited Gsteig in August 1928 (*Letters*, vi. 519 and n. 3).

first yellow leaves are falling. Fruit is cheap – pears and plums especially – and a friend sent us a basket of peaches. But it seems to me the fruit here has not much taste this year – whereas in Italy it was especially good. Curious how things vary. – Well, I shall send a p.c. when we have a new address. I never feel in a good humour here in Germany, I don't know why.

love. DHL

5278. To Nancy Pearn, 21 August 1929
Text: MS UT; Unpublished.

Hotel Löwen. Lichtental, Baden Baden
21 Aug 1929

Dear Nancy Pearn

Murry is bluffing you – being incommunicative on purpose.[1] Of course he remembers perfectly well the little series of essays he published in the winter and spring of 1924 – wasn't it 1924? – when I came to C[urtis] B[rown]? – Essays entitled: 'On Being a Man', 'On Being Religious', and several others. But I will ask Koteliansky.

I continue to be in a bad humour – unusual for me – so I don't do a single thing. I don't know if the fools' mess over the pictures has put me out of joint, or whether it's Germany, or what. I really like it here in the Löwen – but am in a bad temper all the time. However, we are leaving on Sunday for Bavaria, where we have some friends. I shall send the address. Meanwhile would you tell the mail dept. please to hold the letters – and tell Pollinger. He has lapsed into complete silence this last fortnight – can you tell me why?

I suppose you got the article 'Men and Women' for the *Star Review?*[2]

Well, perhaps I'll be my own sweet self again soon.

ever D. H. Lawrence

[1] Nancy Pearn had written to DHL on 15 August (TMSC UT), quoting Murry:

Either Mr. Lawrence or you are under a misapprehension. There is nothing, or practically nothing of Mr. Lawrence's in the early numbers of the *Adelphi* that has not been published in book form. We published one or two chapters of *Fantasia of the Unconscious*, some poems from *Birds, Beasts and Flowers,* and some *Mornings in Mexico*. Possible there may have been one or two scraps besides but if there are, they would not amount to 3 – 4 pages in all.

Murry had also published 'Indians and an Englishman' and 'The Proper Study' in 1923, and 'On Being Religious', 'On Human Destiny' and 'On Being a Man' in 1924 (Roberts C112–13, C116–17, C121).

[2] Pearn acknowledged its arrival in her letter of 7 July 1929.

5279. To Max Mohr, 22 August 1929
Text: MS HMohr; Mohr 172.

Löwen. Lichtental, BadenBaden

22 Aug 1929

Dear Mohr

Also wir reisen Sonntag um 10.28 ab und kommen um 17.55 an München
– lang, nicht? Wir bleiben die Nacht in München und kommen mit der Bahn
an Tegernsee am Montag Morgen – wenn meine Schwägerin nicht andere
Pläne mit dem Auto macht: sie könnte uns bringen. Ich werde von München
oder telefonieren oder telegrafieren. Nett dass Sie am Bahnhof sein werden,
mit Wagen. – und das altes Bauernhaus klingt schön. Ich hoffe nur es wird
nicht regnen – hier haben wir drei grauen Tage, ziemlich kalt, aber ohne
Regen.

Die Frieda und ich haben unseres Zusammenleben in Beuerberg im Isartal
angefangen – in Mai, 1912 – und wie schön es war! ach Gott – und ich hatte
nur 26 Jahren. Vielleicht wird Bayern uns wieder gut sein, wie es war damals.

Also viele Grüsse bis wir uns sehen.

DHL

[Well, we're leaving on Sunday at 10.28 and arriving in Munich at 17.55 –
long, isn't it? We're staying the night in Munich and coming to Tegernsee by
train on Monday morning – if my sister-in-law doesn't make other plans for
the car: she could be bringing us. I will either telephone or telegraph from
Munich. Nice that you'll be at the station, with transport. – and the old
farmhouse sounds fine. I only hope it won't rain – here we've had three grey
days, rather cold, but without rain.

Frieda and I started our life together in Beuerberg in the Isar valley – in
May, 1912 – and how lovely it was! oh God – and I was only 26. Perhaps
Bavaria will be kind to us again, as it once was.

So, many greetings until we see each other.

DHL]

5280. To Maria Chambers, 23 August 1929
Text: MS StaU; cited in Schorer 65.

c/o Sig. G. Orioli. 6 Lungarno Corsini, Florence. Italy.

23 Aug. 1929

Dear Maria Cristina

I got your letter at the Ludwig-Wilhelmstift today. Well really it's monstrous, dragging you to Ellis Island. No, I don't want to come to America, you
are quite right. A robot inhumanity!

I'm not surprised at your feelings about Rich. Myself, I have very little faith in him. Before, they had an Englishman, a Yorkshireman called Barmby, whom I did like, though he was slow and indifferent. But I don't care for the idea of Rich. In fact, I think the whole New York office of Curtis Brown is a bit of a failure.

But the case is difficult. You see the head office is in London, and there, I really think they do their best for me. The Magazine dept. manager, a woman, believes in my work, and works for it accordingly: the same with Pollinger, who looks after my books. They have all my affairs in their hands, and do a great deal for me that I could not possibly do for myself. – I have a contract with them, that all my work shall pass through their hands. Of course they were scared stiff of *Lady C.*, and didn't handle that at all – yet they did help me even there, that is, Pollinger did in London, and without being paid. So of course I can't grumble about the English side. Unfortunately the American side is really unsatisfactory – and yet it is the same firm. Rich has been manager only for about a year – and I know they don't think much of him. I know the London office now supervises all my *American* contracts. But of course, they can't supervise periodical stuff.

You see how it is. I can't suddenly declare that I will deal with the London office but not with the New York. I'm afraid all my things will have nominally to go through their hands, and payments will have to be made to them – it is my contract. If you try to go behind it, you will find all the editors will turn you down, and refuse to deal with you at all. But what you can do is to make a deal with the editors, as occasion arises, get their written statement in a letter, then refer them to Curtis Brown. If you succeed you ought, naturally, to take a percentage – you *must not* work for nothing. You ought to have the Curtis Brown 10% – as it is, we must pay it to them, and you must have something further.

But let us try the thing out for a little while. The *Skirmish with Jolly Roger* was of course arranged by Titus, who gave me half, $150., of the 300 dollars he received from Random House. Curtis Browns were not handling *any Lady Chatterley* stuff – only as soon as they think there is money in it, they begin to rouse up. – The *Skirmish* is now free for magazine publication, if anybody wants it. – About the 'Introd. to the Paintings' I will ask again. When an expensive limited edition like the *Paintings* Book comes out, they usually insist there shall be no re-publication till a year has elapsed. But this does not apply to magazine or periodical publication, necessarily. I will make sure, and have a copy of the Essay sent to you. – I will also order you a copy of the *Criterion* containing 'Mother and Daughter'.

Now as to new material: it is very difficult. You see I must send everything to the London office, and they forward a duplicate to New York. Now it would never do to have you and Rich – or his magazine manager – going round the editors with the same MS. and getting into a rare muddle. I could ensure you a copy of each new thing I send in, if you could work, at least for the time being, in conjunction with the Curtis Brown N. York office. Else I can't see what's to be done, as I can't make a grand break with Curtis Brown.

About the actual books, like *Lost Girl*, there I doubt if you can help. Thomas Seltzer possesses the rights – he is virtually bankrupt, and has nominally transferred his rights to Alfred Boni – or is it Albert Boni. If the books are out of print for more than 6 months, the right lapses back to me – each book individually, of course. Curtis Brown in London is scheming to get hold of the rights, for me, and then have a more reliable publisher publish a complete edition of me. Albert Boni would publish this edition, but Curtis Brown is against him – there seems to be something wrong with him, as a publisher, although he now has money. – But his returns – or Seltzer's,[1] – which I just received, was $49 on nine books. That is, in six months the sales of *nine* books had brought me in only 49 dollars. Which is monstrous. Of course a really good agent would have straightened out this affair sooner – but there are difficulties – you see how many. And Rich is useless, if not worse. Now solve the puzzle. I could if I threw my whole self into it – but then I should neither write nor paint nor even live any more. La vie à tout prix.[2] What I want is to get my books out of the hands of Seltzer-Boni and into the hands of some sound American publisher who will publish a decent uniform edition and properly supply the demand. At the moment this is all a muddle. Boni and Seltzer will let my sales be as low as possible – I believe many of the books are out of print – and nothing doing.

Well, we leave here on Sunday for Bavaria. It is rather cold, rather wet – just the reverse of your poor garden. Here everything is intensely green, the geraniums intensely red, the air always bluish, and a little chill in the languor. I am not very happy here, and want to go away, south, south. The doctor who usually examines me here says he is content with my lung, it's all right – but the asthma very bad. And asthma is basically nerves, chagrin. I take a drop of amber oil, because I like the taste, and my wife shows the feathers to everybody.

There was a great row in London about the pictures – and at the trial they consented not to burn them, but they burned instead four of the books of paintings, one a vellum copy. As if they'd done them any harm! I am very sick about it altogether, and a little weary of the outward world and all its messes. – But I have managed to have published in London, sub rosa, an unexpurgated edition of the *Pansies*, 500 copies at 2 guineas. These are all safely sold.

[1] Seltzer's] Boni's   [2] 'Life at any price.'

I would send you a copy if only it would come through the post – but I doubt
if it would – they'd confiscate it. – Did they say anything about the
reproductions of the pictures, by the way, when you 'entered'? A mercy you
didn't have any of the books – nothing criminal forsooth!

Well, I hope it is cooler and has rained on your dry lawn. Here is already
autumn, in Baden Baden. I shall send you whatever news there may be.

DHL

5281. To Charles Lahr, [23 August 1929]
Text: MS Lazarus; Postmark, Baden-Baden 23.8.29; Unpublished.

Puss-Puss!
   – Oh Auntie, isn't he a beauty! And is he a gentleman or a lady?
   – Neither, my dear! I had him fixed. It saves him from so many
                                                      undesirable associations.

London Mercury
Oh when Mercury came to London
they 'had him fixed.'

And now all the Aunties love him
because, you see, he is 'neither, my dear!'

My little critics
My little critics must all have had Aunties
who petted them, and 'had them fixed'
to keep them from undesirable associations.

It must be so. Otherwise
the sight of a normal Tom wouldn't send them into such silly hysterics,
my little critics, Auntie's dear plump pussies!

Never had a Daddy.
When Mercury and Love and Death
and even the great horse of Physical Energy
have all, by Mr Watts[1] and the Victorians, been carefully emasculated –

So that all our Daddies were quite British 'pure,'
they never did anything –
all dear Daddy-do-nothings!

---

[1] George Frederic Watts (1817–1904), painter, on whose work DHL had commented adversely
over twenty years before: see 'Art and the Individual', in *Study of Thomas Hardy and Other
Essays*, ed. Bruce Steele (Cambridge, 1985), pp. 139, 142 and *Letters*, i. 107. DHL had in view
here Watts's painting *Love and Death* (1874) and his sculpture *Physical Energy* (1902).

What are we, oh what are we
immaculately conceived
Daddyless
children of Daddy-do-nothing?

Little boy blue
come blow up your horn –

Editorial Office

Applicant for post as literary critic: Here are my credentials, Sir!
Editor: Er – quite! But – er – biologically! – have you been fixed? – *arrangé?* –
you get what I mean?
Applicant: I'm afraid I don't.
Editor (sternly): Has everything objectionable been removed from you? Have
you been made[1] safe for the great British Public?
Applicant: Er – I trust so, Sir! But – er – in what way in particular?
Editor: Did your parents have you sterilised? – by surgical operation –
Applicant: Er – I don't think so, Sir. I'm afraid not –
Editor: Good-morning! Don't trouble to call again. We have the welfare of
the Great British Public at heart.

The Great Newspaper Editor and his Subordinate
Mr Smith, Mr Smith
haven't I told you to take the pith
and marrow and substance out of all
the articles passing beneath your scrawl!

And now look here what you've gone and done!
You've told them their lives are not much fun!
When you know they must always be told they are happy
as happy as happy, *full* of fun, you sappy!

Think of the effect on Miss Harrison
When she reads that her life is not really much fun!
What will she do? she'll put down the paper
as if it was giving off poison vapour.

And she'll avoid it, she'll go and order
The Morning Smile, knowing it will afford her
comfort in reading, sure that it will tell her
she's a charming, delightful, high-spirited feller.

Tell her she's happy, tell her she's happy
spoon it out to her, slippy and pappy,
let her believe she's the A. 1. It!
Don't suggest that she's miserable – she'll have a fit!

[1] you been made] from you

When it comes to what ought or ought not to be said
There's but one safe criterion: a serious[1] old maid!
Give them just what a squeamish[2] old maid can swallow
and you're safe – you're quite safe – all the rest will follow.

Chop up your articles, make them pappy
and easy to swallow: always tell them they're happy;
always suggest how pure they are,
what a sense of humour they've got, ha-ha!

Mr Smith, Mr Smith
have you still to learn that pith
and marrow and substance are sure to be
indigestible to Miss Allenby?

Mr Smith, Mr Smith
if you stay in my office, you've got to feel kith
and kin with Miss Jupson, whose guts are narrow
and won't pass things like[3] substance and marrow.

Mr Smith, Mr Smith
Consider Miss Wilks, or depart forthwith.
For the British Public, once more it be said
is summed up in a nice, narrow-gutted old maid.[4]

Löwen.
23 Aug.

Dear L[ahr]

Your letter just come – so glad all has gone off safely. I don't think Steph[ensen] is very safe – keen on self-advertisement and puffing up big enterprises *and* getting in the cash. – He told me about Kot's insisting on £100. down – furious. The Mandrake, like the frog, will blow itself up too big, too quickly, and will burst.

I enclose a few nettles. I *wish* the *Mercury* would print them while Squire is away. But of course they won't.

There is a good deal of underneath sympathy, my way, really. – The *Nottingham Evening News* came out with quite a nice little article backing up the pictures.[5]

---

[1] serious] nice   [2] squeamish] nice   [3] things like] substance like
[4] 'Never had a Daddy', an early version of 'Emasculation', first appeared in *Complete Poems*, ii. 658–9; the others were included – with substantive variants – in *Nettles*.
[5] The 'little article' appeared in the *Nottingham Evening News*, 16 August 1929. The writer reported that the pictures which had been supplied to fill gaps left on the walls of the Warren Gallery by the police raid came from DHL's earlier period and, though they lacked 'the strength of intellectual force' evident in the later pictures, they were 'notable for qualities of composition, harmony of colour, and delicacy of touch'.

We leave here on Sunday. You can get me if you write to
Dr Max Mohr. Wolfsgrube. *Rottach-am-Tegernsee*, Oberbayern.
I had a p. c. from Fred Carter this morning. I shall write him – I liked
him. I believe Titus is risky, but all right with me so far. He has sold 3000
Paris copies. – By the way, have you seen the Random House: *Skirmish with
Jolly Roger* – pamphlet? I don't know how they had the cheek to charge $3.50
for it – but I believe they've sold out the 600.
I shall write from Bavaria. Try to make the vellum copies look nice.
Printer seems a bit of a muddler.

L.

5282. To Frederick Carter, 23 August 1929
Text: MS UT; Unpublished.

Hotel Löwen, Lichtental
23 Aug 1929

Dear Carter
    Glad to hear of you a free lance, and growing younger. As for me, I've
spent the last two years being ill and growing tired of it.
    Yes, things have changed – become more broken up, like my health. What
about your wife? – you don't mention her.[1] – I once saw a notice of your book,
the *Dragon*, and I wanted to buy it. But when one is ill things slip away. But
still I want to buy it? Can I get a copy? I shall order it to be sent to Florence.
And what sort of success did it have?[2]
    We are leaving here on Sunday, going to Bavaria for a bit. I am not sure of
the address, but
    c/o Dr Max Mohr, 'Wolfsgrube'. *Rottach-am-Tegernsee*, Oberbayern
that will find me. And always
c/o Curtis Brown, 6 Henrietta St. W.C. 2
gets me.
    What are your pen drawings like nowadays, and where do you place them,
who prints them? Do you still astrologise, or have you given up?
    I think we shall go to Italy for the winter, and find a permanent house
there; or try to. But we may be in Paris – or you may come our way. In either

---

[1] Nothing is known of her; Carter included no reference to his marriage in his *Who's Who* entry.
[2] In 1926 Carter had published *The Dragon of the Alchemists*, but it was not identical with the
MS DHL had seen in 1923 (see also *Apocalypse* 11–24). Carter said later in *D. H. Lawrence and
the Body Mystical* (1932), p. 42:

> Then I had to explain that the title, *The Dragon of the Alchemists*, had been used for the designs
> done to decorate the *Magnum Opus*. These had been made into a picture-book of figures, of
> symbols, taken from astrological and alchemical ideas; bound up with these drawings as
> prefatory essays were a few of the introductory pages of our old friend, the much-discussed
> manuscript that he had read in Mexico.

case, I hope we shall meet, I should like to see you again. I liked your *Dragon* writing very much. I *must* get the book.

Yrs   D. H. Lawrence

If you see Titus, tell him we are leaving and for where.

5283. To Laurence Pollinger, 23 August 1929
Text: MS UT; Unpublished.

Hotel Löwen
23 Aug 1929

Dear Pollinger

Yours last night – sorry you are so bunged up with work.

Cheque was *not* enclosed with the Seltzer (Boni) account. Boni is artful, because he offered me that $1000. on account of Seltzer's debt to me, irrespective of any agreement, and he wanted to write me a cheque there in the hotel bedroom in Paris – only I wouldn't have it so.

I can't think of any other books of mine published by Seltzer – except *Little Novels of Sicily* – a Verga translation.

I should like Secker to do a 7/6 *Collected Poems*, when Cape is agreeable. Also I should like him to do a 3/6 *Pansies*, perhaps in the spring.[1]

I should like to know where, exactly, the 'Man Who Loved Islands' libels poor Compton Mackenzie. – I don't know what other story Heinemann's might do,[2] unless it were the first half of the *Escaped Cock*. – But the complete thing is due to appear in Paris this autumn, 500 copies, to be shipped, I believe, in bulk to U.S.A. – so that wouldn't touch England.

As for Mr Adams, let him whistle[3] – although that story 'The Rocking Horse Winner', which Lady Cynthia Asquith had for her first collection of stories, must be free now[4] – But I don't know if Cynthia's book appeared in USA. – But that story would be just the sloppy sort to appeal to Mr Adams and his public.

Stephensen didn't actually print this *Pansies* – merely lent his name. I got a little man to do them – a bit of a muddle – but I am due to get £500. Think of it! They are all sold, every one. Now the printer is trying to scrape together a few out-of-series copies to give to my friends. You will get one shortly. Would tell you all about it if I could see you. – Poor Stephensen gets nothing but the réclame.[5] But he is a bit doubtful. – I hear he is selling the picture books to the trade at 12 guineas.

---

[1] Secker published *Collected Poems* in one volume, at 10/6, in August 1932; he published a 3/6 edn of *Pansies* in April 1930.
[2] Cf. p. 381 n. 4, and Letter 5296.   [3] Cf. Letter 5226 and n. 1.
[4] It was included in *The Ghost-Book* (1926) compiled by Lady Cynthia Asquith (1887–1960), a friend since 1913 (see *Letters*, ii. 41; v. 400 and n. 1).   [5] 'advertisement'.

By the way, that *Skirmish with Jolly Roger*, why shouldn't somebody do it in England – not so dear as Random House – I don't know how they had the cheek to charge 3½ dollars – have you seen a copy? – But in a letter to Titus written just after publication they said they would quite soon sell out. 600 copies. Why shouldn't someone do it in England – it is a good vindication of *Lady C*. I would add a little to it, and make it a more complete exposé of my position, if necessary. I wouldn't mind doing that.[1] – Have you seen the Titus edition of the novel? He has already sold the first printing of 3000.

Dorothy Warren seems rather in a woe-begone state. She says she will close the exhibition on the last day of the month, and I sincerely hope she will, to have done with it all. Somehow the false fuss over the pictures got me sick.

We leave here on Sunday, and you can get me

c/o Dr Max Mohr, 'Wolfsgrube', *Rottach-am-Tegernsee*, Oberbayern, Germany.

DHL

5284. To Giuseppe Orioli, [24 August 1929]
Text: MS UCLA; cited in Moore, *Intelligent Heart* 415.

Hotel Löwen
Sat. 24 Aug.

Dear Pino

We leave in the morning for Bavaria and you can write to me

c/o Dr Max Mohr, Wolfsgrube, *Rottach-am-Tegernsee*, Oberbayern.

I've forgotten if I sent the address to Vallombrosa.

I can't make out if I have to pay this muddley bill for the gramophone or not.[2] If I have, would you pay it for me, and I'll send the fifty Liras. I hope Maria will deposit the gramophone with you.

A lovely day, sunny and warm today – I don't know why I've been so sore and miserable here. I think too many large German women of heavy years sitting on top of me. But I feel quite wretched – health too. But I'm packing my bag and tomorrow we go.

I sent all Lasca proofs and everything to Vallombrosa – hope you had them all.

I had a long letter from Maria Cristina – she had a terrible time landing in New York – sent to Ellis Island like a criminal, and all that. But now she's buzzing round. I think her husband was very sorry to see her come back.

Well, I feel Bavaria is a good stride nearer Italy.

a rivederci   DHL

[1] This idea led to the extension of *My Skirmish* into *A Propos of "Lady Chatterley's Lover"*, published by the Mandrake Press on 24 June 1930, at 3/6 (Roberts A48b); it is included in the Cambridge edn of *Lady Chatterley's Lover*.   [2] Cf. Letters 5272 and 5275.

5285. To Charles Lahr, [24 August 1929]

Text: MS UNYB; Postmark, Baden-Baden 24 8 29; cited in Moore, *Intelligent Heart* 415.

Hotel Löwen

Sat.

Dear L[ahr]

I got the paper this morning with the Earp cackle.[1] It arouses me to a squib, which I enclose. Please circulate it.

I am thinking, why don't we start a little fortnightly magazine, about ten pages and about as big as this sheet of paper – called 'The Squib' – and just fire off squibs in it. Do let's do that. Get Davies to help, and a few spunky people, and let us put crackers under their chairs, and a few bent pins under their bottoms. It can be done quite cheap, and without any pretensions – and we can all have *noms de plume* – a bit of fun!²

We leave tomorrow. Did I give you Max Mohr's address –

Wolfsgrube, Rottach-am-Tegernsee, Oberbayern

L.

I heard a little chicken chirp:
My name is Thomas, Thomas Earp,
and I can neither paint nor write,
I can only put other people right.

All people that can write or paint
do tremble under my complaint.
For I am a chicken, and I can chirp,
and my name is Thomas, Thomas Earp.³

5286. To Rhys Davies, 24 August 1929

Text: TMSC NWU; Huxley 818–20.

Hotel Löwen – Lichtental, Baden-Baden.

24 Aug 1929.

Dear Davies,

Your letter this morning – and what a dismal picture of the Welsh country-side! Do you think people are going to die away into a sort of mushroom

---

[1] In 'Mr. Lawrence on Painting', Thomas Wade Earp (1892–1958), art critic and translator, reviewed the exhibition and *The Paintings*, in *New Statesman*, xxxiii (17 August 1929), 578 (see Draper, *The Critical Heritage*, pp. 306–8). While he admired DHL as a novelist and poet, and found the 'Introduction to These Paintings' interesting, Earp accused him of 'a basic inability in mere picture-making ... the pictures ... were really shocking from the point of view of art ... The offensiveness lay [not in their obscenity but] in the bad painting.'

² DHL had floated the idea for 'a little magazine to laugh a few things to death', to William Gerhardie, in November 1928 (*Letters*, vi. 617 and n. 1).

³ The 'squib' was collected (without title) in *Last Poems*, p. 294; see *Complete Poems*, ii. 680.

state, or, when they get low enough, will a new sort of life come in and make them tackle their conditions? Only God knows. But I loathe this mushroomy, fishy apathy. What's the good of despair unless it's lurid!

I'm worried about your novels. The problem is, would the big, bloated public swallow you anyhow, at this state of affairs. If Gollancz doesn't come across, then come to terms pretty quick with the Mandrake for one of your books: ask for at least £150 down, *on receipt of manuscript*. They ought to give it you at once. And urge that they publish before Christmas. It seems to me, that if you catch them on the rise of the wave, the Mandrake ought to serve your purpose very well. They have aroused a certain interest – and there is a big public waiting to get anything which they think is not orthodox, does not come via the 'good' publishers. There is the enormous 'proper' public, of Heinemann or Gollancz. But I believe the 'improper' public is almost as big, if not bigger, so long as they are fairly safe. For men like you and me the 'proper' public is already a dead horse – certainly so, in my case. But then I am amazed to realise how huge, and how much more potent the improper public is. And it is on this the Mandrake will draw. And they may have a run of real success – I would risk them, if I were you. But I don't think they'll have a long run. Stephensen is another sort of mushroom – he grows too fast. And the big publishers, after a while, will quash them. But for the moment they may just be your ticket. That's how it looks to me. I'd gladly write any sort of foreword for you – but better not. In the first place because of the police, in the second, its not really good for your reputation. But if you or Stephensen think of any way in which I could be of use, let me know. I could certainly do a review.

I want Charlie Lahr to start a little fortnightly rag called 'The Squib', or something like that – just to rag them all, to get at them and lampoon them, make fun of them, jeer at them and altogether have a good time. We would have a little thing of about ten pages, not much bigger than this note-paper in size, and we'd all have *noms de plume* – I'd be David Dolittle – and sell it at anything up to sixpence – do a few numbers just for fun, and if it got really started, put it on a money basis – a business basis. For the beginning we'd find the money between us – costs ought to be very slight – I'd stand a few quid. The trouble is a good editor. Would you like to try it? – perhaps with Mrs. Lahr to help. We want short little peppery things, pansies, tiny articles. I'm sure you'd be good at squibs. Your idea of the lily-white policemen of London fainting with shock at the sight of one of my nudes would make an A.1. squib.[1] The thing to do would be to

---

[1] Cf. Letter 5329.

seize on the ridiculous points in politics, literature and newspapers – and people – and just ridicule them – watch the press and the books and just get a laugh out of them.

We leave here tomorrow for Bavaria, and I'm glad. Baden is quite lovely in its way, and everybody quite nice, in their way, yet one feels that the Germans, underneath, *aren't* nice. And these huge German women sitting round one like mountains that would never even know if they sat *on* one – I'm sure their bottoms would be too tough for my poor pinching – they simply give me the horrors. I want to go somewhere where the women are a bit *smaller*: and where their hats don't sit so menacingly on their heads. You can get me in Bavaria

c/o Dr Max Mohr, 'Wolfsgrube', *Rottach-am-Tegernsee*, Oberbayern.
But I shall send an address.

In Sept. we want to go down to Italy to look for a house – and let's hope the gods will guide us.

Tell your mother and sister I'm very glad they stick up for me. They are quite right, I'm quite a nice person, really. God knows why I should have so much mud poured over me.

The poor young man of the faggots and peas[1] (what a good pansy there is there!) *have* you seen any of his stories or poems? And *what* are they like?

If you get much more boost in the Welsh papers you'll soon be able to pose as the national bard, and wear a crown of leaks – or is it written leeks? *porri.*[2]

DHL

5287. To Ada Clarke, [28 August 1929]
Text: MS Clarke; PC v. Kaffee Angermair, Rottach a./Tegernsee; Postmark, Rottach 28 AUG 29; Lawrence–Gelder 198.

Kaffee Angermeier, *Rottach-am-Tegernsee*, Bavaria
[28 August 1929]
Very nice here, so sunny and still – I like it much better than Baden – and we have friends here.

Love   DHL

[1] Unidentified. Cf. Letter 5464.   [2] 'leeks'.

5288. To Baroness Anna von Richthofen, [c. 28 August 1929]

Text: MS Forster; PC v. Café Angermeier bei Rottach am Tegernsee; Postmark, Rottach [. . .]; Unpublished.

Kaffee Angermeier, Rottach am Tegernsee, Oberbayern
[c. 28 August 1929]

Da sind wir denn – und herrlicher Sonnenschein so schön. Die Else Kommt Samstag. Grüsse Annie.

DHL

[Here we are – and splendid sunshine, so beautiful. Else comes Saturday. Greet Annie.

DHL][1]

5289. To Caresse Crosby, [c. 28 August 1929]

Text: TMSC NWU; PC; Unpublished.

Kaffee Angermeier, *Rottach-am-Tegernsee*, Oberbayern
[c. 28 August 1929]

Why haven't I heard from you – hope you got the proofs and pictures – throw the latter aside if unsuitable.[2]

DHL

5290. To William Hopkin, [29 August 1929]

Text: MS NCL; Postmark, Rottach 29 AUG 29; Huxley 821.

Kaffee Angermeier, *Rottach-am-Tegernsee*, Oberbayern
30 Aug 1929[3]

Dear Willie

I got the proofs[4] of Col Hutchinson's novel out of customs the day we left Baden – tell me whether you want me to send them back.[5]

I read the book here – sorry, but I don't think it's very good. Nobody who knows Germany at all will believe in the German part of the book – and nobody who knows women will believe in Rosa and Frau Müller: and nobody

---

[1] Frieda's translation contained in a letter to Albert F. Green, registrar of Mansfield Technical College, on 2 September 1952 (MS Forster).

[2] Caresse Crosby acknowledged the proofs of *The Escaped Cock* and water-colours, on 27 August 1929, but her letter had to be forwarded from Baden. See Letter 5313 and n. 3.

[3] The postmark contradicts this date and may cast doubt on the accuracy of DHL's dating of the nine letters which follow.

[4] proofs] MS

[5] Lt.-Col. Graham Seton Hutchison (1890–1946), professional soldier and prolific author, pseudonym 'Graham Seton'. The book was *The W Plan* (October 1929 and in a third impression in the same month); a spy novel, set principally in Germany during World War I. (Hopkin may have received a proof copy for review in his local paper: see *Letters*, i. 176 n. 2.)

who knows any German will ever believe that Duncan Grant knew much.[1] However, it doesn't matter – the yarn is all right as a yarn, if you forget there is any such place as Germany or such people as the Germans. Col. Hutchinson, though, is terrifically Narcissistic – But the spirit of the book is friendly and human.

We are here among the mountains – rather lovely place – and very peaceful, a little inn smelling terrifically of cows – but we eat out of doors under the trees, and live in a little house to ourselves. It is much more the old Germany here. I simply can't stand the new Germany – it's awful, so empty and depressing and in a hurry to get nowhere.

I think in about a fortnight's time we shall go down to Italy again. Give me the South, the Mediterranean.

I'm sure Eastwood is a dreary place now – and it will go on getting drearier, unless something happens – if anything *can* happen, in happy England.

Hope you had a good time with Stephensen – you two are sure to get on together. – But you have to face the fact that the Socialists dislike the *Pansies* much more than the aristocrats or even the cultured bourgeois do: ergo, the socialists are merely little bourgeois over again.

All good wishes from us both, also to your wife.[2]

D. H. Lawrence

5291. To Edward Titus, 30 August 1929
Text: MS UT; Unpublished.

Kaffee Angermeier. Rottach-am-Tegernsee, Oberbayern
30 Aug 1929

Dear Titus

Thanks for note and bill.[3] It's not so bad, 6.50 a copy. – In their last letter Curtis Brown's people told me they had just sent the agreement to Gallimard

[1] In the novel Col. Duncan Grant is ordered to obtain intelligence to ensure the success of the 'W Plan'.

[2] Hopkin, m. 1925, Olive Lizzie Slack (1895–1988).

[3] DHL was responding to a letter from Titus of 24 August 1929 (TMSC SIU):

Dear Mr. Lawrence,

Fred Carter has just been in and gave me your new address. I take the occasion by the famous forelock and enclose a review from the New Republic, which I think will please you.

I also enclose statement from the printers covering our indebtedness for the printing of Our Lady. I paid this bill yesterday. As you see I have done a much better bargain than I thought in the beginning of our pour parler. I knew that for sometime of course, but I thought I would enjoy the luxury of a pleasant surprise for you.

I hope my book keeper will be able to prepare a statement in the course of next week of sales to date which I shall take pleasure in forwarding to you as soon as ready.

I am still very anxious to hear if any further developments have take[n] place regarding the French edition, as my order for the next impression would depend on whether the French

to sign, and expected it back in a day or two. I shall let you know if I get it –
when it comes to me it will already have the publisher's signature – so – we'll
see if dear M. Maurois has effectually interfered.

Would you please send a copy of *Lady C.* to

John Cournos – c/o Thomas Cook, Place de la Madeleine. Paris.
I promised he should have one on his arrival from America. Or do you
know him? – he writes novels. You could send him a note to Cooks asking
him to call for his copy, if that is easier: and tell him I'll write in it when
we meet.

I hear Charlie Lahr has actually sold all his 500 *Pansies* – sold them in a
week – have you seen a copy? – I wanted ten out-of-series copies, but the
printer seems to have got into a muddle, and they don't appear. I wonder if it
would be worth while doing a Paris edition of them!

D. H. Lawrence

Rather lovely here in the mountains – so still!

5292. To Edward Titus, 30 August 1929
Text: MS UT; Unpublished.

Kaffee Angermaier. *Rottach-am-Tegernsee*, Oberbayern.

30 Aug 1929

Dear Titus

I just received Gallimard's signed contract for *Lady C.* – very mean contract – 7% on first 10,000, 8% on all copies up to 20,000, and 9% after.
Brilliant! But I suppose it's the best one can get out of France: a faithful and
accurate translation and no abbreviations or alterations in the text – date of
publication, within 18 months of this contract.[1] – Curtis Browns are acting
through

W. A. Bradley, 5 rue St. Louis-en-l'Isle. IVe
So if you want to know how it goes you can ask him.

ever   D. H. Lawrence

edition will appear. – I was told, whether the statement is based on truth, I am unable to tell, –
that André Maurois was consulted by Gallimard on the advisability of bringing out Our Lady
in French, and he advised against it. I meant to go to see him about it, but I was told he was out
of town. – Keep me informed, please.

Yours very sincerely,

In the *New Republic* (3 July 1929), Edmund Wilson said *Lady Chatterley's Lover* was among
DHL's 'most vigorous and brilliant' writings.

[1] Cf. Letter 5060 and n. 1.

5293. To Sonia Chapter, 30 August 1929
Text: MS UT; Unpublished.

Kaffee Angermaier. *Rottach-am-Tegernsee*, Oberbayern.

30 Aug. 1929

Dear Miss Chapter

Here is the agreement for Gallimard – a very shabby agreement, but I suppose the best one can do with la belle France.

I am glad to know about Kippenberg – now I will see from this end, what is doing.

Greetings to Miss Watson – her trip was short, but I hope merry.

D. H. Lawrence

Shall be here about two weeks more.

5294. To John Cournos, 30 August 1929
Text: Moore 1187.

Kaffee Angermaier, Rottach-am-Tegernsee, Germany

30 August 1929

Dear Cournos:

Ridiculous of you to send that ten shillings[1] – I tore up the cheque, of course. I got *O'Flaherty* and we both liked it – though it's a bit narcissus but I like the kind of fantasy through it. Damn Knopf anyhow!

I asked Titus – 4 rue Delambre – to send you or give you a copy of his *Lady C.*, and I want to write in it when we meet, or when we are a bit settled and you can send it to me. I suppose we are here about two more weeks, then back to Italy. I find I can live best near the Mediterranean. I was quite happy last winter in Hôtel Beau Rivage, Bandol, near Toulon – did my *Pansies* there. And I was quite happy in Majorca in April, May and June, though it's a winter place – and it's nice here, but not for long. I want soon to go south of the Alps – and we want to find a house and settle down a bit – though whether it will come off is a bit doubtful. I feel I don't care much about the outside world any more – with my cough, my awful asthma, I can't walk much – so given a sunny climate and peasants or common people nice and natural around, I don't bother about much else. I like Florence *neighbourhood* very much – but its climate is bad for bronchials. There is a tiny house called La Massa near Florence which you could rent for not much money, especially for the winter months – and I think it's lovely there.[2]

Well, I don't know when you arrive, but I hope you'll be happier this time

---

[1] Presumably for a copy of the Paris edn of *Lady Chatterley's Lover* (see Letter 5232).
[2] See p. 347 n. 3.

in France. I can't stand big cities – they kill me – but I like French people in
the south. I already long to see the Mediterranean, and am only six weeks
away from it.

5295. To Giulia Pini, 30 August 1929
Text: MS UT; Unpublished.

Kaffee Angermaier, *Rottach-am-Tegernsee*, Oberbayern, Germania

30 agosto 1929

Cara Giulia

Ho ricevuto la tua lettera a Baden Baden, con la descrizione dell'appartimento della Villa Palagio. Mi pare che sarebbe bello, l'appartimento:
solamente, sai, vorremmo una casa tutta a noi. La signora non vuole più
un'appartimento, vuole una piccola villa tutta a se. Però vogliamo venire a
vedere la Villa Palagio subito dopo l'arrivo a Firenze, che deve essere verso
il 20 settembre: e forse il Signor Orioli verrà prima, per scrivere a noi come
la trova lui.

Stiamo bene, ma la Signora ha fatto male al piede, e va zoppicando un poco,
che è molto scommodo. Speriamo che sia presto guarito, ma possono durare
molto tempo, questi mali del piede storcio.

Sarà bello di vedervi tutti un'altra volta – e il podere nuovo, e tutte le
bestie; mi farà proprio piacere. Ti scriverò quando arriviamo a Firenze – in
venti giorni, più o meno.

Con molti saluti.   D. H. Lawrence

[Dear Giulia

I received your letter in Baden Baden, with the description of the flat in the
Villa Palagio. I think it would be beautiful, the flat: only, you know, we would
like an entire house to ourselves. My wife doesn't want a flat any longer, she
wants a small villa all to herself. But we want to come and see the Villa Palagio
shortly after we get to Florence, which should be around the 20th September:
and perhaps Mr Orioli will come to see it earlier, in order to write us what he
thinks about it.

We are very well, but my wife hurt her foot and limps a little, which is very
uncomfortable. We hope that it can be cured soon, but these foot sprains can
last a long time.

It will be nice to see you all again – and the new farm, and all the animals; I
shall be very pleased. I'll write to you when we arrive in Florence – in about
twenty days, more or less.

With my best greetings.   D. H. Lawrence]

5296. To Giuseppe Orioli, 30 August 1929

Text: MS UCLA; cited in Moore, *Intelligent Heart* 415–16.

Kaffee Angermaier. *Rottach-am-Tegernsee*, Oberbayern
30 Aug 1929.

Dear Pino

Here we are up among the mountains again. It is quite beautiful, and very peaceful, cows and haymaking and apples on tall old apple-trees, dropping so suddenly. We eat in the little inn – such a smell of cows – and it's quite nice. I believe you'd like it. But I find even this altitude makes my heart go too fast – we are about 800 metri. Tell me how it is in Italy – and if it's not too hot, we shall come down about Sept. 15th – which is only a fortnight.

I enclose a letter from Giulia. Would you care to go one day and look at the place? The trouble is, it is only an appartimento – we'd be sharing the house with some woman or other – and I don't want to share a house with anybody any more, after Zaira.[1] – I wish you would make an account, and put down all the expenses you have on my behalf – Then if you make the trip to see this place of Giulia's, charge all the expenses to me. I really wish you would do that.

I expect to be hearing from you soon – since you are due to be down from Vallombrosa. – I am writing to a man I used to know in the past, about a book of his, 'The Dragon of the Apocalypse' in my opinion very interesting. I think you might publish it one day.

Heinemann offered me £300. to let him print an edition of 500 copies of 'The Man Who Loved Islands' – and I agreed, and all was ready. Heinemann announced the book, and Mackenzie wrote and said that if it appeared he would at once take proceedings for libel. So Heinemann withdrew rather than have a law-suit. – Aren't these little authors beyond belief, with their vanity!

Frieda still limps quite badly with her foot – my cough is about the same as ever – so we make a bright couple.

DHL

Did you get the MS of *Lady C.* – and *Ermengarde?* The cost of printing the Paris *Lady* was francs 6.50.

5297. To Frederick Carter, 30 August 1929

Text: MS UT; cited in Carter, *D. H. Lawrence and the Body Mystical*, p. 43.

Kaffee Angermaier. *Rottach-am-Tegernsee*, Oberbayern
30 Aug 1929

Dear Carter

I'm sorry you are separated from your wife; she was nice and you seemed to get on. I suppose marriage itself is the difficulty.

[1] See Letter 5080 and n. 1.

And somehow I guessed Elkin Mathews would only do half a *Dragon*. But as soon as I can get to Italy where I can sit down, I'll send him my guinea. One can't carry books around.

Yes, I was, and am still, really interested in the 'Dragon': in fact, I liked your prose better than your drawings: it seemed to be feeling for something bigger. Tell me:
1. Have you got the original MS. – more or less what I saw?[1] – and how big is it? – how many words?
2. Do you really think the second version, on Ritual and Myth, better? – and how long is this?

Because I should really like to read the whole thing again, and see if my first impression holds good. I should like to read the second version too. And if I like the 'Dragon' as much as I originally did – though I admit it was a bit tough and tangled – I'm sure we can find a way of printing it complete, even if I have to write a real spangled foreword to it (perhaps you'd refuse to let me). There was something in that Dragon of the Cosmos lying across the heavens that has never left me. But I feel mistrustful of your second version, coming a few steps down the ladder, to more comprehensible levels. But let us see. I believe we could put the 'Dragon' across – 500 or even 1000 copies at two guineas. I hope you haven't lost or messed up the original MS. that I saw: and the celestial mechanism. Don't make a picture-book of the Apocalypse for a common publisher. The idea is to make a series of *really* illustrative designs for the Revelations, and reveal them a bit more: print them with the Revelations itself, with notes on the mystical purport: and again, sell a thousand at 2 guineas. We'll make Stephensen or Random House print it – if not, we'd do it with Orioli in Florence – But be sure and write good notes on the mystical import – and if you like, I'll add what I can to the notes – or even take yours[2] over and write them up. You ought to clear £300. on this – and it is so interesting. I do wonder what your designs are like now. Have you one or two loose ones? – But that's a splendid idea to print the Apocalypse with notes and prolegomena and a few vivid designs that carry out the mystical meaning and are not too gnashingly baroque. You are more sincere when writing than when drawing, I believe.

Anyhow tell me about the 'Dragon'. – We expect to be here two more weeks at least, then to Italy.

D. H. Lawrence

[1] Carter's manuscript 'had been reconsidered, rewritten in parts, rejected in others as too complicated and esoteric, too occult. And, moreover, it had been put on one side as a subject over-difficult for more than a small public and unprofitable to publish for lack of a popular audience' (Carter, *D. H. Lawrence and the Body Mystical*, p. 42).
[2] yours] them

5298. To Blair Hughes-Stanton, 30 August 1929
Text: MS Hughes-Stanton; 'The D. H. Lawrence Letters', *Samphire*, iii (Spring 1978), 23.

Kaffee Angermeier. *Rottach-am-Tegernsee*, Oberbayern, Germany
30 August 1929

Dear Blair[1]
Your letter reached me only today. So sorry about the house and cash. Perhaps you aren't quite bold enough, in your work: one has to be either downright take-it-or-leave-it, or else one has to love 'em and give 'em what they want. So damned difficult anyhow.

But I am very pleased for you to make drawings for *Birds Beasts*. Don't know anything about the Cresset Press – but if they are going ahead, tell them *not* to approach Secker direct, but to write to

L. E. Pollinger. Curtis Brown Ltd. 6 Henrietta St. W. C.2

and get him to arrange it. He will fix better terms all round, for me and you as well. Tell me the scheme – how many copies, at what price, how many signed – and tell them, if they like I'll do them a new foreword, on the essential nature of poetry or something like that. Tell them that if they print in front: These poems are printed from the *Collected Poems of D.H.L.*, published by Martin Secker – or something to that effect, that goes a long way with Martin Secker: but not to say it if it harms the new edition – yours.

Yes, you must work for the limited-edition people now – it's the only way to make money. And I must keep my eye open for any book that you might do. Perhaps later on, another unexpurgated *Pansies* – that sells.

Well, I'm glad you like your children,[2] for most modern parents emphatically don't, no matter how they wash and comb 'em.

We are here for about two more weeks – then presumably Italy. Frieda limps with her foot – I cough – the scenery is very nice.

Which of my pictures didn't you like, and why?

Regards to you both – and for god's sake, don't go into a *cellar*. If it must be among the corpses, let it at least be a modest above-ground mausoleum!

D. H. Lawrence

No news of Barby lately – have you any?

---

[1] Blair Rowlands Hughes-Stanton (1902–81), distinguished wood-engraver and book illustrator; at art school he had been a contemporary of Barbara Weekley (see *Letters*, vi. 411 n. 3). Illustrated Cresset Press edn of *Birds, Beasts and Flowers* (1930) and *The Ship of Death and Other Poems* (1933). m. 1925, Gertrude Hermes. See Penelope Hughes-Stanton, *The Wood-Engravings of Blair Hughes-Stanton* (1991).
[2] Judith (b.1926) and Simon (b.1928) Hughes-Stanton.

5299. To Amy Dawson Scott, 30 August 1929
Text: MS UT; Unpublished.

Kaffee Angermaier, *Rottach-am-Tegernsee*, Oberbayern
30 Aug 1929

Dear Mrs Scott[1]

I should have thought the P.E.N. would by this time have become
ashamed of me – you can't be good British citizens, surely. But let me know
when you do, and I can countermand the little yellow paper.

Sincerely   D. H. Lawrence[2]

5300. To Ada Clarke, 1 September 1929
Text: MS Clarke; cited in Pinto, *D. H. Lawrence after Thirty Years*, p. 48.

Kaffee Angermaier. *Rottach-am-Tegernsee*, Oberbayern, Germany
1 Sept. 1929.

My dear Sister

I was glad to know you were safely home and glad to be home – you have so
much more room and scope, with your own house and garden. – I also had a
letter from Stephensen: I'm afraid he's a bit of a wind-bag, a real match to
Willie Hopkin – and he needn't talk about Dorothy Warren, for he's by no
means too dependable himself, very slack in his payments, owes Rhys Davies
money for months and now Davies is stone broke. But Dorothy certainly is an
undependable creature – she won't close the show and won't make any definite statement of any sort, but writes most lovingly and says they are coming
out here to meet us in about a fortnight. I expect in the end I shall have to get
the lawyer to settle things up.

I am very much interested to hear you have found the MS. of the *Rainbow*.
Is it the original hand-written MS., from which the book was printed? I wish
you would compare it with the copy of the book which you have, Methuen's

---

[1] Catherine Amy Dawson Scott (1865–1934), poet, novelist and editor; founded P.E.N. in 1921
(see p. 196 n. 2 and *Letters*, v. 88 and n. 1).
[2] Scott replied on 6 September 1929 (TMSC UT):

Dear Mr. Lawrence,
   Many thanks for sending the Banker's Order for your subscription. I hope we are *not* 'good
British citizens' in the silly sense of the term. In any case, if the day comes for asking you to
countermand the Banker's Order, my own resignation will be concurrently submitted to the
committee!
   But I wish we could see you sometimes. You may have heard of the existence of the Young
P.E.N. On the 7th January, a Tuesday, there will be a joint dinner of the P.E.N. and the Young
P.E.N. Is there any likelihood of your being in England, and if so, would you preside, or at any
rate come to the dinner?

Yours sincerely

edition, and see if it is pretty much the same. I know I wrote the novel several times. Do you remember how the MS came into your hands?[1]

As for the final disposal of these things, books and pictures, I don't feel very sentimental about them myself. I want to keep them for the present, because they increase in value and they represent my capital. But of course if ever I want a fair sum of money for any enterprise whatsoever, I shall put them up to auction in the proper way. We only live once, and must use every opportunity of living. Again, if I died, the MSS and pictures would have to be sold to secure something of an income for Frieda. And finally, if it comes to heirlooms, I've got no children of my own – at least at present – and George is the head of the 'family', if you talk of family, and Ernest is the legal heir of heirlooms.[2] No, I've no use for family and heirlooms. As for Jackie and Bertie, I can't see them getting any thrill out of the MSS. of the *Rainbow* and *The Trespasser*, unless it were for that very 'monetary gain' you speak of. No no, hoarding things up for other generations is not my line at all. One should use things while one lives. At the same time, since I am in no need of money, I don't want to sell any of the MSS. or pictures just now, and shall be glad if you will hold for me those that you have got. – Only tell me what the MS. of the *Rainbow* looks like – if it's hand-written, on what sort of paper, if it's clean and *complete* and the *final* MS. from which the book was printed. – Manuscript is handwritten, what is type-written is called type-script, and proofs are *printed*, the print on which one makes corrections. Proofs and type-script also have value, especially if there are corrections on them, but of course written MS. is best.

I suppose we shall stay here another fortnight. I like it, it is beautiful, sunny and peaceful among the mountains, but the altitude tries me a bit, though it's under 3000 ft.

When you have time make me a full list and a bit of a description of the MSS, typescripts and proofs – or let Gertie do it.

love! DHL

Frieda had a bone setter come from the next village. He said the bone was

[1] The MS of *The Rainbow* (Roberts E331a), predominantly in DHL's hand and now at UT, was not the setting-copy for Methuen's first edn, 1915; that edn was set from a heavily revised typescript made from the MS (Roberts E331b). (For further details see *The Rainbow*, ed. Kinkead-Weekes, pp. li–liv.) How the MS came into Ada Clarke's possession is uncertain. The probable explanation is that the MSS returned to DHL by Lady Ottoline Morrell on 1 April 1918 (*Letters*, iii. 230) included *The Rainbow* which he had sent her in November 1915 (*Letters*, ii. 435). Four days after receiving the MSS DHL went to Ripley to stay with his sister; it is highly likely that he took some or all of the MSS with him, deposited them with Ada and then forgot their whereabouts.
[2] George Arthur Lawrence (1876–1967) – DHL's elder brother – and George's elder son Ernest (1897–1972).

off the centre, resting on the side of the socket. He shoved it back with a click, and now she begins to go all right. But I feel mad when I think of the Park Lane specialist whom I paid 12 guineas, and the important doctor in Baden who is not yet paid.

5301. To Enid Hilton, 3 September 1929
Text: MS UCLA; Unpublished.

Kaffee Angermaier. *Rottach-am-Tegernsee*, Oberbayern
3 Sept 1929

Dear Enid

Yes, the proofs were rather a bore – getting them out of Customs and all that.[1] And then the book is about as bad as it could be, really: such foolish narcissism! – These army officers like little boys imagining themselves so brave, so clever, so wonderful, that they save the whole British army all by themselves, and the women crawl at their feet – while they are only full of themselves and their own importance. The book is puerile – pathetic – But don't say anything. I shall only make more enemies. I put it as mildly as I could to your father.

Stephensen wrote from Eastwood, full of raptures – how vital and alive the colliers are, how fresh and unspoiled and inviting the collier lasses! Let us hope so! He wants me to declare myself an active socialist. Meanwhile the socialists are more hostile to me than the conservatives.

It's a nice place here – the people very nice. But I am not well and having to stay in bed again – so tired of it.

I don't know what to say about bringing pictures to Paris. Orioli wants to buy *Dandelions* for £20. – but then it would have to go to Italy. You might ask Dorothy again what she thinks.

Ever   DHL

Frieda had a bone-setter from the next village. He set her foot in one minute – the bone was off the centre, resting on the side of the socket. – And I paid 12 gns. to the man in Park Lane, and the Baden doctor is not yet paid! – Now she goes with confidence, and is only stiff.

5302. To Emily King, 3 September 1929
Text: MS Lazarus; Unpublished.

Kaffee Angermaier. *Rottach-am-Tegernsee*, Oberbayern.
3 Sept 1929

My dear Pamela

Lovely weather we are having here among the mountains – and people very

[1] See Letter 5290 and n. 5.

nice – only damn it all, I'm not very well, and must stay in bed a day or two. I am really getting fed up with my health.

Frieda is happy because the bone-setter came from the next village – just a farmer – and in one minute pushed her foot into its socket. He said the bone was off the centre and resting on the side of the socket – and if one had left it another two months it would have been too late, because the socket gets filled in. – Now she can really walk, though still limping a little – but only from stiffness. – Imagine those beastly doctors, 12 guineas I paid the one in London, and the one in Baden not yet paid. It makes one mad.

Yesterday Else came over in the car from Irschenhausen – where we stayed two years ago. It is only about 30 miles away. And we have friends here – a German writer, a doctor and his wife – and people come from Munich to see me – If only I wasn't always knocked out!

I ordered you a copy of the private edition of the *Pansies*, but the man is a very long while sending them out. The edition itself sold out in three days, but for gift copies he wants unnumbered copies, 'out of series', and the printer made a muddle and printed some short. However, I suppose they will come along in time.

I hope Dorothy Warren will shut the show and send back the pictures now. She talks of coming abroad to see us in middle of September – we might meet in Venice for a few days. She's very vague, but by no means as bad as Stephensen says – he is a very imaginative person.

Joan is at school again, I suppose. And Ada is glad to be home. I shall be glad to go to Italy and find a house.

love   DHL

5303. To Charles Lahr, 3 September 1929
Text: MS UNYB; Postmark, Rottach 4 SEP 29; Unpublished.

Kaffee Angermaier. *Rottach-am-Tegernsee*, Oberbayern
3 Sept. 1929

Dear L[ahr]

Thanks for yours and the bank receipt. I suppose it is the Mandrake who have not yet paid up. When they do pay, give Davies £10. from me towards his new editorial job. And do stop his money from your payments to them – it is inexcusable that they don't pay him.

I don't mind my name going as editor to 'The Squib', if you think it's any use. Let me know how the thing develops.

Do try and send out the gift copies of the Poems. You can cross out Max Mohr's name, because I gave him No. 15. And please put in my sister:

Mrs S. King, 16 Brooklands Rd. Sneinton Hill. Nottingham.

But it seems to me you could send out those copies whose covers are only printed in one colour. The inside is all right, isn't it? – And when do you expect to come out with the vellum copies?

Suppose we'll be here about another fortnight.

ever   L

5304. To Laurence Pollinger, 3 September 1929
Text: MS UT; Unpublished.

Kaffee Angermaier. Rottach-am-Tegernsee, Oberbayern
3 Sept 1929

Dear Pollinger

Thanks for the Random House information – Titus informed me correctly: though I believe he felt very noble giving me half the proceeds of my own work[1] –

You don't say whether you think the same *Jolly Roger* pamphlet could appear to advantage in England. I could of course get it done myself, privately.

I can't readily think of anything else for Random House to do, unless it were the 'Introduction to my Paintings'. I don't know how Stephensen feels about that – whether he would object to that Essay appearing by itself, in the late autumn – I don't see how he could. And then we should secure the American copyright finally. It's a good essay for a limited edition, and they need only omit one sentence. – Another smaller thing – rather 'sweet' – which would do for limited publication is the 'Flowery Tuscany' articles, which Nancy Pearn liked so much. The *New Criterion* published three of the sketches – I thought there were four.[2] But the magazine dept. has them.

The thing to do is to make the most of this boom of limited editions – it's the only way to make money, and without so much fuss. I shall get much more from my 500 *Pansies* than from Secker's 3000 – and no taxes and all that. The queer thing is that one can sell out these limited editions so quickly. In three days the *Pansies* are gone: and really, as a specimen of book-making, it is not worth two guineas. Odd, the sort of esoteric public within the great stupid exoteric public – it comes down to that. – It's all very well for Rich to complain that he didn't have the handling of the *Jolly Roger* – but his attitude to *Lady C.* was one of sheer funk, and of not wishing to touch pitch lest he

[1] Cf. Letter 5269.
[2] *New Criterion* published the first three parts in October, November and December 1927 (Roberts C159, C161 and C164); Part IV is published for the first time with the others in *Sketches of Etruscan Places and Other Essays*, ed. Simonetta de Filippis (Cambridge, 1992). For Nancy Pearn's enthusiasm for the 'Flowery Tuscany' sketches see *Letters*, vi. 52 n. 1.

should be defiled. I must say, I don't think much of Edwin Rich. He's no good: and from what I hear, not even trustworthy. Barmby may have been slow, but he was much better. There's no life at all in your New York office: and they want to be genteel, the fools. This is no moment for Knopfian gentility. The game is all slipping past them.

Ever   D. H. Lawrence

5305. To Achsah and Harwood Brewster, 5 September 1929
Text: MS UT; Brewster 211–12.

Kaffee Angermaier, *Rottach-am-Tegernsee*, Oberbayern
5 Sept 1929

Dear Achsah and Harwood

We have moved on to upper Bavaria – in the mountains like Kesselmatte – and we have the best part of an old peasant house like Kesselmatte, only it's bigger – and we eat in the little inn one minute below the garden. It's really very nice – balconies, apple trees, apples falling, dahlias, cows, women making hay. But I've had such a nasty sort of cold, laid me out, and am as weak as a rat and no happier – rats never look happy.

I'm but a stranger here
Heaven is my home?[1]

We want to stay till about Sept 15th then take a motor to Innsbruck – not very far – and so down to Verona. We *may* go to Venice for a few days – friends – but then to Florence to cast around finally for a house. It must be done – I can't drag around any more. I am writing to Earl – perhaps I shall see him in Florence, and we can make plans. I don't want to go to Capri – it's not my line. But I should like it if we had houses within reach of one another. Let's try to be inspired, and make it so.

As for the child, so she's not going to be a doctor.[2] Well, she's not a child any more either, so it'll be quite a vocation[3] being a woman: God help us all. And perhaps school is a bit futile at this point, if there is no vocational end in view. Dum vivemus vivamus[4] – but how to live.

Frieda is glad because she had a bone-setter from a neighbouring village – a farmer – and he set her foot in one minute. The bone was off the centre and resting on the side of the socket – and in another month or two the socket would have filled in and it would have been too late. And I paid 12 guineas to

---

[1] Hymn by the Congregationalist, Thomas Rawson Taylor (1807–35). DHL may have encountered it in *Psalms, Hymns and Passages of Scripture for Christian Worship* (1853, and often reprinted), popularly known in Congregational circles as the *Leeds Hymn Book*.
[2] Cf. Letter 5122 and p. 317 n. 1.   [3] vocation] vacation   [4] 'Whilst we live, let us enjoy life'.

a Park Lane specialist, and the long-bearded Medizinalrat in BadenBaden is still to pay. Doctors should all be put at once in prison.

Well – after the 15th write c/o G. Orioli, 6 Lungarno Corsini, Florence, and let's be neighbours if we can, for we're all at our wits ends.

love   DHL

5306. To Edward Titus, 5 September 1929
Text: MS UT; Unpublished.

Kaffee Angermaier, *Rottach-am-Tegernsee*, Oberbayern
5 Sept. 1929.

Dear Titus

Would you be so good as to send a copy of the 'Introduction' to our Paris *Lady C.* to:

Curtis Brown Ltd. Foreign Dept, 6 Henrietta St, Covent Garden W.C. 2 Please send the introduction only – if you have no copy of it, then best tear it out of a copy of *Lady C* – and please send by *letter post*, sealed: and charge all expenses to me. They talk of making a pamphlet of it in England now, since Random House sold out all their 600 copies before day of publication – but nothing definite is settled.

You had mine saying the Gallimard contract is signed. What now about the new 3000? – let me know.[1]

Ever   D. H. Lawrence

5307. To Earl Brewster, 5 September 1929
Text: MS UT; Brewster 212–14.

Kaffee Angermaier, *Rottach-am-Tegernsee*. Oberbayern, Germany
5 Sept 1929

Dear Earl

We are here in the mountains of Bavaria, a bit like Kesselmatte, only more spacious and more people – and we have friends here. It's really very nice, but I've had a fierce cold or something, and feel a rag. How tired I am of my ill-health. – But my ill-health is the same as your loss of energy – it's a sort of masculine change of life. It's a change of the whole psychic rhythm, and of most of the psychic values. It means, not only a maladjustment to the present system, but a whole conflict and finally a break with the present system. And we have to accept the ill-health and the loss of energy. Because all the energy that ran concurrent with the present system now leaves us, drains away, like an up-rooted tree, and will not come back till we make new roots in a new

---

[1] Cf. Letters 5268 and n. 3, 5271 and 5292.

emotion. I agree with you entirely about India – but I feel I don't belong to the actual India of today. I love the Indian art, especially Brahmin, more every time I see it – and I feel Hindu philosophy is big enough for anything. Yet we have to bring forth some different thing, in harmony with the great Hindu conceptions – which need carrying out. You couldn't hate the 'western' machine world more than I do. Only it's no good running back into the past.

Our plans are to leave here about Sept. 15th – take a Motor to Innsbruck, then down to Verona – perhaps go for a few days to Venice – then on to Florence – c/o G. Orioli. 6 Lungarno Corsini. – Then we *must* find a house. I don't think the climate is so bad, if one goes right away from the Arno valley, among the hills. It can be very lovely. But we are not fixed – open to any suggestion. We might try Lerici, near Spezia – we once spent a winter there[1] – or to[2] Cassis, near Marseilles – we must see. If you and Achsah are leaving Capri, then let us try this time to settle down as neighbours, Africa is tempting, but I *know*, after a while, one would get stale and exhausted, too much cut off. Italy or S. of France is best – because I'd like to settle down *for good* – have a permanent place, and only go away for a while, and come back. People do manage to be very happy in the Lucca country, and the Siena, and the valleys of Tuscany. The sea is not far. But we must see what we *can* do. Let us be neighbours if possible. And let us meet if possible. Orioli will have all my news.

It's been lovely weather here. I've written to Achsah.

a rivederci   DHL

5308. To Aldous Huxley, [5 September 1929]
Text: Huxley 821–3.

Kaffee Angermaier, Rottach-am-Tegernsee, Oberbayern.

5 Sept.

Dear Aldous, –

Had your letter – also Maria's – glad all goes gaily. Here we've been so-so. On Sunday Frieda had a bone-setter from a neighbouring village – a farmer. He felt her foot, said: *Na! 's ist 'raus!*[3] – shoved with his thumbs, a little click. *Fertig!*[4] he said, and so it was. It was really funny. The bone was off the centre, resting on the side of the socket. He just pushed it back, the whole thing took a minute. But he said if it had gone a few more months it would have been too late, as the socket fills in to fit itself up to the displaced bone. –

---

[1] October 1913–June 1914.   [2] MS reads 'to to'.   [3] 'Hey! it's out!'
[4] 'Done!'

And I had paid 12 guineas to the Park Lane specialist, [   ]:[1] and four guineas
to the masseuse in Baden: and there is still the bill of the long-bearded *Herr*
Medizinabrat [   ] to pay – also a sort of specialist. *Voilà les médecins!*[2] I call it
monstrous. If she hadn't come here she'd have limped all her life, and now
already she goes quite normal, only a little bit of stiffness. '*Ach!* wear it off
like a rusty key!' said the man.

The next is, I've been in bed all week feeling a wreck – and two doctors,
freundlich,[3] descended on me. One is a new, very modern one, who was a
Pfarrer – a priest – and has a *Klinik* in München and does wonders, chiefly
with diet and breathing. He wasn't the ordinary *Artz*[4] at all – says that in a
few weeks, with diet and a bit of breathing, I ought to be well. He says that we
are all undergoing a great change in our animal man – that includes woman, of
course. But especially men between 42 and 49 are in a state of change. The
new animal man will be different from the old – and already demands
different food and different rhythms – but he is given only old food and old
rhythms, and so gets poisoned. He says mine is partly poison from unwanted
food – and I know that's true. Especially heavy German food is poison to me.
He says, go back to simple food. The Roman legions conquered the world on
millet porridge – he says he gets amazing results by substituting millet
porridge for bread and potatoes, etc. Then as much raw food as possible –
fruits, salads, etc. – no coffee, but tea if you like it – no vinegar or strong acid
– otherwise pretty well anything plain – roast beef and so on – beer – a little
wine – but no cake and pastry – and no rich sauces. The great thing is, if you
can, to live mainly on the good, rather solid porridges – millet, oatmeal, barley
– then raw fruits and vegetables – then yaourt and sour milk and light cheese
– and nuts. He says my asthma comes from the vagus nerve, which controls
the expansion of the blood-vessels – and the vagus nerve is in a constant state
of reaction, from the stomach's recoil from constant food which it *doesn't*
really want, and consequent constant poisoning. He says this causes my
cough, in a large measure, and I believe him. He says much more important
than climate is not to be poisoned by wrong food. And any food you feel you
don't really want is wrong.

Now I feel that this, on the whole, is true. I feel I don't want most of the
food I eat, merely because it is the kind of food it is: even the bread. – So now
for a new diet and a new man. – I write it out in detail because I think it
applies a good deal to Maria, and also to you, as well as to me.

We wanted to leave about 15th. Motor to Innsbruck – then to Verona –
then perhaps to Venice for a few days to meet Dorothy Warren and settle

[1] See p. 239 n. 1.   [2] 'So much for the doctors!'   [3] 'friendly'.   [4] 'doctor'.

about the pictures – then finally Florence, to cast round for a house. But this
doctor threatens not to let me go till I am better – so we may be detained here
a bit. Anyhow, I feel this is the right track, doctor or no doctor.

So heaven knows when we shall see you – we'll have to leave it on the knees
of the gods.

Grüsse!   DHL

5309. To Laurence Pollinger, [5 September 1929]
Text: MS UT; Unpublished.

Kaffee Angermaier. Rottach-am-Tegernsee, Oberbayern
Thursday 5 Sept.

Dear Pollinger

First, would you please ask the mail dept to hold, send back, burn, or do
anything they like with the MS which this horrible Schmalhausen threatens
me with – but *not* to bother me with it.[1]

Knopf is a damn fool with his *Pansies* – I hear Secker's edition is selling
even in Los Angeles.

I'll send you my copy of *Jolly Roger*, if you'll send it me back.

I don't know if I'll do the Faber article – what's the good! I'm sick to death
of the British Public, all publishers, and all magazines – and feel I never want
to see a word of mine in public print again. But I'll read the 'Obscenity' article

---

[1] DHL's letter was written on one he had received from Samuel Daniel Schmalhausen who
wrote, on 22 August 1929, using headed notepaper of the New York publishers, the Macaulay
Company. In September 1928 Schmalhausen had sent DHL a copy of his *Why We Misbehave*;
DHL forwarded the 'stupid book' to Kot with instructions either to sell it or 'throw it in the
dust-bin' (*Letters*, vi. 564 and n. 2). In August 1929 Schmalhausen wrote as follows:

Dear D. H. Lawrence:
   I am not at all certain that I have the right to impose this task upon you, and yet, your
wonderful interest in psychoanalysis and psychological wisdom gives me a kind of right.
   I am attempting what you most likely will agree is of great importance in thinking, namely, a
combination of the scientific and artistic attitudes toward life, especially the life of the
emotions. This more creative conception of human nature is precisely what science so desperately lacks.
   In my new book, OUR CHANGING HUMAN NATURE, I am arrogantly assuming that
you as poet and philosopher will discover some provocative ideas and a general critical outlook
that represents more adequately than most psychologies the deeper aspects of our minds.
   Your old friend, Thomas Seltzer, has encouraged me to send my manuscript for your
judgment.
   I shall appreciate greatly indeed your interest in my work.
                                                        Sincerely yours,
   P.S. The enclosed pamphlet will give you a bird's-eye view of the reactions of scholars and
poets to my previous work, 'Why We Misbehave', the first attempt in America to interlink the
various dynamic and vital psychologies, and to apply, as Aldous Huxley pointed out in his
appreciation of my work, the artist's approach to human nature.

over, and if it interests me in itself, I'll lengthen it.[1] Random House might
publish it as a pamphlet. As for Faber & Faber – I should get about £10. – out
of them and a batch more insults – What's the point! But I'll let you know
finally about this, this week.

Am interested in Boni developments and the rescue of all my books from
that morass.

Of course I hate the thought of coming out in[2] a series of Mr Jix and Mr
Wells and all that lot.[3] Why should I put pepper in their stale stew!

DHL

5310. To P. R. Stephensen, 5 September 1929
Text: MS Anon; Munro 313–14.

Kaffee Angermaier. *Rottach-am-Tegernsee*, Oberbayern
5 Sept. 1929

Dear Stephensen

I'm glad you got a kick out of Eastwood and the miners and all. They were
alive when I was a lad, so they can't be so very dead. And if they produced me,
they must be a bit like me, somewhere.[4]

But as for coming out a socialist – the very nastiest attacks on me in the
papers come from the socialists and the Clyneside[5] 'workers' sort of people.
The miners of Eastwood aren't really socialists, any more than I am, really –
and they never will be. The socialist always kills the man, in a man. It did
Willie Hopkin a lot of harm. Look at Bernard Shaw! What I care about, in a
man, is the man, not the socialist. And that very capacity for joy, for real *fun*,
that I care about. Becoming self-conscious kills joy and fun only because we
don't become genuinely aware of ourselves, right through. We stop short, and

[1] DHL referred here to his article, 'Pornography and Obscenity', published in Titus's periodical
This Quarter (see Letter 5057 and n. 1). He was responding to an invitation from Faber & Faber
to contribute an essay on censorship to *Criterion Miscellany*; it appeared – a revised and
lengthened version of the original article – as No. 5 in that series on 14 November 1929, under
the title *Pornography and Obscenity* (Roberts A49).
[2] in] with
[3] William Joynson Hicks, created 1st Viscount Brentford on relinquishing his office as Home
Secretary in June 1929, had been invited to contribute to the Faber series. (E. M. Forster later
remarked: 'It was a happy and indeed a witty thought of the publishers to induce the most
remarkable of our novelists and our most notorious Home Secretary to write pamphlets on the
subject of indecency' (Draper, *The Critical Heritage*, p. 318).) His pamphlet, *Do We Need a
Censor?*, appeared in November 1929; H. G. Wells's *Imperialism and the Open Conspiracy* was
published in the same month in the same series.
[4] Stephensen's account of his visit to Eastwood may have prompted DHL to write 'Nottingham
and the Mining Countryside' (*Adelphi*, June–August 1930), which begins: 'I was born nearly
forty-four years ago' (Roberts C202).
[5] Possibly a deliberate conflation of 'Clydeside' and 'Tyneside'.

substitute a narcissus image, and *that* is the real death of all joy. The bane of socialists is that they are half-self-conscious, and for the other half substitute a narcissus image of their own perfect rightness etc, which is hell. – And that's the trouble with Willie Hopkin – he never got down to the bed-rock of himself, as a man, so has footled all his life with a narcissus image of himself, and each of his two wives has been the better man of the marriage. Poor Sallie – she was the better man, indeed! And he says of her now 'she had a mournful outlook on life.'[1]

I should be glad if I could have those two copies of the *Paintings* Book in Florence. I asked Enid Hilton to take them over to Paris, and send them from there. But I may be too late – she may have gone. I suppose it wouldn't be safe to post them to Orioli. If not, I must find somebody else to take them.

I had a letter asking if the 'Introduction to These Paintings' could be used in America, in a magazine. Have you any objection? It seems to me there can be nothing against it. – Another letter asking if it could be done over there in a limited edition. Any objection to that? It seems to me American editions don't really affect the English one. And several times I have been asked for photographs of the pictures – odd ones. Have you got photographs of them all? I think I ought to be able to arrange an American limited edition with or without a few photographs, if the English edition is all sold. It would rouse American interest. There can be no question of replica. I suppose never again will the whole colour-book appear, like yours.

Frieda had a bone-setter who set her foot in one minute, after we've spent pounds on specialists, and now she walks all right. I've got a doctor in Munich who declares I ought to be well in a few weeks – with *diet*. So there you are.

I want to write you one day about your Mandrake list. I'm a bit sorry you've got Aleister Crowley at such heavy tonnage, I feel his day is rather over.[2] You need to be selective, not in too big a hurry with the Mandrake books, to build the thing up. You've a good thing there, but I'm afraid you'll overload it.

DHL

[1] See pp. 46 n. 1 and 451 n. 2.
[2] Edward Alexander ('Aleister') Crowley (1875–1947), diabolist and prolific author; not one of DHL's favourites (see *Letters*, i. 169, 171). In June and July 1929 Stephensen had contracted to publish five Crowley titles including a volume of short stories – *The Stratagem, and Other Stories* (September 1929); a novel – *Moonchild* (September 1929); and *The Spirit of Solitude: An Autohagiography, Subsequently re-Antichristened The Confessions of Aleister Crowley* in six volumes (of which only the first two were published, November–December 1929). See Munro, *Wild Man of Letters*, pp. 89–91.

5311. To Enid Hilton, [6 September 1929]

Text: MS UCLA; Huxley 823-4.

Kaffee Angermaier, *Rottach-am-Tegernsee*, Oberbayern

Friday

Dear Enid

I wonder if you've gone – and if not, if you could ask Stephensen to give you the two extra copies of the *Paintings* Book which he says he has got for me – and bring them to Paris, and from Paris send them to G. Orioli. 6 Lungarno Corsini. Florence. It's rather an awful bother to put you to, but perhaps you'd do it.

I've been so seedy this week – and in bed most of the time – but now a new doctor has descended on me – in fact three doctors – and they say I can soon be well, with proper regime and diet: that the animal man is in a state of change, and needs a whole corresponding change of food and rhythm. I feel this is true, and shall start in. They also say eliminate *salt* as much as possible, as there is excess of chlorine in the body – and substitute some other salt in place of NaCl: the common salt. I feel that may be true. They say I can get well in quite a short time. I hope it's true – It may be, really.

It's very nice here, and if ever you want a fairly cheap place in the mountains – we have practically a house to ourselves for 3/6 a day, and take our meals in the little Gasthaus to which this house belongs.

If these doctors don't make me stay longer for a cure, we want to leave about the 15th. for Italy. But they may hold on to me a bit longer. We *must* go soon and see about a house.

I told you, didn't I, that Frieda had the village bone-setter for her foot – last Sunday. He set it in a minute, and now already she walks *almost* normal: just a bit of stiffness, no more.

DHL

5312. To Laurence Pollinger, 8 September 1929

Text: MS UT; Unpublished.

Kaffee Angermaier, *Rottach-am-Tegernsee*, Oberbayern

8 Sept 1929

Dear Pollinger

Here is the conclusion of the article on *Obscenity and Pornography*. It now makes about ten thousand words. You can give it to Faber & Faber if you like, for their monthly criterion and their rather silly little shilling books. They are almost sure to reject it: which will be perhaps just as well.

If they accept, they may leave out small bits, if they want to,[1] but they must tell me first.

Anyhow it will now make a very nice pamphlet for somebody to do in a private edition –[2]

Did you get the 'Introduction' to the Paris *Lady C.* – I asked Titus to send it. I suppose you don't need my copy of the *Skirmish* as well?

ever   DHL

5313. To Caresse Crosby, 9 September 1929
Text: MS SIU; Lacy, *Escaped Cock* 82–3.

Kaffee Angermaier, *Rottach-am-Tegernsee*, Oberbayern
9 Sept 1929

Dear Caresse

Your letter came on in time,[3] and I had your telegram. Glad you liked the pictures, but I still wish I had done a sort of plain one for the front.

I want you particularly to tell me what you are doing about copyright. It is very important to secure it, at least for the continent of Europe, and if possible, provisionally for America. Please don't overlook it.

Will you print me half a dozen out of series copies, to give away to friends? And what about the sheets to sign?

We want to leave here in about another week or so, and go south to Italy, perhaps a short while to Venice, then to Florence. Shall let you know exactly. But if you have sheets you want me to sign, can't you get them to me here?

---

[1] want to] will

[2] The 'article' is not known to have appeared (in DHL's lifetime) other than in the shilling *Criterion Miscellany* (cf. Letters 5309 and p. 468 n. 1 and 5354).

[3] See Letter 5289 and n. 2. DHL here acknowledged Caresse Crosby's letter of 27 August 1929 (TMSC SIU) which read as follows:

Dear Loronzo,

   The proofs and watercolors came, the book will be marvellous! Thank you so much. Only we will probably have to send the frontispiece over separately to be put in there. Mr. Marks says they are getting stricter and stricter and more and more troublesome at the Douane. Since I had your letter I wrote him to ask him about prices for he had just sailed. I am sure I can sell to him high enough so that we will clear considerably more than I told you in my last letter – of course it will sell wonderfully, only he does have to give ⅓ off to the bookshops and pay 25% duties and tax de luxe as well, so that the book must retail for *over* twice as much as I sell to him for and I have to consider that in making my prices – at any rate it will be $10 retail at least for the regular copies.

   I will be able to send you an advance copy about the middle of September.

   When are you coming back to the Mill?

Love from   Caresse

   P.S. As *soon* as I have definite figures as to cost of publication and sales price I will let you know exactly what the book will net you.

Love to Freda   C.

How are you both? and how are Harry's loves? One can only speak of them, like his drinks, in the plural. And how is Narcisse? and the ânes sang-pur?[1] It must be lovely at the Mill now. Lovely here, but of course I've been in bed with a chest. I don't really like mountains, so I think they don't like me.

belle cose!   D. H. Lawrence

5314. To Hon. Dorothy Brett, 9 September 1929
Text: MS UCin; Postmark, Rottach 10 SEP 29; Moore 1191–2.

Rottach-am-Tegernsee. Germany
9 Sept 1929

Dear Brett

Your letter with lists of MSS. today – and many thanks. But it is as I felt – there must be some missing. There were two complete MSS. of *The Plumed Serpent*, I think in four complete books. These I remember in the little cupboard – and they are not on the list. They are of course much the most valuable MS. I left, and worth the whole ranch itself. Don't you remember them too? – Edwin Rich has no *Plumed Serpent* MS. on his list from New York. And I have always said: I hope those *Plumed Serpent* MSS are safe! I suppose someone just stole them. Or, more probably, stole the final and complete MS. But if it is gone, we can always put the police on it if it appears for sale.

That MS. of *Sea and Sardinia* in New York can only be a typescript or a forgery, as I destroyed the original with my own hands.

About your other letter, and plan for selling the ranch to you for $2000 down and $500 per annum, it's perfectly all right to me, but Frieda has got to decide for herself. She will write in due course. And anyhow I'll see that nothing is done without telling you first.

I hope you got your copy of *Collected Poems*, and a copy of *Pansies* is ordered for you. Also I have, or Stephensen, the publisher, is holding for you a copy of the Book of *Paintings*, which I hope you'll get one day.

We are here in the mountains for a little longer, then going down to Italy. The doctors all say I am better – but my asthma is acute – that sea-level is best for me and I should never go above 3000 ft. At the moment I don't feel particularly well, but it varies. The fuss over the pictures and the burning of the four books made me very sick – I am so weary of falseness and hypocrisy in the world.

I hope you got the claim to the ditch fixed all right. – Tell Spud I ordered him a copy of *Collected Poems* and *Pansies*, hope he gets them. – I am not short

[1] A whippet and 'pure-bred asses'. Cf. Letter 5091 and n. 3.

of money, *Lady C.* made me over £1000 last year – so there is not that worry. And don't imagine that I believe for a moment in lurid suggestions of my Manuscripts sold from the ranch etc etc.[1] I'm afraid, since it hasn't showed up on your list, that the real and complete MS of *Plumed Serpent* has been stolen – and a beautiful MS. But if so, then I'm sure some American 'admirer' has sneaked it. But perhaps it will turn up.

I saw Mrs Chambers this summer – and what a horrible time *she* had re-entering U S A! No, it's impossible – I want to take a nice house in Italy now, and settle down a bit – then we'll see.

Meanwhile I hope you'll live peacefully and pleasantly, in Taos and the ranch.

DHL

5315. To S. S. Koteliansky, 10 September 1929
Text: MS BL; Postmark, Rottach 10 SEP 29; Moore 1193–4.

Kaffee Angermaier, Rottach-am-Tegernsee, Oberbayern
10 Sept 1929

My dear Kot

I have not written for so long because I knew, with all the police and pictures fuss, you preferred not to receive letters. However, that idiocy has died down again, and everybody knows once more what idiocy it was. – And as a matter of fact, in spite of Hutchinson and the rest, I don't believe my mail is interfered with at all. Hutchinson's letter to me was returned to him simply because he failed to put the name of the city – Baden Baden – on the address. So it could not be delivered.

I suppose you have seen the Lion[2] and his edition of the poems. As a piece of book-making, I confess I was disappointed with it – as I told him. But I suppose he must live and learn. Only he has no experience in matters of *taste*. He is a good man, but a wee bit of a muddler, and careless in details. Still he is a man in ten thousand, and I am very grateful to him for his pluck and energy. – I wish though, that he would wind up soon with the poems. He talks of holding over the vellum copies till towards Christmas. And I wish he would produce the few out-of-series copies to give away. Have you had a copy, by the way? I asked him to give you one. He never tells me in any detail what he does.

We are here in the mountains – and I really don't like mountains. But we want to go down to Italy next week, perhaps for a little while to Venice, then really to look for a house to settle down. I feel I am really fed up with moving

---

[1] See Letter 5158 and n. 2.   [2] Lahr. Cf. p. 23 n. 1.

about, and should be glad to have a place of my own. My health is about the same – a curse and a nuisance. The doctor says I am really better. New and different doctors descended on me from München, and say I only need diet – and no salt. It's a great stunt, the no-salt and Rohkost, raw food diet. I suppose there is something in it.

Frieda's foot is better. The bone-setter, a farmer, came from a near village and pushed the bone into place in half a minute. Now she goes all right. And I paid that specialist in Park Lane 12 guineas and the Medizinalrat in Baden another lot – Swine, these doctors.

I was thinking, one day we must rescue the Shestov translation from Martin Secker.[1] If the Mandrake have any success with Rozanov, we ought to follow it up with a new edition of *All Things are Possible*. I suppose Secker has let the thing lapse out of print long ago, and no intention of re-printing. One day you must write a letter and ask him.

Let me know how you are. If you don't care to write direct to me, you can enclose me a letter addressed

Dr Max Mohr. Wolfsgrube. Rottach am Tegernsee

yrs   DHL

5316. To Hon. Dorothy Brett, 12 September 1929
Text: MS UCin; Postmark, [. . .]; Irvine, *DHL Review*, ix. 97–8.

Rottach-am-Tegernsee. Oberbayern
12 Sept 1929

Dear Brett

I have been thinking over those MSS. at the ranch, and looking down your list again, and am amazed to see that nearly all the hand-written manuscripts must have disappeared. All those you give as typewritten manuscripts, 'Love', 'Taos', 'Life' – the Dance essays – and all the essays from the *Porcupine* book – all these should be there in handwritten manuscript, in various books. Why, I can *see* some of the books still, in that cupboard – the grey ones with perforated sheets,[2] the black ones – I can see them there. Then the whole MS of *David*. Then stories, 'The Last Laugh', 'Jimmy and the Desperate Woman' – these were all left in that cupboard in handwritten manuscript.[3]

---

[1] In 1920 Secker had published the translation by Kot and DHL of Leo Shestov's *All Things Are Possible*, with 'Foreword' by DHL; Secker's handling of some financial aspects of the publication had been a source of irritation to both Kot and DHL (see *Letters*, v. 483 and n. 1, 624 and n. 1, 627–8). On Kot's translation of Rozanov's *Fallen Leaves* see Letter 4830 and n. 3.
[2] MSS of 'The Dance of the Sprouting Corn' and 'Indians and Entertainment' are on perforated paper.
[3] DHL's diary entry for 30 September 1924 reads: 'Sent to Barmby (Curtis Brown) – *St. Mawr*: also MSS of the same, & of *Woman who Rode Away. Last Laugh. Jimmy & the Desperate*

Then the three or four complete books of *The Plumed Serpent*. – Why, Brett,[1] wherever are they all? They can't all have been stolen, without your ever noticing. It means that at least half of the whole cupboard-ful is gone – and surely that couldn't happen without your seeing. No, there is something wrong somewhere – and I wish you'd tell me. I feel also that you are hiding something from me.

If you think the MSS you typed should all be yours – surely, it's going a bit[2] far. Those you've got must be worth towards a thousand dollars, and did you do so much typing.

I wish all this business were settled up. I feel that things aren't straight – and I hate to feel it. You have written so much about loyalty. – And if an MS has been stolen, I am not one to break my heart. – But there is more than that.

When you do send the MSS. to New York, will you put in among them also that little bundle of the page proofs of *The Rainbow* tied up with two old passports. That was with the MSS. in the cupboard.

I think I'd rather you didn't deposit anything in the Taos bank.

I hear Rachel and William are buying Del Monte.[3] Quite a big speculation for them.

I want Frieda to write to you about the ranch itself. And she is writing to Rachel about Azul[4] – either selling him to her or giving him to her for good.

Well – somehow I feel depressed about it all.

                                                                        DHL

I heard from Younghunter – he said you didn't even let him come to the ranch for a day.[5]

5317. To Edward Titus, 12 September 1929
Text: MS UT; Unpublished.

                                          Rottach-am-Tegernsee. Oberbayern
                                                                12 Sept 1929
Dear Titus

Thanks for sending that 'Introd.' to London.[6]

I'm afraid it's useless to look to me for stories just now, long or short – I've

Woman   Border Line. Dance of the Sprouting Corn. Indians & Entertainment' (E. W. Tedlock, *The Frieda Lawrence Collection of D. H. Lawrence Manuscripts*, Albuquerque, 1948, p. 98, corrected from MS). See Letter 5335.
[1] MS reads 'Brette'.   [2] a bit] abit
[3] William Hawk (1891–1975) and his wife Rachel (1898–1992) ran a dairy farm on his parents' ranch, near Kiowa Ranch (cf. *Letters*, iv. 343–4; v. 39 nn. 1 and 3).
[4] Frieda's grey horse.   [5] Cf. Letters 5088 and 5089.
[6] DHL was replying to Titus's letter, 9 September 1929 (TMSC SIU):

not written one for a year, and simply can't get myself to begin. If you knew how I am hunted for short stories – in vain – and the prices they begin to offer! – But I'm 'off' – It's a dead period. – I thought *This Quarter* was better than most magazines, though.

No, I am not in need of money, but shall be glad to know what has come in for the first 3000 of Our Lady, when you can tell me.

If you see Michael Arlen, give him my regards, and tell him to send me a line c/o Orioli.[1]

I think we shall leave here next week – perhaps to Venice.

ever   D. H. Lawrence

5318. To David Lederhandler, 12 September 1929
Text: MS Rosenbach; Postmark, Rottach 13 SEP 29; Huxley 824.

(6. Lungarno Corsini. Florence)
Rottach am Tegernsee, Oberbayern
12 Sept 1929.

Dear Mr Lederhandler

Thanks for your letter and the $15. There is no hurry about that, anyhow.

I will remember you when I want to do something *really* privately in U.S.A. – Which might be fairly soon.

Yes, the paralysis of Sir Clifford is symbolic – all art is *au fond* symbolic, conscious or unconscious. When I began *Lady C.* of course I did not know

Dear Mr. Lawrence:

I have just sent to Curtis Brown a copy of the introduction to Lady C. as you requested. I have ordered another three thousand copies of her Ladyship to be printed and I am going to-morrow evening for an eight or ten days vacation. My address up to the 18th will be Hotel du Cap d'Antibes, Antibes, A.M.

I have two propositions to make to you, to both of which I would like to hear from you as soon as possible. I would like to bring out three or four plaquettes consisting of long, short stories one of which I would like to be by you. These editions will consist of about three hundred to five hundred copies, signed by the author. Can you have something of that kind for me, say about fifteen or twenty thousand words long, for which I would pay 75 guineas? The story would have to pass the censor. My second proposition is to pay you 25 guineas for a story for my magazine.

If you need money I can let you have an advance payment on Lady Chatterly. The money is slow in coming in but, as I say, if you must have it don't hesitate to let me know.

I entertained, one afternoon, Michael Arlen, and one evening himself and his wife. They are both now going to live in Paris for at least a year. We spoke about you. Mike is a tremendous admirer of you and he feels greatly elated at having served you as one of the characters in Lady Chatterly. He keeps you on a pedestal and he seemed very happy when I told him I would mention him to you when next writing.

Yours very sincerely,

[1] Dikran Kouyoumdjian (1895–1956), the original name of Michael Arlen, novelist, whom DHL knew from late 1915 and whom he last saw in Florence in 1927 (see *Letters*, vi. 220 n. 5). m. 1928, Countess Atalanta Inarcati. He served as the model for Michaelis in *Lady Chatterley's Lover*, ed. Michael Squires (Cambridge, 1993), p. 20 and n.

what I was doing – I did not deliberately work symbolically.[1] But by the time
the book was finished I realised what the unconscious symbolism was. And I
wrote the book three times – I have three complete MSS – pretty different,
yet the same. – The wood is of course unconscious symbolism – perhaps even
the mines – even Mrs Bolton.

Sincerely   D. H. Lawrence

5319. To Giuseppe Orioli, 13 September 1929
Text: MS UCLA; Moore, *Intelligent Heart* 416–17.

Kaffee Angermaier, Rottach-am-Tegernsee, Oberbayern
13 Sept. 1929 Friday.

Dear Pino

Here are the proofs of the Notes, and now for the moment addio! a Anton
Francesco, and may heaven smile on him.

Glad you have the gramophone. Does it play loudly and scratchily, or soft
and smooth? I don't really like them.

I have been doing my cure – first taking arsenic and phosphorus twice a
day. This made me feel I was *really* being poisoned, so I gave it up. Now I am
only doing the diet – no salt, and much raw fruit and vegetables, and porridge
in place of bread. I must say I don't feel much better – in fact I have been
rather worse these last two weeks. Perhaps it is the altitude doesn't suit me.
The place itself is very nice, and everybody charming, but I feel rather rotten.
I know I shall be better when we come lower down. But that would be foolish
while the heat wave lasts. I hear there is a heat-wave everywhere – and even
here it is close and rather heavy, but not hot. Today has come cloudy, so I
expect the weather will soon break. And then no doubt it will turn cold, so we
shall want to come down. But we can take a motor-car to Jenbach, which is
near Innsbruck, so we shall soon be down in Verona.

And I am still waiting to hear from the Trotters about meeting them in
Venice. They are perfect demons to have anything to do with: never answer,
never come to the point. The picture-show is still going on. I feel it is all
bewitched. – They wanted us to meet them in Venice and stay in Victor
Cunard's palazzo. But I don't know Victor Cunard. Still, if they *are* going to
Venice, then we will go too, in order to get hold of them and make some sort
of settlement about the pictures. And if we go, then *do* come too. It would be

---

[1] Cf. *A Propos of "Lady Chatterley's Lover"*: 'I have been asked many times if I intentionally
made Clifford paralysed, if it is symbolic . . . Certainly not in the beginning, when Clifford was
created. . . . But the novel was written, from start to finish, three times. And when I read the
first version, I recognised that the lameness of Clifford was symbolic . . . ' (*Lady Chatterley's
Lover*, ed. Squires, p. 333).

great fun. I shall let you know immediately I hear from the Trotters, where
we are to meet them.

No, the Sguanci villa doesn't sound much good. I don't want to share with
a padrone and a padrona, and the thought of a common kitchen makes me
shudder. No no! – Have you spoken with the fattore of the Mirenda yet? I
believe he would really know something. And we might ask the estate agents
just across the Arno there – I forget their name. – Otherwise we might, when
we come, try Lerici, on the Golfo di Spezia. We once spent a winter there,
and liked it. How difficult it seems – and I haven't the energy of a mouse, just
now.

I suppose Frieda told you her foot is better – she limps a bit out of habit,
nothing else. The bone-setter came from a neighbouring village – just a
well-to-do contadino. He felt with his thumb, said: Yes, it's out! – gave a
shove, and it was done, in less than a minute. The bone was resting on the side
of the socket, and couldn't slip back to place. And the socket was filling in,
in a couple of months she would have been lame for life. And I paid 12
guineas to the specialist in Park Lane, and there is a bill in Baden Baden. – So
much for doctors! a great fraud.

Well, dear Pino, I shall be very glad to come south and to see you. Let's
hope I shall revive a bit, for there's not much of me here.

                                                  Hasta la vista!   DHL
Remember me to Douglas – and Reggie.

5320. To Achsah Brewster, 13 September 1929
Text: MS UT; Brewster 214.

                              Kaffee Angermaier. Rottach-am-Tegernsee, Oberbayern
                                                         13[1] Sept 1929
Dear Achsah

Many thanks for the three pretty hankies. Do you know, you were the only
person in the world who wrote me a line for my birthday. Even my sisters
forgot this time.

Doctors came and started a cure on me with arsenic and phosphorus and
raw food and no salt. I feel rather the worse for it, so am avoiding the arsenic
and phosphorus. I find, though, I am becoming by choice rather a vegetarian
– that is, not much meat.

Where shall we meet and where shall we find houses and be neighbours? I
wish the good gods told us. – We shall probably leave here next week –
perhaps Venice a bit – and then – inspire me O Lord!

---
[1] 13] 12

Where is Harwood staying at school?
Send news.

                                                                    DHL

5321. To Muriel Moller, 13 September 1929
Text: TMSC NWU; Huxley 825–6.

                    Kaffee Angermaier, Rottach-am-Tegernsee, Oberbayern
                                                            13 Sept? 1929
Dear Miss Moller.

So after lying low and economising, you are going to fly off into the wildest
extravagances! Anyhow it sounds a most wonderful trip, and I hope you'll
enjoy it tip-top.

Here we are still in the mountains, lovely weather – but as soon as it turns
cold we shall descend. As usual, I don't like altitude, and Frieda does. Her
foot is better – the bone was on the side of the socket. A bone-setter, a farmer,
came on Sunday morning from a neighbouring village, put his thumb on the
place, and said: It's out! He gave it a shove, and it was in. The bone was
resting on the side of the socket, the socket was filling in, and in couple of
months she would have been lame for life. Which is pretty awful, considering
I had a bill for 12 guineas – and paid it, alas – from a Park Lane specialist for
her – and there is another 'famous' doctor unpaid still in Baden Baden. They
all said, it was strained ligaments, and ordered massage. The farmer knew in
the first touch. Why didn't they? She now goes all right – limps a bit out of
habit, and scare.

I too had a doctor – and they prescribed me arsenic and raw carrots. The
arsenic made me feel worse, so I left it off, but I gnaw a carrot now and then.
They say with diet I ought soon to be well. Contentissimo! if only it were so.

We are again uncertain in our movements. We are due to meet Dorothy
Warren and her husband – of my picture show – perhaps in Venice. But they
don't give any date, so we are hung up. I should like to see them, to settle
about the pictures. But they are the hardest birds to lay hold of.

When we have seen them we shall come on to Florence, and I hope you
won't have flown. We are most anxious to find a house to settle down in – but
where oh where! I wish heaven would point me a finger. A place like that of
your friends near Lucca sounds awfully good – but how is one to find such a
place – I wonder if Nelly Morrison knows of anywhere. I would like a villa,
not too big, but all to ourselves this time. I have lost your letter so haven't
Nelly's address. Do ask her if there is anything in the region where she now is.
And I'll send her a line Via de Bardi. I wish there was something possible – I
am really tired of hotels.

Now I hope you have had rain, and it is cooler. Frieda will be able to mount up to your terrace this time, if you are still there   and I, poor broken-winded wretch, shall try. So meanwhile don't get too excited over your trip – and many greetings.

D. H. Lawrence

5322. To Giuseppe Orioli, [14 September 1929]
Text: MS UCLA; cited in Moore, *Intelligent Heart* 418–19.

[Kaffee Angermaier, Rottach-am-Tegernsee, Oberbayern]

Saturday

Dear Pino

There was a telegram from the Trotter's last night – they are in Würzburg, about 5 hours from here, and are on their way to that place in Hungary where they buy that beastly jade – and they say they are writing and sending a cheque. Which means of course that they don't want to see me, because they don't want to answer my questions. So they are slipping past. – But I have wired[1] them to come here – we'll see if they do it.

Anyhow that puts Venice out of the question – and the doctors and everybody urge that I should *not* go to Florence, but to the sea, and insist that if Bandol suited me so well all winter, I should go back there. So I give in, and we will go to Bandol straight from here, and not come to Florence now. Perhaps later, for the trunks. Or perhaps you could bring them, even. I have an idea to take or even buy a small house at Bandol or Cassis – not far away – and then in May or June come to Italy and look for another small house near Cortina or near Bormio, which one could buy or rent, and keep always for summer. I think that would be best.

We want to leave here on Tuesday, get to Marseille on Thursday or Friday. We may try Cassis first, as it is a little nearer Marseille. But I shall send you the address at once. – And then, in the winter, you'll come and stay.

love   DHL

5323. To Ada Clarke, [14 September 1929]
Text: MS Clarke; PC v. Tegernsee, Überfahrt mit Blick auf Egern und Wallberg; Postmark, Rottach 14 SEP 29; Lawrence–Gelder 199.

Rottach.

Sat.

We are leaving here next Tuesday, and going to S. of France – probably Bandol again for the winter. Shall write –

DHL

[1] wired] written

5324. To Emily King, [14 September 1929]

Text: MS Sagar; PC v. Auf der Alm; Postmark, Rottach 14 SEP 29; Unpublished.

                                                                    Rottach.
                                                                        Sat.

We are leaving here next Tuesday, and going to South of France, Bandol or somewhere just near. I shall send you the address.

                                                              love –   DHL

5325. To Laurence Pollinger, 14 September 1929

Text: MS UT; Unpublished.

                                                                    Rottach.
                                                              14 Sept 1929

Dear Pollinger

We leave here next Tuesday, for the south of France. I really want to go to Italy, but they all insist I should be on the sea, and since I was very happy last winter[1] at Bandol, we'd better go somewhere there again. So will you please stop the mail in all the departments – cancel this address.

I suppose you got the continuation of the 'Obscenity' article – and the *Lady C.* 'Introduction', which Titus says he sent you.[2]

As for work, I've been very much off since I came to Germany. Germany depresses me and makes me irritable – I rather hate it. I shall feel better by the Mediterranean, then perhaps I shall write some stories – and perhaps re-cast *The Virgin and the Gipsy.* I haven't felt well here either.

                                                              ever   DHL

5326. To Earl Brewster, [14 September 1929]

Text: MS UT; Brewster 216–17.

                                                        Rottach am Tegernsee.
                                                                     Saturday

Dear Earl

I had your 'birthday' letter yesterday. You will have had mine.

This is a note to say we have decided to go straight to Cassis or Bandol, from here. We leave for Marseille on Tuesday, and should be there on Thursday or Friday. I was so well and so cheerful in Bandol last winter, there seemed such a pleasant cheerfulness in the air, that though the place is in parts *ugly*, etc. – still, I am sure it is best to go back there. Cassis is a little nearer Marseille than Bandol, and there are more houses, I think – it is more scattered. So I think we shall stop there first, and look for a small house, to

¹ winter] year   ² Cf. Letters 5312 and 5317 and n. 6.

rent or buy. They are not at all dear. If we dont find what we want, go on to Bandol, to the Hotel Beau Rivage, which is very nice and cheap. – I want to have a small house, permanent, that I can live in or shut up, but that I can keep, to save this fret of nowhereness. And I *know* that that is a good place.

I heard from Achsah – she is pining to get back to you. I am writing to her now to suggest she might meet you in the Hotel Beau Rivage, Bandol, Var, and we could try and arrange a nice neighbourly winter. But if you think she won't be happy away from Capri, stay on the island.

And will you write me

c/o Thomas Cook & Son. La Canebière. Marseille.

I think John Cournos will be in the Hotel Beau Rivage Bandol – on the 20th or so – and I shall write him: he'll have letters. He's a dark rag of a miserable Jew, in some respects *awful* – in some respects, nice. He writes novels.

Well – we *may* meet in the South of France – the winter was lovely there last year, and it is utterly unlike Nice etc.

so au revoir.   DHL

am writing Achsah *just* what I write you.

Your birthday! shall we still celebrate it together.[1]

5327. To Achsah Brewster, [14 September 1929]
Text: MS UT; Brewster 215–16.

Rottach.
Saturday

Dear Achsah

I wrote you c/o Cook. Piccadilly – thanking you for the *very* pretty hankies. – It's true, you and Earl are the only people in the world who wished me a birthday wish.

We are leaving here on Tuesday, to go to the south of France. I was so well and so cheerful in Bandol last winter – such a sunny winter – that, all things considered, it is perhaps madness to go to Italy. We ought to be in Marseille by Friday at latest. I have written Earl today asking him if he wouldn't like to meet you in the Hotel Beau Rivage. Bandol. Var. – It is very nice, cheap, we liked it. And then we should arrange a nice neighbourly winter. We want to look round first at Cassis, to see if we can't find a nice small house there, that we can keep permanently. Cassis is two stations nearer to Marseille than Bandol. – Bandol is, I think, about an hour from Marseille, in a slow train. – Anyhow write me

c/o Thomas Cook. La Canebière, Marseille

[1] 21 September 1929 was to be Earl Brewster's 51st birthday.

and if you come to Bandol, we can join one another in an hour or two, even if we find something in Cassis and decide to stay on there. If Cassis is unpromising, we shall come on to Bandol, which I know I like. It has its ugly side – the French make their places ugly – but somehow the little port is so friendly and nice – I was happy there.

Well give my blessings to Harwood, and I hope this will catch you in Totnes. – Earl won't have his letter till Wednesday, I'm afraid – perhaps Tuesday. But don't rush to Capri unless you feel you must.

My blessings to Harwood – I'm glad she's having a spell of school on her own –

love from both   DHL

5328. To John Cournos, [14 September 1929]
Text: MS StaU; Postmark, Rottach [. . .] SEP 29; Unpublished.

Rottach.
14 Sept

Dear Cournos

Glad you are safely in Europe. – Remember me to Madame Douillet in the Beau Rivage.

We shall probably be coming also to S. of France soon – doctors say, not to trust Florence winter climate – and I was very happy in Bandol. So probably we'll come back somewhere there. But I want to find a house – we are tired of hotels. A house either at Cassis or Bandol. I shall write you to the Beau Rivage.

And perhaps our friends the Brewsters will turn up there – E. H. Brewster, from Capri – and his wife. She is at present in England, and he in Capri – but I want them to meet in the Beau Rivage – If they come before we do – either of them – talk to them.

Thanks about the publisher. I'll tell Curtis Brown.

ever   D. H. Lawrence

5329. To Charles Lahr, [14 September 1929]
Text: MS StaU; Postmark, Rottach 14 SEP 29; Schorer 66–7.

Rottach.
Saturday

Dear Lahr

What a damn fool that Jackson – he seems a prize one. I do hope the thing will go no further.[1] Vorsicht![2]

---

[1] Obscure, but see Letter 5366.   [2] 'Caution!'

We leave here on Tuesday for the South of France – think we shall winter in or near Bandol, I was so well there last winter. – I shall send you an address.

A monthly 'Squib' at 6d. 12 pp. seems good. But I'd rather it were all anonymous – all *noms de plume* – and a *nom de plume* editor too. It would be so much more fun. We don't want to label it with my name. – I have one or two good nettles about the pictures – and one or two about the govt. Glad you have a caricature – You must ask Fredk Carter too if he can't do squibby-drawings. We want drawings and squibby bits of poetry

> Lately I saw a sight most quaint:
> London's lily-like policemen faint
> in virgin outrage as they viewed
> the nudity of a Lawrence nude.[1]

But what about the prose? Tell me a good subject of the moment to let off a prose squib against: something impersonal.

Life of JMM. by J.C.[2]

John Middleton was born in the year of the Lord 1891. It happened also to be the most lying year of the most lying century since time began, but what is that to an innocent babe!

———

But I cant myself go for Murry – or have him slanged too hard under my name. I have known him too intimately.

What one *might* have is a column of imaginary reviews 'Shorter Notices.' *Life of JMM by J.C.* This is a work which cannot be lightly dismissed. The author has gazed into the flowing stream of introspection, and seen, as in a glass, darkly, the great image of – himself. etc.

Do get some critic to do a column of imaginary shorter notices.

'The Loneliness of Wells' by Susan Kapp.[3] – This book, which was suppressed on its first appearing in 1927, is now re-issued by tacit consent of the Home Secretary –

'The Sighs of Lord Brentford' (is that Jix's title?) by Viscount Poppup. At

---

[1] Cf. Letter 5286. The poem – under the title '"Gross, Coarse, Hideous" (Police description of my pictures)' – was collected in *Last Poems*, p. 295; see *Complete Poems*, ii. 680.

[2] Lahr printed *The Life of J. Middleton Murry by J[esus] C[hrist]* – consisting of the paragraph which follows – in a limited edn in October 1929 (Roberts A51). Murry had published a *Life of Jesus* (1926).

[3] Cf. p. 115 n. 2.

the risk of appearing facetious, we might call these the unsuppressed sighs of the Late Home Sec. etc –

'Hughie and the Hump' by Arthur Figgybaum. This extraordinary book by a child of eleven contains a child's complete appreciation of Mr Hugh Walpole. Mr Walpole studied the child, but here the child has studied Mr Walpole etc.[1]

I will send address as soon as I have one.

DHL

I told Vere Collins to come to you for a book – He is in the Oxford University Press – have known him many years – he might be useful with suggestions.

5330. To Willard Johnson, 14 September 1929
Text: MS YU; Huxley 826–7.

Rottach – Bavaria.
14 Sept 1929.

Dear Spud

Thanks for your letter and the countersigned list of MSS. – and thanks for sending the parcel. I enclose a little cheque to pay postage and my contribution to *The Horse*.[2] I'm sad about those MSS. because many are missing, the complete hand-written manuscript of *The Plumed Serpent* has gone – that part that remains is merely duplicate – and many other things. It seems strange they should all have been stolen – and very depressing.

You ought to pay no customs on the poems at all, as it is the American edition pub. in New York by Cape at $5. So what do the fools want charging customs? There is no duty on books produced in USA. – I ordered you also a copy of *Pansies* – from Knopf.

I knew Idella had a baby, but never knew it died.[3] That's *triste* –

How does the *Horse* go?

My health is still pretty bad – and I don't know when we'll get back to U.S.A. and New Mexico. I think we shall winter in S. of France. We'll be going down to Marseille next week.

---

[1] (Sir) Hugh Seymour Walpole (1884–1941), novelist and critic; he had written stories for children: *Jeremy* (1919), *Jeremy and Hamlet* (1923) and *Jeremy at Crale* (1927).

[2] Johnson's periodical, *The Laughing Horse*, in which DHL had published several times.

[3] Idella Purnell (1901–82), American poet whom DHL had met in Guadalajara, May 1923; she edited *Palms: A Magazine of Verse*, to which DHL contributed. See *Letters*, iv. 435 n. 2. m. 1927, John M. Weatherwax.

Write to me and tell me all the news. I read about Manby – very horrible. What was the final decision? – was he murdered?[1] If you send Idella's address I will send her the collected *Poems*.

Best from us both   D. H. Lawrence

5331. To Maria Huxley, 15 September 1929
Text: Huxley 827–8.

Rottach.

Sunday 15th September, 1929.

Dear Maria, –

To-day you are supposed to be starting off for Paris – hope you'll have a nice trip – wonder if it's hot? Poured with rain in the night, but still quite warm, for here: they say, not been so warm for 105 years – why 105? We want to leave on Tuesday. I have come to the conclusion that I loathe all mountains, and never want to be among them again. Also I feel as if wild horses would never again drag me over the German frontier. *Never* come – at least, not now. Yet everybody here is extraordinarily nice, and the place quite beautiful – a few years ago I should have loved it. And now, unfortunately, I hate it – for no apparent reason.

We intend to go straight to the South of France – Cassis or Bandol. When I compare how cheerful and well I was there in Bandol, to what I am here, then I decide to go straight back and look for a house, there near Marseilles. I shall send you an address.

I began the cure, with rhythmic doses of arsenic and phosphorus. At the end of a week I was nearly dead (the new man! the animal basis!). So I dropped the drug side of the cure absolutely, and feel much better. But I go on fairly with the porridge and *Rohkost* – raw fruit and vegetables – and I'm sure that's good for me. I feel in better tone already. But in Germany I feel so feeble, and as if I hardly want to live. Now I hate it!

I feel I don't want to go to Spain this winter – don't want to make the effort. And at present I'm a bit fed up with travelling: should like a quiet winter, and if I have the energy and initiative, paint.

Dorothy Warren and her husband were due to meet us, and settle up about the pictures, etc. . . . But yesterday I had a wire from Würzburg saying they

[1] DHL had encountered Arthur Rockford Manby (1859?–1929), an eccentric Englishman, in Taos (cf. *Letters*, v. 550 and n. 2). On 3 July 1929 Manby's decapitated body had been discovered in Taos. Greatly hated, Manby may have been murdered to silence him after involvement in robbery and murder; he may have been killed by one of his savage Alsatians; it has even been suggested that he faked his own death. The mystery has never been solved. See Frank Waters, *To Possess the Land: A Biography of Arthur Rockford Manby* (Chicago, 1974).

couldn't possibly come, must go on to Hungary to buy that jade stuff they sell in their Gallery – ugly stuff. . . .

That was a horrible affair of Rose's *prétendant*, poor devil![1] I must say, your family is unlucky in its men – your sisters. What a mercy the poor wretch is dead! One can't really stand these horrors!

I suppose you've still not got your *Pansies*! More muddle. But I've had £300 for it, anyhow – and another £200 due. You'll get a copy in Paris, in time.

Oh, how many liras did you pay for that gramophone? I'd no idea you paid that bill – but if you paid that, I'm sure there were other bits as well. Don't forget to tell me.

I do hope you'll get your *North Sea*. The Warren has it at her house in Maida Vale.

Remember me to Jehanne, and I do hope she's all right.

I wish I was south of the Alps.

Love,   DHL

5332. To Caresse Crosby, 16 September 1929
Text: MS SIU; Lacy, *Escaped Cock* 83–4.

Rottach-Egern.

16[2] Sept 1929

Dear Caresse

I have signed and numbered 50 vellum sheets, and signed six extra in case of accident – packed them up as they came – and now I hope they will reach you safely and without damage. I shall have them sent off tomorrow.

I am very anxious to see the book, and so is Frieda. I wish you had sent me proofs of the colour reproductions – I expect you have them by now.

I am thinking, perhaps when Marks has sold this edition – which ought to take only a very short time – he might make another, cheaper edition, without pictures, and copyright in the ordinary way. He could hold this cheaper edition back a few months, if he liked, the copyright secured. And he could make an agreement direct with me. This would save us from pirates, and would be to his interest. – Otherwise I might get another publisher in America to take it up. Have you any objection to a cheaper American edition appearing, say, in November? Don't forget to let me know about this.

If the printers spoil too many copies in press – or colour-process – then save me some of the imperfect copies, they will do at a pinch to give away.

---

[1] The identity of Rose Nys's suitor is not known (she married Baron Eric de Haulleville in 1935).
[2] 16] 17

And I think I shall have to arrange for an English edition immediately yours is gone – have you any objection?

We are leaving here on Wednesday – day after tomorrow – for South of France. I shall write immediately I have an address. But if you need to get me quickly, write

c/o Thomas Cook. La Canebière, Marseille.

If it weren't such a long way up to Paris, I'd love a few sunny days at the Mill. What about Madame de Jumiac, by the way? – and the red-haired man from Cannes? Did they affect a – I mean *effect* – a marriage? And how is Harry's erotic temperature?

You know, by the way, Marks can secure a temporary U. S. A. copyright (for 3 months) by sending a copy of the French edition to Washington.

Yes I should like to read the story of your eight weeks – what a mercy it's not six! I expect my hair will curl, but even if it does itself up into knots I shall stand by you. Or is it only Harry's 'advice to his wife' – I hope that makes part of the eight weeks' record – which will make hair-curlers in the book (I hope it's a long book)?

Love from Frieda and from Lorenzo   DHL

5333. To Charles Lahr, 16 September 1929
Text: MS UNYB; Postmark, Rottach 17 SEP 29; cited in Moore, *Poste Restante* 102.

Rottach.
16 Sept 1929

Dear L[ahr]

I have your letter and the book. The latter looks very nice, I really prefer it to the others. The only trouble really is my publishers, in London and New York. They might seriously object if I authorised another 500, and I should hate to do them down. So I shall not speak to Tite[1] yet, and will you please do nothing for the moment, unless necessary. We must hold back for a while, then ask Poll[inger] for his opinion on the matter. K[ot] might perhaps take him his copy – if you have not sent it – and ask his advice, telling him everything, and putting my scruples before him. I don't want even to *seem* to swindle my publishers.

I think in France there is no law requiring a publisher's or printer's imprint on a book. There is nothing on the novel. T. was afraid. He has ordered another 3000 copies, and I want to see if he will put his name on that. He is at present in S. of France. – There is a man Bradley in Paris, connected with my London agents, and I think of getting him to handle my Paris matter.

[1] Edward Titus (subsequently 'T.').

He might deal better with Galignani than with T. – it remains to be seen what my agents think.

Perhaps it would be better to send sheets only to France, and bind there. We must think of it.

On the cover, yes, I think there might be a little more space between the title and the word *Poems*. But not much. I don't mind it's being pushed up together.

We leave here Wed. morning, and I shall write from S. of France.

K. thinks the 'Squib' is a bad idea – perhaps it is. Perhaps one would only collect a little bunch of not very nice people. I don't know. I'm not on the spot to judge.

Well, I hope things are quiet. I do *not* want any more notoriety.

L.

5334. To Philip Trotter and Dorothy Warren, 16 September 1929
Text: MS UN; Moore 1199–1200.

Rottach.
Monday. 16 Sept 1929

Dear Philip and Dorothy

Your letter and cheque today. I wrote you crossly to Würzburg – but really, you do exasperate one. You *never* come to the point, you *never* simply answer what one asks you, and you *never* mind leaving one dangling in the thin space of uncertainty, for indecent lengths of time. You are *most* exasperating.

But this in haste: Stephensen has *never* written me a word against you, and I have *never* written him a word against you. If I have said – and my God, I have said it – that I was fed up with the show – then you know what I mean. The whole nauseous business of the public. I have said the same to you. – That false, vile fuss over the pictures got me sick. – But of course I know Stephensen raves against you – (from Enid Hilton, who knows just how to take him, and from my sister, who is impressed) – But I hate people who rave with unreasonable antipathies. And I have my own idea of Stephensen. Goldston I have never written to. So don't think for a moment I am concerned, even for one word, in Stephensens fulminations – which I dislike intensely, and which he senses, hence his complete silence about you to me.

For the rest, thank you for the cheque. It seems very few sold – I wonder nobody at all wanted to buy after the Krach.[1] But I am just as well pleased. I don't want to sell. And I am not hard up for money either – not at all. It wasn't the cheque I wanted. It was a simple and definite winding up of the

---

[1] 'row'.

business. – And I don't want any share in the shillings at the door – but perhaps they will balance a bit the cost of framing and transport, which you bore. I don't want you to bear unfair expenses either.

Now you will remember I gave you *Contadini*, for love – and though the love feels rather cross, it is the same. And then there is *North Sea* to give to Hutchinson for Maria Huxley. Then I told Jack Hutchinson that Mary, his wife, could have a picture at her own price. And Enid Hilton is to have *Fire Dance* for ten pounds – paid in instalments: she won't take it as a gift. And when somebody goes to Florence, perhaps they will take *Dandelions* to Orioli. This disposes of ten, perhaps eleven pictures. The final disposal of the rest we will arrange as soon as you are back in London.

I *must* go to the sea – my health is certainly worse here, and wears me out. Partly it is altitude, it doesn't suit me. We leave on Wednesday for Marseille – you can get me

c/o Thomas Cook. La Canebière, Marseille

and you'll have to swallow my other cross letter, because really, you *do* ask for it. But I should hate you to think there was any Mandraking.

DHL[1]

5335. To Hon. Dorothy Brett, [19 September 1929]
Text: MS UCin; PC v. München: Karlsplatz Rondell; Postmark, München 19 9 29; Irvine, *DHL Review*, ix. 98.

Munich
– 19 Sept

Had a list from London of MSS. in the New York Office of C[urtis] B[rown] – and find that several things are there, which I thought were still at the ranch[2] – so glad – will write fully – we are on the way to South of France.

in haste   DHL

5336. To Emily King, [23? September 1929]
Text: MS Sagar; PC v. La Côte d'Azur. Bandol (Var). – Vue Générale; Postmark, Bandol [...]; Unpublished.

Hotel Beau Rivage, Bandol. Var
[23? September 1929]

So – we are back here – and very lovely – so glad to see the Mediterranean.

DHL

[1] In a note accompanying this MS, Philip Trotter wrote: 'There were jangled nerves at both ends, & for an account of *our* preoccupations at this moment, see Section "Philip Trotter", pp 399/400 – Ed. Nehls III'.
[2] See p. 474 n. 3.

5337. To Charles Lahr, 23 September 1929
Text: MS UNYB; Postmark, Ba[ndol] 24 –9 29; cited in Moore, *Poste Restante* 102.

[GRAND HOTEL BEAU RIVAGE, BANDOL][1] Var, France
23 Sept 1929.

Dear L[ahr]

This is the address – the old place – but very nice – so glad to be back. There was no letter at Marseilles. Send news if any.

L.

The Huxleys are back at Suresnes.[2]

5338. To Caresse Crosby, 23 September 1929
Text: MS UT; Postmark, Bandol 24–9[...]; cited in Moore, *Poste Restante* 102.

Hotel Beau Rivage, *Bandol*, Var
23 Sept 1929

Dear Caresse

We are back at the winter address – hope you had the signed sheets safely – Lovely here!

D. H. Lawrence

5339. To Laurence Pollinger, 23 September 1929
Text: MS UT; Unpublished.

[GRAND[3] HOTEL BEAU RIVAGE, BANDOL] Var. France
23 Sept 1929

Dear Pollinger

This is the address for the time being – I am so glad to be back by the Mediterranean, so lovely here – perhaps one can thaw out again from that tension of the north.

There was no letter at Marseille

Ever   D. H. Lawrence

5340. To Baroness Anna von Richthofen, [24 September 1929]
Text: MS PM; PC v. La Côte d'Azur. Bandol (Var.) – Vue de la Terrasse de l'Hôtel Beau-Rivage; Postmark, Bandol 24[...]9; Unpublished.

Hotel Beau Rivage, *Bandol*. Var.
[24 September 1929]

Da sind wir wieder, und wunderschön!

DHL

[There we are again, and it's marvellous!

DHL]

---

[1] For this letter and Letter 5339 DHL used the hotel's headed notepaper.
[2] DHL added this message on the verso of the envelope.
[3] DHL deleted 'Grand'.

5341. To Giuseppe Orioli, [24 September 1929]

Text: MS NWU; PC v. La Côte d'Azur. Bandol (Var.) – Vue de la Terrasse de l'Hôtel
Beau-Rivage; Postmark, Bandol 24 –9 29; Unpublished.

Hotel Beau Rivage, Bandol. Var.

[24 September 1929]

Back here – and very lovely –

DHL

5342. To Ada Clarke, [26 September 1929]

Text: MS Clarke; Postmark, Toulon 27[. . .]; Unpublished.

Hotel Beau Rivage, *Bandol.* Var.

Thursday

My dear Sister

We got here Monday night – seems the best place, since it suited me so
well. – Frieda has taken a house – one of those chalet-bungalow affairs along
the cliffs towards the pines – where the bulbs were thrown away, if you
remember. It has six rooms, and bath-room, and central-heating, and water –
all very nice – so we ought to be all right for a winter. Perhaps you'll come and
see us again. Shall write properly soon. The house is Villa Beau-Soleil – and I
expect we shall move in on 1st. Oct. – Everybody so pleased to see us here, so
nice, such welcomings!

love   DHL

5343. To Giuseppe Orioli, 27 September 1929

Text: MS UCLA; Unpublished.

Hotel Beau Rivage. *Bandol.* Var

27 Sept 1929

Dear Pino

The sheets came on today, and I have signed them and am sending them. I
signed six extra – hope that is enough for binders' errors. You will see I had to
put brackets in the printed heading, as it was worded to suit the numbered
1000 copies only.[1] I suppose it will do now.

Frieda has taken a house here – Villa Beau-Soleil – and I expect we shall
move in on Tuesday. It has six rooms, bath, water, central heating, is on the
sea in a nice place, about ten minutes from here – so I think I shall like it all
right. But I would just as leave have stayed in this hotel. – There will be a

---

[1] The statement of limitation on the signed copies of *The Story of Doctor Manente* reads as
follows, with DHL's brackets inserted: 'Twelve hundred copies have been printed of this
edition: Two hundred Special copies signed on Binda hand-made paper, (and one thousand
numbered on Lombardy paper,) of which this is No.'

room for you in the winter, when you want to come, and we are getting a good femme de ménage,[1] so I hope we can make you comfortable. I should like the trunks as soon as possible – what a tiresome job for you, as they really need re-packing. I think you can throw the broken trunk away, all the things ought to go in the others. The box of books can stay – perhaps it might go in your cellar. Only I would like my red English dictionary from it. And the type-writer and the gramophone perhaps can be packed in one of the trunks. As for my winter hat, that can stay till you come. Ask Egidi if it would not be better to send all the things from Livorno to Marseille by ship. We are only an hour from Marseille, and could go to the port and get the trunks through customs if necessary. Or perhaps Egidi's men would manage better without our going. Anyway ask him, will you. – I'm awfully sorry to give you this beastly bother. The signing of sheets is nothing in comparison. – We have taken the house for six months, till end of March, at 1000 francs a month. But we can have it longer if we like. – It is very nice here, but I still feel a bit worn out from Germany. However, I am already much better, and becoming my own self slowly. I still find it rather lovely here, and I like the hotel – feel a house a bit of a burden, but Frieda wants it.

The enclosed letter was sent on by Miss Moller, from the Istituto Britannico.[2]

Lahr got in a muddle with the presentation copies of the *Pansies*, and now is afraid to post them, I believe. But you and Douglas will get your copies, in time – perhaps you have them now.

Remember me to everybody. I still feel tired, from the north – never will I go again. Tell me how you are. It is lovely weather here.

DHL

5344. To Earl Brewster, 27 September 1929
Text: MS UT; Brewster 219–20.

Hotel Beau Rivage. Bandol. Var.
27 Sept 1929

Dear Earl

Your letter came this morning. I couldn't write you because I felt sure you would move north to meet Achsah, and I really half expected to find you both here. But I remembered your birthday. – Achsah was the *only* person who remembered mine – and you and Harwood. My mother-in-law was reminded three days later, by Harwood's writing – books and greetings – which I'm

---

[1] 'housekeeper'.
[2] The enclosure – forwarded from the British Institute of Florence – is missing.

going to write thanks for now. But nobody else, not even my sisters, has mentioned one word of happy birthday. Queer that my sisters ignored it so completely, after so many years.

We arrived Monday evening – three days ago. It seemed very lovely – so full of light and a certain newness. I am already much better. In Germany I felt I should certainly die – awful – It was psychic depression. The Germans are in an *awful* state, inwardly – but horrible. I feel that *nothing* will ever again take me north of Lyon. I dread and hate the north, it is full of death and the most grisly disappointment. I feel already nearly myself again here – the sun and sea, the great light, and the *natural* people. I can breathe. In the north, I can't breathe.

We have taken a house for six months – Villa Beau-Soleil. Write there. It is on the sea – rather lovely – a smallish bungalow, six rooms, terrace – bath, central-heating – some neglected garden – costs 1000 francs a month – about 730 Liras. It is ordinary – but not poky – and wonderfully in the air and light. We could probably find you something cheaper – perhaps 600 Liras a month. But this hotel is nice, at least I like it – for 45 francs a day – about 35 Liras. I'm not very keen on going into a house, but Frieda wants it.

We should both be very glad if you came and joined us. There are no English people here – a few French visitors – and a very few English or German drift through the hotel. But the place is on the whole very natural. And the country behind, a mile away, quite wild, pine forests. It is half-an-hour to Toulon, and 1½ hrs to Marseille. You might sail to Marseille. – But *don't* take Achsah from Capri if she clings to it.

From here, one feels Africa. It is queer – but the direct vibration seems to be from Africa. Next winter we'll go.

We have got to get our trunks from Florence – a bore. But I suppose Orioli will send them.

I hope Achsah reached you safely, not too tired. I will write to Harwood.

Love from both   DHL

5345. To Harwood Brewster, 27 September 1929
Text: MS Holt; Brewster 217–19.

Hotel Beau Rivage – Bandol. Var. France
27 Sept 1929.

Dear Harwood

I haven't thanked you yet for your birthday present, because I haven't seen it. My mother-in-law hasn't sent it to me yet. But now we are here, and your Aunt F[rieda] has taken a house – the Villa Beau-Soleil – for six months, I shall have them sent, and look to heaven for inspiration – or at least, strength.

At present I feel as weak as a kitten, and not a nice fluffy bouncy little kitten, but a poor weak-legged miauling brat, that ought to fall down a well. I don't know why Germany made me feel so ill and worn-out this time, but it did.

However, it is lovely here by the sea – about an hour from Marseille. I had a letter from your father this morning, and he says that if we can find him a house, he and Achsah will probably come for the winter. I am almost sure we can find a house, not very dear, so I hope they will come. It is just a small place with fishermen and not many tourists, quite nice – and warm in winter. And it would not be far for you – only 12 hours from Paris. So it would seem to be all right.

I wonder how you like your school. It will seem strange at first, but I'm sure after a while you'll love it.[1] And I do hope you'll get a footing in the world among other people, and independent of your father and mother. Thank goodness it is not too late. Then you can come back to Earl and Achsah with a new outlook, and a new energy, and give them a share in a new Harwood. You are a good sporting child, you always try to make the best of everything, so I'm sure you'll get real experience and something really worth having, out of this new move.

I expect we shall move into the Villa Beau-Soleil on Tuesday. It is just a bungalow with six rooms, and bath, and even a little central-heating plant that looks like a toy. But they say it works. I expect I shall blacken my face and my soul making it work this winter – somehow I feel we shall get real cold spells. But you will be warm enough in Darlington Hall – how grand it sounds!

Well, have a nice time, and tell me if ever there is anything I can send you or do for you.

                                                    love from us both.   DHL

5346. To Maria Chambers, 28 September 1929
Text: MS StaU; cited in Schorer 65, 66.

                                    Villa Beau-Soleil. *Bandol. Var.* France
                                                              28 Sept 1929
Dear Maria Cristina

Your long letter this morning. First, the pictures for *Vanity Fair*.[2] It was a wonder you wrung so much as $100. out of them – as you say, they pay only what they are *forced* to pay. – I want you to keep the hundred dollars for your

---

[1] Harwood Brewster later recalled that Dartington Hall 'was a very progressive school. It had only been functioning for two years when I went to it. There were only 18 children there with a big range in age and a lot of individual attention in study' (Harwood Brewster Picard, 'Remembering D. H. Lawrence', *DHL Review*, xvii, Fall 1984, 210).

[2] See Letter 5354 and p. 504 n. 1.

running-about expenses. *Please don't gainsay me.* And if you try to pay them to me, I shall have to let the matter go through Curtis Brown, whereas if you keep the money I shall merely say you lent your reprods. for a small fee.

I knew Rich would try to scotch you. Of course there are various stories they could have let you have for the *Year-Book* – 'The Blue Moccassins' – printed in a Virginia magazine last winter[1] – 'Things' – from the *Atlantic Monthly* – and *Rawdon's Roof* – done in a small private edn. by Elkin Mathews this spring. By the way, *Rawdon's Roof* was, I think, never sold in America. I think the proof-sheets are in a trunk in Florence – I'll send them. – I've done very little work lately, but I shall order for you things that are appearing in England – some articles – you may find likely places for them in America, if Rich fails. – Curtis Browns are now thinking about placing[2] the 'Introd. to These Paintings' – I'll let you know result. They are also, very clumsily, tackling Seltzer-Boni, demanding confirmation that ten books are out of print, and wanting to know if they intend to re-print. I'm afraid Boni is going to be too smart for them, and it will be a bigger muddle than ever. – By now Knopf's *Pansies* will be out.[3] But if you will tell me the address of your friend sailing from Paris, I will send you a copy of the unexpurgated *Pansies* (private). – You will have seen, also, that Random House did the *Skirmish with Jolly Roger* – (Paris *Lady C.* Introd.) – 600 copies at $8. and all ordered before issued. – I might send you also a couple of copies of *Lady C. 1st edition* – now worth $40 or $50 at least, if your friend is reliable. Pino has about 50 copies (this is strictly private) and we could sell them if we could only get them over.

I wonder if you could have a tiny book-shop. Or better, if someone would let you be a partner in a shop, and you could have a little section for yourself, to deal only with special authors – say me, Norman Douglas, and others of Pino's connection. Then you could collect *all* things, the magazines, the newspapers, with articles and stories in, and sell them, as well as the books – and perhaps even have two or three pictures for sale. We would root out all possible available stuff from the past. You would soon get a connection. – Now Harry B. Marks, another Jew bookseller of New York, is going to get the whole Paris edn. of *The Escaped Cock – Part I and Part II.*, from the Black Sun Press. God knows at what price he will sell it. I shall ask them to send over in the bulk a gift copy for you, and he must give it you. I expect he'll be selling the book in November. Curtis Brown has nothing to do with this, as it is 'improper'!! – This book must be re-published six months after date of 1st edition – or even sooner, if pirates threaten. You see if only I had had

---

[1] It appeared in *Plain Talk*, February 1929 (Roberts C183).   [2] placing] publishing
[3] It had been published the previous day.

someone in N. York to print *Lady C.* for me at once, we could have forestalled
the pirates. Now that chance is lost – and all is lost, as far as *Lady C.* in U.S.A.
goes. – I don't want this to happen over *Escaped Cock*. Perhaps you might
carefully talk to Harry Marks.

Well, I cant think of anything else at the moment.

DHL

5347. To Caresse Crosby, 28 September 1929
Text: MS SIU; Lacy, *Escaped Cock* 86.

Villa Beau-Soleil. *Bandol.* Var
28 Sept. 1929

Dear Caresse

Glad to hear from you,[1] and looking forward to the book. We've taken this
little house on the sea for the winter, bang in the sun. I find strong sunlight
has a soothing and forgetful effect on one.

When you send the books to Marks, will you include in the shipment a gift
copy from me to Mrs Maria Cristina Chambers, and ask him to hand it over
to her. Can't trust the post – so she will call on Marks with a note from me,[2]
and he can give her the book.

And will you send me his address. I must write to him about that copyright
business. In six months *Lady Chatterley* had been pirated at least four times,
in U.S.A. – and I lost at least $15,000. It is ridiculous for me to abstain from
publishing, if the pirates are going to rush in – and rush in they will, with this

---

[1] DHL was responding to Caresse Crosby's letter, 23 September 1929 (TMSC SIU):

Dear Lorenzo,

I have received the Japan sheets back again – Thank you very much for the many signatures.

I couldnt send you examples of the color because they are only now (after the printing of the
text) being done and you will so soon have the completed book – I had the frontispiece
interpreted in fewer colors (as you said I might) and also reduced in size so as not to over-
balance the type – it will look very well and not being quite so flaming it should not offend the
civil authorities!

I will write Mr. Marks your suggestion about a cheaper edition later on, but I must ask you
not to have the English or the U.S. edition done until *six months* after our publication – as this
has always been our agreement with Mr. Marks, and has been the case with all our other first
editions (Joyce, Kay Boyle, Hart Crane) he will not have the book on sale before November, as
it takes several weeks for shipment and it will be another week at least before it is ready to send.

The Gramophone is on its return trip to Paris, when can Frieda meet with it?

Harry has just shot a pheasant cock in the garden – first game of the season – with a beautiful
flaming tail. They come over the fence to eat our "corn on the cob".

Best love to you both. I hope this oppression cast by the Mountains has lifted and that all is
well with you.

Love from   CC

[2] The letter following (presumably enclosed with Letter 5346).

story. Marks must meet the situation, or leave me to handle it. Anyhow please send me his address.

And send me that lurid frontispiece to the *Cock*, when the printer has done with it. I suppose you don't want to keep it? – I hope they kept the man red enough, or it loses its point.

                                                    ever   D. H. Lawrence

5348. To Harry Marks, 28 September 1929
Text: MS SIU; Lacy, *Escaped Cock* 87.

                                        Villa Beau Soleil. *Bandol.* Var. France
                                                            28 Sept. 1929
Dear Mr Marks

I asked Mrs Crosby please to include a gift copy of *The Escaped Cock* in her shipment to you. I hope the thing comes safely in – and if it does, will you please give the said gift copy to Mrs Maria Cristina Chambers, who will bring you this note.

I am anxious about the copyright of the *Cock*. I don't want the whole thing pirated from me, as *Lady Chatterley* was. The best thing would be to have a cheap edition ready to forestall the pirates – and I must do that in[1] England. Will you assure me that you will protect me in the United States?

                                        Yours Sincerely   D. H. Lawrence

5349. To Charles Lahr, 28 September 1929
Text: MS StaU; Postmark, Bandol 28 -9 29; Lacy, *Escaped Cock* 85–6.

                                                Villa Beau-Soleil. *Bandol.* Var
                                                            28 Sept. 1929
Dear L[ahr]

Had yours last night. All right, we'll let the poems lie. – Orioli and Douglas are moaning that they haven't received their copies. Douglas is
                    c/o Thomas Cook. Via Tornabuoni. Florence.
Do send them if you can. – Aldous Huxley is in London for a few days – catch him if you can via Jack Hutchinson. 3 Albert Rd. Regents Park. and give him his *Pansies*. And ask him about the 'Squib'. – Kot. can telephone Hutchinson if you don't want to. – I know Aldington very well, but don't want to write him. If the 'Squib' *begins*, then you write and ask him for some venomous trifle, and tell him I said I wanted him to come in. – Tell Aldous the same. And I'll write him. – I think the 'Squib' is fun: but *no names*: all

---

[1] in] now

noms de guerre – and advertise it: The most famous among the young authors writing under *noms de plume*. – A good fetch.

Do give Davies the £10. – I've got things for the 'Squib' whenever it will be ready. – Aldous is

3 rue du Bac. Suresnes. Seine.

Fredk. Carter might do something.

The *Black Sun Press* edn. of *Escaped Cock* is nearly ready. They are shipping all to U.S.A – 500 copies – and expect to sell it in November – Harry B Marks, the bookseller. But don't talk about it – the quieter the better. – They stipulate a six months interval after the first edn. But I say, if there is a threat of pirates, we must forestall them, six months or no six months. So I shall send you a set of proofs.

But I should like to wind up completely with the poems before doing another book. Do you think Stephensen has sold all those copies? And can you get him to pay, and then you send me the accounts, all settled up and finished? – All, that is, apart from these new red ones. And these we will pay for from Mandrake payments – so really all will be settled. But I shall give you 10% on the red ones, if you think it is enough.

If the 'Squib' starts, give Davies his £10 and another £10. in a months time, and if the 'Squib' fizzles out, it's my loss, I don't want any re-payment.

I wish you would keep for me a copy of my articles and stories – newspaper stuff and magazine stuff – a copy of each thing as it appears – and charge me a bill – but keep me the things together on a shelf. Would it bore you? Or any *really* interesting criticism too.

Start the 'Squib' if you're going to – and tell me, and I'll write a little editorial.
                                                                        DHL

5350. To Emily Lutyens, 28 September 1929
Text: MS UTul; Unpublished.

Villa Beau-Soleil. *Bandol.* Var. France
28 Sept. 1929.

Dear Miss Lutyens

I am glad you liked the article.[1] Would you please send two copies of the Nov. issue (containing the article) to

Mrs Maria Cristina Chambers, 43 Hillside Rd, Elm Point, *Great Neck.*
N.Y. U.S.A.

Also a copy to me here, and a copy to

Signor G. Orioli, 6 Lungarno Corsini, *Florence.* Italy

I hope this is not putting you to too much trouble.

                                        Yours Sincerely   D. H. Lawrence

[1] See Letter 5244 and n. 1.

5351. To Nancy Pearn, 28 September 1929
Text: MS UT; Unpublished.

Villa Beau Soleil. *Bandol.* Var. France
28 Sept. 1929

Dear Nancy Pearn

Yes – we are here – and taken this little house on the sea for the winter. It is very sunny, and I like it, and I hope I shall feel like work. I never felt so low and so dead off everything, as I did in Germany. Hope it was the low-water mark, for I don't want to go any lower.

Could you order a copy of *The Criterion* with 'Mother and Daughter'[1] for Mrs Maria Cristina Chambers. 43 Hillside Rd. Elm Point, *Great Neck*, Long Island. N.York.

And a copy of that article 'The Risen Lord', when it appears in *Everyman*[2] (was it *Everyman?*)[3] I suppose that article is not placed in U.S.A. – neither the *Star Review* one?[4]

Did you have a nice holliday in Scotland?

D. H. Lawrence

5352. To Maria Huxley, [29 September 1929]
Text: Huxley 831–3.

Beau Rivage
Sunday

Dear Maria, –

We've taken a little house, on the west shore – a sort of bungalow something like yours at Forte, only bigger – six rooms, bath, little central heating plant, hot and cold water – town supply of water, quite good and apparently abundant – bare garden, good garage – 1000 fra. a month – and really rather lovely position. We expect to move in on Tuesday – *Villa Beau Soleil.* I think it will be nice and easy. There is a *femme de ménage,* Camille, said to be very good. We have it till end of March – can keep it on if we wish. – You think you might come? – But there are no big old stone villas in great gardens, like Italy. One would have to hunt hard in the country to find a bit of a *château* place – it *might* be possible. These villas – modern, are much easier. And does one, after all, *want* a great stone house? Aren't they a weariness? Here, where one is so much out of doors, a small house is so much more convenient – one opens the door on to a *terrasse* or balcony – we've got a big one – and there one has room. It is sunny and still. Already the visitors are nearly every one gone – the village is nearly as last year. But somehow a bit stunned by the mob of town

---

[1] See Letter 4926 and p. 170 n. 1.   [2] *Everyman*] *Time and T*   [3] See Letter 5239 and n. 1.
[4] DHL's letter was annotated, probably by Nancy Pearn: 'Both on offer in U.SA.'

people that have been here – it was a full season. They will come to life in another fortnight or so. The palm trees are recovered, nearly all, and have new green leaves. But the eucalyptus trees, that were so lovely and tressy, are dead, sawn off, they are now monuments of wood. So the place seems paler, and a bit bare, but Frieda says she likes it better. It is a very still afternoon, the sea very still, blue, but autumn slatey blue, and nothing moving at all – men sitting motionless near the dark nets. I'm fond of the place.

Madame, in the hotel, loves us and is almost bitter that we are leaving her. – Max Mohr is here, but not in this hotel, in Les Goëlands. He is rather like a bewildered seal rolling round. The Brewsters, he and she, *may* come. The girl is at school in England. – I am already feeling better, I felt very *low* in Germany. Frieda's foot almost well, but a bit stiff. She bathes now every day, and says it is lovely. I think I shall bathe from the house.

Do they have, in Paris, that new food Bemax, English – the Vitamin B food? Nichols gave me a tin in Mallorca – it's just like bran, but I've an idea it did me good. It costs only 2/6 or so in England – but would be more in Paris. If you happen to be in the sort of shop that would have it, ask them to send me a tin *by post*, to Villa Beau Soleil, will you? And if you happen to put your nose in a likely book-shop, ask if they have a little brochure on *The Olive Tree* and *The Vine*. I want to write essays on various trees, olive, vine, evergreen oak, stone-pine, of the Mediterranean, and should like a bit of technical *Encylopaedia Britannica* sort of information. But in both cases, don't go out of your way, it doesn't really matter a bit.[1]

I wish Aldous had gone to see Charlie Lahr in London, and got his copy of *Pansies*. Also we talk of making a little magazine, 12pp., called 'The Squib' – which is merely to put crackers under people's chairs. Little sarcastic or lampooning poems, tiny mocking articles, 50 or 100 words, a series of 'mock' reviews – one man wanted to do a tiny 'shorter notice' on the life of M[iddleton] M[urry], by [Jesus Christ][2] – that sort of thing – all anonymous, all *noms de plume*. All short, some caricature, drawings – once a month, 12 pp. – 6d. Just squibs to have little darts of revenge and send little shots of ridicule on a few solemn asses: but good-tempered. Rhys Davies and Charles Lahr would edit it, and I think it would be rather fun. It's badly needed. A squib or two at the old women in government. I'm sure, Aldous, you would be A1 at it.

If you decide seriously you would like a house here, we will tell the agent and look. And we might then take a permanency too. It is an easy

---

[1] Maria Huxley made some notes (see Letter 5371), but if the essays were written they have not survived.
[2] See p. 239 n. 1. See also Letter 5329.

place. One can sail from Marseilles to anywhere. And one is in the sun. But I daren't for my life persuade you. Only I think the north is death, I really do.

How long do you think to stay in Spain? I am so thankful for the thought of sitting still, quite still, for a winter. I don't even want to go to Toulon. Nowhere.

Enclose £1 for the gramophone – you didn't tell me how much. Regards to Rose and to Jehanne, she will take things too seriously – what does a little religion matter nowadays!

DHL

5353. To Giuseppe Orioli, [29? September 1929]
Text: MS UCLA; Unpublished.

[Hotel Beau Rivage, Bandol, Var.]
[29? September 1929]

Dear Pino

When will Lasca be ready? Would you like me to ask Curtis Brown (Pollinger) about a contract with an ordinary publisher – say Oxford University Press – for the whole series? If so, just send Pollinger two copies *after* I have asked him, and I will tell him to make all the agreements with you direct. But I shall have to tell him about the book – and they will be a bit cross because they have not made the agreement between you and me – but I won't have them do that. They can make the agreement with a London publisher – and New York – if you wish. Let me know about this, as I shall have to be telling them as soon as you send your circular out.

DHL

5354. To Laurence Pollinger, 29 September 1929
Text: MS UT; cited in Huxley 828–9.

Hotel Beau Rivage, *Bandol.* Var, France
29 Sept 1929

Dear Pollinger

Your letter this morning: I'll answer it in order.

I expect Secker wants to go straight into a cheap edition because he only printed 3000 (I believe) *Pansies,* and so he would be saved a second printing if he made the cheap edn. now. If you stop him with the cheap edition, he is quite capable of letting the book lapse for the time (he has done so over and over again with the other books) – so watch him. He *won't* push any book beyond the easy point – he just won't, or can't. He told me some time ago he had sold 2,600 of the 10/6 edn.[1] – I expect he is about sold out – So watch him, that he doesn't leave the poems out of print.

I am a bit surprised that Faber & Faber risk the obscenity article – don't mind if they leave out Galsworthy and Barrie, why so much as mention them?[2] – No, if the thing appears publicly, I don't want it to come as a private edition at all. But I want it to appear in U.S.A. – very important to me there – let me know about this.

Don't push the Cressett Press too hard about *BirdsBeasts*. I particularly want them to do the job, for the sake of Blair Hughes-Stanton, who is doing the illustrations, and is a friend, and is very hard up, and he is the important point, for me, in the matter. So do please accommodate the Cressett all you can, as far as I am concerned.

I might do a few more Tuscany articles[3] – *attendons!*

I am very anxious about the Seltzer books. The time is ripe again for me to put my work before the American public – it has never had the ghost of a chance with Seltzer. And I feel that Boni is going to be a tough nut. Do you think it is quite impossible to deal with him? What is there against him, except that he's rather awful altogether? – But I do wish the books could be rescued. I wish, for example, that *The Lost Girl* could be re-issued this coming spring, and properly advertised. It would almost certainly go well, as it would meet the nascent desire for romance, in America.

The *Paintings* 'Introduction' would probably be accepted by *Art and Decoration* (is it?) – the American equivalent – or was – of the *Studio*.[4] But isn't it in Albert Boni's hands? Nevertheless, I'm almost sure he'd print it. – The *Vanity Fair* people are printing four reprods. of the pictures in the Novem. issue. Crownieshields saw a set of proofs of the pictures, which I gave to a friend, and wanted to reproduce four, so I agreed, and he'll pay the fee to the friend – hard up one, as usual – I expect they'll be printing the 'Wall-Pictures' article also then. But they pay very poorly – Aldous Huxley

---

[1] That number represented the entire printing (Roberts A47b).

[2] The passage in the MS reads: 'And this minority public knows well that the books of [Sir James Barrie and Mr. Galsworthy, not to mention the mass of] lesser fry, are far more pornographical than the liveliest story in the *Decameron*: because they tickle and excite to private masturbation, which the wholesome Boccaccio never does.' In all published texts the bracketed words are replaced by: 'many contemporary writers, both big and'.

[3] Cf. Letter 5304 and n. 2.

[4] DHL was probably confusing the American *Art and Progress* (1909–15) which had become the *American Magazine of Art* (1916–36), with the French *Art et Décoration: Revue mensuelle d'art moderne* (1897–1914, 1919–39).

gets a good deal more from them – I suppose partly because he is contracted
to them, which I would never be.[1]

Dorothy Warren is in Austria – she sent me a cheque for the pictures sold.
The others are stored in her house in Maida Vale. I will see about them when
she gets back to London – don't know when.

The two limited editions of the *Pansies* are due entirely to the dirty Police.
If I had been free, of course, all the poems would have gone into the Secker
edition. – But I will not be kept out of print. – Only I wish I had not signed
any copies for Secker – I ought to have kept him to the unlimited and public
edition only, since the other *had* to be sub rosa. – For the rest, I more or less
agree with you. But when a thing *can't* appear publicly, it shall appear
privately, and that's all. And the people who look for something *strong* or
Bluey, as you put it, must keep on looking. I'm not at all anxious to put out
limited editions. But I'll bet Random House could have sold that *Jolly Roger*
pamphlet twice over – and look at it! – I don't mind a bit whether it appears in
England as a limited or unlimited essay. But I should like it to appear, as I
insist on my position. Only for England I should like to make it longer – a few
more things I should like to say. I am not very anxious for Stephensen to do it
– but don't mind particularly.

The Black Sun Press in Paris have got their 500 edn. of *The Escaped Cock*
just about ready. They will ship it over to U.S.A. *en bloc* – and I suppose it
will be sold there in November. I didn't ask you to do anything about this
because I know you do not want any more complications with authorities.

The other thing is Orioli's new little venture – a bit unexpected. I did the
translation for him a year ago, to launch him on a series of translations. I
believe they'll be nice. Aldous Huxley is at work on a Machiavelli play for the
next volume, and Richard Aldington is doing another. – As concerns Orioli's
edition, that is just between him and me, like *Lady C*. But I have asked him if
he will let you arrange, if possible, for public sales. *Doctor Manente* is
absolutely 'proper' – and very suitable for college reading. The other vols.
will be the same. So that I think some firm like *The Oxford Press* might
profitably take up the whole series. – However, we must wait a day or two to
see if Orioli is willing for you to handle the matter. – Properly handled,
though, the series could be sold very well, especially to American colleges and
universities.

We have taken a little house here for six months – the Villa Beau-Soleil –

---

[1] The November *Vanity Fair* (editor, Frank Crowninshield) was to carry 'The Censor' by
Aldous Huxley (reprinted in *Music at Night* as 'To the Puritans All Things are Impure') and
reproductions of DHL's *Fauns and Nymphs*, *Red Willow Trees* and *A Holy Family*. DHL's
'friend' was Maria Cristina Chambers: see Letter 5346.

and expect to move in on Tuesday. I feel much better in the strong light of this sea. But still the thought of the Great British Public puts me off work entirely – either painting or writing. I *cannot* work for that G.B.P. I feel sick at the thought.

Very still and sunny here – olvidar – vergessen – oublier – dimenticare – forget – So difficult to forget –

DHL

5355. To Hon Dorothy Brett, 29 September 1929
Text: MS UCin; Postmark, Bandol 30 –9 29; Huxley 829–31.

Villa Beau-Soleil. *Bandol.* Var. France
29 Sept. 1929

Dear Brett

You will have had my letters – and the one where I suddenly got a slump, feeling there was a great loss of MSS.[1] Fortunately came that list from Curtis Brown, showing most of those which I remembered at the ranch, are now in New York. I was very relieved. It's not so much the loss, as the sense of being robbed, which one minds. That little cupboard was utterly unsafe. And even while I was at the ranch myself, my books were stolen from the shelves. – Of course I knew quite well you would not sell my MSS, in spite of what anybody said. But your visitors are another matter: same as anybody's visitors. – And the MSS. I gave you, of course you do as you like with. Only I wish you'd tell me. – By the way, is my copy of *The Rainbow* still there? – bound in blue, the 1st edition (Methuen).

Glad you are painting – I've had a blank summer – felt perfectly miserable in Germany, and ill, and couldn't do a thing. Now, thank god, we are back at the sea, have taken this little house till end of March, and I feel better. I hope my élan or whatever it is will come back. I felt very down and out this summer. Not money, I've got plenty of money. Nowadays I can easily earn with my writing. But health and spirits. That disgusting affair in London over the pictures got me sick, real sick.

I hear an American dealer got 120 of the *Paintings* books, and apparently got them in all right. Wonder what he sells them at. Yours is in London – worth 12 guineas now.

An awful bore about your copy of *Collected Poems*. But it's the Customs fault. A book produced in U.S.A. should not be held up for Customs. Bynner got *his* copy straight through. – I hope you had the *Pansies* from New York.

Shall be interested to see photographs of your paintings. When you *do* see

---

[1] Cf. Letter 5316.

mine, you won't like them. They take a different line. But *Vanity Fair* will produce four in November: though you can't judge from black and white.

I expect you'll be in Taos by now. Here it's still quite warm, bright sun, very still and soothing. Feel I need it. People are queer everywhere, and the world is going quite insane. But there are still a few quiet places that are livable.

Glad you had the rights of the ditch fixed. One day, when you can get a chance, do try and get someone to fix the real boundaries of the ranch – locate them, I mean. If some old-timer can remember the corner-tree, then you can take the sights. Old Willie Vandiver[1] might know. You know the ranch-property is really a *square*, and is quite a bit bigger than the present enclosure. And the piece above the house, up towards the raspberry canyon, is really inside the bounds, and I should like that secured especially, as it keeps us private. If we could find out the corner marks, we could fence bit by bit.

Hope your hand is better, that you cut clearing the ditch.

Hope all goes well!

DHL

5356. To Charles Lahr, 1 October 1929
Text: MS UNYB; Postmark, Bandol 1 –10 29; cited in *Apocalypse* 12.

Villa Beau Soleil. *Bandol.* Var. France
1st Oct 1929

Dear Lahr

I want to do some work on the Apocalypse, more or less in conjunction with Frederick Carter, and I've asked him to give you a list of the books I should read. I want also a good annotated edition of Revelations – or of New Testament. Do send me the books, as you get them and the bill.

And do get for me if you can Frederick Carter's 'Dragon of the Apocalypse', published by Elkin Mathews at a guinea.[2]

And tell me if you know any books, really good, on civilisation in the Eastern Mediterranean, before the rise of Athens – on Tree and Pillar cult –

---

[1] Vandiver] Berryman (Vandiveer was the blacksmith at San Cristobal: cf. *Letters*, vi. 551 and n. 1.)

[2] Carter's book was entitled *The Dragon of the Alchemists* (1926); his second book, for which DHL wrote the 'Introduction', was originally entitled 'The Dragon of the Apocalypse' but Carter changed the title to *The Dragon of Revelation* (1931).

on the Chaldean and Babylonian myths – Sir Arthur Evans on Crete is so huge and expensive.[1]

We move into our house today – hope we'll have a good winter.

DHL

If a woman Frau Francisca Ewald, writes to you from Berlin to send her stories of mine[2] – from those two Cynthia Asquith books – or the *Criterion*, or *Eve*,[3] or that Elkin Mathews *Rawdon's Roof*, do send them if you can, and charge her the normal charge.

5357. To Frederick Carter, 1 October 1929

Text: MS UT; cited in Moore, *Intelligent Heart* 423.

Villa Beau-Soleil. *Bandol.* Var. France

1 Oct 1929

Dear Carter

The 'Apocalypse' came yesterday, and I have read it. And again I get a peculiar pleasure and liberation out of it. It is very fragmentary – I suppose it is natural to you to be fragmentary. But in fragments fascinating. – Only it's not what the vulgar public calls 'readable.' It is, really, a rather mixed bunch of comments. But myself, I like it extremely. Send me whatever remaining MS. there is, and we will see how we can arrange. We'll get it published. What I shall have to do is to write a comment on the Apocalypse also, from my point of view – and touching on yours – and try to give some sort of complete idea. Then the public will be able to read you. As it is, you will be to them like an old-fashioned book of Euclid, Problem I, Problem II – Theorem III – all difficult and all disconnected.

But you do give one a peculiar and glad liberation into the living cosmos, the big old pagan cosmos, the macrocosm. It was the same in the old MS. – something splendid. Usually you are a muddle and your style is often so bad. But then, in moments, it is so good, and there is the grand liberation into the big world, the vital relation to the cosmos. One must take what one gets. – Only, of course, the public[4] will get nothing out of it, unless it's put before them with a sort of guide or approach.

---

[1] *The Mycenaean Tree and Pillar Cult and its Mediterranean Relations* (1901) by the distinguished archaeologist Sir Arthur John Evans (1851–1941) was neither 'huge' (120pp) nor 'expensive' (6s).

[2] Later (Letter 5425) described as 'a friend', Francisca Ewald was proposing to translate one or more of DHL's stories into German (see Letters 5359 and 5386); nothing came of her plans.

[3] 'The Rocking-Horse Winner' in *The Ghost Book* (1926) and 'The Lovely Lady' in *The Black Cap* (1927); 'Mother and Daughter' in *Criterion* (April 1929); 'The Blue Moccasins' in *Eve* (November 1928).

[4] MS reads 'pubic'.

The drawings, I'm sorry, I don't like. Just what you get, in snatches, in your prose, the wonder of the great cosmos, you seem to me to miss entirely in a drawing like 'Silence in Heaven'.[1] It is modern, and all things modern are merely shallow. It is Blake, without *Blake's* substantial quality, his solidity. That face with the fingers is cheap, modern, and slightly vulgar. The illustration to Tourneur is also rather cheap and vulgar.[2] I'm not speaking of craftsmanship, merely of *concept*. In both, the concept is trivial and a little vulgar. You have a vulgar side to your drawings. – I preferred the older drawings, in line and much more abstract. But I don't think you *are* a good artist with the pen, because your *concepts* are rather trashy. I think this is because you are working all the time from wrong impulse-sources. The first impulse to your drawings is either Greek (Athens) or else Jewish. You make a greater mess with the Jewish even than with the Greek inspiration. But both are really false to you. You are working, in your drawings, with a false inspiration all the time. What fascinates you essentially is the great pagan vision of the eastern Mediterranean, pre-Athenian. I wonder you don't take your inspiration from that world – the Mycenean, Cretan, Etruscan things. The winged bulls, the panthers rampant at the altar, the winged horses with strange bearded heroes, the heroes at the wells, the dogs that bite the thighs of the struggling hero, the bulls that attack, the bulls that rest, the wild boar of the north – and all the time that queer *otherness*, with none of that boring Greek 'beauty', nor that Jewish nasal ethics. Do you know the paintings and sculptures of the Etruscan tombs in Italy? fascinating, especially the older ones. Go to Alinari's and look at the photographs of the tombs in Tarquinia (Corneto) and Cerveteri – all the Etruscan photographs – and catch that curious magic, Cretan or whatever it is, and leave the Parthenon frieze and gothicised Blake alone. I hate allegory in drawings – one wants *experience* revealed, not allegory.

Forgive me if all this is impertinent.

I have ordered your Elkin Mathews book, perhaps I shall like the drawings in that.

Would you be so good as to give Charles Lahr a list of one or two books on the Apocalypse that you think are really interesting? And is there a good annotated edition of Revelations itself, or of the New Testament? or the Bible. Charles Lahr would send them me, if you gave him the titles. I hate

[1] Reproduced in *Library Chronicle of the University of Texas at Austin*, xxxiv (1986), 49.
[2] The Fanfrolico Press published *The Works of Cyril Tourneur*, ed. Allardyce Nicoll, with decorations by Carter, in April 1930.

reading German, but will do so if necessary. The two French books you mention I will order in Paris.[1]

We will make a joint book. I very much want to put into the world again the big old pagan vision, before the *idea* and the concept of personality made everything so small and tight as it is now. Do you insist on your drawings as illustrations?

We have taken this house for six months, and are moving in today. Perhaps you will be coming this way, some time during the winter.

ever   D. H. Lawrence

5358. To Laurence Pollinger, 3 October 1929
Text: MS UT; Unpublished.

Villa Beau Soleil, *Bandol.* Var. France
3 Oct 1929

Dear Pollinger

Thanks for the *Obscenity and Pornography* typescript, with letter. Will you tell Faber & Faber they can make the deletions they specify. –

We are living in this villa now – will you take the address – quite nice, and peaceful – sound of the sea.

ever   D. H. Lawrence

5359. To Else Jaffe, 4 October 1929
Text: MS Jeffrey; Frieda Lawrence 295–6.

Villa Beau-Soleil. Bandol. Var. France.
4 Oct 1929

Dear Else

Here we are already in a house of our own, a nice little bungalow villa right on the sea – and with bathroom and all conveniences – and a nice woman to cook and clean. It is very easy, and I like it. I still love the Mediterranean, it still seems young as Odysseus, in the morning.[2] And Frieda is happy. The only trouble is my health, which is not very good. For some reason, which I don't understand, I lost a lot of strength in Germany. I believe Germany would kill me if I had to stay long in it. Now it has killed Stresemann[3] – whom

---

[1] Cf. Letter 5365 and n. 3.   [2] Cf. 'The Argonauts' (*Complete Poems*, ii. 687).

[3] Gustav Stresemann (1878–1929), Chancellor (1923) and Foreign Minister (1923–9) of the Weimar Republic, had died on 3 October. He achieved a rapprochement in Anglo-German and Franco-German relations, negotiated the Locarno Pact (1925) and Germany's admittance to the League of Nations in 1926, in which year he was awarded the Nobel Peace Prize.

will it not kill? – everybody except the Hindenburgs[1] and the old women in the Stifts. Those ancient ones are the terrible fungi, parasites on the younger life.

It is very lovely, the wind, the clouds, the running sea that bursts up like blossom on the island opposite. If only I was well, and had my strength back! But I am so weak. And something inside me weeps black tears. I wish it would go away.

Max Mohr is quite near in the Goëlands hotel – always very nice and willing to do anything he can to help. But also his voice says the same thing over and over again: Alles ist nichts![2] Why must everybody say it? – when it is only *they* who are nothing: and perhaps not even they. When the morning comes, and the sea runs silvery and the distant islands are delicate and clear, then I feel again, only man is vile.[3] But man, at the moment, is very vile.

Perhaps a woman Francisca Ewald, whose husband is brother of the Salem Ewald woman, will write to you about translating some short story of mine. Do advise her all you can.

The Huxleys say they want to come and take a house here – I rather hope they won't. The Brewsters also may come for the winter – their girl is in school in England.

I do hope Marianne is well from her Ischia, and that everything goes pleasantly. Frieda's foot is *nearly* better – still a little stiffness.

ever DHL

5360. To Emily King, 4 October 1929
Text: MS Lazarus; Unpublished.

Villa Beau-Soleil. *Bandol.* Var. France
4 Oct 1929

My dear Pamela

Ada says you aren't very well – I'm sorry about it. Better see your doctor and ask if there is anything he can do for you. I enclose £5. for the purpose. And do get yourself anything you think would do you good.

It is a great trial, this health. Mine went down with a slump, in Germany – I don't know why. But I felt awfully ill there, and though I feel better here, I'm not nearly so well as I was last winter. But I suppose it will come back.

[1] Paul von Beneckendorff und von Hindenburg (1847–1934), a general recalled from retirement to lead Germany in World War I, and again to become President in 1925. In 1933 he appointed Hitler as Chancellor.
[2] 'All is nothing!'
[3] 'Though every prospect pleases,/And only man is vile': 'From Greenland's Icy Mountains', ll. 11–12, the hymn by Bishop Reginald Heber (1783–1826). Cf. *Letters*, iv. 110.

Only it's very bitter, losing ground as I did in Germany. Never will I come north again. – And the doctors, they can do nothing for one. They are merely a fraud.

We are already in this house – very nice, a bungalow right on the sea, and a woman who comes in to do for us. It is very sunny and fresh, I ought to get well again, and I hope to heaven I shall. But I feel so weak, can't make any effort, and want only to be left alone. I've not done any work all summer – but I don't care about that.

Dorothy Warren paid me for the pictures sold, but she is still in Hungary, so I don't know yet about the delivery of the pictures themselves. That is the main point.

Max Mohr is here – in an hotel – and the Brewsters are probably coming for the winter. Harwood is at school in Devon, and the parents are terribly restless. Everybody seems the same, restless and out of sorts. But I hope I can have a really quiet good winter, and get better. We have got the house till end of March, but can keep it longer if we like. Later you might come for a while – if I can chirp up. I'm not really much worse, I don't think – only no strength, and everything is an effort.

I do hope you'll be better. Tell me if there is anything I can do for you – be sure to let me know.

love from us both   DHL

5361. To Earl Brewster, 4 October 1929
Text: MS UT; Unpublished.

Villa Beau Soleil. Bandol. Var, France
4 Oct 1929

Dear Earl

Just a line to say we are in our little house – like it, though it is quite commonplace – people seem nice – and food is good – good yogurt. I think we shall be all right for the winter.

So there we are, and I shan't say a word to persuade you to come, because you *might* not like it – or Achsah might not. Toulon is 25 minutes in the train, Marseille is 1 hour 20 minutes – so the odds are small.

It is windy and rather scirocco – has been lovely –

DHL

4 October 1929

5362. To Nancy Pearn, 4 October 1929
Text: MS UT; Huxley 834.

Villa Beau-Soleil. *Bandol*, Var. France

4 Oct 1929

Dear Nancy Pearn

Herewith the proofs of article for the *Star Review*.[1]

About a contract for a year with *Vanity Fair*:[2] I am quite willing to write articles for them, but it's not much good my promising one a month – I'd be sure to have a perverse period when I couldn't turn one out. And my health, alas, went down rather with a slump in Germany: am feeling feeble. But I like it here, I feel more myself, and if the gods are with me I'll pick up soon, and do you articles and stories. I wish I felt better.

ever   DHL

5363. To Enid Hilton, 5 October 1929
Text: MS UCLA; cited in Moore, *Intelligent Heart* 419.

Villa Beau Soleil. Bandol. Var.

5 Oct 1929

Dear Enid

Yours today. We are here in this bungalow villa – not bad, right on the sea – and a nice woman to cook. I went down in my health badly in Germany, spite of doctors: don't know why.[3] But I felt awful. Here I feel better, but it will take me some time really to recover. Don't go to Germany, it makes one *ill*.

Yes, of course you are to have the *Fire Dance* for £10. – I told Dorothy Warren[4] – and you are not to pay in cash, but, one day, in kind: a weaving or something. The Warren paid me for the sold pictures. – They are in Austria: didn't come to see us. – As for the final disposal of the pictures themselves, I don't know what I shall do about it. – But when the Warren comes back, just demand the *Fire Dance* from her.

Could you send me a copy of *Everyman* with 'The Risen Lord'. I too am surprised they printed it. And would it trouble you to send a copy to Mrs Maria Cristina Chambers, 43 Hillside Rd, Elm Point, *Great Neck*. N. Y.

USA

It has been sunny as usual here, but this morning heavy rain. Now it's

[1] Cf. Letter 5244 and n. 1.
[2] DHL was responding to Nancy Pearn's letter, 23 September 1929 (TMSC UT): '"*Vanity Fair*", I hear, are keen to discuss a contract for a year. Such a contract would entail the delivery of probably one article a month on subjects to be agreed upon, at a sum in the neighbourhood of £40, and would leave us free to negotiate separately over here. Does the idea attract you?'
[3] why] while   [4] Cf. Letter 5334.

coming sunny again already. I really loathe the north, after Germany. Yes, do come here in the spring. We might find you a tiny house – or would your time be too short?

Now the sea is blue again, and the terrace full of light, so I'll get up – having written a newspaper article[1] – and it's nearly noon. – Ada and the 'family' seemed to me rich. I asked her, which family? *I* never married Eddie Clarke, nor yet Sam King. – Excuse beastly letter-card.

DHL

5364. To Rebecca West, 7 October 1929
Text: MS UTul; Unpublished.

Villa Beau Soleil. *Bandol.* Var, France
7 Oct. 1929

Dear Rebecca West

Titus laments to me that you haven't done for him the article on me which you promised for his magazine *This Quarter*, and wants me to ask you if you will do it.[2] And I don't want to bother you. Because of course if you felt like doing it you'd have done it; and why bother about a thing, if you don't feel like it! And don't trouble to answer this letter either, if you don't want to. I shall just say to Titus, if there is no reply, that you didn't feel up to it.

We came down here a fortnight ago, from Germany, where I felt so ill I saw myself entering the New Jerusalem: in handcuffs. Why does one lose one's bit of strength struggling with an abysmal crass world! But I do hope you are better and feeling chirpy. Terrible, how nauseous the world of man can become to one! But the sea helps me to forget – especially the Mediterranean. I swear I'll never go north of Lyon again: the north kills me dead.

Tell me if ever I can do anything for you, in any way. I'm sadder and wiser, and perhaps might.

Sincerely   D. H. Lawrence

---

[1] Probably 'We Need One Another', one of the articles sent to Nancy Pearn on 4 November 1929 for *Vanity Fair*.

[2] Rebecca West wrote nothing on DHL for *This Quarter*. However, he was apparently unaware of her 'Letter from Abroad' in *Bookman* (New York), lxx (September 1929), 88–91, in which she commented on DHL as a painter and on 'six policemen among D. H. Lawrence's pink pictures'. She had described his pictures as 'real paintings . . . England has a right to be proud of him.'

5365. To Edward Titus, 7 October 1929
Text: MS UT; Unpublished.

Villa Beau-Soleil. *Bandol.* Var
7 Oct 1929.

Dear Titus

Your duplicate letter today – the one from Florence has not come on yet.[1]
Orioli may be in Rome, he hasn't written for the last fortnight. – We came
here because the doctors said I ought: since it suited my health so well last

---

[1] Titus wrote DHL on 5 October 1929 (TMSC SIU):

Dear Mr. Lawrence:
  I had a messenger from Lahr in this morning who left a package here that I shall send on to you registered to Bandol.
  Yesterday I wrote to you to Florence and I send you a copy of that letter enclosed.
                                                                    Yours very sincerely,
The enclosure, dated 4 October, reads as follows:

Dear Mr Lawrence,
  I enclose my cheque for Frcs 10,000 on account of your share in the Lady Chatterley venture. You will be good enough to acknowledge the receipt.
  I can now make you this payment because money has begun to come in, and I hope in the course of the current month or sometime next month a more considerable portion will reach the treasury. – The accounts between us will be a very simple matter. As soon as the proceeds of the impression will have been collected, your share, as agreed, will be remitted to you in its entirety, except that I shall retain in hand (if I am dyspeptically inclined at that particular time, – otherwise I shall probably not do it) your share of the cost of the second printing, which, by the way, is not yet completed.
  I hope this procedure will be satisfactory to you.
  You will please let me know, about when the French version will be ready, so that I may make arrangements accordingly.
  What has happened to the Heinemann crowd that they decided not to publish your The Man who Loved Islands? I understand Secker is to do it now. If there is any further difficulty in the matter I might be willing to do it either on a fifty-fifty basis or make you an advance payment as either Heinemann or Secker were to have made you.
  If the Island story is not available I would repeat my former request for a novelette, for which you may name your own price, and if it is at all within current limits, I shall pay it. I have just secured a story from Hemingway for the quartette that I plan, – each novelette to form a nice little volume by itself.
  Rebecca West, who I wrote you promised to let me have an article on you for This Quarter failed thus far to live up to her promise. If it had been on any other theme, I would not take the matter to heart quite so much, – but I would like to keep the Lawrence ball rolling. I have been wondering whether if you know her well enough, you would not give her a hint diplomatically, – or have some one else do it.
  One more thing and I have done:
  If my memory serves me right, you have two or three version of Our Lady in manuscript. Would you consider selling them or either of them, and at what price? Would you be willing to dispose of any other manuscript of your books? Let me know what you have, and the amount asked.
                                                                    Yours very sincerely,

winter. So we have taken this little house for six months. But we both wanted really to go to Italy.

Yes, do retain my share of the cost of the second printing from my share of the profits of the first. But when the accounts for the first printing are in, you will send me a proper statement, won't you!

Gallimards have paid their half-advance on rights for *Lady C.* – about 1,500 francs – so they must be going ahead. They'd never pay such a noble sum into the void, the darlings.

Heinemann even signed the contract for 'Man Who Loved Islands' – and was giving me £300. down, when in shrieked Compton Mackenzie and said *he* was the man who loved islands, but it was a gross libel on him, and he would take instant proceedings. He may have loved islands, but where the libel or the further likeness comes in, I dont see. However, Heinemanns stood back, and I didn't want any more fuss. I doubt *very much* if Secker will be doing the story – unless Compton McK. has given him a special licence. Have heard nothing. Curtis Brown handles the affair. – If you thought you might do a Paris edition, you could write to him – to L. E. Pollinger, that is.

I enclose a letter to Rebecca West;[1] have not seen her for years, and don't know her address. We occasionally, and rarely, exchange a line. But I like her. She is rather ill, I'm afraid, and down.

I'm not very keen on selling my MSS. A man in New York offered me $3,000 for the MS. of *Lady C.*[2] – but I didn't want to part with it. – A fortnight ago my sister wrote she had discovered the MS. of *The Rainbow*, which I thought utterly lost. It was in one of her attics. I haven't told anybody yet.

Could you send me a couple of books – I dont know the publishers – and send me the bill here, or charge me on account, I don't care which – hope it's not a bother

Rituel Journalier en Egypte. – A. Moret.[3]

L'Apocalypse de Jean. Alfred Loisy. Paris 1923

ever   D. H. Lawrence

The book you forwarded from C. Lahr was a copy of *Pansies*. He embarassed me a bit by confessing, a fortnight ago, that when he had the 500 copies of the limited and unexpurgated edition printed, secretly, he ordered at the same time 400 or so copies on cheaper paper, in case the 500 were seized.[4] I knew nothing of this 400. Now there he has them, in London, quite

---

[1] See preceding letter.   [2] The offer came from Barnet B. Ruder (cf. Letter 5217).
[3] Alexandre Moret, *Le Rituel du Culte Divin Journalier en Egypte* (Paris, 1902).
[4] The 400 copies were most probably of the 'so-called popular edition [Roberts A47c]... issued in heavy pink covers' (Roberts 131). See also Letter 5370.

nice. But I can't possibly let them out, it is too mean to Secker and Knopf and the buyers of the 500. So there they must lie, and perhaps some time next year we might sell them at a moderate price. Would you perhaps sell them for me, later on? they could be carried over to Paris by hand. – Or shall I tell Lahr to destroy them? – But please keep this a secret.

5366. To Charles Lahr, 7 October 1929
Text: MS UNYB; Postmark, Bandol 8–10 29; cited in Moore, *Intelligent Heart* 421.

Villa Beau Soleil. *Bandol.* Var.

7 Oct 1929

Dear L[ahr]

I had the book with your letter from Titus this morning. The book looks very nice. I have mentioned to Titus the 400 odd copies and the question of their disposal some time next year. Shall let you know what he says.

No, I don't want to fill a squib all with myself. I *don't want* to figure prominently. I mentioned the subject to Aldous Huxley, but he is both cautious and timid. You might ask Richard Aldington. And you might ask Rebecca West, Sheila K. Smith[1] – a smart woman or two. Let Davies get Sara Salt[2] to work a bit – and Stephensen. Contributions any length, from ten words up: but preferably not more than 100 words, or at most 500. Squibs, not cannon. All anonymous. Don't run my name: don't run anybody's name. Not too much Stephensen. – And if contributions don't come in, we drop the idea: I mean, of course, material contributions, not money. – And give Davies another £10. on 1st Nov.

About the *Gallo Scappato* – the *Verflogene Hahn*[3] – I still haven't got a copy from Paris: they are hitching. The Black Sun is under contract to allow no other edition till after 6 months. But I tell them, they must watch it, and if Pirates threaten, I'll come out with an edition at any moment. I don't want to do a second *limited* edition – one limited edition is enough, in the world. The *Hahn* is not very risky – mildly – rather[4] Gotteslästerung[5] – same idea as in 'The Risen Lord' – But rather lovely. My decorations are a frontispiece, and four other bits, among the text. I shall order you a copy in Paris, so give me the name of someone who will bring it over to you – no danger. – But I *don't want* my decorations reproduced on any but this Black Sun edition. I'd want the Blue Moon (the astrological opposite is the Red Moon) edition to have no[6] decorations. – The Black Sun edition ought to be ready now – and sell in

---

[1] Sheila Kaye-Smith (1887–1955), Sussex novelist, poet and essayist.
[2] Sarah Salt, pseud. for Coralie (von Werner) Hobson (1891–   ), novelist and short-story writer; she was the wife of the 'ripping fellow', Harold Hobson, whom DHL knew in 1912–13 (see *Letters*, i. 443 and n. 3).
[3] *The Escaped Cock.*   [4] rather] more   [5] 'blasphemy'.   [6] no] any

N. York in Nov. If no pirates threaten, we could sell quietly 'but firmly' in April. I don't believe there'd be much risk. However, you can judge. –

Was there anything further with Jackson and the authorities, or did it end there? please tell me.

The Red Lion is the sign of the sun in his destructive or wrathful aspect. Let us hope he'll bite well, he has cause to be wrathful.

I shall do a lovely sign of a Red Lion with a blue moon in his paw. – The blue moon is the moon in triumph – the body ascendant –

L.

5367. To Jean Watson, 9 October 1929
Text: MS UT; Unpublished.

Villa Beau Soleil. *Bandol.* Var. France.
9 Oct 1929

Dear Miss Watson

I'm afraid those German publishers are having a game with you – and with each other – the chief villain in the piece being old Anton Kippenberg, who is falser than seventeen hells. I am waiting to see which of them will pirate the book first – in intense secrecy. Perhaps one of them has already done it – or they are doing it as a joint affair. Anyhow they all know they can buy a copy of *Lady C.* in Berlin, or any of the big towns, for Mark 10. – the Paris edition. It has sold a lot in Berlin – as they know perfectly well. If they are not willing to spend ten Marks, let them whistle. – And there is never any need for you to put yourself to trouble over getting a copy. If you write to

Edward W. Titus. 4 rue Delambre. Paris. XIV

he will forward a copy wherever you wish. – 60 francs – and he can charge it direct to me, just as you like. But the falseness and treachery of German 'business' just now is almost comic. – No, I don't think much of Prince Lœwenstein either.[1] But I'll see what effect I can have direct, and let you know.

I think I must write to Gallimards and ask them to let me see the translation as it proceeds – I'd rather keep an eye on it. Shall I write them direct? – who is their representative? and what sort of people are they? French publishers are weird creatures, too: in another way.

The Italian books haven't come yet. How amusing to get them, after all these years of travail![2] The Italian mountain certainly takes a long time to bring forth a mouse.

Sincerely   D. H. Lawrence

[1] Cf. p. 333 n. 1.
[2] Among the books Jean Watson may have included a copy of Linati's translation: see Letter 5222 and n. 1.

5368. To S. S. Koteliansky, 10 October 1929
Text: MS BL; Postmark, Bandol 11–10 29; Moore 1208–9.

Villa Beau Soleil, Bandol, Var
10 Oct 1929

My dear Kot

Yes, I had your two letters at Rottach – didn't I answer? But there was nothing to say – and I felt so *awfully* ill in Germany – in spite of doctors and attention – they gave me arsenic, the beasts – of course pure poison – that I wonder I ever managed to crawl away. Here I feel much better, and we have got a nice little house on the sea, and I sit on the terrace in the sun, and there is a good woman to cook – so I feel much serener and better. I never want to come north again, while I live.

Curtis Browns seem very huffed with me for making money on the private editions, apart from them. But they had such a scare over *Lady C.* how can they possibly handle the stuff I do in private. Did I tell you Heinemann's wanted to do 'Man Who Loved Islands' – signed contract, and were paying me £300 down – for a private ed. of 500 – when Compton Mackenzie descended on them with a shriek, threatening a suit for libel, and they withdrew.

Do you still have that book *Early Greek Philosophers* which I bought when I was last in London?[1] if so, would you send it me, I want to do some work on the Apocalypse, and consult it. If you haven't got it, no matter.

So there is now Smerdyakov on God![2] I feel it's about time the Great Dragon swallowed that small fry of treachery. But England will stand hypocrisy for ever.

DHL

5369. To Frederick Carter, 10 October 1929
Text: MS UT; cited in Moore, *Intelligent Heart* 423.

Villa Beau Soleil. *Bandol.* Var, France
10 Oct 1929

Dear Carter

I received 'Apocalyptic Images', and am reading it.[3] It is now quite an

---

[1] DHL had been acquainted with John Burnet's *Early Greek Philosophy* (Edinburgh, 1892) since at least 1915 (see *Letters*, ii. 364 and n. 4). For the significance of the book to his present concerns see *Apocalypse* 13–14.

[2] Murry had just published his *God: An Introduction to the Science of Metabiology* (October 1929). Smerdyakov is a slimy and hypocritical character in Dostoievsky's *The Brothers Karamazov.*

[3] Carter's MS which DHL was reading contained an essay with this title.

argumentative work, if you go on you will equal Archdeacon Charles.[1] It
interests me very much – but as it becomes more scientific and 'adequate' it
tends to lose some of the magic. But I have only read about a third, so far –
and I love reading it.

I have also got your Elkin Mathews book – and I read that with great
pleasure too – keep turning back to it.[2] It is queer, you have such a nice
sensitive feeling for the wonder of the world – and yet you tend, more
nowadays, to kill it with a certain intellectual hardness. Let the damned
dead fuddled scholars be scholastic – what we want is the magic of the deep
world, and you can give it, especially in glimpses. – It is funny, but your
drawings don't give it a *bit* – they are hard, insensitive, done from the will,
in a way *forced* out – and no delicate feeling at all – but none – all bullying
and unreal. One has to be very sensitive to draw the human body – and still
more sensitive, to draw it as indicating the movement of the soul. I'm afraid
you are going hard and monkish. [...][3] – But send me all the MS., and then
we can decide what is to be done. – The older – more amateurish *Dragon*
might be dressed for the great public – But the 'Heaven and Hell' would
have to be in the list of scholastic or serious works, higher criticism, I am
afraid.

I have got 'Charles' from Lahr – two fat vols – and have ordered Moret
and Loisy in Paris. I do hate John's Jewish nasal sort of style – so uglily
moral, condemning other people – prefer the way Osiris rises, or Adonis or
Dionysus – not as Messiahs giving 'heaven' to the 'good' – but life-bringers
for the good and bad alike – like the falling rain – on the just and unjust[4] –
who gives a damn? – like the sun. Spring doesn't only come for the moral
Jew-boys – for them perhaps least.

DHL

Poor Machen, that was a feeble introd. to your book. He never *read* you.

---

[1] Robert Henry Charles (1855–1931), Archdeacon of Westminster and a distinguished biblical
scholar, author of the two-volume *Critical and Exegetical Commentary on the Revelation of St
John* (Edinburgh, 1920).

[2] See Letter 5356 and p. 506 n. 2. Carter's book had an introduction by Arthur Llewelyn Jones
Machen (1863–1947), novelist.

[3] A sentence is scored out in a different ink; it may have read: 'That poor wife of yours'.

[4] Matthew v. 45.

5370. To Edward Titus, 10 October 1929
Text: MS UT; Unpublished.

Villa Beau Soleil, *Bandol.* Var.

10 Oct 1929

Dear Titus

Thanks for yours – to which I reply at once.[1] – Yes, my affairs in U.S.A. are a mess. My royalties from Seltzer, on, I think, nine books – mostly novels – was $49. – for the last six months. There's where I am. You know Seltzer went virtually broke – and joined with Albert Boni. Since then (three years ago) they have let many of my books go out of print, so they can't be bought at all in America. – I have worried Curtis Brown all along to get me away from Seltzer – and they are still fuddling. In the spring Albert Boni was in London when I was in Paris – when I saw you. Boni saw Pollinger (of Curtis Brown)

[1] Titus wrote on 9 October 1929 (TMSC SIU):

Dear Lawrence:
    I received your letter and I hope Auriol will send you the check in due course. In case there is more than the usual delay I can easily send you another check to Bandol and cancel the first. Just as you like.
    After I wrote my last letter to you it so happened that I had a visit from Mr. Reeves, one of the big men at Heinemann's in London. He, Nelson Doubleday, the head of the big publishing house in American, and Michael Arlen called together. They came again two days later and we had an afternoon together at Ernest Hemingway's.
    While at my house they spoke of you. You have a great friend in Arlen and if I must take second place to him so be it. In the course of the conversation we all thought that you were not getting anything like what you should out of your American affairs. I hope sincerely that you will not think I am butting in where I have no place to be. But I venture to enclose a letter which I just received from Reeves of Heinemann's, strictly for your private information. Please return it to me. The letter speaks for itself.
    The question arose whether your relations with any agents or agent would not preclude an outsider to take this matter up. The point is that if Doubleday himself were to try to buy out the interests of American publishers he would be asked a monstrous price. It was then that I suggested submitting propositions, and being a publisher in a small way, the American publishers pretensions might be correspondingly reduced. This accounts for the letter. I must add that this letter is apparently the result of further conversations on this subject between the three men mentioned. They all went to London together the other day and the letter enclosed puts it up to both you and me. You might as well understand that I seek nothing for myself in the proposition, but if I can do anything it will make me very happy.
    Reeves told me the whole story regarding the MAN WHO LOVED ISLANDS and your letter coincides completely with what he said. I might add that he even offered the sheets to me. No conditions were mentioned. I have since discovered that the story had already been published in book form in America which, of course, would measurably decrease my interest in it as a commercial proposition.
    I am terribly sorry over what you have said regarding PANSIES. I think it is a dirty trick. The book probably could be sold provided the point is made clear. If it were, in some way, clearly distinguished, perhaps the trouble might be cured. You haven't signed the cheaper impression?
    Thanks for the letter to Rebecca West. It will be forwarded.
    Wishing you the best of health, I am,   Yours,   Sincerely and devotedly,
[Frere-Reeves' letter is missing.]

and said he would very much like to bring out a new uniform edition of my work in America, if he could have the promise of future books:[1] and he also promised to pay off Seltzer's debt to me of $4,000-odd. Pollinger wrote me all this to Paris, told me Boni was coming to see me, and said to me – be nice to him, because we shall perhaps fix up this deal with him. – So Boni came – a little Jew in a big overcoat – a bit furtive – and we talked – and he seemed to be in some way under a cloud – but obviously really keen on doing my books in America: He said, had I any objections: I said No, I hadn't. But I could say no more than that, as it was Curtis Brown's affair. Then he wanted to pay me a thousand dollars off the Seltzer debt – pulled out his cheque-book to write a cheque there and then in that little bedroom in the Hotel de Versailles. But it is repugnant to me to have money shoved at me in that way, so I refused, and said would he please do all that with my agent. So he put his cheque book back, and insisted again: was I *sure* I had no objections to his being my publisher in America? – and I said: No, I hadn't. – He said: Well, I go away a much happier man than I came! – He also said, in *any case*, whether I came to him as my publisher or not, he would pay me that outstanding debt of 4000 odd. – So he went. I felt puzzled – I still don't understand why he seemed so under a weight, and why he was so genuinely relieved and restored, when I said I wouldn't mind if he were my publisher. Because he had plenty of money – he said so. – However, I wrote Pollinger just how it was, told him just what I had said, and added that Boni didn't make a *very* good impression on me. Pollinger replied that he agreed entirely, that Boni would *never* do as my publisher in New York; that we must get the books away from him at any cost – and that Jonathan Cape would be the man to do my collected works in America. – Since then, things have fizzled on. Boni has paid not one cent of the debt – Pollinger writes him 'stinging' letters.[2] The last thing Pollinger did

---

[1] books] works
[2] For example, Pollinger wrote to Boni on 5 September 1929 (TMS YU):

... It was clearly and definitely understood by Lawrence and myself that you were sending him, without delay, a cheque for $1000.00 on account of Seltzer's debt to him, and irrespective of any fresh agreement being arrived at for his future work. Lawrence tells me you were prepared to write a cheque for this amount in his hotel bedroom in Paris.

I told you when you were here that Lawrence was very keen to have someone issue a Uniform Edition of his work in America, and stated that if you would do this, I thought Lawrence might be willing to sign a contract with you covering his future work. You stated that you would be happy to publish Lawrence in this form, and would be seeing Cape that afternoon with a view to getting him to transfer "THE COLLECTED POEMS" to you. I also understood you could secure from Knopf the books by Lawrence, on his list.

We have not received your cheque for $1,000.00, nor any word from you that Cape and Knopf would transfer their books to you. Is it to be wondered at, therefore, that we have never sent you a contract for his future work, and have approached another publisher about the publication Lawrence so much desires ...

was to write and ask him if a certain seven of my books were out of print (they are, anyhow), and if he was going to re-print them? – No answer to this. – Now I *know* Boni will never deal with Pollinger – Pollinger hasn't treated him quite right – and Boni is a sort of rat in a corner, not so easy to handle. It is impossible for me to do anything – Boni would just say: Have you still any objections to my being your publisher? – and I should have to say: Personally, no! but my agents seem to think there are insuperable objections.

So there we are. Curtis Browns are simply incompetent to deal with my case in New York. Their New York office is a *dud*. I have a friend over there who has been finding things out. – I have told Pollinger plainly what I think of their New York end – and he is offended with me – also offended because [. . .] I arrange *Lady C.* and the [. . .] limited *Pansies* apart from them. Well, they were so terrified over *Lady C.* when the fuss came, I spare them any more danger – and then they take offense because I manage my own affairs when these affairs fall outside their scope. – Pollinger is pretty good, on the English side – but how *can* he handle the New York thing? And Edwin Rich, the New York manager of Curtis Brown, must be a sort of kitten who only wants to be loved: a real dud, who loathes my 'compromising' connection. He 'disapproves.' He must be genteel: he loves Alfred Knopf!!! – Knopf, who has been mean to me, promised to publish anything I offered and then when I asked him particularly, please to get my poems collected (they also lay dead, with Huebsch, Kennerley and Seltzer), said it wasn't worth his while – so Cape collected the *Poems* in America, and is quite satisfied with having done so, and will no doubt publish my collected works when the chestnuts have been pulled out of the Boni-Seltzer-Knopf fire. He won't pull them himself – I suppose it *is* difficult for another publisher. And Knopf, after going very cold about me, now goes hot again, won't release me, sends verbal messages saying I may name my own price and have the money down if I will only go over to him in London as well as New York – etc. (This is all private, please).

Now you are no doubt bored stiff, as I am – but if you can do anything further, I shall be glad. – You would of course have to tell Pollinger. I wonder why Doubledays didn't talk to him either? – But agents are only useful when things are all straight sailing – they can't handle a difficult problem. And they sort of prevent me from doing anything myself –. But I don't want to quarrel with Pollinger, I like him. It's not his fault if their New York office doesn't function properly.

I still haven't heard from Orioli – can't imagine what's happened to him.

Yes, a bore about those 400 *Pansies*.[1] Of course I've not signed them – and they are on more ordinary paper – and bound in red stiff paper – and the drawing is not included – no, they are quite different from the proper 500. And there is no suggestion that they are a limited edition – just ordinary. But still they are a nuisance. Let them lie, however.

Do you know Albert Boni? I didn't really dislike him. But I can't bear it when men are sort of furtive.

My affection to Michael Arlen – I always stick up for him, too – in Germany, battles.

I suppose you'll get me those two books –

lovely weather here, and I feel better.

D. H. Lawrence

We are in a house now – no longer in the hotel.

The letter is sure to come on from Orioli in due course.

5371. To Maria Huxley, [10 October 1929]
Text: Huxley 833.

Villa Beau Soleil. Bandol
Thursday

My dear Maria, –

Your letter this morning – awfully good of you to do the notes – they'll do nicely.[2] Was writing a few poems: then the essays. They have so neglected the olives here, that the oil is bad and bitter.

So you are off to Spain! Spain is *hard*, so don't let it tire you. I shrink from it at the moment. But you'll be thrilled to your marrow, I'm sure. How long will you be gone?

Here we shall sit, thank God, pray God! – still. And if you *seriously* think you want a house, say just what and how, and we can tell the agent, nice man, to scout around and have something ready for you to look at.

Sitting on terrace, the sun goes so early in the west – but lovely and warm, wind a bit cold, but I don't get it – sea blue and troubled, splashing white foam up on the islands. We are not on Bandol harbour, but to the west, more open.

Think of us in the Ramblas at Barcelona.

Such dark paw-marks of the wind on the sea! Here, to me, it is something like Sicily, Greek, or pre-Roman. Yet think how bored you might get with it!

Allora, buon' viaggio e buon' divertimento,[3] and always be content to *miss* something rather than get really tired.

---

[1] Cf. Letters 5365 and 5366.   [2] Cf. Letter 5352 and n. 1.
[3] 'So, have a good journey and a good time'.

Frieda has got a piano.

Foam on the islands, and a far-off sail of a ship.[1] I feel like John on Patmos, and am just as frightened of the Beast-mystic number 666 – was it?[2]

DHL

5372. To Richard Johns, 10 October 1929

Text: MS UD; *A Return to Pagany*, ed. Stephen Halpert (Boston, [1969]), p. 21.

Villa Beau Soleil. *Bandol. Var.* France
10 Oct 1929

Dear Mr Johns

I had your letter today. There's nothing on hand I can find for *Pagany* – my health has been so bad lately. But if you are a 'sincere speculative venture' and not a new flower of literary artifice, you might like the 'Risen Lord' article – which has not appeared in America – at least I suppose not.

Edwin Rich – Curtis Brown Ltd. 116 West 39th St. New York City will tell you for sure. They are my agents. It is an article most magazines would jib at. If you want it, tell Rich I accept your terms. And if you do take it, would you be so good as to tell

Mrs Maria Cristina Chambers. 43 Hillside Rd. Elm Point. Long Island, N.Y.

But you may not want a thing that has appeared in England. – I might send you a couple of poems.

Yours Sincerely   D. H. Lawrence[3]

5373. To Maria Chambers, 11 October 1929

Text: MS StaU; cited in Schorer 66.

Villa Beau Soleil. *Bandol. Var.* France.
11 Oct. 1929

Dear Maria Cristina

Your letters to us both today, also cheque for $100. The cheque I have torn up, as I intend you to keep those hundred dollars for your running about expenses.

---

[1] See 'The Greeks Are Coming!' (*Complete Poems*, ii. 687).   [2] Revelation xiii. 18.

[3] Richard Johns – editor of the new 'Little Magazine' – read 'The Risen Lord' attentively but decided that, despite the temptation to have DHL's name on the cover of the first issue of *Pagany*, 'if all that was available from an established and honored author was an unimportant Sunday Supplement sort of piece', something 'fresh, exciting, and young in imagery' should be preferred. 'The article was returned with thanks and regret that it would not be used. Thus the name of Lawrence never appeared as a contributor, for he died soon after *Pagany*'s inception' (*A Return to Pagany*, ed. Halpert, p. 20).

So sorry about the scratched leg, and do hope it will heal soon. Now you want your stone back. Shall I send it?

I enclose two photographs – You can get them reproduced quite cheaply at any photographers – many as you like.

Yes, your man could have any number of the Paris *Lady C* if he could get them in – there's the rub.

Yes, I had my money all right for the *Skirmish* – quite apart from Rich. And Curtis Browns in London want to handle it on this side! – But I think Mencken is right,[1] and a magazine won't publish it now that it has appeared in an edition of 500. – I told CB.'s also about the *Vanity Fair* reproductions, and that it was my affair. – I don't think Crownieshields would mind[2] your offering the other pictures to other people *after* his four have appeared. – He wants, through Curtis Brown, to make a contract with me to give him an essay a month – I couldn't trust myself to write one every month, I'm afraid.[3]

I saw the review of *Lady C.* in the *New Republic*[4] – Brett sent it. – There will be a review of the book in Jan. in *Pagany* (Boston).[5] By the way, I offered the editor 'The Risen Lord' article which has appeared in *Everyman*, a copy of which you will receive – and I asked him to let you know if he accepted it. (Richard Johns, 94 Revere St. Boston)

I am waiting still for a copy of *The Escaped Cock* from Paris – and for an answer to my letter. They are very high-handed, these precious little people. – Don't give my letter to Harry Marks just yet – unless you've done so – Spy out his land a bit first.

We have got this little house on the sea for six months, so the address is good. It is a rocky sea, very blue, with little islands way out, and mountains behind Toulon – still a touch of Homer, in the dawn – we like it – and it is good for my health. The Moros[6] are setting off today for Spain in the Morrrra's car. They want to come and take a house here also in Dec!!

I do hope all goes well.

DHL

[1] Probably Henry Louis Mencken (1880–1956), American literary editor and critic.
[2] mind] my
[3] Maria Chambers later recalled:

I had persuaded my friend Frank Crowninshield, Editor of *Vanity Fair*, to reproduce some of Lawrence's paintings in his magazine; and had his formal assurance to give Lawrence a year's contract for a monthly essay. But, alas! In one of Lawrence's last letters he surprised me with the news that he found himself unable to accept the magazine contract because of his health's "being a nuisance."' (Chambers 119)

Cf. Letters 5362 and n. 2, 5471 and n. 1.
[4] A review by Edmund Wilson, 'Signs of Life: *Lady Chatterley's Lover*' in *New Republic*, liv (3 July 1929), 184–5. Wilson considered the novel one of DHL's 'most vigorous and brilliant ... Lawrence has written the best descriptions of sexual experience which have yet been done in English.'
[5] No such review is known.   [6] I.e. the Huxleys.

5374. To Laurence Pollinger, 11 October 1929
Text: MS UT; Unpublished.

Villa Beau Soleil. *Bandol.* Var. France
11 Oct. 1929

Dear Pollinger

Herewith the signed contract for Faber & Faber[1] – wonder what we'll make on that little venture – if 100/-! (shillings, I mean).

Orioli writes he is willing for you to arrange the public sale of the Lasca translation – and, I presume, of all the others of the Lungarno Series. He will send you two copies of *Doctor Manente* as soon as he has the book from the binder: and he says, if some publisher undertakes to publish the book – or the series – wouldn't it be as well to sell the rights for a lump sum: that is, I suppose, sell each book outright as it appears. It might be better, save a lot of fuss with little royalties. At the same time, if we managed to get a *scholastic* sale, it might be unwise. But you can judge.

Yes, that looks a bit of an impasse with Albert Boni – I must also put my wits to it.

I'm glad Dahlberg's *Bottom Dogs* is really coming out. I felt a bit mean hooking that £20, as it has to be subtracted from his royalties. – Then he wrote me from New York, a wee bit spitefully, that my Introduction was doing him harm, Huebsch saying it was a 'bad sales' letter' – whatever that may mean. – What are Simon & Schuster like? do you know?[2]

As for *Birds Beasts* – Secker will try to get half, you'll see. – And the only person with any rights now in U.S.A. is Cape – whether you need his permission or not, I don't know. Perhaps better mention it to him.

Hope my wife doesn't bother you – I ask her to leave my affairs alone, but she feels the usual 'call.'

ever   D. H. Lawrence

5375. To Giuseppe Orioli, 11 October 1929
Text: MS UCLA; Unpublished.

Villa Beau Soleil. Bandol. Var. France
11 Oct. 1929

Dear Pino

I thought you were in Rome – what a *nuisance*, that passport! – I have the two letters – Titus with 10,000 frs. for *Lady C.* – 'on account.' – I do hope the trunks won't be an awful trouble to you. And ask[3] Egidi if it would be better to send them by sea, Livorno to Marseille –

---

[1] Cf. Letter 5309 and p. 468 n. 1.   [2] New York publishers; they published *Bottom Dogs* in 1930.
[3] MS reads 'as'.

Pollinger says he will be glad to find a publisher for the *Lungarno Series* – so will you send him *direct* the two copies of *Doctor Manente* when the book is ready – to

> 6 Henrietta St. Covent Garden. W.C. 2.

I have asked him about selling the book outright – and he will give his opinion when he has read Lasca now. – Then I shall ask him to make the final agreement with you: and I suppose it will be for the whole series – provisionally. – I don't let them come in between you and me on the private edition.

We are in our little house – and it's very nice, so sunny, right on the sea. And the sea is not like Forte – there are mountains and little islands and is still, in the dawn, a bit Homeric. You must come and see. Frieda, of course, is pining for her things.

Maria and Aldous are setting off for Spain today. Then in November she too wants to come and look for a house here: hates the Suresnes house.

I don't at all know how much you should ask for *Lady C.*. What price have you put in your catalogue? £4. or £5.? Do as you think best. – I suppose you had the letter from Milan.

love from both.   DHL

5376. To Edward Titus, 11 October 1929
Text: MS UT; Unpublished.

Villa Beau Soleil, Bandol, Var.
11 Oct 1929

Dear Titus

I heard from Orioli this morning – been in Rome – and he sent me your cheque – many thanks.

At the risk of boring you, I enclose part of a letter from my agents this morning.[1] You will see how successful they are. In my opinion, if they are going to stick absolutely stuck in the Boni rut, then they'd better have made a proper wholesome contract with him to handle my work – and I believe he'd have done his best. But you see how things stand. I should be glad to hear what you think.

Ever   D. H. Lawrence

I have told Pollinger, anyhow, I am going to act direct in the matter, if I can – so I feel quite free now to take steps.

---

[1] Enclosure missing.

5377. To Charles Lahr, 11 October 1929
Text: MS UNYB; cited in Moore, *Intelligent Heart* 421.

Villa Beau Soleil. Bandol. Var.
11 Oct. 1929

Dear L[ahr]

I got Carter's book, and the two vols of Charles' 'Apocalypse' – and I've ordered two French books in Paris. So now don't send me any more Apocalypse or I shall feel stuffy about it. How they jaw-jaw-jaw! these scholars! But many thanks for the books – and send me a bill – Oh, send me a good New Testament with notes, if there is such a thing. That's all. Please!

Not a word from Paris about the *Hahn.*[1] Tricky people! Wait a bit.

I don't believe the post is opened, and I don't believe there is any 'perfect espionage' either. I heard the packets were in Mallorca – but they wouldn't deliver them to the friend whose address I gave them – though they handed all letters over – but not *parcels*. Parcels are sacrosanct, because you can *claim* on them. And you[2] *must* have put a sender's address on the voucher which accompanies every foreign parcel – you must have put his address – the slip with senders name and address is delivered abroad with the parcel itself, and *you have* to fill it in – so there is no mystery: no need to write to Postmaster – and of course charge me the postage. But they are very fussy about foreign parcels.

Absurd of Davies to balk at those ten quid. Tell him no such nonsense. He is quite right to be independent with publishers, but what's the point of being independent with you and me!

The cartoon of the swooning policemen is amusing![3] – I've got poems to fix, exactly. – But I feel the squib is not going to go off. There *must* be more than me to it.

Kot loves to feel Russian and spied upon. Nothing in it.

ever.   DHL

I think Harcourt Brace are pretty good – but not always – and who is their connection on this side? Tell him to ask them how much they'll give him for the English rights, *outright.*[4]

---

[1] Cf. Letter 5366 and n. 3.
[2] And you] And Davies had sent something registered to Frau Frieda – and you
[3] Cf. Letter 5329.   [4] they'll ... *outright.*] they'll sell him the English rights for, *outright.*

5378. To Douglas Goldring, [14 October 1929]
Text: MS UTul; Postmark, Bandol 16 –10 29; Douglas Goldring, *Odd Man Out* (1935), pp. 261–2.

Villa Beau Soleil, Bandol. Var.
Monday

Dear Goldring[1]

How amusing to hear from you again. I always asked after you and had bits of your news, so knew all, except the new wife. As for Betty and Brian, we had dinner with them in Manchester Square or somewhere, three years ago: and I laughed to myself, for Mistress Betty had put her foot in it, the bourgeois trap had got her by the hind leg, and she was already pulling. We talked of you, and I could tell she was longing for the old days of Douglas and poverty and woes: Brian Lunn chipping in – 'Er – what kind of wine do you prefer, Lawrence?' – that inestimable English voice. He is one of those English gentlemen (surely!) who make one want to flip a serviette in his face and say: Shut up, you! – Poor Betty – poor Brian! But I knew she'd go once she could get her leg out.

We've got this little house for the winter, I'm hoping my health will be better – it's devilish bad. If only I knew what to do about it. – Am miserable.

If we come Nice way – not likely, but you never know – I shall write you first – and if you come this way, do come and see us. The house is too little for guests, but the village is nice. It would be fun to talk things over – must be ten years since we met.[2] – Aunt Ada and Uncle Fritz have just sailed to India, where he is to sit in the Chair of Arabic in Delhi. But since *Lady C.* we are not on writing terms. But I feel I *must* make the peace. I *must* hear Aunt Ada on Delhi!! Do you remember them? – Hermitage?[3]

If only I was well, I'd come to Nice for a week.

Greetings from both   D. H. Lawrence

[1] Douglas Goldring (1887–1960), novelist, playwright and editor, whom DHL had met through Kot in 1919. Goldring was then married to Beatrix ('Betty') Duncan, an actress whom DHL admired and wanted to play the lead in *The Widowing of Mrs Holroyd* (*Letters*, iii. 483). The Goldrings had subsequently divorced. Douglas married Malin Nordström in 1927; Betty married Brian Lunn (1893–) with whom she translated several works from French and German. See *Letters*, iii. 371 n. 3.

[2] Goldring was as eager as DHL to renew their friendship, but was prevented by temporary poverty from making the short trip from Nice. See Goldring, *Odd Man Out*, p. 262.

[3] Goldring recalled meeting Ada and Fritz Krenkow (cf. Letter 4956 and n. 2) in 1919 when he visited Hermitage in Berkshire:

[DHL's] Aunt Ada and his rich and respectable uncle, who owned a stocking factory somewhere in East Anglia, were coming to lunch and Lawrence and I went off to the pub to buy them some beer. He was determined to tap the uncle for enough money to enable him and Frieda to bolt for Italy ... and throughout the meal he was at his chirpiest. During the afternoon, when the relatives had returned to the inn, after inviting him to dinner, we went for a walk and hatched plans for extracting the necessary cheque ... He returned triumphant, in a few hours' time, waving a cheque for £10 and we had an evening of rejoicing! (ibid., p. 251)

5379. To Caresse Crosby, 15 October 1929
Text: MS UT; Postmark, Bandol 16 –10 29; cited in C. Crosby, *The Passionate Years*, p. 232.

Villa Beau Soleil. Bandol. Var.

15 Oct. 1929

Dear Caresse

Yes, I like it very much indeed – The picture came out very well, considering – which is luck. I do hope it goes through all right. Let me know if you
hear from Marks that it is arriving safely.

I want to know how many copies you have kept for me. And surely you will
give me one of the vellum copies, for myself. But I *must* have some of the
others, out of series, to give away. Let me know how many I can have.
Perhaps you would post me one or two from Paris? I mean, to my sisters and
friends, if I sent you the address.

You didn't give me Marks' address, but I wrote him all the same. And are
you enclosing that copy for Mrs Chambers, as I asked you, and telling Marks
to give it her? Please do!

I am having the book set up in London – no decorations – just an ordinary
unlimited edition at, perhaps, 7/6. But I shan't release it till next March or
April, unless there is a pirate appearance.

The gramophone is in Florence, and will probably be sent on here – but it's
quite safe –

We've got this little house till end of March, and are installed, with a
decent cook. But alas, my health is so bad, it went all to pieces in Germany,
and I am in bed again here, feeling pretty rotten. I expect I shall have to go
into a sanatorium for a time, unless I pick up very soon. No use dying just yet.
Do you know a good sanatorium on this coast? – or near Cannes or Nice? Am
thoroughly miserable. Should have loved a marvellous party of celebration.
But it will have to wait a bit. Anyhow we'd have to wait till we knew it was all
safely landed in New York. Perhaps I'll pick up again.

Lovely weather, still sea, soft sun – I lie and look out. But I am miserable
about my health.

How is Harry? how are you? Frieda is pretty well, but a wee bit lame still
from a sprained foot – done in Mallorca.

D. H. Lawrence

5380. To P. R. Stephensen, 15 October 1929
Text: MS Anon; Munro 314–15.

Villa Beau Soleil. *Bandol.* Var.

15 Oct 1929.

Dear Stephensen

The little books came today, two parcels, and thank you very much. We

haven't a thing to read in the house, they are most welcome. I like the look of
them very much.[1]

I am doing the extension of *Jolly Roger*, and shall be pleased to have it come
in this series of little books.[2] And I agree, one doesn't want to overload the
world with unnecessary limited editions. I shall send the MS. to Curtis
Brown in a day or two, and they will let you have the type-script. Am doing a
sort of key to the whole novel – the basic idea.

My *Escaped Cock* story is just out in Paris – just coming – Black Sun Press
– 500 in all – but they are shipping them all to U.S.A. I shall try to send you a
copy – or if anyone is coming from Paris, they might bring you one – It looks
very nice, I think, with colour decorations by me.

I am so miserable, my health went all to pot in Germany, and I am in bed
again, feeling rotten. I'll have to go into a sanatorium if it doesn't pick up.
Frieda still limps a bit – Meanwhile the weather is lovely, with a silent sea and
a soft sun. I lie and look at it. – We are in this little house till end of March.
It's just on the sea – very nice – and a good cook. But I'm down about my
health.

Hope you are well.

                                                                    DHL

5381. To Ada Clarke, 17 October 1929
Text: MS Clarke; Postmark, [. . .]; cited in Lawrence–Gelder 199–200.

                                          Villa Beau Soleil. Bandol. Var.
                                                           17 Oct 1929
My dear Sister

I should have written before, but had a bad cold and been in bed, but
getting up a bit tomorrow. I somehow went all wrong in Germany, in my
health – and this little bout is a result. But it is also a getting straight again – I

---

[1] Stephensen had sent DHL several of the recently published *Mandrake Booklets* (and was to
send three more a fortnight later).

Stephensen's own *Bushwhackers* helped to launch these booklets, along with Rhys Davies's
sensual and horrific story set in a Welsh mining community, *A Bed of Feathers*, and O'Flaherty's sharply satirical *A Tourist's Guide to Ireland*. Other literary friends, including Jack
McLaren, Thomas Burke and Edgell Rickword, contributed stories to the series [Burke's was
A Bloomsbury Wonder] . . . Although the booklets were mostly fiction . . . there was a sprinkling
of what Stephensen described in the first Mandrake catalogue as *belles lettres*: some Dostoevsky
letters translated by Lawrence's friend Koteliansky, an essay on New York by W. J. Turner,
and translations from Gaelic tales by the Hon. Ruaraidh Erskine of Marr. The London
Observer praised the series as beautiful and original, presenting a range of work 'remarkable in
its catholicity.' (Munro, *Wild Man of Letters*, pp. 88–9)

See also Letter 5410 and n. 1.

[2] See Letter 5283 and p. 446 n. 1. *A Propos* was not included in the Booklets series.

shall be better after. Max Mohr is here – the one who lives in Rottach – and he is a doctor, so Frieda doesn't have to bother about that. We have a really good cook for once, so that we can really have excellent light food. The food in the market is so good in itself.

We've been in our little house two weeks now, and like it. It's right on the sea – I lie and watch the sea and the islands, so lovely, this blue, still autumn weather, like a dream.

Tomorrow I expect the Brewsters will arrive. They are coming by Ship from Naples, and will no doubt spend the winter here. I'm glad, it is good to have someone near. The Huxleys have gone to Spain, but say they'll be back in November, and want to come here too. But they are always so restless and unsatisfied. – If we really like it here for this winter, we shall get a house for a permanency – this or another.

About the MSS. – leave them a while, because Pollinger is arranging a safe-deposit box for me, where they can lie and I can have control of them. But the matter isn't settled yet. That little MS. book of poems I would like to have sent to me – but not just now. That I shall neither sell nor give away, it is too intimate.[1]

Dorothy Warren paid for the pictures – but I havent heard a word from her since. I suppose she's still abroad.

The man who printed *Pansies* got in a muddle at the end, and hadn't enough copies. But you'll get your copy eventually, – perhaps on vellum – and Emily hers. And when there is an opportunity I shall send you a copy of *The Escaped Cock* which rich friends have just brought out in Paris – 500 copies, but all going to New York – It is very beautifully done. I don't want it to go to England at all. Did you see 'The Risen Lord' in last week's *Everyman*? or the week before. They asked me for an article, but I was surprised they printed it.

I want my health to get better now – and I feel it will. Germany was curiously bad for me – so was Paris last spring. The fact of the matter is, I shouldn't come north. It always makes me ill. We'd better get a permanent place somewhere down here. – I wrote to Pamela – she says she's feeling better. – If you hear from Aunt Ada do tell me. I want so much to know how she re-acts to India. It'll be a bit hard on her, I'm afraid. It's very trying, that change. Glad I needn't go.

Love to all.   DHL

[1] Probably the Nottingham University College Notebook (Roberts E320.1) which contained early poems, some addressed to his mother and to Ada herself, among others.

5382. To Laurence Pollinger, 17 October 1929
Text: MS UT; Unpublished.

Villa Beau Soleil, Bandol. Var.
17 Oct 1929

Dear Pollinger

I told Stephensen I'd do the *Jolly Roger* enlargement for one of his 3/6 series – and it's nearly done – but it will be *so* unsuitable in that series, with Aleister Crowley and the other Murder stories.[1] Perhaps he'd do it separate, at 3/6. – Shall send MS. in a day or two.

About Boni – will you leave him alone, then, for a bit – let matters stand as they are – and I'll see what I can do myself. I'll let you know the result, if there is any result. Might as well try, anyhow.

Ever   D. H. Lawrence

5383. To Edward Titus, 17 October 1929
Text: MS UT; Unpublished.

Villa Beau Soleil, Bandol, Var
17 Oct 1929

Dear Titus[2]

I have written Pollinger to ask him please to leave the Boni matter alone now, and to let me try what I can do myself – and that I will report the result to

---

[1] Cf. Letter 5310 and n. 2.

[2] DHL was responding to Titus's letter, 15 October 1929 (TMSC SIU):

Dear Mr. Lawrence:

I am obliged to you for the additional information you so fully supplied. I have since heard again from Mr. Frere-Reeves of Heinemann's. I enclose his note for your information. Please return it.

I think a tactical error was committed by Curtis Brown when they wrote to Seltzer that unless new editions are published the books would be sold to another publisher. A remark like that would naturally get a man's back up instantly. They could have had that in mind without saying so. I am going right ahead with an offer to acquire the various copyrights. I will make my proposition in a very modest sort of a way and rather casually, showing no very keen interest. I will say that the price being agreeable to me, payment will be made in cash right off the bat. I only ask you to be good enough to give me your promise that as far as you may be concerned, you will let nobody, no agent, or anybody else meddle with the affair, unless my efforts have failed and I am obliged to throw up the sponge. On the other hand, I shall get a promise from the prospective purchasers of the copyrights that they will stand by me and agree to take over the copyrights in case I have been successful, subject naturally to any further agreement that may have to take place between you and them as to the future.

... Whatever you may think of Cape as a successful publisher I personally do not believe he will set the Thames on fire in America. I should leave him quite alone for the present.

I want you to understand that personally I seek no emolument in this matter for myself. I am not wallowing in wealth by a long shot but I am not out for any compensation in this particular affair. I will only ask you to do as little correspondence on the subject with others as you consistently can. I would not even let Curtis Brown know that Titus [h]as anything to do with the

him. That seems all that is necessary for the time being. I'll ask him what he thinks of Doubledays on some other occasion, à propos of something else.

Many thanks indeed for your help. It'll be a good thing if we can get that American side straightened out. Of course there's Alfred Knopf.

I shan't tell anybody at all that you are moving in the matter.

ever   D. H. Lawrence

5384. To Käthe Mohr, 21 October 1929
Text: MS HMohr; Mohr, *Briefe* 535–6.

Villa Beau Soleil. Bandol. Var.
Monday 21 Oct 1929

Dear Frau Käthe

You wrote about sunshine, and it is raining hard, the mistral is blowing cold and bitter, the sea is grey-green, the waves splash white and spiteful against the island, the clouds move on and on, in layers, and this is the Land wo die Citronen blühen – und dein Mann fährt heute fort.[1] Blessed is he that expecteth little, for he shall not be disappointed.[2] So don't expect much of the sunny South, and you may even get a blue sky. – Ich bin im Bett – war erkältet, und hatte schlechtes Blut in der Brust, von Deutschland (!) Jetzt aber ist es weg, und ich fühle mich leichter und mehr mich. Doch ärgere ich mich über meine Gesundheit.[3] – But I can't go to Toulon with Mohr, so Frieda and Achsah are going. They start off in a taxi at two o'clock, and they want to buy things in Toulon. When the wind blows and the rain rains, Toulon is perhaps the coldest and most uncomfortable place on earth, so *there*'s a nice start for home and Wolfsgrube!

But we are sad that Mohr is going. It seems so natural, so familiar here, so easy. It's a pity you didn't come with us and have a house, then you would have stayed *all* the winter, and we would even have played bridge. But come in January – really, don't wait till February. Come in January, and have a house and forget all the north, even your beloved Wolfsgrube. It is so good to

business. Let it for the present remain a little secret between you, Doubleday, Heinemann's and myself. Arlen know[s] about it and Ernest Hemingway also, as the matter was touched upon at his place one day when we were all of us calling on him.

The two French books that you want me to get for you I am trying to get. I have already asked my Paris jobber to find them for me. As soon as I get them they will be forwarded to you.

If the Rainbow manuscript is for sale let me know what you would ask for it.

Yours very sincerely,

[1] 'land where the lemons blossom [Goethe, "Mignon Lied", l. 1; "Kennst du das Land, wo die Zitronen blühn"] – and your husband is leaving today.'
[2] Proverbial: see *Oxford Dictionary of English Proverbs*, ed. F. P. Wilson (Oxford, 1970), p. 66.
[3] 'I am in bed – had a cold, and had bad blood in the chest, from Germany (!) Now it's gone, however, and I feel lighter and more myself. But all the same I'm angry about my health.'

forget. You will see from Mohr: er schimpft nicht mehr über Berlin, Gott sei
dank. Ich auch nicht. Wie zwei Ringtauben *roucoulen* wir.[1]

Wolfsgrube and the Angermaier seem so far, and the Frau Marie ist wie
eine Persone aus einem Bauerngeschichte[2] – Why do I keep dropping into
German? – And Vroni lebt nur in einem Mohrdrama. – Oh weh! das Wetter
wird schlechter, das Meer ist halb verschwunden im Regen, und der Mohr
hat weder Mantel oder Schirm. Höre mal, das Regen ist wie geärgert,
spukt auf das Fenster wie eine wutende Katze. Und es ist schon halb Zwei.
Gott sei dank, ich bin warm in Bett, ich schaue aus, und sehe, wie furchtbar
ist die Welt, und mache keinen Schritt dahin. Gott sei dank, ich fahre nicht
heute Nacht nach Paris.

Gruss die Eva.[3] It will be good for her to come out of Germany and see that
there are all sorts of people in the world. Now she thinks there are only
Bürger and Bauern[4] – when she finds there are Französer und Gott weiss
was, wird sie ganz neue Ideen bekommen.

Also auf Wiedersehen, im Neujahr, und leb' wohl, und wenn etwas
schweres kommt, wo ich helfen könnte, sag' es mir nur.[5]

DHL

5385. To Laurence Pollinger, 21 October 1929
Text: MS UT; Unpublished.

Villa Beau Soleil, Bandol, Var.
21 Oct 1929.

Dear Pollinger

I haven't got a copy of *Birds Beasts and Flowers* here, but will get one, and
see if there is any point or amusement in a hundred-word caption before each
of the nine parts. If I see any point, and can do it, I'll do it, but at present feel
perfectly blank before the idea.

[1] 'he doesn't grumble about Berlin any more, thank God. I don't either. We *coo* like two
ring-doves.'
[2] 'Frau Marie is like a person out of a folk-tale'.
[3] 'Vroni lives only in a Mohr-play. – Alas! the weather is getting worse, the sea has half-
disappeared in the rain, and Mohr has neither coat nor umbrella. Listen to it, the rain sounds
enraged, spits on the window like an angry cat. And it is already half-past one. Thank God, I'm
warm in bed, I look out and see how dreadful the world is, and don't take one step into it.
Thank God I'm not travelling to Paris tonight. Greetings to Eva.' (Eva was the Mohrs'
daughter.)
[4] 'bourgeois and peasants'.
[5] 'French people and God knows what, she will acquire completely new ideas. So auf wiedersehen, till the New Year, and goodbye, and if any difficulty comes up, where I could help, just
tell me.'

I bet[1] Secker was mad at being cut down to 50 gns. – good for him.

Of course I can't remember in detail what Boni said or I said last March in Paris. All I remember is that he asked me if I would write an article about the pictures for *The Studio* – and, though a bit surprised, I said I'd try. There was certainly no mention of terms – and I believe there was no mention whatever of *Creative Art* – because I didn't know till the summer, from an American friend, that there was such a paper. Certainly, however, I made no terms whatsoever with Boni – and that's the point. If he prints in his magazine naturally he ought to pay. And if *The Studio* made no mention of acquiring the Amer. rights, when they bought the English rights – well, then they didn't acquire them.[2]

Orioli will send you copies of the Lasca translation. As for my health, it is no better, and I hate it.

ever   D. H. Lawrence

5386. To Caresse Crosby, 23 October 1929
Text: MS SIU; Unpublished.

Villa Beau Soleil. *Bandol.* Var.
23 Oct 1929

Dear Caresse

I haven't heard anything further from you about the book – do let me know.

The Fischer Verlag want to translate it into German – so they say. Could you send a copy of the text to

Frau Francisca Ewald, Nestorstrasse 16. *Berlin – Halensee*

It doesn't matter if the copy is imperfect in other ways, so long as the text is complete.

I've been in bed these last ten days, but am feebly getting up a bit in the afternoon. How I hate this ill health.

Hope you are both flourishing.

D. H. Lawrence

5387. To Aldous and Maria Huxley, 23 October 1929
Text: Huxley 834–5.

Villa Beau Soleil, Bandol, Var.
23 Oct., 1929, Wed.

Dear Aldous and Maria, –

Yours from Barcelona. Glad you like it, but sorry about the cold – which,

---

[1] MS reads 'get'.

[2] See Letter 5042 and n. 1. Nancy Pearn annotated DHL's letter at this point: 'Exactly!'

however, is prevalent here just the same, and I've been in bed with it. I expect your weather has changed – we've had wind and rain since Friday – but calmer and warmer to-day. The Brewsters arrived suddenly from Naples, and are also looking round for a house. She is very *nervosa*, poor dear.

Aldous's book of essays came[1] – and many thanks. I haven't read them all, but 'Baudelaire' seemed to me very good. All needs saying, badly: Wonder what sort of a press it will get.

No news here – Max Mohr has gone back to Germany, but says he'll return here with wife and child in January. The little house – this – which Achsah finds truly terrible because it is so lacking in '*Beauty*,' is quite pleasant, for the time being, and I believe will be cosy enough. It was the 'love-nest' (Frieda's word) of a *femme-tenue*,[2] hence the sunk-in marble bath and rather expensive plumbing, including the central heating. But it is, none the less, a rather hard square box. I mind the hardness most – it's not flimsy. Maria, you may have the stoniest house in the world, if you can find it. When I'm up and about we're going scouting along the coast-plain a bit, with the Brewsters, who love nothing better. Achsah buys every 'beautiful' house that is not for sale. But we'd get a bit of an idea of what's available.

We've got a cat – a young yellow 'marmalade' cat with a white breast, who simply forced himself on us. He is very nice, but I never knew a French cat before – sang-froid, will of his own, *aimable*, but wasting no emotion. I like him very much, but I don't love him – which is perhaps as it should be. He simply abandoned his French home, and howled like a lion on the terrace till I let him live here – he's about eight months, I suppose.

I hope you'll get this – if so, it'll be at Granada, which everybody says is so lovely. Do hope you are cured of the cold and able to enjoy it all, both of you.

Love, DHL

Brewsters having a bad time with their vegetables in the Beau Rivage.[3]

5388. To S. S. Koteliansky, 25 October 1929
Text: MS BL; Postmark, [. . .]; Zytaruk 391.

Villa Beau Soleil. Bandol. Var.
25 Oct 1929

My dear Kot

Thanks for your letters. About coming to England to be near Mundesley, I

---

[1] *Do What You Will* (October 1929).   [2] 'kept woman'.
[3] As Buddhists, the Brewsters were vegetarians.

could never do it.[1] But if my health gets very tiresome, I could go to live near some sanatorium down here, if I knew of a good one, and be under supervision. I would do that. But you see it's quite different supervising lungs, which are straightforward, from supervising what is my real trouble, chronic inflammation of the bronchials and all the breathing passages. The doctors say they think the lung is healed again – the local doctor here said the same – but the bronchitis and asthma are bad – and they don't know what to suggest.

I feel as you do about the Lion. In fact I had already asked him to make a proper bill and square up and finish altogether with the poems. But for some time I haven't heard from him at all. I know he's perfectly honest – but not calm enough. I don't think I shall have him print anything else. I wonder why he's not written lately.

Stephensen sent me the 3/6 books – so I suppose Rosanov will come along in time.[2] I still think, if Rosanov goes, we might rescue Shestov from Secker. I could do it.

We are settled in our little house – very pleasant – We have for once all the conveniences, bath-room, and central-heating plant. They say it works well. The Brewsters – friends from Capri – are here, and probably will take a house for the winter – and the Huxleys, who are now in Spain, say they will come in November. I haven't heard again from Frederick Carter.

I should be quite happy if only my health were better – my miserable bronchials.

My regards – and I hope you are all right.

DHL

5389. To Maria Chambers, 25 October 1929
Text: MS StaU; Unpublished.

Villa Beau Soleil. Bandol. Var.
25 Oct 1929

Dear Maria Cristina

Just a word to say I have your air-letter – (cable) – about Marks, but I can't do anything, as the whole arrangement is made between Mrs Harry Crosby, of the Black Sun Press, Paris, and this bookseller, Marks, and I have nothing to do with it. Moreover Mrs Crosby seems determined I shall have nothing to do with it. But the edition is being posted – or sent some way – to New York,

---

[1] The Mundesley Sanatorium, Norfolk, specialised in the treatment of tuberculosis and other chest diseases; DHL's friends Gertler and Gertrude Cooper had been patients there (see *Letters*, v. 311 and n. 2; vi. 25 n. 1). See also Letter 5428 and n. 3.
[2] See Letter 4830 and n. 3.

in small batches. I have got *one copy* only, and it looks rather lovely, beautifully done. – But keep as quiet about this story as you can – I await now the letter by the *Bremen*.[1]

Hope you managed to hide the moth-bites in your husbands blacks[2] –

DHL

5390. To Edward Titus, 25 October 1929
Text: MS UT; Unpublished.

Villa Beau Soleil, Bandol, Var.
25 Oct 1929

Dear Titus[3]

Thanks for the *Apocalypse*, which came today.

The catalogue of Davis & Orioli is, I suppose, the London catalogue – Davis' – with which Orioli has nothing to do. Anyhow I know nothing about that MS. (typescript) of *Women in Love*. It is another of the MSS. stolen from me, I suppose – by Thomas Seltzer, no doubt. He had the final typescript. – I have never put any MS. on the market – I have sold two small ones only, and given a couple away – but those exposed for sale are all stolen.

No, I *haven't* heard that Heinemanns are doing 'Man Who Loved Islands'. Not a word from Pollinger about it.

Neither have I heard from Gallimards at all. I think they should have their translator collaborate with me – and I want to suggest it. I feel I ought to see

---

[1] *S. S. Bremen*, transatlantic liner of the North German Lloyd line.
[2] I.e. his black or dress trousers.
[3] DHL was replying to Titus's letter, 23 October 1929 (TMSC SIU):

Dear Mr. Lawrence:

   Today's post takes away to you one of the books ordered, – St. Jean, L'Apocalypse. The other has not as yet been received ...

   I have just received a catalogue from Davies & Orioli, wherein I find advertised for sale you[r] original typescript of Women in Love, – "literally full of corrections, additions and alterations in the author's autograph." For which they asked the hefty sum of £275.

   Have you heard again from Pullinger? I have had occasion to see the Gallimard people. They are rather in trouble getting the right kind of people to do the job for them. They want to find a man of letters of some recognized moral standing, to write the introduction to the book. One or two have refused and they finally took my suggestion, which they found a very good one, to try to get Paul Morand, who, as you know, is one of your admirers. I think he is a sufficiently independent man to be able to do what he likes. He is now at Villefranche and I have already asked a mutual friend to write him in a casual sort of way that in case there should be any question as to his writing the introduction, would he please act favorably. So there you are.

   I saw Michael Arlen again yesterday. He told me that Heinemann's have again changed their mind and *are* bringing out The Man Who Loved Islands, but I suppose you know this already. As soon as the second issue of my magazine is ready I may run down South for two or three days, in which case, if I may, I would like to spend a day or two in Bandol.

Yours very sincerely,

that translation as it proceeds. – Huxley told me that Paul Morand was an admirer – but a queer sort of chap to introduce *Lady C.* – I suppose all the other 'moral' ones have turned catholic, like Mauriac and Gabriel Marcel. One could understand better their turning to the bosom of the church if one felt the church had any bosom.

It will be nice to see you here. I expect the Huxleys will be here in November, on their way back from Spain. So you'd see them too.

ever   DHL[1]

5391. To Giuseppe Orioli, 25 October 1929
Text: MS UCLA; Unpublished.

Villa Beau Soleil. *Bandol.* Var
25 Oct. 1929

Dear Pino

No sign of the trunks yet – I will let you know as soon as they arrive. – About the music, the song-books are the chief thing. And when you have time, would you send my English dictionary and the Italian dictionary. I don't want my winter coat – but Frieda would like hers. I think you have to make a special declaration for it: personal property, worn clothing of addressee, or something like that. But don't be in any hurry. It's a shame to bother you.

I think, nevertheless, it is a pity that the Lungarno Series is not offered to one publisher. *If* there was a scholastic sale, it would be very profitable. I have no doubt Aldous and Aldington could easily tell their agents that you were disposing of the public rights of the whole series. I don't see why you shouldn't have a share in the royalties from the public edition, since you do all the work, and the book is only translation. Certainly if you find special introductions, or special notes, then you have a right to a share in the book containing the introduction or notes. – But you must ask Aldous and Aldington. If you can arrange with them, that would establish the rule for the whole series. This series could be made very profitable, if sold *as a series*. If sold as odd little books, there is not much in it. You might put the matter to Aldous

---

[1] Titus wrote again on 31 October 1929 (TMSC SIU):

Dear Mr. Lawrence:

Just a line to straighten things out. I wrote to you in my last note that I heard of the change of mind of Heinemann's regarding the publication of the MAN WHO LOVED ISLANDS. This apparently has been a false alarm. Frere-Reeves of Heinemann's was again in Paris the other day. He came in to see me and when I asked him about it said that they are not publishing it: that in fact the type has been distributed. Michael Arlen from whom I had the news originally, was quite evidently wrong . . .

and Aldington, and say that I propose you should have a share in *public* royalties. – Aldous and Maria are in Spain – they gave me Poste Restante, Granada, as the address. But in November they are coming here to Bandol, and we can talk it over. If we settle the procedure for the first two books, Lasca and Machiavelli, that will bring the others into line. So just tell Pollinger to wait till you have settled matters with the other translators. Of course you can fix a time limit for the public edition – not before three months, or six months, as you like. – We could probably find somebody to write a good essay on Syphilis, once you decide and Aldington agrees to do the poem.[1]

I don't want to sell the MSS. of *Lady C.* – and I don't much want to sell the proofs, though those are not so important. Titus tells me that in Davis & Orioli's catalogue is advertised the type-script of *Women in Love*, for £275. Is that Davis' catalogue? and where did he get the typescript? This must be a stolen thing too – how sickening! Can't one stop this business? – I hear from my sister she has discovered the MS of the *Rainbow* in her attic. Boris was very keen to have that MS. three years ago.[2]

The Brewsters are here from Capri, also looking for a house. I have been in bed with a cold – the weather is rather bad. Frieda has got a piano, but no music yet. I do hope my health will improve this winter – it's been very bad since Germany.

love DHL

Find out what the man would give for the proofs.[3]

5392. To Jehanne Moulaert, 26 October 1929
Text: Huxley 835–7.

Villa Beau Soleil, Bandol, Var.
26 Oct 1929

Dear Jehanne, –

The typescript has just come, and thank you very much. But the bill for typing is not enclosed. Do send it me, please.[4]

Yes, I have often thought of you, and of our talks. I like you because you seem to me quite honest, you say what you mean, and nearly all people equivocate when a subject really touches them, so I think that in the end you will come out all right, after this horrible period of frustration.[5] You must

---

[1] See Letter 5418 and n. 2.   [2] Cf. p. 78 n. 2.   [3] Unidentified.
[4] She had arranged for the typing of an article on the almond tree for DHL: see Letters 5352 and n. 1 and 5459.
[5] Jehanne's husband René Moulaert had deserted her for another woman in the summer of 1928. She went to live with her sister Maria, and Aldous Huxley, at Suresnes:

remember that all your life you have been revolting against your special bourgeois *milieu* in which you were brought up, because it was so moral, so *loveless*; and so materialist, while it pretended to be ideal and loving. I do think that morality combined with lovelessness is *hateful*, so you have rebelled, because you are by nature affectionate, yet you have never been able to trust your own affection. You almost deliberately chose a man you could not trust, because you didn't want to trust. You felt it was all a swindle, trust, affection, morality, ideals, all a bourgeois swindle, and perhaps in the bourgeoisie; so it is. And yet affection and trust and even morality are not in themselves a swindle. One can't live without them. One *must* be honest about money and those things, or one loses one's self-respect. It is a pity that the bourgeoisie, with their greedy dead materialism, have made morality and family and affection and trust all suspicious and repulsive.

I think, if you would only remember, when you feel so hostile and bewildered: 'Now I am only tangled up in my hatred of my *bourgeois* self, which comes from my bourgeois, bad upbringing. But in my own individual self, I don't care. I am honest because I am naturally honest, I am affectionate because I am naturally affectionate, and I must be careful, when I'm fighting my nasty bourgeois nature.' Then you'll have more peace. Maria, too, has a real nature, and a bad, bourgeois nature and perhaps one's own family bring out the bad side of one's nature more than anybody. So perhaps it is well if you are not too much together.

Well, there's a sermon. But I have thought of you so often, and the torments I could see in you. But now I'm sure you are beginning to accept the *real* individual side of your nature, which is the nice side, and to get free of the nasty bourgeois side, which comes from upbringing. And if one can only be real and at peace with oneself, that is about all that matters. Other people don't matter very much. The chief thing is to be one's own real self, and to be at peace with oneself. Then life comes easily again. While one is in conflict with oneself, life holds back and is difficult all the time.

Well, never mind if I preach at you, I suppose it is my nature, too. A card

---

Jeanne, at Suresnes, was a married woman with a child of her own whose life had just gone to pieces. She was unhappy, and not particularly sociable. She was setting out to earn her own and Sophie's living. France ... was in a state of financial instability; it was a hard time for an untrained young woman who had wanted to be an artist. She turned to hand-painting scarves and dress materials which for a while sold well. (Bedford, *Aldous Huxley*, i. 197)

The sisters were profoundly attached but very different: 'Jeanne very straight, blunt at times; Maria, "toute souplesse, charme et savoir faire (avec un côté bourgeois si on veut). Je n'aimais pas les formes extérieures," ["quite relaxed, with charm and savoir faire (though with a somewhat bourgeois side to her perhaps). I didn't much take to her outward appearance,"] Jeanne says of herself' (ibid.).

from Maria this morning from Valencia – she says they are happy. We are installed in this commonplace little bourgeois house, that was made by a *femme entretenue*, and is her ideal: awful. But it is right on the edge of the sea; I can lie and look out through the open doors at the sun on the water, and the foam against the islands, so I like it all right – why bother about this house. Perhaps you will come to Bandol some time and we can have more talks. My wife kept your shawl, she loves it. Have you done any more nice ones? If only we were nearer to see them, I should buy one for my sister-in-law.

Belle cose,   D. H. Lawrence

5393. To Max Mohr, [27 October 1929]
Text: MS HMohr; Unpublished.

Bandol
Sunday
Dear Mohr

Here is a long Geschwätz that amounts to nothing.[1] Wir lassen diese Hunden bleiben, und ihre eigenen Flöhe kratzen.[2]

Had your note from Paris – I'm sure it's no fun. Here we have had great storms, the waves looked as if they were rushing into the house, frightening – and they burst right over the island, enormous.[3] I have never seen them so big. Also it poured in torrents of rain. Today is quieter and sunny, but cold. When the Madame Martinse[4] comes she will light the central-heating. Because the Brewsters are coming to dinner tonight, and they are always cold. – We shan't have a duck, nor even tripe, only an omelette souflée and pommes Pont Neuf. – They have run everywhere looking for houses, to Sanary and Tamaris and Toulon. But they don't find anything that is *cheap* and nobel – *noble*: and it must be *both*; rather difficult. There is a nice house here for you,

---

[1] The 'long natter' so summarily dismissed was an enclosed letter, dated 24 October 1929 (in reply to DHL's missing letter of 19 October), in which the Fischer Verlag explained that they never had any intention of publishing a limited edn of *Lady Chatterley's Lover*. They had asked the Rowohlt Verlag and the Kiepenheuer Verlag their plans; both had thought of doing the book but had given up the idea: Rowohlt because of DHL's cheap Paris edition and Kiepenheuer because the Insel Verlag (DHL's usual German publisher) had expressed an interest in doing it. The Insel Verlag had eventually offered the book to Kiepenheuer, but the latter had turned down the idea of publishing just a single work; they would have agreed to publish *Lady Chatterley's Lover* only if DHL had contracted with them for the future publication of all his work.

[2] 'We'll leave these dogs alone, and they can scratch their own fleas.'

[3] See 'Mana of the Sea' (*Complete Poems*, ii. 705).

[4] Hitherto DHL has always referred to his femme de ménage as Camille. In Letter 5481 he calls her 'Mme Martens' (a not uncommon surname in the area). It may be that in the early days he misheard 'Martens' (spoken by a Provençale) as 'Martinse'.

for 500 frs a month,[1] rooms rather small but I believe really quite nice. So when you have had enough of Wolfsgrube, you can just pack up and come back here with Frau Käthe und Kind und Kegel.[2]

Your Nelken[3] are just dead – they have lasted all week, beautiful.

Yes the *douche* is all right, I duly douche my nose and choke myself. Achsah massages F[rieda]'s foot, and slaps it with sharp little slaps. She is still very *nerveuse*, but better than when she came. Poor man, he suffers in silence. But tomorrow he is going to Cannes to see a friend and ask about houses *there* – so perhaps they will leave us.

Regards to you all   DHL

5394. To Frederick Carter, 29 October 1929
Text: MS UT; cited in Moore, *Intelligent Heart* 423.

Villa Beau Soleil, *Bandol*, Var
29 Oct 1929

Dear Carter

I have received and carefully read 'The Visionary Way': and am still racking my brains to know how to make a book for the public out of your various MSS. But we'll find a way in the end. I'm beginning to hate St. John the Divine and his bloody Revelations. The more one gets used to him the more Jewish he smells, like paraffin – with a moral smell of paraffin everywhere that we know so well from chapel, and loathe. It would be interesting to have a chapter on the special Jewish-Jewy symbolism and *aim* of apocalypse – because the very aim is moral rather than re-vivifying, as in pagan mystery. Personally, I don't care much about the bloody Revelations, and whether they have any order or not – or even any meaning. But they are a very useful start for other excursions. I love the pre-Christian heavens – the planets that became such a prison of the consciousness – and the ritual year of the zodiac. But I like the heavens best *pre-Orphic, before* there was any 'fall' of the soul, and any redemption.[4] The soul only 'fell' about 500 B.C. or thereabouts, with the Orphics and late Egypt. Isn't that so? Isn't 'fall' and 'redemption' quite a late and new departure in religion and in myth: about Homer's time? Aren't the great heavens of the true pagans – I call all these orphicising 'redemption' mysteries half-christian – aren't they clean of the 'Salvation' idea, though they have the re-birth idea? and aren't they clean of the 'fall',

---

[1] MS reads 'months'.   [2] 'Frau Käthe and the whole family'.   [3] 'carnations'.

[4] 'The Orphic religion which arose in Greece between the sixth and third centuries B.C. saw the soul as a fallen god, and sought to release it from this "wheel of birth", from further reincarnation in a physical form, and thus enable it to become once more a god living in eternal bliss' (*Apocalypse* 15).

though they have the descent of the soul? The two things are quite different. In my opinion the great pagan religions of the Aegean, and Egypt and Babylon, must have conceived of the 'descent' as a great triumph, and each Easter of the clothing in flesh as[1] a supreme glory, and the Mother Moon who gives us our body as the supreme giver of the great gift, hence the very ancient Magna Mater in the East. This 'fall' into Matter (matter wasn't even conceived in 600 B.C. – no such idea) this 'entombment' in the 'envelope of flesh' is a new and pernicious idea arising about 500 B.C. into distinct cult-consciousness – and destined to kill the grandeur of the heavens altogether at last. The Jews were particularly pernicious, for their regeneration,[2] instead of being vital and hyacinthine, was always moral and through the nose. So I wish you would always look for the great heavens, and damn the candlesticks. I like so much in the old *Dragon* – which I saw some years ago – all that about the great man of the skies upon the cross, and the foot of the Cross moving into Pisces and now moving out, the gradual shifting of the Pole. – Just as at the end of this MS. I like the divine John on his back really *in* the heavens – (I'm afraid he never did it – but the Chaldeans did, so what's the odds!) – And I wish you'd put a few little chapters of real astrology in – the Planets, their meanings, metals etc – and if possible figures diagrams [3] – do the *astrology* of the book, it's all you're interested in – and so you need to set up again the astrological vision that remained in the first centuries around Jesus. – But I agree with Eisler[4] – or I mean, I feel he's right – the Zodiac was the year's rhythm of Sacrifice and attainment of the *Mana* of the creatures – the great effort of pre-spiritual man was to get himself the *powers* – the *honours and powers and might* – the Mana – of the vivid beasts – and the Mana of all was consummated in Man – or God. This is John's idea too – the association of the vivid attributes of the great Creatures into the human One Might and Power (or divine). – But do a few little chaps. of explanatory astrology and diagrams or figures – to make it *real*.

If you come to Paris perhaps you'll run down here and we can talk it over. Pity this beastly little house is so small: and my health so tiresome.

I wonder why Charlie Lahr hasn't written lately – have you seen him. Hope you're all right.

D. H. Lawrence

---

[1] as] of   [2] regeneration,] salvation,
[3] DHL wrote 'figures', then added 'diagrams' above without deleting the first word; he clarified his intentions at the end of the paragraph.
[4] Robert Eisler, *Orpheus the Fisher: Comparative Studies in Orphic and Early Christian Cult Symbolism* (1921).

5395. To Laurence Pollinger, [ante 29 October 1929]
Text: MS UT; Unpublished.

[Villa Beau Soleil, Bandol, Var]
[ante 29 October 1929]

Dear Pollinger

Yes, it explains itself.[1] The envelope is addressed *Mrs Mabel Henderson*: this letter is headed *Mrs Mabel Lulran*: the real name is *Mrs Mabel Luhan (LUHAN)*. But perhaps the book was correctly addressed – I know she has got a copy of the *Poems*, but she may have bought it, as she never said 'thanks'. I'll ask her. – The other people, I heard, were having difficulty getting the book through customs, because the value was not declared. – Bore, these americans!

DHL

5396. To Mabel Dodge Luhan, 29 October 1929
Text: MS Brill; Luhan 348–50.

Villa Beau Soleil. *Bandol*, Var, France.
29 Oct 1929

Dear Mabel

It's true it's a long time since I wrote you. But my health went down with such a slump in Germany, and I got depressed too. The doctors seem to think the lung is not troubling – it is never very much – but the bronchials and asthma are awful, and affecting my heart a bit, so I sympathise with you. However, I'm so glad to know you are better, and at last feeling your real self. There seemed to come a bit of the real you out of your last letter.[2] It's quite true, as you say, this being 'mad' with people isn't one's own real self functioning, it is something mysteriously superimposed. I say, as the ancients said, there is an evil world-soul which sometimes overpowers one, and with which one has to struggle most of the time, to keep oneself clear. I feel so strongly as if my illness weren't really me – I feel perfectly well and all right, *in myself.* Yet there is this beastly torturing chest superimposed on me, and it's as if there was a demon lived there, triumphing, and extraneous to me. I do feel it extraneous to me. I feel perfectly well, even perfectly healthy – till the devil starts scratching and squeezing, and I feel perfectly awful. So what's to be done! Doctors frankly say – they don't know.

We've taken this little house till end of March, right on the edge of the sea. This place suited me so well last winter, I thought we'd better come back.

---

[1] This letter is written on one from Pollinger to 'Mrs Lulran' dated 25 July 1929, telling her that a copy of *Collected Poems* has been sent to her under separate cover, at DHL's request.

[2] Mabel Luhan annotated DHL's letter: 'I wrote him I had got over my irritations!'

Frieda seems happier and more peaceful, but of course not so strong, and sometimes unstrung – but on the whole, more restful. She likes the little house, and all the bits of curtains and so on. – The Brewsters are here, and are looking for a house for the winter. Harwood, the girl, is in school in England. I heard from Ida Rauh from Geneva yesterday – I suppose she will come and see us here. – I liked Maria Cristina, but only saw her one week. She is 'working' for me now in New York. Did you get a copy of my *Collected Poems*, from me? It was sent you by Curtis Brown, London. And a copy of *Pansies* from New York. I hope you have them both – Let me know. Because the mail in America is so insolent.

I think these violent antipathies between people are in themselves a sign of nervous unbalance. Nobody matters all that; unless it's somebody very very near. So I'm glad you and Brett are friendly – so long as you keep cool about it, it is the best way, I think. Some things are inevitable, even some people. One can accept the bit then that is inevitable, and keep clear of all the tiresome accidental part of a relationship: as far as possible.

The Manby story was horrible. It somehow spoils Taos for me. I should always have to think of it. – And Nina would of course be too late with her floral tribute. Tell her to lay it, and the message, on her own grave: 'from myself to myself: a tribute etc.' – That's spiteful – but Nina makes me feel so. So absolutely self-important to herself, on the golden pedestal of her money. As I grow older, money bores me, and one smells it in people like a bad smell. Which is not because I'm hard up at all, because I'm not. I put myself on my feet by publishing *Lady C.* for myself.

Well – when shall I come to New Mexico again? God knows. At present it seems further off than Babylon or Nineveh, which are dreams in the sand. But the cycle of the greater year still goes round, and as it turns, it will probably bring us back. One has to wait for the auspicious day. I find one has to lean a great deal on destiny, when one's own will has been so thoroughly curbed by illness and things, and one finds one can't do anything, hardly, as one likes.

Regards from us both, and I do hope now you'll keep well and happy.

DHL

Of course I want you to do just as you think best with your MSS. – publish if you can.[1]

---

[1] In the summer of 1926 Mabel sent DHL MSS of various sections of her autobiography (*Intimate Memories*, 4 vols., New York, 1933–7). He gave detailed criticisms but advised against publication in her mother's lifetime (see *Letters*, v. 510).

5397. To Giuseppe Orioli, 1 November 1929
Text: MS UCLA; Unpublished.

Villa Beau Soleil, *Bandol*, Var
1 Nov. 1929

Dear Pino

I am sending you a copy of *The Escaped Cock* – hope you get it safely.

I have just heard, the trunks are in Ventimiglia, and they want to know, will I pay about 460 francs duty – chiefly the gramophone and the typewriter.

Yes, if I were you I would give at least 20% discount on the Lungarno books.

My health not very good – am sick of it. Hope you are well –

D. H. Lawrence

5398. To Caresse Crosby, 1 November 1929
Text: MS SIU; Huxley 837.

Villa Beau Soleil, *Bandol*, Var
1 Nov 1929

Dear Caresse

I have got the four vellum copies, and the ten others, and very many thanks indeed. I am so glad to have them. – I haven't received any imperfect copies. Did you send any?

Thanks also for sending that copy to Berlin. It was enthusiastically received.

Have you heard anything of the copies sent to New York? I do wonder how they will fare. Tell me as soon as you hear. – If they are stopped, we must make a plan for getting them to England.

An aeroplane! Is Harry really tired of life?[1] Do try it first on all your venturesome enemies – though of course *he* would want to send up Armand[2] first, and *you* would want to let one of the innumerable best girls try her chances in the sky. Don't you set foot in it – nor let Narcisse.

So you are going to New York for a fortnight! Is that for a rest, or for a change?

We are quiet here – have some American friends in the hotel – and expect the Huxleys shortly. The weather varies between very lovely and rather fidgetty.

Greetings from us both   D. H. Lawrence

---

[1] Harry Crosby was learning to fly and was determined not to return to USA until he had flown solo (which he did on 11 November 1929). See Wolff, *Black Sun*, p. 262.

[2] Cf. p. 324 n. 1.

5399. To Laurence Pollinger, 1 November 1929
Text: MS UT; Unpublished.

Villa Beau Soleil – *Bandol*. Var. France.
1st Novem 1929

Dear Pollinger

I enclose the agreement for the Cresset Press.[1] I haven't got a copy of *Birds Beasts*, but when my trunks come, I'll see if I can put in those bits in front of the separate sections – as Hughes-Stanton wants – though I don't in the least know how to begin.[2]

I enclose proofs of the *Obscenity* article. Yes, I'm glad they're not doing a limited edition.

I enclose also the MS. of the continuation of the *Jolly Roger* sketch. I don't know what has got Stephensen – he hasn't answered my last two letters – seems to be a[3] bit 'off' somewhere – and I know it's not unfriendliness. I know he has spent rather too much of Goldston's money, and Goldston is tightening the strings: how tight, I *don't* know. But Stephensen is very hasty and lavish at a start, and very apt to fizzle out, so watch the Mandrake. I don't a bit care about publishing this Sketch – though it's quite a beautiful sketch, in its way. But I don't care if it is never published. I feel as if I don't want to publish anything any more.

Would you answer this *Smart Set* man and let him have what he wants as far as possible, because *Smart Set* used to give me money for poems when I was very poor.[4]

I'm glad Secker sells the pocket editions[5] – though the reduction of £146 to £99 by taxes makes one lose interest in Royalties money. I was wondering, if Stephensen does *Jolly Roger* whether we should sell him the rights outright for, say, two years. But perhaps not – I believe Goldston would tighten up.

About a Spring book of newspaper articles,[6] if it was left to me, I should say don't do it. I've got a real revulsion from the thought of things coming out before the public – the nausea of it. But if you think I ought to have this book out, then do as you like, I don't care. But there are several articles – essays – from the *Adelphi* which could go in, if you want – Nancy Pearn sent me a list of them – and there is a 'Nightingale' sketch – several others – which are somewhat shorter and more newspapery than 'Making Pictures' and 'Pic-

---

[1] Cf. Letters 5298 and n. 1, 5354.   [2] See Letter 5416 and n. 1.   [3] a] be
[4] The enclosure is missing. *Smart Set* had published three of DHL's stories and one poem in 1913–14, and another story in 1924 (Roberts C27, 30.5, 31, 34.5, 123), but nothing subsequently.
[5] For the past two years Secker had been bringing out most of DHL's fiction in cheap pocket edns.
[6] I.e. *Assorted Articles*.

tures on the Walls' – which don't quite seem to fit the rest. Let me know about this. I'll think of a title.

No, my health is bad – but the weather is pretty good –

Sincerely   D. H. Lawrence

5400. To Charles Lahr, [2 November 1929]

Text: MS UNYB; Postmark, Bandol 2 –11 29; cited in *Apocalypse* 17.

Villa Beau Soleil.

2 Nov.

Dear L[ahr]

It's a long time since I heard from you – is there any reason? Also I can't get a word out of Stephensen lately. Do let me know if anything is wrong.

We heard from Rhys – I wish he'd not be so silly about that cheque, and *spend* it.

I have got one or two copies of the *Hahn* – looks very nice indeed. Shall I post one?

Did I thank you for the Bible and *Testament*? I like that Moffat translation.[1]

Well write a word –

ever   DHL

5401. To Maria Chambers, 2 November 1929

Text: MS UT; Unpublished.

Villa Beau Soleil. *Bandol.* Var

2 Nov. 1929

Dear Maria Cristina

Your long letter today. *The Escaped Cock* is ready and some have been sent off to New York, and one copy for you is supposed to go to Marks. It is a lovely little book. – I don't have any part in fixing the price etc. of this edition of 500 – Mrs Crosby does all that direct with Marks – and I let it be so. She, Mrs Crosby, is coming to New York this month, so I suppose she will tackle Marks direct. There are only 500 copies in this edition. If you dont get your copy (gift) from Marks, then I will send you one of mine and risk the customs. Today I am sending you by reg. book post a complete set of proofs – they are not likely to stop that – It is disarranged, but you can easily re-arrange it. I particularly want you to find out from Marks about the pirates and the *public* edition.

If there were a way of getting them in, then I'm sure you could have the 50

[1] James Moffatt, *The New Testament: A New Translation* (1913).

first editions of my novel *L[ady] C[hatterley]* – and later as many of the Paris edition as you wish. It is a question of the entry into America. Are you sure you trust your friend Mr Parke?[1] How far do you know him, in business? His figures are all wrong – Random House only did 600 of *Jolly Roger*, and I think they came down to $2½., considering the tiny size of the book. So their whole sales would be only $1500 – of which $300. would be 20%. – I *know* they paid Titus just the $300. –

Then the picture-book – I only know that an American speculator bought 150 copies – not 250. Probably he took them all to U.S.A. – as the customs did *not* stop the copy Curtis Brown sent to Rich for copyright at Washington. That passed all right, and the provisional copyright was secured. If your friend Mr Parke knows the booksellers – like the Holliday Bookshop – he knows whether any of the picture books have been offered for public sale in New York. – I don't know, but will ask. Anyhow I don't want an Amer. edition of the picture book till about a year after the other appeared – last July.

I don't believe he could get $75. for each copy of the first edition of *L.C.* And 40% is very high for booksellers discount – his suggestion is really

$$\begin{cases} 40\% \text{ to the bookseller} & = \$30 \\ 20\% \text{ to you} & = \$15 \\ 40\% \text{ to me.} & = \$30 \end{cases}$$

it is usually 25% to $33\frac{1}{3}$%. Are you *sure* of your friend? And of course you must have a discount on all sales – that is definite. Pino is offering the 1st edit. of *L.C.* in his catalogue at $50.

Ida Rauh wrote from Geneva. I suppose she will come here.

Don't bother about Mabel's questions – she is such a nosy Parker. Always wanting to *find out*.

I'm sorry about [. . .][2]. Such experimentalism is an inevitable preliminary to insanity. Let us hope there is more talking than doing. But be very careful. A neurotic cannot be cured – and one of the most infectious things is insanity, particularly incipient insanity. So be very careful – don't ever get tangled up in the neurotic processes – *believe* in something, and *do* something, and don't think very much about yourself. Thinking a lot about oneself is the beginning of neurosis. – Oh, it is very necessary to keep sane and sound, *at any price*. At any price, keep sane and sound if you can. And for the time being, *personally* be quiescent.

Rich has been trying to sell 'The Risen Lord' – so far, without success. You needn't tell him anything about the pictures or the *Gallo* – but you'll have, for the time, to let him receive payment for all the *public* things.

---

[1] Unidentified.   [2] The rest of this sentence is inked out and cannot be recovered.

I hope things are going pretty well. – I don't know whether there are any more sets of proofs of the pictures – ours is incomplete – and I don't know of any other than yours.

Let me know if you get your copy of the *Gallo*, and the proofs I now send.

Los Moros – La Mora wrote today from Granada, not very happy, not liking the people. I think they *won't* come here.

belle cose!   DHL

5402. To Brewster Ghiselin, 3 November 1929
Text: MS Ghiselin; Postmark, Bandol 4 –11 29; Nehls, iii. 408.

Villa Beau Soleil. *Bandol*. Var. France
3 Novem 1929

Dear Ghiselin

We had your letter yesterday, and you see where it finds us. We were in Germany the summer, very bad for my health, I was ill as could be, and am still rather wretched. However, I am thankful to be back in Bandol, where the sun shines and the sea sparkles. We have got this very ordinary little house right on the sea – on the Marseille side of the village, near the pine-grove. It is unpretentious but comfortable enough, my wife likes it, hangs up curtains and buys chairs – and I lie in bed and look at the islands out to sea, and think of the Greeks, and cough, and wish either that I was different or the world was different. No, but I really do wish my health was better – and I hope yours is perfectly good.

The Brewsters are here, also looking round for a house. They have left Capri for good (for the moment) and Mrs Brewster wants to find a house she can buy and live in for ever and ever. As for Earl, I think he feels, as I do: 'heaven is my home.'[1] We were talking about you just before your letter came, wondering about you as a married man, wondering if you hated Europe as much at a distance as you did at close quarters, wondering if you minded teaching, if you were more content, and what you were doing besides teach. Your letter answers a little of the wonderings, but not all.

I'm doing nothing at the moment. What with my health, and the stupidity over my pictures and the *Pansies*, I feel sort of fed up. – I suppose, by the way, you've seen Knopf's *Pansies*. I see they are out, but I haven't received a copy yet. I suppose there'll be another stupid press. How boring it all is!

I was once in Salt Lake City for a few hours –[2] Such a clean, respectable place with a glorified chapel! But the country round was weird – seemed to

---

[1] Cf. Letter 5305 and n. 1.
[2] When he was en route for Los Angeles from Buffalo, on 29 August 1923.

me a bit macabre. One day you must run down to Taos, you are not far off. Mabel Luhan is there, and Miss Brett, and they'd be nice to you.

Do you remember the little fishes you painted here?[1] Madame at the *Beau Rivage* recalled them and said what bijoux they were. And do you remember the drawing I was doing when you left? It became the painting *Spring*, which I liked very much. Perhaps you'll see the reproduction one day – the original is sold.[2]

Souvenirs: D. H. Lawrence

5403. To Martin Secker, 3 November 1929
Text: MS UInd; Postmark, Bandol 4 11[...]; Secker 123–4.

Villa Beau Soleil. Bandol. Var. France
3 Novem 1929

Dear Secker

Can you please send me a copy of *The Plumed Serpent*. My sister-in-law is doing the German translation, and wants me to help her with the hymns, and I haven't got a copy.[3] And send me at the same time please a copy of *Fantasia of the Unconscious*, for a friend. This – *Fantasia* – has just appeared in German under the title *Spiel des Unbewussten* – done by a Munich firm.[4] I shall be interested to see how the Germans take it.

I have been feeling rather down, because my health has been so bad. It went down with a slump in Germany, and stayed down. We've been here a month, and I've been most of the time in bed, feeling very cheap. Frieda still has some trouble with her foot, and bothers about it. So altogether it's a poor show. However, I am feeling better and going out a bit. We've got a commonplace little house on the sea, but it is pretty comfortable, a good bathroom, and a central-heating system that warms up very quickly. But mostly we don't need it, because the sun shines in warm off the sea, rather lovely. I'm thankful to be here and not in the north. – And for once we've got a good cook. So once I begin to get better I expect I shall be all right. But as for work, I haven't felt like doing anything at all, and I am still that way. I neither write nor paint – which I suppose is best for my health.

I am glad the 3/6 edition sells fairly well. Perhaps it will gradually increase.

---

[1] Ghiselin's *Mediterranean Fishes* is reproduced in Nehls, iii. facing p. 161.

[2] Perhaps sold from the Warren Gallery; the purchaser is not known.

[3] Else Jaffe's ambition to translate *The Plumed Serpent* had roots four years deep (see *Letters*, v. 332; vi. 199); it was never to be realised.

[4] The book, translated by Walter Osborne, was published by Dornverlag G. Ullman (Roberts D79).

I wish there could have been a cheap *Pansies*, but apparently we must wait. And I must see what the winter brings me.

I hope you are all well and fairly peaceful. It seems a long time since we were at Spotorno,[1] yet being on the same coast, I often think of it. I wish I were as strong as I was then!

                                                    Ever.   D. H. Lawrence

5404. To Nancy Pearn, 4 November 1929
Text: MS UT; Unpublished.
                                               Villa Beau Soleil. *Bandol. Var.*
                                                                4 Nov. 1929
Dear Nancy Pearn

I'm sending you three articles which I wrote with an eye to *Vanity Fair*, but I don't know if they are suitable.[2] When they are typed will you read them, and *don't* offer them to *Vanity Fair* if you think them unsuitable. – About a contract – ask them if they want anything special – and I expect I can turn out a dozen articles, in spasms – but I don't want to make them pay for anything they don't want. I don't like that. But if I agree to give them an article a month, to the best of my ability, and leave them free to refuse it if they like, then I think they ought to pay $200. – because I know they *do* pay that sum.

My health a bit better – am hoping to God it's going to pick up

                                                                Ever   DHL

Tell Pollinger I sent the Faber proofs etc on Saturday – and hope he has them. And I think there is a bit of a breach between Stephensen and Goldston, and a bit of a halt in the Mandrake.

5405. To Frederick Carter, 7 November 1929
Text: MS UT; cited in Moore, *Intelligent Heart* 423.
                                               Villa Beau Soleil, *Bandol*, Var
                                                                7 Nov. 1929
Dear Carter

The last batch of Apocalypsis – and the last chapter of it very interesting. I think you are right, not to do any more of this MS. We must try and put a

---

[1] November 1925–April 1926.
[2] The three articles (none of which was published in *Vanity Fair*) were 'We Need One Another', 'The Real Thing' and 'Nobody Loves Me' (see Roberts C198, 201 and 203). Nancy Pearn had written to DHL on 21 October 1929 (TMSC UT) about the proposed contract with *Vanity Fair* (cf. Letter 5362 and n. 2), telling him that the editor was prepared to sign a contract which did not insist on 'any specific dates of delivery' and guaranteed $150 per article.

book together out of these four MSS.[1] The difficulty is, you see, that for the general reader nothing hangs together, and many chapters are absolutely dry and without live interest – you have got much drier and colder than you were some years ago – whereas for the scholar there is not enough developed argument and scholarship. We must see what we can do – it will be difficult to get a publisher – and now the Mandrake Press seems to be dying off.[2] I rather wish you would do a bit of purely astronomical and astrological explanation – the planets, their signs, metals, qualities etc. – the zodiac, and its signs: the meaning of the Houses – and the exaltation and fall – and the ecliptic, and the inclination of the ecliptic to the horizon: those simple things which ordinary people *don't* know, even the people who are going to read this book. And I wish you did a few purely geometric or formal designs – a simple plan of the heavens – a diagram if possible of the ecliptic –

[sketch]

just simple beautiful *diagrams*, astronomical and astrological. They would help a lot. If you want to be read by the public you must give the public something it *can* read: and something that will make it seem worth while. A good chapter with good diagrams, on the astronomy and astrology of John's day, would be worth a great deal of exposition of the astrological movement of the apocalypse – which isn't very convincing because it isn't very interesting. – I wish we had had the old 'Dragon', because it was more human and more

---

[1] The MSS were those which DHL had received during October and which eventually formed parts of Carter's *Dragon of Revelation* (1931): 'Apocalypse' (Letter 5357); 'Apocalyptic Images' and 'Heaven and Hell' (5369); and 'The Visionary Way' (5394).

[2] For a full account of DHL's collaboration with Carter see *Apocalypse* 17–22. Carter himself summarised it in a letter to the *London Mercury*, xxii (September 1930), 451:

... In the beginning [DHL] had intended to take a more conspicuous part in the publication of the essays on the symbols in the *Revelation* of St. John which I had in preparation, and at one period indeed had suggested making a joint book of it.

In fact, this idea held until the end of last year, and he informed me when I was his guest in December that he was writing a long introductory section to my MS. which had then attained the dimensions, I believe he said, of twenty to thirty thousand words. He was still engaged on this when he was compelled to cease writing on his departure to the sanatorium.

In place of this long introduction, however, early this year he sent me the typescript of the present shorter one, and suggested that I should go forward with arrangements for the publication of my part, for he was in difficulties about the other, and its suitability to the purpose was doubtful.

The Mandrake Press then undertook the publication of my manuscript, together with a series of designs to illustrate or decorate the text of the book of *Revelation* itself. This, of course, they advertised as an edition of the *Revelation* of St. John the Divine for which I had made decorations, and to which, in addition to my commentary on the symbolism, there was an introduction by D. H. Lawrence...

The Mandrake Press did not survive long enough to complete the promised publication. DHL's 'introduction', intended for Carter's book, appeared in the *London Mercury* in July 1930 (Roberts C204); the 'long introduction' became *Apocalypse*, published by Orioli (1931).

interesting. Now you are more learned, in a narrow sense, and more scientific, but I doubt if you are as readable. Your theory is all right up to the point, but the moment one really reads Revelation again, it is obvious how much of it is *not* astrological.

However, perhaps you don't want to do any of the things I suggest, so I must ask you to excuse my suggesting them. I'm afraid you have grown stiff-necked and obstinate[1] – and in these matters it's no good. If you want to be published you want to be read, and if you want to be read you must be readable, and even a little entertaining and instructive (in this case). It is fairly obvious that even Arthur Machen never even read the book he introduced:[2] which is all wrong, and *his* fault this time. But if you want the public to read your text, then you mustn't offer them pictures that they can look at and avoid the text. You must give them diagrams that will send them to the text.

However, you will be tired of all this

Ever   D. H. Lawrence

5406. To Nancy Pearn, 7 November 1929
Text: MS UT; *Apocalypse* 18.

Villa Beau Soleil, Bandol. Var. France
7 Nov 1929

Dear Nancy Pearn

Here is an article on Rozanov's *Fallen Leaves* and I wish you would find somebody to publish it, for the book's sake.[3]

Hope you got the MS. of the other three articles.[4]

Sincerely   D. H. Lawrence

[1] Both adjectives have a biblical source: e.g. Deuteronomy ii.30, x.16.
[2] Cf. Letter 5369 and p. 519 n. 2.
[3] Stephensen had written to DHL on 31 October 1929 (TMSC Munro):

Dear Lorenzo,
    I am sending you three more MANDRAKE BOOKLETS and also a copy of FALLEN LEAVES. I hope you enjoy reading them. Dear old Kot. is hoping that somebody will read Rozanov. I am completely pessimistic, and don't suppose we shall sell fifty copies … Anyway, I only published FALLEN LEAVES to do Kot. a service because I like him. On looking at the book, I am becoming more and more impressed by it. Rozanov really had something to say! Nevertheless the book will not sell, because *Solitaria* made hardly any headway at all. Why is this? …

DHL's article, 'A Remarkable Russian', appeared in *Everyman*, 23 January 1930 (Roberts C196).
[4] Nancy Pearn acknowledged them on 7 November (TMSC UT).

5407. To Caresse Crosby, [9 November 1929]

Text: MS SIU; Unpublished.

Villa Beau Soleil. Bandol. Var.

Sat.

Dear Caresse

You will be off to New York just now. Do drop me a line first and tell me if you have heard that the book has passed in or not, I am anxious to know.

Could you just send a line to

Pino Orioli. 6 Lungarno Corsini. Florence

to tell him the name of the colour-printer who reproduced the frontispiece to the *Cock*, and the cost per 100 reproductions. I'm afraid it is collotype and rather dear. But he has a frontispiece he wants to reproduce. – I shall send you a copy of the *Doctor Manente* story he has just got out.

Beastly weather today, lovely yesterday – The gramophone is at the station – imagine!!

belle cose!   DHL

5408. To Giuseppe Orioli, 9 November 1929

Text: MS UCLA; cited in Moore, *Intelligent Heart* 393.

Beau Soleil. *Bandol.* Var

9 Nov 1929

Dear Pino

The four Lasca's came, and are very nice – molto distinto[1] indeed! I like the get-up very much. I think if people ever *see* the book they will buy it, especially America. Don't be in a hurry, because once the book gets over there, you'll see the orders will come in: and once they see there is no fear of the customs or police interference.

It is Mrs Caresse Crosby who does the books:

19 rue de Lille. Paris. 7e.

– She is just going to New York. They are rich people, so I don't know if she'd bother about Lasca – you could ask her. But don't bother, it will go.

Will you send a copy to each of my sisters:

Mrs L. A. Clarke. Broadway. Ripley near Derby. England.

Mrs. S. King. 16 Brooklands Rd. Sneinton[2] Hill. Nottingham.

And just send me two more copies. – Have you sent to Charles Lahr – he is a very good man for introducing the book to people. – I believe Stephensen has made a mess of the Mandrake Press – published far too much – printed 3000

[1] 'very distinguished'.

[2] Thinking, perhaps, that 'Sneinton' might not be fully legible, DHL repeated it above his first attempt.

copies of Aleister Crowley, and sold 200. So there is a bit of a split between him and Goldston, I rather think the end of the Mandrake for the moment.

I am feeling a lot better – my illness was the remains of Germany. This place seems really to suit me. We've been motoring round with the Brewsters looking for a house for them – the country is really quite lovely, and once one leaves the coast, less spoiled than Italy.

Today came the notice of the trunks, arrived at the station, and 1,148 francs to pay. I think there must be some mistake, as the total cost from Ventimiglia here is only 56 francs. So why more than 1000 frs. in Italy? I am writing to the agent at Ventimiglia. There is a swindle somewhere. I wonder what Egidi's charges are – do you know? – and do you know if they are on this bill?

The music has not come yet.

The weather varies – today rainy, yesterday lovely. I hope it'll be a good winter, but am afraid. It will be fun if you get your passport, and can come at Christmas time. Then the weather is usually good.

I will let you know about the trunks.

Probably the reproduction of the *Cock* is rather expensive – you could get
      Dr Max Mohr, Wolfsgrube, Rottach-am-Tegernsee, Oberbayern
– to ask in Munich. Tell him I told you – and if you ask him, send him a Lasca. – Oh, send Aldington one, please. He did not send us his novel[1] – we had it in MS. at the Vigie last year – and I disliked the first part *intensely*. But since the Vigie I don't write to him[2] – that's a long story.

                                                   au revoir then!   DHL
Huxleys not coming here – going via Biarritz to Paris.

I had to write Caresse Crosby, so have asked her to send you name of the color-printer, and terms.

5409. To Emily King, 9 November 1929
Text: MS Lazarus; Postmark, Bandol 9 11 29; Unpublished.

                                   Villa Beau Soleil. Bandol. Var.
                                   9 Novem. 1929

My dear Pamela

Just a line to say all well here – I'm feeling quite a lot better – really picking up. We've been several motor-rides with the Brewsters – and I am taking my walks along the coast again – though not far. The weather changes – yesterday lovely, we motored inland, the vineyards all red and yellow, a riot of colour, beautiful. It is lovely country, a bit back. The Brewsters are looking for a

[1] *Death of a Hero* (September 1929).   [2] See p. 17 n. 3.

house, and I think have found what they want – alone on a hill about 4 miles
from here – a bit too lonely really. I think we shall go into a permanent house
after Christmas – either here or in the next village – a bit bigger than this –
though this is very comfortable, the central heating makes it all warm in half
an hour, and the bath gets boiling hot. Frieda likes it. And now we hear the
trunks from Florence are at the station.

Ada said you were better – and I hope you keep up. – Orioli will send you a
little book from Florence – a translation – and I expect you will receive my
pamphlet on *Obscenity*, against Jix. Always lots of things to do, and so many
letters to write, I get tired to death of them. So if I'm rather long answering,
don't worry.

The Huxleys are in Spain – right down at Seville – and she driving – I'm
sure she'll be worn out. Now she's got to motor all the way back to Paris –
awful! I hate motoring, hate it.

Tell me if ever you want anything, and love to you all.

DHL

5410. To Charles Lahr, [9 November 1929]
Text: MS StaU; Postmark, Bandol 10 –11 29; Lacy, *Escaped Cock* 89–90.

Beau Soleil.
Saturday.

Dear L[ahr]

Thanks for letter and enclosure. That's bad news of Stephensen. He wrote
me that he was having to leave London to be in the country for three months,
and the Mandrake would be at a standstill, but he hoped it would put forth
new shoots in the spring. Meanwhile he sent me a copy of Rozanov – and
three more of the 3/6 series. He is afraid Rozanov won't sell. I wrote an article
on it and sent it to Curtis Brown, but don't know if anyone will print it. I
didn't think the 3/6's very good – a W. J. Turner, and an Edgell Rickword,
and a *Smiling Faces*.[1] But I can't believe people break their necks to buy such
little stuff. If *only* Stephensen weren't in such a hurry! – Tell me, do you
think Goldston has *actually* sold all the painting books, and all the *Pansies?* –
It is rough on Davies if the Mandrake dies, but then we'd have to publish his
novels ourselves, and he'd have to sell them. He wrote to Frieda from Wales,
chewing the cud of misery and rather liking the taste of it. I believe success
would make him feel quite ill. – You don't tell me if you think it would be safe
for me to send you the *Hahn* through the post. It is quite a lovely little book –

[1] Brinsley Macnamara's *Smiling Faces and Other Stories* and Rickword's *Love One Another* were
published in October 1929, W[alter] J[ames] Turner's *A Trip to New York; And a Poem*
appeared in November.

in get-up. I am still waiting to hear if it has passed through into U.S.A. –
Look out for my *Obscenity and Pornography* pamphlet in Faber & Faber's
series – should be out soon. – I am not in any hurry over the Goldston money
and the Jackson, except that it would be nice to get the thing all finished up
and done with. But please deduct your proper share, and all the costs of
sending me books – like the Bible etc – very useful. And if you can see a good
translation of Hesiod: *Homeric Hymns, Works and Days, Fragments* – then
please send it me. I don't know if the Loeb is the best. And if you come across
a second-hand Plutarch – I think in Bohn's library – send me that. But be
sure to take the money for[1] them all from my payments.

We must discuss a plan for publishing Davies' novels, if you and he think it
wise. But he would have to look after it properly.

And the *Hahn* we will discuss when I know it is in New York all right. –
Shall I mail you a copy, reg. letter post – or how?

Tell Davies to spend that £10. for God's sake, or I shall throw it in the sea.

ever   DHL

Have you got *The Story of Doctor Manente* from Orioli? I think it ought to
sell – and absolutely 'safe.'

5411. To Aldous and Maria Huxley, 9 November 1929
Text: Huxley 837–8.

Beau Soleil, Bandol.
Saturday, 9 November, 1929

Dear Aldous and Maria, –

I didn't write to Seville, thought it was too late. Hope you're not *dead* tired.
Rather changesome weather here – yesterday lovely, to-day raining. We've
motored a bit with Brewsters, looking at houses. The country is lovely –
yesterday, the lovely wide valley full of brilliant vines, beautiful, beautiful! I
think they will take a little *stone* house, just like a smaller Mirenda on a
hill-top, Château Brun – about 5 miles from here – quite lovely situation,
lovely – but lonely, and no light nor bath nor water-closet – and water from
wells – but very nice – and unfurnished, only two thousand five hundred
francs a year – a pleasant old place. But hunting, one could find all sorts of
things – and fascinating country. But I don't want to be so *isolated*. We shall
get a bit bigger house in the spring – perhaps here – perhaps at St. Cyr-s.-mer
or Les Lecques – about 7 miles nearer Marseilles from here. But it's easy and
pleasant living here, suits me.

Our trunks – 4 – at the station, and a charge of 1148 frs. Monstrous!

[1] for] from

I'm feeling a good bit better – Frieda pretty well. From the outside world, little or no news. I'm so anxious when I think of that *enormous* way from S. of Spain by Biarritz to Paris. Too much, too much. Hope you won't go to Gibraltar. When we've motored for one morning, I'm so thankful to have done.

Pino may come for Xmas – seems very hopeful about the passport. The *Doctor Manente* story looks awfully well.

Very Novemberish to-day – wish you were safe at home!

Must send this to Suresnes.

Love from both to both.   DHL

5412. To Giuseppe Orioli, 11 November 1929
Text: MS UCLA; Unpublished.

Villa Beau Soleil, Bandol. Var.
Monday 11 Nov. 1929

Dear Pino

The trunks are here – came this afternoon – I had to pay 1,148 francs – of which 643 were for Italy, 326 for dogana,[1] and only about 90 for France altogether. Egidi must have charged. The music has also come – and the dictionary and Misericordia. Now when Frieda's coat is here, it is all for the time being, because perhaps you will bring my coat and hat, later.

I wrote to you on Saturday, so there is no news – except Lahr says he is giving your copy and Douglas' of the *Pansies* to Frederick Carter – vellum copies too – to bring to Paris this week – and they will be posted from Paris.

Thank you so much for sending all these things – what a bother it must have been – I shall write to Carletto.

Poor Scott Moncrieff, I hope it's *not* cancer.[2]

ever   DHL

5413. To Emily King, [11 November 1929]
Text: MS Lazarus; Postmark, Toulon 12 11 29; Unpublished.

Beau Soleil. Bandol. Var.
Monday 11 Nov.

My dear Sister

Your letter and the cake came this morning – imagine your having a silver

---

[1] 'customs'.

[2] Charles Kenneth Scott-Moncrieff (1889–1930), Scottish translator of Stendhal, Proust and Pirandello. A friend of Orioli; DHL had enjoyed his witty conversation (cf. *Letters*, vi. 214 and n. 5). See *Times* obituary, 3 March 1930.

wedding! – it means grey hairs, alas. When my [turn?]¹ comes round I shall most carefully forget it is coming. We are having the cake for tea – at least Brewster and I are having my half, all to ourselves. Frieda has gone off with Achsah to Marseille to ask about a house for them, but they'll be back this evening. It's been a sunny day, very blue, but a cold wind from the mountains. – I am feeling better, as I said. – No more news, and I hope you're all well and chirpy. What a terror thaᵗ old Mrs King!²

love   DHL

5414. To Charles Lahr, 11 November 1929

Text: TMSC ULon; Postmark, Toulon 12 11 29; Unpublished.

Villa Beau Soleil, Bandol, Var.
11 Nov. 1929

Dear L[ahr]

The vellum book came this morning, and many thanks. – I think I would like best the *bright blue* calf for the fifty³ – I only wish it were a little less shiny.

I shall expect Carter down here soon, then.

Let me know how to send you a *Hahn* – have you anybody crossing from Paris?

Any further news of the Mandrake?

ever   DHL

5415. To Frederick Carter, 11 November 1929

Text: MS UT; Unpublished.

Villa Beau Soleil. Bandol. Var.
11 Nov. 1929

Dear Carter

I hear you will soon be in Paris. Good! Then you will come down here and we will lay our heads together about the *Dragon* – alas, he's Prolegomena now. – I get worried trying to think how to prepare him for a public emergence – difficult.

I want you to be my guest for a week or so in the Hotel Beau Rivage here, as this house is so small. I shall arrange it myself with Mme. Douillet. So let me know the day you will come. And my health is rotten, so I can't walk much – but perhaps you can amuse yourself – and our friends the Brewsters are in the hotel – and my wife is here.

au revoir then   D. H. Lawrence

¹ MS reads 'my comes'.   ² Emily's mother-in-law, Ann King (1852–1940).
³ Lahr had ten copies of *Pansies* bound in green vellum (Roberts 132); 50 copies of the definitive edn were bound in blue leather (Roberts A47d).

5416. To Blair Hughes-Stanton, [12 November 1929]
Text: MS UT; Unpublished.

Villa Beau Soleil, *Bandol*, Var
12 Nov.

Dear Blair

Here are the nine bits[1] – I hope they will do – if not don't use them – just put them in the fire – I only did them because you wanted them, so you and the publishers can do as you like.

Hope the drawings progress – no, never teach school if you can avoid it – anyhow I never would. Glad you and Gertie have got niceish things to do for the moment.

regards   D. H. Lawrence

5417. To Martin Secker, 13 November 1929
Text: MS UInd; Postmark, [. . .]; Secker 124.

Villa Beau Soleil, *Bandol*. Var, France
13 Nov 1929

Dear Secker

Many thanks for the books – only you sent me *Sons and Lovers* instead of *Plumed Serpent* which I asked for, because I want to translate the hymns into German. Will[2] you send it me then? – Thanks also for the two translations – how German you have become! I read the Thomas Mann[3] – and he is exactly like the Germans – except that he leaves out the shady side. He is so good – and yet I feel, ultimately, he is nothing.

Sorry Bridgefoot is a bit of a trial. There's no home like the office, as a man said to me. Here it's pretty quiet – house small, cook good but wasteful – but I cant bother. My health a nuisance – very poor. We have this place till March – and we may find a permanent place here – it is easier, somehow, than Italy, and a good climate as a rule. The Brewsters are taking a house about four miles off, and the Huxleys want to come after Christmas and find a permanent house.

It will be amusing to see the *Lit. Supp.* and *Illustrated* again, but don't

---

[1] For each of the nine sections of *Birds, Beasts and Flowers* DHL wrote a prefatory note for inclusion in the Cresset Press edn illustrated by Hughes-Stanton. On the contents of the notes see Letter 5426. The 'nine bits' were reprinted in *Phoenix* 65–8 and in *Complete Poems*, i. 277, 295, 303, 319, 331, 348, 368, 376, 406.

[2] Will] Then

[3] Secker was publishing translations of works by Lion Feuchtwanger and Gerhart Hauptmann, as well as by Thomas Mann; Mann's *Early Sorrow* appeared in November 1929, and in the same month his *Death in Venice* had been published in Secker's *New Adelphi Library*.

bother if it's a nuisance. – There's a nice little hotel here, 45 frs., if you want a change for a bit in the winter – we are about ten minutes away.

Regards from both to you all.   DHL

5418. To Laurence Pollinger, 13 November 1929
Text: MS UT; Unpublished.

Villa Beau Soleil, *Bandol*. Var. France
13 Novem. 1929

Dear Pollinger[1]

I heard from Stephensen, no answer to *anything* I asked him, just saying briefly he must retire to the country for three months, to the sun and quiet, and the Mandrake would die down temporarily, but he hoped it would revive in the spring – no word of 'business.' But I hear from other sources he has spent *far* too much of Goldston's money, printed 3000 Aleister Crowley novels and sold 200, and an action for libel was impending – and altogether it looks as if Stephensen had run away with himself. – I have never written to Goldston, but he sends friendly messages, so if you like you can speak to him – just as you think best. I believe he'd be friendly. I think he's lost no money over me, but owes me some.

About Orioli, he is waiting till Huxley gets back from Spain – next week: then he will get definite dates from him and from Aldington. He thought of asking Aldington to do the famous Renaissance book on syphilis – *Syphilida*, or whatever it's called – it's a Latin book.[2] – He says he's afraid Aldington and Huxley may want to contract with their own agents for these books, but I say, they cannot, if he is really making a *series*, and supplying wood-cuts etc.

---

[1] DHL was replying to Pollinger's letter, 12 November 1929 (TMS UCLA):

Dear Lawrence,

I have written Orioli three letters about 'The Lungarno Series', but up to the time of writing have not received any word from him. Is there anything you can do to stir him into sending me a reply.

I know we can place the Series advantageously both here and in America, if Orioli will only let me know the approximate length of each book, the titles he is planning to add to the Series in the future, when your book, Huxley's book, and Aldington's book will be ready, and any other information he thinks might be of use to me in negotiating the sale of the Series.

Stephensen is rather an illusive bird these days. I have tried several times during the last few days to establish contact with him, but have not been successful. I will get some word from him about JOLLY ROGER in the next day or two, or die in the attempt.

Yours sincerely,

[2] DHL most probably had in mind Girolamo Fracastoro's *Syphilis, Sive Morbus Gallicus* (Verona, 1530), a versified account of the disease; it was translated into several languages: into English, by Nahum Tate – *Syphilis; or, A Poetical History of the French Disease* (1686); into Italian, *La Sifilide* (Bologna, 1738); etc.

as in *Doctor Manente*. Didn't you think it a nice little book? – But he now realises how good it would be to place the whole series with one publisher, so he will try to arrange it so – and will write to you shortly.[1]

Would you hand enclosed to Miss Watson.[2]

My health, like the sea, choppy and a bit sickening.

ever   DHL

5419. To Giuseppe Orioli, [13? November 1929]
Text: MS UCLA; Unpublished.

[Villa Beau Soleil, Bandol, Var]
[13? November 1929]

Dear Pino[3]

Aldous will be in Suresnes next week – write to him – and write Aldington. It will be very much to your advantage to fix up for the series. I have written Pollinger to tell him you are waiting for Aldous – they are in Madrid – on their way to Paris now. I don't think they *loved* Spain; but Aldous, no doubt, will write *articles* on it. They are not coming here till after Christmas, then they will find a permanent house here, if they can. The Brewsters have already taken a house for a year.

It is nice having all our things – Egidi packed very well – only one little thing broken, and I think nothing stolen. The weather varies very much – now suddenly *cold* – but we have good central heating.

I was wondering if you could put the cookery book in the Lungarno Series. Perhaps not.[4]

I have no word from Mrs Crosby. She may have left already.

Hope Lasca goes. This Wall Street smash will hinder you now.[5] – Do you think Italian money is safe? if not, I'd transfer my sterling from Haskard.

ever   DHL

---

[1] Pollinger annotated DHL's letter for Curtis Brown: 'Decent of *DHL* to try to steer this Series our way'; Curtis Brown agreed: 'Yes. No doubt we'll be thanking him'.

[2] The enclosure is missing.

[3] DHL sent Pollinger's letter, 12 November 1929 (p. 564 n. 1) to Orioli, writing this letter on it.

[4] See Letter 4874 and n. 1.

[5] The US stock market had shown persistent weakness for several months; there was panic selling of shares on Wall Street on 25 October, a further collapse on 29th, more heavy selling on 7 November and another fall on 12th. DHL had invested in stocks and shares – at least $6,000 – via Curtis Brown's New York office, but he does not appear to have lost very much (John Worthen, *D. H. Lawrence: A Literary Life*, 1989, pp. xx and n. 1, 162).

5420. To Max and Käthe Mohr, 14 November 1929
Text: MS HMohr; Mohr, Briefe 536–7.

Villa Beau Soleil, *Bandol*, Var.

14 Nov 1929

Dear Mohr und Käthe Mohr

Well how is it now at Wolfsgrube? Here, this evening it is cold, with a cold mistral blowing – but the house is warm, the central heating works very well. The morning was cold but lovely, very bright, with dark blue sea – tonight there is a big moon in thin clouds. The Brewsters were here for tea – they have just gone. They have taken a house – a little Château Brun, for 2,500 frs. a *year* – without furniture. It is very nice, a square stone house standing on a little hill between here and St. Cyr – in the Marseille direction – about four miles along the road – and with vineyards all round. It is very cheap – so they are having it whitewashed, and buying furniture, and at the end of next week they want to move in. Achsah is very happy to have a chateau and be a châtelaine. She says even *Var* is not elegant enough – so she will put the address:

Chateau Brun, St Cyr. *Provence*

– That will sound very romantic – I say she should be Madame la Comtesse Brewster, since he is already Earl. – He is not very happy – feels again like a *prisoner*.

Our trunks have come from Florence – but they cost 1,148 francs. But Frieda is happy – she is now singing Schubert at the piano; but the gramophone – 'Kiss your hand, Madame' — I only allow in the kitchen, with the doors shut. I do mortally hate it. Then we have pictures on the walls, covers on the 'divan' etc. etc. – and Frieda is proud of her little house, though I call it a little railway station, and Achsah despises it terribly, calls it a vulgar box. She, however, is only too happy to come to it. – The Huxleys are in Madrid, shivering, but admiring El Greco. They will not come here until February, when they also will look for a *château* for five francs. I think I must be a châtelain à deux sous.[1]

There is no news in the world – our world. I was better, and taking my little walks, but mostly through the pine trees towards the English-woman's house. Now I've got a chill – a touch of grippe – so am staying indoors a day or two. The country looks very lovely, the vines all red and yellow – we have been motoring several times with the B's. – We had a very special octopus for supper on Saturday evening – *not* with the B's – and it was quite good, but still I had to shut my eyes. I wonder if you have had *tripe* yet.

---

[1] 'twopenny lord'.

Well, tell us how the Tirol is behaving. The Cote d'Azur is sometimes grey.

Many greetings from us both.   DHL

5421. To Jean Watson, 16 November 1929
Text: MS UT; Unpublished.

Villa Beau Soleil. *Bandol.* Var.

16 Nov 1929

Dear Miss Watson

Like all the rest of them, Kiepenheuer is a liar[1] – I have had no communication with him whatsoever, I have only found out, privately, what that little witches' kitchen have been doing – Kippenberg, Fischer, Kiepenheuer, Rowohlt. Old Anton Kippenberg is of course the frustrator. He is terribly afraid of bourgeois prejudice – they take the whole thing *Lady C.* as anti-bourgeois and subversive – Curtius, the Foreign Minister, gassed a long time to my sister-in-law: ein erschütterndes Buch![2] – Kippenberg, the old pasha, is privately determined if possible to prevent a german translation – and the others are afraid of going counter to him. Tell Kiepenheuer I have no arrangement with them *at all* (If I had, I should tell you at once) – and then go ahead as you wish. I too was approached by the Vienna firm[3] – indirectly – but made no answer. Privately, after my summer in Germany, I too am left with very little desire to see a German translation of *Lady C.* The germans are in an unpleasant sort of state, God knows how they'd take the book. Kippenberg says that all the really educated people read it in English, and the uneducated ought not to read it at all. So much for him and his education – erzogen[4] indeed! Even then he may be right.

So sorry your having such a lot of bother.

Sincerely   D. H. Lawrence

Does the Vienna firm propose a *limited* edition, or unlimited? and if the former, how many copies and at how much?

[1] Gustav Kiepenheuer, publisher in Berlin. Cf. p. 543 n. 1.
[2] Julius Curtius (1877–1948), formerly Minister of Economic Affairs (1926–9), had become Minister of Foreign Affairs in October 1929. Presumably he had muttered: 'a shocking book!'
[3] The Vienna firm, E. P. Tal, were to publish Herberth E. Herlitschka's translation of *Lady Chatterley's Lover*, for subscribers only, in 1930 (Roberts D80).
[4] 'educated'.

5422. To Laurence Pollinger, 18 November 1929
Text: MS UT; Unpublished.

Beau Soleil. *Bandol.* Var. France
18 Nov 1929

Dear Pollinger

I've mislaid the list of material intended for the new book of sketches, but I *believe* it did not include these essays from the *Adelphi*: 'Education and Sex', 'Love and Marriage', 'Proper Study', 'On being religious', 'On Human Destiny', 'On Being a Man' – that is six essays.[1] These are all topical newspaper stuff – and could be included, if they are quite suitable. If Miss Pearn has no copies, and Murry says he can supply none, probably Koteliansky has copies.

It would be a good thing if Knopf could get the books from Boni. A friend of mine who knows Albert was trying to get an answer from him about releasing the books he has, but so far no result. Shall let you know if anything comes.

Why does Alfred love me again, after refusing *Collected Poems*?[2] How are *Pansies* doing in America, I wonder.

I'm glad *Obscenity* is biting through their skin, as I intended it should. Mr Lawrence not only believes what he says, he knows it's true.[3]

Ever   D. H. Lawrence

5423. To Edward Titus, 20 November 1929
Text: MS UT; cited in Titus, *Times Literary Supplement*, 16 July 1931, p. 564.

Beau Rivage, *Bandol*, Var
20 Nov. 1929

Dear Titus[4]

Thanks for your letter and the cheque for 10,000 francs, for *Lady C.* – But do make me a statement one day.

[1] 'Education and Sex' was the title given to chapter VIII of *Fantasia of the Unconscious* when it was printed in *Adelphi*, July 1923; extracts from chapters XI and XII appeared there under the title 'On Love and Marriage' in September 1923. 'The Proper Study' and 'On Being Religious' (see Letter 5278 and n. 1) were not included in *Assorted Articles*; 'On Human Destiny' and 'On Being a Man' (see p. 400 n. 3) were collected in that volume.

[2] See letter following.

[3] DHL appears to be alluding to some notice of *Pornography and Obscenity* sent him by Pollinger; the source is not known.

[4] DHL was replying to Titus's letter, 18 November 1929 (TMSC SIU):

Dear Mr. Lawrence,

  I enclose check for 10,000 francs on account of LADY CHATTERLEY. Kindly acknowledge receipt.

  I am sorry that the other French book has not turned up yet. I am afraid that if you want it very badly, it will have to be advertised for.

Don't bother about the Moret book if it's difficult. I believe I haven't given you the complete title – though that *should* be enough.

Carter is here, looking a good bit older – I haven't seen him for six years. We are talking about his Apocalyptic work. – Charlie Lahr is 68 Red Lion St. W.C. 1. I'm glad you'll pay Rhys Davies now, he's pretty hard up. – They haven't sent me *Bottom Dogs* – The last time Dahlberg[1] wrote from New York he was a bit peevish, because Ben Huebsch had said my introd. was a bad 'sales letter', whatever that is, for his novel.

I have heard nothing of the seizure of *This Quarter* in England: there is certainly nothing official, as the 'Obscenity' article is printed intact in a 1/- pamphlet by Faber & Faber (only lengthened) in England, and the people hate it. – If any copies of *This Quarter* are lost, it is little post-office clerks who steal them hoping for something they can sell high. The only redress is to register the parcels, and then claim.

We shall be pleased to see you – it's brilliant weather, for the moment.

Sincerely   D. H. Lawrence

I suppose you have nothing from Albert Boni? Curtis Brown writes that A. A. Knopf is in London, is interested in publishing my collected books in U. S. A. and is approaching Boni to secure the copyrights. Hope there'll be no clash, but I think not.

DHL

5424. To Max Mohr, [21 November 1929]
Text: MS HMohr; Mohr, Briefe 537–8.

Bandol. Var.
Thursday. 20 Novem.

Dear Mohr

The Etruscan book came safely,[2] and the other books, and many thanks. But why oh why will you spend your money, when you are such a Wolf in a

I have just received your DOCTOR MANENTE from Orioli and also Dahlberg's BOTTOM DOGS with your introduction. Both will form my next Sunday's reading.

I saw your friend Carter once or twice. He tells me he is going South to pay you a visit.

I wonder if you can give me Lahr's address. I have to pay him for a story by Rhys Davis, which I accepted through him and for which I now want to pay.

Carter told me, but I have not heard anything myself on the matter, that my magazine, containing your article ['Pornography and Obscenity'], has been seized in England. As I said, I have heard nothing direct in the matter; although one firm informed me that they had received only half the quantity of copies I sent them. Now, the next thing you are going to do about it, is to get one of your high and mighty friends in Parliament to ask for an explanation.

I am still thinking of taking a run down South for a few minutes, in which case I shall certainly pay you "mes hommages."

Yours sincerely

[1] Dahlberg] he   [2] Possibly Fritz Schachermeyr, *Etruskische Frühgeschichte* (Berlin, 1929).

grube!¹ – But I like the Etruscan book very much, and am reading it in spite of the tiresome and jaw-cracking style. *Why* must these Wissenschafter² write such long sentences, it is worse than Brewster's yoga exercises, which make him hold his breath till his brain goes silly. But the man takes a really sensible view of the Etrusker, as far as I have read. He seems to have some real feeling for them.

Here all goes very quietly. Frederick Carter, the man who writes on the Offenbarung Johannis³ is here, staying in the Beau Rivage. It is six years since I have seen him, and he seems much older and sadder, and no wiser, only a little more dead. He is separated from his wife, and everything has gone wrong. He is not really interested in Apocalypse or Astrology any more – but of course he would like to get published this work he has already done. So I must see if I can manage it.

Yesterday Madame Douillet and her daughter – from the Beau Rivage – came to tea, and she talked of Earl and Achsah, in all respect, but it was rather funny. Pourquoi, Monsieur, pourquoi mangent-ils comme ça? pourquoi? C'est manger sans vouloir manger, n'est-ce pas?⁴ – It was a serious problem to her. And when I said: Voyez-vous, ils sont Bouddhistes, les dévotés du dieu Bouddha, de l'Inde⁵ – she was all the more astonished and mystified. Can't get it at all. She brought us a pretty little palm tree in a pot, saying: J'ai pensé à Monsieur⁶ – and she is going to send us some little *gold-fish* – alive and swimming: also for Monsieur, I suppose. I'm afraid Monsieur Mickie Beau Soleil, le chat jaune, la trouvera fort à son gout.⁷

The Brewsters have taken the Château Brun, and paid 1,200 francs for six months rent. Now the workmen are white-washing the inside, for 700 frs. – and Earl and Achsah are⁸ supposed to be painting the doors and windows, also white. The whole interior is to be snow-white, like a pure, pure lily: imaginez-vous, Monsieur, comme un tombeau!⁹ But Earl does not want to go to the house, he is afraid of being there all alone with his Achsah, so when they go to paint the doors, after an hour he has a head-ache, and must come home. I'm afraid it is going to be very difficult. – They have bought two old chairs and a set of fire-irons (for 6 frs) so far. I don't know how they'll ever really move in to the house: they really worry me.

I have been better lately, taking my little walks. We have had three lovely

¹ The Mohrs' house was called 'Wolfsgrube': 'wolf-hole' or 'wolf-trap'.   ² 'academics'.
³ 'Revelation of John'.
⁴ 'Why, Monsieur, why do they eat like that? why? It's eating without wanting to eat, isn't it?'
⁵ 'You see, they are Buddhists, devotees of the god Buddha, from India'.
⁶ 'I thought of Monsieur'.
⁷ 'Monsieur Mickie Beau Soleil, the marmalade cat, will find it very much to his taste' (cf. Letter 5387).
⁸ Achsah are] Achsah and I are   ⁹ 'imagine, Monsieur, like a tomb!'

brilliant days, very blue, with a yellow sun sinking down in the sea at four oclock. The wind is rather strong, but from the east, and warm. We light the chauffage centrale at tea-time, but all the day is warm. On Monday we baked bread, five loaves only, and white bread, because one cannot buy Vollkorn Mehl.[1] But Mme Douillet is getting us some – she calls it farine de seigle, which is Roggenmehl,[2] but I hope it won't be, because that is so difficult to bake. Madame Martinse, our femme de ménage, was very jealous when we baked the bread, and bounced about the kitchen, and burnt Frieda's Apfelkuchen[3] black. But I sat in the kitchen like a lion and watched my bread bake safely. It is very good, but nearly all eaten.

The Huxleys will be almost in Paris now. They went back by Madrid and Bourges and Biarritz, and won't come here till after Christmas. Will you really stay in Wolfsgrube till February? it seems a long time. And what work are you doing? – Thank you for the article on *Fantasia*[4] – I hope they'll manage to sell some copies. And I hope Eva's cold is better, and you are well and cheerful. And again many thanks, but *don't* spend money on these things.

ever   DHL

5425. To Herberth Herlitschka, 25 November 1929
Text: MS UR; Unpublished.

Villa Beau Soleil, *Bandol.* Var. France
25 Nov 1929

Dear Mr Herlitschka[5]

Since you write frankly, I will answer in the same spirit.[6] – Kippenberg kept hesitating a long time over *Lady Chatterley* – Rowohlt was prepared to do

---

[1] 'wholemeal flour'.   [2] 'rye flour'.   [3] 'apple cake'.

[4] Not known; presumably written with reference to the German translation of *Fantasia* (cf. Letter 5403).

[5] Herberth Egon Herlitschka (1893–1970), b. Vienna; professional translator of recent English literature into German, including works by Charles Morgan, Virginia Woolf, Thornton Wilder, Aldous Huxley, W. B. Yeats and David Garnett.

[6] Herlitschka had written, 19 November 1929 (TMSC UR), that he had recently read *Lady Chatterley's Lover* for the Insel Verlag, and had recommended that

A general (ordinary) edition [was] out of the question unless several passages were toned down and however carefully and skillfully this might be done by the translator it would falsify the tenor of the book and would certainly be quite against the author's wishes and intentions . . . So there remain nothing but an exact German Version to be published in a private edition . . . At the same time I strongly advised them to bring out the book not only on account of its literary merits but also because it does apply as well to the psychic and mental attitude of Germans as of English men and women though perhaps not to the same degree . . . To my great regret the Insel-Verlag . . . decided not to take it because for the time being they do not like to bring out private editions.

Being anxious to translate the book, Herlitschka had then recommended it to Tal, who very much wanted to take it, but were being obstructed by Curtis Brown's Leipzig sub-agent.

it – Kiepenheuer also *said* they wanted it – Kippenberg prevented them, and then at last turned the book down – afraid – and afraid of the 'subversive' anti-bourgeois note! Then Curtis Browns Foreign Manager – Miss Jean Watson – apparently began to look to Vienna – I said to her, wait a moment and let me find out what has happened between Kippenberg, Fischer, Rowohlt and Kiepenheuer. I found out all I wanted to know, and told Miss Watson to go ahead with what she was doing, but I wasn't very keen on seeing a German translation. I was in Germany all summer, and at the end I rather felt, *damn Germany! They're sure to misunderstand, anyhow.* – Frau Ewald is a friend. I asked her to ask in Berlin certain questions about *Lady C.*, but I did *not* commission her to act in any way for the book: in fact I asked her to leave it alone. My agents, Curtis Brown, have the responsibility for the book. I *believe* they are negotiating with the *Phaidon*: but Miss Watson is a difficult person. What would you like me to say to her? I know nothing about either the Phaidon or Mr Tal, – and I'm afraid she doesn't know much.

As for my translations, don't say anything. For the very first book, *The Rainbow*, Kippenberg used to send me proofs to consider. But the translation made my blood run cold.[1] It wasn't me at all. I don't care about little mistakes and mistranslations, if only the *spirit* of the original can be preserved. But oh dear, what a horrible pompous-commonplace spirit filled the German translation of *The Rainbow*. I lamented in vain to Kippenberg, the old Pasha seemed to like pompous commonplace. Then he did change, and his new translator[2] gave me a sort of Proustian tone, utterly unreal. As the least of these literary evils, I begged for my sister-in-law to translate me – and after some years' refusal, Kippenberg agreed. She is now doing *The Plumed Serpent*, and I tremble in my shoes. Because though Frau Jaffe understands me fairly well, yet she has not the peculiar *mastery* a translator needs, to give a work its own life in a new language.

Well – I almost wish I need never be translated. But since that is fultile,

Herlitschka had just received a telephone call from Dr Horovitz of the Phaidon-Verlag who said he had been offered the book by Frau Franziska Ewald, claiming to be the only person authorised by DHL to offer the book in Germany. Herlitschka went on to warn DHL against the many incompetent translators working in Germany:

That even a first class firm of publishers may make a grave mistake in the choice of their translators is borne out by the German editions of your own books, I regret to say ... The translations of your books are all equally unsatisfactory even that of the volume entitled "Die Frau die davon ritt" [*The Woman Who Rode Away*] which was done, I understand, by a relative of yours [Else Jaffe] upon your special request; but you will, I hope, forgive me, if I am quite candid in these matters.

He enclosed a list of mistranslations from one of DHL's volumes.

[1] By Franz Franzius.   [2] Thesi Mutzenbecher (translated *Women in Love*).

let me know now about *Lady C* and if there is anything you would like me to do.

                        Sincerely   D. H. Lawrence

5426. To Laurence Pollinger, 25 November 1929
Text: MS UT; cited in *Apocalypse* 14.

                        Villa BeauSoleil, Bandol. Var. France
                        25 Novem 1929
Dear Pollinger

Seems to me Percy Robinson's charges are pretty stiff – damn all lawyers. I enclose cheque for their amount, and am thankful to forget them.

About the Cresset Press: the 'bits' to go in front of the *Birds Beasts* sections are part original and sometimes quotations from the fragments of Xenophanes and Empedokles and others, but I should like it all put in inverted commas, and let them crack their wits (the public) to find out what is ancient quotation and what isn't. (It is nearly all of it me.)

By the way, those ten copies of the *Obscenity* Pamphlet. Would you send four to me here – and then one to my sisters (poor things)

1. Mrs L. A. Clarke. Broadway. *Ripley nr. Derby.*
1. Mrs S. King. 16 Brooklands Rd. Sneinton Hill. Nottingham.
1. Sig. G. Orioli. 6 Lungarno Corsini. Florence.
1. Mr Edward W. Titus. 4 rue Delambre. Paris. XIV.
1. Dr Max Mohr. Wolfsgrube. *Rottach-am-Tegernsee*, Oberbayern. Germany.
1. Rhys Davies Esq. c/o Charles Lahr. 68 Red Lion St. W. C. 1.

Don't bother about Orioli and the Lungarno Series – he is a very vague person with regard to business beyond his little shop, but I will get him to nail Aldous, Aldington and Douglas definitely, and that is enough on which to base negotiations. In fact I'll write Huxley myself. – And later I shall do a second vol. of Lasca. Wait a little bit.

I hear that Stephensen says he wants to float off the Mandrake into a limited company, as they have £6000-worth of stock to sell. Well it's none of it me. But it seems as if there was a quite definite breach between Stephensen and Goldston, so perhaps the Mandrake is already a withered root. Too bad! but no wonder, with half a ton of Crowley on top of it. – I hear this Sideways – Stephensen writes no more, sends affec. messages –

                        Amitiés   D. H. Lawrence

5427. To Witter Bynner, 26 November 1929
Text: MS HU; Witter Bynner, *Journey with Genius* (New York, 1951), pp. 339–40.

Villa Beau Soleil. *Bandol.* Var. France
26 Nov 1929

Dear Bynner

I meant to answer you long ago, but the flesh is very weak.[1] My health is *very* tiresome, and I don't feel like doing a thing: unusual for me. But I do believe the root of all my sickness is a sort of rage. I realise now, Europe gets me into an inward rage, that keeps my bronchials hellish inflamed. I believe I'd get better in no time in New Mexico, because I'm not really weak. But I can't digest my inward spleen in Europe – that's what ails me. And in New Mexico I can. – Now I have really come to this conclusion, I shall try all my might to arrange getting back, in the New Year. I wish there weren't all these passport difficulties. – And if we can come we should probably try to take some little furnished place in Santa Fe for the first month or so, to get me used to the altitude – and also to look round for a winter house near Santa Fe, and just summer at the ranch. That is what *Frieda* wants.

No, I'm sure I'm flattered if you dedicate your poems to me: but you haven't sent me the poems. And I am all agog to hear of you writing a novel.[2] I hope by now it's done. What a great lark, a novel after all! And I was sorry to hear of you so ill. But illness seems to be one's portion nowadays. I feel I'm a chastened bird – but perhaps I'm not.

We have got this little house on the sea near Marseille until end of March – then I really wish we could come west. Ida Rauh is in Geneva, and I think she is coming down here, so perhaps she can help it. I don't quite know whether I'm *persona grata* in U.S.A. just now – after *Lady C.* etc. But I dont suppose anybody really cares. It's the emigration question which is most difficult – and so silly. – Frieda is prepared to come back: but warily.

I do really and firmly believe, though, that it's Europe that has made me so ill. One gets so innerly angry with the dull sort of hopelessness and deadness there is over here. Anyhow in New Mexico the sun and the air are alive, let man be what he may. But here they've killed the very sun, the very air.

Tell Christine Hughes I will write to her, and Mary Christine I will give her a wedding present if she is still married and not minding. I never give wedding presents till two years after. Wait and see, is my English motto, with

---

[1] Cf. Matthew xxvi. 41.

[2] Bynner subsequently sent the poems, *Indian Earth*; Frieda later told him that she 'could almost *smell* Chapala' in them (*Journey with Genius*, p. 345). He never published a novel.

regard to young marriages. – Frieda, by the way, has her elder daughter 'safely' married, and seems hugely relieved at the fact.[1]

Well – I'm really quite an aimiable person underneath, even if I'm catty as you say. But cats are really very easy animals. I feel a rather bedraggled one at present – wish a few people would stroke my fur the right way and make me purr. Perhaps when we come to Santa Fe.

                                                  So au revoir   D. H. Lawrence

5428. To S. S. Koteliansky, [27 November 1929]
Text: MS BL; Postmark, Bandol 28 11 29; Moore 1217.

                                                              Beau Soleil.
                                                              Wed.
Dear Kot

Didn't I answer your letter? – I got Rosanov, and some of it I think really good – the latter half. I did a small article on it, and sent it to Curtis Brown, but probably they'll not be able to place it.[2] I said in it that Rosanov died a few years later than *Fallen Leaves* – 1912 – That's right, isn't it?

I don't know what to say about your doctor.[3] It's a great bore for him to get out at Toulon and come back here – about 8 miles – and then next day or so go on to Cannes or wherever he is going – some hours from Toulon. And I simply don't want to make a three or four hours' journey to talk with a doctor who will want to talk about lungs when the trouble is bronchials. If I knew a doctor who understood bronchials! – but they are much more difficult than lungs!

Carter is here, and we've had various talks about everything going. He makes me feel that all is very dreary and dead in that literary London, and the young have no life in them at all.

I'm glad you could let Curtis Browns have the *Adelphi* copies. Murry was trying to frustrate me there. You will know by now they want to publish those essays in a vol. of collected newspaper and magazine articles. – I don't want any more limited editions of me to appear just now. – There is *Manente* and the *Escaped Cock* – people will be tired. I wish I could have sent you a *Cock*, but I myself only got one or two. I shall try to secure others. It will have to

---

[1] Cf. p. 69 n. 2.   [2] Cf. Letter 5406 and n. 3. (Rozanov d. 1919.)
[3] Dr Andrew John Morland (1896–1957), resident physician at Mundesley Hospital, near Norwich; author of *Pulmonary Tuberculosis in General Practice* (1932); and subsequently head of the Department of Chest Diseases at University College Hospital, London. m. 1928, Dorothy Saunders. He had been persuaded by his friends Kot and Gertler to offer to break his journey in southern France in January 1930 to examine DHL. See Nehls, iii. 423–5; G. Zytaruk, 'The Last Days of D. H. Lawrence: Hitherto Unpublished Letter of Dr Andrew Morland', *DHL Review*, i (Spring 1968), 44–50.

appear in England later – but I am not arranging anything so far with C[harles] L[ahr]. The Mandrake is, I believe, as good as dead. – Carter is taking a copy of the *Cock* to the Lion – promised from the first, so I must keep my promise.

I'm glad Murry has decided there is no God. It makes one know that there *is*.

I shall have to think of somebody for an edition of the *Cock* next year. Do you ever hear of Margaret Radford?[1]

ever   DHL

5429. To Aldous and Maria Huxley, [27 November 1929]
Text: Huxley 840–1.

Beau Soleil, Bandol.
Wed.

Dear Aldous and Maria, –

So you are safely back – that's one mercy, anyhow, and we needn't think of you on rainy, windy days and imagine the little red car ploughing on, ploughing on. Ugh! – I feel I don't want to feel any bad weather or see one single ugly or frightening thing just now – and Spain seems full of frightfulness. As for weather, we get mixed – blue and windy just now, turning colder, I think.

No news here. I sent you a copy of *Pansies*, which [Frederick Carter][2] brought from London. He does etchings and drawings, and writes on the Apocalypse – I knew him in the past – he is staying at the Beau Rivage for the moment. But he fills me with the same savage despair with the young Englishman – so without fire, without spark, without spunk – so *ineffectual*. What's the good of such people, though they are clever. They think the whole end of living is achieved if they talk, with a drink, rather amusingly and cleverly for an evening. Bores me – somehow so fatuous.

Yesterday Frieda went to Toulon with [Achsah], and she bought six snowy-white cups and saucers, and six snowy-white plates – very inexpensive – after having demanded *des tasses de Limoges*.[3] Then she went to the carpet dept. – *Dames de France* – floated down on the salesman and demanded *des tapis de Bokhara, s'il vous plaît!*[4] – and bought, of course, a straw mat for 70 frs. But said to Frieda: 'Frieda, *isn't* it rather lovely, *quite* oriental design – and won't [Earl] appreciate it – a touch of the East.' – It was Jap, of course. – They want us to look for a house very near them – but for the moment, the sight of their flurries is enough for me. I am thankful for this unredeemably

---

[1] Daughter of DHL's war-time friend Dollie Radford (1864–1920); DHL's references to her over the years were often uncomplimentary (e.g. *Letters*, iii. 226, 228, 277; v. 426).
[2] See p. 239 n. 1.   [3] 'cups in Limoges china'.   [4] 'carpets from Bokhara, please!'

modern and small Beau Soleil, taken for 6 months and no more, and am thankful to God to escape anything like a permanency. 'Better fifty years of Europe than a cycle of Cathay.'[1] Well, I've had nearly fifty years of Europe, so I would rather try the cycle of Cathay. – Douglas sent me his *What About Europe?*[2] – a bit rancid, perhaps, and sometimes fatuous, but on the whole he's right – Europe is as reesty[3] as he says.

DHL

5430. To Giuseppe Orioli, [27 November 1929]
Text: MS UCLA; Moore 1214–15.

Beau Soleil, *Bandol*, Var
Wednesday

Dear Pino

I haven't thanked you for the other copies of *Manente* – they came safely. Today comes the notice that the other parcel – Frieda's coat – has arrived at the station, so that will be the last. Now do send me a bill of all the charges and costs. – I found out from the agent that Egidi charged *Lire 100 for storage* and Lire 100 for imballaggio[4] – surely we didn't owe 100L. for storage.

Today I got *What About Europe?* – I have read it, and really, it's true what Norman says about Europe – in fact I begin to feel hopeless. There's *no* spunk in anybody today, and the young Englishmen are every one Willy-Wetlegs. Frederick Carter is here – the Apocalypse man – another quite clever ineffectual blighter – No fire, no courage, no spunk – It drives me mad.

The Brewsters have taken their little Chateau Brun for 2,500 frs. a year – and are having it done up, and are going to buy furniture. They say they have no money, so the first thing they do is to hire a grand piano: a horizontal grand – I don't believe they'll ever stay in that lonely house – it's about five miles from here.

I don't hear a word from the Crosbys – so I expect she has gone to America. I heard they advertised the *Cock* in *Transition*, but haven't seen a copy.[5]

I hope you got the copy of *Pansies*, and one for Douglas, which I sent last week: nice vellum copies.

Aldous wrote from Suresnes – they are back, rather tired. I don't think

---

[1] Tennyson, 'Locksley Hall' (1842), l. 184.
[2] Douglas published his *How about Europe: Some Footnotes on East and West*, privately (550 copies), in Florence in 1929; Chatto & Windus republished it in June 1930.
[3] 'rancid' (English dialect).   [4] 'packing'.
[5] Together with other new Black Sun Press editions, *The Escaped Cock* was advertised in *transition*, No. 18, November 1929; purchasers were referred to Harry F. Marks, 31 West 47th Street, New York.

they liked Spain *very* much, but no doubt he will get a vol. of essays out of it.
– Try and fix up the date etc. of the Machiavelli volume with him, and give
Pollinger approximate dates for Aldington's translation, and Douglas' – so
that he can do something about the series. Was Richard Aldington in
Florence? Is Douglas back? How is Scott-Moncrieff?

Mixed weather here – not bad – but I don't feel in a very good way – I
don't want to work or paint or do anything: feel somehow cross with
everything.

How about your passport?

How is *Manente* going now? The Wall Street Crash has hit the Americans
hard – it will make selling more difficult. Everything will be tight.

I ordered you a copy of my *Obscenity* pamphlet – They hate it in England.
– Tell me if you got the *Pansies*.

                                                                        DHL

[Frieda Lawrence begins]

Am writing a long letter soon!

                                                                 Love   F–

5431. To Charles Lahr, [27 November 1929]
Text: MS UNYB; Postmark, Bandol 28 11 29; Unpublished.

                                                                 Beau Soleil
                                                                         Wed
Dear Lahr

I got *Hesiod* all right – many thanks – and Carter brought the 3 copies of
the poems. I haven't heard from anybody in England, that they have received
their copies – but I suppose it's all right.

Your letter two days ago. I talked to Carter about the 'Squib'. He damps
it out considerably – says that nobody will ever do anything if it's
anonymous, and anyhow there's not enough young people eager and willing
to make anything of it. I am dead against doing a one-man show. To me
the 'Squib' meant an opportunity for some young people to make some
elder people jump. If the young haven't enough gun-powder in them, all
right – I can fire *my* squibs in pamphlets like *Obscenity*. That seems to
annoy them hard enough. If I'm going to be alone I'll be alone. – As for
material, I have nothing but a little set of poems, and they can go elsewhere.

I am sending you a *Hahn* by Carter. Mrs Crosby has apparently gone off
to New York with the 500: so I must wait till she comes back before making
any move.

It's rather a bore about the Mandrake. Goldston doesn't seem quite the

Sabbath Jew I thought he was. I must certainly not let them do any limited edition for me again.

Just got Douglas' *What About Europe?* It's disgruntled, but Europe is quite as bad as he says. And Carter makes me feel that all young Englishmen are willy-wetlegs, if not worse. How very dreary!

I'm glad Davies is appearing in the *London Mercury* – now he'll be in at the tea-party of all the Aunties, god bless him! I want to write to him, but somehow haven't got the right word to say.

ever   DHL

5432. To Ada Clarke, [27 November 1929]
Text: MS Clarke; Postmark, B[andol] 27 11 29; cited in Lawrence–Gelder 203–4.

Beau Soleil, Bandol, Var
Wed

My dear Sister

You mustn't mind if it is a long time between letters – nowadays I find it simply an effort to write – In fact I don't really do anything, writing or painting or anything else – unusual for me, but I suppose it's a mood. My health is better, but not very good – and I simply don't want to do anything on earth, not even read. I try to persuade Frieda to write, but she never was a good correspondent.

Did you get a copy of the *Pansies?* – very nice, on vellum, and bound in white calf. Let me know if you have it – and Emily hers. Also the copy of *Dr Manente* from Florence, and the *Obscenity* pamphlet. There is still another thing I shall send you when I have a chance.

Everything very quiet here – a sunny day, but windy, and turning colder. The Brewsters have gone off to paint the inside doors of their house. They've taken an old, I'm afraid cold house on a hill about 5. miles away – lovely situation – for £20 a year. It's only an old smallish house, but it's called Château Brun, so Achsah is very proud. They say they have no money at all, but they always take a taxi to the house, and the first thing Achsah has done is to hire a horizontal grand piano. Then they've bought two sets of fire-irons for 6 frs. – 1/- – and two old stripped chairs. It'll be *some* place, by the time they move in. Meanwhile they are still in the Beau Rivage. – Frederick Carter is there too – do you remember, the man I went to stay with in the Deanery, Pontesbury nr. Shrewsbury, when I left you in Ripley about five years ago[1] –

---

[1] On 3 January 1924 (see *Letters*, iv. 554).

and we missed the train in Derby? He looks _so_ much older, and disgruntled: separated from his wife for good, and everything gone to pot. But he earns enough by his drawings to live on.

Stephensen apparently has made a mess of the Mandrake Press by bringing out far too many books – which he can't sell – and so spending far more money than he makes. So he and Goldston, his financial backer, have had some sort of split, and I'm afraid the Mandrake is about at the end of its running.

Many people seem angry over my _Obscenity_ Pamphlet, but Charlie Lahr said he had sold three dozen, and only 3 copies of Jix's. People need something to scrap about.

Poor Rhys Davies, the Mandrake were going to publish his two novels, and now they're off. He gets very bitter. But Jack Squire has accepted one of his stories for _The London Mercury_, so that cheers him up a bit.

We've got our trunks from Florence, so have our own things around us again. The Brewsters want us to take a permanent house near them, but I don't much want to. Why be tied down to these permanencies!

Well I hope all goes well. The yellow narcissus are many of them out in the little field next us – and in the country the green peas are up – seems queer. The femme de menage brings us lovely roses and pink carnations – they are cheap just now.

Even if I don't write, send me a line now and then –

love   DHL

5433. To Earl and Achsah Brewster, [28? November 1929]
Text: MS UT; Brewster 223–4.

BeauSoleil.
Thursday

Dear Earl and Achsah

We laid tea for you, and had home-baked bread and cakes fit to send any liver crazy – we're so sorry you weren't feeling well enough to come – Carter told us he thought you might. I hope it'll be better tomorrow. Anyhow the pump-motor is still broke, and we can't have any chauffage. But struggle around if you can, or I shall have to stagger to you. The wind makes one feel a bit stupid.

I do hope you'll both be feeling all right tomorrow.

DHL

5434. To Emily King, 30 November 1929
Text: MS Lazarus; cited in V. de S. Pinto, 'D. H. Lawrence: Letter-Writer and Craftsman in Verse', *Renaissance and Modern Studies*, i (1957), 9.

Beau Soleil, *Bandol*, Var
30 Nov. 1929

My dear Pamela

I am writing by return to say we should love a Christmas pudding and a little cake and a bit of mincemeat, and half a pound of tea and Harwood Brewster will bring it, if you put it in a good shut-up basket that she can travel with easily, and easily open for the customs. Dont send anything that *won't keep*, as the trains are very hot – no pork pie or anything with meat – and no chocolate, because they might charge duty. They won't charge on a pudding and a cake, I don't think. Harwood leaves her school on 17th Dec., so see she has it in time.

Miss Harwood Brewster. Dartington Hall. *Totnes*, Devon.
And you might ask Ada to send to Harwood for Frieda
2 large meridian undervests.
2 knickers.[1]

Myself I don't need any underclothing or anything at all. – We shall have to pretend the mince-meat and pudding are made with nut-fat, as the Brewsters will [. . .] be having a Christmas dinner with us, and would faint at the thought of suet.

They have taken a house about five miles away, a lovely situation, but a bit lonely, and the house a bit cold. They have taken it unfurnished for a year, and are buying odds and ends of furniture. They say they have no money: but Achsah has already hired a horizontal grand piano. They want us to find a permanent house in their neighbourhood, – it's near St. Cyr, the next village – but I still feel disinclined for a permanency. Anyhow we've got this till end of March.

Maria Huxley also wants to come in January, to find a house – and they want to *buy* one, somewhere near here.

Frederick Carter has been staying at the Beau Rivage this last two weeks, but he leaves today. He comes every day – and the Brewsters come every day to tea, so we've not been lonely. We expect a friend from Santa Fe soon[2] – she'll stay in the Beau Rivage.

The weather is poor – grey, uneasy, but not much rain – and my health is only middling. But I just stay comfortably in bed, and don't bother. The femme de ménage cooks quite good meals.

---

[1] Ada jotted the address and the requests on the verso of the envelope to Letter 5432.
[2] Ida Rauh (see Letters 5442 and 5447).

I ordered you my *Obscenity* article – but you needn't read it. Stirs them up
a bit. That Jix is a mealy-mouthed worm – but I saw the *New Statesman*
standing up for me boldly this week.[1] – I haven't sent you the *Escaped Cock*
yet. It is out, and very beautifully printed. I think they have shipped all the
500 copies from Paris to New York: but now America is really very hard hit
by the Wall Street crash, trade really very bad over there, and books hardly
selling at all. So we must go slow for a time.

Don't send any parcel by post here – it takes at least three weeks, and
everything smashed.

love   DHL

5435. To Edward Titus, 30 November 1929
Text: MS UT; cited in *Apocalypse* 18.

Beau Soleil, *Bandol*, Var
30 Nov 1929

Dear Titus[2]

I don't quite see your reasons for selling 200 copies of *Lady C*. to your
traveller at 50% discount. What is the point, exactly? Why should you *sell* the

---

[1] The review of *Pornography and Obscenity*, by R. A. Barclay, appeared in the *New Statesman* on
23 November 1929 (reprinted in Draper, *The Critical Heritage*, pp. 314–17):

It is a real masterpiece of fundamental analysis written by a man of genius from the very
bottom of his heart ... it is one of the most powerful and sane and penetrating pieces of writing
that we have read for very many years ... His pamphlet ... may well mark an epoch in the
history not only of censorship but of the reasonable appreciation of the realities of sexual
morality and sexual honesty and decency.

[2] DHL was replying to a letter from Titus, 28 November 1929 (TMSC SIU):

Dear Mr. Lawrence:

Will you let me know by return of post whether you will permit me to sell 200 copies of "Our
Lady" at a 50% discount? Frankly, I do not like to do it, but it might perhaps be advisable in
this particular instance for the following reason: I have had a disagreement with my traveller.
These disagreements, of course, are not, properly speaking, your affair. As you know, he has
been getting 15% on all sales made by him. As he did not cover territory which should have
been covered by him, I decided to fill orders from such uncovered territory. I thought there
was no reason why any sales should be lost just because he could not or would not travel in
these particular parts. I am decidedly within my rights, but he could not see it this way. To
obviate these disagreements, he now proposes to buy direct from me 200 copies to be delivered
to him, thus relieving me from shipping to various bookdealers, on condition that I allow him
50%. If business should be smoother, it might perhaps be advisable to agree to his terms.

There is this danger, however, that we might run: He might, having such a big discount, be
able to undersell us. This apprehension is perhaps exaggerated on my part; but I feel it my duty
to put it before you just the same. Will you have the goodness to let me know what you think
about it?

While I am writing to you, I might perhaps mention that the other day a young man at my
place of business told me that he had seen you at Bandol and that you mentioned that you
intended bringing out another and more expensive edition of "Lady Chatterly" in France. The

books to a traveller? – It seems to me, if there is some dispute between you, he would most certainly use his opportunity to get his own back on you, by underselling, or by some other means which you have not thought of. Unless there is a *good* reason for selling him 200 copies at 50% discount, I should say, don't do it.

As for Tombazis,[1] I think people deliberately tell lies. Young men are always going round inventing things 'I have said.' – I may have mentioned to him that I had heard that a new, more expensive, *illustrated* edition of *Lady C.* was coming out, *pirated*, in U.S.A. And see what he twists it to! Of course it's all nonsense.

No, we are still in BeauSoleil –

I wish you would send me a statement of sales and expenses for *Lady C.* up to now, so I can see where we are.

Frederick Carter leaves today, and will call in and see you.

Ever   D. H. Lawrence

I ordered you a copy of my *Obscenity* pamphlet.

5436. To Laurence Pollinger, 30 November 1929
Text: MS UT; Unpublished.

Beau Soleil, *Bandol*, Var, France
30 Novem 1929

Dear Pollinger

Yes, the Mandrake is in a bad way – but Goldston has money all right. – He owes us £250 on the Book of *Paintings*, shortly, doesn't he?[2] – I hear he cleared £2000, about that, on the book. – I *believe* he will pay his debts – but Stephensen is a complete uncertainty. It's no good their doing *Jolly Roger* if they are really finished. – Yes, I would like it done cheap – 2/- or 3/6.[3]

Can you tell me why Eyre & Spottiswood should have 30 pages of *Kangaroo* for £5-5-0, when you make Harold Munro pay £10. for two pages of poetry?[4] It means I should get fifty shillings – and not for fifty shillings, by a long chalk, would I bother to [. . .] cut down a chapter of a novel from fifty to

young man's name escapes me; but I think it was a Greek name, maybe Tombazis. I was naturally amazed to hear this and I told him I thought he was mistaken.

I hope you are enjoying good health.

Yours very sincerely,

[1] Unidentified.
[2] DHL's letter was annotated in Curtis Brown's office: 'Advance £250. 0. 0. £50 Pd. Apr 3/29. £200 Pd. July 3/29.'
[3] Cf. p. 446 and n. 1.   [4] Cf. Letters 5164 and n. 2, 5171.

30 pages. But why this strange cheapness and solemnity about five guineas, of which Secker gets half? Is there some other point? – Kudos?

I have seen one or two papers about the *Pornography* article – today came the *Everyman* – what a mealy-mouthed maggot that Jix is![1]

Do you really think Secker is a good person for the Lungarno Series? I don't: though the terms are all right.

No, I don't want any more Limited Editions of any sort, just now. – I should like to see the complete MS of the suggested book of newspaper articles as soon as it is ready. Shall we call it 'Orts and Slarts'! It means the beaux restes – pieces left over from a meal, etc.[2] It's dialect – but Orts is in the dictionary.

Yes, it would be good if Alfred A. [Knopf] rescued us from the slough of Albert [Boni]. I can't imagine why he – Knopf – suddenly loves me. Have you seen any American cuttings – reviews – of *Pansies?* I've only had one.[3] Wonder how they take them.

Bandol is about half an hour from Toulon, and Toulon is about 14 hours from Paris, by the Riviera express trains.

The weather is poor, my health is ditto.

ever   DHL

5437. To Muriel Moller, 1 December 1929
Text: TMSC NWU; Huxley 839.

Villa Beau Soleil, Bandol, Var. France.
1 Dec. 1929.

Dear Miss Moller

Many thanks for your letter and for sending on those addresses. But here we are, and have taken a house for six months. The doctors said, as I found

---

[1] *Everyman*, 28 November 1929, carried an article, 'HOW THE CENSORSHIP WORKS' by ('Jix') Lord Brentford. He expressed satisfaction with the reception of his pamphlet, *Do We Need a Censor?*, except from 'a certain section of the community who prefer to put liberty before decency'. Having stated his confidence that 'the Englishman is a decently minded person', he wondered 'what the average father of a family would say if he found his daughter reading Mr. D. H. Lawrence's latest pamphlet on pornography'. Brentford (without specifying) alluded to 'an exhibition of pictures ... which it was alleged were indecent ... and the exhibition was closed'. Finally, he recalled how 'two poems by a well-known man were caught in the post, quite accidentally – not under the Home Secretary's warrant, but simply on the haphazard opening by the Customs authorities of a parcel to see whether it contained anything contraband. It was found to contain a most pernicious poem.'

[2] DHL used 'orts and slarts', with this meaning, in two early poems: 'Whether or Not': vii (a group of dialect poems) and 'Rose of all the World' (*Complete Poems*, i. 82, 219; ii. 924).

[3] The review to which DHL refers has not been traced. The earliest known American review was by Mark van Doren in *New York Herald Tribune Books*, 15 December 1929. He felt that many of the poems were 'distressingly flat', but concluded that if it were not taken too seriously

this place, and the sea, suited me so excellently last winter, it would be folly not to come back again this winter. So I obeyed. We'd both rather have come to Italy – but if only I can get my infernal chest better, then we'll be *free* to come and to take a house where we like.

It is very quiet here, a tiny port,[1] village, aimiable and careless people. It somehow is more cheerful than Italy, more free of care. It does not put weights on one, as Italy does sometimes. – The house is just an ugly six-room bungalow, but it has bath and water and central heating, a big terrace, a wilderness garden, and stands in a rather lovely position on the sea, so let's hope the gods will be good to us and I shall get strong and Frieda will be happy having a new place to play with.

And you will soon be gone! it will be most thrilling. But don't get too tired. Somehow I think travelling becomes more tiring. – And we will meet in spring in Florence, when your terrace is full of flowers, and it will be lovely. – And if by any chance you come this way, *come and see us.*

affectionately from both.   D. H. Lawrence

5438. To Richard de la Mare, 3 December 1929
Text: MS Faber; Unpublished.

Villa Beau Soleil, *Bandol*, Var, France
3 Dec 1929

Dear Mr de la Mare[2]

I am sending four poems to Miss Pearn of Curtis Brown, and she will let you see them.[3] I think 'Neptune' is the best for your purposes, but of course you please yourself. If you do choose one, do let me see the decorations. I didn't mind the futuristic ones to Eliot's poem, but I thought those to Yeats poem pretty stiff, especially the cover with the baby.

I think I'd rather have *no* limited edition, personally.

Sincerely   D. H. Lawrence

Pansies 'turns out to be one of the sincerest books which this strangely interesting man has published'.

[1] TMSC reads 'post'.

[2] Richard Herbert Ingpen de la Mare (1901–86), son of Walter de la Mare, was director of Faber & Faber from 1929, and eventually chairman (1960–71). He had apparently invited DHL to submit a poem for inclusion in the *Ariel Poems* series, and had sent as examples T. S. Eliot's *A Song for Simeon* (November 1928), illustrated with a boldly schematic single black figure by E. McKnight Kauffer (who designed the cover for *Look! We Have Come Through!*, see *Letters*, iii. 184 n. 1, 187), and W. B. Yeats's *Three Things* (November 1929), with drawings by Gilbert Spencer. (On Kauffer see *Artists at the Curwen Press*, Tate Gallery, 1977, pp. 74–80.)

[3] On 13 December 1929 (TMSC UT) Nancy Pearn acknowledged the receipt of 'Bells', 'The Triumph of the Machine', 'Father Neptune's Little Affair with Freedom' and 'The Man in the Street'. *The Triumph of the Machine* was published as *Ariel Poems*, No. 28 in October 1930, with illustrations by Althea Willoughby, in a limited edn of 400 copies, as well as an ordinary edn (Roberts A58).

5439. To Maria Chambers, 4 December 1929
Text: MS UT; Unpublished.

Beau Soleil, *Bandol*, Var, France
4 Dec 1929

Dear Maria Cristina

Your express letter this morning! – so the man Marks at least received the first copies sent, which looks as if customs were not stopping them. Selling at $25 too! I'm glad you extracted that bit of information. I know they'd have told me a lie. I suppose he's a worm. – He's right, that *some* of the pirates are in prison. He's not right, that he can't copyright: he can secure provisional copyright, for three months. But since the crash, I really don't believe they'll pirate the book in any hurry. There isn't enough money going. But we can watch out. Of course it'll take him some time now to sell 500 copies at $25. – since the crash people aren't buying books. Orioli and Norman Douglas have hardly any orders at all from America – only from England. So we won't do anything about Osiris[1] at the moment. If Marks sells out, I'll bring out a cheap edition in London, and perhaps find someone to do the same in America. We want to see how the book goes, what is the attitude of the public to it, and what is the attitude of the trade. Your friend Parke might help you with this information. But I'm sure he's not trustworthy, even for information. And his per-centage demands are absurdly high.

Alas, your *Cameronian*[2] scheme is no good, as it is[3] just as difficult to send copies of *Lady C.* to Glasgow as to New York, perhaps more so. One needs an Italian ship – or French.

Ida Rauh hasn't appeared yet – she is in Switzerland. Los Moros are back in Paris.

The weather here has stayed very warm, but rather cloudy. The garden next us is full of yellow narcissus, and in the room are big bowls of roses, yellow and pink, and big orange marigolds, and even the little blue iris. The green peas in the fields are about five inches high.

My health remains tiresome – I wish it was better.

Glad you are fairly chirpy – hope it will continue. The thing to do is to keep as steady as you can, not enter into nervous strains.

Get your copy of Osiris from Marks.

Ever   DHL

[1] *The Escaped Cock.*
[2] Cameronian] Camerronian (The *S. S. Cameronian* belonged to the Anchor Line which was based both in Glasgow and New York.)
[3] MS reads: 'it just'.

5440. To Edward Titus, 8 December 1929
Text: MS UT; Unpublished.

> Beau Soleil. Bandol. Var.
> 8 Dec 1929

Dear Titus[1]

Here is the copy of the agreement you asked for. It says statements every three months, but if that is too tiresome, let us make it six months, and stick to it. Also apparently we ought to have made a little new agreement for the new three thousand copies, but this letter will do instead. We will continue with the original agreement for this second three thousand copies of *Lady Chatterley's Lover*, if you are willing. If you are, please confirm this.

I expect business will be bad for a time, especially American. But after all, we haven't done so badly, do you think?

> Sincerely   D. H. Lawrence

What does one do to a typewriter – a Remington portable – when it suddenly doesn't print the top half of capital letters? – do you know?

5441. To Laurence Pollinger, 8 December 1929
Text: MS UT; Unpublished.

> Beau Soleil, Bandol, Var.
> 8 Dec. 1929.

Dear Pollinger

You must decide about *Jolly Roger* and the Mandrake. Is there anything against the *Jolly Roger* title being changed?[2] It doesn't fit very well any more. But perhaps to change the title would cause confusion. Would it be easy for

---

[1] DHL was replying to Titus's (partly illegible) letter, 6 December 1929 (TMSC SIU):

Dear Mr. Lawrence:

Mr. Carter was in the other day and brought greetings from you.

I am about to prepare for you a statement of account, but just at the moment I am unable to lay my hands on my copy of our agreement. I have lately changed secretaries [   ] but as I have no wish to delay sending you a statement longer than is absolutely necessary, perhaps you might be good enough to send me a copy of yours. I am awfully sorry to trouble you about something that is purely clerical and hope that you will forgive me.

Regarding the fifty per cent discount, I fully agree with you, especially when you say that by according this discount to the agent, he might be in a position to undersell us. If you will refer to the contents of my letter, you will find that I stated that. I thought it, however, my duty to put both views before you, leaving the final decision to your judgment, with which, I repeat, I concur fully.

Business is pretty bad just now and I am afraid that as a result of the New York crash, we shall see some very quiet times for some months to come. I have just paid for the second printing of "Lady Chatterley"; but money is very slow in coming in.

> Yours very sincerely,

[2] Cf. p. 446 n. 1.

you to send me the complete typescript, before it goes any further? I'd like to look it over. – I feel very mistrustful of the Mandrake – and wish this little book could have come out now, following the Faber pamphlet.

Thanks for sending out the copies of the pamphlet.

Orioli's authors, from Huxley down, seem to be frightened of going into a series, for fear – of God knows what. So leave 'em – nothing to me.

I saw the two Knopfs were in Paris.

I don't care one bit whether they put me in their little anthologies or not – but rather resent being made use of.

Do come after Christmas and be my guest in the Hotel Beau Rivage. But let us know in time to secure a decent room.

ever   D. H. Lawrence

I think most of Orioli's authors hate Secker. They might have swallowed Knopf – both for England and U.S.A.

5442. To Giuseppe Orioli, [9 December 1929]
Text: MS UCLA; Unpublished.

BeauSoleil, *Bandol*, Var
9 Dec

Dear Pino

Thanks for the Lasca accounts. It's not so bad, considering – everybody complains that the book trade is dead, entirely dead in New York. But wait a bit, it will revive. Will you make up the accounts at the end of every month, and send me a cheque – there is never any hurry. But don't pay the money into Casardi's bank, as I will use it here in France.

Don't bother then about the Lungarno series and Pollinger – let it go. I don't care at all, personally. But the others are fools, since they want money, and a series would sell at least five times as much as single vols. But of course Aldous is a greedy one – somehow he irritates me. – And a series that *sold* would make your series famous and *give* it a cachet. – But truly, personally I don't care a bit.

Did you get my *Obscenity* pamphlet – I ordered it for you. It made quite a stir – sells 1200 copies a week!

It will be great fun if you come for New Year. Probably you will have to be my guest in the Beau Rivage, as either my sister or Frieda's sister will be here, and the house is tiny. But we'll see. In the Beau Rivage are the di Chiaras from Capri – do you remember she ordered 3 copies of *Lady C.* at the very first – she is American, he is Napolitano. Also Ida Rauh, a Taos friend is in the Hotel – and the Brewsters still there – so we aren't lonely.

My health is better, but I can't *walk* – I just can't.

But we will have a good time when you come.

a rivederci   DHL

5443. To Charles Lahr, [9 December 1929]
Text: MS UNYB; Postmark, Bandol 1[. . .] 12 29; Moore 1220.

Beausoleil.
9 Dec.

Dear L[ahr]

Many thanks for the bank receipt and for the Plutarch[1] – Plutarch *very* acceptable – What a mercy the stone is, after all, a gold stone!

But you must soon be making an account and taking your share and paying yourself for all the books you have sent me. What about the 50 vellums?

I am getting those *Nettles* ready – Faber & Faber want to do them in a pamphlet, like *Obscenity*, and I might as well let them, don't you think, since the 'Squib' is damp. If the 'Squib' ever starts to pop, I'll be there. – The *Nettles* are about twenty in number. – The *Obscenity* pamphlet has sold over 6,000 – more than any of the others –

Tell Davies I am really writing him – We're always talking about him.

You'll have seen Carter by now. I know some of the *Hahns* got to the bookseller Harry Marks in New York, but haven't heard yet about the bulk. He is selling the ordinary copies at $25.

Again thanks for the book.

DHL

5444. To Laurence Pollinger, 9 December 1929
Text: MS UT; Unpublished.

Beau Soleil, Bandol. Var
9 Dec 1929

Dear Pollinger

Sorry Richard dela Mare is such a wet rag – is he Walter's son? – The arrangement for the *Ariel* (save the mark!) poem is all right[2] – though I rather dislike their 400 at 7/6 business – *signed* – How I hate signing!

I will send the *Nettles* – twelve or twenty poems with a sting – in a few days. I don't want a limited edition of them, but you'll see the publishers will.

You didn't send me *Dante* by T. S. Eliot, so I don't know quite what the *Poets on the Poets* series is like.[3] And what damn poet would they want me to be 'on'?

Lovely sunny days, yesterday and today – hope same over there.

ever DHL

---

[1] Cf. Letter 5410. It is not known which of Plutarch's works in the Bohn edn Lahr had sent; the *Morals* (1848, etc.) or the *Lives* (1853, etc.) were perhaps the most likely.

[2] Cf. Letter 5438 and nn. 2 and 3. (DHL did not sign them.)

[3] Eliot's *Dante*, in Faber's *Poets on Poets* series, was published in an ordinary (3/6d) and a limited edn (21/–), September and October 1929 respectively.

5445. To Madame Douillet, [ante 10 December 1929]
Text: Huxley 838–9.

Beau Soleil.
[ante 10 December 1929]

O Madame Douillet, –

Merci bien pour les poissons – ils sont si jolis, comme un petit soleil couchant et une petite lune levante dans leur ciel courbé. Je les regarde pendant des heures, s'agrandir et se diminuer comme par magique, et toujours en mouvement, toujours.

Aussi Madame Douillet, la mère, était-elle très gentille de nous les apporter.

Veuillez payer la note de Monsieur Carter avec ce billet de mille francs – et aussi le pain, et les deux jolis poissons. Je préfère beaucoup ce pain de seigle au pain du village, qui est quelquefois un peu aigre.

Salutations!   DHL

[Many thanks for the fishes – they are so pretty, like a little setting sun and a little rising moon in their curved sky. I watch them for hours, getting larger and smaller as if by magic, and always moving, always.

Also Madame Douillet, your mother was very kind to bring them to us.

Please pay Mr Carter's bill with this thousand franc note – and also the bread, and the two pretty fishes. I much prefer this rye bread to the village bread, which is sometimes a little bitter.

Greetings!   DHL]

5446. To Maria Huxley, 10 December 1929
Text: Huxley 841–2.

Beau Soleil, Bandol.
10 Dec., 1929.

Dear Maria, –

We've got two goldfish or one gold and one silver – sent to me by Madame Douillet, of the hotel – and they are the bane of the cat's life,[1] for he thinks they are demons or phantasmagoria as they go round and gleam and become unnaturally huge in the glass.

How are your little kittens? Is the grey colour of earth descending on them? They must be fun. Our yellow Beau Soleil gets huge.

Do you still think of coming in January? You know I expect every letter to give a different plan.

---

[1] Cf. Letter 5387.

We have got my sister Ada coming after Xmas, Frieda's sister Else, and Barby [Weekley][1] shall have to fit them in in turn, the house is impossible for two visitors. Really, it's too small for one – everybody hears everybody brushing their teeth, and I hate it. But you'll be all right in the Beau Rivage, won't you? – Pino will probably be there – and the Brewsters will be gone. It's quite near.

I believe by dint of looking you might find the sort of house you want – and the countryside is lovely. But I'm in a sort of despair – my health is very tiresome, and I'm sick of it altogether. I sort of wish I could go to the moon. Meanwhile, this little place is quite comfortable and all right; we've had some marvellous sunny days, rather too warm – the peasants are picking the narcissus – all in bloom.

I'd be all right if I felt better. It's beginning to irritate me. Not that I'm thinner or weaker – only the asthma is so maddening.

Well, I'm glad the rue du Bac sounds cheerful, and that Jehanne is well. She is nice, really, and soon she'll get a real chance, I feel.

Did you get the flowers Frieda sent?

DHL

5447. To Ada Clarke, 10 December 1929
Text: MS Clarke; Postmark, Bandol 11 [. . .] 29; cited in Lawrence–Gelder 201.

Beau Soleil, *Bandol*, Var
10 Dec 1929

My dear Sister

Your parcel was surely the prize foreign parcel – it actually arrived yesterday, safe and sound, and cost only nine francs. The cake, pudding and mincemeat are quite safe, though I'm afraid the basin is broken – and the braces and sewing-companion are there, and the three pretty cards. You sent me two pairs of braces in the summer, so I shall give a pair to Brewster for Christmas.

They are still in the hotel – waiting for their money to come from America before they can buy a bit of furniture for the house – they are hard up. Ida Rauh, from Santa Fe, is also in the Beau Rivage – also the di Chiaras from Capri – and they all troop over, so we are by no means lonely.

My health is rather a nuisance – doesn't recover very well from the set-back in the summer. But I hope the turn of the year will improve it. Walking is the worst – I hardly go a stride – much worse than last year. Yet in myself I don't think I'm worse. But what a weariness it is!

When do you think you will come? Give us an approximate date, because

[1] See p. 239 n. 1.

Frieda's sister wants to come, and perhaps Barby – and Maria Huxley, but she must stay in the hotel. Would you like to bring Jackie? – he would have to sleep in the sitting-room, but he'd be all right. If you bring him you could travel second all the way, if you wish, and if it's worth it. I could pay his ticket.

We shan't have such a quiet time for Christmas as last year – Frieda has been trying your paper table-cloth already. But I'm afraid I'm rather unsociable – these attempts at festivity are a bit tiring.

I enclose a pound each for Christmas for the boys, they are to get what they want – and the rest is for you, and to pay for the meridian vests and drawers which Frieda wants – has Emily told you? – two pairs of each, and Harwood Brewster will bring them. She leaves her school on the 17th. I told Emily to ask you.[1]

We've had a few lovely sunny days, but really rather too warm. The yellow narcissus are full in flower – and the fresh young radishes and new potatoes are very good – grown since the rain. On the whole we get very pleasant food here.

Well it's still early for Christmas greetings – but many thanks for the parcel.

love   DHL

That *Obscenity* pamphlet has already sold over 6,000 – quite a stir.

5448. To Laurence Pollinger, [10 December 1929]
Text: MS UT; Unpublished.

Beau Soleil. Bandol. Var
10 Dec.

Dear Pollinger

I am sending you this wearisome letter of Koteliansky's.[2] If it is true, it hits

---

[1] Cf. Letter 5434 and n. 1.
[2] Kot wrote as follows on 7 December 1929 (MS UT):

My dear Lawrence,
    I saw Goldston (of the Mandrake Press) yesterday and he told me that a man had offered him 60 copies of Pansies, a pirated edition of the unexpurgated poems, at 7/6 each. I asked the name of the man, but G said the man had three names. I said I would write to you advising to institute proceedings against the pirate, in the following manner: Secker, who holds the copyright of the "Pansies" (the unexp. edition contains only a few poems; and therefore the copyright law cannot be invalidated, – this is my legal reasoning which I think is correct) will bring a case in court demanding that Goldston should reveal the name of the person who had offered him the pirated edition; and from that man it will be easy to discover who the original scoundrel is. Goldston tried to persuade me that the pirated edition, being made from the unexp. edition, has no defence in law. But I think it would be advisable to instruct Pollinger to have a good talk with G. and to find out who the pirate is. When the name of the pirate is found out, then you may, if you like, institute proceedings, – this of course to be done by Secker.

Secker's and Knopf's *Pansies*. I suppose the easiest way to kill the pirate would be a 3/6 *Pansies* from Secker – But what do you think, altogether?

DHL[1]

5449. To Emily King, 12 December 1929
Text: MS Lazarus; Unpublished.

Beau Soleil. Bandol. Var
12 Dec 1929

My dear Sister

When you wrote, your cake was in the oven – I hope it turned out all right. Ada's parcel came two days ago – very quick – and quite safely, except the pudding-basin was broken. So if your basket comes too, we shall have a pudding for Christmas and one for New Year: which is very nice, I like plum pudding. I don't know whom we shall invite – Ida Rauh is in the hotel, from Santa Fe – and the di Chiaras from Capri – they all troop over. And the Brewsters are still there, waiting for some money to come from America before they can buy a few sticks of furniture and move into their house. They've been very silly about their money – and they always say they've got none – yet they live in hotels, and spend about £7 a week, apart from Harwood's costs: and now they haven't a bean, till some comes.

I read about the bad weather in England, and it's rather curious, because we've had lovely sunny days, only too warm. Tonight is a brilliant moonlit night over a clear sea, and quite a wind, yet warm as late spring. It doesn't feel right altogether. – My health is rather better, but it's not behaving very well this year. Perhaps it'll be better when the year turns.

The flowers are so nice in the room, great big double marigolds, orange like suns, and pale yellow roses, and pink stocks and narcissus. The narcissus have just come, but the other flowers are having the last flush of their autumn-

G. also told me as a sort of rumour that someone in U.S.A. had published your Introduction of the Book of Paintings.

I dislike bothering you with these news, but I think you ought to know, particularly as regards the pirated Pansies. Personally I think that Secker, as original publisher of Pansies, can institute proceedings against the pirate. At any rate, if G. is approached by Pollinger and told strictly that he, G., will be implicated if he does not divulge the name of the man who offered him 60 copies, – the pirate will be intimidated and perhaps stop selling his edition.

What a horrible crew all these people are! Just little petty thieves.

I had no time to go and see Lion about it; but I shall call one day next week and tell him the news of the pirated edition. Perhaps he, too, knows about it.

Yours K.

[1] Nancy Pearn annotated this letter with a query to Pollinger: 'Need I read Koteliansky? Don't much like that man! N.P.'

winter season, and are very lovely. We have fresh young radishes too, and lettuce, and young potatoes. Things grow after the autumn rains.

I'm glad you are keeping better. You don't mention the shop – I suppose it drags on as ever. The season has been very slack down here too, but places are beginning to fill up now.

I send you this little cheque which came for some poetry. Give Peg a pound and a pound for Joan, and then get yourself something. It's too soon really to be wishing Christmas wishes, but perhaps the children will like to have time to spend their cash.

love   DHL

5450. To Hon. Dorothy Brett, 12 December 1929
Text: MS UT; Moore 1221–2.

Villa Beau Soleil. *Bandol.* Var, France
12 Decem. 1929

Dear Brett

Ida Rauh is in the hotel here, so of course we talk about New Mexico all the time, and get a great longing to come back. Tonight is a brilliant clear night with a moon over the sea, but warm, really too warm. I can imagine the desert under the moon. How far away it seems! – so far – and requires, somehow, a whole change in one's feeling. I think Ida is really happier over here – she seems quite chirpy. She belongs to civilisation and to society, she is not a person for isolation, or for roughness or for wildness. I think the *tempo* of the S. of France just suits her: easy, pleasant, no efforts and no excitements, an old civilisation jogging along on its income.

The Brewsters, as perhaps you know, have taken a house about four miles from here. But they are still in the hotel, hung up as usual for lack of money. Apparently their resources get lower and lower, and dribbles come from America to keep them just going. Now they can't move into their house till they've bought a few sticks of furniture – and not a sou to buy them with – altogether their money problems are a bit of a nuisance. People who don't work, and who live in comfortable hotels, shouldn't have money problems.

The di Chiaras are also in the hotel – did you know them in Capri? She gets smaller and older, and he more glum. Oh these married people!

Ida says you are going to New York and having a show. I wonder if it's true. I hope it won't be a mere disappointment again – but never say die. My pictures are still stacked in London, I'm sick at the thought of them – and I don't paint a stroke – quite gone out of me. Oh, if you are fairly happy in America, don't come to Europe – it takes all the life out of one. – I really think I shall try to come back in the spring. I begin to believe I shall never get well over here. My health is no better this year than last – it's really worse – and I hardly walk a stride. I'm so sick of it. Somewhere I am not ill, but my bronchials and asthma *get me down*. How I hate it. Perhaps if I came back to New Mexico I would get up again. Frieda sometimes says she wants to come – then again not. I would do anything now to get really on my feet again, and not be this semi-invalid. I really do stick to the thought of coming back in March or April – What's the good of dragging on over here!

Well, I do hope things go well with you – no complications and unnecessary difficulties. Remembrances for Christmas.

DHL

5451. To Laurence Pollinger, 13 December 1929
Text: MS UT; Unpublished.

Beau Soleil, Bandol, Var
13 Dec 1929

Dear Pollinger

Orioli certainly wrote a stupid letter. He is riled because 'his authors' suggest that he's trying to make money out of them on the public edition, so he's in a rage, and doesn't distinguish between one person and another. Very Italian. – But drop the Lungarno Series, at least for the time. Nothing like little authors for self-importance.

I don't care one damn about Jonathan's £2-2-0, one way or another.[1]

I believe that about the *Pansies* piracy isn't a real alarm – but I *wish* we could get from Goldston the name of the man who offered the sixty copies at 7/6.[2] Do you think you could?

I enclose MS of *Nettles*: should like them done at 1/–, *no* 'limited edition'. Tell me what you think of them.

I suppose you have my other letters.

DHL

---

[1] Perhaps connected with the eventual inclusion of DHL's 'Triumph of the Machine' (cf. p. 585 n. 3) in *The Best Poems of 1930* to be published by Cape in September 1930 (Roberts B29).
[2] Cf. Letter 5448 and n. 2.

5452. To Herberth Herlitschka, 14 December 1929
Text: MS UR; Unpublished.

Beau Soleil. *Bandol.* Var. France
14 Dec 1929

Dear Mr Herlitschka[1]

Of course Prince Löwenstein had no authorisation to deal with *Lady C.* – he had merely talked to my wife, who is a friend of Mrs Trotter. But basta! they are all too tiresome.

The manager of the Foreign Dept of Curtis Brown is a certain Miss Watson, and in the summer she married old Curtis Brown's son.[2] She was a high-handed young lady before – but now there's no holding her. She simply infuriates everybody – especially in Germany. She wants, of course, to be absolute *boss*: that's why nobody must write to me. But it is all silly – I will ask her now to conclude negotiations with Tal as soon as possible.[3] If you are still waiting for a copy of *Lady Chatterley*, please write to

Edward W. Titus. 4 rue Delambre, Paris XIV

---

[1] Herlitschka had written on 9 December 1929 (TMSC UR):

When in Berlin recently Tal told a friend of his, Mr. Beermann-Höllriegl, a well-known author and journalist, about his difficulties in trying to acquire the German rights in "Lady Ch." Beerman then offered to invoke the help of an acquaintance of his, Mrs. Dorothy Trotter, whom he knew to be a friend of yours ... After his return to Vienna Tal received a letter from a Prince Loewenstein-Wertheim of London ... He said that Mrs. Trotter had written to him – we thought, of course, she would write to you direct but probably she has done that as well – of Tal's interest in the book but that at the moment he could do nothing about it. He pointed out that he and he only had been appointed by you to handle the German rights in Lady Ch. and that your authorisation had lately been confirmed by your friend and travelling companion Herr Max Mohr. He himself had offered the book to Kiepenheuer who, however, was still hesitating to take it as it had been offered to him by various other people as well. The Prince neither offered the book to Tal nor did he explicitly decline to do so.

[2] See p. 32 n. 1.

[3] Herlitschka continued:

Herr Fiedler of Leipzig [Curtis Brown's sole agent for Germany] with whom Tal was already in correspondence since August last ... wrote a day or two later that Tal could now have the book if he wanted to and he also said that he was sending him a copy for examination – which copy has not arrived up til now. As this letter was not in the shape of a firm offer Tal thought it best under the circumstances to ask for one and also for an exclusive option for a short period within which to accept it. Before a reply to this came Tal received a letter from Curtis Brown. They said that you had instructed them to offer the book to him and that they supposed their Leipzig man had already done so on their behalf. They also reproached Tal bitterly for having applied to you direct. In fact they took him to task like a naughty boy for having gone behind their back and added something like "don't do it again". They also asked him for an immediate decision as they could not tolerate any further delay. Mark, please, that Tal had applied for the rights as early as August last and had not up til then got a firm offer of terms nor a copy of the book from either Curtis Brown or their Leipzig representative! So the delay is hardly his fault, and I think the way they wrote to a client who has done business with them on several occasions

and ask him please to send you a copy on my account – and I will mention the matter to him when I write. He published the Paris edition. – If Miss Watson makes the contract with Tal, I think you can be quite sure there will be no complication: she will not have promised anything to someone else, and certainly I have promised nothing.

I shall ask my sister-in-law about showing you her translation of *Plumed Serpent*.

And I will try to find out if Kippenberg will really release *White Peacock*, *Lost Girl*, and *Aaron's Rod*: but I doubt if he will.[1]

I think 12 M. for a paper-covered book of this sort is about right – I don't like high prices. I suppose the Paris edition sells for about the same.

I shall be pleased to see the translations you are sending me.

Yours Sincerely   D. H. Lawrence

5453. To Jean Watson, 14 December 1929
Text: MS UT; Unpublished.

Villa Beau Soleil. *Bandol.* Var, France
14 Dec 1929

Dear Miss Watson

If you can do so, I wish you would conclude negotiations with Tal quickly. If he is a little afraid for his advance – well, perhaps you can accommodate him. It would be a very good thing to settle up as quickly as possible now, for this book: there seems such a stew. And apparently Prince Löwenstein is once

---

is highly objectionable.
Herlitschka went on to explain that Tal did not wish to pay the whole advance immediately, in order to protect himself against being undersold by pirates.
[1] Herlitschka concluded his letter:

As for the translation, I can fully understand your attitude after your experiences with your other books. All I can say is: please try me. I shall be pleased to submit the manuscript of my translation of Lady Ch. to you for your approval as soon as it will be ready. And I am sure you will be satisfied though I shall be glad of any comments you might care to make on it. In the meantime I am going to send you tomorrow three of my translations the originals of which are widely different in style ... As for your future books I should not like to ask you to let me translate them before you had seen the German version of "Lady Ch." In the meantime, however, I should be glad to help you with "The Plumed Serpent". If the manuscript translation has not yet gone to the publishers ... I will work through it and make the alterations I might find necessary ... if it can be managed, that is, without offence to Frau Jaffe.
I gather from a remark old K. once made to me that the Insel people do not intend to bring out "Aaron's Rod", "The White Peacock" and "The Lost Girl". Could you get K. to say definitely whether he wants these books or whether he does not? If he declines them officially Tal would most likely take them – in fact he would like to make an agreement with you by which all books of yours which the Insel-Verlag does not want should be offered to him immediately. Would you care to give Curtis Brown the necessary instructions to bring about such an arrangement? ...

more butting in – God knows why: because he once talked for five minutes with my wife, I suppose. Anyhow I believe that man Herlitschka, who translates for Tal, is really competent – and that's a lot. If Tal can come out with a really good translation, *quickly*, then the advance on royalties is not so all-important.

I heard a rumour too, that Kippenberg says he does not intend to bring out translations of *The*[1] *White Peacock*, *The Lost Girl*, and *Aaron's Rod*. I can't believe this, but you might ask Dr. Fiedler if it is true.

But the thing to do now is to settle up as soon as possible about *Lady C.*, so that the German translation can appear.

Yours Sincerely   D. H. Lawrence

5454. To Else Jaffe, 14 December 1929
Text: MS Jeffrey; Frieda Lawrence 297–8.

BeauSoleil, *Bandol*, Var, France
14 Dec 1929

Dear Else

I got a copy of *Plumed Serpent* and tried to translate a hymn – but you might as well ask me to translate into Hottentot – I can't even *begin*. So that's that. – I think Tal of Vienna is going to do *Lady C.* – and the translator
            Herberth E. Herlitschka, Wiedner Gürtel 6. Wien. IV
has written me several times. He seems a competent and experienced translator – and his criticism of the translation of *Women in Love* made my blood feel chill. He says he would be glad to help you with *Plumed Serpent* if there is any difficulty, or to go over the manuscript if you could send him a carbon copy. You must please yourself about it.

You are coming to see us in the New Year – I wish you would send an approximate date, as my sister Ada also wants to come, and Barby Weekley. There is only one little extra bedroom.

We've had lovely sunny weather all week – today is a most beautiful day, still and sunny. The narcissus are in full flower in the tiny field next to us – so yellow.

My health has been a great nuisance – not so good as last winter – and it wearies me. Then I don't want to do anything.

The Brewsters are still in the hotel – and Mr and Mrs di Chiara from Capri (she is American) and Ida Rauh (Mrs Max Eastman – the socialists wife) from Santa Fe – and they all come trooping along, so we are by no means alone. Frieda loves her little house – though it's very commonplace – but it is

[1] of *The*] of Women in *The*

sunny and warm and easy, so one doesn't grumble. Her foot still troubles her a bit.

Have you seen Dr Osbornes translation of *Fantasia*[1] – quite good, in my opinion.

I shall write again directly.

love DHL

5455. To Frederick Carter, 15 December 1929
Text: MS UT; Moore, *Intelligent Heart* 424.

Beau Soleil, Bandol, Var
15 Dec 1929

Dear Carter

Thanks for *Enoch*, who came yesterday.[2] I have read a good deal of him, and some parts are rather nice.

I have roughly finished my introduction, and am going over it, working it a bit into shape.[3] I'm hoping I can get Brewster's daughter to type it – she comes this week. – God knows what anybody will think of it. When you have done your chapter, send me a copy – I'll send *Enoch* back.

We've had the most beautiful weather lately – brilliant sunny days, and warm. This morning is another calm and lovely morning. – The Brewsters are still in the hotel – had no money to go to their house with – not a sou even to pay the hotel: but thank goodness, some has come at last – or almost come – so are a little nearer. Today the grand piano is being sent up from Toulon, and they are going to welcome it. It will be the first piece of furniture in the *chateau*! – all alone. – We are quite a party – Mr and Mrs di Chiara, from Capri, are in the hotel – also Mrs Eastman, from New Mexico. They all troop along to tea, so the BeauSoleil resounds with voices, and the cat goes away in disgust.

We are fairly well – a little better. – I was sorry to hear from Charlie Lahr of his motor-accident.[4] What a world!

Saluti. D. H. Lawrence

[1] See Letter 5403 and n. 4.

[2] 'The Ethiopic Book of Enoch' exists in many translations; Carter may have sent a copy of the most recent: *The Hebrew Book of Enoch*, ed. and tr. Hugo Odeberg (Cambridge, 1928). *Enoch* would be of interest to Carter and DHL since it is a compilation of several apocalyptic writings, the oldest – 'Apocalypse of Weeks' – dated c. 160 BC.

[3] The introduction was intended for Carter's 'Revelation of St. John the Divine' and Harwood Brewster typed it; it 'grew beyond bounds' (Brewster 307) and eventually became *Apocalypse* (Roberts A57 and C204).

[4] Lahr, his daughter Sheila and Rhys Davies were involved in a minor car accident caused by unlighted roadworks; Davies suffered broken ribs, the Lahrs only cuts and bruises. Cf. Letter 5463.

5456. To Giuseppe Orioli, [18 December 1929]

Text: MS UCLA; cited in Moore, *Intelligent Heart* 421, 422.

Beau Soleil. *Bandol.* Var. France
Wed.

Dear Pino

Many thanks for the cheque for £95..17..6. It seems quite a nice sum of money already. And perhaps America will rouse up a bit.

I had also your other letter with Aldington's cheque for £4.

Pollinger sent me the letter you wrote him. It certainly was a rude letter. Why did you get the wind up against him, he was only doing his best? However, I tried to soothe him down, and told him to drop the idea of the Lungarno Series finally.

As for Aldous, he won't come here at Christmas. Maria talks of coming alone in the New Year. Something seems to have gone wrong between him and her, I don't know what. Anyhow I shall never ask him for anything, neither for myself nor anybody else, any more. He takes not the slightest notice. He annoys me. – I doubt if ever you will get anything out of him.

We had lovely warm sunny weather all last week, till yesterday, when the wind came cold. I think perhaps it is going to turn colder now, though the sun is warm in the shelter. Do you think you might bring me another blue jacket from the shop in Via Tornabuoni, the same blue as the one I've got now. I love the colour so much.

And would it trouble you to look in the wooden box for copies of newspaper articles by me. They want to publish a volume of my newspaper articles in spring, and some are missing. I know they are there in the wooden box – at least I put them there. There is one 'The Nightingale' and another 'Fireworks' – I want those two especially[1] – and perhaps there are one or two more. I don't want stories or long articles – only these short things. Would you post them to me?

Tell me when you will come, and we'll have a room ready for you. The di Chiaras too are so relieved to be away from Italy for a bit. I do hope the weather will be good when you come – and we'll take some drives around.

You haven't told me how much I owe you for all the parcels posted and everything. You must take it off the next account.

Did you see that Harry Crosby committed suicide in New York last week – shot himself and another young woman[2] – very horrible – the last sort of

---

[1] Neither piece (Roberts C155 and C158) appeared in *Assorted Articles.*

[2] On 10 December 1929 Crosby killed his mistress, Josephine Rotch Bigelow, and then committed suicide; he had told DHL about the 'sun-maid' in August 1928 (see *Letters,* vi. 504 and n. 2); she married Albert Bigelow in June 1929. For a full account of the incident see Wolff, *Black Sun,* pp. 278–94.

cocktail excitement. The wife is on her way back to Paris already with the ashes (his only) in a silver jar. – He had always been *too* rich and spoilt: nothing to do but to commit suicide. It depressed me very much.

Au revoir then. Frieda is just off to Marseilles with the Brewsters – in a car. Thank goodness I need not go.

ever   DHL

5457. To Edward Titus, [18 December 1929]
Text: MS UT; Unpublished.

BeauSoleil, *Bandol*, Var.
Wed.

Dear Titus

Thanks for *This Quarter*, which has just come. I see Rebecca West didn't keep her promise.[1] – I'll see if I can rake up a couple of poems for the next issue.

I didn't see the review of *Lady C.* in *Nouvelles Litteraires* – could you send it me?[2] – But I don't suppose it'll have any effect any more. The book is becoming, like *Ulysses*, an accepted fact. A man called Guillaume Lerolle wrote me from Paris wanting to translate it. Do you know anything of him?

If a man called Herlitschka writes from Vienna for a copy of *Lady C.*, please send it him, and charge it to me. – By the way, you haven't sent me a copy of the accounts for the first edition yet!

I wish you would tell me if you had any answer at all from Albert Boni about releasing my books.

Horrible the Harry Crosby business!

ever   D. H. Lawrence

You were right about my typewriter ribbon – I needed only to push it up to 'red' –[3]

[1] Cf. Letter 5364 and n. 2.
[2] The review by André Levinson, under the title 'Immoraliste Virtueuse', appeared on 14. December 1929 in *Les Nouvelles Littéraires, Artistiques et Scientifiques*, issue 374, p. 6. See Letter 5466 and n. 2.
[3] Titus had written on 11 December 1929 (TMSC SIU), acknowledging DHL's Letter 5440. He thanked DHL for the copy of the agreement and responded at length to the query in his postscript:

My diagnosis is that probably you need a new ribbon, and if that does not turn the trick, try something else. You will find at the right-hand side of your machine . . . a little slot with a lever which serves for the reversal of the ribbon from blue or black to red. Just throw over the lever to the opposite direction in which you find it now. This will have the effect of using the upper part of the ribbon . . .

Titus answered the present letter on 20 December 1929 (TMSC SIU):

5458. To Jean Watson, 18 December 1929
Text: MS UT; Unpublished.

Beau Soleil, *Bandol*, Var, France
18 Dec 1929

Dear Miss Watson

Herewith the Tal agreement – yes, I'm glad it's settled up. – It is true, Orioli didn't secure the copyright – European – on the first edition, but Titus says he secured it for the second: and I hope it holds good. However, we must watch the Germans.

Sincerely   D. H. Lawrence

5459. To Maria Huxley, [19 December 1929]
Text: Huxley 842.

Beau Soleil, Var, Bandol.
Thursday, Dec., 1929.

Dear Maria, –

Well, here's Xmas in a day or two! – I rather hate it. Why make merry when one doesn't feel merry. However, my sisters have sent plum pudding and cake, so I suppose we'll invite the friends and eat it appropriately. – Don't send anything, by the way – don't bother. Because I don't know what I should send you and Aldous; I've got nothing – and there *is* nothing. So don't send anything except *amore, amore!* And before I forget do tell me what Jehanne paid for the typing of that almond-tree article[1] – so nice it is – but tell me.

It was very warm, lovely, and sunny here till Tuesday! When it went cold. To-day is sunny and clear, but cold, the sun has no strength. I keep mostly indoors. It's a bit too sharp for me.

Dear Mr. Lawrence,

Herewith the article which appeared in the Nouvelles Litteraires. – Guillaume Lerolle, at first impression, might be one of the editors of Gringoire [a Parisian literary journal founded in November 1928]. I shall enquire to make sure. –

Frere-Reeves, of Heinemann's went to New York recently, and he will get in touch with a friend of mind whom I have asked to handle the Boni matter. One cant afford to be too forward. We shall soon hear from New York.

You will have your statement of account as soon as my stupid accountant recovers from the flue.

You knew, I believe, Crosby rather well. So did I. The news was shocking, but not surprising. Too much silver spoon, and no balance.

You have helped me to discover myself the possessor of another talent, – that of curing ailing typewriters by correspondence.

Good luck to you

[1] Cf. Letters 5352 and 5392 and n. 4.

No news – except, I suppose, you saw about Harry Crosby – that upset me very much.

The cat made an attack on the goldfish to-day, and a few small brilliant gold scales are floating loose. I spanked him, and he looked like a Chinese demon. Now he's trying to make up to me, but I'm cold.

The sun is just going down: coldly, from a milk-blue sea.

There come the friends.

DHL

You really ought to get your picture from Dorothy Warren now.[1] She's distributed all the sold ones.

5460. To Max and Käthe Mohr, 19 December 1929
Text: MS HMohr; Mohr, Briefe 538–9.

Beau Soleil, Bandol, Var, France
19 Dec 1929

Dear Mohr and Käthe Mohr

Christmas nearly here – I wish I had the energy to go to the village and find you something and send it – but I haven't, so I can only write a letter. There isn't even a really nice book – only dull books – and I won't send those. So please don't mind if there is no Weihnachtsgabe[2] – anyhow I don't like Weihnacht.

Wie geht's? Hier nicht schlecht. Es war so schön und warm, wie Frühling – wunderbar – bis Dienstag, dann ist's kalt geworden. Heute war kalt und sonnig – aber die Sonne hatte sehr wenig kraft – merkwürdig – weil letzte woche war sie so stark. Jetzt fällt die Nacht, das Meer ist blau, die Bergen weit und kalt, Himmel ist primmel-gelb und auch weit. Es ist winter. Ich sitze auf dem Bett und schreibe bis die Freunde zum Thee kommen: und der M. Beausoleil schläft auf meinen Füssen. Er ist aber *in disgrace*. Heut Morgen ist er fischen gegangen im Goldfischvase – hat beinah einen gefangen – jetzt flotten im Wasser ein Paar goldnen glanzenden Fischmünzer – fishscales[3] – but the wounded one seems all right, though scarred. I spanked M. Beau-

---

[1] The picture was *North Sea* (cf. Letter 5200).   [2] 'Christmas-gift'.

[3] 'How are things? Here it's not bad. It was so lovely and warm, like spring – wonderful – until Tuesday, then it went cold. Today was cold and sunny – but the sun had very little strength – strange – because last week it was so strong. Now the night is falling, the sea is blue, the mountains far-off and cold, sky is primrose-yellow and also far-off. It is winter. I sit on the bed and write until friends come for tea: and M. Beausoleil sleeps on my feet. He is however *in disgrace*. This morning he went fishing in the goldfish vase – almost caught one – a few golden glittering scales are now floating in the water – fishscales'.

soleil well, and he twisted round at me like a Chinese dragon, so I spanked him more. Now he wants to *kosen*,[1] but I refuse. He is in disgrace!

We are still quite a colony here – the Brewsters still in the hotel – kein Geld, kein Geld, immer kein Geld – sie haben aber verlorenen Stühlen gekauft, und wollen Samstag ins Haus ziehen.[2] The daughter comes today from England: and on Saturday Ida Rauh's son[3] comes from Geneva: the di Chiaras are still in the hotel: so we have parties. I went to lunch at the hotel on Tuesday, but had a headache after, drinking Chablis, I suppose, so I shan't go again. My sister has sent plum-pudding and cake and mincemeat, so I expect we shall have a little Christmas party.

Did you read of Harry Crosby – the American in Paris who printed *Escaped Cock*? – He shot himself in New York, and shot a young woman along with him. Horrible! The wife is bringing his ashes back to Paris.

Did you know Tal of Vienna has signed a contract to publish *Lady C.* in translation – in Papierband[4] at 12 Mark. His translator Herlitschka seems quite good. Kiepenheuer once more wanted the book – but I'm glad it has gone to Vienna. I am tired of those Berliners.

The world is certainly mad: and worse than ever.

Maria Huxley wants to come down here alone in January. There is something wrong too between her and Aldous – some sort of krach.[5] How wretched everything is!

The pamphlet on *Obscenity* which I wrote at Rottach, at the Angermeier – has made the old ones hate me still more in England, but it has sold very well, and had a very good effect, I think. Toujours la guerre.[6]

Well I do hope you'll have a good Christmas – wish you could be here to eat duck and Christmas pudding. Will you really come in February?

Many greetings   DHL

5461. To S. S. Koteliansky, [23 December 1929]
Text: MS BL; Postmark, Bandol [. . .]; Moore 1225–6.

Beau Soleil – Bandol. Var.
23 Dec

Dear Kot

Well here is Christmas! We had a great storm yesterday, so today is grey

---

[1] 'cuddle'.
[2] 'no money, no money, always no money – but they have bought some forlorn chairs, and want to move into their house on Saturday.'
[3] Daniel Eastman (1913/4–69).   [4] 'paperback'.   [5] 'row'.
[6] 'Always a fight.'

and sulky. I am in bed, as usual, my bronchials really behaving very badly this winter. Am so tired of them.

I shall be pleased to see Dr Morland if he stops off here – but don't at all like the thought of troubling him and interrupting his journey. It is very kind of him to say he will see me.

I wrote Pollinger about *Pansies* pirates and he has tried to see Goldston, without success. Goldston is getting a difficult bird too.

There is nothing new in the world. I wish my health was better: hope yours is all right. There are various friends here in the hotel, so we shall have a certain amount of Christmas fun. I hate it, but Frieda seems to think it is essential.

Excuse this poor letter –

DHL

5462. To Mark Gertler, 23 December 1929

Text: MS SIU; Postmark, Bandol 23 12 29; Huxley 843.

Beau Soleil, Bandol, Var.
23 Dec 1929

Dear Gertler[1]

Sorry you are feeling low in spirits. Don't worry, it is very common with men when they pass forty – or when they draw near forty. Men seem to undergo a sort of *spiritual* change of life, with really painful depression and loss of energy. Even men whose physical health is quite good. So don't fret. Often an *entire* change of scene helps a lot – But it's a condition which often drags over several years. Then, in the end, you come out of it with a new sort of rhythm, a new psychic rhythm: a sort of re-birth. Meanwhile it is what the mystics call the little death, and you have to put up with it. I have had it too, though not so acutely as some men. But then my health is enough to depress the Archangel Michael himself. My bronchials are really awful. It's not the lungs.

I shall be pleased to see Dr Morland, if he really wants to take the trouble to stop off here. But I don't like the thought of troubling him.

And we shall be pleased to see you later. The Hotel Beau Rivage is really very nice, Bandol is a quiet little place, but usually sunny and pleasant. Yesterday there was a great storm, the first, so today is grey and a bit stunned, but quiet. I hope it will soon clear again – we get so used to the sun, we miss it worse than ever.

All good wishes from us both – and au revoir   DHL

---

[1] Mark Gertler (1892–1939), painter, friend of DHL's since 1914 (see *Letters*, ii. 214 and n. 1); he suffered from tuberculosis, had himself been to Mundesley Hospital for treatment and endured frequent bouts of depression. Cf. Letter 5428 and n. 3.

5463. To Charles Lahr, 23 December 1929
Text: MS UNYB; Postmark, Bandol 23 –12 29; Unpublished.

Beau Soleil, Bandol, Var
23 Dec 1929

Dear Lahr

I was very sad about the motor accident and your child and Davies. I do hope everything is mending up well, and no serious results. Why have motor-cars taken to turning over so easily – ? seems a regular habit.

Anyhow they can't upset me, for I'm in bed with my bronchials, and linseed poultices and all the miseries. A real seasonal Christmas!

Did you see that Harry Crosby shot himself in New York – and a mistress? Dismal affair. The wife is on her way back to Paris. The books were all landed safely in New York – and taken to Harry Marks' bookshop – I told you he was asking $25 a copy.

And have you seen the enclosed?[1]

And have you heard any more about the *Pansies* piracy? I hear Pollinger can't get hold of Goldston, anyhow.[2]

I sent my *Nettles* to be offered to Faber & Faber for a pamphlet-booklet. Was rather sad, really.

Thanks for your card. Oh, if only Jesus *had* been a turnip (turnips did not exist, by the way) and the ass had eaten him!

Let me know if all is well.

DHL

5464. To Rhys Davies, 23 December 1929
Text: TMSC NWU; Huxley 844–5.

Beau Soleil, Bandol, Var.
23 Dec. 1929.

Dear Davies,

I have been wanting all this time to write – but my bronchials have been giving me such a bad time. Now I'm in bed with linseed poultices, so can't go much lower. There was a great storm yesterday – huge seas – today is quiet, but grey and chill and forlorn: imagine me the same.

We were so sorry to hear of that motor-car accident and those two ribs. I believe ribs aren't terribly important – witness Eve – so I hope you're about better now. But it was too bad. And I always thought Charlie Lahr was a

---

[1] The enclosure is missing.
[2] This remark, taken in conjunction with Letter 5448 and n. 2, and the existence of an envelope addressed to Lahr and postmarked 'Bandol 10 –12 29', suggests that DHL wrote to Lahr on 10 December about the *Pansies* piracy and that his letter has been lost.

lucky man – now one must doubt it. Anyhow there's no luck in the wide world at present.

I read your story in *This Quarter* – quite amusing.[1] What does your mother say to it? la jeunesse! And you are coming out in the *London Mercury*! Oh beware, they'll be putting a little blue ribbon round your neck, tied in a blue bow at the side.

Did you read that Harry Crosby, the rich young American in Paris who printed *Escaped Cock* for me, shot himself and his mistress in New York. Very horrible! Too much money – and *Transition surréalisme* –

We've got altogether seven friends in the Beau Rivage, and they all come to tea. I tell you it's a jorum.[2]

Frieda says she is writing to you.

Tell me if there is anything I could order you for Christmas – any book or books you'd specially like – or a pen or something. Do tell me.

Remember us warmly to your mother, and to your sister. I wish we could come in and have a mince-pie with you – do you have mince-pie in Wales.

I'm disappointed about the chips and faggots young man.[3]

I thought of calling my book of collected sketches: 'Chips and Faggots'.

Well, I won't say Merry Christmas, but I do hope you are feeling chirpy, all the same. And do let me know if there is anything I can do for you.

DHL

---

[1] Referring to their visit to Paris together in the spring, Davies recalled that DHL

was unexpectedly helpful with a short story of mine when he had met Edward Titus for discussion of an edition of *Lady Chatterley*. Titus, prosperous husband of Helena Rubinstein, edited a magazine in Paris, *This Quarter*; Lawrence took him my short story, and, calling later at the editor's office in a street behind the Dôme, I received a generous cheque. In pursuance of my policy of ridding Anglo-Welsh writing of flannel and bringing some needed flesh tints to it, my story had to do with a naked bourgeois wife opening the front door of her house and finding there, instead of her expected husband, a startled young miner whose own Baptist chapel wife had never granted him such a dazzling treat. Called 'Revelation', I had written the story one evening after listening to Madame S's rites of Venus in the room next to mine in Nice. (*Print of a Hare's Foot*, p. 159)

[2] I.e. a large number, group.   [3] See Letter 5286.

5465. To Aldous Huxley, 23 December 1929
Text: Huxley 843–4.

Beau Soleil, Bandol.
23 Dec., 1929.

Dear Aldous, –

Many thanks for Maillol, which has just come.[1] He has a certain tender charm.

I haven't sent a thing to anybody, as I am in bed with a bout of bronchitis, and feel I can't make any efforts. Wonder how Maria got on in San Remo – futile sort of journey – futile business! Expect she had the storm yesterday same as here. The world very grey and stunned to-day. I'm rather the same, as I had to put a linseed poultice on my broncs. Hope your rheumatism is better. It is indeed a curse, being ill.

I hope you've got good news of Julian.[2] Somehow, I feel he'll dodge through, and the tsetse flies won't bite him. But let me know, as I shall go on wondering.

I think you're lucky to escape the Christmassing. Why do we do it! But I suppose the children like it. – I'm keeping ours down to a mere tea-party, so not much harm done. But the friends in the hotel are now seven!

No news in our world. I am doing practically nothing – haven't touched a paint-brush. Sad!

Did you get the painting from Dorothy Warren? You could claim it any time now.

Gertler talks of coming down here in January.

DHL

The cat has killed the silver goldfish – nothing less than a tragedy.

---

[1] Huxley had written to Robert Nichols on 14 December 1929 (Smith 322): 'I think Maillol is the only artist of modern times – since Chaucer and Boccaccio anyhow – to recapture the pre-Platonic quality of feeling. His sculpture springs quite genuinely from the same roots as the best archaic Greek or (better) Etruscan – the Apollo of Veii, for example, at Rome.' He had doubtless written in the same terms to DHL and, for Christmas, sent him a book of reproductions – perhaps *Aristide Maillol: vingt-huit reproductions de sculptures et dessins* (Paris, 1926).
[2] Julian Huxley was in East Africa.

5466. To Herberth Herlitschka, 26 December 1929
Text: MS UR; cited in *Apocalypse* 20.

Beau Soleil, *Bandol*, Var. France
26 Dec 1929

Dear Mr Herlitschka

I have not yet thanked you for the books, which came safely.[1] I liked the Butler best, and thought the translation excellent. Poor Yeats, his shoddiness shows up rather badly in translation. I like him, and I like some of his things very much. But there is a certain shoddy quality in nearly all the Irish, which they cover with an 'Irish' style, but which shows badly in another language. Why is it that belles lettres are so rarely beautiful in translation? is it because they are not *really* beautiful in the original? – As for Thornton Wilder, you make him better in German than he is in his high-school American. He is nothing – empty affectation.

I hope that Tal has by now received the agreement for *Lady C.*, which I signed and sent on to Curtis Brown.[2] Now I really hope all will go smoothly.

---

[1] Herlitschka appears to have sent three of his translations: Samuel Butler, *Der Weg alles Fleisches* (Vienna, 1929); W. B. Yeats, *Die Chymische Rose* (Hellerau, 1927); Thornton Wilder, *Die Brücke von San Luis Rey* (Leipzig, 1929).

[2] DHL here turns to answer Herlitschka's letter, 22 December 1929 (TMSC UR):

Dear Mr. Lawrence,

   Thank you for your letter of the 14th. Tal received a letter from Courtis Brown since in which, thanks to your intervention, they were rather apologetic and friendly indeed. They also sent a draft agreement for Tal to sign. He did so and returned it, and he is now awaiting the counterpart which I suppose Curtis Brown have in the meantime submitted to you for signature. I do hope no hitch will occur at the last moment . . .

   I hope to hear from you again when you have received a reply from your sister-in-law and from Kippenberg. I shall gladly avail myself of your kind offer and ask your Paris publisher for a copy of "Lady Ch." By the way – there was a long article on the book in "Les Nouvelles Litteraires" No. 374 of December 14th. Did you see it? Rather hopeless and idiotic. How ridiculous this comparison with Martin Maurice "Amour, Terre inconnue"! Of course, the theme is the same, but Maurice treats it just as it should not be treated, and his book seems to me cold and conventional and almost banal. The writer of the article entirely fails to grasp what you were out to do. But then it is even more difficult for the French than for the Germans to understand a book like "Lady Ch." You are quite right by saying the Germans will not understand it – the many, that is. The few will – and I still believe its worth it doing things for them. Do you think that the many in Germany understand Aldous Huxley or Samuel Butler or appreciate Yeats for that matter? But I feel I must keep on trying to make them understand. No good being disheartened, and I will not believe you really are though your first letter sounded as if you were just a little.

   I enclose two cuttings about Katherine Mansfield you might perhaps like to have as I suppose you were good friends . . . I have now been trying to find a German publisher for her work since 1925. They all fight shy of an author who has written no long novel . . . I offered [Insel-Verlag] K. M's work ages ago and urged them again and again for years. Now they promised to re-consider the matter.

   I have been commissioned by Kippenberg to write a little pamphlet on the modern English novel and the authors he is publishing in particular. For this purpose I require some data about

– I saw the review in *Nouvelles Litteraires,* but it didn't cut any ice.
Second-rate little critics have said all that before.

I will send you an autobiographical sketch in a day or two. I have only one
copy, and it has gone to a man who wants to lecture on me, but he will send it
back, and I will forward it to you at once.

Poor Katharine Mansfield! – it's a pity they defer publishing her, as she
belongs to her day and will fade. I knew her too well, though, to accept her as
a saint!

I heard from Kippenberg that he will not release *any* of my novels to
anybody – nor *White Peacock* nor any other. Very emphatic.

David Herbert Lawrence – born at Eastwood, Nottinghamshire
11 Septem. 1885.

For dates of publication, if you need them, you could write to Curtis Brown. I
can't remember. – But you shall have that autobiographical sketch in a few
days.

My sister-in-law was huffy when I suggested she should let you see her
translation of *Plumed Serpent.* People are always so easily offended.

I am working on a little book about the Apocalypse – Offenbarung
Johannis – which I suppose will annoy everybody who reads me. –

ever   D. H. Lawrence

5467. To Emil von Krug, 28 December 1929
Text: MS UT; Unpublished.

Beau Soleil, *Bandol,* Var, France.
28 Dec 1929

Dear Emil

The pen came at last yesterday – quite safe and sound, and very handsome.
I feel at once I ought to have a noble study with a mahogany desk, to fit it. But
the pen writes very nicely, and will be very useful. It comes at the right
moment, as my old one is Kaput. So very many thanks.

Christmas passed quietly, thank God. I don't like a lot of festivity, it's such
hard work and always rather false. We have half a dozen friends in the hotel
here – and other friends have taken a house not far away. So we are by no
means alone: every day somebody.

---

you and your work which my available sources dont give exactly enough. If it is not too much
bother please let me have the information by opportunity, i.e. date and place of your birth and
the correct order in which your books (prose and poetry) were published – with dates if
possible. Any additional details you would care to give I should very much appreciate –
particularly about your plans for the next future and what you are working on just now ...

The weather has been bad, for here – stormy and grey. Even the sun no longer loves the Christian festivals, he stays away.

We have this house till end of March, and after that, I don't know what we shall do. But as you say, we will never stay so long in Baden any more. Frieda must go alone – it is no place for a man. Perhaps we might come to Berlin – it would be an experience. If only my health would be better! It is really very trying. I should be so glad to be really well again, to be able to move about freely.

France is a very easy country to live in, very free and on the whole very aimiable. But it isn't inspiring. There is a certain petit-bourgeois quality everywhere, one can't escape it. And it is rather deadening. I'm sure no one will ever do *great* work in France, as it is now: only clever work, or smart work. So I would hate to have to live here always.

Well I do hope you and Nusch will have a real good year in 1930, with a bit of inward peace and warmth, that's the chief thing.[1]

5468. To Martin Secker, 28 December 1929
Text: MS UInd; Postmark, Bandol 29 –12 29; Secker 125.

Beau Soleil, *Bandol.* Var
28 Dec 1929
Dear Secker

I have sent back the MSS of the book of articles to Pollinger. I put the title *Assorted Articles* as that seemed to me just what they are. I found two more sketches – and I included two of the *Adelphi* articles, as they seem to wind up on the right note.[2] Two I omit, as being out of key. Now tell me if you think it is all right, or if there is anything else you would suggest.

Christmas is over – passed very quietly, thank god – with rather bad weather. We have half a dozen friends in the hotel, so are by no means alone. But I managed to have a bit of extra bronchitis, and was in bed. Very trying, my health.

I'm glad Rina is in Alassio – she will probably enjoy it, and you will have a bit of peace. I felt very chilly when I heard of Bridgefoot with no servant at all. Dio mio! how awful is a dissatisfied woman!

All good wishes for New Year.   D. H. Lawrence

Would you please send me galley proofs of the *Articles*, so that I can make alterations or stick bits in if I want to – to keep the book in harmony.

---

[1] Complimentary close and signature have been cut from MS.   [2] See p. 400 n. 3.

5469. To Edward Titus, 3 January 1930
Text: MS UT; Unpublished.

Villa Beau Soleil, *Bandol*, Var.
3 Jan 1930[1]

Dear Titus[2]

Thanks for your letter of Dec. 31st. with cheque for ten thousand francs for *Lady C.* – and the statement of sales of the first 3,000 copies. The reckoning is all right as far as I can count.

About an advertisement in the local English press – do you mean the Paris *Herald* and the *Mail*? I doubt if it would make much difference, but do it if you think it is worth while.

I'll tell them to keep you a room at the Beau Rivage next week – I expect the New Year visitors will mostly have left. I hardly go out at all – so you will have to walk here to see me – but it is only ten minutes. And the weather is lovely just now.

Curtis Browns' want to start an action against Seltzer-Boni, for recovery of plates of my novels, and for payment of debt: putting it in the hands of the lawyer Stern.[3] I am waiting a day or two before deciding: but I feel something has got to be done, drastically.

All good wishes for New Year   D. H. Lawrence

---

[1] 1930] 1929
[2] DHL was replying to Titus's letter, 31 December 1929 (TMSC SIU):

Dear Mr. Lawrence,
    My book-keeper is still unavailable, but as you asked for a statement, and quite justly, I am myself gathering, unskilfully perhaps, the figures, and am giving them to you enclosed herewith, errors excepted, together with another cheque for Frcs. 10,000.00.
    The 8/15 and 7/15th percentage worried me a little; and if there is an error in the calculation (I am very poor at figures), forgive, and my book-keeper will straighten this out on her return. –
    The best of luck to you in the New Year, and keep your pecker up.
                                                                Yours sincerely,
    What do you think of the idea of a small advertisement in the local English press, – simply mentioning that D. H. Lawrences Lady Chatterley's Lover is obtainable at all English Booksellers at 60 Frcs the copy, – or words to that effect? Say once a week. It might help along, especially as things are rather slack now? – If it should not be any trouble to you, I shall send you a wire sometime next week asking you to reserve a room for me at a hotel at Bandol for two or three days. I need a change, – but that is all the time I can spare. –

The statement concerned the sale of 2978 copies of the first printing, at 40 francs per copy. The total profit was 77,537.20; DHL's share (8/15ths) was 41,352.80; he had been paid 30,000, and was now being paid 10,000 on account.
[3] Benjamin H. Stern, of the New York legal firm, Stern & Ruben, had been used before by Curtis Brown on DHL's behalf: see *Letters,* iv. 182 n. 2; v. 18 and n. 3.

5470. To Frederick Carter, 6 January 1930
Text: MS UT; Moore 1228–9.

Beau Soleil, *Bandol*, Var. France.
6 Jan. 1930

Dear Carter

I meant to write before – but I waited, getting bothered by my Intro-duction. It became so long and somehow unsuitable to go in front of your essays. So at last I laid it aside, and have written you now a proper intro-duction, about 5000 words, I think, which is really quite good and to the point, I feel. So I shall send it tomorrow or the next day to Curtis Brown to be typed, and they will send you a typescript copy. I shall not say anything to them about placing the book: then if you can do it yourself, well and good. – For such an introduction I usually get £20 or £25,[1] as outright payment, with right to include the introd. in a book of collected essays later on: which is quite simple, and leaves you free to arrange all terms yourself; the publisher merely paying me the £20. down for his[2] right to use the introd. for, say, a term of two years. – Probably I shall publish my first Introd., which grew to 25,000 words nearly, later on, as a small book.[3] But I am in no hurry, and hope you'll have yours out first. I too thought of *Dragon of Revelation*: it seems to me a good title. If the publishers don't like it, we can think of another. Chattos would be good people, but I doubt if they'll catch on. I shall be very much interested to see your new chapter, and most interested to see the drawings.

Weather rather stormy – has been very good. Health so-so. Brewsters are in their Chateau Brun, and seem to like it. My wife is all right, and sends her good wishes. We had quite a number of visitors – now most are gone, but still three in the hotel, and more coming. Do you still think of coming down?

All good luck for the New Year   DHL

5471. To Nancy Pearn, [6 January 1930]
Text: MS UT; cited in *Apocalypse* 25.

Beau Soleil, *Bandol*, Var. France.
6 Jan. 1929

Dear Nancy Pearn

Will you please have this 'Introduction' typed out and send one copy to
Frederick Carter, 45 Norfolk Square. W. 2.
He has written a book on Revelation and wants to find a publisher. I have told him, if he finds the publisher, he can pay £20. for the 'Introd.' But I

---

[1] £25,] £25, but we could arrange that: [2] his] the   [3] *Apocalypse.*

think he'll have hard work getting anyone to take his book. – This 'Introd.' might possibly be serialised.

Ask *Vanity Fair* to suggest me some titles: it works better that way, gives me a lead away from myself.[1]

Tell Pollinger I shall be writing him, and I'm so sorry he's not well, hope he'll be better. He must stay longer down here.

All very quiet – my health mediocre – but I hear from a man telling me he has some of my old MSS. with one or two unpublished things. I might work over and send them you – it might turn out quite nice. The man used to type for me years ago – Edward Garnett's nephew.[2] Lucky he is honest.

All good wishes for the new year.

ever   D. H. Lawrence

5472. To Maria and Aldous Huxley, 6 January 1930
Text: Huxley 845–6.

Beau Soleil, Bandol.
6 Jan., 1930.

Dear Maria and Aldous, –

I'm rather better but don't get on much. Still, I think I'm better – warily. Frieda's got a cold for a change.

Already the year is changing round. Ida Rauh being here, we talk, of course, of Taos and the ranch, and plan to go back in the spring. It might pick me up again: who knows?

Pino and Douglas were very sweet, but rather on the holiday razzle, so rather dêpressing. I find that people who are on the razzle, enjoying themselves, are so inwardly miserable and *agacé*,[3] they are a real trial.

How are you both after the festivities? – I don't suppose you razzled much, anyhow. What about your plans? Are you coming down as you said about the

---

[1] Donald Freeman, managing editor of *Vanity Fair*, was still hoping to persuade DHL to sign a year's contract as a regular contributor to the magazine (cf. Letter 5362 and n. 2). Freeman regarded him as an 'ideal writer' (letter from Nancy Pearn to DHL, 22 November 1929, TMSC UT), and though he rejected the essays DHL sent on 4 November (cf. Letter 5404 and n. 2), he continued to pursue the matter of a contract. Nancy Pearn told DHL on 1 January 1930 (TMSC UT) that *Vanity Fair* were inviting him to propose titles for essays which might be written in association with a contract.

[2] Douglas Clayton (1894–1960), DHL's regular typist 1913–15 (see *Letters*, ii. 30 n. 3), was the nephew of Edward Garnett (1868–1937), DHL's close friend and patron during his early years as a writer (see *Letters*, i. 15–18, 297 n. 2). An envelope postmarked 'Ba[nd]ol 26 – 12 29' is extant (MS UT), addressed to Clayton in DHL's hand; it establishes that DHL had already replied to him about the MSS; the letter itself is missing.

[3] 'on edge'.

20th? That is only a fortnight ahead. When one does nothing, how time seems to vanish away!

Weather has been so warm, unnaturally so, and sunny. These last two days it is stormy from the sea, but still not at all cold. Perhaps we are not going to have any real cold this winter.

What is the latest news of Julian and Juliette? I wondered so often, but Aldous did not tell me. And Yvonne, is she still errant?

Margaret Gordon[1] wants us to go and stay with her in her house near Grasse, but I think not. I hear [Wells][2] and [Maugham][3] and Co. were rolling their incomes round Nice for Xmas, rich as pigs, [Hugh Walpole] sunning himself in the glow of their lucre, Pino Orioli the obscure satellite, being the guest of the obscure [Douglas?]. So we climb down the steps of the hierarchy, from a pinnacle of [Wells] to the lowest rung of a Pino! *Scala degli angioli!*[4]

[Brett Young] says his income is an 'easy' four thousand a year. So he has got a 'hall' in the lake district in England, a Georgian hall in which he can become a little more damp than he already is, to be a last lake poet, instead of a mere puddle poet.[5]

I feel very spiteful against them all, for being mere incomes on two legs.

Well, I can't write letters any more, but am not depressed. Tell us the news, and about your coming.

DHL

5473. To Prince Leopold Löwenstein, 6 January 1930
Text: MS Besterman; Moore 1231.

Villa Beau Soleil, *Bandol*, Var, France.
6 Jan. 1930

Dear Prince Löwenstein

I am so sorry there has been all this trouble over *Lady C.*[6] The real cause was Kippenberg, holding up the book and then changing his mind and upsetting everybody. However, it is over now, so I hope we can all forget the endless annoyances. I am very grateful to you for all the trouble you have taken, and

---

[1] Unidentified.   [2] See p. 239 n. 1.

[3] DHL's earlier references to the novelist William Somerset Maugham (1874–1965), whom he met in Mexico City in 1924, had been less than complimentary: see *Letters*, v. 157–8, 160–2, 166, 446.

[4] 'Ladder of the Angels!'

[5] Francis Brett Young (1884–1954), doctor and novelist; he and his wife Jessica had known DHL in Capri, 1919–20 (see *Letters*, iii. 438 and n. 2; Keith Sagar, 'Three Separate Ways', *Review of English Literature*, vi (July 1965), 93–105). The 'Georgian hall' was Esthwaite Lodge where 'life was full of memories of Wordsworth, Coleridge, de Quincey and all the other Lakeland writers' (Jessica Brett Young, *Francis Brett Young*, 1962, p. 169).

[6] Cf. Letters 5143 and n. 1, 5452 and n. 1, 5453.

very sorry you should have had so much irritation over the matter. But Miss Jean Watson seems a thoroughly good hand at irritating *everybody*, myself included – and now she is Mrs Curtis Brown Junior there seems to be no holding her.

However, we can let it rest now.

My wife sends her greetings, I mine.

Sincerely   D. H. Lawrence

5474. To Mabel Dodge Luhan, 6 January 1930
Text: MS Brill; Luhan 350–1.

Villa Beau Soleil, *Bandol*, Var, France.
6 Jan. 1930

Dear Mabel

Ida says she has written you about our coming to Taos in the spring. I think, if I felt safe about it, I have the energy to get up and start, and I feel that once I got there, I should begin to be well again. Europe is slowly killing me, I feel.

Ida seems pretty well. She goes around here with various friends of ours, and seems to enjoy herself all right. In fact I think she's really in a healthier state of mind than when I saw her last in New Mexico. We talk and make plans: plans of coming back to the ranch and having places near one another – and perhaps having a sort of old school, like the Greek philosophers, talks in a garden – that is, under the pine-trees. I feel I might perhaps get going with a few young people, building up a new unit of life out there, making a new concept of life. Who knows! we have always talked of it. My being ill so long has made me realise perhaps I had better talk to the young and try to make a bit of a new thing with them, and not bother much more about my own personal life. Perhaps now I should submit, and be a teacher. I have fought so against it.

For my own part, though I am perhaps *more* irascible, being more easily irritable, not being well, still, I think I am more inwardly tolerant and companiable. Who knows! Anyhow people's little oddities don't frighten me any more: even their badnesses. I think we might get on easily together. Frieda is suspicious, but I think even she is weary of the old watchful and hostile attitude, and doesn't care very much when people affront her a bit. As Brett says, she might quite easily like even Brett. So many of our feelings are illusion. We don't *really* have them. I think we might all be a great soothing and support to one another – I do really. I think we might even trust one another, sufficiently. It would be very good to have a real togetherness.

I wish we could start afresh with this year. You have never really trusted *anybody*, and you have never felt any real togetherness with anybody. Perhaps we might begin, and then do our best. We are too much cut off. I am too much cut off.

I hope you are feeling well, and fairly serene. I had your story. Of course it was *all* about yourself: just yourself. But I suppose, while you remain alone, you cannot escape yourself.

Well, here's to the spring, and a little new hope.

DHL

5475. To Hon. Dorothy Brett, 8 January 1930
Text: MS UT; Moore 1231–2.

Villa Beau Soleil, *Bandol*, Var.
8 Jan. 1930

Dear Brett

Your letter a couple of days ago. I suppose you had mine too.[1] Glad all goes well, and you're beginning to *sell*. I've not touched a brush since we were in Spain: have been very low. But am trying with all my might to bite on and get better sufficiently to come back to New Mexico. This winter makes me know I shall just die if I linger on like this in Europe any more: and what's the good of my dying! and anyhow it's so wearying and painful, being ill. So at the week-end, when Earl comes down and tells me the name and address of the American Consul in Marseille, I shall write him and ask his advice about our coming over in March or April, and about the quota and all that. I hope he'll be friendly. We could sail Dollar Line from Marseille, and land either in New York or even San Francisco:[2] I wouldn't mind a long sea trip. But I do want to do something about my health, for I feel my life leaving me, and I believe it's this old moribund Europe just killing one.

I shall let you know how I get on with the Consul etc.

Maria Cristina Chambers cabled she would come over in Feb. Frankly, I don't like her very much, but *don't* say so to anybody, as she seems to slave for me – for my books – in New York. Not that much is achieved.

But I believe we might all of us fit together and make a life. I have always said that Frieda's hate was at least half illusory, all the time – and now she begins to feel it. I don't believe there'd be any squabbling – with a bit of patience. As for me, I doubt if I've the strength to quarrel with anybody.

I hope I can get strong enough to sail in March or April, and there won't be much difficulty. For I realise I'm at the end of my tether over here – And they

---

[1] Unless (as seems unlikely) DHL was referring to Letter 5355, this letter to Brett is missing.
[2] From 1924 the Dollar Steamship Line (founded in 1910 by Capt. Robert Dollar) provided a round-the-world service including the ports of Marseille, New York and San Francisco.

all so eagerly *expect* me to die – Murry and the London lot. How they want to bury me! Oh God!

Send us your New York address, so I can write there.

DHL

5476. To S. S. Koteliansky, 9 January 1930
Text: MS BL; Postmark, [. . .]; Moore 1233.

Beau Rivage, *Bandol,* Var
9 Jan. 1930

Dear Kot

I was just writing about the impossibility of fitting the Christian religion to the State – Send me the *Grand Inquisitor*, and I'll see if I can do an introduction.[1] Tell me how *long* you'd like it. I did about 6,000 words for Carter's Apocalypse book. For the Introd. to Dahlberg's *Bottom Dogs* I got £20 – but that is a bit low. It depends on the publisher and the price of the edition etc. Tell me what the plan is. We can arrange all right.

Dr Morland is due to arrive here on the 15th – and so is Pollinger, travelling straight from London. Pollinger is staying about a week – he's not well either. I don't know whether he'd like to travel with the Morlands –

Weather rather bad – health so-so. I do hope you're feeling better than in your other letter, and no serious troubles. I do hope too that Sonia is better. Everybody seems to be ill.

Send me your translation.

DHL

5477. To Martin Secker, 9 January 1930
Text: MS UInd; Postmark, Bandol 11 –1 30; Huxley 846–7.

Beau Soleil, *Bandol,* Var.
9 Jan 1930[2]

Dear Secker

Count Keyserling asked my sister-in-law to give him a copy of *Plumed Serpent* because he wants to write an article on it.[3] Mean swine won't buy a copy! I leave it to you whether you send one – you have my sister-in-law's address:

Frau Dr Else Jaffé, Bismarckstr. 17. Heidelberg.

---

[1] Kot's translation of *The Grand Inquisitor* (a chapter from Dostoievsky's novel *The Brothers Karamazov*) together with DHL's introduction, was published in July 1930 (Roberts B28).
[2] 1930] 1929
[3] Count Hermann Alexander Keyserling (1880–1946), a popular philosopher whom DHL did not hold in high regard (cf. *Letters,* v. 390 and n. 3, 639 and n. 2).

Hope the MSS of *Assorted Articles* was all right – and title – I haven't heard anything. You'll send me galley proofs, won't you.

All quiet here – had a number of visitors, including the Brett Youngs, on £4000 a year, so they say. (Bit[1] of spite – cross it out.)

Hope all goes well.

DHL

5478. To Laurence Pollinger, 9 January 1930

Text: MS UT; Unpublished.

Villa Beau Soleil, Bandol, Var.
9 Jan 1930

Dear Pollinger

I'm sorry about that cold – do hope the sun will shine here – You must arrange to stay longer than six days. I'm no good at walking so shan't come to the station – but you'll find the hotel bus there waiting – Hotel Beau Rivage – just get in – and if by any chance the bus should *not* be there, take a taxi – it's only a few minutes. Madame Douillet will be expecting you at the hotel, and perhaps my wife will be there. If not, she will come about 4.0 to fetch you here – and perhaps that will be best, for then you can rest, you will be dead tired. Everything is very easy. I have told Madame Douillet you will be my guest – she is used to the arrangement. She'll look after you all right.

Perhaps you'll be able to settle with Faber & Faber about the *Ariel* poem and the *Nettles* before you come.

Take care of the journey: the beastly trains are either boiling or icy, as a rule. I do hope they won't be *late*.

And I do hope you are feeling better.

D. H. Lawrence

It is possible Dr Morland and his wife will be coming on your very train – they are just calling to see me, staying one night, then going on. But I myself don't know them personally, yet. Mark Gertler sends them. You could ask Koteliansky, if you feel you'd like to travel with them. They are due to arrive on the 15th.

---

[1] say. (Bit] say. How are the puny risen! (Bit

5479. To Stephen Potter, 9 January 1930

Text: MS Jenner; Stephen Potter, *D. H. Lawrence: A First Study* (1930), pp. 7, 159.

Villa Beau Soleil, *Bandol*, Var.

9 Jan 1930

Dear Mr Potter[1]

I believe my books are published pretty well in the order in which they were written: I don't think there are any serious divergencies. Only *Women in Love* was finished by end of 1916 and didn't get published till some years later – was it 1922? – I haven't got any important unprinted works: and I don't think any exist.

We are here till end of March, and I shall be pleased to see you if you really want to come down – though I hate reading about myself and my 'works.' The Hotel Beau Rivage here is quite pleasant, costs about 45–50 francs a day – and is ten minutes distant from here.

About a photograph – perhaps my sister would lend you one that was taken for my 21st birthday, clean-shaven, bright young prig in a high collar like a curate – guaranteed to counteract all the dark and sinister effect of all the newspaper photographs.[2]

I don't know the name of your novel, or I would order it. Please tell me.

All good wishes   D. H. Lawrence

5480. To S. S. Koteliansky, 15 January 1930

Text: MS BL; Postmark, Ban[dol] 16 –[. . .] 30; Zytaruk 396.

Beau Soleil, *Bandol*, Var

15 Jan. 1930

Dear Kot

Just a word to say I have the *Inquisitor* and will try to do a nice little introduction – though I shall never be able to squash myself down to a thousand words.

Pollinger arrived today, but we haven't talked business at all yet. He says he must leave Monday. Dr Morland arrives with his wife on Friday. Shall let you know what he says.

ever   DHL

---

[1] Stephen Meredith Potter (1900–69), author, critic and humorist; lecturer in English, University of London. He had recently published a novel, *The Young Man* (October 1929). He wished to discuss with DHL his book – to be published in March 1930 – *D. H. Lawrence: A First Study* (written apparently in ignorance of Herbert J. Seligmann's *D. H. Lawrence, An American Interpretation*, 1924). His planned visit did not take place because of DHL's death. Shortly after the publication of his book, Frieda Lawrence visited Potter to thank him for such a sympathetic study. He later achieved fame as the author of books on 'gamesmanship' and 'one-upmanship'.

[2] Potter borrowed this photograph from Emily King and used it facing p. 38 in his book.

By the way, how do we stand with regard to copies of my novel? Did the Lion have them all? and did he sell them all?

5481. To Ada Clarke, 15 January 1930
Text: MS Clarke; Postmark, [...]; cited in Lawrence–Gelder 203.

Beau Soleil, *Bandol*, Var.
15 Jany 1930

My dear Sister

Time I wrote again – one of my notes. We've had rather a run of visitors – Pollinger, of Curtis Brown's, now at the hotel – and Frieda's sister Else arrives here on Friday, to stay a week or so. I hope it will be fine, for today is grey and depressing as England.

My health has been rather better. On Friday also arrives Dr Morland and his wife – from Mundesley. He will stay in the hotel a day or two – don't suppose he'll be able to tell me much. I shall let you know.

So you and Pamela will come at the end of February. That should be all right. Frieda might go to Germany to see her mother while you two are here to look after me. But we can arrange that later. – And Jack is going on a swell trip to the chateaux – he'll just enjoy that. – How is your French, by the way? Will you be able to do the housekeeping with Mme Martens, the cook? She is a common little dark provençale woman, common, but quite good in her way. – The Brewsters are up in their house – rather uncomfortable, and not very well, either of them. Harwood went back to England yesterday – and delighted to go. I think she loves escaping her parents.

I suppose I shall send Peg money for her 21st – or is there anything you could get for her for me? – or would she rather have the money, £5 or £6. or so? Tell me – and let me know the *date*. Don't forget.

love.   DHL

5482. To Emily King, 15 January 1930
Text: MS Lazarus; Postmark, [...] 16–1 30; cited in Pinto, *Renaissance and Modern Studies*, i. 9.

Beau Soleil, *Bandol*, Var
15 Jany 1930

My dear Pamela

I don't suppose Frieda has answered your letter, so it will be just a note from me. We shall be pleased to see you and Ada at the end of February – it ought to be nice then. And perhaps while you are here to keep house and look after me, Frieda can go to Germany for a while. Do her good to get away from me for a bit. I'm afraid she gets a bit sick of my being so much in bed. But I'm really rather better again – only I never want to walk or move about. I must wait for that to come back. While I lie on the sofa I feel all right: but I'm no good at moving round. The woman who works for us isn't bad, she'll do anything one wants.

I've got Mr Pollinger at the Beau Rivage, and the day after tomorrow Else arrives from Heidelberg, to stay about a week. She'll stay in the house with us – in the little back bedroom. And I do hope it will be fine, for today is as grey as any London. Harwood Brewster went back to England yesterday – she'll be in the train now, nearing Totnes. She said she would write to you. She was delighted to go back to school – loves it so much better than home. That's how the young are. But I like her – and her parents *are* trying. They're not very well, either, in their Chateau Brun.

I asked Ada to tell me whether I should send Peg plain money for her 21st – or whether send the money to Ada to buy something for her. You might talk it over. What day is her birthday – February 20th?[1] I hope she'll have a nice party – and you won't have much fuss, if it isn't in the house.

Love   DHL

5483. To Frederick Carter, 15 January 1930
Text: MS UT; Unpublished.

Beau Soleil, *Bandol*, Var.
15 Jany 1930

Dear Carter

I got the chapter on the 'Antique Heavens' (will you really say *antique?*) and personally like it very much – but wonder where you'll put it, in the book.

I sent the Introduction to Curtis Browns to be typed out, and ordered a copy to be sent to you. Perhaps you have got it by now. I hope it's what you want. I like it myself, and think of it as an introduction really. Now I shall be *most* interested to hear what publishers say of the whole MS. – will you try Chattos first? Be sure to let me know. And tell me if there is anything else you would like me to do. – I shall lay my longer introduction by – not try to publish it now.

Everything quiet here – had rather a run of visitors – now Pollinger, Curtis Brown's man, is at the Beau Rivage – and on Friday comes my wife's sister from Heidelberg. The Brewsters, in the Chateau Brun, are not at all well: I say, too cold, they say no. The daughter has gone back to England to school. The weather really isn't cold, but today is most dismally grey: like London.

Hope you are well and chirpy –

ever   D. H. Lawrence

[1] The date was 9 February.

5484. To Lady Ottoline Morrell, 21 January 1930
Text: MS UT; Postmark, Bandol 21 –1 30; Huxley 848.

> Villa Beau Soleil, *Bandol*, Var
> 21 Jan 1930

My dear Ottoline

Many thanks for sending me Philip's book[1] – I have begun to read it, and shall enjoy it – nice and fat and human, one can keep on with it pleasantly for many a day. Quite a job worth doing, to make such a book accessible. I must say, I like the Englishmen of a hundred years ago. They were still men.

All very quiet here – my health been bad this winter – doctor says perhaps I must go into a sanatorium for a couple of months. Perhaps I will, I am tired of being always defeated by bad health. It has been rather bitter to me, this not being able to get better, for such a long time. But the body has a strange will of its own, and nurses its own chagrin.

Frieda's sister is staying with us – and her daughter Barbara comes next week – so we are not lonely. The weather has been quite lovely – a grey day today, but I don't mind it. It is nice here, but there is something curiously flat and uninteresting about the French – though they are very nice to us here.

What a pity we didn't know, when you were at Aix, so near. It would have been so good to see you again. I don't know when I shall come to England, with my wretched health – but perhaps you will come south.

> With love from us both   DHL

5485. To Maria Chambers, 21 January 1930
Text: TMSC UT and MS StaU; Chambers 119.

> Villa Beau Soleil, *Bandol*, Var
> 21 Jan. 1930

Dear Maria Cristina

I had your letter today – see you sitting on the fence and being calm. There is no news here, except my health is a nuisance. The doctor came from England, and wants to put me in a sanatorium for two months. I *might* go.

The poems I return. They are quite nice, but not very good: a little second-hand. But why not!

I heard from Mrs Crosby. She is in Austria, saying there was perfect love and perfect understanding between her and Harry. Well! As for him, I had not seen him since last Easter, but he was very very *spoilt*. I have no news from her, yet, about Osiris: not a word. We must wait still.

All the essays are collected and are going to appear with Knopf in a volume

---

[1] *Leaves from the Greville Diary* (November 1929), extracts from the diaries of Charles Cavendish Fulke Greville (1794–1865).

of *Assorted Articles* at end of April. I haven't done any more about *Vanity Fair* essays – my health is so tiresome: haven't done anything.

Mabel writes from Taos – rather sad. She wants us to go out there, and if I can get well enough, I shall do so, because I believe my health will never be right, here in Europe. It really gets worse in stead of better – and I believe New Mexico would cure me again.

Ida Rauh was here in the hotel for some weeks – very nice, but a bit at a loose end – wants something *to do*. She is in Nice now, but coming back here, I think. Brett, I believe, will be in New York – but I haven't heard.

I wonder if you will really come to Europe! You might truly like it better.

I can't write letters anymore – and Frieda won't write them – but do send all the news, and I do hope you'll keep lazy and cheerful.

DHL

[1]There is now a law-suit in my name against Boni and Seltzer, to recover the plates and rights of my books. It is being conducted by Stern, the literary lawyer. His address used to be

B. H. Stern. Stern & Ruben, 149 Broadway. N. Y. City

I don't know if it is still the same.

He *might* be glad of this letter about the 'out of prints'. Would you send him a *copy*, and ask him – tell him I asked you.

5486. To Mabel Dodge Luhan, 21 January 1930
Text: MS Brill; Luhan 351–2.

Villa Beau Soleil, *Bandol*, Var. France.
21 Jan. 1930

Dear Mabel

Your letter came yesterday – rather sad – and finds us rather sad. The doctor from England came on Monday – says the bronchitis is acute, and aggravated by the lung. I must lie still for two months – Talks of my going

---

[1] It is possible that these two paragraphs (MS StaU) were a postscript to this letter; or they may have been sent separately, at about the same time, to accompany the now missing enclosure. The following jottings (which form part of MS StaU), were probably given to Maria Cristina Chambers as additional information relating to the problem with which DHL needed her assistance:

My agent in New York
Edwin W. Rich, Curtis Brown, 116 West 39th St, New York

Old publisher Thomas Seltzer transferred his rights in my books to A. C. Boni who now has nine or ten volumes of mine – the point is, to find which are out of print, and have been out of print for six months

into a sanatorium near Nice, but I don't know if it's suitable. And I don't know if I shall go. He says with absolute care for two months – absolute rest from everything – I ought to be well enough to come to New Mexico and there get quite strong. – I believe I *should* get strong if I could be back: but I'm not well enough to travel yet. I must see. As soon as I *can* come I want to come. The thing to do is to take one's hands entirely off the body, and let it live of itself, have its own will. It is by the body we live and we have forced it too much. Now it refuses to live. Yours does the same. Now I have got to lie still till my body moves of itself, and takes its own life. It is very hard to yield entirely. You must do the same – try to give up yourself, try to yield yourself entirely to your body, and let it take its own life at last. You have bullied it so much – even to having your womb removed. Now try to love it, to think tenderly of it, to feel tenderly towards it, and let it come to its own life at last. It is a bit late – but better late than never. – And that is the true way. And it is a thing you can only do by being alone, people will only prevent you. Lie still and gradually let your body come to its own life, free at last of your will. – It is what I have got to do too. – If we can manage it, and I can come to New Mexico there we can begin a new life, with real tenderness in it. Every form of bullying is bad. But you must help me about coming over, when the time comes.

love from us both   DHL

5487. To Edward Titus, 23 January 1930
Text: MS UT; Unpublished.

Villa Beau Soleil, *Bandol*, Var
23 Jan 1930

Dear Titus[1]

Thank you for the cheque for 7,692 francs which you gave me when you

[1] DHL was replying to Titus's letter, 21 January 1930 (TMSC SIU):

Dear Mr. Lawrence,

Just as a matter of form, I will be obliged to you if you would kindly acknowledge the receipt of 7,672 Francs turned over to you the other day.–.

I would like to say that I enjoyed my visit with you and Mrs Lawrence tremendously and if I did not fear that I should have been making too serious inroads on your time and patience, I should have enjoyed nothing better than to have spent a few days more in Bandol.–.

On my return, I found another letter from Komroff. I enclose it for your perusal, I am afraid that Boni has set his mind on continuing the publication of your books. Komroff suggests naming a price, but I am afraid this would lead to no useful end by correspondence from this distance.–.

If no change takes place in the situation I may have an opportunity perhaps in the near future to take a trip to New-York and will then come face to face with Boni. I was rather embarrased to talk business to you to excess and have for that reason not pressed further my proposition to get a long-short story from you to be published in an edition of 500 copies in a series of 4 signed by the author. I mentioned that I could pay you 100 Guineas. This has not been accepted nor refused. May I or may I not consider it a bargain? We have however come to an understanding on the subject of contributions by you to this "Quarter" at the rate of P 20 each.–.

The weather has been wonderful here since my return. It must be glorious your way.

Yours sincerely.

were here last week, also for the 300 francs in notes: makes it eight[1] thousand francs near enough.

The doctor ordered absolute rest for some months – says I must do *no* work, see *no* people, and not even think. Hard task! So that puts the lid on everything for a bit – for I have got nothing ready.

Apparently the suit against Boni is being started by the lawyer Stern of Stern & Rubens. God knows what the result will be. You didn't enclose the Komroff letter, I think.[2]

Well, it's a hard world – I must not ever go to the hotel for lunch again – such a nice lunch –

D. H. Lawrence

They want to put me in a sanatorium.

5488. To Maria Huxley, 23 January 1930
Text: Huxley 848–9.

Beau Soleil, Bandol.
23 Jan., 1930

My dear Maria, –

Your letter came yesterday, and we deciphered it. Glad you had a good time in London – thrilled about the play[3] – hope it'll make you lots of money, then the rest doesn't much matter. It's bound to be horrible to look at, all plays are – so utterly false. But if it settles the money worries, good for it.

We had that doctor – he says I'm to rest absolutely, lie out on the balcony, do nothing, say nothing and above all, see no people. He says it's the people use up the life. Then in two months there should be a decided improvement. So I am obeying – doing nothing, saying nothing, seeing nobody, lying either in bed or on the balcony – and we'll see the result. He said he'd look at a sanatorium above Nice – his chief desire seems to be to remove me from the reach of 'people.' He says the bronchitis is very bad, and the lung is a bit active, and they aggravate one another, but the thing to do is to try to get the bronchitis down, as it is doing most mischief.

Well, if you come here, I shall be – in bed or on the balcony – *Santa Madonna!* possessing my soul in false patience.

[1] it eight] it so 79 eight
[2] Manuel Komroff (1890–   ), American novelist, biographer and religious writer whose *The Voice of Fire* Titus had published in Paris in 1927; two of his books (*The Grace of Lambs*, 1925, and *Juggler's Kiss*, 1927) had been published by Boni & Liveright in New York.
[3] The play was *This Way to Paradise*, adapted by Campbell Dixon from *Point Counter Point*; it opened at Daly's Theatre in London on 30 January. See Letter 5514 and n. 1.

Meanwhile I hope the play will be a great success, and let me know.

DHL[1]

5489. To Charles Lahr, 24 January 1930
Text: MS UNYB; Postmark, Bandol 26 –1 30; Lacy, *Escaped Cock* 90–1.

Beau Soleil, *Bandol*, Var.

24 Jan. 1930

Dear L[ahr]

I haven't written – been so seedy – now the doctor says I must lie quite still, do no work at all, see nobody, and try to get better – not even think of work. So I am obeying.

I have no further news of the *Hahn*: shall let you know. What was your idea about it? To do a public edition, with another title? Tell me.

Tell Davies thanks for his letter, and he must stop off here and see me – I'm not allowed now to read an MS. – but perhaps later. Now I do nothing but lie in bed, kaput!

DHL

5490. To Hon. Dorothy Brett, 24 January 1930
Text: MS UT; Huxley 849–50.

Villa Beau Soleil, *Bandol*, Var. France

24 Jan. 1930

Dear Brett

I saw your father died – apparently it was easy for him – and 78. I hope he has left you better off – if not, never mind.[2] And I wonder if it'll take you to England.

I am lying in bed quite still, cut off from work and everything, trying to get my bronchitis healed a bit – very bad this winter. I want so much to get well enough to be able to start for New Mexico. I feel I'd get better there, and I get worse here. There is the consul to see – I can't do it – perhaps Earl will. Ida went away, when I depended on her a bit. – I was wondering if it would be

---

[1] On the day he read this letter Aldous Huxley wrote to Flora Strousse (American writer, pseudonym Floyd Starkey):

[DHL] has actually consented to see a doctor and, still more extraordinary, talks of following his advice and going into a sanatorium for a bit. It's a bad sign in one way; for it means he must be feeling very ill indeed: otherwise he wd never have consented to such a thing. Let's hope the sanatorium may do him some good and that it's not too late – as I rather fear – to do anything very effective. (Smith 327)

[2] Cf. p. 24 n. 1. Viscount Esher d. 22 January 1930, aged 77. *The Times* printed a lengthy obituary on 23 January; like her father's will, it omitted any mention of Brett.

best to sail on your Dollar line from Marseille right to San Francisco, and land there. Landing might be easier, and the long sea voyage might do me good. But I shall see what Mabel says. And of course I must get better than I am, before I can think of travel. But by end of March, surely, I shall be well enough again – I pray the gods. But I'm bad this winter: much worse than last.

I wonder where you are – you have not written – you should have had two letters – or three – of mine by now.

Frieda must write to you herself.[1] I don't know how she's going to act. But I feel I mustn't stay here to get any worse, or I'm done for. I don't know why I've gone down so this winter – there's no reason. But here I am, almost helpless, and minding it bittterly.

Well – hasta la vista! as you say.

DHL

The doctor says the lung trouble is active, but the bronchitis is the worst, and I must try and get that down first.

5491. To Mabel Dodge Luhan, 24 January 1930
Text: MS Brill; Unpublished.

Villa Beau Soleil, *Bandol*, Var. France
24 Jan. 1930

Dear Mabel

Your letter yesterday – nice of you to move at once for me. I am lying quite still, trying to get the bronchitis to go away – am in good hopes. Myself, I would like to sail as soon as I can – in March if I can. But then of course there's the question of visas, and whether we can come in on the quota. We could have 6-month visas any time, I suppose, but it's not much good. Someone will have to see the consul at Marseille about the quota.

I should be quite happy to stay with you and Tony for a bit – you could let us pay. But I doubt you wouldn't want me very badly, if I'm seedy and in

---

[1] Frieda wrote to Brett about 28 January (MS UCin):

If only you could be simple & natural, Brett, & let things be! I am *not* afraid of you, I am not jealous of you – I get so weary repeating these things – I would be *glad* if you amused Lawrence – I liked your paintings, they are awfully good – but deathly, deathly, *my* world is another world – but I dont want to interfere with yours – dont you interfere with mine – Are you really so unutterably *dense* that you cant see L's & my relationship or is it evil & you dont want to? Then you might as well deny that there is a star Orion or Venus or something like that – And if he grumbles, he is *sick* & so he grumbles at me – You just think I am such small beer! without significance! Your father is dead! You will feel it for all that – I would be quite glad to see you – If you wont try to *boss* & be *hostile*, it's *you*, you know – He is *very* ill, so be careful what you say!
F.

bed: which I hope I wouldn't be, but can't trust myself any more. And Frieda doesn't say what she wants – I think she'll hang back. But I feel I ought to come. It is useless to lie here and die. And there *is* something in New Mexico. Perhaps I should never have left. – And of course I should be quite pleased to see Brett, but then again, Frieda must say what she wants, for we can't stand rows: I can't. As soon as I can get something from the consul I shall write again. I thought Ida would help, but she went away. – I am thinking, perhaps we might sail on a *Dollar* boat from Marseille and keep on right to San Francisco, and land there, like the first time. What do you think? Would it be easier entry? The long sea voyage might set me up. How I wish I was stronger! but I've gone down this winter. – I saw Brett's father died – wonder if it makes any difference! – Glad you are better, hope all goes well.

au revoir.   DHL

5492. To S. S. Koteliansky, [25 January 1930]
Text: MS BL; Postmark, [. . .] 26 –1 30; Zytaruk 397.

Beau Soleil, Bandol, Var
Sat.

Dear Kot

Dr Morland said I must lie still and see no one and do no work – the lung trouble active, but the bronchitis the worst, and I must get it down – they aggravate one another. So I am lying quite still, and already feel rather better.

Pollinger took the Introd. back with him – about 4000 words I suppose.[1] He thinks Mrs Henderson is all right.[2]

I won't write any more – but hope you'll like the Introd.

DHL

5493. To Giuseppe Orioli, 30 January 1930
Text: MS UCLA; Moore, *Intelligent Heart* 426.

Beau Soleil, *Bandol*, Var. France
30 Jany 1930

Dear Pino

Douglas said you were ill, but he didn't say how or what. I do hope it isn't bad. I expect you got yourself thoroughly upset Christmassing at Nice and Menton. When you were here I knew from your *voice* that you were knocking yourself up. Why are you so silly? Why do you think you want to razzle and drink like Douglas? It doesn't agree with you – and you are only miserable. Remember that by family you are born moral, and so you'll always be miser-

[1] Cf. Letter 5476 and n. 1.   [2] Unidentified.

able when you go off the hooks. You'll merely kill yourself if you try to live up to Douglas' festive standards. You're not made that way.

There's a preach! – and all the time, here am I in bed too. The doctor says I must stay in bed for two months absolute rest – no work – no seeing people – then perhaps go to the ranch. – Frieda's daughter Barbara is here – her sister has just gone away. My sisters come in about a fortnight.

The Huxleys are in England, as *Point Counter Point* is being made into a play – first night tomorrow – and Aldous seems to be enjoying himself, figuring among the actors and actresses and being *It*.

Ask Carletto to send me a line to say how you are.

DHL

5494. To Else Jaffe, 30 January 1930
Text: MS Jeffrey; Frieda Lawrence 299.

Beau Soleil, *Bandol*, Var.
30 Jan 1930

Dear Else

So you got back safely – at least as far as Strassburg.

Here all is the same – I lay out today in the mouth of the garage, because the mistral is blowing – a sunny brilliant day with blue sea and sharp white foam. Barby helps Frieda to look after me, and all goes very well. Yesterday the bronchitis was *much* better, but today it is tiresome again – probably the wind.

The doctor sent word about the nursing home at Vence – it is not much of a place – like a little hotel or convalescent home – If I make good progress here, I shall not go to Vence – but if I don't get better, I will. But truly, I am already much stronger for this rest.

It was very kind of you to come all that long way to give us a helping hand – it did Frieda a lot of good, to share the responsibility with you, and I was glad to see you.

I have asked for a copy of *Escaped Cock* for you.

Barby is still in an unhappy state, inside herself. Oh dear o!

Remember me to Friedel.

DHL

5495. To Dr Andrew Morland, 30 January 1930
Text: MS Lazarus; Moore, *Intelligent Heart* 428.

Beau Soleil, *Bandol*, Var. France.
30 Jan. 1930

Dear Morland

Had your letter from Vence – many thanks – I don't much want to go *ad*

astra. I lie still in bed – I don't do any work – see no-one, for there is no-one
to see, except my wife's daughter, who is staying with us: and by yesterday
the bronchitis had subsided a lot – but it's come back a bit today again,
probably the north wind. – If I make good progress as I am, I shan't go to
Vence: if I don't, I shall.

We are both very grateful to you for your advice, which I can see is sound.
I should like to give you a signed copy of the first edition of *Lady Chatterley* –
if you'd care for it. I can get a copy from Florence. But where shall I send it?
– to Mrs Morland? What is her address in Mentone?

Shall report progress again next week.

Sincerely   D. H. Lawrence

5496. To Dorothy Warren, 30 January 1930

Text: MS UN; Nehls, iii. 429.

Villa Beau Soleil, *Bandol*, Var. France.
30 Jany 1930

Dear Dorothy

I am thinking you won't want to be bothered holding my pictures much
longer, and as I never want to show any of them again, and care nothing about
selling them, I think the best thing to do would be to turn them all over to my
sister Mrs Clarke, and let her store them in her attic, where she has lots of
room. So would you give Maria Huxley her *North Sea* – and you take *Contadini* – and then perhaps the others could go in their cases and be sent off to
Ripley (Derby). You have the address:

Mrs. W.E. Clarke, Broadway.

Anyhow let me know. I haven't written my sister yet, about it, but I'll do so.

My health is rotten this winter – Now I'm ordered to stay in bed for two
months, and not budge. Am very tired of it.

I hope you and Philip are well and flourishing – and I hope you think of us
affectionately, as we do of you.

Send a line.

D. H. Lawrence

5497. To Ada Clarke, 30 January 1930

Text: MS Sagar; Unpublished.

Beau Soleil, Bandol. Var. France
30 Jany 1930

My dear Sister

We shall be pleased to see you and Emily on the 18th or so.

The doctor says I must lie quite still for two months – absolute rest. It is true, I've gone down badly this winter – really. He wants me to go into a sanatorium above Nice – If this lying still doesn't help, I shall have to do so. I've been in bed ten days – feel rather better.

Else, Frieda's sister, was here till Sunday – and now Barby Weekley is here – helps to keep things going, and is very nice. Frieda needs someone to keep her balanced.

I am asking Dorothy Warren to send *all* the pictures for you to store in your attic. The doctor says, when I'm well enough, we should go to the ranch, for the climate – I should like to know that the pictures were safe with you.

Did you get a copy of the *Escaped Cock*? I asked for one to be sent you, from London.

Yes, your cake and pudding were very good – eaten up in a twinkling, with all the friends. When you come, bring some *tea*, and some of Pamela's chutney if she's got any.

We keep very quiet – I'm supposed to see no people – and do *no* work at all.

love   DHL

5498. To Douglas Clayton, 30 January 1930
Text: MS UT; Unpublished.

Villa Beau Soleil, Bandol, Var – France
30 Jan. 1930

Dear Clayton

I wondered what had happened to you, that you did not write. I understand you are rushed, and am thinking, the best would be if you sent me *all* the MSS. here for me to look at – except those you have advertised – and then I shall know what they are. They will be perfectly safe if you send by registered mail – and I can return them to you when I have looked them through and decided what would be best to do with them. It may be I shall not even want the typescript of 'Love Among the Haystacks' and 'Once', so if you haven't begun the typing, don't, but just send me all the MSS.

Yes, I think £30 to £40 all right for the MSS you offer. We'll see what the result is. I *might* offer the MS. of *The Rainbow*. A man in America offered me $3000 for the MS. of *Lady Chatterley*, but I refused.

The doctor says I am to stay in bed and do absolutely nothing, for some weeks – so here I am, in bed and writing this note.

Remember me to your mother.[1]

D. H. Lawrence

[1] Katharine Clayton (see *Letters*, ii. 30 and n. 1).

5499. To Max Mohr, 30 January 1930
Text: MS HMohr; Mohr, Briefe 540.

Beau Soleil, *Bandol*, Var. France
30 Jany 1930

Dear Mohr

I had your letter – glad you are working and all goes well. Here all has gone rather badly – my health has been very troublesome all winter. The doctor came from England, and said I must lie in bed for two months, and do no work, and see no people, only rest. So I do that. On sunny days I lie out of doors in the garden on a liegestuhl[1] – otherwise I am in bed. And I get weary in my soul. My cough also is a great nuisance. So this year Bandol has not been much help.

Frieda's sister Else, Frau Jaffé, was here last week: and now F's daughter Barbara is with us: I don't know for how long. In February my two sisters are coming, together. – The Huxleys are in London, because *Point Counter Point* is being made into a play, a drama – the first night is tonight. *She* writes that the play is awful. But let us hope it will bring them plenty of money.

Will you really go to Hamburg? If I can get well, I want to go to America, to the ranch, because I believe I should get better there. I wish it were possible to sail at the end of March.

I finished my little book on Offenbarung Johannis, but I shan't publish it. And of course I am doing nothing at all, now.

The weather is sunny, the almond trees are all in blossom, beautiful, but I am not allowed any more to go out and see them.

Many greetings from us both, and all good wishes.   DHL

5500. To Laurence Pollinger, 30 January 1930
Text: MS UT; Huxley 850.

Beau Soleil, *Bandol*, Var.
30 Jan. –30

Dear Pollinger

Not a sound from you – I do hope you got home safely and are well.

I duly lie in bed – or out on the terrace – and I think I'm really better. I don't do any work, and I see no people, for there is no-one to see – only my wife's daughter Barbara is with us.

I wanted to say, I don't want to publish that *Jolly Roger-extended* essay with the Mandrake[2] – I just feel I don't want to publish it as it stands – so do

---

[1] 'deck-chair'.   [2] Cf. p. 446 n. 1.

suppress the agreement, which I signed.[1]

Weather sunny – they say all the almond blossom is out, lovely up at the Brewsters. I watch the sea and the white foam.

DHL[2]

5501. To Caresse Crosby, 30 January 1930
Text: MS (Photocopy) SIU; Huxley 847.

Beau Soleil, *Bandol*, Var.
30 Jan. 30.

Dear Caresse

Thank you for the dream book.[3] Harry had a real poetic gift – if only he hadn't tried to disintegrate himself so! This disintegrating spirit, and the tangled sound of it, makes my soul weary to death.

I shall be interested to read the diary, later, if you wish me to – or what of it you wish me to.[4] And if I could write a suitable foreword, I'd be glad to. – But for the next two months, I'm not allowed to do *anything*. The doctor came from England, and said I must lie in bed for two months, and do *nothing*, and see no people – absolute rest. Oh dear! – and Harry was really so well, physically. And my nerves are so healthy, but my chest lets me down. So there we are. Life and death in all of us!

Did *Chariot of the Sun* ever appear?[5] I have never seen a copy. I should like very much to have one, if the book exists.

And is it possible for you to send me a couple of imperfect copies of *Escaped Cock*, as you once suggested. I should be glad.

Oh yes, don't you try to recover yourself too soon – it is much better to be a little blind and stunned for a time longer, and not make efforts to see or to feel. Work is the best, and a certain numbness, a merciful numbness. It was too dreadful a blow – and it was wrong.

DHL

---

[1] A copy of the *A Propos* contract, dated 22 January 1930, survives among Stephensen's papers (Munro, '*Lady Chatterley* in London' in *D. H. Lawrence's 'Lady'*, ed. Squires and Jackson, p. 234 n. 10).

[2] Nancy Pearn annotated the letter: 'I'm very depressed about him.'

[3] *Sleeping Together* (Paris, Black Sun Press, 1929). See Wolff, *Black Sun*, p. 245.

[4] Crosby's diaries appeared in three volumes, entitled *Shadows of the Sun*, First, Second and Third Series (Paris, Black Sun Press, 1928–30); DHL was presumably referring to the diary for Crosby's final year, published as 'Third Series' in 1930.

[5] The first edn was published in 1928. The 'Edition de Luxe' with DHL's introduction did not appear until November 1931 (Roberts B33).

5502. To Beatrice Campbell, 2 February 1930

Text: MS UCin; Peter L. Irvine and Anne Riley, 'D. H. Lawrence: Letters to Gordon and Beatrice Campbell', *DHL Review*, vi (Spring 1973), 17.

Beau Soleil, *Bandol*, Var.
2 Feb. 1930

Dear Beatrice[1]

Kot had told me about the *Lady C.* – I was so disappointed, when it came out, that Gordon didn't order a copy: because of course it was a great adventure, and some risk: and he wrote and told me he'd wait and borrow a copy: apparently he did: my copy. Gordon is so often stingy in the wrong place. *You* can have that copy if you buy it with your own money, for the original £2. – but Gordon, if he wants it, must pay the £6.

Here too everything very quiet, but my health a great nuisance, and I think of going into a sanatorium near Nice for a month or perhaps two. Wonder if I can bear it. If Ireland were *dry* I'd come there. Poor Ireland, she was never dry.

You sound quite nice and chirpy – your children growing up. Frieda's daughter Barbara, the younger, is with us: and she's 25. Dio buono! We're the middle-aged people.

D. H. Lawrence

5503. To Margaret King, 2 February 1930

Text: MS Needham; cited in Pinto, *D. H. Lawrence after Thirty Years*, p. 49.

Beau Soleil, *Bandol*, Var.
2 Feb 1930

My dear Peg

Well it is nearly your birthday, and you are nearly a real legal woman. It doesn't make any odds, really: but it is a nice reason for festivating a bit, and having a cake with candles. I send you a little cash to buy some trifle, which I'm sorry I couldn't go and buy myself for you.[2] But perhaps even then you'll know best what you want.

We are changing plans a bit here. I have written to the sanatorium near Nice to say I will go for a month or so, if they have a room ready. I expect their answer tomorrow – and if there is a room, I shall go on Tuesday. It is at Vence, about 15 miles from Nice – or less – and about 1000 ft. above the sea:

---

[1] Beatrice Moss Campbell, née Elvery (d. 1970), wife of Hon. Charles Henry Gordon Campbell (1885–1963), Irish barrister; in 1931 he succeeded to the barony of Glenavy of Milltown (see *Letters*, vi. 191 n. 3). DHL had known the Campbells since 1913; in October 1927 – after a gap of eight years – he had resumed his correspondence with them. He urged Campbell, in March 1928, to 'buy "John Thomas" – and perhaps a few of your friends will too' (ibid., vi. 335).

[2] For her 21st birthday DHL sent her £6 (information from Margaret Needham).

which is better. Of course I hate the thought of going, but I'd best do it and have done with it.

I don't know whether your mother will still want to come here. Frieda will go with me to Vence, stay a couple of days, then come back here and stay with Barby, who is with us this last week. I believe I shall be allowed to see people only twice a week. I'm not really any worse, but Dr Morland assured me I should get better so much more quickly in a sanatorium, and be able to *walk* again – and that is what I want. I want my legs back again.

Well, this is dull for a birthday letter – but I hope you will forgive it – and that you'll have a very jolly party up there at Mapperley.

With love from us both   D. H. Lawrence

5504. To Mabel Dodge Luhan, 2 February 1930
Text: MS Brill; Unpublished.

Villa Beau Soleil, *Bandol*, Var. France.
2 Feby 1930

Dear Mabel

Your letter enclosing one for Ida and also Arthur Brisbane's, came today.[1] Brisbane is not very re-assuring, really: I shall never forget the experience we had last time, coming in at El Paso[2] – how should I risk a repetition, now when my health is so bad. – I am thinking now of going into the sanatorium near Nice, to recuperate, if I can, and be ready for March. I haven't written to the consul yet, because of my health and this sanatorium business making me uncertain. I must see how I pick up. – Frieda was very scared, somehow, of the ranch, and Brett and all – a lamentable business – so she said she would want to stay in, or near Santa Fe. But of course she wouldn't: and I shouldn't. And now the whole thing changes, because her daughter Barbara wants to come with us, so Frieda feels ready for anything. Barby is all right, you'd like her all right. – The real trouble is my health – and I feel the Americans don't really like me. They are afraid of *Lady C.* Brisbane doesn't even mention it – only the pictures – and he must know all about it, especially since this Boston book-seller's case.[3] It's a bad sign that he doesn't mention it. – But they don't

---

[1] Arthur Brisbane (1864–1936), American newspaper editor; publisher of the *New York Journal*. It was through his influence that, in 1917, Mabel Luhan became a syndicated columnist for the chain of newspapers owned by William Randolph Hearst (1863–1951).

[2] See Letter 4896; see also *Letters*, v. 229.

[3] In November 1929 the manager and clerk of the Dunster House Book Shop in Cambridge, Massachusetts, were found guilty of selling a copy of *Lady Chatterley's Lover* to John T. Slaymaker who, under an assumed name, bought the book in order to bring a prosecution on behalf of the Watch and Ward Society. Those convicted appealed against the sentence (fine and imprisonment) and, at the appeal, while both the defence and prosecution lawyers condemned

like me, those Hearstians – they don't like *Pansies*. Somehow, I feel there is a block against my coming – somehow I feel it.

I think I have all your letters – I hope you have mine. I have written several times. It is a long time too since Brett wrote.

Why is the world so difficult!

DHL

Perhaps the idea of coming round to San Francisco in a Dollar Boat is the best.

5505. To Edward Titus, 3 February 1930
Text: MS UT; Postmark, Bandol 3–2 30; cited in Titus, *Times Literary Supplement*, 16 July 1931, p. 564.

Villa Beausoleil, *Bandol*, Var.
3 Feby 1930

Dear Titus

The Komroff letter has got mislaid, so I can't send it back – and I'm in bed – so please forgive.[1] The lawyer Stern of Stern & Rubens is considering Boni.

Your wire this morning.[2] Will you really print so many as ten thousand at a whack? No, I would rather go on three thousand at a time – it is safer. Print another three thousand – that's best. – It[3] means, I suppose, the book is being shipped to England and America – I hope carefully, or there may be trouble.

---

the Society's methods of obtaining evidence, they agreed that the book was obscene under the law. See John Trebbel, *A History of Book Publishing in the United States* (New York, 1978), iii. 407.
[1] Titus had failed to send Komroff's letter when he wrote on 21 January 1930 (see Letter 5487 and n. 1); he wrote again on 29 January (TMSC SIU), enclosed it and requested its return.
[2] Titus's letter of 5 February 1930 (TMSC SIU) clarifies the purpose of his telegram:

Dear Mr Lawrence,

I sent off a wire to you day before yesterday saying that Lady C. is beginning to move again and that I thought the next impression should be about ten thousand copies. I don't think we would be running any risk, and we would be able to shave the cost price down a little more, perhaps sufficient, I can't as yet say for sure, to pay for more prospectuses and a little occasional publicity, should it become necessary to think of it. – Let me have your opinion, please, as soon as you can, so that I may lay my plans accordingly for the approaching season. You never can tell, there may [be] a sudden splurge of demand for the book with the spring, and I would not like to stand empty-handed before it.

You will receive some more money from me, probably as soon as by the end of February. Owing to poor business conditions booksellers are very backward with their payments.

I hope to receive cheering news of your health.

Sincerely,
[3] No, I ... It] Do so if you think best – you know how the thing is going. – It

There's always trouble when one gets too bold. Toujours doucement, ma petite dame!¹

Lahr is worrying me again over those 200 *pansies*. He wants to send them to you by hand. What do you think about it? – will you take them, and put in a new title-page, and sell them at 60 frs. or so, and give me about 30 frs a copy on all sold, and I pay costs of production, and you pay cost of new title page. – Unfortunately I think all the copies are bound up: rather nice really. – I'm open to any suggestion you like to make in the matter.

I have said I will go on Thursday to a sanatorium for a month or so –

Ad Astra. *Vence*. A. M.

It is above Nice. I would like to get better quickly – here I am in bed allowed to do *nothing* – so I may as well make it as short as possible.

I suppose, since there is to be a third printing, we'll soon get the first settled up. You only owe about 3000 frs. on that – isn't it so?

ever   D. H. Lawrence

Will you write Lahr direct about the *pansies?* – or do you prefer not to? I mean about sending them over.

P.S. I decided it's best to print three thousand copies of *Lady C.* at a time – as sure as we get too big, there'll be trouble. So let it be a third three-thousand, will you please?   DHL

Could you send me a copy of *Le Renard* (translation of 'The Fox' my story) here to Bandol.²

5506. To Charles Lahr, 3 February 1930
Text: MS UNYB; Postmark, Bandol 5 –2 30; Moore 1239–40.

Beau Soleil, *Bandol*, Var
3 Feb 1930

Dear L[ahr]

I have asked Titus again about the *pansies* – He thinks to put in a new title-page and sell at 60 frs. I asked him to write you direct. – What about the blue-bound vellum copies? – you don't mention them. I should like to settle up finally and altogether about the *pansies* before we begin the *Cock*.

Yes, the title *The Man Who had died* is all right for the *Escaped Cock*.³ – But I don't want a limited edition – one limited edition of a book is enough. I would like an unlimited edition at 10/6 – Call it a blue moon book if you like –

---

¹ 'Always gently, my little lady!'
² *Le Renard*, tr. L. A. Delieutraz (Paris, 1928) (Roberts D40).
³ The first (approximate) reference to the title – *The Man Who Died* – adopted by both Secker and Knopf for their edns in 1931 (see Roberts A50c). No edn was published by Lahr.

Oflaherty's essay is too slight – too short I mean – it's no good printing such small things alone by themselves.[1]

On Thursday I am going to a Sanatorium above Nice –

Ad Astra, *Vence*, A. M.

Write to me there.

DHL

I'm so afraid you'll get in an awful muddle with accounts, if you go in for publishing: that is, unless you buy the rights outright each time, from the author.

If we come to a decision about the *Hahn*, I can send you a set of proofs to print from – or can you use your copy, without spoiling it?

5507. To Ada Clarke, 3 February 1930
Text: MS Clarke; Postmark, [. . .]–2 30; Lawrence–Gelder 204–5.

Beau-Soleil, *Bandol*, Var.
3 Feb. 30

My dear Sister

I have decided to go to the sanatorium that Dr Morland recommended

Ad Astra, *Vence*, A. M.

It is above Nice. I've arranged to go on Thursday – and Frieda will stay a few days with me, then she will come back here.

But you won't want to come here when I'm in Vence: and they will let me have visitors only twice a week. So wait a bit, till I'm walking about, and then come to Vence – they say it's nice there.

Barby will stay here with Frieda.

Of course I hate going – but perhaps it won't be so bad.

love   DHL

5508. To Laurence Pollinger, 3 February 1930
Text: MS UT; Unpublished.

Beau Soleil, *Bandol*, Var.
3 Feby 1930

Dear Pollinger,

Herewith the contract for *Nettles*. Does the first clause allow me to print them again, in collected edition or otherwise, after a certain time has elapsed – say two years? I want to reserve that right, so do make sure. – No, I don't mind if the poems run on.

---

[1] Two months later Lahr published *Joseph Conrad: An Appreciation* by the Irish novelist, Liam O'Flaherty (1897–1984), as *Blue Moon Booklet 1* (12 pages and costing 1/-).

I shall wait to hear about Stern.

I don't mind if Random House does the Introd. to the *Paintings* – but why do they want it signed if it isn't a limited edition? However, you can tell me particulars later. – And please let Stephensen know of this proposition.

I'll do the *Jolly Roger* extension again later – can't do it now.

I am going on Thursday to the sanatorium that Dr Morland recommended.

Ad Astra, Vence (VENCE), A. M.

It is above Nice.

So sorry about your mother's illness.

DHL

Keep the agreement for me – my copy.

Many thanks for the Priestley book.[1] Proofs of *Nettles* not yet arrived – neither *Bottom Dogs*.

5509. To Frederick Carter, [5? February 1930]
Text: MS UT; PC v. Snarling Tiger; Postmark, Bandol 7 –2 30; cited in Carter, *D. H. Lawrence and the Body Mystical*, p. 62

[Villa Beau Soleil, Bandol, Var]
[5? February 1930]

My wife is sending off the MSS of the Apocalypse, but unfortunately she can't find the last bit, the 'Antique Heavens' – She will send it as soon as it turns up. – Also *Enoch* is being sent now.[2] – I am in bed – and probably going this week into a sanatorium. No luck. Have not finished my longer essay on Revelation – and am abandoning it. Perhaps you'd do better if you offered a shorter MS.

best luck   DHL

5510. To Blair Hughes-Stanton, [7 February 1930]
Text: MS Hughes-Stanton; *Samphire*, iii. 22.

Ad Astra.
Friday.

Dear Blair

So many thanks for yesterday – give Barby this letter – it contains the money for housekeeping and to pay you back.[3]

I mind it a bit less here today than yesterday – Oh *why* is one ill!

DHL

[1] John Boynton Priestley (1894–1984), novelist, playwright and essayist. The book was probably his latest and immediately popular novel, *The Good Companions* (July 1929).
[2] Cf. Letter 5455 and n. 2.
[3] Hughes-Stanton had met the Lawrences at Nice and driven them to the sanatorium. For the enclosure see letter following.

5511. To Barbara Weekley, [7 February 1930]
Text: Nehls, iii. 434.

[Ad Astra, Vence, A. M.]
[7 February 1930]

Blair has been as kind as an angel to me. Here is £10 for housekeeping.

[Frieda Lawrence begins]

Be careful with the money.[1]

5512. To Ada Clarke, [7 February 1930]
Text: MS Clarke; PC v. Vence (Alpes-Maritimes). Altitude 325m., Climat marin atténué, Station touristique. Les Quatre Baons.; Postmark, [. . .] 8 [. . .] 30; Lawrence–Gelder 206.

Ad Astra. Vence. A. M.
[7 February 1930]

Got here yesterday – think I shall be all right – quite nice, and not alarming. Frieda is in the hotel – I have a balcony and see the coast-line and Cannes, five miles off. Shall go downstairs to lunch next week, all being well.

love   DHL

5513. To Emily King, [7 February 1930]
Text: MS Sagar; PC v. Vence (Alpes-Maritimes). – Altitude: 325 m.– Climat marin atténué. Station touristique d'Hiver et d'Eté. – La Place de l'Eglise; Postmark, Ve[nce] [. . .]; Unpublished.

Ad Astra. Vence. A. M.
[7 February 1930]

We came here yesterday – and I am installed – think I shall be all right – was examined today – have been losing weight this winter, but nothing very serious – Frieda is in the hotel – Shall write properly

DHL

5514. To Maria Huxley, [7 February 1930]
Text: Huxley 850–1.

Ad Astra, Vence, A. M.
Friday

I have submitted and come here to a sanatorium – sort of sanatorium – and Frieda is in the hotel – I came yesterday. It doesn't seem very different from

---

[1] Barbara Weekley recalled: 'This admonition impressed me so much, that when Blair and his wife came to see me, I gave them only a few rags of boiled meat from the soup for lunch, and offended them' (Nehls, iii. 434).

an ordinary hotel – but the doctors are there to look after one. – I'll tell you the results. – I heard the play wasn't a success with the public, but perhaps they'll come round to it.[1] Pity if it doesn't make you richer, if not rich. – Maria, do send me a bit of that liver medicine which Aldous found so good.[2] It's quite a nice place here – the air is good, and one is aloft. Shall write properly.

DHL

5515. To Giuseppe Orioli, [7? February 1930]
Text: MS NWU; PC v. Vence (A. M.). – Alt. 325 m. Station touristique. Climat marin atténué. – Vieille Rue; Postmark, Vence 8 –2 30; Moore, *Intelligent Heart* 430.

'Ad Astra.' Vence. A.M.
[7? February 1930]

Have come to a sanatorium here, as I was losing weight. It's not bad. Frieda is in the hotel. Glad to hear you are better – *take care*, don't get really knocked up, like me. – The doctors think they can make me better fairly soon – I hope so, am so tired of this. Write me here –

DHL

5516. To Max Mohr, [7? February 1930)
Text: MS HMohr; PC v. Vence (A. M.), – Alt. 325 m. Station touristique. Climat marin atténué. – Vieille Rue; Postmark, [. . .]; Mohr, *Briefe* 540.

'Ad Astra'. *Vence.* A. M.
[7? February 1930]

I have at last submitted, and come to a sanatorium here – Frieda is in the hotel for the time being, here. – I have been losing weight this winter, so thought I had better do something about it – hope this place will set me up – the air is

[1] Aldous Huxley replied to DHL's postcard on 11 February 1930 (Smith 327–9) and, commenting on the production of his play *This Way to Paradise*, said: ' . . . the play goes on, doing moderate and (surprisingly) slightly improving business. It may run only three weeks, unless the improvement continues.' It closed on 1 March.

[2] In the same letter Huxley wrote:

I am despatching a box of the invaluable *Coréine*. It is not specifically for the liver and only cleared up mine because I was being poisoned by a spot in the intestine and the poison was making trouble in the liver. All that it is is mucilage – which is practically speaking vegetable gum. You swallow it: it swells up in your inside, mixes itself with the food and passes out absorbing on the way all undue moisture (which means in practice all accumulations of toxins) and mechanically pushing along any stagnating matter. In fact, it sweeps and garnishes one's guts, but in a mechanical, not a pharmaceutical way – so doesn't have any of the bad effect of a purge, yet does what the purge does and also other excellent things beside. It may not act on the liver in all cases, for the good reason that the liver may be going wrong on its own account and not because of the intestine. But it can't do any harm to try it: and if there's any tendency to auto-intoxication it can only do good. Old [V. E.] Sorapure, who recommended it to me, is a great believer in it and prescribes it to all his patients, with good results.

better than Bandol – Perhaps you would like to come here, later. – But it is 10 km. from the sea.

Grüsse   DHL

5517. To S. S. Koteliansky, 9 February 1930

Text: MS BL; Postmark, [Ven]ce 10[...] 30; cited in K. W. Gransden, 'Rananim: D. H. Lawrence's Letters to S. S. Koteliansky', *Twentieth Century*, clix (January–June 1955), 32.

Ad Astra, Vence, A. M.
9 Feb 1930

Dear Kot

Well I came here last Thursday – and it's no different from being in an hotel, not a bit – except that a nurse takes my temperature. I have the ordinary hotel food – and do just as I like – and am far less 'looked after' than I was in the Beausoleil. So much for a sanatorium. The doctors don't seem to think my case desperate – they don't seem to think anything of it at all – I have no fever – and weigh under 45 kgr. – 90 lb. But I think I'll be all right.

Yes, we both liked Dr Morland.[1]

If you see Mrs Henderson, thank her for her letter, and tell her I'll answer it – tell her how I'm fixed. Send me her address.

Yes, you can leave out Murry's name – put Katharine's instead, if you like.[2]

It rains today.

DHL

5518. To Charles Lahr, 9 February 1930

Text: MS UNYB; Postmark, Vence 10 –2 30; Lacy, *Escaped Cock* 91.

Ad Astra, *Vence*, A. M.
9 Feby. 30

Dear Lahr

I have never mentioned *Escaped Cock* to Goldston – never written him in my life[3] – I'm afraid this is another piracy trick of his – but the book is sheltered under the Berne convention copyright. I don't want him to do it anyhow – after that *Pansies* affair. – I have written to Pollinger of Curtis

---

[1] See Introduction, pp. 12–13.

[2] At the opening to his Introduction for Kot's translation of *The Grand Inquisitor* by Dostoevsky, DHL had written: 'I remember when I first read *The Brothers Karamazov*, in 1913, how fascinated yet unconvinced it left me. And I remember Middleton Murry saying to me: "Of course the whole clue to Dostoievsky is in that Grand Inquisitor story." And I remember saying: "Why? It seems to me just rubbish"' (*Phoenix* 283). When the book was published in July 1930, the name of Katherine Mansfield had been substituted for Murry's.

[3] DHL had forgotten that he ordered books from Goldston in 1927: see *Letters*, vi. 102, 107.

Brown to see if he'd look after it for me – then if we can fix up, you'd better print quickly, as I mistrust Goldston and Co. I am not bound to those six months – we can come out in March if we like.

I like the poems by the Powys boy.[1]

But don't do like Stephensen, too many little things one after the other.

If I am well I think I shall come to England this summer.

DHL

5519. To Laurence Pollinger, [10 February 1930]
Text: MS UT; Unpublished.

Ad Astra, Vence, A. M.
Monday

Dear Pollinger

Well here I am – not much of a sanatorium – but I think I shall be all right.

I want to ask you about *The Escaped Cock* – which I have not mentioned since you were so shocked by it. It was done in Paris in November, 500 copies, and the whole edition sent safely to New York – and by this time sold, I expect, though I have no news. – Now, to prevent piracy I want to do an edition in England. I heard that Goldston was saying that he is publishing *The Escaped Cock* – whereas I have never even mentioned the name to him – never written to him in my life. I'm afraid he wants to be at his piracy trick again. – But I have written to Chas Lahr of 68 Red Lion St. W.C. 1. – he really did the other *Pansies* – and he wants to do it. He is a bit harum scarum, but quite honest. He says it can be done quite publicly if we change the title – nobody will take offence. I would have 500 copies, *unlimited*, at 10/6. – Let me know if you want to look after this for me, or if you would still rather not handle it. Don't hesitate to say no. But please let me know at once, as I am afraid of Goldston's tricks.

Have you got a real romantic book to send me.

My wife is in the hotel in Vence – rather dull.

DHL

5520. To Achsah Brewster, [12 February 1930]
Text: MS UT; Brewster 230–1.

Ad Astra, *Vence, A-M*.
Wed.

Dear Achsah,

Well here I am – and it's not so bad. I feel better for the change, for the

---

[1] Lahr published *At the Harlot's Burial: Poems*, by Laurence Powys, in March 1930.

higher level, and the escaping from Beausoleil. Here one is in the sky again, and on top of things. There, one was underneath.

The doctors don't insist on rest, like Morland – they suggest I go down to meals, two flights of *steep* stairs, alas! And I have the ordinary hotel food – but good food. Still, I feel better, I feel I've escaped something. The doctors X-rayed me a long while – the lung has hardly moved since Mexico – the broncs. are very bad – and the liver inflamed and enlarged – All very boring. But I believe a certain amount of movement is necessary for me. I don't seem to have any fever.

It was a lovely day. I was out in the garden a bit – and out on my balcony. There is a mimosa tree in blossom. Earl will be coming tomorrow. He looks better and fresher for his change.

Frieda wants to come back to Beausoleil on Saturday, and pack up, and then move into the Casa dei Sogni – I hope she's wise.

What a world it is! But I shall see you soon – and I hope before very long I shall be pitching my tent in the shade of the Château Brun –

love   DHL

5521. To Maria Huxley, [12 February 1930]
Text: Huxley 851–2.

Ad Astra, Vence.
Wed.

Dear Maria, –

Your letter came on – a good letter, made me understand about the play very well.[1] I'm afraid the public wants to be made to feel it is all on the side of the angels. But I hope the run will be longer than you think, and make a bit of money anyhow.

Here I came at last, as I was getting so feeble and so thin. It isn't a sanatorium, really – an hotel where a nurse takes your temperature and two doctors look at you once a week – for the rest, just an hotel. They examined me with X-rays and all that. It is as I say – the lung has moved very little since Mexico, in five years. But the broncs are awful, and they have inflamed my lower man, the *ventre* and the liver. I suppose that's why I've gone so thin – I daren't tell you my weight – but I've lost a lot this winter, can't understand why. Of course they can do nothing for me – food, the food is good, but it's hotel food – they say milk is bad for my liver, and it's true. They don't say rest all the time – I go down to lunch, down two flights of steep stairs, alas – and I'm going to practise walking again. I think they are right and the English

[1] Cf. Letter 5514 and n. 1.

doctor wrong. A certain amount of movement is better. I've got a good balcony and lovely view – and the air is much better than Bandol. If ever you want to live in these parts, try a place like Vence. – Frieda is in the Nouvel Hôtel in Vence – she goes back to the Beau Soleil Saturday – her daughter Barbara is there. They will pack up and go to a little house in Cagnes, which the di Chiaras are giving up. Then they'll come on the bus, about 20 minutes, to see me. – It's dull here – only French people convalescing and nothing in my line. But I'm feeling more chirpy, and shall try to get *on my legs*. It would be fun to see you, end of this month. When I hope I can walk a bit. I wish we could have been somewhere to have a good time like Diablerets. Or I wish I could sail away to somewhere really thrilling – perhaps we shall go to the ranch. What I want is to be thoroughly cheered up somehow – not this rest-cure business.

Well, it all sounds very egoistic – that's the worst of being sick. The mimosa is all out, in clouds – like Australia, and the almond blossom very lovely, especially around Bandol. To-day was a marvellous day – I sat in the garden. Perhaps we might have a few jolly days, if you came down – just jolly, like Diablerets.

DHL

5522. To Emily King, [14 February 1930]
Text: MS Lazarus; Postmark, [. . .] 15 [. . .] 30; Pinto, *Renaissance and Modern Studies*, i. 9.

'Ad Astra', *Vence*, A–M. France
14 Feb.

My dear Sister

I had your letter and Peg's today – glad the dance was a success. – I had to give in and come here – Dr Morland insisted so hard, and I was losing weight so badly, week by week. I only weigh something over six stones – and even in the spring I was over seven, nearly eight. So I had to do something at once. Yet I haven't gained any weight here either – nor lost any – in the 8 days. I have had careful xray examination – the lung trouble is slight, but the bronchial-asthma condition very bad, it uses up my strength – and I've lost my appetite. They try to give me things to pick me up, but as yet there is no change – I'm not in any sudden danger – but in slow danger. I didn't want you both to come there to that little Beausoleil house – it would have upset me too much and been too much for me – and it wouldn't have been much fun for you. Wait and see how I go on here – then in the spring we may meet in some nice place. If I'd waited, as you suggest, heaven knows what might have happened – do you think I come into a sanatorium for the fun of the thing?

And when one feels so weak and down, one doesn't want to see anybody, and that's the truth. – It would have been no fun for you.

Frieda will go back to Bandol on Monday and give up the Beausoleil and come to Cagnes, just below here, and have a house there for a while – so she can come and see me every day. Luckily she will have Barby with her.

Give my letter to Ada, so she understands too.

love   DHL

There is no need for you to worry, either of you. But there is need for me to take care.

5523. To Caresse Crosby, 14 February 1930
Text: MS UT; Postmark, [...] 16 2 30; Moore 1243–4.

'Ad Astra', *Vence*. A–M.
14 Feby 1930

Dear Caresse

I had to come here, to a sort of sanatorium, for my health. I have been losing weight badly, so there is not much left of me, and soon I too should be a goner. I think I am better here, but I've gained no weight: and it is very wearisome.

Your letter came on, with the cheque. But did you really sell that whole edition for $2,250? It seems absurd, for Marks was retailing it at $25 a copy, as I know from two sources. He may have had to come down in price, later. But did you sell the whole edition, *including the vellums*, for $2,250? If you did, you are not the good business woman I should expect you to be: and I resent bitterly those little Jew booksellers making all that money out of us.

I hope you haven't sent Harry's MS. to Bandol. If you have, it will come on all right. If I get it here, I can read it and think about it. I hope it won't upset me too much – I rather dread it.

And I hope time is passing not too heavily for you – time is the best healer, when it isn't a killer.

You didn't say if you could let me have a couple of imperfect copies of *Escaped Cock*. I wish you could.

Frieda is in the Nouvel Hotel here – and sends her love, and her sympathy, with mine.

D. H. Lawrence

5524. To Edward Titus, 14 February 1930
Text: MS UT; Unpublished.

'Ad Astra', *Vence*. A–M.

14 Feby. 1930

Dear Titus[1]

Thanks for letter and cheque for 3,000 frs. You have now paid me 10,000 + 10,000 + 10,000 + 3,000 frs. in cheques on your account, then 7,372 in a transferred cheque, and 300 in notes: total *40,372* frs. There were due to me, if I remember rightly, 41,000 frs. Why didn't you settle up neatly and tidily, deducting what I owe you for further books – then the first 3,000 copies would be accounted for.

I will tell Charles Lahr to send you the *Pansies*.

I had to come into a sanatorium because I was losing weight so badly. There is a very slight tubercular trouble, but the x-ray shows that that would not trouble me at all, if only we could get the bronchial-asthmatic condition better – it is that that eats up my strength. I think I am better here – the altitude – but I haven't gained any weight. It's a great weariness, and I get so tired of myself, not being able to do anything. I wish I could throw the thing off, it's really like a vampire. But the *view* is fine, from my room!!!!

I hope I shall soon pick up, and can do something again.

DHL

5525. To Charles Lahr, 20 February 1930
Text: MS ULon; Postmark, Vence 2 [. . .] 30; Lacy, *Escaped Cock* 91–2.

Ad Astra, *Vence*. A–M.

20 Feb./30

Dear Lahr

Heard from Pollinger – he talks of making a regular contract for *Man Who had Died*. (you must put *Escaped Cock* as a sub-title) – But I don't want you to

---

[1] Titus had replied to Letter 5505, on 12 February 1930 (TMSC SIU):

Dear Mr. Lawrence:

Frankly, it gave me a dreadful shock to hear that you had to go to a sanatorium. I was out of sorts as a result of it for a few days, and lacked the courage to write to you.

I enclose three thousand francs as requested. Will you please acknowledge receipt?

I am not going to argue the point as to whether 10,000 copies of Lady Chatterley's Lover should be printed or whether it is best to stick to the original quantity. It so happens that there is a strike at my printer's; I can only hope that it won't last long.

I am sending out today to get you the translation of your book, which I'll send you as soon as I get it. There have been several seizures, according to the paper, of Lady C. in America; the last one in Philadelphia.

As to your Pensees, Lahr may send them over. I will see what I can do with them to the best advantage. You can trust me. We shan't quarrel as to the "kale".

Arlen was in to see me the other day. He was just back from the south, and he was very sorry

pay any money in advance – I don't want it. Pay at the end of the first month, on all copies sold.

Titus said you could send along the 200 *Pansies*, and he would arrange selling them. But he's very indefinite.

If you do publish *Man Who Had Died*, get it out as soon as possible, will you.

I'm rather worse in this beastly place –

ever   DHL

5526. To Laurence Pollinger, 20 February 1930
Text: MS UT; Huxley 852.

Ad Astra. *Vence. A. M.* France
20 Feb 1930

Dear Pollinger

Do try and stop Rich sending over my presentation copies to London. He does it on purpose. – I enclose list of addresses.[1]

I don't believe Stern is going to get far with Boni.

About Charles Lahr – don't insist on money down – I don't want it. Say accounts made a month after publication. Thank you so much for looking after it.

Oh that Mandrake – vegetable of ill omen!

When will *Nettles?* appear?

Thank you for the books. I read *Mumba* and the Chinese book:[2] the other two, the girl at sea is a feeble fake,[3] and the other man, I'm sick of self-conscious young americans posing before their own cameras.[4]

I've been rather worse here – think I have a bit of flue – pain too. There's nothing in this place – I was better in Beausoleil – have been here fifteen days –

that he didn't know your address; he would have visited you if he had had it.

I certainly hope that your health will improve rapidly and that when I see you again your cheeks will be nice and pink.

Very sincerely,

[1] The enclosure is missing.
[2] Du Bose Heyward, *Mamba's Daughters* (February 1929); the 'Chinese book' may have been Witter Bynner's *Jade Mountain: A Chinese Anthology* which DHL had heard about from Bynner in 1928 (see *Letters*, vi. 278 and n. 3) and which Knopf had published in an English edn, January 1930.
[3] Joan Lowell's *Cradle of the Deep* (New York, 1920) – published in England, June 1929, as *Child of the Deep* – was a hoax, purporting to be an autobiography.
[4] Possibly Thomas Wolfe, *Look Homeward, Angel* (New York, 1929).

Commando hasn't come, from F. V. Morley.[1]

My wife has her daughter Barbara with her – and another friend[2] – not so bad. I'm rather miserable here.

ever   DHL

5527. To Giuseppe Orioli, [21 February 1930]
Text: MS UCLA; Moore, *Intelligent Heart* 432.

Ad Astra, Vence, A M
Friday

Dear Pino

Glad to hear you are better. I am not – rather worse. This place doesn't suit me – Shan't stay long, perhaps another week – Feel wretched. – Perhaps we shall take a house here for a short while.

Will you send me a copy of the first editn. of *Lady C* – I want to give it to my English doctor – he won't take a fee.

Weather bad – I am all the time in bed again – and feel miserable. Will write more later.

DHL

5528. To Earl Brewster, [21 February 1930]
Text: MS UT; Brewster 231–2.

Vence.
Friday

Dear Earl

What woes! – you must tell me if you get into straits – what a bore!

I'm rather worse than better – doesn't suit me here – have awful bad nights, cough and pain – and seems they cant do anything for me. I was better in Beausoleil. Shan't stay long here – perhaps till next Thursday. Perhaps we'll take a house here for a short time. Ida Rauh is here, looking fat. Will write more later.

love   DHL

Beastly weather here.

---

[1] Faber had published Deneys Reitz's *Commando: A Boer Journal of the Boer War* in October 1929; Frank Vigor Morley (1899–) was a miscellaneous writer whose connection with DHL is not known.

[2] Ida Rauh (cf. Letter 5530).

5529. To Ada Clarke, [21 February 1930]
Text: MS Clarke; Unpublished.

Ad Astra, *Vence*, A. M.
Friday

My dear Sister

Philip Trotter wrote they would send the pictures to you the moment they knew you were expecting them. Will you write him or Dorothy Warren.

39A Maddox St. W.

– and take them safely. I'm afraid of the Trotters going bankrupt or something.

I'm not any better – don't think much of this place – shan't stay long – does me no good. Perhaps we'll get a house here for a bit – God knows. – Ida Rauh, from Santa Fe, is here too.

love   DHL

5530. To Maria Huxley, [21 February 1930]
Text: Huxley 853.

Ad Astra, Vence.
Friday.

Dear Maria, –

The two parcels came now – very luxurious. Frieda trying them all – very extravagant of you to send so much. And Coréine and the Browning book. It's interesting, the Browning, yet somehow humiliating – bourgeois.[1] The bourgeois at its highest level makes one squirm a bit.

I am rather worse here – such bad nights, and cough, and heart, and pain decidedly worse here – and miserable. Seems to me like *grippe*, but they say not. It's not a good place – shan't stay long – I'm better in a house – I'm miserable.

Frieda has Barbey with her – and Ida Rauh. When do you think of coming?[2]

DHL

This place no good.

[1] *Elizabeth Barrett Browning: Letters to her Sister, 1846–1859* (November 1929), edited by Maria's father-in-law, Leonard Huxley (1860–1933).
[2] See Letter 5534 and n. 1.

5531. To Emily King, [27 February 1930]

Text: MS Sagar; PC v. l'Hostellerie Provençale 'Ad-Astra'; Postmark, Vence 28 2 [. . .];
Unpublished.

[Ad Astra, Vence, A. M.]

Thursday –

Amusing the photograph of the party! I am about the same – anyhow no
worse. We are moving into a house here in Vence[1] on Saturday and I am
having an English nurse from Nice[2] – I think it will be better.

love   DHL

5532. To Philip Trotter, [27 February 1930]

Text: MS UN; Unpublished.

Ad Astra – Vence. A. M.

Thursday. 20 Feby/30

Dear Philip

I am here this last three weeks in a sanatorium – but doesn't suit me, so we
are moving into a house here in Vence.

The Aga Khan came this afternoon, and wants to take my pictures to Paris
– to show in a private show – perhaps buy some.[3] So will you *not* send them to
Ripley – please – And the Aga Khan will come and see you shortly and
discuss about them – I liked him.

Do hope Dorothy is better – I'm in bed, a bit dismal.

DHL

5533. To Ada Clarke, [27 February 1930]

Text: MS Clarke; PC v. l'Hostellerie Provençale 'Ad-Astra'; Postmark, Vence 28 –2 30;
Lawrence–Gelder 205.

[Ad Astra, Vence, A. M.]

Thursday –

I am about the same, anyhow no worse. We are moving into a house here at
Vence on Saturday, and I'm having a nurse. – I am telegraphing Warren to
hold pictures awhile, because the Aga Khan came with his wife this afternoon

[1] The Villa Robermond.
[2] Possibly Evelyn Thorogood (Nehls, iii. 432, 730 n. 421). There may have been a connection
between her appointment and the concern felt by Dr Morland which he expressed in a letter to
Gertler, 25 February 1930: see Introduction, pp. 13–14.
[3] Aga Khan III (1877–1957), hereditary head of the Ismaili sect; first President of the All-India
Moslem League, in 1906; India's representative at the League of Nations in 1930s. m. (1) 1896,
Shahzadi Begum, (2) 1908, Teresa Magliano, (3) 1929, Andrée Carron. He had visited the
Warren Gallery exhibition on the day of the police raid (Nehls, iii. 344–5). According to
Aldington, after DHL's death the Aga Khan withdrew his offer to buy DHL's paintings when
Frieda asked £20,000 for them (Nehls, iii. 718 n. 220).

and is so keen to show them to artists in a private gallery in Paris. He was very nice – so we'll see.

love   DHL

5534. To Earl Brewster, [27 February 1930]
Text: MS UT; Brewster 232–3.

Ad Astra, Vence, A M
Thursday

Dear Earl

Many thanks for letter and cheque – it's a bit too much, I shall give you some back.

I'm about the same – I think no worse – but we are moving into a house here in Vence on Saturday, and I'm having an English nurse from Nice. I shall be better looked after.

H. G. Wells came to see me Monday – a common temporary soul. – Today the Aga Khan came with his wife – I liked him – a bit of real religion in the middle of his fat face. He wants to take my pictures to Paris – perhaps buy some – we'll see.

The Huxleys are in Cannes – came Tuesday, and coming again tomorrow.[1] Queer – something gone out of them – they'll have to be left now to the world – finished, in some spiritual way. Their play is running its final week. But they are well in health.

How much did those shares bring you, actually? Tell me.

Ida and Barby are both very good. We talk of you. I *do* hope Achsah's face is better – worrying, that is.

It's beastly weather.

– love   DHL

Excuse paper. Frieda took the other to her room.

Joe Davidson (?) came and made a clay head of me – made me tired – result in clay mediocre.[2]

---

[1] The Huxleys were with DHL when he died at the Villa Robermond, at 10 p.m. on Sunday, 2 March 1930.

[2] Jo Davidson (1883–1952), American sculptor best known for his busts of Franklin D. Roosevelt, Einstein, Gandhi, Chaplin, Conrad, Joyce, Wells (who prompted his visit to DHL on 26 February), *et al* (see Nehls, iii. 433–4). His bust of DHL is at UT.

INDEX

No distinction is made between a reference in the text or in a footnote.
All titles of writings by Lawrence are gathered under his name.
For localities, public buildings, etc. in London, see the comprehensive entry under the place-name; all biblical references are collected under 'Bible'.
A bold numeral indicates a biographical entry in a footnote.

Abraham, Dr Felix, 287, 335
Ad Astra (Vence), 2, 12–15, 626, 630–2, 635–6, 638–52
Ada, *see* Clarke, L.
Adams, Eldridge, 233, 236, 239, 272, 390–1, 445
Adelphi, see New Adelphi, The
Adonis, 519
Aegean, 545
Africa, 28, 166, 181, 220, 465, 494
'After the Fireworks', *see* Huxley, A.
Aga Khan III, 15, **652**–3
Agag, 189
Aix-en-Provence, 623
Ajaccio, 183, 190–1
Alassio, 611
Albenga, 164, 167, 169, 171
Albert, *see* Boni, A.
Aldington, Hilda, **349**
letter, to 414–15
Aldington, Richard, **17**, 151, 349, 416, 498, 504, 516, 540–1, 558, 564–5, 573, 578, 600, 652; *Death of a Hero*, 558
Aldous, *see* Huxley, A.
Aleister, *see* Crowley, E.
Alfred, *see* Knopf, A. *and* Weber, A.
Alicante, 273, 276, 282–3, 286
Alinari, Fratelli, 368, 508
All Things Are Possible, see Shestov, L.
Allen & Co., 47–8
Alps, 332, 394, 453, 487
Ambergate (Derbyshire), 261
America, 4, 21, 25–7, 30, 35–6, 38–40, 42, 45, 47–8, 55, 57, 62, 66, 77, 83–5, 89, 94, 96, 98, 105, 108, 113, 115, 129, 131–2, 137, 138–9, 144–5, 158, 160, 168, 172, 182, 184, 186, 192, 197, 202,

203, 205, 207, 210, 213, 217, 219, 226, 231, 234, 238, 241, 243, 250–1, 265–6, 268–9, 272, 274, 277, 279, 286–7, 290, 300, 302, 308, 312, 315–17, 320–4, 326, 334–5, 337, 341, 343–4, 350, 353, 375, 379, 383, 386–7, 392, 401, 404, 423, 426, 438–40, 445, 452, 462, 469, 471, 473, 476, 485, 487–8, 496–500, 503–5, 519–21, 524, 526, 531, 533–4, 536, 546–8, 551, 557, 560, 564, 568–9, 574, 577–8, 582–4, 586–8, 591, 593–4, 600, 609, 617, 633, 636–7, 649
American Caravan, The, see Brooks, V.
Amour, Terre Inconnue, see Maurice, M.
Anacapri, 28, 68, 155, 170
Anchor (Shipping) Line, 586
Anita, Annie, *see* Hinke, A. von
Anton, Francesco, *see* Grazzini, A.
Antonio (hotel boy), 296
Apocalypse de Jean, L'., see, Loisy, A.
Arabella, *see* Yorke, D.
Archer, Esther, *see* Lahr, E.
Architectural Review, The, 4, 269, 295
Archuleta, Trinidad, **277**
Aretino, Pietro, 141
Ariel Poems, see Faber & Faber
Arkansas, 395
Arlen, Michael, *see* Kouyoumdjian, D.
Arno river, 181, 465, 478
Art, see Bell, A.
Art and Progress, 503
Art et Décoration, 503
Art Nonsense, see Gill E.
Asquith, Lady Cynthia, **445**, 507; *The Black Cap*, 507; *The Ghost Book*, 445, 507
At the Harlot's Burial: Poems, see Powys L.
Athens, 506, 508

Kiepenheuer, Gustav, 543, 567, 572, 596, 604

King, Ann, **562**

King, Emily Una ('Pamela', 'Pem'), (sister), 1, 11, 68, 76, 95, 97, 107, 124, 192, 232, 259, 319, 321–2, 330, 346, 347, 352, 360, 398, 461, 478, 494, 530, 532, 557, 573, 579, 592, 602, 620–1, 630–3, 636
letters to, 17, 22, 52–3, 69–70, 127–8, 187, 209–10, 216, 225, 241, 254, 262, 326–7, 331, 338, 351, 364, 366, 378, 393, 418, 436–7, 460–1, 481, 490, 510–11, 558–9, 561–2, 581–2, 593–4, 621–2, 641, 646–7, 652

King, F(rederick) A(llen), 230
letter to, **226**

King, Joan Frieda, (niece), 17, 22, 69, 210, 262, 327, 418, 461, 594

King, Margaret Emily ('Peg', 'Peggy') (niece), 17, 22, 53, 69, 127, 259, 262, 366, 594, 621–2, 646
letters to, 299, 635–6

King, Samuel Taylor, 17, 22, 69, 127–8, 513

Kiowa Ranch, 5, 10–11, 25, 29, 54–5, 96, 138, 183, 195, 197, 203, 205–6, 213, 263, 277, 287–90, 292, 312, 318, 342–3, 345, 360, 385, 472–5, 490, 505–6, 574, 614, 616, 630, 632–3, 636, 646

Kipling, Joseph Rudyard, 85, 198, 234

Kippenburg, Dr Anton, 32, 51, 113–14, 139, 335, 375, 386, 410, 453, 517, 567, 571–2, 597–8, 609–10, 615
letter to, 113
letter from, 139

Kippenberg, Katherina, 113–14

Knopf, Alfred Abraham, 3, **27**, 38, 111, 174, 236, 239–40, 243, 266, 297, 301–3, 305, 308, 312–13, 315, 320, 324, 328, 347, 349, 383, 386, 391, 394–5, 413–14, 453, 463, 467, 485, 496, 516, 521–2, 534, 552, 568–9, 584, 588, 593, 623, 638

Knopf, Blanche, 40, 45, 588
letter to, 37

Komroff, Manuel, 625–6, 637

Koteliansky, Samuel Solomonovich ('Kot'), 1, 12, 47–8, 59, 61–2, 66, 68, 84, 97, 124, 131, 134, 140, 143–4, 151, 154, 198, 233, 278, 296–7, 301, 318–19, 321,

324, 328, 340, 346, 380, 434, 437, 443, 488–9, 498, 528, 531, 556, 568, 592, 619, 635; *The Grand Inquisitor*, 618, 620, 629
letters to, 18, 39–40, 49, 60, 82, 125, 141–3, 147, 162, 167–8, 197, 209, 282, 302–3, 319–20, 330, 473–4, 518, 537–8, 575–6, 604–5, 618, 620–1, 629, 643
letter from, 592–3

Kouyoumdjian, Dikran (Michael Arlen), 476, 520, 523, 534, 539–40, 648

Kra, 245

Kranzler, N., *Joy Go With You*, 42

Krenkow, Ada Rose, **193**, 529, 532

Krenkow, Fritz Johann Heinrich, **193**, 529

Krug, Emil von (brother-in-law), 74
letter to, 610–11

Krug, Johanna von ('Nusch') (sister-in-law), 74, 422, 611

Kugler, Mrs, 75, 422

Kurhaus Plättig, *see* Hotel (Kurhaus) Plättig

Kurpark, 378

La Massa, *see* Villa La Massa

La Rochefoucauld, Armand, Comte de, 323–4, 548

La Vernia, 432

Labour Party, 315, 325, 327, 413

Lago di Garda, 5, 34, 46, 52, 54, 172, 221, 260, 273, 276, 277, 283, 317–18, 327, 332, 347, 354, 391, 394, 435

Lahr, Charles ('Lion'), 1, 3–4, 6, 30–1, 39, 42–3, 45, 47–50, 59–61, 71, 89, 96, 112, 124–6, 134, 140–1, 143, 148, 151, 153, 163, 167, 173, 177, 191, 202, 237, 282, 320, 330, 346, 394, 396, 411, 429, 433, 448, 452, 461, 473, 493, 501, 508, 514–15, 519, 538, 545, 557, 561, 569, 573, 576, 580, 593, 599, 606, 621, 638, 644, 648–9; *Red Lion* edition, 301–2, 319–20, 473, 517
letters to, **23**, 30–1, 43–4, 47–8, 60–1, 88, 110–11, 120–1, 142–4, 147, 154–5, 161–2, 172, 197–8, 233–4, 247, 255–6, 264–5, 278, 300–2, 314–15, 324–5, 328, 333–4, 336–7, 340, 353–4, 361–2, 365, 375, 376–7, 380, 389, 404, 406, 412–13, 434, 441–4, 447, 461–2, 483–5, 488–9,

682 *Index*

0 7 OCT 2020

Printed in Great Britain
by Amazon